American History told by Contemporaries

BY THE SAME EDITOR
A Source-Book of American History

The *Source-Book* is independent of the four volumes of *Contemporaries,* and contains no articles which appear in the larger series.

THE MACMILLAN COMPANY

60 FIFTH AVENUE, NEW YORK

American History told by Contemporaries

VOLUME I

ERA OF COLONIZATION

1492–1689

THE MACMILLAN COMPANY
NEW YORK · BOSTON · CHICAGO · DALLAS
ATLANTA · SAN FRANCISCO

MACMILLAN AND CO., Limited
LONDON · BOMBAY · CALCUTTA · MADRAS
MELBOURNE

THE MACMILLAN COMPANY
OF CANADA, Limited
TORONTO

American History told by Contemporaries

VOLUME I

ERA OF COLONIZATION

1492–1689

EDITED BY

ALBERT BUSHNELL HART

PROFESSOR OF HISTORY IN HARVARD UNIVERSITY
MEMBER OF THE MASSACHUSETTS HISTORICAL SOCIETY
AUTHOR OF "FORMATION OF THE UNION," "EPOCH MAPS,"
"PRACTICAL ESSAYS," ETC.

NEW YORK

THE MACMILLAN COMPANY

LONDON : MACMILLAN & CO., LTD.

1939

24856

Preface

A GENIAL reviewer has said of a book intended to aid students to a convenient use of the material of American history : " they hausmannize the wilderness that their students may sip coffee in an ample boulevard." This work likewise aims to make broad the highways for those who would visit their forefathers. It is an attempt to combine two objects not easily harmonized : first, to put within convenient reach of schools, libraries, and scholars authoritative texts of rare or quaint writings in American history, contemporary with the events which they describe ; and, in the second place, to give, in a succession of scenes, a notion of the movement and connection of the history of America, so that from this work by itself may be had an impression of the forces which have shaped our history, and the problems upon which they have worked. The limitations of space, however, make it imperative to clip and gouge most of the pieces selected ; and explanations and connections must be omitted. Nevertheless the author believes sincerely that a half-loaf baked in the oven of the times, is better than all the spiced buns of modern writers, for carrying to the mind a flavor of the life which our ancestors lived, and the motives which guided them ; he hopes that the reader may find in these lively, human, brief extracts, the real spirit of his countrymen.

A few words should be said on the principles of selection and arrangement. First of all, pains have been taken to use the first authoritative edition of each work in English ; and a faithful translation of pieces in foreign languages. Next, the copy is meant to be exact. A mighty historian like Sparks may correct the spelling and grammar of his ancestors ; lesser men had better leave the corrections to the reader.

Words not easily recognized are, however, repeated in modern dress in brackets. Next, the quotations are meant to be exact, all omissions being indicated, and the place where the extract was found being noted at the end.

No effort has been made to select writers especially for their literary value; and where there are two equally credible authorities on the same subject, that one is usually chosen who does not appear elsewhere in the volume. Nevertheless, no reader can fail to admire the literary crispness and sparkle of men like John Smith, William Bradford, John Hammond, Sir William Berkeley, Gabriel Thomas, and Dankers and Sluyter. There has not been space for long accounts of the writers, such as will be found in Tyler's *History of American Literature*, and in the introductions to special editions; but a few words are prefixed on each person, and a few references are added intended to lead to other sources, and to secondary works.

In making up this volume the difficulty has not been to find suitable extracts, but to choose out of the wealth of material; doubtless much has been left out that would have been as interesting as anything which here appears: it is the editor's hope, however, that nothing has been admitted that has not a distinct significance, and that as many elements of Colonial history are here presented as the space allows.

The uses to which such a volume may be put in schools and elsewhere are set forth at large in the *Practical Introduction* below. The editor's thought is that it may be an adjunct to the regular text-book teaching, may serve as material for topical study, and may open up to readers the field of delightful narratives in which American history abounds. Almost no constitutional documents are included: they are to be found in many collections; and they have not the persuasive power of the writings addressed by men to men.

An acknowledgment is due to the Harvard College Library for its generous grant of special privileges without which the book could hardly have been prepared.

ALBERT BUSHNELL HART.

CAMBRIDGE, May 1, 1897.

Contents

PART I

PRACTICAL INTRODUCTION
FOR TEACHERS, LIBRARIES, AND STUDENTS

CHAPTER I — THE SOURCES

CHAPTER II — USE OF SOURCES

PART II

DISCOVERY AND EARLY VOYAGES, 1000–1600

CHAPTER III — NORSE AND SPANISH DISCOVERIES

PART III

CONDITIONS OF COLONIZATION

CHAPTER VI — REASONS FOR COLONIZATION

CHAPTER VII — REGULATION OF COLONIZATION

CHAPTER XI — MARYLAND

CHAPTER XII — THE CAROLINAS

CHAPTER XIII — SOUTHERN COLONIAL LIFE

PART V

NEW ENGLAND

CHAPTER XIV — CONDITIONS

CHAPTER XV — PLYMOUTH

CHAPTER XVI — EARLY MASSACHUSETTS

PART VI

MIDDLE COLONIES

CHAPTER XXII — CONDITIONS

CHAPTER XXIII — NEW YORK

CHAPTER XXIV — PENNSYLVANIA AND DELAWARE

American History told by Contemporaries

PART I

PRACTICAL INTRODUCTION
FOR TEACHERS, PUPILS, STUDENTS AND LIBRARIES

CHAPTER I—THE SOURCES

1. What are Sources?

IN the current discussions on the teaching and study of history, one of the most frequent expressions is " the sources," or " original material." What do these words mean? As history is an account of the past actions of men, every historical statement must go back to the memory of those who saw the events, or to some record made at the time. Tradition is the handing down of memories from one person to another; and one of the most famous of the pieces in this volume — the Norse Sagas on the discovery of America (No. 16) — were thus transmitted for three centuries before they were finally put into writing. Such transmissions are likely to get away from the first form as years go on, and may change into legends. The more exact form of transmitting earlier memories is by autobiography, and by reminiscence written out in later life ; and even they are apt to be twisted by the lapse of the years between the event and the making of the record. Hence in preparing this volume such works have been rarely used. Perhaps Edward Johnson's book (No. 105) is the nearest approach to an example.

Much more important are the records and memoranda made at or very near the time of the event. Sometimes silent monuments may be all that is left ; the Great Serpent Mound in Ohio is a striking contem-

B   I

porary record, — if anybody could interpret it ; and the house of Governor Cradock in Medford, Massachusetts, still stands to tell us that its builder was a man of taste and substance.

Laws, proclamations, and other public documents are sources of a high order, because they not only describe, but constitute the event; they bear the signatures, the affixing of which gives them validity ; they are drawn up before the event takes place. An example is the Bull of Alexander VI (No. 18) and the Connecticut laws (No. 144). Of greater literary interest are the narratives of explorers, travellers, and visitors, in which American history is rich ; an instance is De Vries' trading voyages (No. 151). As travellers have, however, a lively sense of the importance of their own impressions, a more valuable kind of source is the contemporary journal, written from day to day during the events described. When written by men who were the helmsmen of a Commonwealth, like John Winthrop (No. 107), they have the highest historical value ; for they are forged fresh from the mint, and reveal what even the official records may conceal. Even when written without any expectation of publication, they furnish valuable evidence ; no better example can be found than the Diary of Samuel Sewall, "The Puritan Pepys" (No. 149). The letters of public men, or even of private men, have the same double value of an unvarnished tale, written at the moment ; and they also reveal the writer's character. Such are the familiar letters of Colonel Fitzhugh (No. 87). More elaborate are the arguments or controversial pamphlets intended for circulation at the time, such as Butler's attack on the Virginia government (No. 66), and the accounts of the Andros Revolution (No. 136). Narratives composed immediately after events have passed, like Quentin Stockwell's account of his Indian captivity (No. 147) have a sober value.

Historical sources, then, are nothing less nor more than records made at or near the time of the events, described by men who took part in them, and are, therefore, qualified to speak.

---◆---

2. Educative Value of Sources

L IKE other literature, the office of history is to record, to instruct, and to please. It is a subject which has natural claims on the interest of a student or reader, for it deals with stirring events, with human character, and with the welfare of the race. There must be in history something to arouse the minds of young and old, and to develop them when aroused. The training element of history as a school subject has been discussed in many places, and a list of references to such discussions appears in Channing and Hart's *Guide to the Study of American History*, § 15. The value of sources, as a part of that study, has long been in the minds of the scholars and antiquarians who have painfully preserved and reprinted the old narratives; but they are less appreciated by the reading or teaching public.

As a record, sources are the basis of history, but not mere raw material like the herbaria of the botanist, or the chemicals of a laboratory, stuffs to be destroyed in discovering their nature; as utterances of men living when they were made, they have in them the breath of human life; history is the biology of human conduct. Nobody can settle any historical question without an appeal to the sources, or without taking into account the character of the actors in history.

Nobody remembers all the history he reads; the bold and striking events seize hold of his mind, and around them he associates the rest. But a source gives that bold and striking event in its most durable form. Volumes about the Iroquois will not tell us so much that we shall remember as Father Jogues' account of their cruelty to him (No. 40).

Hence the instructing power of history goes back in considerable part to the sources. They do not tell all their own story; they need to be arranged and set in order by the historian, who on the solid piers of their assurances spans his continuous bridge of narrative. But there are two sides to history : the outward events in their succession, with which secondary historians alone can deal; and the inner spirit, which is revealed only by the sources. If we could not know both things, it would be better to know how Mary Dyer justified herself for being a Quakeress (No. 140), than how her trial was carried on. The source, therefore, throws an inner light on events; secondary writers may go over them, collate them, compare them, sometimes supplement them; but can never supersede them.

As for entertainment, the narratives of discovery are the Arabian Nights of History for their marvels and adventures. The quiet unassuming tale of the Conquest of the great country of Peru by a handful of Spanish adventurers (No. 22), the story of Pocahontas (No. 64), are part of the world's library of romantic literature. Other pieces please by their quaintness, such as Harrison's account of England in 1586 (No.

44), and John Josselyn's malicious account of New England (No. 145). Others of these selections are milestones in the growth of a national literature — all the way from Bradford's beautiful account of the Puritan exiles from England (No. 149) through the *Bay Psalm Book's* rugged measures (No. 138) to Cotton Mather's sounding brass and tinkling cymbal (No. 148). As an account of bold spirits engaged in desperate adventures, of the planting of a civilization in the wilderness, of the growth of free government, the sources of American history are a contribution to the world's literature.

———◆———

3. Classification of Sources on Colonization

ASSUMING that the use of sources needs no further argument, the next important question is, What sort of material is available on the period covered by this volume?

Among the " monuments " are the Pueblos of the southwest, and the mounds of the Mississippi Valley. But the most important unwritten records stand along the seacoast. These consist of old forts, such as that at St. Augustine, Florida ; of public buildings, of which very few date from the seventeenth century ; of churches, as the little Roger Williams building (1634) in Salem, Massachusetts, and St. Luke's in Smithfield, Virginia (1632) ; and of dwelling houses, of which the Fairbanks House in Dedham, Massachusetts, and the Whitefields' in Guilford, Connecticut, are good examples. Such remains can be used by visiting them, or by showing photographs of them. In several parts of the country, as the National Museum at Washington, the Field Museum in Chicago, and the Peabody Museum in Cambridge, there are collections of the implements and arts of the aborigines of North and South America.

Manuscript records ordinarily appeal only to the investigator, for whose benefit are the suggestions in Winsor's *Narrative and Critical History*, VIII, 413 *et seq. ;* and in Channing and Hart, *Guide to American History*, § 35. Two classes of written records may, however, sometimes be used by beginners : family papers and local records. From the unpublished town records of Brookline, Massachusetts, pupils in the high schools have drawn some interesting material. It is worth while to make pupils acquainted with the handwriting of the sixteenth and seventeenth centuries, and many facsimiles are to be found in Winsor's *Narrative and Critical History* and in many other places.

Official public records have been little used in this volume, because they seldom give a résumé of the previous history ; examples have, however, been introduced of governors' reports (Nos. 70, 116, 156) ; of minutes of a colonial council (No. 74), and of colonial legislatures (Nos. 65, 104, 121, 131, 160) ; of colonial statutes (Nos. 84, 144) ; of a colonial constitution (No. 120) ; of colonizing corporations' proceedings (Nos. 50, 128) ; of royal proclamations (Nos. 53, 83) ; of a charter (No. 158), and instructions (No. 54) ; of the proceedings of a colonial federation (Nos. 129, 170) ; of an Indian deed (No. 123), and an Indian treaty (No. 92) ; of a colonial court (No. 141), and a county court (No. 143) ; and of a papal bull (No. 18).

Such records have been printed in elaborate collections for nearly all the twelve colonies formed before 1700. Sets of the charters are printed in Ben: Perley Poore, *Federal and State Constitutions;* in H. W. Preston, *Documents relative to American History;* in many numbers of the *American History Leaflets* and *Old South Leaflets;* and in other collections. Lists of these collections, with exact titles, may be found in Channing and Hart, *Guide to American History,* § 29.

In the same place may be found a list of the printed colonial laws, of which hardly any state has made up a full set; the best collections are Hening's *Statutes* for Virginia and various editions of Massachusetts laws. Many early laws are printed as appendices to histories of the colonies (enumerated in Channing and Hart, *Guide to American History,* § 23).

The printed records of the colonial councils and assemblies are also enumerated in Channing and Hart, § 29. Part of the earliest of these records — Virginia, 1619 — is reprinted below (No. 65). The best printed records are those of New Hampshire, Massachusetts, Connecticut (and New Haven), Pennsylvania, Maryland, and North Carolina.

Narratives of the explorers and discoverers are among the most fascinating sources for American history, and they have been freely drawn upon for this volume. Among the writers thus cited are the Icelandic Sagas (No. 16), Columbus (Nos. 17, 19), Gómara (No. 21), Hernando Pizarro (No. 22), a Gentleman of Elvas (No. 23), Jarimillo (No. 24), Philips (No. 25), Hawkins (No. 29), Pretty (No. 30), Drake (No. 31), Barlowe (No. 32), Ralegh (No. 33), Verrazano (No. 34), Cartier (No. 35), Laudonnière (No. 36), Lescarbot (No. 37), Juet (No. 38), Champlain (No. 39), Jogues (No. 40), Le Clercq (No. 41), Marquette (No.

42), Membré (No. 43), John Smith (Nos. 62, 90), Strachey (No. 60), Lechford (Nos. 91, 110), Hamor (No. 64), Andrew White (No. 73), Hammond (No. 75), Alsop (No. 76), Wilson (No. 81), Johnson (Nos. 105, 119), Josselyn (Nos. 125, 145), Dankers and Sluyter (Nos. 145, 172), De Vries (No. 151), Thomas (No. 168), Michaelius (No. 169).

Hardly distinguishable from the explorers in many cases are the contemporary accounts left by commonwealth builders. Extracts from the records of colonization companies may be found in Nos. 50, 52, 67, 128 ; of proprietors' instructions in Nos. 72, 78, 164. Narratives by the following colonial governors have been used : Columbus (No. 19), Bradford (Nos. 49, 97, 99, 100, 117), Keift (No. 95), John Smith (No. 62), Wingfield (No. 63), Gates (No. 61), Penn (Nos. 77, 161, 162), Berkeley (Nos. 68, 70), Bennett (No. 69), John Winthrop (No. 107), Calvert (Nos. 72, 77), Winslow (No. 107), Dongan (No. 156), Endicott (No. 132).

Other colonists, hardly less important than the governor, have left many letters or narratives. Such are Woodward (No. 79), Wilson (No. 81), Fitzhugh (No. 87), Clayton (No. 88), Hartwell, Blair, and Chilton (No. 89), Child (No. 111), Ward (No. 112), Gorton (No. 113), Weare (No. 126), Nowell and others (No. 139), Sewall (No. 149), Van der Donck (No. 154), Ten Hove (No. 155), Hudde (No. 159), Pastorius (No. 163), Barclay, Forbes, and Lawrie (No. 167), Thomas (No. 168). With them may be included some colonial biographies, as Norton's *Cotton* (No. 96), and Cotton Mather's *Phips* (No. 148).

The great trading and planting companies are here represented by extracts from the records or the missives of the Virginia Company (Nos. 50, 67), the Council of New England (Nos. 51, 128), the Massachusetts Company (No. 52), the Dutch West India Company (No. 150).

Accounts of the Indians and their relations with the colonists, come in incidentally in many of the above, and especially in the following pieces : Jogues (No. 40), Strachey (No. 60), Lechford (No. 91), treaty (No. 92), Megalopolis (No. 152), Underhill (No. 127), Randolph (No. 133), Hutchinson (No. 134), Stockwell (No. 147), deed (No. 123).

Contemporary English and European discussions of colonization are quoted from Waldseemüller (No. 20), Pasqualigo and Soncino (No. 26), Anonymous (Nos. 27, 48), Hakluyt (Nos. 28, 46), Hayes (No. 47), Harrison (No. 45), Werden (No. 166).

Ecclesiastical affairs and toleration are discussed especially in Robinson (No. 55), Berkeley (No. 70), Maryland (No. 84), "R. G." (No. 85), John Calvin (No. 93), Davenport (No. 94), Child (No. 111), Ward (No. 112), Williams (No. 115), Bulkeley (No. 130), Mary Dyer (No. 140), Michaelius (No. 169).

Special discussions of emigration may be found in Peckham (No. 45), Higginson (No. 56), Clapp (No. 57), Charles I (No. 53), Butler (No. 66), Gates (No. 61). Slavery was the special interest of Godwyn (No. 86). Education comes into the accounts of William and Mary (No. 89), and of Harvard College (No. 137).

Discussions of popular government are quoted from Butler (No. 66), Hammond (No. 75), Calvin (No. 93), Davenport (No. 94), Mayflower passengers (No. 98), Bradford (No. 100), Winslow (No. 101), Roger White (No. 102), Saltonstall (No. 106), Norton (No. 96), Winthrop (Nos. 107, 118), Child (No. 111), Johnson (No. 119), Connecticut (No. 122), Arnold (No. 114), Danforth (No. 136), Van der Donck (No. 154), "Gentlemen of N. Y." (No. 157), Newark (No. 165).

The above narratives, and others like them not quoted in this volume, are printed in many different fashions. Of many there are original editions, now very rare, as Edward Johnson's *Wonder-working Providence* (No. 105). Some of these have been reprinted in the original, or in the translation, often with critical notes; for instance, Trumbull's edition of Lechford's *Plain Dealing*. Many others appear in the transactions of the various learned societies (see A. P. C. Griffin, *Bibliography of American Historical Societies*, republished from the *Annual Report of the American Historical Society*, 1895 ; and Channing and Hart, *Guide to American History*, § 31) ; in collections of state executive documents (*Guide*, § 29), or as appendices to local histories (*Guide*, § 23). Collected reprints will be mentioned below (No. 5). The works of some of the early writers have been collected, as those of William Penn. Many interesting and valuable sources are reprinted in historical periodicals (*Guide*, § 26) ; but there were no newspapers or gazettes in the colonies before 1689.

Illustrative sources may be found in the colonial poetry of which the *News from Virginia* (No. 82) and the *Bay Psalm Book* (No. 138) are here used, and in sermons and the few books of general literature for which Moses Coit Tyler's *History of American Literature* is the best guide. Lists of historical novels and poems appear in Channing and Hart, *Guide to American History*, § 36.

4. Libraries of Sources in Colonial History

NO library has anything approaching a complete set either of originals or reprints of the historical writings of colonial times. Nevertheless, one who examines the books in a special library of Americana
is amazed at the number, variety, and interest of the material. Six
great libraries deserve special mention — all growing collections, and
several of them purchasers of rarities at great prices. The John Carter
Brown Library in Providence, kept up as a private collection, but under
the direction of a trained specialist librarian ; the Lenox Library in
New York, also made by a private man, but now a part of the great New
York Public Library ; the Boston Public Library, containing the Prince
Collection and other valuable accumulations of many private gifts, supplemented by purchases ; and the Harvard College Library, which contains a well classified collection, abounding in rarities ; the fifth is the
Library of Congress, which contains great treasures of early books, as
yet uncatalogued and almost unexplored ; the sixth is the library of the
American Antiquarian Society in Worcester, especially rich in colonial
and later newspapers.

Of many early reprints there are but half a dozen copies extant, and
it is almost impossible for later libraries to secure sets equally complete
with the older collections. Nevertheless, there are numerous and valuable Americana in the libraries of Cornell University, Columbia University, and the University of Pennsylvania. In each state a special
historical society is likely to contain early printed works and reprints
on the history of that state. Some libraries will lend rare books direct,
or through a local librarian who makes himself responsible.

Abroad, the largest collection of Americana is that of the British
Museum, containing some unique pamphlets not to be found in Amer-
ica ; and there are also rare pamphlets in the Bodleian Library of Oxford.
In England also is a great reservoir of colonial manuscript material,
chiefly in the Public Record Office. Transcripts of many of these docu-
ments have been made and transferred to America ; for instance, the
Minutes of the Lords of Trade in the Pennsylvania Historical Society.
Continental archives have also material on discovery and colonization,
especially those of Simancas in Spain, and those of France, Genoa, and
Venice.

5. Reprints of Collected Sources

NEARLY all the important early works have been reprinted, some·
times verbatim, oftener with corrections of spelling and grammar.
Many such reprints are made by historical societies ; others are gathered
in series, as Rider's *Rhode Island Historical Tracts*, and the *Publications*
of the Narragansett Club.   Others appear in special reprint editions,
with introduction and notes by a special editor.   A few have been fac-
similed, notably Bradford's *History* (Nos. 100–102).   For making transcripts or verifying a passage, the original edition is always preferable.

For many of the separate colonies there are collections of documents.
They may be found through Channing and Hart, *Guide to American
History*, §§ 23, 29 ; and Winsor, *Narrative and Critical History*, II–V.
There are also several valuable collections of related documents, of which
the following may be mentioned.   The two colonial collections specially
mentioned contain documents concerning other colonies.   These titles
do not include collections of sources on the history of a single colony,
nor colonial archives, nor the many valuable collections of state and
local historical societies ; such material may be found through Channing
and Hart, *Guide*, §§ 23, 29, 33, 34, 77–130.

Peter Force, *Tracts and Other Papers relating to the Colonies in North
    America*. 4 vols. Washington, 1836–1846. — A very interesting set,
    freely used in compiling this volume.

Gorges Society [*no general title*]. 5 vols. Portland, 1884–1893. — Reprints
    in New England history.

Richard Hakluyt, *The Principal Navigations, Voyages, Traffiques, and Discov
    eries of the English Nation* (Edmund Goldsmid, editor). 16 vols. Edir ·
    burgh, 1885–1890. — Reprint modernized of the original editions of 1589
    (one volume) and 1599–1600 (3 vols. in 2, folio) ; also a reprint edition of
    1809–1812), with additions. — Very interesting and valuable ; supplemented
    by the next title.

Hakluyt Society [London], *Works issued by the Hakluyt Society*. London,
    1847–1896. — About one hundred volumes now issued ; edited reprints and
    transcripts of manuscripts not before printed, and invaluable translations.

Ebenezer Hazard, *Historical Collections ; consisting of State Papers and Other
    Documents*. 2 vols. Philadelphia, 1792–1794. — Very useful.

Albert Bushnell Hart and Edward Channing, editors, *American History Leaf·
    lets*. 30 numbers. New York, 1892–1896. — Includes many colonial docu
    ments.

Edwin Doak Mead, editor, *Old South Leaflets.* 75 numbers, bound in 3 vols Boston, 1888–1896. — Many historical pieces; texts not carefully collated. Valuable for schools.

Joel Munsell, editor, *Historical Series.* 24 vols. Albany, 1857–1895.

Edmund Bailey O'Callaghan and Berthold Fernow, editors, *Documents relative to the Colonial History of the State of New York.* 15 vols. Albany, 1856–1887. — Much matter not relating exclusively to New York; includes a useful index volume. Vols. I–III, IX, XII–XIV on the period before 1689.

William Stevens Perry, editor, *Historical Collections relating to the American Colonial Church.* 5 vols. Hartford, 1870–1878. — A very small edition, and therefore rare.

Ben: Perley Poore, compiler, *The Federal and State Constitutions, Colonial Charters, and Other Organic Laws of the United States.* 2 parts. Washington, 1877. — A much-needed reprint is in preparation (1897).

Prince Society, *Publications.* 21 vols. Boston, 1865–1894. — Reprints of rare publications or of manuscripts.

Samuel Purchas, *Hakluytus Posthumus, or Purchas his Pilgrimes.* 5 vols. London, 1625–1626. — Reprints of early voyages; now very rare.

William L. Saunders, editor, *The Colonial Records of North Carolina.* 10 vols. Raleigh, 1886–1890. — Very inconveniently arranged, without contents or index, but abounding in general material. Vol. I on colonization.

Edwin Clarence Stedman and Ellen Mackay Hutchinson, *A Library of American Literature from the Earliest Settlement to the Present Time.* 11 vols. New York, 1888–1890. — Vol. I and part of Vol. II on colonization; very well chosen, though not with immediate reference to the historical value of the pieces. An excellent set for a school library.

———————

6. Select Library of Sources on Colonization

THIS volume contains examples of many colonial writers, but only a short extract from most of them, and many do not appear here at all. For careful study of colonial history and for extensive topical work the student or pupil needs a greater range of material; and every library and high school ought to have at least a few of the sources in complete editions.

First in importance are the general printed collections mentioned in the preceding section (No. 5), or so many of them as the library can afford. Next may come selections from the records of one colony out of each of the three groups of Southern, New England, and Middle Colonies. Virginia, Massachusetts (including Plymouth), and New York were the oldest in each group, and have the completest literature. Next to them in historical interest come Maryland, Connecticut, and Pennsylvania.

Below will be found a list of the most useful sources and general books containing sources on the three typical colonies. Most of the volumes may be readily purchased new or at second hand, though the large sets are expensive. To these should be added such other colonial records, laws, collections, and histories containing documents as the library may afford (Lists in Channing and Hart, *Guide*, §§ 23, 29, 95–130), especially of that colony which has the closest relation with the state or place in which the library is situated. The local records (if printed) should of course be included ; and a few of the typical town records, as Worcester, Lancaster, Watertown, Providence, East Hampton (L.I.).

VIRGINIA

The Virginia material is scattered, and difficult to bring within moderate compass. The list here given should be increased by adding some of the individual narratives, found in such collections as Force's *Tracts*, Hakluyt's *Voyages*, and Hazard's *Collections* (see No. 5 above). This list is of course brief and incomplete.

[Robert Beverly], *The History of Virginia, in Four Parts* (1584–1720). London, 1705 (and later editions). — Beverly's memory went back of 1689.

Alexander Brown, *Genesis of the United States.* 2 vols. Boston and New York, 1890. — Valuable material, including some interesting documents translated from the Spanish archives.

John (Daly) Burk, *The History of Virginia from its First Settlement to the Present Day.* 3 vols. Petersburg, Va., 1804–1805. — With appendices of documents.

Ralphe Hamor, *A Trve Discovrse on the Present Estate of Virginia . . . till June,* 1614. London, 1615; (reprint, Albany, 1860).

Hartwell, Blair, and Chilton, *The Present State of Virginia and the College.* London, 1727.

William Waller Hening, *The Statutes-at-Large, being a Collection of all the Laws of Virginia* (1619–1792) ; 13 vols. Philadelphia and New York, 1823. — Perhaps the most important set of colonial statutes printed.

Edward Duffield Neill, *Virginia Carolorum: The Colony under the Rule of Charles the First and Second.* Albany, 1886. — Includes interesting documents.

Edward Duffield Neill, *Virginia Vetusta, during the Reign of James the First.* Albany, 1885. — Includes interesting documents.

Conway Robinson and R. A. Brock, *Proceedings of the Virginia Company*, 1619–1624. 2 vols. (in the Virginia Historical Society, *Collections, New Series*, VII, VIII). Richmond, 1888, 1889.

John Smith, *Generall Historie of Virginia, New England and the Summer Isles from* 1584–1626. London, 1626 (also later editions). — Indispensable for its information and its style, but less trustworthy than earlier books by the same author.

William Stith, *The History of the First Discovery and Settlement of Virginia*. New York, 1865 (Joseph Sabin, *Reprints*, VI). — Includes reprints of documents.

Virginia Historical Society, *Collections, New Series*. 11 vols. Richmond, 1882–1892. — Many valuable reprints of documents.

The Virginia Magazine of History and Biography. Richmond, 1893. — The present publication of the Virginia Historical Society. Includes the invaluable Fitzhugh papers.

Thomas Hicks Wynne and W. S. Gilman, editors, *Colonial Records of Virginia* ([*Virginia*] *Senate Doc. Extra*). Richmond, 1874.

MASSACHUSETTS

The colony about the history of which we have most first-hand information is Massachusetts; her records were well kept and well preserved; her public men felt that they were making history of which an account ought to be left for posterity; her historical society is the oldest and perhaps the most active in the Union. The list below is meagre, when compared with the available material.

Boston Town Records from 1634–1789. Almost 30 vols. Boston, 1876–1896. — Very full and characteristic.

William Bradford, *History of Plymouth Plantation* [to 1645], (edited by Charles Deane) in Massachusetts Historical Society, *Collections*, III; also in a separate facsimile reprint. London, 1896. — The foundation of our knowledge of early Plymouth.

William Hubbard, *A Narrative of the Troubles with the Indians in New England*. Boston, 1667. (Revision, edited by S. G. Drake, Boston, 1865.)

Thomas Hutchinson, *A Collection of Original Papers Relative to the History of the Colony of Massachusetts Bay* [1628–1750]. Boston, 1769. — A useful set.

Edward Johnson, *Wonder Working Providence of Sion's Savior* in New England. London, 1654. (Reprint edited by W. F. Poole, Andover, 1867.)

John Josselyn, *Account of Two Voyages to New England*. London, 1675. (Reprint, Boston, 1875.)

Thomas Lechford, *Plain Dealing, or News from New England*. London, 1642. (Reprint edited by Trumbull, Boston, 1867.)

Massachusetts Historical Society, *Collections*. 6 series (about 60 vols.)
Boston, 1792–1896. — Abounds in important sources, including the Sewall
diary, and the letters of Sewall and Winthrop.

Massachusetts Historical Society, *Proceedings*, 1791–1883. 20 vols. Boston.
Second series, 1883–1896. 10 vols. Boston.

Cotton Mather, *Magnalia Christi Americana: or, The Ecclesiastical History
of New England.* London, 1702. (Reprint edition. 2 vols. Hartford,
1820.)

Prince Society, *Publications*. 21 vols. Albany and Boston, 1865–1892.

Samuel Sewall, *Diary* [1674–1729]. 3 vols. (In Massachusetts Historical
Society, *Collections*, 5th series, Vols. V–VII). Boston, 1878–1882. — The
best colonial diary extant.

Nathaniel Bradstreet Shurtleff and others, compilers, *Records of the Colony of
New Plymouth in New England* [1620–1692]. 12 vols. Boston, 1855–
1861. — The official publication.

Nathaniel B. Shurtleff, editor, *Records of the Governor and Company of the
Massachusetts Bay in New England* (1628–1686). 5 vols. Boston, 1853–
1854. — The official publication.

John Winthrop, *History of New England* [1638–1648]. 2 vols. Edited by
James Savage, Boston, 1825–1826; new edition, also edited by James
Savage, 1853. — A source of the highest value, but too coarse for children.

Alexander Young, *Chronicles of the First Planters of the Colony of Massachusetts Bay* (1623–1636). Boston, 1846. — A valuable and correct compilation.

Alexander Young, *Chronicles of the Pilgrim Fathers of the Colony of Plymouth* (1602–1625). Boston, 1841. — A valuable and correct publication.
Includes Mourt's *Relation*, not elsewhere printed.

NEW YORK

The two official collections of documents, supplemented by the transactions of the local societies, contain most of the valuable material on
this colony, so that reprints of individual narratives are less necessary.

John Romeyn Brodhead, *History of the State of New York*. 2 vols. — Vol.
I, 1609–1664, New York, 1853; Vol. II, 1664–1691, New York, 1871.—With
documents.

Long Island Historical Society, *Memoirs*. 4 vols. Brooklyn, 1867–1889. —
Includes several pieces indispensable for New York history.

New York Historical Society, *Collections* (about 30 vols. to 1890). New
York, 1811. — Very important and useful in both Dutch and English New
York.

New York Historical Society, *Proceedings*. 7 vols. in 4. New York, 1844.

John Warner Barber and Henry Howe, *Historical Collections of the State of New York*. New York, 1845. — Local history; hardly scientific.

Edmund Bailey O'Callaghan, *The Documentary History of the State of New York*. 4 vols. Albany, 1849–1851. — Not many pieces.

Edmund Bailey O'Callaghan and Berthold Fernow, editors, *Documents relative to the Colonial History of the State of New York*. 15 vols. Albany, 1856–1887. — One of the best sets ever published on colonial history; includes documents of all kinds, conveniently arranged, printed, and indexed; valuable on all the colonies.

Edmund Bailey O'Callaghan, compiler, *Laws and Ordinances of New Netherland*, 1638–1674. Albany, 1868.

William Smith, *The History of the late Province of New York, from its Discovery to 1762*. 2 vols. (New York Historical Society, *Collections*, Vols. IV and V.) New York, 1829–1830. — With documents.

SMALL COLLECTION

For a small library which can afford only a scanty collection of sources, the following works are most important for the period of discovery and colonization.

American History Leaflets. 30 numbers. New York, 1892–1896.

George Alsop, *Character of the Province of Maryland*. London, 1666. (New edition, edited by T. G. Shea, New York, 1869.)

Samuel Greene Arnold, *The History of Rhode Island*. 2 vols. New York, 1859. — With many documents.

John Leeds Bozman, *History of Maryland* (1632–1660). 2 vols. Baltimore, 1837. — With documents.

William Bradford, *History of the Plymouth Plantation* [to 1645], (edited by Charles Deane) in Massachusetts Historical Society, *Collections*, III; also in a separate facsimile reprint, London, 1896.

B. R. Carroll, compiler, *Historical Collections of South Carolina* (1492–1776). 2 vols. New York, 1836. — Many interesting papers on the South.

Benjamin Franklin French, *Historical Collections of Louisiana*. 5 vols. New York. 1846–1853. — Covers the French relations in the Southwest.

R. Hakluyt, *Principal Navigations, Voyages, Traffiques, and Discoveries of the English Nation*. Edited by Edmund Goldsmid. Edinburgh, 1885–1890. — Of the 16 vols., those which bear on America are VII (England's naval exploits), XII–XV (America), XVI (circumnavigation). — The older 3-volume editions (quarto) may also be picked up. A treasury of adventurous narrative.

John Hammond, *Leah and Rachael; or, The Two Fruitfull Sisters, Virginia and Maryland*. London, 1656. Reprinted in Force, *Tracts*, III.

Francis Lister Hawks, *History of North Carolina.* 2d edition. 2 vols. Fayetteville, 1857–1858. — With documents.

Samuel Hazard, *Annals of Pennsylvania from the Discovery of the Delaware, 1609–1682.* Philadelphia, 1850. — Many extracts in one bulky volume.

Edward Duffield Neill, *The Founders of Maryland.* Albany, 1861. — Resembles his *Virginia* in plan.

Edward Duffield Neill, *Virginia Carolorum; The Colony under the Rule of Charles the First and Second.* Albany, 1886.

Edward Duffield Neill, *Virginia Vetusta during the Reign of James the First.* Albany, 1885.

Edmund Bailey O'Callaghan and Berthold Fernow, editors, *Documents relative to the Colonial History of the State of New York.* 15 vols. Albany, 1856–1887. — The most important volumes for the seventeenth century are I, II, IX, XII.

Old South Leaflets. 75 numbers bound in 3 vols. Boston, 1888–1896.

Samuel Sewall, *Diary* (in Massachusetts Historical Society, *Collections*, 5th series, vols. V–VII). — Inexhaustible in reference and its view of Puritan society.

William Strachey, *The Historie of Travaile into Virginia Brittania* (Hakluyt Society, *Works*). London, 1849.

Benjamin Trumbull, *Complete History of Connecticut, Civil and Ecclesiastical, from 1630 to 1764.* 2 vols. New Haven, 1818.

John Winthrop, *History of New England* [1638–1648]. 2 vols. Edited by James Savage, Boston, 1825–1826. (New edition, also edited by James Savage, 1853.)

Alexander Young, *Chronicles of the First Planters of the Colony of Massachusetts Bay* (1623–1636). Boston, 1846.

Alexander Young, *Chronicles of the Pilgrim Fathers of the Colony of Plymouth* (1602–1625). Boston, 1841. — These books are out of print and quoted at high prices.

CHAPTER II — USE OF SOURCES

7. How to find Colonial Sources

TO the accumulating mass of original material there was till a few years ago no general guide. The histories of the eighteenth century (from which quotations will be made in Vol. II) used what they could find. The second group of historians, headed by George Bancroft and Jared Sparks and Francis Parkman, made elaborate collections of transcripts of documents. Winsor, Charles Francis Adams, Bruce, and others, the present school of historians, have liberally used the printed records and can be tracked through their foot-notes.

There are now three methods of reaching sources which bear on colonial history. First, and most convenient for a quick search to verify a particular point, the elaborate foot-notes in general or local histories. A list of serviceable secondary works will be found later (No. 15). Most important for this purpose are J. A. Doyle, *English in America;* J. G. Palfrey, *History of New England;* George Bancroft, *History of the United States* (original edition); W. B. Weeden, *Economic and Social History;* P. A. Bruce, *Economic History of Virginia.* Most such books contain a bibliography of the books cited. In the monographs on colonial history and institutions, especially in the *Johns Hopkins University Studies*, will also be found reliable foot-notes.

The second method is through the catalogues of libraries containing valuable collections. The most important are those of the Boston Public Library (*Bates Hall*) and *Supplement;* Boston Athenæum, Peabody Institute (Baltimore); and the card catalogue of the Harvard College Library. The catalogues of the state libraries and state historical societies are also sometimes valuable.

The third method is by special bibliographies of the subject. Most elaborate is Joseph Sabin, *Dictionary of Books relating to America* (20 vols., New York, 1867-1894), which is an attempt to give the titles (alphabetically by authors) of all the books printed on America up to

1867, with many references to the libraries in which particular rarities are found. When completed the work is to have an index by subjects ; it includes no comparison of the value of books mentioned. The most remarkable contribution to the knowledge of sources is Justin Winsor, *Narrative and Critical History of America* (Boston, 1886–1889). This monument of learning and well-directed industry devotes eight large volumes to narrative and to critical statements as to the bearing and value of authorities, both original and secondary ; and makes many mentions of libraries in which the books are to be found. It is invaluable to the student of sources, for it searches out and discriminates between editions, it mentions reprints, and it is arranged in a convenient method and indexed.

The most recent book (in which the authors acknowledge the help they have gained from Winsor) is Channing and Hart, *Guide to the Study of American History* (New York, 1896). This is a brief work, covering in 500 small pages the field of Winsor's volumes, and extending on down to 1865 ; the sources mentioned are selected out of the mass and arranged in successive paragraphs. In Part I are various classified lists, chiefly of sources ; and under each of the topical headings is a special selection of sources.

With these aids, students who can have the use of a large library may go direct to the sources most important for their purpose. There are also special guides to the voluminous collections of the state historical societies ; viz., A. P. C. Griffin, *Bibliography of American Historical Societies*, republished from the *Annual Report of the American Historical Association*, 1895 ; a selected list in Channing and Hart, *Guide*, § 31. Colonial records are enumerated in the *Guide*, § 29.

To locate a particular book in a library is often a matter of patience and dexterity. The first thing is to get the exact title from the catalogue or from some other printed list ; and to be sure that there is no confusion of editions. A critical reprint is an aid in understanding the bearing of the source, and Winsor is an unfailing aid on critical points. The first authoritative edition of a source is usually to be preferred.

In making notes and citing references, the rule is absolute that every extract which is in the words of the author should be set off by quotation marks ; and that all omissions within such a quoted extract should be shown by points or stars (. . . ＊ ＊ ＊). Exact dates should be noted, with especial observance of the fact that dates between January 1 and March 25 fall in one year in "Old Style" reckoning, and in the

c

following year in " New Style." In 1752 England accepted the new
calendar ; and all later dates are in " New Style." In old documents,
since March is the first month, September is the seventh (as the name
suggests), and December is the tenth. A common precaution (some-
times found in the original) is to give both years ; as February 1, 16$\frac{31}{32}$.

---

8. Use of Sources by Teachers

OF the three offices of sources in teaching — furnishing material, furnishing illustration, and giving insight into the spirit of the times —
all are important. It is not to be expected that any but the most highly
trained specialist will found all or his chief knowledge of history on
sources ; but parts of the field may thus be underlaid by actual contact
with the material. For example, such topics as the mishaps of the first
Virginia Colony (Nos. 64–69), the quarrels of Plymouth and Merry-
mount (No. 103), the Revolution of 1689 (No. 136), may be readily
worked up from the narratives of the time ; and even such a limited
collection as this volume throws light upon them.

For illustrations and additions in class work, some study of the sources
greatly enlivens the exercise and interests the pupil. For instance, the
quotations from the *Bay Psalm Book* (No. 138) add a quaint side light
to a lesson in the Puritan church system. De Vries' account of his
voyage to America (No. 151) brings out the trading side of the Dutch
settlements. Philips' story of his life in Mexico (No. 25) is a supplement to any account of the Spanish Colonies. Brief extracts from such
originals, or a paraphrase of their narrative, will serve to rivet the more
general events in the minds of the pupils.

Perhaps the most important service which sources perform for the
teacher is to fill his mind — and through him the pupil's mind — with
the real spirit of the age described. John Smith (Nos. 62, 90), whatever his truthfulness, was a man writing to fellow-men, and we cannot
help sharing his experiences while reading. The Connecticut laws
(No. 144) have in their rugged chapters the sternness of Puritan character. The gossip of Samuel Sewall (No. 149) is a sample of the daily
table talk of his generation. William Penn's letters (No. 162) reveal
the compound of shrewd self-interest and broad public spirit which made
up his character. In the exuberant and prosperous correspondence of

Colonel Fitzhugh (No. 87), we get an insight into plantation life, which is heightened by Clayton's methodical account of tobacco planting (No. 88) ; and the whole wretchedness and heartlessness of the persecution of the Quakers are set forth in the records of the trials (Nos. 140–142). Contact with the sources has some of the effects of visiting the scenes, in the way of leaving in the mind a clear-cut impression.

Sources will therefore bear reading several or many times, so that the mind may be permeated with them. The teacher cannot be too familiar with the earliest statements of actual discoverers, as those of Columbus (No. 17), of Verrazano (No. 34), and of Hudson (No. 38). The sharp words which passed between king and colonies under Charles II (No. 132) are the expression of whole lines of policy. Of course the teacher will also use connecting secondary matter, so as to know how one event follows another, and what is the relation between events.

Some very successful teachers deliberately choose what may be called the episodic method, especially with young classes ; they present a series of intellectual pictures of stirring events, without trying to make a complete narrative. Such a method has much to commend it, and is aided by the use of brief selected sources.

---

9. Use of Sources by Pupils

ONE of the main objects of this work is to bring together in convenient form a body of material suitable for use by pupils, even though immature. Hence pieces have been selected which have an interest in themselves, though taken out of their connection ; and there has been care to exclude numerous passages which are suitable enough for older students, but which are too strong and plain spoken for children. Pupils cannot be expected to found their knowledge of history on sources, because they have not the judgment to distinguish between the different kinds of material. But it is believed that the use of such a collection as this — or such parts of it as there may be time to read — will fix many of the most important events and tendencies mentioned in the text-book. For instance, no second-hand account of the Indians can compare in " holding power " with the narratives of Jogues (No. 40) and Megapolensis (No. 152), or of Quintin Stockwell (No. 147). The steady and calculating pressure of the whites on the Indians is the thing best worth remembering in the Indian wars; and what could more clearly set it forth than such a narrative as Captain Underhill's (No. 127).

Perhaps the principal value of the educational side of sources for pupils is in the aid such material gives to intelligent topical work and to the preparation of "special reports." Of course many of the advantages of topical study (which is discussed at large in Channing and Hart, *Guide to American History*, §§ 67, 68) may be had from the use of good secondary books, new to the user. But such work does not teach the most important lesson of all: that history is the search for truth, and that truth must depend on the ultimate sources. No pupil by the use of this volume or any other collection can overset a conclusion of Parkman's; but he may learn that Parkman's greatness lies in his graphic and effective grouping of what he learned from sources.

A topic prepared with access to sources is therefore to the pupil's mind a creation, or rather a building up from materials known to be sound; it is an exercise in the kind of work which every historian must do, but which, in an elementary form, may be done by all just beginning the subject. It often may stimulate the pupil to learn more about the picturesque men whose narrative he reads, — the Quakers who protest (Nos. 140–142), and the seamen traders who open up the country (No. 151). It is therefore natural that the requirements in history for entrance to college, drawn up by a conference at Columbia University in February, 1896, should suggest sources as a part of the pupil's material.

As extracts for reading, many of the pieces in this volume have unique value. Crabbed and misspelled English, like that in Eden (No. 27), may at least suggest the growth of the language; while Harrison (No. 44), Josselyn (No. 125), Hamor (No. 64), and Thomas (No. 168), are examples of good, racy, joyous English, and are a real addition to the reading books.

To sum up briefly: the pupil may get a foothold in the world of colonial thought by reading properly chosen and related extracts from sources; he may get a peculiar and valuable training by working out some particular point. For instance, a very good exercise might be to ask him, from the material in this volume, to work up the condition of slaves; or the nature of colonial schools; or the dealings of the colonists with Indians; or the methods of royal control.

10. Use of Sources by Students and Investigators

TWO theories of historical teaching contest for the field of education through history; the first, or English method, is to ground students in well-chosen secondary books which they are to read, assimilate, and compare, and the divergences between which they must note, though they have not the means to reconcile them. Even in English universities, historical students use sources rather as illustrative than as a part of their study and training.

The opposing method expects some knowledge of the original material. The student's work is based upon some rather brief text-book or combination of books, but requires from all students collateral use of sources. The English method may be compared to an orderly ship canal, going straight to the end, with an ascertained depth of water, but always shallow and confined : the other method, to a natural river, abounding in deep pools, and joined by a multitude of branches which one cannot explore ; with many unfordable places ; but winding among human habitations, and giving glimpses of human life.

For study through sources has been devised a variety of written exercises, in which students gather and compare original evidence on important points. The merits of this system have been set forth above (Nos. 8, 9), but, while applicable to all ages, the use of sources becomes more and more valuable as the student advances ; and when he reaches the highest stage of the student's work, — the preparation of materials for a thorough-going account of some episode or period, — sources are the reservoirs from which he must draw most of his knowledge.

Such a collection as this book may serve as a beginning to the ambitious student ; but it will have served less than its design if it do not lead him to wish for the full texts from which these extracts are taken ; for additional information in some one question which interests him ; and for that acquaintance with original material and the methods of using it which give a student at once an insight into past times and a power to reproduce them before the minds of his readers.

Former historians have had to collect and organize their material in painful and expensive fashion. Jared Sparks and Francis Parkman each accumulated a costly set of transcripts of manuscripts. For future historians, much of the most valuable material is now in print ; and while no one will ever again set himself to George Bancroft's task of writing a

general history of the United States from sources, the special works
which are to be the foundation of new views must rest wholly on such
materials. Although large collections of printed sources are now available, many of them have not yet been examined by competent writers,
and discoveries of great importance are still to be made by the investigator. For instance, Alexander Brown in his comparatively recent
Genesis of the United States was the first to publish the despatches
which show how much Spain resented the planting of Virginia, a territory
which Spain claimed.

----

11. Use of Sources by Readers

FOR the numerous class of persons who have not the opportunity to
be students, or the inclination to investigate, sources are useful by
arousing the imagination and filling up the sketch made by the secondary
writer. All that has been said about the usefulness of materials for the
teacher and pupil applies equally to the self-taught. Sources alone are
one-sided, because they lack perspective and comparison of views, and
because they leave great gaps. Secondary works alone are also one-sided,
because they tell us about people, instead of letting the people tell us
about themselves. The ideal method is to read a brief sketch of colonial history such as Professor Fisher's *Colonial Era ;* then some illustrative extracts from sources ; then a fuller work like Doyle's *English in
America*, or John Fiske's books, with a larger collateral use of sources.
Upon the general subject of home study of American history, Channing
and Hart have a discussion in the *Guide to American History*, § 13.

Among the reprints in this book most useful to readers are : Columbus'
letters (Nos. 17, 19), Hawkins and Drake's adventures (Nos. 29, 30,
31), English claims (No. 48), Champlain and Jogues (Nos. 39, 40), Calvin's ideas of government (No. 93), the Virginia assembly (No. 65),
Berkeley (Nos. 68, 70), Edward Randolph (No. 133), Godwyn on
slavery (No. 86), Clayton on tobacco (No. 88) ; Governor Bradford
(Nos. 97–100, 117), Edward Johnson (Nos. 105, 119), Winthrop (No.
107), Lechford (No. 110), Davenport (No. 94) ; Roger Williams
(No. 115), New England Confederation (No. 129), the Quaker documents (Nos. 140–142), Cotton Mather (No. 148), Sewall's Diary (No.
149), De Vries (No. 151), Van der Donck (No. 154), Dankers and
Sluyter (Nos. 146, 172), Gabriel Thomas (No. 168).

12. Use of Sources by Libraries

THE triple object of most libraries is to inform, to entertain, and to instruct. Sources — as has been said above — fulfil all these objects. Boys who like Robinson Crusoe will certainly like Drake (No. 31), Captain John Smith (No. 62), Champlain (No. 39), and John Josselyn (No. 125), discoverer of the famous " Pilhannaw bird which ayries over the high hills of Ossapy." Girls who enjoy Strickland's *Queens of England* will like the courageous Ann Hutchinson as she faces and outwits her tormentors (No. 108). The student of the Dutch Republic will be glad to follow the Hollanders into the new world (Nos. 150-155, 169-172); the admirer of the Roman proconsuls should enjoy Lord Berkeley's power and loyalty (Nos. 68, 70). The colonial writers ooze with rugged, genuine human nature, interesting to those who are interested in their kind. Who can read of Ralegh's desperate expedition into Venezuela (No. 33), or of John Cotton (No. 96), or Pastorius and his Germans (No. 163), without wishing to know more of these men and their writings?

The other functions of the library — to inform and to instruct — are equally provided for by proper use of sources They are the adjunct of the teacher, the reservoir of the pupil, and the nutritious intellectual food of the general reader. Of the extracts in this volume, those from works like John Smith's (No. 62), Bradford's (Nos. 97-100), and Winthrop's (No. 107) are available in many libraries in the full text. But many of the extracts in this volume are hard to come at, and for a person whose time is limited, such a selection as this may be more useful. As regular standard reading matter, the libraries may well provide some sources.

In those larger libraries which aim at general completeness, or at special historical collections, it is an obvious duty to put abundant sources on their shelves, for the benefit of the students and investigators who must have a large range. The sources are scientific material comparable with the fossils of the palæontologists, by the use of which the popular books are to be written, as well as the general scientific treatises. Not to have them is to give up one of the principal objects of libraries, — the preservation of accumulated knowledge from age to age.

For libraries especially are intended the list of most valuable sources above (Nos. 5, 6), which may suggest purchases in this field.

13. Cautions in using Sources

VALUABLE as are original records, they must be used intelligently or they will mislead. First of all, they are not all of equal authority or of equal value. To turn an inexperienced student unguided among sources is to invite errors, for sometimes even sources are untruthful. For instance, how is the tyro to know that a New Hampshire Indian Deed, gravely printed by Hazard in his *Collections*, was a forgery made to substantiate land claims? Sometimes a writer bears internal evidence of malice or untruthfulness, as in Morton's *Revels of New Canaan* (No. 103), in which his animus against the Pilgrims is plain enough. But, without warning, how is one to know that Edmund Randolph (No. 133), shrewd observer as he was, was sent to the colonies with the mission of finding something wrong, and was bound to justify his employment. For many sources, the value depends on the writer's truthfulness, which cannot be attacked without training and sifting of later evidence : most reprints of old pieces, especially in the proceedings of historical societies, include a critical account of the writer. Other criticisms may be found in Moses Coit Tyler, *History of American Literature* (2 vols. published, New York, 1878) ; in Justin Winsor, *Narrative and Critical History* (Boston, 1886–1889) ; in Henry T. Tuckerman, *America and her Commentators* (New York, 1864) ; in S. Austin Allibone, *Critical Dictionary of English Literature and British and American Authors* (3 vols., Philadelphia, 1858–1871). Extracts from records and formal documents may usually be relied upon (as in Nos. 104, 106, 160), but even such a document as the address of Massachusetts to Charles II (No. 132) is a special plea, and does not state the whole truth.

In the next place, even contemporaries had not all the same opportunities for seeing things, or the same knack of describing them. Captain Underhill was a man whom nobody in his time believed ; but he was in the midst of the Pequot war which he describes (No. 127), and probably states nearly the truth. Alexander VI in his Bull of Demarcation (No. 18) was influenced by the hearsay of the Spanish and Portuguese ambassadors. Nearly all the pieces in this volume are chosen from the writings of eye-witnesses, but there is a wide difference between the twittering observations of Gabriel Thomas on New Jersey (No. 168) and the keen eye and truthful pen of Francis Higginson (No. 56).

Some allowance must always be made for national prejudices. Miles

Philips (No. 25) had no reason to love the Spanish Mexicans whom he describes. The Dutch hated the New Englanders (No. 95), and were hated by them (No. 170).

Many of the most interesting sources are also written rather as arguments than as narratives. Such are the glowing incitements to emigration (Nos. 32, 45, 46, 47, 59, 167) ; and the attacks on the colonial governments (Nos. 66, 102, 111, 154).

But while secondary writers correct the errors of the original writers, and show the relation of one event with another, they have also their prejudices and make their errors. One of the first lessons to be learned by a child beginning history is that it is difficult and often impossible to get at the exact truth, just as it is hard to get at the facts of everyday current events. To the secondary book one must look for a survey of the whole field, and that is an indispensable service ; to sources we must still turn for that reality, that flavor of real human life and thought, which can be had only by reading the words written while history was making.

---

14. Use of Secondary Works

FOR the indispensable background of narrative history there is a large literature. The best way of teaching a young class is by a text-book, the ground as fast as traversed to be extended by the use of sources for reading — perhaps for reading aloud (No. 9, above) — and for simple topical work. The pupil should go beyond the material in this volume, if libraries be available. For older classes there should be a fuller text-book (one to be preferred which has brief specific bibliographies), and pupils may be encouraged to make little studies of the biography of writers in this volume, and of the events of which they relate a part, using additional sources so far as available. For college classes a more extended book may be used as the basis, and the reading of all the selections in this volume be required and enforced by proper examinations ; in addition there should be written work. For the most advanced students of American history this is only a nucleus around which to group their studies from sources.

The secondary book has then two functions : to cover the whole field, bridging over the gaps between sources ; and to furnish a starting-point from which sources may be examined, in order to extend the text-book, to check its statements, and to enliven them.

15. Select List of Secondary Works on Colonization

A LARGE list might be made of secondary books suitable to accompany such a volume of texts as this. Fortunately there has been a recent output of scholarly brief books, and also of more detailed general works. A few of them are selected to be named here. Winsor, in the *Narrative and Critical History*, discusses the general historians, as does Charles Kendall Adams in his *Manual of Historical Literature* (New York, 1882).

SCHOOL HISTORIES

Out of the legion of school histories the following are chosen, as being especially well written or especially useful in colonial history : —

Edward Channing, *School History of the United States*. New York (in preparation, 1897). — The work of an accomplished scholar; very well illustrated.

Edward Eggleston, *A History of the United States and its People for the Use of Schools*. New York, 1888. — Very strong on colonial life.

John Fiske, *A History of the United States for Schools*. Boston, 1894. — Delightfully written, but very brief.

Thomas Wentworth Higginson, *Young Folks' History of the United States*. New York, revised to 1891. — A very popular and successful book.

Allen C. Thomas, *A History of the United States*. Boston, 1894. — A good, plain, sensible book.

BRIEF GENERAL HISTORIES

Edward Eggleston, *The Beginners of a Nation, a History of the Source and Rise of the Earliest English Settlements in America, with Special Reference to the Life and Character of the People*. New York, 1896. — A very careful and thoughtful book.

George Park Fisher, *The Colonial Era* (American History Series, I). New York, 1892. — This book and Thwaites' have much the same purpose, of giving a brief, compact account of colonial history.

Thomas Wentworth Higginson, *A Larger History of the United States*. New York, 1886. — A charming study of American life.

Henry Cabot Lodge, *A Short History of the English Colonies in America*. New York, Harpers, 1881. — Deals particularly with the eighteenth century.

Reuben Gold Thwaites, *The Colonies* (Epochs of American History, I). New York (8th edition), 1895.

DETAILED GENERAL HISTORIES

George Bancroft, *A History of the United States*. (10 vol. edition.) London and Boston, 1834–1874. — This first edition is much better on the colonies than the later ones.

Philip A. Bruce, *Economic History of Virginia in the Seventeenth Century*. 2 vols. New York, etc., 1896. — Most recent study of its subject.

John Andrew Doyle, *The English in America*. 3 vols. London, 1882–1887. — The most recent general work, based on sources. Middle Colonies not yet issued.

John Fiske, *The Beginnings of New England*. Boston, 1889.

John Fiske, *The Discovery of America*. 2 vols. Boston, 1892.

Richard Hildreth, *The History of the United States*. 6 vols. New York, 1851–1856. — Full and accurate, though dry. Vol. I covers colonization.

Francis Parkman, *France and England in North America, a Series of Historical Narratives*. 9 vols. Boston, Little, 1865–1892. — Unrivalled for style and impartiality.

William B. Weeden, *Economic and Social History of New England*. 2 vols. Boston, 1890. — Valuable side-lights on colonial history.

Justin Winsor, editor, *The Narrative and Critical History of America*. 8 vols. Boston, 1886–1889. — Narratives and bibliography on the period before 1689, in Vols. I–V.

John Gorham Palfrey, *History of New England*. 5 vols. Boston, Little, 1858–1890. — A standard painstaking work.

PART II

DISCOVERY AND EARLY VOYAGES
(1000–1600)

======

CHAPTER III — NORSE AND SPANISH DISCOVERIES

16. Norse Discoveries of Greenland and Wineland the Good (about 1000)

BY HAUK ERLENDSSON (ABOUT 1300)

(TRANSLATED BY A. M. REEVES, 1890)

These Sagas were the accounts composed at the time and handed down by oral tradition for about three centuries, when the version used below was written down in Icelandic by Erlendsson, a Norwegian knight and "lawman" of Icelandic birth. The narrative is trustworthy, but does not go into details enough to identify the places mentioned. — Bibliography in Justin Winsor, *Narrative and Critical History of America*, I, ch. ii; P. B. Watson, *Bibliography of Pre-Columbian Discoveries*, in Anderson's *America not discovered by Columbus;* Channing and Hart, *Guide to the Study of American History*, § 81.

ERIC THE RED FINDS GREENLAND

THERE was a man named Thorvald; he was a son of Asvald Ulf's son, Eyxna-Thori's son. His son's name was Eric. He and his father went from Jaederen to Iceland, on account of man-slaughter, and settled on Hornstrandir, and dwelt at Drangar. . . .

Eric and his people were condemned to outlawry at Thorsness-thing. He equipped his ship for a voyage, in Ericsvag; while Eyiolf concealed him in Dimunarvag, when Thorgest and his people were searching for him among the islands. He said to them, that it was his intention to go in search of that land which Gunnbiorn, son of Ulf the Crow, saw when he was driven out of his course, westward across the main, and discovered Gunnbiorns-skerries. He told them that he would return again to his friends, if he should succeed in finding that country. Thorbiorn, and Eyiolf, and Styr accompanied Eric out beyond the islands, and they parted with the greatest friendliness; Eric said to them that he would render them similar aid, so far as it might lie within his power, if they should ever stand in need of his help. Eric sailed out to sea from Snaefells-iokul, and arrived at that ice mountain which is called Black-sark. Thence he sailed to the southward, that he might ascertain whether there was habitable country in that direction. He passed the first winter at Ericsey near the middle of the Western-settlement. In the following spring he proceeded to Ericsfirth, and selected a site there for his home-stead. That summer he explored the western uninhabited region, re-maining there for a long time, and assigning many local names there. The second winter he spent at Ericsholms beyond Hvarfsgnipa. But the third summer he sailed northward to Snaefell, and into Hrafnsfirth. He be-lieved then that he had reached the head of Ericsfirth. The following summer he sailed to Iceland, and landed in Breidafirth. He remained that winter with Ingolf at Holmlatr. In the spring he and Thorgest fought together, and Eric was defeated; after this a reconciliation was effected between them. That summer Eric set out to colonize the land which he had discovered, and which he called Greenland, because, he said, men would be the more readily persuaded thither if the land had a good name. . . .

CONCERNING LEIF THE LUCKY AND THE INTRODUCTION OF CHRISTIANITY INTO GREENLAND

Eric was married to a woman named Thorhild, and had two sons; one of these was named Torstein, and the other Leif. They were both promising men. Thorstein lived at home with his father, and there was not at that time a man in Greenland who was accounted of so great promise as he. Leif had sailed to Norway, where he was at the court of King Olaf Tryggvason. . . .

He was well received by the king, who felt that he could see that Leif was a man of great accomplishments. Upon one occasion the king came to speech with Leif, and asks him, 'Is it thy purpose to sail to Greenland in the summer?' 'It is my purpose,' said Leif, 'if it be your will.' 'I believe it will be well,' answers the king, 'and thither thou shalt go upon my errand, to proclaim Christianity there.' Leif replied that the king should decide, but gave it as his belief that it would be difficult to carry this mission to a successful issue in Greenland. The king replied that he knew of no man who would be better fitted for this undertaking, 'and in thy hands the cause will surely prosper.'

' This can only be,' said Leif, ' if I enjoy the grace of your protection.'
Leif put to sea when his ship was ready for the voyage. For a long
time he was tossed about upon the ocean, and came upon lands of
which he had previously had no knowledge. There were self-sown wheat-
fields and vines growing there. There were also those trees there which
are called ' mausur,' and of all these they took specimens. Some of the
timbers were so large that they were used in building. Leif found men
upon a wreck, and took them home with him, and procured quarters
for them all during the winter. In this wise he showed his nobleness
and goodness, since he introduced Christianity into the country, and
saved the men from the wreck ; and he was called Leif the Lucky ever
after. Leif landed in Ericsfirth, and then went home to Brattahlid ;
he was well received by every one. He soon proclaimed Christianity
throughout the land, and the Catholic faith, and announced King Olaf
Tryggvason's messages to the people, telling them how much excel-
lence and how great glory accompanied this faith. . . .

BEGINNING OF THE WINELAND VOYAGES

About this time there began to be much talk at Brattahlid, to the
effect that Wineland the Good should be explored, for, it was said, that
country must be possessed of many goodly qualities. And so it came to
pass that Karlsefni and Snorri fitted out their ship, for the purpose of
going in search of that country in the spring. Biarni and Thorhall
joined the expedition with their ship and the men who had borne them
company. . . .

Thorhall was stout and swarthy and of giant stature ; he was a man
of few words, though given to abusive language, when he did speak, and
he ever incited Eric to evil. He was a poor Christian ; he had a wide
knowledge of the unsettled regions. He was on the same ship with
Thorvard and Thorvald. They had that ship which Thorbiorn had
brought out. They had in all one hundred and sixty men, when they
sailed to the Western settlement, and thence to Bear Island. Thence
they bore away to the southward two ' dœgr.' Then they saw land, and
launched a boat, and explored the land, and found there large flat
stones [*hellur*], and many of these were twelve ells wide ; there were
many Arctic foxes there. They gave a name to the country, and called
it Helluland [the land of flat stones]. Then they sailed with northerly
winds two ' dœgr,' and land then lay before them, and upon it was a
great wood and many wild beasts ; an island lay off the land to the

southeast, and there they found a bear, and they called this Biarney
[Bear Island], while the land where the wood was they called Markland
[Forest-land]. Thence they sailed southward along the land for a long
time, and came to a cape ; the land lay upon the starboard ; there were
long strands and sandy banks there. They rowed to the land and found
upon the cape there the keel of a ship, and they called it there Kialarnes
[Keelness] ; they also called the strands Furdustrandir [Wonder-strands],
because they were so long to sail by. Then the country became indented with bays, and they steered their ships into a bay. . . . Now
when they had sailed past Wonder-strands, they put the Gaels ashore,
and directed them to run to the southward, and investigate the nature
of the country, and return again before the end of the third half-day.
They were each clad in a garment, which they called ' kiafal,' and which
was so fashioned, that it had a hood at the top, was open at the sides,
was sleeveless, and was fastened . . . with buttons and loops, while
elsewhere they were naked. Karlsefni and his companions cast anchor,
and lay there during their absence ; and when they came again, one
of them carried a bunch of grapes, and the other an ear of new-sown
wheat. They went on board the ship, whereupon Karlsefni and his
followers held on their way, until they came to where the coast was
indented with bays. They stood into a bay with their ships. There
was an island out at the mouth of the bay, about which there were
strong currents, wherefore they called it Straumey [Stream Isle]. There
were so many birds there, that it was scarcely possible to step between
the eggs. They sailed through the firth, and called it Straumfiord
[Streamfirth], and carried their cargoes ashore from the ships, and established themselves there. There were mountains thereabouts. They
occupied themselves exclusively with the exploration of the country.
They remained there during the winter, and they had taken no thought
for this during the summer. The fishing began to fail, and they began
to fall short of food. . . . The weather then improved, and they could
now row out to fish, and thenceforward they had no lack of provisions,
for they could hunt game on the land, gather eggs on the island, and
catch fish from the sea.

CONCERNING KARLSEFNI AND THORHALL

It is said, that Thorhall wished to sail to the northward beyond
Wonder-strands, in search of Wineland, while Karlsefni desired to proceed to the southward, off the coast. . . .

It is now to be told of Karlsefni, that he cruised southward off the coast, with Snorri and Biarni, and their people. They sailed for a long time, and until they came at last to a river, which flowed down from the land into a lake, and so into the sea. There were great bars at the mouth of the river, so that it could only be entered at the height of the flood-tide. Karlsefni and his men sailed into the mouth of the river, and called it there Hóp [a small land-locked bay]. They found self-sown wheat-fields on the land there, wherever there were hollows, and wherever there was hilly ground, there were vines. Every brook there was full of fish. They dug pits, on the shore where the tide rose highest, and when the tide fell, there were halibut in the pits. There were great numbers of wild animals of all kinds in the woods. They remained there half a month, and enjoyed themselves, and kept no watch. They had their live-stock with them. Now one morning early, when they looked about them, they saw a great number of skin-canoes, and staves were brandished from the boats, with a noise like flails, and they were revolved in the same direction in which the sun moves. Then said Karlsefni, 'What may this betoken?' Snorri, Thorbrand's son, answers him : 'It may be, that this is a signal of peace, wherefore let us take a white shield and display it.' And thus they did. Thereupon the strangers rowed toward them, and went upon the land, marvelling at those whom they saw before them. They were swarthy men, and ill looking, and the hair of their heads was ugly. They had great eyes, and were broad of cheek. They tarried there for a long time looking curiously at the people they saw before them, and then rowed away, and to the southward around the point.

Karlsefni and his followers had built their huts above the lake, some of their dwellings being near the lake, and others farther away. Now they remained there that winter. No snow came there, and all of their live-stock lived by grazing. And when spring opened, they discovered, early one morning, a great number of skin-canoes, rowing from the south past the cape, so numerous, that it looked as if coals had been scattered broadcast out before the bay ; and on every boat staves were waved. Thereupon Karlsefni and his people displayed their shields, and when they came together, they began to barter with each other. Especially did the strangers wish to buy red-cloth, for which they offered in exchange peltries and quite grey skins. They also desired to buy swords and spears, but Karlsefni and Snorri forbade this. In exchange for perfect unsullied skins, the Skrellings would take red stuff a span in length,

which they would bind around their heads. So their trade went on for
a time, until Karlsefni and his people began to grow short of cloth, when
they divided it into such narrow pieces, that it was not more than a
finger's breadth wide, but the Skrellings still continued to give just as
much for this as before, or more.

It so happened, that a bull, which belonged to Karlsefni and his
people, ran out from the woods, bellowing loudly. This so terrified the
Skrellings, that they sped out to their canoes, and then rowed away to
the southward along the coast. For three entire weeks nothing more
was seen of them. At the end of this time, however, a great multitude
of Skrelling boats was discovered approaching from the south, as if a
stream were pouring down, and all of their staves were waved in a direction contrary to the course of the sun, and the Skrellings were all uttering loud cries. Thereupon Karlsefni and his men took red shields and
displayed them. The Skrellings sprang from their boats, and they met
them, and fought together. There was a fierce shower of missiles, for
the Skrellings had war-slings. Karlsefni and Snorri observed that the
Skrellings raised upon a pole a great ball-shaped body, almost the size
of a sheep's belly, and nearly black in colour, and this they hurled from
the pole up on the land above Karlsefni's followers, and it made a
frightful noise, where it fell. Whereupon a great fear seized upon
Karlsefni, and all his men, so that they could think of nought but flight,
and of making their escape up along the river bank, for it seemed to
them, that the troop of the Skrellings was rushing towards them from
every side, and they did not pause until they came to certain jutting
crags, where they offered a stout resistance. Freydis came out, and
seeing that Karlsefni and his men were fleeing, she cried : ' Why do you
flee from these wretches, such worthy men as ye, when, meseems, ye
might slaughter them like cattle. Had I but a weapon, methinks, I
would fight better than any of you ! ' They gave no heed to her words.
Freydis sought to join them, but lagged behind, for she was not hale ;
she followed them, however, into the forest, while the Skrellings pursued
her ; she found a dead man in front of her ; this was Thorbrand, Snorri's
son, his skull cleft by a flat stone ; his naked sword lay beside him ; she
took it up and prepared to defend herself with it. The Skrellings then
approached her, whereupon she . . . slapped her breast with the naked
sword. At this the Skrellings were terrified and ran down to their
boats, and rowed away. Karlsefni and his companions, however, joined
her, and praised her valour. Two of Karlsefni's men had fallen, and a

D

great number of the Skrellings. Karlsefni's party had been overpowered by dint of superior numbers. They now returned to their dwellings, and bound up their wounds, and weighed carefully what throng of men that could have been, which had seemed to descend upon them from the land; it now seemed to them, that there could have been but the one party, that which came from the boats, and that the other troop must have been an ocular delusion. The Skrellings, moreover, found a dead man, and an axe lay beside him. One of their number picked up the axe, and struck at a tree with it, and one after another [they tested it], and it seemed to them to be a treasure, and to cut well; then one of their number seized it, and hewed at a stone with it, so that the axe broke, whereat they concluded that it could be of no use, since it would not withstand stone, and they cast it away.

It now seemed clear to Karlsefni and his people, that although the country thereabouts was attractive, their life would be one of constant dread and turmoil by reason of the [hostility of the] inhabitants of the country, so they forthwith prepared to leave, and determined to return to their own country. They sailed to the northward off the coast, and found five Skrellings clad in skin-doublets, lying asleep near the sea. There were vessels beside them, containing animal marrow mixed with blood. Karlsefni and his company concluded that they must have been banished from their own land. They put them to death. They afterwards found a cape, upon which there was a great number of animals, . . . which lay there at night. They now arrived again at Streamfirth, where they found great abundance of all those things of which they stood in need. Some men say that Biarni and Freydis remained behind here with a hundred men, and went no further; while Karlsefni and Snorri proceeded to the southward with forty men, tarrying at Hóp barely two months, and returning again the same summer. Karlsefni then set out with one ship, in search of Thorhall the Huntsman, but the greater part of the company remained behind. They sailed to the northward around Keelness, and then bore to the westward, having land to the larboard. The country there was a wooded wilderness, as far as they could see, with scarcely an open space; and when they had journeyed a considerable distance, a river flowed down from the east toward the west. They sailed into the mouth of the river, and lay to by the southern bank. . . .

Saga of Eric the Red in Arthur Middleton Reeves, editor and translator, *The Finding of Wineland the Good* (London, 1890), pp. 29–49 *passim*.

17. Discovery of America (1492)

BY CHRISTOPHER COLUMBUS

ABRIDGED BY LAS CASAS (TRANSLATED BY H. L. THOMAS, 1880)

The journal kept by Columbus, a Genoese navigator in the service of Spain, has disappeared, but the extant abridgment evidently contains many of the original phrases. The narrative is colored by the desire to make as much as possible of his own part in the expedition. — Bibliography in Justin Winsor, *Narrative and Critical History*, II, 46–69, and *Columbus*, chs. i, ii; Henry Harrisse, *Christophe Colombe*, I; Channing and Hart, *Guide to American History*, § 82; *American History Leaflets*, No. 1.

WEDNESDAY OCTOBER 10th.

HE sailed west-southwest, at the rate of ten miles an hour and occasionally twelve, and at other times seven, running between day and night fifty-nine leagues ; he told the men only forty-four. Here the crew could stand it no longer, they complained of the long voyage, but the Admiral encouraged them as best he could, giving them hopes of the profits that they might have. And he added that it was useless to murmur because he had come to [in quest of] the Indies, and was going to continue until he found them with God's help.

THURSDAY OCTOBER 11th.

He sailed to the west-southwest, had a high sea, higher than hitherto. They saw pardelas and floating by the vessel a green rush. The men of the Pinta saw a reed and a stick, and got a small stick apparently cut or marked with an iron instrument, and a piece of cane, and some other grass which grows on the land, and a small board. Those of the Caravel Niña also saw other indications of land and a little stick loaded with dog roses. In view of such signs they breathed more freely and grew cheerful. They ran until sunset of that day twenty-seven leagues. After sunset he sailed on his first course to the West ; they went about twelve miles an hour, and two hours after midnight they had run about ninety miles, that is twenty-two and a half leagues. As the Caravel Pinta was a better sailer and had the lead, she made land and showed the signals ordered by the Admiral. The land was first seen by a sailor called Rodrigo de Triana ; as the Admiral at ten o'clock at night standing on the castle of the poop saw a light, but so indistinct that he did not dare to affirm that it was land ; yet he called the attention of Pero Gutierrez, a King's butler, to it, and told him that it seemed to be a light, and told him to look, he did so and saw it ; he did the same with

Rodrigo Sanchez de Segovia, whom the King and Queen had sent with the fleet as supervisor and purveyor, but he, not being in a good position for seeing it, saw nothing. After the Admiral said this it was seen once or twice, and it was like a small wax candle that was being hoisted and raised, which would seem to few to be an indication of land. The Admiral however was quite convinced of the proximity of land. In consequence of that when they said the *Salve*, which they used to say and sing it in their way, all the sailors and all being present, the Admiral requested and admonished them to keep a sharp lookout at the castle of the bow, and to look well for land, and said that he would give to him who first saw land a silk doublet, besides the other rewards that the King and Queen had promised, namely an annual pension of ten thousand maravedis to him who should see it first. Two hours after midnight the land appeared, about two leagues off. They lowered all the sails, leaving only a storm square sail, which is the mainsail without bonnets, and lay to until Friday when they reached a small island of the Lucayos, called *Guanahani* by the natives. They soon saw people naked, and the Admiral went on shore in the armed boat, also Martin Alonso Pinzon and Vincente Anes, his brother, who was commander of the Niña. The Admiral took the Royal standard and the captains with two banners of the Green Cross, which the Admiral carried on all the ships as a distinguishing flag having an F and a Y : each letter surmounted by its crown, one at one arm of the cross, and the other at the other arm. As soon as they had landed they saw trees of a brilliant green abundance of water and fruits of various kinds. The Admiral called the two captains and the rest who had come on shore, and Rodrigo Descovedo, the Notary of all the fleet, and Rodrigo Sanchez de Segovia, and he called them as witnesses to certify that he in the presence of them all, was taking, as he in fact took possession of said island for the King and Queen his masters, making the declarations that were required as they will be found more fully in the attestations then taken down in writing. Soon after a large crowd of natives congregated there. What follows are the Admiral's own words in his book on the first voyage and discovery of these Indies. " In order to win the friendship and affection of that people, and because I was convinced that their conversion to our Holy Faith would be better promoted through love than through force ; I presented some of them with red caps and some strings of glass beads which they placed around their necks, and with other trifles of insignificant worth that delighted them and by which we have got a

wonderful hold on their affections.   They afterwards came to the boats
of the vessels swimming, bringing us parrots, cotton thread in balls, and
spears, and many other things, which they bartered for others we gave
them, as glass beads and little bells.   Finally they received everything
and gave whatever they had with good will.   But I thought them to be a
very poor people. . . .   I saw but one very young girl, all the rest being
young men, none of them being over thirty years of age ; their forms
being very well proportioned ; their bodies graceful and their features
handsome : their hair is as coarse as the hair of a horse's tail and cut
short : they wear their hair over their eye brows except a little behind
which they wear long, and which they never cut : some of them paint
themselves black, and they are of the color of the Canary islanders,
neither black nor white, and some paint themselves white, and some
red, and some with whatever they find, and some paint their faces,
and some the whole body, and some their eyes only, and some their
noses only.   They do not carry arms and have no knowledge of them,
for when I showed them the swords they took them by the edge, and
through ignorance, cut themselves.   They have no iron ; their spears
consist of staffs without iron, some of them having a fish's tooth at the
end, and the others other things.   As a body they are of good size, good
demeanor, and well formed ; I saw some with scars on their bodies,
and to my signs asking them what these meant, they answered in the
same manner, that people from neighboring islands wanted to capture
them, and they had defended themselves ; and I did believe, and do
believe, that they came from the mainland to take them prisoners.   They
must be good servants and very intelligent, because I see that they repeat
very quickly what I told them, and it is my conviction that they would
easily become Christians, for they seem not to have any sect.   If it
please our Lord, I will take six of them from here to your Highnesses
on my departure, that they may learn to speak.   I have seen here no
beasts whatever, but parrots only."   All these are the words of the
Admiral.

SATURDAY OCTOBER 13th.

" At dawn many of these men came down to the shore, all are, as
already, said, youths of good size and very handsome : their hair is not
wooly, but loose and coarse like horse hair, they have broader heads and
foreheads than I have ever seen in any other race of men, and the eyes
very beautiful not small, none of them are black, but of the complexion
of the inhabitants of the Canaries, as it is to be expected, for it is east

[and] west with the island of Hierro in the Canaries. in the same line. All without exception have very straight limbs, and no bellies, and very well formed. They came to the ship in canoes, made out of trunks of trees all in one piece, and wonderfully built according to the locality, in some of them forty or forty-five men came, others were smaller, and in some but a single man came. They paddled with a peel like that of a baker, and make wonderful speed ; and if it capsizes all begin to swim and set it right again, and bail out the water with calabashes which they carry. They brought balls of spun cotton, parrots, spears, and other little things which would be tedious to describe, and gave them away for anything that was given to them. I examined them closely and tried to ascertain if there was any gold, and noticed that some carried a small piece of it hanging from a little hole in their nose, and by signs I was able to understand that by going to the south or going around the island to the southward, there was a king who had large gold vessels, and gold in abundance. I endeavored to persuade them to go there, and I afterwards saw that they had no wish to go. I determined to wait, until tomorrow evening, and then to sail for the southwest, for many of them told me that there was a land to the south and to the southwest and to the northwest, and that those from the northwest came frequently to fight with them, and so go to the southwest to get gold and precious stones. This island is very large and very level and has very green trees, and abundance of water, and a very large lagoon in the middle, without any mountain, and all is covered with verdure, most pleasing to the eye ; the people are remarkably gentle, and from the desire to get some of our things, and thinking that nothing will be given to them unless they give some thing, and having nothing they take what they can and swim off [to the ship] ; but all that they have they give for any thing that is offered to them ; so that they bought even pieces of crockery, and pieces of broken glass, and I saw sixteen balls of cotton given for three ceotis of Portugal, which is equivalent to a blanca of Castile, and in them there must have been more than one arraba of spun cotton. I forbad this and allowed no one to take any unless I ordered it to be taken for your Highnesses should it be found in abundance. It grows in the island, although on account of the shortness of time I could not assert it positively, and likewise the gold which they carry hanging in their noses is found here ; but in order to lose no time I am now going to try if I can find the island of Cipango. At this moment it is dark and all went on shore in their canoes."

SUNDAY OCTOBER 14.

" At dawn I ordered the boat of the ship and the boats of the Caravels
to be got ready, and went along the island, in a north-northeasterly direction, to see the other side, which was on the other side of the east, and
also to see the villages, and soon saw two or three and their inhabitants,
coming to the shore calling us and praising God; some brought us water,
some eatables; others, when they saw that I did not care to go on shore,
plunged into the sea swimming and came, and we understood that they
asked us if we had come down from heaven; and one old man got into
the boat, while others in a loud voice called both men and women saying : come and see the men from heaven : bring them food and drink.
A crowd of men and many women came, each bringing something, giving
thanks to God, throwing themselves down, and lifting their hands to
heaven, and entreating or beseeching us to land there : but I was afraid
of a reef of rocks which entirely surrounds that island, although there is
within it depth enough and ample harbor for all the vessels of christendom, but the entrance is very narrow.   It is true that the interior of that
belt contains some rocks, but the sea is there as still as the water in a
well.   And in order to see all this I moved this morning, that I might
give an account of everything to your Highnesses, and also to see where
a fort could be built, and found a piece of land like an island, although
it is not one, with six houses on it, which in two days could easily be cut
off and converted into an island; such a work however is not necessary
in my opinion, because the people are totally unacquainted with arms, as
your Highnesses will see by observing the seven which I have caused to
be taken in order to carry them to Castile to be taught our language, and
to return them unless your Highnesses when they shall send orders
may take them all to Castile, or keep them in the same island as captives,
for with fifty men all can be kept in subjection, and made to do whatever
you desire ; and near by the said little island there are orchards of trees
the most beautiful that I have seen, with leaves as fresh and green as
those of Castile in April and May, and much water.   I observed all that
harbor, and afterwards I returned to the ship and set sail, and saw so
many islands that I could not decide to which one I should go first, and
the men I had taken told me by signs that they were innumerable, and
named more than one hundred of them.   In consequence I looked for
the largest one and determined to make for it, and I am so doing, and
it is probably distant five leagues from this of *San Salvador*, to others
some more, some less : all are very level, without mountains and of great

fertility, and all are inhabited, and they make war upon each other, although these are very simple hearted and very finely formed men."

Report of the Superintendent of the U. S. Coast and Geodetic Survey, etc. (Washington, 1882), pp. 353–358.

———◆———

18. Papal Bull Dividing the New World (1493)

BY POPE ALEXANDER VI

(Translated by Richard Eden, 1555)

Alexander VI (Borgia) was a Spaniard. This bull was the result of rival claims of Portugal and Spain to new discoveries, and was intended to secure to the Spaniards and Portuguese the new western and eastern roads to India. Eden's translation from the Latin into Black-letter English is in itself a good example of the crabbed English of the time. — For bibliography see Justin Winsor, *Narrative and Critical History*, II, 13, 44, 592, 596, and *Columbus*, 252–254; Channing and Hart, *Guide to American History*, § 82.

The coppie of the Bull or donation, by th[e]autoritie wherof, Pope Alexander the syxte of that name, gaue and graunted to the kynges of Castyle and theyr successours the Regions and Ilandes founde in the Weste Ocean sea by the nauigations of the Spangardes

ALEXANDER byshoppe, the seruante of the seruantes of God: To owre moste deare beloued sonne in Christ Kynge Ferdinande, And to owre deare beloued daughter in Chryste Elyzabeth Queene of Castyle, Legion [Leon], Aragon, Sicilie, and Granata, most noble Princes, Gretynge and Apostolical benediction.

Amonge other woorkes acceptable to the diuine maiestie and accordynge to owre hartes desyre, this certeinely is the chiefe, that the Catholyke fayth and Christian religion, specially in this owre tyme may in all places bee exalted, amplified, and enlarged, wherby the health of soules may be procured, and the Barbarous nations subdued and brought to the fayth. And therefore wheras by the fauoure of gods clemencie (although not without equall desertes) we are cauled [called] to this holy seate of Peter, and understandynge you to bee trewe Catholyke Princes as we haue euer knowen you, and as youre noble and woorthy factes haue declared in maner to the hole worlde in that with all your studie, diligence, and industrye, you haue spared no trauayles, charges, or perels, aduenturynge euen the shedynge of your owne bludde, with applyinge yowre hole myndes and endeuours here unto, as your noble expeditions achyued in recouerynge the kyngdome of Granata from the tyrannie of the Sarracens in these our dayes, doo playnely declare your factes with so great glorye of the diuine name. For the whiche

as we thinke you woorthy, so owght we of owre owne free wyl [will] fauor-
ably to graunt you all thynges whereby you maye dayely with more feruent
myndes to the honoure of god and enlargynge the Christian empire, prosecute
your deuoute and laudable purpose most acceptable to the immortall God.
We are credably informed that whereas of late you were determyned to seeke
and fynde certyne Ilandes & firme landes farre remote and vnknowen (and
not heretofore found by any other) to th[e]intent to bringe th[e]inhabi-
tauntes of the same to honoure owre redemer and to professe the catholyke
fayth, you haue hetherto byn much occupied in th[e]expugnation and recou-
erie of the kyngedome of Granata, by reason whereof yowe coulde not
brynge yowre sayde laudable purpose to th[e]ende desyred.   Neuerthelesse
as it hath pleased almyghty god, the forsayde kyngedome beinge recouered,
wyllyng t[o]accomplyshe your sayde desyre, you haue, not without great
laboure, perelles, and charges, appoynted owre welbeloued sonne Christopher
Colonus (a man certes wel commended as moste worthy and apte for so
great a matter) well furnyshed with men and shippes and other necessaries,
to seeke (by the sea where hetherto no manne hath sayled) suche firme landes
and Ilandes farre remote and hitherto vnknowen.   Who (by gods helpe)
makynge diligente searche in the Ocean sea, haue founde certeyne remote
Ilandes and firme landes whiche were not heretofore founde by any other.
In the which (as is sayde) many nations inhabite lyuinge peaceably and
goinge naked, not accustomed to eate fleshe.   And as farre as yowre messengers can coniecture, the nations inhabitynge the foresayde landes and
Ilandes, beleue that there is one god creatoure in heauen: and seeme apte
to be brought to th[e]imbrasinge of the catholyke faythe and to be imbued
with good maners: by reason whereof, we may hope that if they be well
instructed, they may easely bee induced to receaue the name of owre sauiour
Iesu Christ.   We are further aduertised that the forenamed Christopher
hathe nowe builded and erected a fortresse with good munition in one of the
foresayde principall Ilandes in the which he hath placed a garrison of certeine
of the Christian men that wente thyther with him: aswell to th[e]intent
to defende the same, as also to searche other Ilandes and firme landes farre
remote and yet vnknowen.   We also vnderstande, that in these landes and
Ilandes lately founde, is great plentie of golde and spices, with dyuers and
many other precious thynges of sundry kyndes and qualities.   Therfore al
thinges diligently considered (especially th[e]amplifyinge and enlargyng of
the catholike fayth, as it behoueth catholike Princes folowyng th[e]exem-
ples of yowre noble progenitours of famous memorie) wheras yowe are
determyned by the fauour of almightie god to subdue and brynge to the
catholyke fayth th[e]inhabitauntes of the foresayde landes and Ilandes.

We greatly commendynge this yowre godly and laudable purpose in owr
lorde, and desirous to haue the same brought to a dewe ende, and the name
of owre sauioure to be knowen in those partes, doo exhorte yowe in owre

Lorde and by the receauynge of yowre holy baptisme wherby yowe are bounde to Apostolicall obedience, and ernestely require yowe by the bowels of mercy of owre Lorde Iesu Christ, that when yowe intende for the zeale of the Catholyke faythe to prosecute the sayde expedition to reduce the people of the foresayde landes and Ilandes to the Christian religion, yowe shall spare no labours at any tyme, or bee deterred with any perels, conceauynge [conceiving] firme hope and confidence that the omnipotent godde wyll gyue good successe to yowre godly attemptes.   And that beinge autorysed by the priuilege of the Apostolycall grace, yowe may the more freely and bouldly take upon yowe th[e]enterpryse of so greate a matter, we of owre owne motion, and not eyther at yowre request or at the instant peticion of any other person, but of owre owne mere liberalitie and certeyne science, and by the fulnesse of Apostolycall power, doo gyue, graunt, and assigne to yowe, yowre heyres and successours, al the firme landes & Ilandes found or to be found, discouered or to be discouered toward the West & South, drawyng a line from the pole Artike to the pole Antartike (that is) from the north to the Southe : Conteynynge in this donation, what so euer firme landes or Ilandes are founde or to bee founde towarde *India* or towarde any other parte what so euer it bee, being distant from, or without the foresayd lyne drawen a hundreth leagues towarde the Weste and South from any of the Ilandes which are commonly cauled *De Los Azores* and *Cabo Verde*.   All the Ilandes therefore and firme landes, founde and to be founde, discouered and to be discouered from the sayde lyne towarde the West and South, such as haue not actually bin heretofore possessed by any other Christian kynge or prynce vntyll the daye of the natiuitie of owre Lorde Iesu Chryste laste paste, from the which begynneth this present yeare beinge the yeare of owre Lorde M. LLLL. lxxxiii. when so euer any such shalbe founde by your messingers & capytaines,

Wee by the autoritie of almyghtie God graunted vnto vs in saynt Peter, and by the office which we beare on the earth in the steede of Iesu Christe, doo for euer by the tenoure of these presentes, gyue, graunte, assigne, vnto yowe, yowre heyres, and successoures (the kynges of Castyle and Legion) all those landes and Ilandes, with theyr dominions, territories, cities, castels, towres, places, and vyllages, with all the ryght and iurisdictions thereunto perteynynge : constitutynge, assignynge, and deputynge, yowe, yowre heyres, and successours the lordes thereof, with full and free poure, autoritie, and iurisdiction.   Decreeinge neuerthelesse by this owre donation, graunt, and assignation, that from no Christian Prince whiche actually hath possessed the foresayde Ilandes and firme landes vnto the day of the natiuitie of owre lorde beforesayde theyr ryght obteyned to bee vnderstoode hereby to be taken away, as that it owght to be taken away.

Furthermore wee commaunde yowe in the vertue of holy obedience (as yowe haue promysed, and as wee doubte not you wyll doo vppon mere deuotion and princiely magnanimitie) to sende to the sayde firme landes and Flandes, honeste, vertuous, and lerned men, such as feare God, and are able to instructe th[e]inhabitauntes in the Catholyke fayth and good maners, applyinge all theyre possible diligence in the premisses.

We furthermore streightly inhibite all maner of persons, of what state, degree, order, or condition so euer they bee, although of Emperiall and regall dignitie, vnder the peyne of the sentence of excommunication whiche they shall incurre yf they doo to the contrary, that they in no case persume without speciall lycence of yowe, yowre heyres, and successours, to trauayle for merchaundies or for any other cause, to the sayde landes or Flandes, founde or to bee found, discouered, or to bee discouered, toward the west & south, drawing a line from the pole Artyke to the pole Antartike, whether the firme lands & Flandes found and to be found, be situate toward *India* or towarde any other parte beinge distant from the lyne drawen a hundreth leagues towarde the west from any of the Flandes commonly cauled *De Los Azores* and *Cabo Verde :* Notwithstandynge constitutions, decrees, and Apostolycall ordinaunces what so euer they are to the contrary : In him from whom Empyres, dominions, and all good thynges doo procede : Trustynge that almyghtie god directynge yowre enterprises, yf yowe folowe yowre godly and laudable attemptes, yowre laboures and trauayles herein, shall in shorte tyme obteyne a happy ende with felicitie and glorie of all Christian people. But forasmuch as it shulde bee a thynge of great difficultie these letters to bee caryed to all suche places as shuld bee expedient, we wyll, and of lyke motion and knowleage doo decree that whyther so euer the same shalbe sent, or wher so euer they shalbe receaued with the subscription of a common notarie therunto requyred, with the seale of any person constitute in ecclesiasticall courte, or suche as are authoryzed by the ecclesiasticall courte, the same fayth and credite to bee gyuen therevnto in judgement or else where, as shulde bee exhibyted to these presentes.

It shall therefore bee lawefull for no man to infringe or rashely to contrarie this letter of owre commendation, exhortacion, requeste, donation, graunt, assignation, constitution, deputation, decree, commaundement, inhibition, and determination. And yf any shall presume to attempte the same, he owght to knowe that he shall thereby incurre the indignation of almyghtie God and his holye Apostles Peter and Paule. (∴) (:) (∵)

Gyuen at Rome at saynt Peters : In the yeare of th[e]incarnation of owre Lord M.CCCC. Lxx.xxIII. The fourth day of the nones of Maye; the fyrste yeare of owre seate. ( ) ( ) ( )

Peter Martyr, *The Decades of the newe worlde or west India* (London, 1555), pp. 171–173.

19. The Thirst for Gold (1503)

BY CHRISTOPHER COLUMBUS

(TRANSLATED BY R. H. MAJOR, 1847)

Columbus, the author of No. 17 above, is here a prejudiced writer in his own behalf. — Bibliography in Winsor, *Narrative and Critical History*, II, ch. i, and *Columbus*, 450–461; Channing and Hart, *Guide*, § 82.

A Letter written by Don Christopher Columbus, Viceroy and Admiral of the Indies, to the most Christian and mighty Sovereigns, the King and Queen of Spain, in which are described the events of his voyage, and the countries, provinces, cities, rivers and other marvellous matters therein discovered, as well as the places where gold and other substances of great richness and value are to be found.

MOST serene, and very high and mighty Princes, the King and Queen our Sovereigns : — My passage from Cadiz to the Canary occupied four days, and thence to the Indies, from which I wrote, sixteen days. My intention was to expedite my voyage as much as possible while I had good vessels, good crews and stores, and because Jamaica was the place to which I was bound. I wrote this in Dominica ; and until now my time has been occupied in gaining information. . . .

Such is my fate, that the twenty years of service through which I have passed with so much toil and danger, have profited me nothing, and at this very day I do not possess a roof in Spain that I can call my own ; if I wish to eat or sleep, I have nowhere to go but to the inn or tavern, and most times lack wherewith to pay the bill. Another anxiety wrung my very heart-strings, which was the thought of my son Diego, whom I had left an orphan in Spain, and stripped of the honour and property which were due to him on my account, although I had looked upon it as a certainty, that your Majesties, as just and grateful Princes, would restore it to him in all respects with increase. I reached the land of Cariay, where I stopped to repair my vessels and take in provisions, as well as to afford relaxation to the men, who had become very weak. I myself (who, as I said before, had been several times at the point of death) gained information respecting the gold mines of which I was in search, in the province of Ciamba ; and two Indians conducted me to Carambaru, where the people . . . wear golden mirrors round their necks, which they will neither sell, give, nor part with for any consideration. They named to me many places on the sea-coast where there were both gold and mines. The last that they mentioned was Veragua [Venezuela ?] which was five-and-twenty leagues distant from the place where we then were. I started with the intention of visiting all of them, but when I had reached the middle of my journey I learned that there were other mines at so short a distance that they might be reached in two days. I determined on sending to see them. It was on the eve of St. Simon and St. Jude, which was the day fixed for our departure; but that night there arose so violent a storm, that we were forced to go wherever it drove us, and the Indian who was to conduct us to the mines was with us all the time. As I had found everything true that had been told me in the different places which I had visited, I felt satisfied it would be the same with respect to Ciguare, which according to their account, is nine days' journey across the country westward : they tell me there is a great quantity of gold there, and that the inhabitants wear coral ornaments on their heads, and very large coral bracelets and anklets, with which article also they adorn and inlay their seats, boxes and tables. They also said that the women there wore necklaces hanging down to their shoulders. All the people agree in the report I now repeat, and their account is so favourable that I should be content with the tithe of the advantages that their description holds out. They are all likewise acquainted with the pepper-plant; according to the account of these people, the inhabitants of Ciguare are accustomed to hold fairs and markets for carrying on their commerce, and they showed me also the mode and form in which they transact their various exchanges; others assert that their ships carry guns, and that the men go clothed and use bows and arrows, swords and cuirasses, and that on shore they have horses which they use in battle, and that they wear rich clothes and have most excellent houses. They also say that the sea surrounds Ciguare, and that at ten days' journey from thence is the river Ganges; these lands appear to hold the same relation to Veragua, as Tortosa to Fontarabia, or Pisa to Venice. When I left Carambaru and reached the places in its neighbourhood, which I have above mentioned as being spoken of by the Indians, I found the customs of the people correspond with the accounts that had been given of them, except as regarded the golden mirrors : any man who had one of them would willingly part with it for three hawks'-bells, although they were equivalent in weight to ten or fifteen ducats. These people resemble the natives of Española in all their habits. They have various modes of collecting the gold, none of which will bear comparison with the plans adopted by the Christians. . . .

On the sixth of February, while it was still raining, I sent seventy men on shore to go into the interior, and, at five leagues' distance they found several mines. The Indians who went with them, conducted them to a very lofty mountain, and thence showing them the country all round, as far as the eye could reach, told them there was gold in every part, and that, towards the west, the mines extended twenty days' journey; they also recounted the names of the towns and villages where there was more or less of it. I afterwards learned that the cacique Quibian, who had lent these Indians, had ordered them to show the distant mines, and which belonged to an enemy of his; but that in his own territory, one man might, if he would, collect in ten days a great abundance of gold. I bring with me some Indians, his servants, who are witnesses of this fact. The boats went up to the spot where the dwellings of these people are situated; and, after four hours, my brother returned with the guides, all of them bringing back gold which they had collected at that place. The gold must be abundant, and of good quality, for none of these men had ever seen mines before; very many of them had never seen pure gold, and most of them were seamen and lads. . . .

This is the account I have to give of my voyage. The men who accompanied me were a hundred and fifty in number, among whom were many calculated for pilots and good sailors, but none of them can explain whither I went nor whence I came; . . . The pilots thought we had come to the island of St. John, whereas it was the land of Mango, four hundred leagues to the westward of where they said. Let them answer and say if they know where Veragua is situated. I assert that they can give no other account than that they went to lands, where there was an abundance of gold, and this they can certify surely enough; but they do not know the way to return thither for such a purpose; they would be obliged to go on a voyage of discovery as much as if they had never been there before. . . . The nation of which Pope Pius writes has now been found, judging at least by the situation and other evidences, excepting the horses with the saddles and poitrels [breastplates] and bridles of gold; but this is not to be wondered at, for the lands on the sea-coast are only inhabited by fishermen, and moreover I made no stay there, because I was in haste to proceed on my voyage. In Cariay and the neighbouring country there are great enchanters of a very fearful character. They would have given the world to prevent my remaining there an hour. . . .

. . . when I discovered the Indies, I said that they composed the richest lordship in the world; I spoke of gold and pearls and precious stones, of spices and the traffic that might be carried on in them ; and because all these things were not forthcoming at once I was abused. This punishment causes me to refrain from relating anything but what the natives tell me. One thing I can venture upon stating, because there are so many witnesses of it, viz., that in this land of Veragua I saw more signs of gold in the two first days than I saw in Española during four years, and that there is not a more fertile or better cultivated country in all the world, nor one whose inhabitants are more timid ; added to which there is a good harbour, a beautiful river, and the whole place is capable of being easily put into a state of defence. All this tends to the security of the Christians and the permanency of their sovereignty, while it affords the hope of great increase and honour to the Christian religion ; moreover the road hither will be as short as that to Española, because there is a certainty of a fair wind for the passage. Your Highnesses are as much lords of this country as of Xerez or Toledo, and your ships that may come here will do so with the same freedom as if they were going to your own royal palace. From hence they will obtain gold, and whereas if they should wish to become masters of the products of other lands, they will have to take them by force or retire empty-handed ; in this country they will simply have to trust their persons in hands of a savage.

I have already explained my reason for refraining to treat of other subjects respecting which I might speak. I do not state as certain, nor do I confirm even the sixth part of all that I have said or written, nor do I pretend to be at the fountain-head of the information. The Genoese, Venetians, and all other nations that possess pearls, precious stones, and other articles of value, take them to the ends of the world to exchange them for gold. Gold is the most precious of all commodities ; gold constitutes treasure, and he who possesses it has all he needs in this world, as also the means of rescuing souls from purgatory, and restoring them to the enjoyment of paradise. They say that when one of the lords of the country of Veragua dies, they bury all the gold he possessed with his body. There were brought to Solomon at one journey six hundred and sixty-six quintals of gold, besides what the merchants and sailors brought, and that which was paid in Arabia. . . . Who will offer himself for this work ? Should any one do so, I pledge myself, in the name of God, to convey him safely thither, provided the Lord permits me to return to Spain. The people who have sailed with me have passed through incredible toil and danger, and I beseech your Highnesses, since they are poor, to pay them promptly, and to be gracious to each of them according to their respective merits; for I can safely assert, that to my belief they are the bearers of the best news that ever were carried to Spain. With respect to the gold which belongs to Quibian, the cacique of Veragua, and other chiefs in the neighbouring country, although it appears by the accounts we have received of it to be very abundant, I do not think it would be well or desirable, on the part of your Highnesses, to take possession of it in the way of plunder; by fair dealing, scandal and disrepute will be avoided, and all the gold will thus reach your Highnesses' treasury without the loss of a grain. . . .

. . . The lands in this part of the world, which are now under your Highnesses' sway, are richer and more extensive than those of any other Christian power, and yet, after that I had, by the Divine will, placed them under your high and royal sovereignty, and was on the point of bringing your majesties into the receipt of a very great and unexpected revenue; and while I was waiting for the ships, to convey me in safety, and with a heart full of joy, to your royal presence, victoriously to announce the news of the gold that I had discovered, I was arrested and thrown, with my two brothers, loaded with irons, into a ship, stripped, and very ill-treated, without being allowed any appeal to justice. Who could believe, that a poor foreigner would have risen against your Highnesses, in such a place, without any motive or argument on his side; without even the assistance of any other prince upon which to rely; but on the contrary, amongst your own vassals and natural subjects, and with my sons staying at your royal court? I was twenty-eight years old when I came into your Highnesses' service, and now I have not a hair upon me that is not grey; my body is infirm, and all that was left to me, as well as to my brothers, has been taken away and sold, even to the frock that I wore, to my great dishonour. I cannot but believe that this was done without your royal permission. The restitution of my honour, the reparation of my losses, and the punishment of those who have inflicted them, will redound to the honour of your royal character; a similar punishment also is due to those who plundered me of my pearls, and who have brought a disparagement upon the privileges of my admiralty. Great and unexampled will be the glory and fame of your Highnesses, if you do this; and the memory of your Highnesses, as just and grateful sovereigns, will survive as a bright example to Spain in future ages. . . .

Select Letters of Christopher Columbus, in Hakluyt Society, *Works issued, 1847* (London, 1847), 169–202 *passim*.

20. First Use of the Name America (1507)

BY MARTIN WALTZEE-MÜLLER (HYLACO-MYLUS)

(TRANSLATED BY EDWARD G. BOURNE, 1892)

Waltzee-Müller (or, as he called himself in classical form, "Hylaco-mylus") was a schoolmaster in St.-Dié, in Alsace, and member of a coterie interested in the new discoveries, and especially in Vespuccius. — On the author see Winsor, *Narrative and Critical History*, II, 163–171. On the subject see Winsor, II, 153–179; Henry Harrisse, *Discovery of North America*, 274–280; Channing and Hart, *Guide*, § 84.

. . . AND the fourth part of the world having been discovered by Americus, it may be called Amerige; that is, the land of Americus or America.

. . . Now truly, as these regions are more widely explored, and another fourth part is discovered, by Americus Vesputius, as may be learned from the following letters, I do not see why any one may justly forbid it to be named Amerige, that is, Americ's Land, from Americus the discoverer, a man of sagacious mind, or America, since both Europe and Asia derived their names from women.

Martin Waltzee-Müller, *Cosmographiae Introductio cum quibusdam Geometriae*, extract translated in Winsor, *Narrative and Critical History of America* (Boston, 1886), II, 147–148 *passim*.

---

21. How Cortez took Montezuma Prisoner (1519)

BY FRANCISCO LOPEZ DE GÓMARA (1552)

(TRANSLATED BY THOMAS NICHOLAS, 1578)

Gómara was Cortes' chaplain and secretary after 1540. — On the author, Winsor, *Narrative and Critical History*, II, 412. Bibliography on the subject, Winsor, *Narrative and Critical History*, II, 397–430; Channing and Hart, *Guide*, § 83; H. H. Bancroft, *Mexico*, I (*Pacific States*, IV).

HERNANDO CORTEZ and his company, were five daies in beholding and perusing the scituation of the Citie and secrets of the same, with yᵉ notable thinges before rehearsed: they were often visited by Mutezuma, and the Gentlemen of his Court, and abundantly provided of things necessary for his vse, and the Indians of his company.

Likewise his Horses were cherished and serued with greene barley and grasse, whereof there is plentie all the yeare: likewise of corne, meale, roses, and of all thinges that their owners would request, in so

E

much that beddes of floures were made for them in place of litter.   But
yet notwithstanding, although they were in this sorte cherished, and also
lodged in so riche a Countrey, where they mighte fill their purses, they
were not yet all contente and merrie, but rather with great feare and
care, especially Cortez, who hadde the onely care as head and chief
Captaine for the defence of his fellowes, hee (I say) was pensiue, noting the scituation of the Citie, the infinite number of people, the state
and maiestie of Mexico, yea and some disquietnesse of his owne com-
panye, who woulde come and laye vnto his charge the snare and nette
that they were in, in thinking it a thing vnpossible that anye of them
coulde escape, if Mutezuma, were thervnto determined, or else with the
least muteny in the worlde, that mought be raised in the Citie, although
that euery inhabitant shoulde throw but one stone at them, or else to
breake vp the drawbridges, or withdrawing their victuals, things very
easie to bee done.   With this greate care that he had of the preseruation
of his fellowes, and to remedie the perill and daunger that he stoode
in, he determined to apprehēd Mutezuma, and to builde foure Foystes
[forts] to haue the lake in subiection, which he hadde before imagined,
and without the apprehension of the King, he coulde not come by the
Kingdome : he would very gladly haue built the Foystes out of hand,
but he left off that pretence, only because hee would not delay the
imprisonment of Mutezuma, wherein consisted the effect of all his
businesse, so that forthwith he minded to put in execution his intent,
without giuing any of his company to vnderstand thereof.

The quarrell wherewith he had armed himselfe for that purpose, was,
that the Lord Qualpopoca hadde slaine nine Spaniardes : likewise encouraged him the great presumption of his letters written to the
Emperour Charles his king, wherein he wrote that he would take
Mutezuma prisoner, and dispossesse him of his Empyre.   These causes
considered, he tooke the letters of Pedro Hircio, wherin was written,
howe Qualpopoca was the cause of the death of nine Spaniardes, put
those letters into his pocket, and walking vp and downe his lodging,
tossing too and fro these imaginations in his brayne, full of care of the
greate enterprise that he had in hande, yea he himselfe iudging the
matter doubtfull, and his head beeing in this sort occupied, he chanced
to espie one wall more whiter than the rest, and beholding the same, he
sawe that it was a dore lately dammed vp, and calling vnto him two of
his seruaunts (for all the residue were a sleepe) because it was late in
the **nighte,** he opened that dore, and went in, and there found sundry

halles, some with Idols, some with gallant feathers, Jewels, precious stones, plate, yea and such an infinite quantitie of golde, that the sight thereof amazed him, and other gallant things that made him to maruell. He shutte this doore againe as well as he moughte, without touching any part of that treasure, because he woulde not make any uprore there-aboute, nor yet to delaye the imprsonment of Mutezuma, for that treas-ure was alwaies there to be had.

The next daye in the morning came certpine Spaniards vnto him, and manye Indians of Tlaxcallon saying that the Citizens did goe about to conspire their deathe, and to breake downe the bridges of the calseyes, [causeways] to bring their purpose the better to passe. So that with this newes, beeing true or false, Cortes left the one halfe of his men to defende and keepe his lodging, and at euery crosse streete he planted mê[n], and the residue he sent to the Court by two and two, and three and three, and he himselfe came to the pallaice, saying that hee must talke with Mutezuma of matters that did emport their liues. Cortez was secretly armed. Mutezuma hearing howe Cortez attended for him, came foorth and receiued him, taking him by the hande, and placed him in his seate thirtie Spaniards waited vpon Cortez, and the residue abode without at the doore.

Cortes saluted Mutezuma according to his accustomed manner, and began to iest and talke merrily as hee was wont to doe. Mutezuma being carelesse of the thing that Fortune hadde prepared againste him, was also very merrie, and pleased with that conuersation. he gaue vnto Cortez Jewels of golde, and one of his daughters, and other noble mens daughters to others of his company. Cortez receiued the gift, for otherwise it had beene a frent vnto Mutezuma. But yet he enformed him, that he was a married man, and that he coulde not marrie with his daughter, for the Christian law did not permitte the same, nor yet that any Christian mought haue more then one wife, vppon paine of infamy, and to be marked in the forehead.

After all this talke ended, Cortes tooke the letters of Pedro Hircio, and caused them to be interpreted vnto Mutezuma, making his grieuous complainte againste Qualpopoca, who hadde slaine so many Spaniardes through his commaundement, yea and that his subiects had published, that they would kill the Spaniardes, and breake downe the bridges.

Mutezuma excused himselfe earnestly, as well of the one as of the other, saying, the report giuen out againste his subiectes was false and vntrue. and as for Qualpopoca who had slaine the Spaniardes, he was

innocent therof: and because that he shoulde see the troth, he called
incontinent certaine of his seruauntes, commaunding them to goe for
Qualpopoca, and gaue vnto them his seale, which was a stone that he
ware at his wrest, engraued with the figure of the God Vitzilopuchtli,
and the messẽgers departed therewith incontinent [forthwith].

Cortez replied and said, My Lord, your highnesse must goe with me
to my lodging, and there abide, vntill your messengers returne with
Qualpopoca, and the certaintie of the deathe of my men: In my lodging youre highnesse shall rule and commaund as you doe heere in Court,
your person shall bee well vsed, wherefore take you no care, for I will
haue respecte vnto youre honor, as to mine owne proper, or the honor
of my King, beseeching you to pardon me in this my request, for if I
should do otherwise, and dissemble with you, mine own company would
be offended with me, saying that I doe not defende them according
to dutie. Wherefore commaund your householde seruantes to repose
themselues without alteration, for be you assured that if any hurt come
vnto mee, or vnto anye of mine, youre person shall pay the same with
life, considering that it lieth in youre hande to goe quietly with me.

Mutezuma was sore amazed, saying, Sir, my person is not fitte to be a
prisoner, yea, and though I woulde permitte the same, my subiectes
would not suffer.

They abode arguing the matter neere foure houres, and at length
Mutezuma was content to goe, hauing promise that he shoulde rule and
gouerne as he was wont to do. Cortez commaunded a place in his
lodging to be trimmed for him, and he went forthwith thither with
Cortes. There came many noble men bare footed, weeping and lament-
ing the case, carrying their best garments vnder their armes, and brought
a rich seate, wheron Mutezuma was placed, they carried him vppon their
shoulders.

When it was blowen abroade in the Citie that Mutezuma was carried
prisoner to the Spaniardes lodging, all the Citie was on an vprore: but
yet Mutezuma did cõfort the Gentlemen that carried and followed him
weeping, praying them to cease their lamentation, saying that he was
not prisoner, nor yet went with the Christians againste his will, but for
his onely pleasure. Cortes appointed a Spanish garde for him, with a
Captaine, the which he chãged, and had Spaniards alwaies in his cõpany
to make him pastime. Also poore Mutezuma was cõtented with their
conuersation, gaue thẽ stil rewards. He was serued with his owne
seruãts Indians, as at home in his pallace. Cortes, alwaies intreated

him to put of sadnes, to be merrie, permitting him to dispatch suters, to deale in all affaires of his estate, and to comune and talke openly or secretly with his noble men as he was wont to do, and that was but onely a baite to bring them to the hooke.   There was neuer Greeke nor Romaine, nor any other nation since the name of kings was ordeined, did giue yᵉ like interprise as Hernando Cortez did, in taking Mutezuma prisoner in his owne house, beeing a most mightie King, in a most strong fort among infinite people, he hauing but only 450. companions.

Francisco Lopez de Gómara, *The Pleasant Historie of the Conquest of the West India, now called New Spaine* (London, 1596), pp. 207–212.

---

22. The Story of Pizarro's Conquest (1531)

BY HERNANDO PIZARRO

(TRANSLATED BY CLEMENTS R. MARKHAM, 1872)

By the brother of the commander of the expedition. — Bibliography: Winsor, *Narrative and Critical History*, II, 563–568; Channing and Hart, *Guide*, § 85.

MAGNIFICENT lords, — I arrived in this port of Yaguana on my way to Spain, by order of the Governor Francisco Pizarro, to inform his Majesty of what has happened in that government of Peru, to give an account of the country, and of its present condition; . . .

The Governor, in the name of his Majesty, founded a town near the sea-coast, which was called San Miguel.   It is twenty-five leagues from that point to Tumbez.   Having left citizens there, and assigned the Indians in the district to them, he set out with sixty horse and ninety foot, in search of the town of Caxamalca, at which place he was informed that Atabaliva then was, the son of old Cuzco, and brother of him who is now Lord of that land.   Between the two brothers there had been a very fierce war, and this Atabaliva had conquered the land as far as he then was, which, from the point whence we started, was a hundred and fifty leagues.   After seven or eight marches, a captain of Atabaliva came to the Governor and said that his Lord had heard of his arrival and rejoiced greatly at it, having a strong desire to see the Christians; and when he had been two days with the Governor he said that he wished to go forward and tell the news to his Lord, and that another would soon be on the road with a present, as a token of peace.   The Governor continued his march until he came to a town called *La*

Ramada. Up to that point all the land was flat, while all beyond was very rugged, and obstructed by very difficult passes. When we saw that the messenger from Atabaliva did not return, he wished to obtain intelligence from some Indians who had come from Caxamalca; so they were tortured, and they then said that they had heard that Atabaliva was waiting for the Governor in the mountains to give him battle. The Governor then ordered the troops to advance, leaving the rear guard in the plain. The rest ascended, and the road was so bad that, in truth, if they had been waiting for us, either in this pass or in another that we came to on the road to Caxamalca, they could very easily have stopped us; for, even by exerting all our skill, we could not have taken the horses by the roads; and neither horse nor foot can cross those mountains except by the roads. The distance across them to Caxamalca is twenty leagues.

When we were half way, messengers arrived from Atabaliva, and brought provisions to the Governor. They said that Atabaliva was waiting for him at Caxamalca, wishing to be his friend; and that he wished the Governor to know that his captains, whom he has sent to the war of Cuzco, had taken his brother prisoner, that they would reach Caxamalca within two days, and that all the territory of his father now belonged to him. The Governor sent back to say that he rejoiced greatly at this news, and that, if there was any Lord who refused to submit, he would give assistance and subjugate him. Two days afterwards the Governor came in sight of Caxamalca, and he met Indians with food. He put the troops in order, and marched to the town. Atabaliva was not there, but was encamped on the plain at a distance of a league, with all his people in tents. When the Governor saw that Atabaliva did not come, he sent a Captain, with fifteen horsemen, to speak to Atabaliva, saying that he would not assign quarters to the Christians until he knew where it was the pleasure of Atabaliva that they should lodge, and he desired him to come that they might be friends. . . . He said that, four marches from that spot, there were some very rebellious Indians who would not submit to him, and that the Christians might go there to help his troops. I said that the Governor would send ten horsemen, who would suffice for the whole country, and that his Indians were unnecessary, except to search for those who concealed themselves. He smiled like a man who did not think so much of us. The Captain told me that, until I came, he had not been able to get him to speak, but that one of his chiefs had answered for him, while he always kept his head down. He was seated in all the majesty of command, surrounded by all his women, and with many chiefs near him. . . .

That night a good look-out was kept. In the morning he sent messengers to put off his visit until the afternoon ; and these messengers, in conversing with some Indian girls in the service of the Christians, who were their relations, told them to run away because Atabaliva was coming that afternoon to attack the Christians and kill them. Among the messengers there came that Captain who had already met the Governor on the road. He told the Governor that his Lord Atabaliva said that, as the Christians had come armed to his camp, he also would come armed. The Governor replied that he might come as he liked. Atabaliva set out from his camp at noon, and when he came to a place which was about half a quarter of a league from Caxamalca, he stopped until late in the afternoon. . . . The Governor sent a Christian, and presently Atabaliva moved, leaving the armed men behind him. He took with him about five or six thousand Indians without arms, except that, under their shirts, they had small darts and slings with stones.

He came in a litter, and before him went three or four hundred Indians in liveries, cleaning the straws from the road and singing. Then came Atabaliva in the midst of his chiefs and principal men, the greatest among them being also borne on men's shoulders. When they entered the open space, twelve or fifteen Indians went up to the little fortress that was there and occupied it, taking possession with a banner fixed on a lance. When Atabaliva had advanced to the centre of the open space he stopped, and a Dominican Friar, who was with the Governor, came forward to tell him, on the part of the Governor, that he waited for him in his lodging, and that he was sent to speak with him. The Friar then told Atabaliva that he was a Priest, and that he was sent there to teach the things of the Faith, if they should desire to be Christians. He showed Atabaliva a book which he carried in his hands, and told him that that book contained the things of God. Atabaliva asked for the book, and threw it on the ground, saying : " I will not leave this place until you have restored all that you have taken in my land. I know well who you are, and what you have come for." Then he rose up in his litter and addressed his men, and there were murmurs among them and calls to those who were armed. The Friar went to the Governor and reported what was being done, and that no time was to be lost. The Governor sent to me ; and I had arranged with the Captain of the artillery that, when a sign was given, he should discharge his pieces, and that, on hearing the reports, all the troops should come forth at once.   This was done, and as the Indians were unarmed, they were defeated without danger to any Christian.   Those who carried the litter, and the chiefs who surrounded Atabaliva, were all killed, falling round him.   The Governor came out and seized Atabaliva, and, in protecting him, he received a knife-cut from a Christian in the hand.   The troops continued the pursuit as far as the place where the armed Indians were stationed, who made no resistance whatever, because it was now night. All were brought into the town, where the Governor was quartered. . . . The Governor said that he had not come to make war on the Indians, but that our Lord the Emperor, who was Lord of the whole world, had ordered him to come, that he might see the land and let Atabaliva know the things of our Faith, in case he should wish to become a Christian. The Governor also told him that that land, and all other lands, belonged to the Emperor, and that he must acknowledge him as his Lord.   He replied that he was content, and, observing that the Christians had col- lected some gold, Atabaliva said to the Governor that they need not take such care of it, as if there was so little ; for that he could give them ten thousand plates, and that he could fill the room in which he was up to a white line, which was the height of a man and a half from the floor. The room was seventeen or eighteen feet wide, and thirty-five feet long. He said that he could do this in two months. . . .

After returning to Caxamalca and reporting my proceedings to the Governor, he ordered me to go to Spain, and to give an account to his Majesty of this and other things which appertain to his service.   I took, from the heap of gold, 100,000 *castellanos* for his Majesty, being the amount of his fifth.   The day after I left Caxamalca, the Christians who had gone to Cuzco returned, and brought 1,500,000 of gold.   After I arrived at Panama, another ship came in, with some knights.   They say that a distribution of the gold was made ; and that the share of his Majesty, besides the 100,000 *pesos* [Spanish dollars] and the 5000 *marcos* [8 ounces] of silver that I bring, was another 165,000 *castellanos* [$\frac{1}{6}$ ounce] and 7000 or 8000 *marcos* of silver; while to all those of us who had gone, a further share of gold was sent.

After my departure, according to what the Governor writes to me, it became known that Atabaliva had assembled troops to make war on the Christians, and justice was done upon him.   The Governor made his brother, who was his enemy, lord in his place.   Molina comes to this city, and from him your worships may learn anything else that you may desire to know. The shares of the troops were, to the horsemen 9000 *castellanos*, to the Governor 6000, to me 3000. The Governor has derived no other profit from that land, nor has there been deceit or fraud in the account. I say this to your worships, because if any other statement is made, this is the truth. May our Lord long guard and prosper the magnificent persons of your worships.

Letters from Hernando Pizarro to the Royal Audience of Santo Domingo, in Hakluyt Society, *Works issued, 1872* (London, 1872), pp. 113–127 *passim*.

———————◆———————

23. From the Ocean to the Mississippi (1539–1542)

BY "A PORTUGALL GENTLEMAN OF ELUAS"

(TRANSLATED BY RICHARD HAKLUYT, 1609)

The name of this writer is not known (perhaps Alvaro Fernandez); but he was a member of this expedition. — Bibliography: Winsor, *Narrative and Critical History*, II, 289; Channing and Hart, *Guide*, § 86.

CAPTAINE *SOTO* was the son of a Squire of *Xerez* of *Badaioz*. He went into the Spanish *Indies* when *Peter Arias* of *Auila* was Gouernour of the West *Indies:* And there he was without any thing else of his owne, saue his sword and target : and for his good qualities and valour, *Peter Arias* made him Captaine of a troope of horsemen, and by his commandement hee went with *Fernando Pizarro* to the conquest of *Peru:* where (as many persons of credit reported, which were there present) as well at the taking of *Atabalipa*, Lord of *Peru*, as at the assault of the citie of *Cusco*, and in all other places where they found resistance, wheresoeuer hee was present, hee passed all other Captaines and principall persons. For which cause, besides his part of the treasure of *Atabalipa*, he had a good share : whereby in time he gathered an hundred and foure-score thousand Duckets together, with that which fell to his part : which he brought into *Spaine:* whereof the Emperour borrowed a certaine part, which he repaied againe with 60,000 Rials of plate in the rent of the silkes of *Granada*, and all the rest was deliuered him in the contractation house of *Siuil* [Seville]. He tooke seruants, to wit, a Steward, a Gentleman Vsher, Pages, a Gentleman of the Horse, a Chamberlaine, Lakies, and al other officers that the house of a Noble mã requireth, . . . The Emperour made him the Gouernor of the Isle of *Cuba*, and Ade-

lantado or President of *Florida;* with a title of Marques of a certaine
part of the lands, that he should conquer.

On Sunday the 18. of May, in the yeere of our Lord, 1539, the Adelantado or president departed from *Hauana* in *Cuba* with his fleete,
which were nine vessels, fiue great ships, two carauels, and two brigantines : They sailed seuen daies with a prosperous wind. . . . On Friday
the 30. of May they landed in *Florida,* two leagues from a towne of an
Indian Lord, called *Vcita.* . . .

. . . Hee left Captaine *Calderan* at the Port, with thirtie horsemen,
and seuentie footemen, with prouision for two yeeres, and himselfe with
all the rest marched into the maine land, and came to the *Paracossi,* at
whose towne *Baltasar de Gallegos* was : and from thence with all his
men tooke the way to *Cale.* . . .

This Riuer . . . was that which . . . fell into *Rio grande,* or the
Great Riuer [Mississippi], which passed by *Pachaha* and *Aquixo* neere
vnto the prouince of *Guachoya :* and the Lord thereof came vp the Riuer
in canoes to make warre with him of *Nilco.* On his behalf there came an
Indian to the Gouernour and said vnto him, That he was his seruant, and
prayed him so to hold him, and that within two daies hee would come
to kisse his Lordships hands : and at the time appointed he came with
some of his principal Indians, which accompanied him, and with words
of great offers and courtesie hee gaue the Gouernour a present of many
Mantles and Deeres skinnes.   The Gouernour gaue him some other
things in recompense, and honoured him much.   Hee asked him what
townes there were downe the Riuer?   Hee answered that he knew none
other but his owne : and on the other side of the Riuer a prouince of a
Cacique called *Quigalta.*   So hee tooke his leaue of the Gouernour and
went to his owne towne.   Within few daies the Gouernour determined
to goe to *Guacheya,* to learne there whether the Sea were neere, or
whether there were any habitation neere, where hee might relieue his
companie, while the brigantines were making, which he meant to send
to the land of the Christians.   As he passed the Riuer of *Nilco,* there
came in canoes Indians of *Guachoya* vp the streame, and when they
saw him, supposing that he came to seeke them to doe them some hurt,
they returned downe the Riuer, and informed the Cacique thereof:
who with all his people, spoiling the towne of all that they could carrie
away, passed that night ouer to the other side of *Rio grande,* or the
great Riuer.   The Gouernour sent a Captaine with fiftie men in sixe
canoes downe the Riuer, and went himselfe by land with the rest : hee

came to *Guachoya* vpon Sunday the 17. of Aprill: he lodged in the towne of the Cacique, which was inclosed about, and seated a crossebow shot distant from the Riuer. . . .

The Gouernour fell into great dumps to see how hard it was to get to the Sea: and worse, because his men and horses euery day diminished, being without succour to sustaine themselues in the country: and with that thought he fell sick, . . . being euill handled with feuers, and was much aggrieued, that he was not in case to passe presently the Riuer and to seeke him, to see if he could abate that pride of his, considering the Riuer went now very strongly in those parts; for it was neere halfe a league broad, and 16. fathomes deep, and uery furious, and ranne with a great current; and on both sides there were many Indians, and his power was not now so great, but that hee had need to helpe himselfe rather by flights than by force.

. . . the 21. of May, 1542. departed out of this life, the valorous, virtuous, and valiant Captaine, *Don Fernando de Soto*, Gouernour of *Cuba*, and Adelantado of *Florida*: whom fortune advanced, as it vseth to doe others, that hee might haue the higher fal [fall]. He departed in such a place, and at such a time, as is his sicknesse he had but little comfort: and the danger wherein all his people were of perishing in that Countrie, which appeared before their eies was cause sufficient, why euery one of them had need of comfort, and why they did not visit nor accompanie him as they ought to haue done. *Luys de Moscoso* determined to conceale his death from the Indians, because *Ferdinando de Soto* had made them beleeue, That the Christians were immortall. . . .

Assoone as he was dead, *Luis de Moscoso* commanded to put him secretly in an house, where hee remained three daies: and remoouing him from thence, commanded him to bee buried in the night at one of the gates of the towne within the wall. And as the Indians had seene him sick, and missed him, so did they suspect what might bee. And passing by the place where hee was buried, seeing the earth mooved, they looked and spake one to another. *Luys de Moscoso* vnderstanding of it, commanded him to be taken vp by night, and to cast a greate deale of sand into the mantles, wherein he was winded vp, wherein he was carried in a canoe, and throwne into the middest of the Riuer. . . .

Virginia richly valued, by the Description of the Maine Land of Florida, her Next Neighbour, etc.; in Richard Hakluyt, *The Principall Voyages, Navigations, Traffiques, and Discoveries of the English Nation* (London, 1609), II, 1–131 *passim*.

24. First Expedition to Kansas and Nebraska (1540)

BY CAPTAIN JUAN JARAMILLO

(Translated by George P. Winship, 1896)

Jaramillo's opportunities and character are set forth in his own narrative. — Bibliography: Winsor, *Narrative and Critical History*, II, 498–504 ; Channing and Hart, *Guide*, § 86 ; Geo. P. Winship, *List of Works useful to the Student of the Coronado Expedition ;* H. H. Bancroft, *Arizona and New Mexico* (*Pacific States*, XII).

FROM here we went to another river, which we called the Bermejo, or Red river, in two days' journey in the same direction, but less toward the northeast. Here we saw an Indian or two, who afterwards turned out to be from the first settlement of Cibola. From here we came in two days' journey to the said village, the first of Cibola. The houses have flat roofs and walls of stone and mud, and here was where they killed Steve, or Estevanillo, the negro who had come with Dorantes from Florida and returned with Friar Marcos de Niza. In this province of Cibola there are five little villages besides this, all with flat roofs and of stone and mud, as I described. The country is cold, as is shown by the houses and hothouses (estufas) they have. From this first village of Cibola, facing the northeast and a little less, on the left hand, there is a province called Tucayan, about five days off, which has seven flat-roofed villages, with as good as or better food supply than these, and even a larger population ; and they also have the skins of cows and of deer, and cloaks of cotton, as I said.

All the waterways we found up to this Cibola, — and I don't know but what a day or two beyond, — the rivers and streams, run into the south sea [Pacific], and those from beyond here into the north sea [Gulf of Mexico].

From this first village of Cibola, as I have said, we went to another in this same province, which was about a short day's journey off, on the way to Tihuex [Rio Grande]. It is nine days of such marches as we have made from this settlement of Cibola to the river of Tihuex. Halfway between, I do not know but it may be a day more or less, is a village of earth and dressed stone, in a very strong position, which is called Tutahaco. All these Indians, except the first in the village of Cibola, received us well. At the river of Tihuex there are 15 villages within a distance of about 20 leagues, all with flat-roofed houses of earth, and not stone, after the fashion of mud walls. There are other villages besides these on other streams which flow into this, and three of these are, for Indians, well worth seeing, especially one that is called Chia, and another Uraba, and another Cicuique. Uraba and Cicuique have many houses, two stories high. All the rest, and these also, have corn and beans and melons, skins, and some long robes of feathers which they braid, joining the feathers with a sort of thread ; and they also make them of a sort of plain weaving with which they make the cloaks with which they protect themselves. They all have hot rooms underground, which, although not very clean, are very warm. They raise and have a very little cotton, of which they make the cloaks of which I have spoken above. This river comes from the northwest and flows about southeast, which shows that it certainly flows into the North sea. Leaving this settlement and the said river, we went by two other villages whose names I do not know, and in four days came to Cicuique [Pecos pueblo], which I have already mentioned. The direction of this is toward the northeast. From Cicuique we came to another river [Pecos?], which the Spaniards named Cicuique, in three days ; if I remember rightly, it seems to me that we went rather toward the northeast to reach this river by the way we came, and, after crossing this, we turned more to the left hand, which would be more to the northeast, and began to enter the plains where the cows [buffalo] are, although we did not find them for some four or five days, after which we began to come across bulls, of which there are great numbers, and after going on and meeting the bulls for two or three days in the same direction, after this we began to find ourselves in the midst of very great numbers of cows, yearlings, and bulls all in together. We found Indians among these first cows, who were called, on this account, by those in the flat-roofed houses, Querechos. They live without houses, but have some sets of poles which they carry with them to make something like huts in the places where they stop, which serve them for houses. They tie these poles together at the top and stick the bottoms into the ground, covering them with some cow-skins which they carry around, and which, as I have said, serve them for houses. From what was learned of these Indians, all their human needs are supplied by these cows, for they are fed and clothed and shod from these. They are a people who go around here and there, wherever seems to them best. We went on for eight or ten days in the same direction, along those streams which are among the cows. The Indian who guided us from here was the one that had given us the news about Quivira and Arache (or Arahei) and about its being a very rich country, with much

gold, and other things, and he and the other one were from that country
I mentioned, to which we were going, and we found these two Indians
in the flat-roofed villages. It seems that, as the said Indian wanted to
go to his own country, he proceeded to tell us what we found was not
true, and I do not know whether it was on this account or because he
was counselled to take us into other regions by confusing us about the
road, although there are none in all this region except those of the cows.
We understood, however, that he was leading us away from the route we
ought to follow and wanted to get us on to those plains where he had
got us, so that we would eat up the food, and both ourselves and our
horses would become weak from the lack of this, because if we should go
either back or ahead in this condition we could not make any resistance
to whatever they might wish to do to us. At last as, from the time when,
as I said, we entered the plains and from this settlement of Querechos,
he led us off more to the east, until we came to be in extreme need from
the lack of food. . . . I believe we had been travelling twenty days or
more in this direction. . . . We all went forward one day to a stream
which was down in a ravine in the midst of good meadows, to agree
on who should go ahead and how the rest should return. Here the
Indian Isopete, as we had called the companion of the said Turk, was
asked to tell us the truth, and to lead us to that country which we had
come in search of. He said he would do it, and that it was not as
the Turk had said, because those were certainly fine things which he
had said and had given us to understand, about gold, and how it was
secured, and the buildings, and the style of them, and their trade, and
many other things told for the sake of prolixity, which had led us to
go in search of them, with the advice of all who gave it and of the
priests. He asked us to leave him afterwards in that country, as it
was his native country, as a reward for guiding us, and, also, that the
Turk might not go along with him, because he would quarrel and try
to restrain him in everything that he wanted to do for our advantage ;
and the general promised him this, and said he would be with one of
the thirty, and he went in this way. And when everything was ready
for us to set out and for the others to remain, we pursued our way,
turning all the time after this toward the north, for more than thirty
days' march, although not long marches, without having to go without
water on any one of them, and among cows all the time, some days
in larger numbers than others, according to the water which we came
across, so that on Saint Peter and Paul's day we reached a river which

we found to be there below Quibira, and when we reached the said river, the Indian recognized it and said that was it, and that it was below the settlements. We crossed it there and went up the other side on the north, the direction turning toward the northeast, and after marching three days we found some Indians who were going hunting, killing the cows to take the meat to their village, which was about three or four days still farther away from us. Here where we found the Indians and they saw us, they began to utter yells and appeared to fly, and some even had their wives there with them. The Indian Isopete began to call them in his language, and so they came to us without any signs of fear. . . . Some satisfaction was experienced here on seeing the good appearance of the earth, and it is certainly such here among the cows, and from here on. The general wrote a letter here to the governor of Harahey and Quivira, giving him to understand that he was a Christian from the army of Florida, led astray by what the Indian had said of their manner of government and their general character, which he had made us believe. So the Indians went to their houses, which were at the distance mentioned, and we also proceeded at our rate of marching until we reached the settlements, which we found along good river bottoms, although without much water, and good streams which flow into another, larger than the one I have mentioned. There were, if I recall correctly, six or seven settlements, at quite a distance from one another, among which we travelled for four or five days, since it was understood to be uninhabited between one stream and the other. We reached what they said was the end of Quivira, to which they took us, saying that what there was there was of great importance.

Here there was a river, with more water and more inhabitants than the others. Being asked if there was anything beyond, they said that there was nothing more of Quivira, but that there was Harahey, and that it was the same sort of a place, with settlements like these, and of about the same size. The general sent to summon the lord of those parts and the other Indians whom they said resided in Harahey, and he came with about 200 men — all naked — with bows, and I don't know what sort of things on their heads. . . . He was a big Indian, with a large body and limbs, and well proportioned. After he had got the opinion of one and another about it, the general asked them what we ought to do, reminding us of how the army had been left and that the rest of us were there, so that it seemed to all of us that as it was already almost the opening of winter, for, if I remember rightly, it was after the middle of August, and because there was little to winter there for, and we were but very little prepared for it, and the uncertainty as to the success of the army that had been left, and because the winter might close the roads with snow and rivers which we could not cross, and also in order to see what had happened to the rest of the force left behind, it seemed to us all that his grace ought to go back in search of them, and when he had found out for certain how they were, to winter there and return to that country at the opening of spring, to conquer and cultivate it.   Since, as I said, this was the last point which we reached, here the Turk saw that he had lied to us, and called upon all these people to attack us one night and kill us.   We learned of it, and put him under guard and strangled him that night, so that he never waked up.   With the plan mentioned, we turned back it may have been two or three days, where we provided ourselves with picked fruit and dried corn for our return.   The general raised a cross at this place, at the foot of which he made some letters with a chisel, which said that "Francisco Vazquez de Coronado," general of that army, had arrived here.

This country presents a very fine appearance, than which I have not seen a better in all our Spain nor Italy nor a part of France, nor, indeed, in the other countries in which I have travelled in His Majesty's service, for it is not a very rough country, but is made up of hillocks and plains, and very fine appearing rivers and streams, which certainly satisfied me and made me sure that it will be very fruitful in all sorts of products.   Indeed, there is profit in the cattle ready to the hand, from the quantity of them, which is as great as one could imagine.   We found a variety of Castilian prunes which are not all red, but some of them black and green ; the tree and fruit is certainly like that of Castile, with a very excellent flavor.   Among the cows we found flax, which springs up from the earth in clumps apart from each other, which are noticeable, as the cattle do not eat it, with their tops and blue flowers, and very perfect although small, resembling that of our own Spain (or and sumach like ours in Spain).   There are grapes along some streams, of a fair flavor, not to be improved upon. . . .

Bureau of Ethnology, *Fourteenth Annual Report* (Washington, 1896?), pp. 584-593 *passim*.

25. An Englishman in Mexico (1568)

BY MILES PHILIPS (1582)

Philips was one of Hawkins' men, and was set on shore after the battle at San Juan d'Ulloa (No. 29 below). His truthfulness is somewhat questioned. — Bibliography: Winsor, *Narrative and Critical History*, II, ch. vii; H. H. Bancroft, *Mexico*, II (*Pacific States*, V); Channing and Hart, *Guide*, § 86.

THE gentlemen that thus tooke vs for their seruants or slaues, did new apparell vs through out, with whom we abode, doing such seruice as they appointed vs vnto, which was for the most part to attend vpon them at the table, and to be as their chamberlaines, and to waite vpon them when they went abroad, which they greatly accounted of: for in that countrey no Spaniard will serue one another, but they are all of them attended and serued by Indians weekely, and by Negroes which be their slaues during their life. In this sort we remained and serued in the said citie of Mexico, and thereabouts for the space of a yeere and somewhat longer. Afterwards many of vs were by our masters appointed to go to sundry of their Mines where they had to doe, and to be as ouerseers of the Negroes and Indians that laboured there. In which mines many of vs did profite and gaine greatly : for first we were allowed three hundred Pezos a man for a yeere, which is threescore pound sterling, and besides that the Indians and Negroes which wrought vnder our charge, vpon our well using and intreating of them, would at times as vpon Saturdayes when they had left worke, labour for vs, and blow as much siluer as should be worth vnto vs 3 markes or thereabouts, euery marke being worth 6 Pezos, and a halfe of their money, which 19 Pezos and a halfe, is worth 4 li. 10 s. of our money. Sundry weekes we did gaine so much by this meanes besides our wages, that many of vs became very rich, and were worth three thousand or foure thousand Pezos, for we liued and gained thus in those Mines some three or foure yeeres. As concerning those Gentlemen which were deliuered as hostages, and that were kept in prison, in the Viceroy his house, after that we were gone from out the garden to serue sundry gentlemen as aforesaid, they remained prisoners in the said house for the space of 4 moneths after their comming thither, at the end whereof the fleete being readie to depart from S. Iohn de Vllua, to goe for Spaine, the said Gentlemen were sent away into Spaine with the fleete, where as I haue heard it credibly reported, many of them died with the cruell handling of the Spaniards, in the Inquisition house, as those which haue bene deliuered home after they had suffered the persecution of that house can more perfectly declare.   Robert Barret also master of the Iesus, was sent away with the fleete into Spaine the next yeere following, where afterwards he suffered persecution in the Inquisition, and at the last was condemned to be burnt, and with him one more of our men whose name was Iohn Gilbert.

Now after that sixe yeeres were fully expired since our first coming into the Indies, in which time we had bene imprisoned and serued in the said countreys as is before truely declared.   In the yeere of our Lord one thousand fiue hundred seuenty foure, the Inquisition began to be established in the Indies, very much against the mindes of many of the Spaniards themselues : for neuer vntill this time since their first conquering and planting in the Indies, were they subiect to that bloodie and cruell Inquisition.   The chiefe Inquisitor was named Don Pedro Moya de Contreres, and Iohn de Bouilla his companion, and Iohn Sanches the Fischall, and Pedro de los Rios, the Secretary : they being come and setled, and placed in a very faire house neere vnto the white Friers, considering with themselues that they must make an entrance and beginning of that their most detestable Inquisition here in Mexico, to the terror of the whole countrey, thought it best to call vs that were Englishmen first in question, and so much the rather, for that they had perfect knowledge and intelligence that many of vs were become very rich, as hath bene alreadie declared, and therefore we were a very good booty and pray to the Inquisitors : so that now againe began our sorrowes a fresh, for we were sent for, and sought out in all places of the countrey, and proclamation made vpon paine of loosing of goods and excommunication, that no man should hide or keepe secret any Englishmen or any part of their goods.   By means whereof we were all soone apprehended in all places, and all our goods seized and taken for the Inquisitors vse, and so from all parts of the countrey we were conueied and sent as prisoners to the citie of Mexico, and there committed to prison in sundry dark dungeons, where we could not see but by candle light, and were neuer past two together in one place, so that we saw not one another, neither could one of vs tell what was become of another. . . .

I Miles Philips and William Lowe were appointed to the blacke Friers, where I was appointed to be an ouerseer of Indian workmen, who wrought there in building of a new church : amongst which Indians I learned their language or Mexican tongue very perfectly, and had great

familiaritie with many of them, whom I found to be a courteous and
louing kind of people, ingenious, and of great vnderstanding, and they
hate and abhorre the Spaniardes with all their hearts, they haue vsed such
horrible cruelties against them, and doe still keepe them in such subiection
and seruitude, that they and the Negros also doe daily lie in waite to
practise their deliuerance out of that thraldome and bondage, that the
Spaniardes doe keepe them in.   William Lowe he was appointed to serue
the Cooke in the kitchin, Richard Williams and Dauid Alexander were
appointed to the Grey Friers, Iohn Story and Robert Cooke to the white
Friers : Paul Horsewel the Secretary tooke to be his seruant : Thomas
Hull was sent to a Monastery of priests, where afterward he died.   Thus
we serued out the yeeres that we were condemned for, with the vse of our
fooles coates, and we must needs confesse that the Friers did vse us very
courteously : for euery one of vs had his chamber with bedding and diet,
and all things cleane and neat : yea many of the Spaniards and Friers
themselues do vtterly abhorre and mislike of that cruell Inquisition, and
would as they durst bewaile our miseries, and comfort vs the best they
could, although they stood in such feare of that diuelish Inquisition, that
they durst not let the left hande know what the right doth.   Now after
that the time was expired for which we were condemned to serue in
those religious houses, we were then brought againe before the chiefe
Inquisitor, and had all our fooles coates pulled off and hanged vp in the
head church, called Ecclesia Maior, and euery mans name and iudement
written thereupon with this addition, An heretike Lutheran reconciled.
And there are also all their coates hanged vp, which were condemned to
the gallies, with their names and iudgements, and vnderneath his coat,
Heretike Lutheran reconciled.   And also the coats and names of the
three that were burned, whereupon were written, An obstinate heretike
Lutheran burnt.   Then were we suffered to goe vp and downe the countrey,
and to place our selues as we could, and yet not so free, but that we
very well knew that there was good espiall alwayes attending vs and all
our actions, so that we durst not once speake or looke awry.   Dauid
Alexander and Robert Cooke returned to serue the Inquisitor, who
shortly after married them both to two of his Negro women : Richard
Williams married a rich widow of Biskay with 4000 Pezos : Paul Horse-
well is married to a Mestisa as they name those whose fathers were
Spaniards, and their mothers Indians, and this woman which Paul Horse-
well hath married, is sayd to be the daughter of one that came in with
Hernando Cortes the Conquerour, who had with her in marriage foure

thousand Pezos, and a faire house : Iohn Storie is married to a Negro woman : William Lowe had leaue and license to goe into Spaine where he is now married : for mine owne part I could neuer thoroughly settle myselfe to marry in that countrey, although many faire offers were made vnto me of such as were of great abilitie and wealth, but I could haue no liking to liue in that place, where I must euery where see and know such horrible idolatrie committed, and durst not once for my life speake against it : and therefore I had alwayes a longing and desire to this my natiue countrey : and, to returne and serue againe in the Mines where I might haue gathered great riches and wealth, I very well saw that at one time or another I should fall againe into the danger of that diuelish Inquisition, and so be stript of all, with losse of life also, and therefore I made my choice rather to learne to weaue Grogranes and Taffaties, and so compounding with a Silke-weauer, I bound my selfe for three yeeres to serue him, and gaue him an hundred and fiftie Pezos to teach me the science, otherwise he would not haue taught mee vnder seuen yeeres prentiship, and by this meanes I liued the more quiet, and free from suspition. Howbeit I should many times be charged by familiars of that diuelish house, that I had a meaning to runne away into England, and to be an heretike Lutheran again : To whom I would answere that they had no neede to suspect any such thing in mee, for that they knew all very well that it was impossible for me to escape by any maner of meanes : yet notwithstanding I was called before the Inquisitor, and demaunded why I did not marrie : I answered that I had bound myselfe at an occupation. Well said the Inquisitor, I knowe thou meanest to runne away, and therefore I charge thee here vpon paine of burning as an heretike relapsed, that thou depart not out of this citie, nor come neere to the port of S. Iohn de Vllua, nor to any port : to the which I answered that I would willingly obey. Yea, said he, see thou doe so, and thy fellowes also, they shall haue the like charge. . . .

Discourse, in Richard Hakluyt, *The Principall Navigations, Voyages, Traffiques, and Discoveries of the English Nation* (London, 1599-1600), III, 479-482 *passim*.

CHAPTER IV — ENGLISH DISCOVERIES
(1497–1600)

26. John Cabot and the First English Voyage to America (1497)

BY LORENZO PASQUALIGO AND RAIMONDO DI SONCINO

(TRANSLATED BY CLEMENTS R. MARKHAM, 1893)

Pasqualigo was a Venetian, resident in London. Soncino was Milanese ambassador. — See Winsor, *Narrative and Critical History*, III, 1–58; Henry Harrisse, *Discovery of North America*, 6, 7 ; Channing and Hart, *Guide*, § 92.

A. LETTER FROM LORENZO PASQUALIGO TO HIS BROTHERS ALVISE AND FRANCESCO

LONDON, 23rd AUGUST, 1497.

OUR Venetian, who went with a small ship from Bristol to find new islands, has come back, and says he has discovered, 700 leagues off, the mainland of the country of the Grau Cam [Tartary, *i.e.* China], and that he coasted along it for 300 leagues, and landed, but did not see any person. But he has brought here to the king certain snares spread to take game, and a needle for making nets, and he found some notched trees, from which he judged that there were inhabitants. Being in doubt, he came back to the ship. He has been away three months on the voyage, which is certain, and, in returning, he saw two islands to the right, but he did not wish to land, lest he should lose time, for he was in want of provisions. This king has been much pleased. He says that the tides are slack, and do not make currents as they do here. The king has promised for another time, ten armed ships as he desires, and has given him all the prisoners, except such as are confined for high treason, to go with him as he has requested ; and has granted him money to amuse himself till then. Meanwhile, he is with his Venetian wife and his sons at Bristol. His name is Zuam Talbot, and he is called the Great Admiral, great honour being paid to him, and he goes dressed in silk. The English are ready to go with him, and so are many of our rascals. The discoverer of these things has planted a large cross in the ground with a banner of England, and one of St. Mark, as he is a Venetian; so that our flag has been hoisted very far away.

B. FIRST DESPATCH OF RAIMONDO DI SONCINO TO THE DUKE OF MILAN

24th AUGUST, 1497.

. . . Some months afterwards His Majesty sent a Venetian, who is a distinguished sailor, and who was much skilled in the discovery of new islands, and he has returned safe, and has discovered two very large and fertile islands, having, it would seem, discovered the seven cities 400 leagues from England to the westward. These successes led His Majesty at once to entertain the intention of sending him with fifteen or twenty vessels.

C. SECOND DESPATCH OF RAIMONDO DI SONCINO TO THE DUKE OF MILAN

18th DECEMBER, 1497.

My most illustrious and most excellent Lord, —

Perhaps amidst so many occupations of your Excellency it will not be unwelcome to learn how his Majesty has acquired a part of Asia without drawing his sword. In this kingdom there is a certain Venetian named Zoanne Caboto, of gentle disposition, very expert in navigation, who, seeing that the most serene Kings of Portugal and Spain had occupied unknown islands, meditated the achievement of a similar acquisition for the said Majesty. Having obtained royal privileges securing to himself the use of the dominions he might discover, the sovereignty being reserved to the Crown, he entrusted his fortune to a small vessel with a crew of 18 persons, and set out from Bristo, a port in the western part of this kingdom. Having passed Ibernia, which is still further to the west, and then shaped a northerly course, he began to navigate to the eastern part, leaving (during several days) the north star on the right hand ; and having wandered thus far a long time, at length he hit upon land, where he hoisted the royal standard, and took possession for this Highness, and, having obtained various proofs of his discovery, he returned. The said Messer Zoanne, being a foreigner and poor, would not have been believed if the crew, who are nearly all English, and belonging to Bristo, had not testified that what he said was the truth. This Messer Zoanne has the description of the world on a chart, and also on a solid sphere which he has constructed, and on which he shows where he has been; and, proceeding towards the east, he has passed as far as the country of the Tanais. And they say that there the land is excellent and temperate, suggesting that brasil [dye-wood] and silk grow there. They affirm that the sea is full of fish, which are not only taken with a net, but also with a basket, a stone being fastened to it in order to keep it in the water; and this I have heard stated by the said Messer Zoanne.

The said Englishmen, his companions, say that they took so many fish that this kingdom will no longer have need of Iceland, from which country there is an immense trade in the fish they call stock-fish. But Messer Zoanne has set his mind on higher things, for he thinks that, when that place has been occupied, he will keep on still further to the east, where he will be opposite to an island called Cipango, situated in the equinoctial region, where he believes that all the spices of the world, as well as the jewels, are found. He further says that he was once at Mecca, whither the spices are brought by caravans from distant countries; and having inquired from whence they were brought and where they grow, they answered they did not know, but that such merchandize was brought from distant countries by other caravans to their home; and they further say that they are also conveyed from other remote regions. And he adduced this argument, that if the eastern people tell those in the south that these things come from a far distance from them, presupposing the rotundity of the earth, it must be that the last turn would be by the north towards the west; and it is said that in this way the route would not cost more than it costs now, and I also believe it. And what is more, this Majesty, who is wise and not prodigal, reposes such trust in him because of what he has already achieved, that he gives him a good maintenance, as Messer Zoanne has himself told me. And it is said that before long his Majesty will arm some ships for him, and will give him all the malefactors to go to that country and form a colony, so that they hope to establish a greater depot of spices in London than there is in Alexandria. The principal people in the enterprise belong to Bristo. They are great seamen, and now that they know where to go, they say that the voyage thither will not occupy more than 15 days after leaving Ibernia. I have also spoken with a Burgundian, who was a companion of Messer Zoanne, who affirms all this, and who wishes to return because the Admiral (for so Messer Zoanne is so entitled) has given him an island, and has given another to his barber of Castione, who is a Genoese, and both look upon themselves as Counts; nor do they look upon my Lord the Admiral as less than a Prince. I also believe that some poor Italian friars are going on this voyage, who have all had bishopricks promised to them. And if I had made friends with the Admiral when he was about to sail, I should have got an archbishoprick at least; but I have thought that the benefits reserved for me by your Excellency will be more secure. I would venture to pray that, in the event of a vacancy taking place in my absence, I may be put in possession, and that I may not be superseded by those, who being present, can be more diligent than I, who am reduced in this country to eating at each meal ten or twelve kinds of victuals, and to being three hours at table every day, two for love of your Excellency, to whom I humbly recommend myself. London, 18 Dec. 1497, your Excellency's most humble servant.

Documents relating to the Voyages of Discovery of John Cabot, in Hakluyt Society, *Works issued, 1893* (London, 1893), pp. 201-206.

---

27. First Printed Account of America in English (1511)

ANONYMOUS

This is an extract from a book printed in Antwerp, and is a compilation, with many fanciful additions, from the narratives of Amerigo Vespuccius. — Bibliography: Edward Arber, *First Three English Books on America*, pp. xxv, xxvi.

OF THE NEWE LANDES AND OF YE PEOPLE FOUNDE BY THE MESSENGERS OF THE KYNGE OF PORTYU-GALE NAMED EMANUEL. OF THE R. [5] DYNERS NACYONS CRYSTENED. OF POPE JOHN AND HIS LANDES AND OF THE COSTELY KEYES AND WON-DERS MOLO DYES THAT IN THAT LANDE IS

HEre aforetymes [formerly] in the yere of our Lorde god. M.CCCC.xcvi. [1496] and so be we with shyppes of Lusseboene [Lisbon] sayled oute of Portyngale thorough the commaundement of the Kynge Emanuel So haue we had our vyage For by fortune ylandes ouer the great see with great charge and daunger so haue we at the laste founde oon lordshyp where we sayled well. ix.C. [900] mylee [mile] by the cooste of Selandes there we at ye laste went a

lande but that lande is not nowe knowen for there haue no masters wryten
thereof nor it knowethe and it is named Armenica [America]   there we
sawe meny wonders of beestes and fowles yat [that] we haue neuer seen
before   the people of this lande haue no kynge nor lorde nor theyr god
But all thinges is comune . . . the men and women haue on theyr heed
necke Armes Knees and fete all with feders [feathers] bounden for
their bewtynes [beauty] and fayrenes.   These folke lyuen [live] lyke
bestes without any resenablenes. . . .   And they ete [eat] also on[e]
a nother   The man etethe [eateth] his wyfe his chylderne as we also
haue seen and they hange also the bodyes or persons fleeshe in the
smoke as men do with vs swynes fleshe.   And that lande is ryght full of
folke for they lyue commonly.   iii.C. [300] yere and more as with
sykenesse they dye nat   they take much fysshe for they can goen vnder
the water and fe[t]che so the fysshes out of the water.   and they werre
[war] also on[e] vpon a nother   for the olde men brynge the yonge
men thereto that they gather a great company thereto of towe [two]
partyes and come the on[e] ayene [against] the other to the felde or
bateyll [battle] and slee [slay] on[e] the other with great hepes [heaps].
And nowe holdeth the fylde [field] they take the other prysoners   And
they brynge them to deth and ete them and as the deed [dead] is eten
then fley [flay] they the rest   And they been [are] than [then] eten
also or otherwyse lyue they longer tymes and many yeres more than
other people for they haue costely spyces and rotes [roots] where they
them selfe recouer with and hele [heal] them as they be seke [sick].

Edward Arber, *The First Three English Books on America* (London, 1885),
p. xxvii.

━━━━━◆━━━━━

28. The First English Slave Trader (1530)

BY RICHARD HAKLUYT (1589)

Hakluyt, an English scholar, was from a boy interested in geography; he col-
lected the voyages to stimulate his countrymen to adventure. — Bibliography of
Hakluyt: Winsor, *Narrative and Critical History*, III, 189, 209; on the subject,
Winsor, III; Channing and Hart, *Guide*, § 93.

OLDE M. William Haukins of Plimmouth, a man for his wisedome,
valure [valor], experience, and skill in sea causes much esteemed,
and beloued of king Henry the 8, and being one of the principall Sea
Captaines in the West partes of England in his time, not contented with

the short voyages commonly then made onely to the knowen coastes of Europe, armed out a tall and goodly ship of his owne of the burthen of 250 tunnes called the Pole of Plimmouth, wherewith he made three long and famous voyages vnto the coast of Brasill, a thing in those dayes very rare, especially to our Nation. In the course of which voyages he touched at the Riuer of Sestos vpon the coast of Guinea, where hee traffiqued with the Negroes, and tooke of them Olephants teeth, and other commodities which that place yeeldeth: and so arriuing on the coast of Brasil, vsed there such discretion, and behaued himselfe so wisely with those sauage people, that he grew into great familiaritie and friendship with them. Insomuch that in his 2, [second] voyage, one of the sauage kings of the Countrey of Brasill, was contented to take shipe with him, and to bee transported hither into England: whereunto M. Haukins agreed, leauing behinde in the Countrey as a pledge for his safetie and returne againe, one Martin Cockeram of Plimmouth. This Brasilian king being arriued, was brought vp to London, and presented to King Henry the 8, lying as then at Whitehall: at the sight of whome, the King and all the Nobilitie did not a litle marueile [marvel], and not without cause: for in his cheekes were holes made according to their sauage maner, and therein small bones were planted, standing an inche out from the said holes, which in his owne Countrey was reputed for a great brauerie. He had also another hole in his nether lippe, wherein was set a precious stone about the bignesse of a pease: All his apparell, behauior, and gesture, were very strange to the beholders.

Hauing remained here the space almost of a whole yere, and the king with his sight fully satisfied, M. Hawkins according to his promise and appointment, purposed to conuey him againe into his Countrey: but it fell out in the way, that by change of ayre and alteration of diet, the saide Sauage king died at Sea, which was feared woulde turne to the losse of the life of Martin Cockeram his pledge. Neuerthelesse, the Sauages being fully perswaded of the honest dealing of our men with their Prince, restored againe the saide pledge, without any harme to him, or any man of the companie: which pledge of theirs they brought home againe into England, with their shippe fraighted, and furnished with the commodities of the Countrey. Which Martine Cockeram, by the witnesse of sir John Hawkins, being an officer in the towne of Plimmouth, was liuing within these fewe yeeres.

Richard Hakluyt, *The Principall Navigations, Voiages, and Discoveries of the English Nation* (London, 1589), pp. 520–521.

29. An English Free-booter's Adventures (1568)

BY SIR JOHN HAWKINS

Hawkins is an excellent example of the bold and piratical English sea dog. — Bibliography: Winsor, *Narrative and Critical History;* Channing and Hart, *Guide,* § 93.

THE shippes departed from Plymmouth, the second day of October, Anno 1567. and had reasonable weather, vntil the seuenth day, at which time fortie leagues North from Cape Finister, there arose an extreme storme, which continued foure daies, in such sorte, that the fleete was dispersed, and all our great boates lost, and the Iesus our chiefe shippe, in such case, as not thought able to serue the voyage : . . . but the elevent day of the same moneth, the winde changed with faire weather, whereby we were animated to followe our enterprise, and so did, directing our course with the Islands of Grand Canaries, where according to an order before prescribed, all our shippes before dispersed, mette in one of those Islands, called Gomera, where we tooke water, and departed from thence the fourth day of Nouember, towards the coast of Guinea, and arrived at Cape Verde, the eighteenth of Nouember : where we landed 150. men, hoping to obtaine some Negroes, where we gatte but fewe, and those with great hurte and damage to our men, which chiefly proceeded from their enuenomed arrows ; and although in the beginning, they seemed to be but small hurtes, yet there hardely escaped any, that had blood drawen of them, but died in strange sort, with their mouths shutte, some ten dayes before he died, and after their woundes were whole, where I my selfe had one of the greatest wounds, yet thanks be to God, escaped.   From thence we passed the time upon the coast of Guinea, searching with all diligence, the Rivers from Rio grande, vnto Sierra Leona, till the twelfth of Ianuarie, in which time wee had not gotten together a hundreth and fiftie Negroes : yet notwithstanding the sickness of our men, and the late time of the yeere commanded vs away, and thus hauing nothing wherewith to seeke the coast of the West Indies, I was with the rest of our Companie in consultation to goe to the coast of the Myne, hoping therto haue obtained some golde for our wares, and thereby to have defraied our charge.   But even in that present instant, there came to vs a Negroe, sent from a King, oppressed by other Kings his neighbours, desiring our aide, with promise, that as many Negroes as by these wares might be obtained, as well of his part, as of ours, should be at our pleasure : whereupon we concluded to give aide, and sent 120. of our men, which the fifteenth of Januarie, assaulted a towne of the Negroes of our Allies aduersaries, which had in it 8000. Inhabitants, and very strongly impaled and fenced, after their manner, but it was so well defended, that our men prevailed not but lost sixe men and 40. hurt, so that our men sent forthwith to me for more helpe : whereupon considering that the good successe of this enterprise might highly further the commodotie of our voyage, I went myselfe, and with the helpe of the King of our side, assaulted the towne both by land and sea, and very hardly with fire, (their houses being covered with dry Palme leaues), obtained the towne, and put the Inhabitants to flight, where we took 250. persons, men, women, and children, and by our friend the King of our side, there was taken 600. prisoners, whereof we hoped to haue had our choice : but the Negro (in which nation is seldome or never found truth) meant nothing lesse : for that night he remoued his campe, and prisoners, so that we were faine to content vs with those fewe which we had gotten our selues.   Now had we obtained between 4. and 500. Negroes, wherewith we thought it somewhat reasonable to seeke the coast of the West Indies, and there, for our Negroes, and other our merchandize, we hoped to obtaine, whereof to counteruaile our charges with some gaines, whereunto we proceeded with all diligence, furnished our watring, took fuell, and departed the coast of Guinea the third of Februarie, continuing at the sea with a passage more harde, then before hath beene accustomed, till the 27th day of March, which day we had sight of an Island, called Dominica, vpon the coast of the west Indies, in 14. degrees : from thence we coasted from place to place, making our trafficke with the Spaniards, as we might, somewhat hardly, because the King had straightly commanded all his Gouernours in those partes, by no means to suffer any trade to be made with vs : notwithstanding we had reasonable trade, and courteous entertainment, from the Isle of Margarita vnto Cartagena, without anything greatly worth the noting, sauing at Capo de la Vela, in a towne called Rio de la Hache, from whence came all the pearles : the treasurer who had the charge there, would by no means agree to any trade, or suffer vs to take water, he had fortified his towne with diuers bulwarks in all places, where it might be entred, and furnished himselfe with 100. Hargabusiers, so that he thought by famine to have enforced vs to have put a land our Negroes : of which purpose he had not greatly failed vnles we had by force entred the towne : which (after we could by no means obtaine his favour) we were enforced to do, and so with 200. men broke in vpon their bulwarkes, and entred the towne with the losse only of ii. men of our partes, and no hurte done to the Spanyards because after their volye of shott discharged they all fled.

Thus hauing the town, with some circumstance, as partly by the Spanyards desire of Negroes and partly by friendship of the Treasorer, we obtained a secrete trade : whereupon the Spanyards resorted to vs by night, and bought of vs to the number of 200. Negroes : in all other places where we traded the Spanyard inhabitants were glad of vs and traded willingly. . . .

. . . Shortly after the xvi. of September we entered the Port of St. John de Vllua and in our entrie the Spanyardes thinking vs to be the fleete of Spaine, the chief officers of the Countrey came aborde vs, which being deceived of their expectation were greatly dismayed : but immediately when they saw our demaund was nothing but victuals, were recomforted. I found also in the same Port xii. ships which had in them by the report 200000 li. in golde and siluer all which (being in my possession, with the Kinges Island, as also the passengers before in my way thitherwarde stayde) I set at libertie, without the taking from them the wayght of a grote : onely because I woulde not bee delayed of my dispatch, I stayed two men of estimation and sent post immediately to Mexico, which was 200. miles from vs, to the Presidentes and Counsell there, shewing them of our arriuall there by the force of weather, and the necessitie of the repaire of our shippes and victualls, which wantes wee required as friends to king Philip to be furnished of for our money : and that the Presidentes and Counselle there should with all conuenient speede take order, that at the arriuall of the Spanishe fleete which was daily looked for, there might be no cause of quarrel rise between vs and them, but for the better maintenance of amitie, their commaundment might be had in that behalfe.

This message being sent away the sixteenth day of September at night, being the very day of our arriual, in the next morning which was the sixteenth day of the same moneth, we saw open of the Hauen xiii. great shippes, and vnderstanding them to be the fleete of Spaine, I sent immediately to aduertise the General of the fleete of my being there, doing him to vnderstand, that before I would suffer them to enter the Port, there should some other order of conditions passe betweene vs for our safe being there, . . . and here I began to bewaile that which after folowed, for now said I, I am in two dangers, and forced to receaue the one of them. That was, either I must haue kept out the fleete from entring

the Port, that which with Gods helpe I was very well able to do, or els
suffer them to enter in with their accustomed treason, which they never
faile to execute, where they may haue opportunitie, or circumuent it by
any meanes : if I had kept them out, then had there bin present ship-
warke of al the fleete which amounted in value to sixe millions, which
was in value of our money 1800000. li. [£] which I considered I was
not able to aunswere, fearing the Queens Maiesties indignation in so
weighty a matter. Thus with my selfe reuoluing the doubts, thought
rather better to abide the Jutt [impulse] of the vncerteinty, than the
certeinty. The vncerteine doubt I accompt was their treasure which by
good policy I hoped might be preuented, and therefore as chusing the
least mischief I proceeded to conditions. . . .

. . . these conditions at the first, he somewhat misliked, chiefly the
gard of the Island to be in our owne keeping, which if they had had, we
had soon knowen our fare : for with the first North wind they had cut our
cables and our ships had gone ashore : but in the ende he concluded to
our request. . . . Thus at the end of 3 daies all was concluded, and the
fleete entred the Port, saluting one another as the maner of the sea doth
require. Thus, as I said before, thursday we entred the Port, friday we
sawe the fleete, and on monday at night they entred the Port : then we
laboured ii. daies placing the English ships by themselues, and the Spanish ships by themselues, the captaines of each port and inferiour men
of theyr partes promissing great amity of all sides : which euen with
all fidelity was ment of our part, so the Spanyardes ment no thing lesse
of their partes, but from the maine land had furnished themselues with
a supplie of men to the nomber of 1000, and ment the next thursday,
being the 23 of September, at dinner time, to set vpon vs of all sides,
the same thursday, in the morning, . . . the vice Roy . . . blewe the
trumpet, and of all sides set vpon vs ; our men which warded ashore
being stricken with soden feare, gaue place, fled, and sought to recouer
succour of the shippes, the Spanyardes being before prouided for the
purpose landed in all places in multitudes from their shippes, which
they might easely doe without boates, and slewe all our men a shore
without mercy, a fewe of them escaped aborde the Jesus. The great
shippe which had by the estimation 300 men placed in her secretly,
immediately fell aborde the Minion which by Gods apointment in the
time of the suspition we had, which was only one halfe houre, the Minion
was made ready to auoide and so leesing hir hedfastes, and hayling away
by the stearne fastes shee was gotten out ; thus with Gods helpe she

defended the violence of the first brunt of these CCC. men. The Minion being paste out they came aborde the Jesus, which also with very much adoe and the losse of many of our men weare defended and kept out. There were also two other shippes that assaulted the Jesus at the same instant, so that she had hard getting loose, but yet with some time we had cut our hedfastes, and gotten out by the stearn fastes. Now when the Jesus and the Minion were gotten abroad two shippes length from the Spanish fleete, the fight beganne hot of all sides, that within one houre the Admirall of the Spanyardes was supposed to be suncke their vice Admirall burned and one other of there principall ships supposed to be sunke, so that the ships were little to annoy us.

Then it is to be vnderstood that all the ordinance vpon the Islande was in the Spanyardes handes, which did vs so great annoyance, that it cutt all the Mastes and yardes of the Jesus in such sort there was no hope to carry her away ; also it sunke our small shippes, whereupon wee determined to place the Jesus on that side of the Minion that shee myght abide all the batterie from the lande, and so be a defence for the Minion till night, and then to take such reliefe of victuall and other necessaries from the Jesus as the time would suffer vs, and to leaue her. As wee were thus determining, and had placed the Minion from the shott of the lande, suddenly the Spanyardes had fired two great shippes which were comming directly with vs, and having no meanes to auoide the fire, it bread among our men a marueilous feare, so that some said, let vs depart with the Minion, other sayd, let vs see where the winde will carrie the fyre from vs.

But to be short, the Minion men which had alwayes there sayles in a readinesse, thought to make sure worke, and so without eyther consent of the Captaine or Master cutte their sayle, so that verie hardly I was receaued into the Minion.

The most part of the men that were left a lyue in the Jesus made shift and followed the Minion in a small boat, the rest, which the little boate was not able to receaue, were inforced to abide the mercy of the Spanyards (which I doubt was very little); so with the Minion onely and the Judith (a small barke of fiftie tunne) wee escaped, which barke the same night forsooke vs in our great myserie : wee were nowe remooued with the Minion from the Spanyshe shippes two bowe shootes and there roade all that nyght : the next morning wee recoouered an Ilande a myle from the Spanyardes, where there tooke vs a north winde, and being left onely with two Ankers and two cables (for in this conflicte wee loste three Cables and two Ankers) wee thought alwayes vpon death which euer was present, but God preserued vs to a longer tyme.

The weather waxed seasonable, and the Satturday we set sayle, and having a great nomber of men and lyttle victuals our hope of life waxed lesse and lesse : some desired to yelde to the Spanyardes, some rather desired to obtayne a place where they might giue themselues to the Infidels, and some had rather abide with a little pittance the mercie of God at Sea : so thus with manie sorrowfull hearts wee wandred in an unknowen Sea by the space of fourteene dayes, tyll hunger inforced vs to seeke the lande, for birdes were thought very good meate, rattes, cattes, mise, and dogges, none escaped that might be gotten, parrates and monkeys that were had in great prise, were thought then very profitable if they serued the tourne one dinner : thus in the ende the eyght day of October wee came to the lande in the botome of the same bay of Mexico. . . .

And such as were willing to land I put them apart, and such as were desirous to goe homewards, I put apart, so that they were indifferently parted a hundred of one side and a hundred of the other side : these hundred men we set a land with all diligence in this little place before said, which being landed, we determined there to refresh our water, and so with our little remains of victuals to take the Sea. . . .

But yet God againe had mercie on vs, sent faire weather, had aborde our water, and departed the sixteene day of October, after which day wee had faire and prosperous weather till the sixteene day of Nouember, which day God be praysed wee were cleere from the coast of the Indians and out of the Channell and Goulfe of Bahama, which is betweene the Cape of Florida and the Islandes of Cuba. After this growing neere to the colde Countrie, our men being oppressed with Famine, died continually, and they that were left, grewe into such weaknes that wee were scantly able to . . . [manœuvre] our ship, and the wind being alwaies yll for vs to recouer England, determined to go with Galicia in Spaine, with intent there to releeue our company and other extreame wants. And being arriued the last day of December in a place near vnto Vigo called Ponte vedra, our men with excess of freshe meate grew into miserable diseases, and died a great part of them. This matter was borne out as long as it might be, but in the end although there was none of our men suffered to goe a lande, yet by accesse of the Spanyardes, our feblenes was knowen to them. Whereupon they ceased not to seeke by all meanes to betraie vs. but with all speede possible we departed to Vigo, where we had some helpe of certaine English ships and xii. fresh men wherewith we repaired our wants as we might, and departing the xx. day of Januarie 1568, arriued in Mounts bay in Cornewale the xxv. of the same moneth, praised be God therefore.

If all the miseries and troublesome affaires of this sorrowfull voyage should be perfectly and thoroughly written, there should neede a payn-full man with his penne, and as great a time as hee had that wrote the liues and deathes of the martirs.

The Hawkins Voyages, in Hakluyt Society, *Works issued, 1878* (London, 1878), pp. 70–81 *passim*.

30.　The Famous Voyage of Sir Francis Drake about the Whole Globe (1577–1580)

BY FRANCIS PRETTY (1589)

Pretty was a Suffolk gentleman, one of Drake's company. — Bibliography : Winsor, *Narrative and Critical History*, III, ch. iii; Payne, *Voyages of Elizabethan Seamen*, 141–169; Channing and Hart, *Guide*, § 93.

THE 15. day of Nouember, in the yeere of our Lord 1577. M. Francis Drake, with a fleete of fiue ships and barkes, and to the number of 164. men, gentlemen and sailers, departed from Plimmouth, giuing out his pretended voyage for Alexandria : but the wind falling contrary, hee was forced the next morning to put into Falmouth hauen in Cornewall, where such and so terrible a tempest tooke vs, as few men haue seene the like, and was in deed so vehement, that all our ships were like to haue gone to wracke : but it pleased God to preserue vs from that extrem-itie, and to afflict vs onely for that present with these two particulars : The mast of our Admirall which was the Pellican, was cut ouer boord for the safegard of the ship, and the Marigold was driuen ashore, and somewhat bruised : for the repairing of which damages wee returned againe to Plimmouth, and hauing recouered those harmes, and brought the ships againe to good state, we set forth the second time from Plimmouth, and set saile the 13. day of December following.

The 25. day of the same moneth we fell with the Cape Cantin, vpon the coast of Barbarie, and coasting along, the 27. day we found an Island called Mogador, lying one mile distant from the maine, betweene which Island and the maine, we found a very good and safe harbour for our ships to ride in, as also very good entrance, and voyde of any danger.

G

On this Island our Generall erected a pinnesse, whereof he brought out of England with him foure already framed. . . .

Our pinnesse being finished, wee departed from this place the 30. and last day of December, and coasting along the shore, wee did descrie, not contrary to our expectation, certaine Canters which were Spanish fishermen, to whom we gaue chase and tooke three of them, and proceeding further we met with 3. Carauels and tooke them also.

The 17. day of Ianuary we arriued at Cape Blanco, where we found a ship riding at anchor, within the Cape, and but two simple Mariners in her, which ship we tooke and caried her further into the harbour, where we remained 4. dayes, and in that space our General mustered, and trayned his men on land in warlike manner, to make them fit for all occasions.

In this space we tooke of the Fishermen such necessaries as wee wanted, and they could yeeld vs, . . .

Being departed from these Islands, we drew towards the line, where wee were becalmed the space of 3. weekes, but yet subiect to diuers great stormes, terrible lightnings and much thunder: but with this miserie we had the commoditie of great store of fish, as Dolphins, Bonitos, and flying fishes, whereof some fell into our shippes, wherehence they could not rise againe for want of moisture, for when their wings are drie, they cannot flie.

From the first day of our departure from the Islands of Cape Verde, wee sayled 54. dayes without sight of land, and the first land that we fell with was the coast of Brasil, which we saw the fift of April in ye height of 33. degrees towardes the pole Antarctike, . . .

From hence we went our course to 36. degrees, and entred the great riuer of Plate, and ranne into 54. and 53. fadomes [fathoms] and a halfe of fresh water, where wee filled our water by the ships side: but our Generall finding here no good harborough, as he thought he should, bare out againe to sea the 27. of April, . . .

. . . the twentieth of Iune, wee harboured our selues againe in a very good harborough, called by Magellan Port S. Julian, where we found a gibbet standing vpon the maine, which we supposed to be the place where Magellan did execution vpon some of his disobedient and rebellious company. . . .

In this Port our Generall began to enquire diligently of the actions of M. Thomas Doughtie, and found them not to be such as he looked for, but tending rather to contention or mutinie, or some other disorder,

whereby (without redresse) the successe of the voyage might greatly
haue bene hazarded : . . . our Generall saw, although his priuate
affection to M. Doughtie (as hee then in the presence of vs all sacredly
protested) was great, yet the care he had of the state of the voyage, of
the expectation of her Maiestie, and of the honour of his countrey did
more touch him, (as indeede it ought) then [than] the priuate respect
of one man : so that the cause being thoroughly heard, and all things
done in good order as neere as might be to the course of our lawes in
England, it was concluded that M. Doughtie should receive punishment
according to the qualitie of the offence : and he seeing no remedie but
patience for himselfe, desired before his death to receive the Communion, which he did at the hands of M. Fletcher our Minister, and our
Generall himselfe accompanied him in that holy action : which being
done, and the place of execution made ready, hee hauing embraced our
Generall and taken his leaue of all the companie, with prayer for the
Queenes maiestie and our realme, in quiet sort laid his head to the
blocke, where he ended his life. . . .

The 17. day of August we departed the port of S. Iulian, and the 20.
day we fell with the streight or freat [strait] of Magellan going into the
South sea, at the Cape or headland whereof we found the bodie of a
dead man, whose flesh was cleane consumed.

The 21. day we entred The streight, which we found to haue many
turnings, and as it were shuttings vp, as if there were no passage at all,
by meanes whereof we had the wind often against vs, so that some of
the fleete recouering a Cape or point of land, others should be forced
to turne backe againe, and to come to an anchor where they could.

In this streight there be many faire harbors, with store of fresh water,
but yet they lacke their best commoditie : for the water is there of such
depth, that no man shal find ground to anchor in, except it bee in some
narow riuer or corner, or betweene some rocks, so that if any extreme
blasts or contrary winds do come (whereunto the place is much subiect)
it carieth with it no small danger. . . .

The 6. day of September we entred the South sea at the Cape or head
shore. . . .

Our Generall seeing this, stayed here no longer, but wayed anchor,
and set sayle towards the coast of Chili, and drawing towards it, we
mette neere to the shore an Indian in a Canoa, who thinking vs to haue
bene Spaniards, came to vs and tolde vs, that at a place called S. Iago,
there was a great Spanish ship laden from the kingdome of Peru : for

which good newes our Generall gaue him diuers trifles, whereof he was glad, and went along with vs and brought vs to the place, which is called the port of Valparizo. . . .

They of the towne being not aboue 9. housholds, presently fled away and abandoned the towne. Our Generall manned his boate, and the Spanish ships boate, and went to the Towne, and being come to it, we rifled it, and came to a small chappell which wee entred, and found therein a siluer chalice, two cruets, and one altar cloth, the spoyle whereof our Generall gave to M. Fletcher his minister. . . .

When we were at sea, our Generall rifled the ship, and found in her good store of the wine of Chili, and 25000. pezoes of very pure and fine gold of Baldiuia, amounting in value to 37000. ducats of Spanish money, and aboue. So going on our course, wee arriued next at a place called Coquimbo, where our Generall sent 14. of his men on land to fetch water : but they were espied by the Spaniards, who came with 300. horsemen and 200. footemen, and slewe one of our men with a piece [firearm], the rest came aboord in safetie, and the Spaniards departed : wee went on shore againe, and buried our man, and the Spaniards came downe againe with a flag of truce, but we set sayle and would not trust them.

From hence we went to a certaine port called Tarapaça, where being landed, we found by the Sea side a Spaniard lying asleepe, who had lying by him 13. barres of siluer, which weighed 4000. ducats Spanish ; we tooke the siluer, and left the man.

Not farre from hence going on land for fresh water, we met with a Spaniard and an Indian boy driuing 8. Llamas or sheepe of Peru which are as big as asses ; euery of which sheepe had on his backe 2. bags of leather, each bagge conteining 50. li. weight of fine siluer : so that bringing both the sheepe and their burthen to the ships, we found in all the bags 800. weight of siluer.

Here hence we sailed to a place called Arica, and being entred the port, we found there three small barkes which we rifled, and found in one of them 57 wedges of siluer, each of them weighing about 20 pound weight, and euery of these wedges were of the fashion and bignesse of a brickbat. In all these 3. barkes we found not one person : . . .

To Lima we came the 13. day of February, and being entred the hauen, we found there about twelue sayle of ships lying fast moored at an anker, hauing all their sayles caried on shore ; for the masters and marchants were here most secure, hauing neuer bene assaulted by enemies, and at this time feared the approch of none such as we were. Our generall rifled these ships, and found in one of them a chest full of royals of plate, and good store of silkes and linnen cloth, and tooke the chest into his owne ship, and good store of the silkes and linnen. In which ship hee had newes of another ship called the Cacafuego which was gone towards Paita, and that the same shippe was laden with treasure : whereupon we staied no longer here, but cutting all the cables of the shippes in the hauen, we let them driue whither they would, either to sea or to the shore, and with all speede we followed the Cacafuego toward Paita, . . . It fortuned that Iohn Drake going vp into the top, descried her about three of the clocke, and about sixe of the clocke we came to her and boorded her, and shotte at her three peeces of ordinance, and stroke downe her Misen, and being entered, we found in her great riches, as iewels and precious stones, thirteene chests full of royals of plate, foure score pound weight of golde, and sixe and twentie tunne of siluer. The place where we tooke this prize, was called Cape de San Francisco, about 150. leagues from Panama.

The Pilots name of this Shippe was Francisco, and amongst other plate that our Generall found in this ship, he found two very faire guilt bowles of siluer, which were the Pilots : to whom our Generall sayd : Senior Pilot, you haue here two siluer cups, but I must needes haue one of them : which the Pilot because hee could not otherwise chuse, yeelded vnto, and gaue the other to the steward of our Generals ships.

When this Pilot departed from vs, his boy sayde thus vnto our Generall : Captaine, our ship shall be called no more the Cacafuego [Spitfire], but the Cacaplata [Spit-treasure], and your shippe shall bee called the Cacafuego : which pretie speach of the Pilots boy ministred matter of laughter to vs, both then and long after.

When our Generall had done what hee would with this Cacafuego, hee cast her off, and wee went on our course still towards the West, and not long after met with a ship laden with linnen cloth and fine China-dishes of white earth, and great store of China-silks, of all which things wee tooke as we listed.

The owner himselfe of this ship was in her, who was a Spanish Gentleman, from whom our Generall tooke a Fawlcon of golde, with a great emeraud in the breast thereof, and the Pilot of the ship he tooke also with him, and so cast the ship off. . . .

And while wee were here, we espied a shippe, and set saile after her, and tooke her, and found in her two Pilots and a Spanish Gouernour, going for the Islands of the Philippinas: wee searched the shippe, and tooke some of her marchandizes, and so let her goe. Our Generall at this place and time, thinking himselfe both in respect of his priuate iniuries receiued from the Spaniards, as also of their contempts and indignities offered to our countrey and Prince in generall, sufficiently satisfied, and reuenged: and supposing that her Maiestie at his returne would rest contented with his seruice, proposed to continue no longer vpon the Spanish coasts, but began to consider and to consult of the best way for his Countrey.

He thought it not good to returne by the Streights, for two speciall causes: the one, lest the Spaniards should there waite, and attend for him in great number and strength, whose hands, hee being left but one ship, could not possibly escape. The other cause was the dangerous situation of the mouth of the streights in the South sea, where continuall stormes reigning and blustering, as he found by experience, besides the shoalds and sands vpon the coast, he thought it not a good course to aduenture that way: he resolued therefore to auoyde these hazards, to goe forward to the Islandes of the Malucos, and therehence to saile the course of the Portugals by the Cape of Buena Esperança.

Upon this resolution, hee beganne to thinke of his best way to the Malucos, and finding himselfe where he now was becalmed, he saw that of necessitie hee must be forced to take a Spanish course, namely to sayle somewhat Northerly to get a winde. Wee therefore set saile, and sayled 600. leagues at the least for a good winde, and thus much we sailed from the 16. of April, till the 3. of Iune.

The 5. day of Iune, being in 43. degrees towards the pole Arctike, we found the ayre so colde, that our men being grieuously pinched with the same, complained of the extremitie thereof, and the further we went, the more the colde increased vpon vs. Whereupon we thought it best for that time to seeke the land, and did so, finding it not mountainous, but low plaine land, till wee came within 38. degrees towards the line. In which height it pleased God to send vs into a faire and good Baye, with a good winde to enter the same [coast of California]. . . .

Our Generall called this Countrey Noua Albion, and that for two causes: the one in respect of the white bankes and cliffes, which lie towards the sea: and the other, because it might haue some affinitie with our Countrey in name, which sometime was so called.

There is no part of earth heere to be taken vp, wherein there is not some probable shew of gold or siluer.

At our departure hence our Generall set vp a monument of our being there, as also of her Maiesties right and title to the same, namely a plate, nailed vpon a faire great poste, whereupon was ingrauen her Maiesties name, the day and yeere of our arriuall there, with the free giuing vp of the prouince and people into her Maiesties hand, together with her hignesse picture and armes, in a peece of sixe pence in current English money under the plate, whereunder was also written the name of our Generall. . . .

After we had set saile from hence, wee continued without sight of land till the 13. day of October following, which day in the morning wee fell with certaine Islands 8. degrees to the Northward of the line, . . .

The 14. of November we fell with the Islands of Maluco, . . . For of all other dayes vpon the 9. of Ianuarie, in the yeere 1579. wee ranne suddenly vpon a rocke, where we stucke fast from 8. of the clocke at night, til 4. of the clocke in the afternoone the next day, being indeede out of all hope to escape the danger : but our Generall as hee had always hitherto shewed himselfe couragious, and of a good confidence in the mercie and protection of God : so now he continued in the same, and lest he should seeme to perish wilfully, both he, and we did our best indeuour to saue our selues, which it pleased God so to blesse, that in the ende we cleared our selues most happily of the danger.

We lighted our ship vpon the rockes of 3. tunne of cloues, 8 peeces of ordinance, and certaine meale and beanes : and then the winde (as it were in a moment by the speciall grace of God) changing from the starreboord to the larboord of the ship, we hoised our sailes, and the happy gale droue our ship off the rocke into the sea againe, to the no litle comfort of all our hearts for which we gaue God such prayse and thanks, as so great a benefite required. . . .

From Iaua [Java] Maior we sailed for the cape of Good Hope, which was the first land we fell with all : neither did we touch with it, or any other land, vntill we came to Sierra Leona, vpon the coast of Guinea : notwithstanding we ranne hard aboord the Cape, finding the report of the Portugals to be most false, who affirme, that it is the most dangerous Cape of the world, neuer without intolerable stormes and present danger to trauailers, which come neere the same.

This Cape is a most stately thing, and the fairest Cape we saw in the whole circumference of the earth, and we passed by it the 18. of Iune.

From thence we continued our course to Sierra Leona, on the coast of Guinea, were we arriued the 22. of Iuly, and found necessarie prouisions, great store of Elephants, Oisters vpon trees of one kinde, spawning and increasing infinitely, the Oister suffering no budde to grow. We departed thence the 24. day.

We arriued in England the third of Nouember 1580. being the third yeere of our departure.

Richard Hakluyt, *Principall Voyages, Traffiques and Discoveries of the English Nation* (London, 1599-1600), III, 730-742 *passim*.

———— ◆ ————

31. The Piety of a Sea Rover (1578)

BY SIR FRANCIS DRAKE

This letter, written by the famous Captain, shows how little he looked upon the capture of vessels in time of peace and the looting of towns as inconsistent with religion. — Bibliography as in No. 30.

MASTER *WINTER*, if it pleaseth God that you should chance to meete with this ship of Sant *Iohn de Anton*, I pray you vse him well, according to my word and promise giuen vnto them, and if you want any thing that is in this ship of *Sant Iohn de Anton*, I pray you pay them double the value for it, which I will satisfie againe, and command your men not to doe her any hurt : and what composition or agreement we haue made, at my returne into *England* I will by Gods helpe perfourme, although I am in doubt that this letter will neuer come to your hands : notwithstanding I am the man I haue promised to be : Beseeching God, the Sauiour of all the world, to haue vs in his keeping, to whom onely I giue all honour, praise and glory. What I haue written, is not only to you M. *Winter*, but also to M. *Thomas*, M. *Charles*, M. *Caube*, and M. *Anthoine*, with all our other good friendes, whom I commit to the tuition of him that with his blood redeemed vs, and am in good hope, that we shal be in no more trouble, but that he will helpe vs in aduersitie, desiring you for the Passion of Christ, if you fall into any danger, that you will not despaire of Gods mercy, for hee will defend you and preserue you from all danger, and bring vs to our desired hauen, to whom bee all honour, glory, and praise for euer and euer. Amen. Your sorrowfull Captaine, whose heart is heauy for you :

Letter of Sir Francis Drake to his Company, in Hakluyt, *The Principall Voyages, Navigations, Traffiques and Discoveries* (London, 1599-1600), III, 748.

32. First Voyage to Virginia (1584)

BY CAPT. ARTHUR BARLOWE

"The first voyage made to the coasts of *America*, with two barks, wherein were Captaines M. *Philip Amadas*, and M. *Arthur Barlowe*, who discouered part of the countrey now called *Virginia, Anno* 1584. Written by one of the said Captaines, and sent to sir *Walter Ralegh* knight, at whose charge and direction, the said voyage was set forth." — Bibliography: Winsor, *Narrative and Critical History*, III, ch. iv; Channing and Hart, *Guide*, § 95.

THE 27 day of Aprill, in the yeere of our redemption, 1584 we departed the West of England, with two barkes well furnished with men and victuals, hauing receiued our last and perfect directions by your letters, confirming the former instructions, and commandements deliuered by your selfe at our leauing the riuer of Thames.   And I thinke it a matter both vnnecessary, for the manifest discouerie of the Countrey, as also for tediousnesse sake, to remember vnto you the diurnall of our course, sayling thither and returning : onely I haue presumed to present vnto you this briefe discourse, by which you may iudge how profitable this land is like to succeede, as well to your selfe, (by whose direction and charge, and by whose seruants this our discouerie hath beene performed) as also to her Highnesse, and the Common wealth, in which we hope your wisedome wilbe satisfied, considering that as much by vs hath bene brought to light, as by those smal meanes, and number of men we had, could any way haue bene expected, or hoped for.

The tenth of May we arriued at the Canaries, and the tenth of Iune in this present yeere, we were fallen with the Islands of the West Indies. . . .

The second of Iuly, we found shole water, wher we smelt so sweet and so strong a smel, as if we had bene in the midst of some delicate garden abounding with all kinde of odoiferous flowers, by which we were assured, that the land could not be farre distant : and keeping good watch, and bearing but slacke saile, the fourth of the same moneth we arriued vpon the coast, which we supposed to be a continent and firme lande, and we sayled along the same a hundred and twentie English miles before we could finde any entrance, or riuer issuing into the Sea.   The first that appeared vnto vs, we entred, though not without some difficultie, & cast anker about three harquebuz-shot within the hauens mouth, on the left hand of the same : and after thankes giuen to God for our safe arriual thither, we manned our boats, and went to view the land next adioyning, and " to take possession of the same, in the right of

the Queenes most excellent Maiestie, as rightfull Queene, and Princesse
of the same, and after deliuered the same ouer to your vse, according to
her Maiesties grant, and letters patent, vnder her Highnesse great Seale.
Which being performed, according to the ceremonies vsed in such enterprises, we viewed the land about vs, being, whereas we first landed,
very sandie and low towards the waters side, but so full of grapes, as the
very beating and surge of the Sea ouerflowed them. . . .

We passed from the Sea side towardes the toppes of those hilles next
adioyning, being but of meane higth, and from thence wee behelde the
Sea on both sides to the North, and to the South, finding no ende any
of both wayes. This lande lay stretching it selfe to the West, which
after wee found to bee but an Island of twentie miles long, and not
above sixe miles broade. Vnder the banke or hill whereon we stoode,
we behelde the vallyes replenished with goodly Cedar trees, and hauing
discharged our harquebuz-shot, such a flocke of Cranes (the most pat
[part] white) arose vnder vs, with such a cry redoubled by many
ecchoes, as if an armie of men had showted all together.

This Island had many goodly woodes full of Deere, Conies, Hares,
and Fowle, euen in the middest of Summer in incredible abundance.
The woodes are not such as you finde in Bohemia, Moscouia, or Her-
cynia, barren and fruitles, but the highest and reddest Cedars in the
world, farre bettering the Ceders of the Açores, of the Indies, or
Lybanus, Pynes, Cypres, Sassaphras, the Lentisk, or the tree that beareth the Masticke, the tree that beareth the rine of blacke Sinamon, of
which Master Winter brought from the streights of Magellan, and many
other of excellent smell and qualitie. We remained by the side of
this Island two whole dayes before we saw any people of the Countrey :
the third day we espied one small boate rowing towardes vs, hauing in
it three persons : this boat came to the Island side, foure harquebuz-
shot from our shippes, and there two of the people remaining, the
third came along the shoreside towards vs, and wee being then all
within boord, he walked vp and downe vpon the point of the land next
vnto vs : then the Master and the Pilot of the Admirall, Simon Ferdinando, and the Captaine Philip Amadas, my selfe, and others rowed to
the land, whose comming this fellow attended, neuer making any shew
of feare or doubt. And after he had spoken of many things not vnderstood by vs, we brought him with his owne good liking, aboord the
ships, and gaue him a shirt, a hat, & some other things, and made him
taste of our wine, and our meat, which he liked very wel : and after

hauing viewed both barks, he departed, and went to his own boate
againe, which hee had left in a little Coue or Creeke adioyning : assoone
[as soon] as hee was two bow shoot into the water, he fell to fishing,
and in lesse then halfe an houre, he had laden his boate as deepe, as
it could swimme, with which hee came againe to the point of lande,
and there he deuided his fish intc two parts, pointing one part to the
ship, and the other to the pinnesse : which, after he had (as much as
he might) requited the former benefites receaued, departed out of our
sight.

The next day there came vnto vs diuers boates, and in one of them
the Kings brother, accompanied with fortie or fiftie men, very handsome and goodly people, and in their behauiour as mannerly and ciuill
as any in Europe.   His name was Granganimeo, and the king is called
Wingina, the countrey Wingandacoa, and now by her Maiestie Virginia. . . .

The King is greatly obeyed, and his brothers and children reuerenced :
the King himselfe in person was at our being there, sore wounded in a
fight which hee had with the King of the next countrey. . . .   A day
or two after this, we fell to trading with them, exchanging some things
that we had, for Chamoys, Buffe, and Deere skinnes : when we shewed
him all our packet of merchandize, of all things that he sawe, a bright
tinne dish most pleased him, which hee presently tooke up and clapt
it before his breast, and after made a hole in the brimme thereof
and hung it about his necke, making signes that it would defende
him against his enemies arrowes : for those people maintaine a deadly
and terrible warre, with the people and King adioyning.   We exchanged
our tinne dish for twentie skinnes, woorth twentie Crownes, or twentie
Nobles : and a copper kettle for fiftie skins woorth fifty Crownes.
They offered vs good exchange for our hatchets, and axes, and for
kniues, and would haue giuen anything for swordes : but wee would
not depart with any.   After two or three dayes the Kings brother
came aboord the shippes and dranke wine, and eat of our meat and of
our bread, and liked exceedingly thereof : and after a few dayes ouer-
passed, he brought his wife with him to the ships, his daughter and two
or three children : his wife was very well fauoured, of meane stature
and very bashfull : shee had on her backe a long cloake of leather, with
the furre side next to her body, and before her a piece of the same :
about her forehead shee had a bande of wite Corall, and so had her
husband many times : in her eares shee had bracelets of pearles hang-

ing downe to her middle, (whereof wee deliuered your worship a little bracelet) and those were of the bignes of good pease. The rest of her women of the better sort had pendants of copper hanging in either eare, and some of the children of the kings brother and other noble men, haue fiue or sixe in either eare : he himselfe had vpon his head a broad plate of golde, or copper, for being unpolished we knew not what mettal it should be, neither would he by any meanes suffer vs to take it off his head, but feeling it, it would bow very easily. His apparell was as his wiues, onely the women weare their haire long on both sides, and the men but on one. They are of colour yellowish, and their haire black for the most part, and yet we saw children that had very fine auburne, and chestnut coloured haire.

. . . Their boates are made of one tree, either of Pine, or of Pitch trees : a wood not commonly knowen to our people, nor found growing in England. They haue no edge-tooles to make them withall : if they haue any they are very fewe, and those it seemes they had twentie yeres since, which, as those two men declared, was out of a wrake which happened vpon their coast of some Christian ship, . . . The manner of making their boates is thus : they burne downe some great tree, or take such as are winde fallen, and putting gumme and rosen vpon one side thereof, they set fire into it, and when it hath burnt it hollow, they cut out the coale with their shels, and euer where they would burne it deeper or wider they lay on gummes, which burne away the timber, and by this meanes they fashion very fine boates, and such as will transport twentie men. Their oares are like scoopes, and many times they set with long poles, as the depth serueth.

The Kings brother had great liking of our armour, a sword, and diuers other things which we had : and offered to lay a great boxe of pearle in gage for them : but we refused it for this time, because we would not make them knowe, that we esteemed thereof, untill we had vnderstoode in what places of the countrey the pearle grew : which now your Worshippe doeth very well vnderstand. . . .

The soile is the most plentifull, sweete, fruitfull and wholsome of all the worlde : there are aboue fourteene seuerall sweete smelling timber trees, and the most part of their vnderwoods are Bayes, and such like : they haue those Okes that we haue, but farre greater and better. After they had bene diuers times aboord our shippes, my selfe, with seuen more went twentie mile into the Riuer, that runneth towarde the Citie of Skicoak, which Riuer they call Occam : and the euening fol-

lowing, wee came to an Island, which they call Raonoak, distant from
the harbour by which we entred, seuen leagues : and at the North end
thereof was a village of nine houses, built of Cedar, and fortified round
about with sharpe trees, to keepe out their enemies, and the entrance
into it made like a turne pike very artifically : when wee came towardes
it, standing neere vnto the waters side, the wife of Granganimo, the
kings brother came running out to meete vs very cheerefully and
friendly. . . .

After we had thus dryed our selues, she brought vs into the inner
roome, where shee set on the boord standing along the house, some
wheate like furmentie, sodden Venison, and roasted, fish sodden, boyled
and roasted, Melons rawe, and sodden, rootes of diuers kindes, and
diuers fruites : their drinke is commonly water, but while the grape last-
eth, they drinke wine, and for want of caskes to keepe it, all the yere
after they drink water, but it is sodden with Ginger in it, and blacke
Sinamon, and sometimes Sassaphras, and diuers other wholesome, and
medicinable hearbes and trees. We were entertained with all loue and
kindnesse, and with as much bountie (after their maner) as they could
possibly deuise. We found the people most gentle, louing, and faithfull,
voide of all guile and treason, and such as liue after the maner of the
golden age. The people onely care howe to defend themselues from
the cold in their short winter, and to feed themselues with such meat as
the soile affoordeth : there meate is very well sodden and they make
broth very sweet and sauorie : their vessels are earthern pots, very large,
white and sweete, their dishes are wodden platters of sweet timber :
within the place where they feede was their lodging, and within that their
Idoll, which they worship, of whome they speake incredible things. . . .

Beyond this Island there is the maine land, and ouer against this
Island falleth into this spacious water, the great riuer called Occam by
the inhabitants, on which standeth a towne called Pomeiock, & sixe
dayes iourney from the same is situate their greatest citie, called Skicoak,
which this people affirme to be very great : but the Sauages were neuer
at it, only they speake of it by the report of their fathers and other
men, whom they haue heard affirme it to bee aboue one houres iourney
about.

In to this riuer falleth another great riuer, called Cipo, in which there
is found great store of Muskles in which there are pearles : likewise
there descendeth into this Occam, another riuer, called Nomopana. . . .
Towards the Southwest foure dayes iourney is situate a towne called

Sequotan, which is the Southermost towne of Wingandacoa, neere vnto which, sixe and twentie yeres past, there was a ship cast away, whereof some of the people were saued, and those were white people, whom the countrey people preserued. . . .

. . . other then these, there was neuer any people apparelled, or white of colour, either seene, or heard of amongst these people, and these aforesaid were seene onely by the inhabitantes of Secotan, which appeared to be very true, for they wondred maruelously when we were amongst them at the whitenes of our skins, euer coueting to touch our breasts, and to view the same. Besides they had our ships in maruelous admiration, & all things els were so strange vnto them, as it appeared that none of them had euer seene the like. When we discharged any piece, were it but an hargubuz, they would tremble thereat for very feare, and for the strangenesse of the same : for the weapons which themselules vse are bowes and arrowes : the arrowes are but of small canes, headed with a sharpe shell or tooth of a fish sufficient ynough to kill a naked man. Their swordes be of wood hardened : likewise they vse wooden breastplates for their defence. They haue beside a kinde of club, in the end whereof they fasten the sharpe hornes of a stagge, or other beast. When they goe to warres they cary about with them their idol, of whom they aske counsel, as the Romans were woont of the Oracle of Apollo. They sing songs as they march towardes the battell in stead of drummes and trumpets : their warres are very cruell and bloody, by reason whereof, and of their ciuill dissentions which haue happened of late yeeres amongst them, the people are maruelously wasted, and in some places the countrey left desolate.

Adioyning to this countrey aforesaid called Secotan, beginneth a countrey called Pomouik, belonging to another king whom they call Piamacum, . . . and these two haue oftentimes since persuaded vs to surprize Piemacum his towne, hauing promised and assured vs, that there will be found in it great store of commodities. But whether their persuasion be to the ende they may be reuenged of their enemies, or for the loue they beare to vs, we leaue that to the tryall hereafter.

Beyond this Island called Roanoak, are maine Islands very plentifull of fruits and other naturall increases, together with many townes, and villages, along the side of the continent, some bounding vpon the Islands, and some stretching vp further into the land.

When we first had sight of this countrey, some thought the first land we saw to bee the continent : but after we entred into the Hauen, we

saw before vs another mighty long Sea : for there lyeth along the coast
a tracte of Islands, two hundreth miles in length, adioyning to the
Ocean sea, and betweene the Islands, two or three entrances : when
you are entred betweene them (these Islands being very narrow for the
most part, as in most places sixe miles broad, in some places lesse,
in fewe more) then there appeareth another great Sea, containing in
bredth in some places, forty, and in some fifty, in some twenty miles
ouer, before you come vnto the continent : and in this inclosed Sea
there are aboue an hundreth Islands of diuers bignesses, whereof one is
sixteene miles long, at which we were, finding it a most pleasant and
fertile ground, replenished with goodly Cedars, and diuers other sweete
woods, full of Corrants, of flaxe, and many other notable commodities,
which we at that time had no leasure to view. . . .

Thus Sir, we haue acquainted you with the particulars of our discouery
made this present voyage, as farre foorth as the shortnesse of the time
we there continued would affoord vs to take viewe of : and so content-
ing our selues with this seruice at this time, which wee hope hereafter to
inlarge, as occasion and assistance shalbe giuen, we resolued to leaue
the countrey, and to apply our selues to returne for England, which we
did accordingly, and arriued safely in the West of England about the
middest of September.

And whereas wee haue aboue certified you of the countrey taken in
possession by vs, to her Maiesties vse, and so to yours by her Maiesties
grant, wee thought good for the better assurance thereof, to record
some of the particular Gentlemen, & men of accompt, who then were
present, as witnesses of the same. . . .

We brought home also two of the Sauages being lustie men, whose
names were Wanchese and Manteo.

Richard Hakluyt, *The Principall Voyages, Traffiques, and Discoveries of the
English Nation* (London, 1599–1600), III, 246–251 *passim.*

33. Expedition to El Dorado (1595)

BY SIR WALTER RALEGH

Ralegh was the most determined of the explorers and colonizers of the time; this
narrative shows the credulity of the age; the " lady " mentioned is of course Queen
Elizabeth. — Bibliography: Winsor, *Narrative and Critical History*, III, 121–126;
Channing and Hart, *Guide*, § 95.

ON Thursday the 6. of Februarie in the yeare 1595. we departed
England, . . .

Meeting with the ships at *puerto de los Hispanioles*, we founde at
the landing place a company of Spaniardes who kept a gard at the
descente. . . . Taking a time of much adūantage, I set vpon the *Corp
du guard* in the euening, and hauing put them to the sword, sent Captain
Calfield onwards with 60. soldiers, & my selfe followed with 40. more &
so toke ther new city which they called S. *Ioseph*, by breake of day: . . .

We then hastened away towards our purposed discouerie, & first I
called all the Captaines of the Iland together that were enemies to the
Spaniards, for ther were som which *Berreo* had broght out of other
countries, & planted there to eat out & wast those that were natural
of the place, & by my Indian interpreter, which I caried out of England, I made them vnderstand that *I* was the seruant of a Queene, who
was the great *Casique* of the North, and a virgin, and had more *Casiqui*
vnder her then were trees in that *Iland :* that shee was an enemy to the
Castelani in respect of their tyranny and oppression and that she deliuered all such nations about her, as were by them oppressed, & hauing
freed al the coast of the northern world from their seruitude had sent
me to free them also & with all to defend the countrey of *Guiana* from
their inuasion and conquest. *I* shewed them her maiesties picture which
they so admired and honoured, as it had beene easi to haue brought
them *I*dolatrous thereof.

I sent Captain *Whiddon* the yeare before to get what knowledge he
could of *Guiana*, and the end of my iorney at this time was to discouer
& enter the same, but my intelligence was farre from trueth, for the
country is situate aboue 600. English miles further from the sea, then I
was made beleeue it had been, which afterward vnderstanding to be true
by *Berreo*, I kept it from the knowledge of my companie, who else would
neuer haue beene brought to attempt the same, of which 600. miles I
passed 400. leauing my shippes so farre from me at ancor in the sea,
which was more of desire to performe that discouery, then of reasō,

especially hauing such poore & weake uessels to transport our selues in;
for in the bottom of an old *Gallego* which I caused to be fashioned like
a Galley, & in one barge, two wherries, and a ship bote of the Lions
whelpe, we caried 100. persons and their victuals for a moneth in the
same, being al driuen to lie in the raine & weather, in the open aire, in
the burning sun, & vpon the hard bords, and to dresse our meate, and to
cary al maner of furniture in them, wherewith they were so pestred &
vnsauery, that what with victualls being most fish, with the wet clothes
of so many men thrust together and the heate of the sunne, I will vndertake there was neuer any prison in England, that coulde be founde more
vnsauory and lothsome, especially to my selfe, who had for many yeares
before beene dieted and carred for in a sort farre more differing. . . .

The Empyre of *Guiana* is directly east from *Peru* towards the sea,
and lieth vnder the Equinoctiall line, and it hath more abundance of
Golde then any parte of *Peru*, and as many or more greate Cities then
euer *Peru* had when it flourished most: it is gouerned by the same
lawes, and the Emperour and people obserue the same religion, and the
same forme and pollicies in gouernment as was vsed in *Peru*, not differing in any part: and as I haue beene assured by such of the *Spanyardes*
as haue seene *Manoa* the imperiall Citie of *Guiana*, which the *Spanyards*
cal *El Dorado*, that for the greatnes, for the riches, and for the excellent seate, it farre exceedeth any of the world, at least so much of the
world as is knowen to the spanish nation: it is founded vpon a lake of
salt water of 200. leagues long like vnto *mare capsiũ*.

. . . I had knowledge of all the riuers between *Oreonque* and *Amazones*, and was uery desirous to vnderstand the trueth of those warlike
women, bicause of some it is beleeued, of others not: And though I
digresse from my purpose, yet I will set downe what hath beene deliuered me for the trueth of those women, and I spake with a *Casique* or
Lorde of people that told me he had been in the riuer, and beyond it
also. The nations of these women are on the south side of the riuer in
the prouinces of *Tapago*, and their chiefest strengths and retraicts are
in the Ilandes scituate on the south side of the entrance, some 60.
leagues within the mouth of the said riuer. . . . It was farther told
me, that if in the wars they tooke any prisoners that they vsed to accompany with those also at what time soeuer, but in the end for certaine
they put them to death: for they are said to be verie cruell and blood-
thirsty, especially to such as offer to inuade their territories. These
Amazones haue likewise great store of these plates of Golde, which

H

they recouer by exchange chiefly for a kinde of greene stones, which the Spaniards call *Piedras Hiiadas*, and we use for spleene stones, and for the disease of the stone we also esteeme them: of these I sawe diuers in *Guiana*, and commonly euery kind or *Casique* hath one, which their wiues for the most part weare, and they esteeme them as great iewels.

. . . *Arwacan* promised to bring me into the great riuer of Oreonoque, but indeede of that which we entred he was vtterly ignorant. . . . and if we went by the Sun or compasse hoping thereby to go directly one way or other, yet that waie we were also carried in a circle amongest multitudes of Ilands, and euery Iland so bordered with high trees, as no man coulde see any further than the bredth of the riuer, or length of the breach. . . .

The farther we went on (our victual decreasing and the aire breeding great faintnes) we grew weaker and weaker when we had most need of strength and abilitie, for howrelie [hourly] the riuer ran more violently than other against vs, and the barge wherries, and ships bote of Captaine *Gifford*, and Captaine *Calfield* had spent all their prouisions, so as wee were brought into despaire and discomfort, had wee not perswaded all the companie that it was but onelie one daies worke more to attaine the lande where we should bee releeued of all wee wanted, and if we returned that we were sure to starue by the way, and that the worlde woulde also laugh vs to scorne. . . .

Our old Pilot of the *Ciawani* (whom, as I said before, wee tooke to redeeme *Ferdinando*), tould vs, that if we would enter a branch of a riuer on the right hand with our barge and wherries, and leaue the Galley at ancor the while in the great riuer, hee would bring vs to a towne of the *Arwacas* where we should find store of bread, hens, fish, and of the countrey wine, and perswaded vs that departing from the Galley at noon, we might returne ere night: . . . But when it grew towardes night, and wee demaunded where the place was, hee tolde vs but fowre reaches more, when we had rowed fower and fower, we sawe no signe, and our poore water men euen hart broken, and tired, were readie to giue vp the ghost; for wee had nowe come from the Galley neere forty miles.

At the last wee determined to hang the *P*ilot, and if we had well knowen the way backe againe by night, he had surely gone, but our owne necessities pleaded sufficientlie for his safetie: for it was as darke as pitch. and the riuer began so to narrowe it selfe and the trees to hang

ouer from side to side, as we were driuen with arming swordes to cut a
passage thorowe the branches that couered the water.   We were very
desirous to finde this towne hoping of a feast, because we had but a
shorte breakefast aboorde the *Galley* in the morning, and it was now
eight a clocke at night, and our stomacks began to gnawe apace : but
whether it was best to returne or to go on, we began to doubt, suspect-
ing treason in the Pilote more and more : but the poore olde Indian
euer assured vs that it was but a little farther, and but this one turning,
and that turning, and at last about one a clocke after midnight we saw
a light, and rowing towardes it, we heard the dogs of the village. . . .

. . . seeking after the Spaniardes, we found the *Armacas* hidden in
the woods which were pilots for the Spaniards, and rowed their *Canoas :*
of which I kept the chiefest for a Pilot ; and carried him with me to
Guiana, by whom I vnderstood, where and in what countries the Spaniards had labored for gold, though I made not the same knowen to all :
for when the springs began to breake, and the riuers to raise themselues
so suddenly as by no meanes we coulde abide the digging of any mine,
especially for that the richest are defended with rocks of hard stone,
which we call the *White spar*, and that it required both time, men, and
instruments fit for such a worke, I thought it best not to houer thereabouts, . . . to staie to dig out golde with our nayles, had beene *Opus
laboris*, but not *Ingen ÿ :* such a quantitie as woulde haue serued our
turnes we could not haue had, but a discouery of the mines to our
infinite disaduantage we had made, and that coulde haue been the best
profit of farther search or stay : for those mines are not easily broken,
nor opened in hast, and I could haue returned a good quantity of gold
ready cast, if *I* had not shot at another mark than present profit.

. . . so the 15. day wee discoured a far off the mountaines of *Guiana*
to our great ioy, and towards the euening had a slent of a northerly
winde that blew uery strong, which brought vs in sight of the great riuer
of *Orenoque*. . . .

That *Casique* that was a stranger had his wife staying at the port
where we ankored, and in all my life I haue seldome seene a better
fauored woman ; she was of good stature, with blacke eies, fat of body,
of an excellent countenance, her haire almost as long as her selfe, tied
vp againe in prittie knots, and it seemed she stood not in that awe of
her husband, as the rest, for she spake and discourst, and dranke among
the gentlemen and captaines, and was uery pleasant, knowing her owne
comeliness, and taking great pride therein.   I haue seene a Lady in

England so like her, as but for the difference of colour I would haue sworne might haue beene the same. . . .

The next morning towardes nine of the clocke, we weied ancor, & the brize encreasing, we sailed alwaies west vp the riuer, and after a while opening the lande on the right side, the country appeered to be champaine [plains], and the banks shewed very perfect red : . . .

The next day we arriued at the port of *Morequito*, and ankored there ; sending away one of our Pilots to seeke the king of *Aromaia* : . . .

After this olde king had rested a while in a little tent, that I caused to be set vp, I began by my interpreter to discourse with him of the death of *Morequito* his predecessor, and afterwarde of the Spaniards, and ere *I* went anie farther I made him knowe the cause of my comming thither, whose seruaunt I was, and that the Queenes pleasure was, I shoulde vndertake the voyage for their defence, and to deliuer them from the tyrannie of the Spaniardes, dilating at large (as *I* had done before to those of *Trinedado*) her Maiesties greatnesse, her iustice, her charitie to all oppressed Nations, with as manie of the rest of her beauties and vertues, as eyther *I* could expresse or they conceiue, all which being with great admiration attentiuelie hearde, and maruellouslie admired, *I* began to sounde the olde man as touching *Guina*, . . . He told me farther that fower daies iourney from his towne was *Macureguarai*, and that those were the next, & nearest of his subiectes of *Inga*, and of the *Epuremei*, and the first towne of apparrelled and rich people, and that all those plates of Golde which were scattered among the borderers and caried to other nations farre and neere, came from the saide *Marcureguarai* and were there made, but that those of the lande within were farre finer, and were fashioned after the *I*mage of men, bestes, birdes, and fishes. I asked him whether hee thought that those companies that *I* had there with me, were sufficient to take that towne or no ; hee told mee that he thought they were. . . . For mine owne part (as we were not able to march it for the riuers neither had any such strength as was requisite, and durst not abide the comming of the winter, or to tarry any longer from our shippes) I thought it were euill counsell to haue attempted it at that time, although the desire of golde will answere many obiections ; But it woulde haue beene in mine opinion an vtter ouerthrow to the enterprize, if the same should be hereafter by her Maiesty attempted : for then (wheras now they haue heard we were enemies to the Spaniards & were sent by her Maiesty to relieue them) they would as good cheape haue ioyned with the Spaniardes at our returne, as to haue yeelded vnto vs, when they had proued that we came both for one errant, and that both fought but to sacke and spoyle them, but as yet our desire of gold, or our purpose of inuasion is not knowen vnto those of the empire : and it is likely that if her Maiesty vndertake the enterprize, they will rather submit themselues to her obedience then to Spaniards, of whose cruelty both themselues and the borderers haue already tasted ; and therefore till I had knowen her Maiesties pleasure, I would rather haue lost the sacke of one or two townes (although they might haue beene uery profitable) then to haue defaced or indangered the future hope of so many millions, and the great good, & rich trade which England may bee possessed off thereby. . . . I after asked the manner how the *Epuremei* wrought those plates of golde, and how they could melt it out of the stone ; he tolde me that they most of the gold which they made in plates and images was not seuered from the stone, but that on the lake of *Manoa*, & in a multitude of other riuers they gathered it in graines of perfect gold and in peeces as big as small stones, and that they put it to a part of copper, otherwise they could not worke it, & that they vsed a great earthen pot with holes round about it, and when they had mingled the gold & copper together, they fashioned canes to the hole, and so with the breath of men they increased the fire till the mettel ran, and then they cast it into moulds of stone & clay, and so make the plants and Images.   I haue sent your Honours of two sorts such as coulde by chaunce recouer, more to shew the maner of them, then for the value : for I did not in any sort make my desire of gold knowen, because I had neither time, nor power to haue a greater quantity. I gaue among them manie more pesoes of Golde then I receiued of the new money of 20. shillings with her maiesties picture to weare, with promise that they would become her seruants thenceforth. . . .

To speake of what past homeward were tedious, . . . about nine of the clocke, we descried the Iland of *Trinedado*, and stearing for the nearest part of it, wee kept the shore til we came to *Curiapan*, where we found our ships at ancor, then which, there was neuer to vs a more ioyfull sight.

W. Ralegh, *The Discoverie of the Large, Rich, and Beavtiful Empire of Gviana*, etc. (London, 1596), 1–90 *passim*.

CHAPTER V — FRENCH AND DUTCH
(1524–1682)

34. A Voyage along the Atlantic Coast (1524)

BY CAPTAIN JOHN VERRAZANO

(TRANSLATED BY JOSEPH G. COGSWELL, 1860)

**Verrazano was a Florentine, sailing under the orders of Francis I, King of France.
— Bibliography: Winsor, *Narrative and Critical History*, IV, 17–29; Channing and Hart, *Guide*, § 87.**

ON the 17th of last January we set sail from a desolate rock near the island of Madeira, belonging to his most serene Majesty the King of Portugal, with fifty men; having provisions sufficient for eight months, arms, and other warlike munition and naval stores. Sailing westward with a light and pleasant easterly breeze, in twenty-five days we ran eight hundred leagues. On the 24th of February we encountered as violent a hurricane as any ship ever weathered, from which we escaped unhurt by the divine assistance and goodness, to the praise of the glorious and fortunate name of our good ship, that had been able to support the violent tossing of the waves. Pursuing our voyage towards the west, a little northwardly, in twenty-four days more, having run four hundred leagues, we reached a new country which had never before been seen by any one either in ancient or modern times. At first it appeared to be very low; but on approaching it to within a quarter of a league from the shore, we perceived, by the great fires near the coast, that it was inhabited. We perceived that it stretched to the south, and coasted along in that direction in search of some port in which we might come to an anchor and examine into the nature of the country; but for fifty leagues we could find none in which we could lie securely. Seeing the coast still stretched to the south, we resolved to change our course and stand to the northward; and as we still had the same difficulty, we drew in with the land, and sent a boat on shore. Many people who were seen coming to the sea-side, fled at our approach; but occasionally stopping, they looked back upon us with astonishment, and some were at length induced, by various friendly signs, to come to us. These shewed the greatest delight on beholding us, wondering at our dress, countenances, and complexion. They then shewed us by signs where we could more conveniently secure our boat, and offered us some of their provisions. That your Majesty may know all that we learned, while on shore, of their manners and customs of life, I will relate what we saw as briefly as possible. . . .

The complexion of these people is black, not much different from that of the Ethiopians. Their hair is black and thick, and not very long; it is worn tied back upon the head, in the form of a little tail. In person they are of good proportions, of middle stature, a little above our own; broad across the breast, strong in the arms, and well formed in the legs and other parts of the body. The only exception to their good looks, is that they have broad faces; but not all, however, as we saw many that had sharp ones, with large black eyes and a fixed expression. They are not very strong in body, but acute in mind, active and swift of foot, as far as we could judge by observation. In these last two particulars they resemble the people of the East, especially those the most remote. We could not learn a great many particulars of their usages on account of our short stay among them and the distance of our ship from the shore.

We found, not far from this people, another, whose mode of life we judged to be similar. The whole shore is covered with fine sand, about fifteen feet thick, rising in the form of little hills, about fifty paces broad. Ascending farther, we found several arms of the sea, which make in through inlets, washing the shores on both sides as the coast runs. An outstretched country appears at a little distance, rising somewhat above the sandy shore, in beautiful fields and broad plains, covered with immense forests of trees more or less dense, too various in colours, and too delightful and charming in appearance to be described. I do not believe they are like the Hercynian forest, or the rough wilds of Scythia; and the northern regions full of vines and common trees; but adorned with palms, laurels, cypresses, and other varieties, unknown in Europe; that send forth the sweetest fragrance, to a great distance; but which we could not examine more closely for the reasons before given, and not on account of any difficulty in traversing the woods; which, on the contrary, are easily penetrated.

As the "East" stretches around this country, I think it cannot be devoid of the same medicinal and aromatic drugs, and various riches of gold and the like, as is denoted by the colour of the ground. It abounds also in animals, as the deer, stags, hares, and many other similar, and with a great variety of birds for every kind of pleasant and delightful sport. It is plentifully supplied with lakes and ponds of running water ; and being in the latitude of 31°, the air is salubrious, pure, and temperate, and free from the extremes of both heat and cold. There are violent winds in these regions ; the most prevalent are the north-west and west. In summer, the season in which we were there, the sky is clear, with but little rain. If fogs and mists are at any time driven in by the south wind, they are instantaneously dissipated, and at once it becomes serene and bright again. The sea is calm, not boisterous, and its waves are gentle. Although the whole coast is low and without harbours, it is not dangerous for navigation, being free from rocks, and bold, so that, within four or five fathoms from the shore, there is twenty-four feet of water at all times of tide ; and this depth constantly increases in a uniform proportion. The holding ground is so good that no ship can part her cable, however violent the wind, as we proved by experience ; for while riding at anchor on the coast, we were overtaken by a gale in the beginning of March, when the winds are high, as is usual in all countries ; we found our anchor broken before it started from its hold or moved at all. . . .

We saw in this country many vines, growing naturally, which entwine about the trees, and run up upon them as they do in the plains of Lombardy. These vines would doubtless produce excellent wine if they were properly cultivated and attended to, as we have often seen the grapes which they produce very sweet and pleasant, and not unlike our own. They must be held in estimation by them, as they carefully remove the shrubbery from around them wherever they grow, to allow the fruit to ripen better. We found also, wild roses, violets, lilies, and many sorts of plants and fragrant flowers different from our own. We cannot describe their habitations, as they are in the interior of the country, but from various indications we conclude they must be formed of trees and shrubs. We saw also many grounds for conjecturing that they often slept in the open air, without any covering but the sky. Of their other usages we know nothing ; we believe, however, that all the people we were among live in the same way.

After having remained here three days, riding at anchor on the coast, as we could find no harbour, we determined to depart, and coast along the shore to the north-east, keeping sail on the vessel only by day, and coming to anchor by night. After proceeding one hundred leagues, we found a very pleasant situation among some steep hills, through which a very large river, deep at its mouth, forced its way to the sea ; from the sea to the estuary of the river, any ship heavily laden might pass, with the help of the tide, which rises eight feet.   But as we were riding at anchor in a good berth, we would not venture up in our vessel, without a knowledge of the mouth : therefore we took the boat, and entering the river, we found the country on its banks well peopled, the inhabitants not differing much from the others, being dressed out with the feathers of birds of various colours.   They came towards us with evident delight, raising loud shouts of admiration, and showing us where we could most securely land with our boat.   We passed up this river, about half a league, when we found it formed a most beautiful lake three leagues in circuit, upon which they were rowing thirty or more of their small boats, from one shore to the other, filled with multitudes who came to see us.   All of a sudden as is wont to happen to navigators, a violent contrary wind blew in from the sea, and forced us to return to our ship, greatly regretting to leave this region which seemed so commodious and delightful, and which we supposed must contain great riches, as the hills showed many indications of minerals.   Weighing anchor, we sailed eighty leagues towards the east, as the coast stretched in that direction, and always in sight of it ; at length we discovered an island of a triangular form, about ten leagues from the mainland, in size about equal to the island of Rhodes, having many hills covered with trees, and well peopled, judging from the great number of fires which we saw all around its shores ; we gave it the name of your Majesty's mother.

We did not land there, as the weather was unfavorable, but proceeded to another place, fifteen leagues distant from the island, where we found a very excellent harbour.   Before entering it, we saw about twenty small boats full of people, who came about our ship, uttering many cries of astonishment, but they would not approach nearer than within fifty paces ; stopping, they looked at the structure of our ship, our persons and dress, afterwards they all raised a loud shout together, signifying that they were pleased. . . .   This is the finest looking tribe, and the handsomest in their costumes, that we have found in our voyage.   They exceed us in size, and they are of a very fair complexion ; some of them incline more to a white [bronze], and others to a tawny colour ; their faces are sharp, their hair long and black, upon the adorning of which they bestow great pains; their eyes are black and sharp, their expression mild and pleasant, greatly resembling the antique. . . .

This region is situated in the parallel of Rome, being 41° 40' of north latitude; but much colder, from accidental circumstances, and not by nature, as I shall hereafter explain to your Majesty, and confine myself at present to the description of its local situation. It looks towards the south, on which side the harbour is half a league broad; afterwards, upon entering it, the extent between the coast and north is twelve leagues; and then enlarging itself, it forms a very large bay, twenty leagues in circumference, in which are five small islands of great fertility and beauty, covered with large and lofty trees. Among these islands any fleet, however large, might ride safely, without fear of tempests or other dangers. Turning towards the south, at the entrance of the harbour, on both sides, there are very pleasant hills, and many streams of clear water which flow down to the sea. In the midst of the entrance there is a rock of freestone, formed by nature, and suitable for the construction of any kind of machine or bulwark for the defence of the harbour.

Having supplied ourselves with everything necessary, on the fifth of May we departed from the port, and sailed one hundred and fifty leagues, keeping so close to the coast as never to lose it from our sight. The nature of the country appeared much the same as before; but the mountains were a little higher, and all, in appearance, rich in minerals. We did not stop to land, as the weather was very favourable for pursuing our voyage, and the country presented no variety. The shore stretched to the east; and fifty leagues beyond, more to the north, where we found a more elevated country full of very thick woods of fir trees, cypresses, and the like, indicative of a cold climate. The people were entirely different from the others we had seen, whom we had found kind and gentle; but these were so rude and barbarous that we were unable, by any sign we could make, to hold communication with them. . . .

Departing from thence, we kept along the coast, steering north-east, and found the country more pleasant and open, free from woods; and distant in the interior we saw lofty mountains, but none which extended to the shore. Within fifty leagues we discovered thirty-two islands, all near the mainland, small, and of pleasant appearance; but high, and so disposed as to afford excellent harbours and channels, as we see in the Adriatic Gulf, near Illyria and Dalmatia. We had no intercourse with the people; but we judge that they were similar in nature and usages to those we were last among. After sailing between east and north the distance of one hundred and fifty leagues more, and finding our provisions and naval stores nearly exhausted, we took in wood and water, and determined to return to France, having discovered 502, that is 700 leagues of unknown land. . . .

Hakluyt Society, *Works issued, 1860* (London, 1860), 200–221 *passim*.

---

35. Discovery of the St. Lawrence (1534–1535)

BY CAPTAIN JACQUES CARTIER

(TRANSLATED BY RICHARD HAKLUYT, 1609)

Cartier was a Breton sailor, perhaps a pirate, made Captain General and Chief Pilot by Francis I. — Bibliography: Winsor, *Narrative and Critical History*, IV, ch. ii; Channing and Hart, *Guide*, § 87.

AFTER that Sir Charles of Mouy knight lord of Meylleraye, and Vice-admirall of France had caused the Captaines, Masters, and Mariners of the shippes to be sworn to behaue themselues truely and faithfully in the seruice of the most Christian King of France, vnder the charge of the sayd Carthier, vpon the twentieth day of Aprill 1534, we departed from the Port of S. Malo with two ships of threescore tun apiece burden, and 61 well appointed men in each one ; . . . The next day being the last of the moneth saue one, the winde blewe South and by East. Wee sailed Westward vntill Tuesday morning at Sunne rising, being the last of the moneth, without any sight or knowledge of any lande except in the euening toward Sunne set, that wee discouered a lande which seemed to be two Ilands, that were beyond vs West southwest, about nine or tenne leagues. All the next day till the next morning at sunne rising wee sailed Westward about fourtie leagues, and by the way we perceiued that the land we had seene like Ilands, was firme land, lying South southeast, and North northwest, to a very good Cape of land called Cape Orleans. Al the said land is low and plaine, and the fairest that may possibly be seene, full of goodly medowes and trees. True it is that we could finde no harborough there, because it is all full of shelues and sands. We with our boats went on shore in many places, and among the rest wee entred into a goodly riuer, but very shallow, which we named The riuer of boats, because that there wee saw boates full of wild men that were crossing the riuer. . . .

VPon Thursday being the eight of the moneth, because the winde was not good to go out with our ships, we set our boates in a readinesse to goe to discouer the said Bay, and that day wee went 25. leagues within it. The next day the wind and weather being faire, we sailed vntil noone, in which time we had notice of a great part of the said Bay, and how that ouer the low lands, there were other lands with high mountaines : but seeing that there was no passage at all, wee began to turne back againe, taking our way along the coast ; and sayling, we saw certaine wilde men . . . and by and by in clusters they came to the shore where wee were, with their boates, bringing with them skinnes and other such things as they had, to haue of our wares . . . til they had nothing but their naked bodies ; for they gaue vs all whatsoeuer they had, and that was but of small value. We perceiued that this people might very easily be conuerted to our Religion. They goe from place to place. They liue onely with fishing. They haue an ordinarie time to fish for their prouision. The countrey is hotter than the countrey of Spaine, and the fairest that can possibly be found, altogether smooth, and leuel. There is no place be it neuer so little, but it hath some trees (yea albeit it be sandie) or else is full of wilde corne, that hath an eare like vnto Rie : the corne is like oates, and smal peason as thicke as if they had bene sowen and plowed, white and red Roses, with many other flouers of very sweet and pleasant smell. There be also many goodly medowes full of grasse, and lakes wherein great plentie of salmons be. They call a hatchet in their tongue Cochi, and a knife Bacon : we named it The bay of heat.

. . . The Saturday following, being the first of August, by Sunne rising, wee had certaine other landes, lying North and Northeast, that were very high and craggie, and seemed to be mountaines : betweene which were other low lands with woods and riuers : wee went about the sayd lands, as well on the one side as on the other, still bending Northwest, to see if it were either a gulfe, or a passage, vntill the fift of the moneth. The distance from one land to the other is about fifteene leagues. The middle betweene them both is 50 degrees and a terce in latitude. We had much adoe to go fiue miles farther, the winds were so great and the tide against vs. And at fiue miles end, we might plainely see and perceiue land on both sides, which there beginneth to spread it selfe. . . .

AFter we had sailed along the sayd coast, for the space of two houres, behold, the tide began to turne against vs, with so swift and raging a course, that it was not possible for vs with 13 oares to row or get one

stones cast farther, so that we were constrained to leaue our boates with
some of our men to guard them, and 10 or 12 men went ashore to the
sayd Cape, where we found that the land beginneth to bend Southwest,
which hauing seene, we came to our boats againe, and so to our ships,
which were stil ready vnder saile, hoping to go forward : but for all that,
they were fallen more then foure leagues to leeward from the place where
we had left them, where so soone as we came, wee assembled together
all our Captaines, Masters, and Mariners, to haue their aduice and opinion what was best to be done ; and after that euery one had said, considering that the Easterly winds began to beare away, and blow, and
that the flood was so great, that we did but fall, and that there was
nothing to be gotten, and that stormes and tempests began to reigne in
Newfoundland, and that we were so farre from home, not knowing the
perils and dangers that were behind, for either we must agree to returne
home againe, or els to stay there all the yeere.   More ouer, we did consider, that if the Northerne winds did take vs, it were not possible for vs
to depart thence.   All which opinions being heard and considered, we
altogether determined to addresse our selues homeward.   Nowe because
vpon Saint Peters day wee entred into the sayd Streite, we named it
Saint Peters Streite. . . .

IN the yeere of our Lord 1535, vpon Whitsunday, being the 16. of
May, by the commandement of our Captaine Iames Cartier, and with a
common accord, in the Cathedrall Church of S. Malo we deuoutly each
one confessed our selues, and receiued the Sacrament : and all entring
into the Quier of the sayd Church, wee presented our selues before the
Reuerend Father in Christ, the Lord Bishop of S. Malo, who blessed vs
all, being in his Bishops roabes.   The Wednesday following, being the
19. of May, there arose a good gale of wind, and therefore we hoysed
sayle with three ships. . . .   We staied and rested our selues in the
sayd hauen, vntill the seuenth of August being Sonday : on which day
we hoysed sayle, and came toward land on the South side toward Cape
Robast, distant from the sayd hauen about twentie leagues Northnorth-
east, and Southsouthwest : but the next day there rose a stormie and a
contrary winde, and because we could find no hauen there toward the
South, thence we went coasting along toward the North, beyond the
abouesayd hauen about ten leagues, where we found a goodly great
gulfe, full of Islands, passages, and entrances, toward what wind soeuer
you please to bend : for the knowledge of this gulfe there is a great

Island that is like to a Cape of lande, stretching somewhat further foorth than the others, and about two leagues within the land, there is an hill fashioned as it were an heape of corne.   We named the sayd gulfe Saint Laurence his bay.   The twelfth of the sayd moneth wee went from the sayd Saint Laurence his Bay, or gulfe, sayling Westward, and discouered a Cape of land toward the South, that runneth West and by South, distant from the sayd Saint Laurence his Bay, about fiue and twenty leagues.
. . . Moreouer I beleeue that there were neuer so many Whales seen as wee saw that day about the sayd Cape.   The next day after being our Ladie day of August the fifteenth of the moneth, hauing passed the Straight, we had notice of certaine lands that wee left toward the South, which landes are full of uery great and high hilles, and this Cape wee named The Island of the Assumption, . . .   The Countreys lying North may plainely be perceiued to be higher than the Southerly, more then thirty leagues in length.   We trended the sayd landes about toward the South : from the sayd day vntill Tewesday noone following, the winde came West, and therefore wee bended toward the North, purposing to goe and see the land that we before had spied.   Being arriued there, we found the sayd landes, as it were ioyned together, and low toward the Sea.   And the Northerly mountaines that are vpon the sayd low lands stretch East, and West, and a quarter of the South.   Our wild men told vs that there was the beginning of Saguenay, and that it was land inhabited, and that thence commeth the red Copper, of them named Caignetdaze.   There is betweene the Southerly lands, and the Northerly about thirty leagues distance, and more then two hundreth fadome depth.   The sayd men did moreouer certifie vnto vs, that there was the way and beginning of the great riuer of Hochelaga and ready way to Canada, which riuer the further it went the narrower it came, euen vnto Canada, and that then there was fresh water, which went so farre vpwards, that they had neuer heard of any man who had gone to the head of it, and that there is no other passage but with small boates. . . .   Vpon the first of September we departed out of the said hauen, purposing to go toward Canada ; and about 15 leagues from it toward the West, and Westsouthwest, amidst the riuer, there are three Islands, ouer against the which there is a riuer which runneth swift, and is of great depth, and it is that which leadeth, and runneth into the countrey and kingdome of Saguenay, as by the two wild men of Canada it was told vs.   This riuer passeth and runneth along very high and steepe hills of bare stone, where uery little earth is, and notwithstanding there is a great quantity of sundry sorts of trees that grow in

the said bare stones, euen as vpon good and fertile ground, in such sort that we haue seene some so great as wel would suffise to make a mast for a ship of 30 tunne burden, and as greene as possibly can be, growing in a stony rocke without any earth at all. . . . The seuenth of the moneth being our Ladies euen, after seruice we went from that Iland to go vp higher into the riuer, and came to 14 Ilands seuen or eight leagues from the Iland of Filberds, where the countrey of Canada beginneth, one of which Ilands is ten leagues in length, and fiue in bredth, greatly inhabited of such men as onely liue by fishing of such sorts of fishes as the riuer affordeth, according to the season of them. . . . The next day following, the Lord of Canada (whose proper name was Donnacona, but by the name of Lord they call him Agouhanna) with twelue boats came to our ships, accompanied with many people, who causing ten of his boates to goe backe with the other two, approched vnto vs with six-teene men. . . . Our Captaine then caused our boates to be set in order, that with the next tide he might goe vp higher into the riuer, to find some safe harborough for our ships : and we passed vp the riuer against the streame about tenne leagues, coasting the said Iland, at the end whereof, we found a goodly and pleasant sound, where is a little riuer and hauen, where by reason of the flood there is about three fadome water. This place seemed to vs very fit and commodious to harbour our ships therein, and so we did very safely, we named it the holy Crosse, for on that day we came thither. Neere vnto it, there is a village, whereof Donnacona is Lord, and there he keepeth his abode : it is called Stada-cona [Quebec] as goodly a plot of ground as possibly may be seene. . . . Hauing considered the place, and finding it fit for our purpose, our Captaine withdrew himselfe on purpose to returne to our ships : . . .

AFter we were come with our boats vnto our ships againe, our Cap-taine caused our barks to be made readie to goe on land in the said Iland, to note the trees that in shew seemed so faire, and to consider the nature and qualitie of it : which things we did, and found it full of goodly trees likes to ours. Also we saw many goodly Vines, a thing not before of vs seene in those countries, and therefore we named it Bacchus Iland. It is in length about twelue leagues, in sight very pleasant, but full of woods, no part of it manured, vnlesse it be in certaine places, where a few cottages be for Fishers dwellings as before we haue said. . . .

THe next day being the 19 of September we hoysed saile, and with our Pinnesse and two boates departed to goe vp the riuer with the flood, where on both shores of it we beganne to see as goodly a countrey as possibly can with eye be seene, all replenished with very goodly trees, and Vines laden as full of grapes as could be all along the riuer, which rather seemed to haue bin planted by mans hand than otherwise.   True it is, that because they are not dressed and wrought as they should be, their bunches of grapes are not so great nor sweete as ours : . . .   From the nineteenth vntill the eight and twentieth of September, we sailed vp along the saide riuer, neuer losing one houre of time, all which time we saw as goodly and pleasant a countrey as possibly can be wished for, . . .

THe next day our Captaine seeing for that time it was not possible for our Pinnesse to goe on any further, he caused our boates to be made readie, and as much munition and victuals to be put in them, as they could well beare : he departed with them, accompanyed with many Gentlemen, that is to say, Claudius of Ponte Briand, Cup-bearer to tne Lorde Dolphin of France, Charles of Pommeraye, Iohn Gouion, Iohn Powlet, with twentie and eight Mariners : and Mace Iallobert, and William Briton, who had the charge vnder the Captaine of the other two ships, to goe vp as farre as they could into that riuer : we sayled with good and prosperous weather vntill the second of October, on which day we came to the towne of Hochelaga, [Montreal] distant from the place where we had left our Pinnesse fiue and fortie leagues. . . .

Richard Hakluyt, *The Principal Navigations, Voyages, Traffiques, and Discoveries of the English Nation* (Edinburgh, 1889), XIII, 77–117 *passim*.

———— ◆ ————

36. A French Huguenot Colony (1564)

BY RÉNÉ LAUDONNIÈRE

(TRANSLATED BY RICHARD HAKLUYT)

The author of this piece was a Protestant gentleman, much esteemed as a marine officer. — Bibliography : Winsor, *Narrative and Critical History*, IV, 295, 316; Channing and Hart, *Guide*, § 88.

AFTERWARD, we passed between *Anquilla* and *Anegarda*, sailing toward New France, where we arrived fifteen days after, to wit : on Thursday, the 22d of June, about three of the clock in the afternoon.
    . . . The next day, the 23d of this month (because that, toward the south, I had not found any commodious place for us to inhabit and to build a fort), I gave commandment to weigh anchor, and to hoist our sails to sail toward the *River of May*, where we arrived two days after,

and cast anchor.   Afterward, going on land with some number of gentlemen and soldiers, to know for a certainty the singularities of this
place, we espied the *paracoussy* of the country which came toward us
(this was the very same that we saw in the voyage of Captain John
Ribault), which, having espied us, cried, very far off, *Antipola! Antipola!*
and, being so joyful that he could not contain himself, he came to meet
us, accompanied with two of his sons, as fair and mighty persons as
might be found in all the world, which had nothing in their mouths but
this word — *amy, amy;* that is to say, friend, friend ; yea, and knowing
those which were there in the first voyage, they went principally to
them to use this speech unto them.   There was in their train a great
number of men and women, which still made very much of us, and, by
evident signs, made us understand how glad they were of our arrival.

. . . I was of opinion, if it seemed good unto them, to seat ourselves
about the *River of May*, seeing, also, that, in our first voyage, we found
the same only among all the rest to abound in maize and corn, besides
the gold and silver that was found there : a thing that put me in hope
of some happy discovery in time to come.   After I had proposed these
things, every one gave his opinion thereof; and, in fine, all resolved,
namely, those which had been with me in the first voyage, that it was
expedient to seat themselves rather on the *River of May* [St. Johns]
than on any other, until they might hear news out of France.   This point
being thus agreed upon, we sailed toward the river, and used such diligence
that, with the favor of the winds, we arrived there the morrow after, about
the break of day, which was on Thursday, 29th of June.

Having cast anchor, I embarked all my stuff, and the soldiers of my
company, to sail right toward the opening of this river, wherein we
entered a good way up, and found a creek, of a reasonable bigness, which
invited us to refresh ourselves a little, while we reposed ourselves there.
Afterward we went on shore, to seek out a place. . . . then we discovered a little hill adjoining unto a great vale, very green, and, in form, flat ;
wherein were the fairest meadows of the world, and grass to feed cattle.
Moreover, it is environed with a great number of brooks of fresh water,
and high woods, which make the vale more delectable to the eye.   After
I had taken the view, thereof, at mine ease, I named it, at the request
of our soldiers, the *Vale of Laudonnière.* . . .

. . . we gathered our spirits together, and, marching with a cheerful
courage, we came to the place which we had chosen to make our habitation in : whereupon, at that instant, near the river's brink, we strewed

I

a number of boughs and leaves, to take our rest on them the night following, which we found exceeding sweet, because of the pain which before we had taken in our travel.

On the morrow, about break of day, I commanded a trumpet to be sounded, that, being assembled, we might give GOD thanks for our favorable and happy arrival. Then we sang a psalm of thanksgiving unto GOD, beseeching him that it would please him of his grace to continue his accustomed goodness toward us, his poor servants, and aid us in all our enterprises that all might turn to his glory and the advancement of our King. The prayer ended, every man began to take courage.

Afterward, having measured out a piece of ground, in the form of a triangle, we endeavored ourselves of all sides — some to bring earth, some to cut faggots, and others to raise and make the rampart; for there was not a man that had not either a shovel, or cutting-hook, or hatchet, as well to make the ground plain by cutting down the trees, as for the building the fort, which we did hasten, in such cheerfulness, that, within a few days, the effect of our diligence was apparent; . . .

Our fort was built in the form of a triangle: the side toward the west, which was toward the land, was inclosed with a little trench, and raised with turns made in the form of a battlement, of nine feet high; the other side, which was toward the river, was inclosed with a palisade of planks of timber, after the manner that gabions are made. On the south side, there was a kind of bastion, within which I caused an house for the munition to be built; it was all builded with faggots and sand, saving about two or three feet high, with turf, whereof the battlements were made. In the midst, I caused a great court to be made, of eighteen paces long and broad, in the midst whereof, on the one side drawing toward the south, I builded a corps de gard, *and an house on the other side, toward the north, which I caused to be raised somewhat too high, for, within a short while after, the wind beat it down;* and experience taught me that we may not build with high stages in this country, by reason of the winds whereunto it is subject. One of the sides that enclosed my court, which I made very fair and large, reached unto the range of my munitions, and, on the other side, towards the river, was mine own lodging, round about which were galleries, all covered. One principal door of my lodging was in the midst of the great place, and the other was toward the river. A good distance from the fort, I built an oven, to avoid the danger against fire, because the houses are of palm-leaves, which will soon be burnt after the fire catcheth hold of them, so that, with much ado, a man shall have leisure to quench them. Lo, here, in brief, the description of our fortress, which I named *Caroline*, in honor of our prince, King Charles.

. . . In the meanwhile, I was not able, with the same store of victuals which I had, so well to proportion out the travel upon the ships which we built to return into France ; but that, in the end, we were constrained to endure extreme famine, which continued among us all the month of May ; for, in this latter season, neither maize, nor beans, nor mast, was to be found in the villages, because they had employed all for to sow their fields, insomuch that we were constrained to eat roots, which the most part of our men pounded in the morters (which I had brought with me to beat gunpowder in), and the grain which came to us from other places. Some took the wood of *esquine*, beat it, and made meal thereof, which they boiled with water, and eat it ; others went, with their harquebuses, to seek to kill some fowl. Yea, this misery was so great, that one was found that gathered up, among the filth of my house, all the fish-bones that he could find, which he dried, and beat into a powder, to make bread thereof.

. . . I leave it to your cogitation to think how near it went to our hearts to leave a place abounding in riches (as we were thoroughly informed thereof), in coming whereunto, and doing service unto our Prince. we left our own country, wives, children, parents, and friends, and passed the perils of the sea, and were therein arrived, as in a plentiful treasure of all our hearts desire. As each of us were much tormented in mind with these, or such like cogitations, the third of August, I descried four sails in the sea as I walked upon a little hill, whereof I was exceedingly well repaid. I sent, immediately, one of them which were with me, to advertise those of the fort, thereof, which were so glad of these news, that one would have thought them to be out of their wits, to see them laugh and leap for joy.

. . . Captain Vasseur and my lieutenant, which were gone to meet them, which brought me word that they were Englishmen ; . . . The general [Sir Francis Drake] immediately understood the desire and urgent occasion which I had to return into France, whereupon he offered to transport me and all my company home ; whereunto, notwithstanding, I would not agree, being in doubt on what occasion he made so large an offer ; for I knew not how the case stood between the French and the English ; and, although he promised me, on his faith, to put me on land in France, before he would touch in England, yet I stood in doubt, lest he would attempt somewhat in Floril, in the name of his mistress ; wherefore I flatly refused his offer. . . .

AS I was thus occupied in these conferences, the wind and the tide served well to set sail — which was the eighth and twentieth of August ; at which instant, Captain VASSEUR, which commanded in one of my ships, and Captain VERDIER, which was chief in the other — now ready to go forth, began to descry certain sails at sea, whereof they advertised me with diligence ; . . .

Being, therefore, advertised that it was Captain RIBAULT, I went forth of the fort to meet him ; and, to do him all the honor I could by any means, I caused him to be welcomed with the artillery, and a gentle volley of my shot, whereunto he answered with his. Afterward, being come on shore, and received honorably with joy, I brought him to my lodging, rejoicing not a little, because that, in this company I knew a good number of my friends, which I entreated, in the best sort that I was able, with such victuals as I could get in the country, and that small store which I had left me, with that which I had of the English general. . . . But, lo ! how oftentimes misfortune doth search and pursue us, even when we think to be at rest ! Lo ! see what happened after that Capt. RIBAULT had brought up three of his small ships into the river, which was the 4th of September. Six great Spanish ships arrived in the road, where four of our greatest ships remained, which cast anchor, assuring our men of good amity. They asked how the chief captains of the enterprise did, and called them all by their names and sirnames. I report me to you, if it could be otherwise ; but these men, before they went out of Spain, must needs be informed of the enterprise, and of those that were to execute the same. About the break of day, they began to make toward our men ; but our men, which trusted them never a deal, had hoisted their sails by night, being ready to cut the strings that tied them ; wherefore, perceiving that this making toward our men of the Spaniards was not to do them any pleasure, and knowing well that their furniture was too small to make head against them, because that the most part of their men were on shore, they cut their cables, left their anchors, and set sail. . . .

After he [Ribault] understood these news, he returned to the fortress, and came to my chamber, where I was sick ; and there, in the presence of Captains LA GRANGE, ST. MARIE, OTTIGNE, VISTY, YONOUILLE, and other gentlemen, he propounded that it was necessary, for the King's service, to embark himself, with all his forces, and, with the three ships that were in the road, to seek the Spanish fleet; whereupon he asked our advice. . . .

. . . Then he told me that he could do no less than to continue this enterprise; and that in the letter which he had received from my Lord Admiral, there was a postscript, which he showed me, written in these words:

"Captain JOHN RIBAULT, as I was enclosing of this letter, I received a certain advice, that DON PEDRO MELENDES departeth from Spain, to go to the coast of *New France*. See that you suffer him not to encroach upon you, no more than he would that you should encroach upon him."

"You see," quoth he, "the charge that I have; and I leave it unto yourself to judge if you could do any less in this case, considering the certain advertisement that we have, that they are already on land, and will invade us." . . . The night between the 19th and 20th of September, LA VIGNE kept watch with his company, wherein he used all endeavor, although it rained without ceasing. When the day was, therefore, come, and that he saw that it still rained worse than it did before, he pitied the sentinels so moiled and wet, and thinking the Spaniards would not have come in such a strange time, he let them depart, and, to say the truth, he went himself unto his lodging. In the meanwhile, one which had something to do without the fort, and my trumpeter, which went up unto the rampart, perceived a troop of Spaniards which came down from a little *knappe*, where, incontinently, they began to cry alarm, and the trumpeter also, which, as soon as ever I understood, forthwith I issued out, with my target and sword in my hand, and got me into the midst of the court, where I began to cry upon my soldiers. . . .

AS I went to succor them which were defending the breach on the south-west side, I encountered, by chance, a great company of Spaniards, which had already repulsed our men, and were now entered, which drove me back unto the court of the fort . . . and, in the meanwhile, I saved myself by the breach, which was on the west side, near unto my lieutenant's lodging and gateway, into the woods, where I found certain of my men, which were escaped, of which number there were three or four which were sore hurt.

. . . being able to go no farther, by reason of my sickness which I had, I sent two of my men, which were with me, which could swim well, unto the ships, to advertise them of that which had happened, and to send them word to come and help me. . . .

The 25th of September, we set sail to return into France. . . .

The indifferent and unpassionate readers may easily weigh the truth of my doings, and be upright judges of the endeavor which I there used. For mine own part, I will not accuse, nor excuse any; it sufficeth me to have followed the truth of the history, whereof many are able to bear witness, which were there present. I will plainly say one thing — that the long delay that Captain JOHN RIBAULT used in his embarking, and the fifteen days that he spent in roving along the coast of Florida before he came to our fort (Caroline), were the cause of the loss we sustained; for he discovered the coast on the 14th of August, and spent the time in going from river to river, which had been sufficient for him to have discharged his ships in, and for me to have embarked myself to have returned into France. I note well that all that he did was upon a good intent; yet, in mine opinion, he should have had more regard unto his charge than to the devices of his own brain, which, sometimes, he printed in his head so deeply, that it was very hard to put them out, which also turned to his utter undoing; for he was no sooner departed from us but a tempest took him, which, in fine, wrecked him upon the coast, where all his ships were cast away; and he, with much ado, escaped drowning, to fall into their hands, which cruelly massacred him and all his company

B. F. French, *Historical Collections of Louisiana and Florida* (new series, New York, 1869), I, 222–346 *passim*.

————◆————

37. The Myth of Norembega (1606)

BY MARC LESCARBOT

(TRANSLATED BY P. EORONDELLES, 1609)

The author was a Parisian lawyer, a friend of De Monts, and his book is much esteemed. — Bibliography: Winsor, *Narrative and Critical History*, III, ch. vi; Channing and Hart, *Guide*, § 94.

THE rough season being passed, *Monsieur de Monts* wearied with his badde dwelling at Saint *Croix*, determined to seeke out another Port in a warmer countrie, and more to the South: And to that end made a Pinnesse to be armed and furnished with victuals, to follow the coast, and discouering new countries, to seeke out some happier Port in a more temperate aire. And because that in seeking, one can-

not set forward so much as when in full sailes one goeth in open sea,
and that finding out baies and gulfes, lying betweene two lands, one
must put in, because that there one may assoone finde that which is
sought for, as else where, he made in this voyage but about six score
leagues, as wee will tell you now.   From Saint *Croix* to 60. leagues forward, the coast lieth East and West ; at the end of which 60. leagues, is
the riuer called by the Sauages *Kinibeki*.   From which place to *Malebarre*
it lieth North and South, and there is yet from one to the other 60.
leagues, in right line, not following the baies.   So farre stretcheth
Monsieur De Monts his voyage, wherein he had for Pilot in his vessell,
Monsieur De Champdore.   In all this coast so farre as *Kinibeki* there is
many places where shippes may be harbored amongst the Ilands, but
the people there is not so frequent as is beyond that : And there is no
remarkable thing (at least that may be seene in the outside of the lands)
but a riuer, whereof many haue written fables one after another, like to
those that they (who grounding themselues, vpon *Hannas* his Com-
mentaries, a Carthaginian captain) haue fained of Townes built by him
in great number vpon the coasts of Africa, which is watered with the
Ocean sea, for that hee plaied an heroycall part in sailing so farre as the
Iles of *Cap Vert*, where long time since no body hath beene, the Nauigation not being so secure then, vpon that great sea, as it is at this day
by the benefit of the Compasse.

Therefore without alleaging that, which the first writers (Spaniards
and Portingals) haue said, I will recite that which is in the last booke,
intituled, *The vniuersall Hiſtorie of the Weſt Indies*, Printed at *Douay*
the last yeere 1607. in the place where he speaketh of *Norombega :* For
in reporting this, I shall haue also said that which the first haue written,
from whom they haue had it.

   " Moreouer, towards the North (saith the Author, after he had spoken
" of *Virginia*) is *Norombega*, which is known well enough by reason of a
" faire towne, and a great riuer, though it is not found from whence it
" hath his name : for the Barbarians doe call it *Agguncia ;* At the mouth
" of this riuer there is an Iland uery fit for fishing. The region that
" goeth along the sea, doth abound in fish, and towards New France
" there is great number of wilde beasts, and is verie commodious for
" hunting ; the Inhabitants doe liue in the same maner as they of New
" France."   If this beautifull Towne hath euer beene in nature, I would
faine know who hath pulled it downe : For there is but Cabanes here
and there made with pearkes, and couered with barkes of trees, or with

skinnes, and both the riuer and the place inhabited, is called *Pemptegoet*, and not *Agguncia*. The riuer (sauing the tide) is scarce as the riuer of *Oyse*. And there can be no great riuer on that coast, because there are not lands sufficient to produce them, by reason of the great riuer of *Canada*, which runneth like this coast, and is not foure-score leagues distant from that place in crossing the lands, which from else-where re-ceiued manie riuers falling from those parts which are toward *Norombega*: At the entrie whereof, it is so farre from hauing but one Iland, that rather the number thereof is almost infinite, for as much as this riuer enlarging it selfe like the Greeke *Lambda* Λ, the mouth whereof is all full of Iles, whereof there is one of them lying very farre off (and the formost) in the sea, which is high and remarkable aboue the others.

But some will say that I aequiuocate in the situation of *Norombega*, and that it is not placed where I take it. To this I answer, that the author, whose words I haue a little before alleaged, is in this my suffi-cient warrant, who in his Geographicall Mappe hath placed in the mouth of this riuer in the 44. degree, and his supposed towne is in the 45. wherein we differ but in one degree, which is a smal matter. For the riuer that I meane is in the 45. degree, and as for any towne, there is none. Now of necessitie it must be this riuer, because that the same being passed, and that of *Kinibeki*, (which is in the same height) there is no other riuer forward, whereof account should be made, tell one come to *Virginia*. I say furthermore, that seeing the Barbarians of *Norombega* doe liue as they of New France, and haue abundance of hunting, it must be, that their prouience be seated in our New France: For fiftie leagues farther to the Southwest there is no great game, be- " cause the woods are thinner there, and the inhabitants setled, and in " greater number than in *Norombega*.   "

True it is that a sea Captaine, named *John Alfonse*, of *Xaintonge*, in the relation of his aduenturous voiages, hath written, that, hauing passed Saint *Iohns* Iland (which I take for the same that I haue called heereto-fore the Ile of *Bacaillos*) the coast turneth to the West, and West South-" west, as far as the riuer of *Norombergue*, newly discouered (saith he) " by the Portugais and Spaniards, which is in 30. degrees; adding that " this riuer hath, at the entrie thereof many Iles, bankes, and rockes, and " that fifteene or twenty leagues within it, is built a great towne, where the " people be small and blackish, like them of the Indies, and are clothed " with skinnes, whereof they haue abundance of all sorts. Item, that the " bank of New found land endeth there: and that, that riuer being passed,

" the coast turneth to the West, and West Northwest, aboue 250. leagues
" towards a countrie, where there is both townes and castels.   But I see
" very little or no truth at all, in all the discourses of this man ; and well
may he call his voiages aduenturous, not for him, who was neuer in the
hundreth part of the places he described (at least it is easie so to
thinke) but for those that will follow the waies, which he willeth mariners to follow.   For if the said riuer of *Norombega* be in thirtie degrees, it must needs be in *Florida*, which is the contrarie to all them
that euer haue written of it, and to the verie truth it selfe.

Marc Lescarbot, *Nova Francia* (London, 1609), 45-48.

———◆———

38. Discovery of the Hudson River (1607)

BY ROBERT JUET

(TRANSLATED BY GEORGE M. ASHER, 1860)

Juet was mate of the Half Moon, in which this voyage was made; this is the only
contemporary account. — Bibliography: Winsor, *Narrative and Critical History*,
III, 103, IV, 416; Channing and Hart, *Guide*, § 104.

ON Saturday, the *five and twentieth of March*, 1609, after the old
account, we set sayle from Amsterdam, and by the *seven and
twentieth* day, we were downe at the Texel : and by twelve of the clocke
we were off the land, it being east of us two leagues off. . . .

The *twelfth* was very foggie, we stood our course all the morning till
eleven of the clocke ; at which time we had sight of the land, which is
low white sandie ground, right on head off us ; and had ten fathoms.
Then we tackt to the southward, and stood off foure glasses: then we
tackt to the land againe, thinking to have rode under it, and as we came
neere it the fog was so thicke that we could not see ; so wee stood off
againe. . . .

The *sixteenth*, in the morning, it cleered up, and we had sight of five
islands lying north, and north and by west from us, two leagues.   Then
wee made ready to set sayle, but the myst came so thicke that we durst
not enter in among them.

The *seventeenth*, was all mystie, so that we could not get into the harbour.   At ten of the clocke two boats came off to us, with sixe of the
savages of the countrey, seeming glad of our comming.   We gave them
trifles, and they eate and dranke with us ; and told us that there were

gold, silver, and copper mynes hard by us; and that the French-men doe trade with them; which is very likely, for one of them spake some words of French. So wee rode still all day and all night, the weather continuing mystie.

The *eighteenth*, faire weather, wee went into a very good harbour, and rode hard by the shoare in foure fathom water. . . .

The *nineteenth*, . . . The people coming aboord, shewed us great friendship, but we could not trust them. The *twentieth*, . . . wee espied two French shallops full of the country people come into the harbour, but they offered us no wrong, seeing we stood upon our guard. They brought many beaver skinnes and other fine furres, which they would have changed for redde gownes. For the French trade with them for red cassockes, knives, hatchets, copper, kettles, trevits, [tripods for cooking] beades, and other trifles.

. . . We kept good watch for fear of being betrayed by the people, and perceived where they layd their shallops.

The *five and twentieth*, very faire weather and hot. In the morning wee manned our scute with foure muskets and sixe men, and tooke one of their shallops and brought it aboord. Then we manned our boat and scute with twelve men and muskets, and two stone pieces or murderers, and drave the savages from their houses, and tooke the spoyle of them, as they would have done of us. . . .

. . . wee steered away north againe, and saw the land from the west by north to the north-west by north, all like broken islands, and our soundings were eleven and ten fathoms. Then wee looft in for the shoare, and faire by the shoare we had seven fathoms. The course along the land we found to be north-east by north. From the land which we had first sight of, untill we came to a great lake of water, as wee could judge it to bee, being drowned land, which made it to rise like islands, which was in length ten leagues. The mouth of that land hath many shoalds, and the sea breaketh on them as it is cast out of the mouth of it. And from that lake or bay the land lyeth north by east, and wee had a great streame out of the bay; . . .

. . . The land is very pleasant and high, and bold to fall withall. At three of the clock in the after-noone, wee came to three great rivers. So we stood along to the northermost, thinking to have gone into it, . . .

. . . This day the people of the countrey came aboord of us, seeming very glad of our comming, and brought greene tobacco, and gave us of it for knives and beads. They goe in deere skins loose, well dressed.

They have yellow copper. They desire cloathes, and are very civill. They have great store of maize or Indian wheate, whereof they make good bread. The countrey is full of great and tall oakes.

The *fifth*, in the morning, as soone as the day was light, the wind ceased and the flood came. So we heaved off our ship againe into five fathoms water, and sent our boate to sound the bay, and we found that there was three fathoms hard by the souther shoare. Our men went on land there, and saw great store of men, women, and children, who gave them tabacco at their comming on land. So they went up into the woods, and saw great store of very goodly oakes and some currants. For one of them came aboord and brought some dryed, and gave me some, which were sweet and good. This day many of the people came aboord, some in mantles of feathers, and some in skinnes of divers sorts of good furres. Some women also came to us with hempe. They had red copper tabacco pipes, and other things of copper they did weare about their neckes. At night they went on land againe, so wee rode very quiet, but durst not trust them.

The *sixth*, in the morning, was faire weather, and our master sent John Colman, with foure other men in our boate, over to the north-side to sound the other river, being foure leagues from us. They found by the way shoald water, two fathoms; but at the north of the river eighteen, and twentie fathoms, and very good riding for ships; and a narrow river to the westward, betweene two ilands. The lands, they told us, were as pleasant with grasse and flowers and goodly trees as ever they had seene, and very sweet smells came from them. So they went in two leagues and saw an open sea, and returned; and as they came backe, they were set upon by two canoes, the one having twelve, the other fourteene men. The night came on, and it began to rayne, so that their match went out; and they had one man slaine in the fight, which was an Englishman, named John Colman, with an arrow shot into his throat, and two more hurt. It grew so darke that they could not find the ship that night, but labored too and fro on their oares. They had so great a streame, that their grapnell would not hold them.

The *eleventh* was faire and very hot weather. . . . wee anchored, and saw that it was a very good harbour for all windes, and rode all night. The people of the country came aboord of us, making shew of love, and gave us tabacco and Indian wheat, and departed for that night; but we durst not trust them.

The *twelfth*, very faire and hot. In the after-noone, at two of the clocke, wee weighed, the winde being variable betweene the north and the north-west. So we turned into the river two leagues and anchored. This morning, at our first rode in the river, there came eight and twentie canoes full of men, women and children to betray us : but we saw their intent, and suffered none of them to come aboord of us. . . .

The *fourteenth*, in the morning, being very faire weather, the wind south-east, we sayled up the river twelve leagues, . . . The river is a mile broad : there is very high land on both sides. . . . The land grew very high and mountainous. The river is full of fish.

The *fifteenth*, in the morning, was misty, untill the sunne arose : then it cleered. So wee weighed with the wind at south, and ran up into the river twentie leagues, passing by high mountaines. Wee had a very good depth, as sixe, seven, eight, nine, ten, twelve, and thirteene fathomes, and great store of salmons in the river. This morning our two savages got out of a port and swam away. After wee were under sayle, they called to us in scorne. At night we came to other mountaines, which lie from the rivers side. There wee found very loving people, and very old men : where wee were well used. Our boat went to fish, and caught great store of very good fish.

The *sixteenth*, faire and very hot weather. In the morning our boat went againe to fishing, but could catch but few, by reason their canoes had beene there all night. . . .

The *seventeenth*, faire sun-shining weather, and very hot. In the morning, as soone as the sun was up, we set sayle, and ran up six leagues higher, and found shoalds in the middle of the channell, and small ilands, but seven fathoms water on both sides. . . .

The *eighteenth*, in the morning, was faire weather, and we rode still. In the after-noone our masters mate went on land with an old savage, a governor of the countrey ; who carried him to his house, and made him good cheere. . . .

. . . Our carpenter went on land, and made a fore-yard. And our master and his mate determined to trie some of the chiefe men of the countrey, whether they had any treacherie in them. So they tooke them downe into the cabbin, and gave them so much wine and *aqua vitæ*, that they were all merrie : and one of them had his wife with them, which sate so modestly, as any of our countrey women would doe in a strange place. In the ende one of them was drunke, which had beene aboord of our ship all the time that we had beene there : and that was strange to them ; for they could not tell how to take it. The canoes

and folke went all on shoare : but some of them came againe, and
brought stropes of beades : some had sixe, seven, eight, nine, ten ; and
gave him. So he slept all night quietly.

The *two and twentieth* was faire weather : in the morning our masters
mate and foure more of the companie went up with our boat to sound
the river higher up. The people of the countrey came not aboord till
noone ; but when they came, and saw the savages well, they were glad.
So at three of the clocke in the afternoone they came aboord, and
brought tabacco, and more beades, and gave them to our master, and
made an oration, and shewed him all the countrey round about. Then
they sent one of their companie on land, who presently returned, and
brought a great platter full of venison dressed by themselves ; and they
caused him to eate with them : then they made him reverence and
departed, all save the old man that lay aboord. This night, at ten of
the clocke, our boat returned in a showre of raine from sounding of the
river ; and found it to bee at an end for shipping to goe in. For they
had beene up eight or nine leagues, and found but seven foot water, and
unconstant soundings. . . .

Hakluyt Society, *Works issued, 1860* (London, 1860), 45–86 *passim.*

———————◆———————

39. Adventures on Lake Champlain (1609)

BY SIEUR SAMUEL CHAMPLAIN

(TRANSLATED BY CHARLES POMEROY OTIS, 1882)

Champlain, "Captain in ordinary to the King in the marine," is one of the most
trustworthy writers of his time. — Bibliography : Winsor, *Narrative and Critical
History*, IV, ch. iii ; Channing and Hart, *Guide*, § 89.

I SET out from St. Croix on the 3d of June with all the savages. We
passed the Trois Rivières, a very beautiful country, covered with a
growth of fine trees. From this place to St. Croix is a distance of fifteen leagues. At the mouth of the above-named river there are six
islands, three of which are very small, the others from fifteen to sixteen
hundred paces long, very pleasant in appearance. Near Lake St. Peter,
some two leagues up the river, there is a little fall not very difficult to
pass. This place is in latitude 46°, lacking some minutes. The savages
of the country gave us to understand that some days' journey up this
river there is a lake, through which the river flows. The length of the

lake is ten days' journey, when some falls are passed, and afterwards three or four other lakes of five or six days' journey in length. Having reached the end of these, they go four or five leagues by land, and enter still another lake, where the Sacqué has its principal source. From this lake, the savages go to Tadoussac. The Trois Rivières extends forty days' journey of the savages. They say that at the end of this river there is a people, who are great hunters, without a fixed abode, and who are less than six days' journey from the North Sea. What little of the country I have seen is sandy, very high, with hills, covered with large quantities of pine and fir on the river border ; but some quarter of a league inland the woods are very fine and open, and the country level.

Thence we continued our course to the entrance of Lake St. Peter, where the country is exceedingly pleasant and level, and crossed the lake, in two, three, and four fathoms of water, which is some eight leagues long and four wide. On the north side, we saw a very pleasant river, extending some twenty leagues into the interior, which I named St. Suzanne ; on the south side, there are two, one called Rivière du Pont, the other Rivière de Gennes, which are very pretty, and in a fine and fertile country. The water is almost still in the lake, which is full of fish. On the north bank, there are seen some slight elevations at a distance of some twelve or fifteen leagues from the lake. After crossing the lake, we passed a large number of islands of various sizes, containing many nut-trees and vines, and fine meadows, with quantities of game and wild animals, which go over from the main land to these islands. Fish are here more abundant than in any other part of the river that we have seen. From these islands, we went to the mouth of the River of the Iroquois, where we stayed two days, refreshing ourselves with good venison, birds, and fish, which the savages gave us. Here there sprang up among them some difference of opinion on the subject of the war, so that a portion only determined to go with me, while the others returned to their country with their wives and the merchandise which they had obtained by barter. . . .

I SET out accordingly from the fall of the Iroquois River on the 2d of July. All the savages set to carrying their canoes, arms, and baggage overland, some half a league, in order to pass by the violence and strength of the fall, which was speedily accomplished. . . .

We set out the next day, continuing our course in the river as far as the entrance of the lake. There are many pretty islands here, low, and containing very fine woods and meadows, with abundance of fowl and such animals of the chase as stags, fallow-deer, fawns, roe-bucks, bears, and others, which go from the main land to these islands. We captured a large number of these animals. There are also many beavers, not only in this river, but also in numerous other little ones that flow into it. These regions, although they are pleasant, are not inhabited by any savages, on account of their wars; but they withdraw as far as possible from the rivers into the interior, in order not to be suddenly surprised.

The next day we entered the lake, which is of great extent, say eighty or a hundred leagues long, where I saw four fine islands, ten, twelve, and fifteen leagues long, which were formerly inhabited by the savages, like the River of the Iroquois; but they have been abandoned since the wars of the savages with one another prevail. There are also many rivers falling into the lake, bordered by many fine trees of the same kinds as those we have in France, with many vines finer than any I have seen in any other place; also many chestnut-trees on the border of this lake, which I had not seen before. . . .

Continuing our course over this lake on the western side, I noticed, while observing the country, some very high mountains on the eastern side, on the top of which there was snow. I made inquiry of the savages, whether these localities were inhabited, when they told me that the Iroquois dwelt there, and that there were beautiful valleys in these places, with plains productive in grain, such as I had eaten in this country, together with many kinds of fruit without limit. They said also that the lake extended near mountains, some twenty-five leagues distant from us, as I judge. I saw, on the south, other mountains, no less high than the first, but without any snow. . . .

When it was evening, we embarked in our canoes to continue our course; and, as we advanced very quietly and without making any noise, we met on the 29th of the month the Iroquois, about ten o'clock at evening, at the extremity of a cape which extends into the lake on the western bank. They had come to fight. We both began to utter loud cries, all getting their arms in readiness. We withdrew out on the water, and the Iroquois went on shore, where they drew up all their canoes close to each other and began to fell trees with poor axes, which they acquire in war sometimes, using also others of stone. Thus they barricaded themselves very well.

Our forces also passed the entire night, their canoes being drawn up close to each other, and fastened to poles, so that they might not get separated, and that they might be all in readiness to fight, if occasion required. . . . After arming ourselves with light armor, we each took an arquebuse, and went on shore. I saw the enemy go out of their barricade, nearly two hundred in number, stout and rugged in appearance. They came at a slow pace towards us, with a dignity and assurance which greatly amused me, having three chiefs at their head. Our men also advanced in the same order, telling me that those who had three large plumes were the chiefs, and that they had only these three, and that they could be distinguished by these plumes, which were much larger than those of their companions, and that I should do what I could to kill them. I promised to do all in my power, and said that I was very sorry they could not understand me, so that I might give order and shape to their mode of attacking their enemies, and then we should, without doubt, defeat them all ; but that this could not now be obviated, and that I should be very glad to show them my courage and good-will when we should engage in the fight.

As soon as we had landed, they began to run for some two hundred paces towards their enemies, who stood firmly, not having as yet noticed my companions, who went into the woods with some savages. Our men began to call me with loud cries ; and in order to give me a passage-way, they opened in two parts, and put me at their head, where I marched some twenty paces in advance of the rest, until I was within about thirty paces of the enemy, who at once noticed me, and, halting, gazed at me, as I did also at them. When I saw them making a move to fire at us, I rested my musket against my cheek, and aimed directly at one of the three chiefs. With the same shot, two fell to the ground ; and one of their men was so wounded that he died some time after. I had loaded my musket with four balls. When our side saw this shot so favorable for them, they began to raise such loud cries that one could not have heard it thunder. Meanwhile, the arrows flew on both sides. The Iroquois were greatly astonished that two men had been so quickly killed, although they were equipped with armor woven from cotton thread, and with wood which was a proof against their arrows. This caused great alarm among them. As I was loading again, one of my companions fired a shot from the woods, which astonished them anew to such a degree that, seeing their chiefs dead, they lost courage, and took to flight, abandoning their camp and fort, and fleeing into the woods, whither I pursued them, killing still more of them. Our savages also killed several of them, and took ten or twelve prisoners. The remainder escaped with the wounded. Fifteen or sixteen were wounded on our side with arrow-shots ; but they were soon healed.

After gaining the victory, our men amused themselves by taking a great quantity of Indian corn and some meal from their enemies, also their armor, which they had left behind that they might run better. After feasting sumptuously, dancing and singing, we returned three hours after, with the prisoners. The spot where this attack took place is in latitude 43° and some minutes, and the lake was called Lake Champlain.

AFTER going some eight leagues, towards evening they took one of the prisoners, to whom they made a harangue, enumerating the cruelties which he and his men had already practised towards them without any mercy, and that, in like manner, he ought to make up his mind to receive as much. They commanded him to sing, if he had courage, which he did ; but it was a very sad song.

Rev. Edmund F. Slafter, *Voyages of Samuel de Champlain* (Prince Society
Publications, II, Boston, 1878), 204–224 *passim*.

———◆———

40. Experiences of a Jesuit Missionary (1643)

BY FATHER ISAAC JOGUES

(Translated by John Gilmary Shea, 1857)

The heroism of this quiet and refined man is set forth in these extracts; the worst
horrors have been omitted. — Bibliography : Winsor, *Narrative and Critical History*,
IV, 295–316; Channing and Hart, *Guide*, § 89.

. . . THE exceeding charity of your Reverence, which in other days overlooked my manifold transgressions, will excuse me if, after eight years' intercourse and residence with savages, nay, a savage now in form and dress myself, aught be here wanting in correctness or decorum. I fear still more, that, rude in language, I may be more so in knowledge, "nor know the time of my visitation," (Luke xix, 44,) nor remember the character imposed on me by God, of preacher of his Gospel, Jesuit and Priest. This induced me to write to you, that if this letter should ever reach your hands, I may, though living here in this hard land amid Iroquois and Maaquas, be helped by your masses and the prayers of your whole province. This aid, I trust, will be more earnestly given, when from a perusal of this letter you shall have seen both how much I am indebted to the Almighty, and in what need I am of the prayers oi the pious, in which, I am aware, I have a powerful shield.

We sailed from the Hurons on the 13th of June, 1642, in four small boats, here called canoes; we were twenty-three in all, five of us being French. . . .

The Superior, conscious of the dangers to which I was exposed on this journey (one, however, absolutely necessary for God's glory,) assigned the task to me in such a way as to leave me at liberty to decline it if I chose. "I did not," however, "resist, I did not go back," (Isaias 1) but willingly and cheerfully accepted this mission imposed upon me by obedience and charity. Had I declined it, it would have fallen to another, far more worthy than myself. . . .

We consequently urged on our way, but had scarcely advanced a mile when we fell into an ambush of the enemy, who lay in two divisions on the opposite banks of the river, to the number of seventy in twelve canoes. . . . We, the four Frenchmen, thus left with a few either already Christians, or at least Catechumens, offering up a prayer to Christ, faced the enemy. We were, however, outnumbered, being scarcely twelve or fourteen against thirty; yet we fought on till our comrades, seeing fresh canoes shoot out from the opposite bank of the river, lost heart and fled. Then a Frenchman named René Goupil, who was fighting with the bravest, was taken, together with some of the Hurons. When I saw this, I neither could nor cared to fly. Whither, indeed, could I escape, barefooted as I was? Conceal myself amid the reeds and tall grass I could indeed, and thus, perhaps, escape; but could I leave a countryman and the unchristened Hurons, already taken, or soon to be? As the enemy, in hot pursuit of the fugitives, had passed on, leaving me standing on the battle-field, I called out to one of those who had remained to guard the prisoners, and bade him place me beside his French captive, that as I had been his companion on the way, so would I be in his dangers and death. Scarce crediting what he heard, and fearful for himself, he advanced and led me to the other prisoners. . . . Last of all, William Couture was dragged in . . .

When I beheld him thus bound and naked, I could not contain myself, but, leaving my keepers, rushed through the midst of the savages who had brought him, embraced him most tenderly; exhorted him to offer all this to God for himself, and those at whose hands he suffered. They at first looked on, in wonder, at my proceeding; then, as if recollecting themselves, and gathering all their rage, they fell upon me, and with their fists, thongs and clubs beat me till I fell senseless. Two of them then dragged me back to where I had been before ; and scarcely had I begun to breathe, when some others, attacking me, tore out, by biting, almost all my nails, and crunched my two fore-fingers with their teeth, giving me intense pain. . . .

Never till now had the Indian scaffold beheld French or other Christian captives. Hence, contrary to usual custom, we were led around through all their villages to gratify the general curiosity. The third indeed [Teonontogen] we entered scatheless, but on the scaffold a scene met my eyes more heart-rending than any torment ; it was a group of four Hurons taken elsewhere by another party and dragged in to swell our wretched company. Among other cruelties, every one of these had lost some fingers, and the eldest of the band his two thumbs. As soon as I reached them, I began to instruct them separately on the articles of faith, then on the very stage itself I baptized two with rain-drops gathered from the leaves of a stalk of Indian corn given us to chew ; the other two I baptized at a little stream which we passed when led to another village. At this place, cold setting in after the rain, we suffered extremely from it as we were entirely uncovered. Often shivering with cold on the stage, I would, unordered, come down and enter some hut, but I could scarcely begin to warm myself when I was commanded to return to the scaffold. . . . Being ordered to sing as other captives do, we at last complied, for alas ! what could we do ; but we " sang the canticles of the Lord in a strange land." . . .

And now the middle of October was come, when the Indians leave their villages to go and hunt deer, which they take by traps, or kill with their guns, in the use of which they are very skilful. This season, to the Indians one of relaxation and enjoyment, brought its new burden of sorrows for me ; for I was given to a party who were at first amazed at me, then ridiculed, and at last began to hate me. Mindful of the character imposed upon me by God, I began with modesty to discourse with them of the adoration of one only God, of the observance of his commandments, of heaven, hell, and the other mysteries of our faith, as fully as I was able. At first, indeed, they listened ; but when they saw me constantly recur to these things, and especially when the chase did not meet with the desired success, then they declared that I was a demon who caused them to take so little game. But what turned their ill-will into perfect rage and fury, so to speak, was this : it is the custom with all these nations to have recourse, in their hunting, fishing, war, sickness, and the like, to a certain demon, whom they call Aireskoi. Whoever desires his fishing, hunting, or other expeditions to be successful, takes meat and other of the better articles of food, and begs the oldest of the house or village to *bless* them for him, if I may use the expression, . . .

The very first time I heard a formula couched in such words, I was filled with a deep detestation of this barbarian superstition, and firmly resolved to abstain forever from meats thus offered. They interpreted this abstinence on my part, and this contempt of their demon, as the cause of their taking little game: "the wicked have hated me without cause." (John xv, 25.) As under the influence of this hate, they would neither listen to my instructions, nor help me to acquire their language in which I refuted their fables, I resolved to devote my time entirely to spiritual exercises. . . .

Although I could in all probability escape either through the Europeans or the Indian nations around us, did I wish to fly, yet on this cross to which our Lord has nailed me, beside Himself, am I resolved by His grace to live and die. For who in my absence would console the French captives? who absolve the penitent? who remind the christened Huron of his duty? who instruct the prisoners constantly brought in? who baptize them dying, encourage them in their torments? who cleanse the infants in the saving waters? who provide for the salvation of the dying adult, the instruction of those in health? Indeed I cannot but think it a peculiar interposition of divine goodness, that while a nation, fallen from the true Catholic religion, barred the entrance of the faith to these regions, on one side, and on the other, a fierce war between savage nations, and on their account with the French, I should have fallen into the hands of these Indians, who by the will of God reluctantly, and I may say against their will, have thus far spared my life, that through me, though unworthy, those might be instructed, believe and be baptized, who are predestined to eternal life. Since the time when I was taken, I have baptized seventy children, young and old, of five different nations and languages, that of "every tribe, and people, and tongue, they might stand in the sight of the Lord." (Apoc. vii, 9.) . . .

New York Historical Society, *Collections* (second series, New York, 1857), III, Part I, 173-205 *passim*.

41. The French Government of Canada (1663)

BY FATHER CHRISTIAN LE CLERCQ (1691)

(TRANSLATED BY JOHN GILMARY SHEA, 1881)

Le Clercq was a missionary of the Recollet monks, who were violent rivals of the Jesuits. — Bibliography: Winsor, *Narrative and Critical History*, IV, 290–292; Channing and Hart, *Guide*, § 90.

THE Church of New France, far from making any progress, could not subsist long unless a more powerful arm than that of the gentlemen of the Company came to her assistance in the extremity to which Canada was reduced in 1663.

The Iroquois, after having defeated and almost entirely destroyed our allies, desolated our habitations. The people were not in security even at Quebec, being unable to resist the enemy, who threatened us with total destruction. The missionaries' route to go and preach the Gospel was closed ; the barbarians having already destroyed a great number of them during this war and the preceding one. The colony, far from increasing, began to diminish. Some returned to France, others were taken and killed by the Indians. Many died of misery ; the clearing and cultivation of lands advanced but little, and they were obliged to expect all from France. The order of police and justice, so necessary for the establishment of the Church, had taken no form. More powerful assistance was needed for the ministers of the Gospel, in order not to be obliged to support themselves by ways forbidden by their institute. Although the colony was so thinly inhabited, division always reigned more and more among the inhabitants. Commerce (the only resource for the country) was entirely ruined.

Till then the king reserved only the sovereign authority, having yielded the domain and the property, seigneury, and commerce of New France to the gentlemen of the Company, on condition that they should pay all charges at their own expense. These gentlemen had doubtless good intentions, and we knew that most had joined only from a zeal for religion. They had made great efforts in the first years, but, being finally weary of so many useless outlays, which produced no return, they had for the last years abandoned the commerce to the inhabitants of the country under certain conditions. These were ruined by several reasons which are no part of my subject.

Involved by its great loans to more than two hundred thousand livres, far from being able to sustain itself or advance, it daily became more embarrassed, although ten per cent. was levied on all merchandise.

Worthy object of the piety of the king [Louis XIV] — who, after having given peace to Europe by the treaty of the Pyrenees, re-established order and felicity in the kingdom ; begun to destroy heresy, which is now entirely annihilated ; obtained from God a successor to the crown in the person of the Dauphin — he wished to turn his zeal towards New France, which his Majesty united to his domain, assumed the debts of the country, undertook to provide all the expenses of the Church, justice, and war, established a company for the sole direction of commerce in a single hand, which has since been so advantageous to the inhabitants, a true father and saviour of Canada. This great prince, from a principle of religion, reserved to himself and his council every care, more with a view of forming a Christian empire than of extending the limits of a temporal kingdom. Of all the effects of protection which his bounty occasioned during the present epoch, the most advantageous was the powerful assistance he sent — intelligent and enlightened ministers and officers capable of giving a form to this rising country, with considerable sums drawn from his treasury, and sparing nothing to establish this colony. He sent also experienced troops to repel the enemy and sustain the inhabitants. . . .

Whilst God gave these blessings to the arms of the king, the intendant gave his attention to the establishment and general good of the country, which soon changed its appearance by the wisdom of so penetrating, so experienced a minister, so zealous for the service of God and the king, as Monsieur Talon has always been, as were, too, his brothers in the intendancies and other employments of distinction.

The colony, which was as yet only a handful of settlers scattered here and there in different cantons, was notably increased by the number of officers and soldiers who chose to settle when the troops were disbanded, and who formed more than three hundred new families. To each soldier the king allowed fifty livres and rations for a year, to a sergeant fifty crowns, and to an officer in proportion. Sixty leagues of land ascending the Saint Lawrence, on the lakes, rivers, and inland, were divided up The lands were erected into seigneuries for the captains and officers, each seigneur granting farms in his district to his soldiers and others who came from France, so that in a few years the clearing and cultivation of the lands having materially increased, they were able to support the settlers. The young women sent over in great numbers by the king in the following years found regular settlements, and were advantageously married according to their degree.

Courts were not as yet fixed and regulated. The king everywhere established royal subaltern seigniorial courts and a superior sovereign council erected by letters-patent at Quebec, composed of a president, dean and councillors, judging as a court of last resort in all cases of appeal, according to the laws of the kingdom.

The intendant endeavored to give some form of administration everywhere as in France, establishing the manufacture of linen, leather, shoes, hats, lace, etc. Potash works and breweries, public edifices in many parts of the country, were the result of his attention, as well as the construction of ships and barks ; the re-establishment of treaties with Indian tribes, free trade for the colonists, the regulation and perfect order of the royal income, attracted merchants from France.

The number of workmen in all trades insensibly increased by means of those whom the king annually sent to aid the colonists, and in the same way the country was supplied with horses and domestic animals of all kinds.

The colony also assumed an entirely new face by the continual favors bestowed by the king and by the application of Monsieur de Courcelles and Monsieur Talon ; but the chief advantage was the restoration of the missions among the Indian nations and the new progress of the Church in the colony, which forms the subject of my history.

The king, forgetting nothing that depended on his piety to contribute to the establishment of the kingdom of God in Canada, assigned considerable allowances to the two seminaries and all the religious communities of both sexes, besides concessions of the best lands and farms in the country to give them means to fulfil their functions, for the spiritual edification of the colony and the Indian nations.

Father Christian Le Clercq, *First Establishment of the Faith in New France* (New York, 1881), II, 52–61 *passim.*

42. Discovery of the Mississippi (1673)

BY FATHER JAMES MARQUETTE

(Translated by J. D. B. De Bow, 1850)

Marquette, a Jesuit, lost his papers on the return journey, and composed this narrative from memory. — Bibliography: Winsor, *Narrative and Critical History*, IV, 190–202, 209–233 ; Channing and Hart, *Guide*, § 90.

I EMBARKED with M. Joliet, who had been chosen to conduct this enterprise, on the 13th May, 1673, with five other Frenchmen, in two bark canoes. We laid in some Indian corn and smoked beef for our voyage. We first took care, however, to draw from the Indians all the information we could, concerning the countries through which we designed to travel, and drew up a map, on which we marked down the rivers, nations, and points of the compass to guide us in our journey. The first nation we came to was called the Folles-Avoines, or the *nation of wild oats*. I entered their river to visit them, as I had preached among them some years before. The wild oats, from which they derive their name, grows spontaneously in their country. . . .

I acquainted them with my design of discovering other nations, to preach to them the mysteries of our holy religion, at which they were much surprised, and said all they could to dissuade me from it. They told me I would meet Indians who spare no strangers, and whom they kill without any provocation or mercy ; that the war they have one with the other would expose me to be taken by their warriors, as they are constantly on the look-out to surprise their enemies. That the Great River was exceedingly dangerous, and full of frightful monsters who devoured men and canoes together, and that the heat was so great that it would positively cause our death. I thanked them for their kind advice, but told them I would not follow it, as the salvation of a great many souls was concerned in our undertaking, for whom I should be glad to lose my life. I added that I defied their monsters, and their information would oblige us to keep more upon our guard to avoid a surprise. And having prayed with them, and given them some instructions, we set out for the Bay of Puan [Green Bay], where our missionaries had been successful in converting them. . . .

This bay [Green Bay] is about thirty leagues long, and eight broad in the greatest breadth ; for it grows narrower and forms a cone at the extremity. It has tides that flow and ebb as regular as the sea. We left this bay to go into a river [Fox River] that discharges itself therein, and found its mouth very broad and deep. It flows very gently, but after we had advanced some leagues into it we found it difficult to navigate, on account of the rocks and the currents; we fortunately overcame all these difficulties. It abounds in bustards, ducks, and other birds, which are attracted there by the wild oats, of which they are very fond. We next came to a village of the Maskoutens, or nation of fire. . . .

The next day, being the 10th of June, the two guides [*Miamies*] embarked with us in sight of all the village, who were astonished at our attempting so dangerous an expedition. We were informed that at three leagues from the *Maskoutens*, we should find a river which runs into the Mississippi, and that we were to go to the west-south-west to find it, but there were so many marshes and lakes, that if it had not been for our guides we could not have found it. The river upon which we rowed and had to carry our canoes from one to the other, looked more like a corn-field than a river, insomuch that we could hardly find its channel. As our guides had been frequently at this portage, they knew the way, and helped us to carry our canoes overland into the other river, distant about two miles and a half; from whence they returned home, leaving us in an unknown country, having nothing to rely upon but Divine Providence. We now left the waters which extend to Quebec, about five or six hundred leagues, to take those which would leads us hereafter into strange lands.

Before embarking we all offered up prayers to the Holy Virgin, which we continued to do every morning, placing ourselves and the events of the journey under her protection, and after having encouraged each other, we got into our canoes. The river upon which we embarked is called Mesconsin [Wisconsin]; the river is very wide, but the sand bars make it very difficult to navigate, which is increased by numerous islands covered with grape vines. The country through which it flows is beautiful; the groves are so dispersed in the prairies that it makes a noble prospect; and the fruit of the trees shows a fertile soil. These groves are full of walnut, oak, and other trees unknown to us in Europe. We saw neither game nor fish, but roebuck and buffaloes in great numbers. After having navigated thirty leagues we discovered some iron mines, and one of our company who had seen such mines before, said these were very rich in ore. They are covered with about three feet of soil, and situate near a chain of rocks, whose base is covered with fine timber. After having rowed ten leagues further, making forty leagues from the place where we had embarked, we came into the Mississippi on the 17th of June [1673].

The mouth of the Mesconsin [Wisconsin] is in about 42½° N. lat. Behold us, then, upon this celebrated river, whose singularities I have attentively studied. The Mississippi takes its rise in several lakes in the North. Its channel is very narrow at the mouth of the Mesconsin, and runs south until it is affected by very high hills. Its current is slow, because of its depth. In sounding we found nineteen fathoms of water. A little further on it widens nearly three-quarters of a league, and the width continues to be more equal. We slowly followed its course to the south and south-east to the 42° N. lat. Here we perceived the country change its appearance. There were scarcely any more woods or mountains. The islands are covered with fine trees, but we could not see any more roebucks, buffaloes, bustards, and swans. We met from time to time monstrous fish, which struck so violently against our canoes, that at first we took them to be large trees, which threatened to upset us. We saw also a hideous monster; his head was like that of a tiger, his nose was sharp, and somewhat resembled a wildcat; his beard was long; his ears stood upright; the color of his head was gray; and his neck black. He looked upon us for some time, but as we came near him our oars frightened him away. When we threw our nets into the water we caught an abundance of sturgeons, and another kind of fish like our trout, except that the eyes and nose are much smaller, and they have near the nose a bone like a woman's busk, three inches broad and a foot and a half long, the end of which is flat and broad, and when it leaps out of the water the weight of it throws it on its back.

Having descended the river as far as 41° 28′, we found that turkeys took the place of game, and the Pisikious that of other animals. We called the Pisikious wild buffaloes, because they very much resemble our domestic oxen; they are not so long, but twice as large. We shot one of them, and it was as much as thirteen men could do to drag him from the place where he fell. . . .

We continued to descend the river, not knowing where we were going, and having made an hundred leagues without seeing anything but wild beasts and birds, and being on our guard we landed at night to make our fire and prepare our repast, and then left the shore to anchor in the river, while one of us watched by turns to prevent a surprise. We went south and south-west until we found ourselves in about the latitude of 40° and some minutes, having rowed more than sixty leagues since we entered the river.

. . . We took leave of our guides about the end of June, and embarked in presence of all the village, who admired our birch canoes, as they had never before seen anything like them. We descended the river, looking for another called *Pekitanoni* [Missouri], which runs from the north-west into the Mississippi, of which I will speak more hereafter. . . .

As we were descending the river we saw high rocks with hideous monsters painted on them, and upon which the bravest Indians dare not look. They are as large as a calf, with head and horns like a goat; their eyes red; beard like a tiger's; and a face like a man's. Their tails are so long that they pass over their heads and between their fore legs, under their belly, and ending like a fish's tail. They are painted red, green, and black. They are so well drawn that I cannot believe they were drawn by the Indians. And for what purpose they were made seems to me a great mystery. As we fell down the river, and while we were discoursing upon these monsters, we heard a great rushing and bubbling of waters, and small islands of floating trees coming from the mouth of the *Pekitanoni* [Missouri], with such rapidity that we could not trust ourselves to go near it. The water of this river is so muddy that we could not drink it. It so discolors the Mississippi as to make the navigation of it dangerous. This river comes from the north-west, and empties into the Mississippi, and on its banks are situated a number of Indian villages. We judged by the compass, that the Mississippi discharged itself into the Gulf of Mexico. It would, however, have been more agreeable if it had discharged itself into the South Sea or Gulf of California. . . .

Having satisfied ourselves that the Gulf of Mexico was in latitude 31° 40', and that we could reach it in three or four days' journey from the *Akansea* [Arkansas River], and that the Mississippi discharged itself into it, and not to the eastward of the Cape of Florida, nor into the California Sea, we resolved to return home. We considered that the advantage of our travels would be altogether lost to our nation if we fell into the hands of the Spaniards, from whom we could expect no other treatment than death or slavery; besides, we saw that we were not prepared to resist the Indians, the allies of the Europeans, who continually infested the lower part of this river; we therefore came to the conclusion to return, and make a report to those who had sent us. So that having rested another day, we left the village of the Akansea, on the seventeenth of July, 1673, having followed the Mississippi from the latitude 42° to 34°, and preached the Gospel to the utmost of my power, to the nations we visited. We then ascended the Mississippi with great difficulty against the current, and left it in the latitude of 38° north, to enter another river [Illinois], which took us to the lake of the Illinois [Michigan], which is a much shorter way than through the River Mesconsin [Wisconsin], by which we entered the Mississippi. . . .

J. D. B. De Bow, *Marquette and Joliet's Account of the Voyage to Discover the Mississippi River*, in B. F. French, *Historical Collections of Louisiana* (Philadelphia, 1850), Part II, 279–296 *passim*.

---

43. La Salle's Exploration of the Mississippi (1682)

BY FATHER ZENOBIUS MEMBRÉ

(TRANSLATED BY JOHN GILMARY SHEA, 1852)

Membré was also a Recollet. His narrative is less satisfactory than Marquette's. — Bibliography: Winsor, *Narrative and Critical History*, IV, 254; Channing and Hart, *Guide*, § 90.

M. LA SALLE having arrived safely at the Miamies on the 3d of November, 1681, began with his ordinary activity and vast mind, to make all preparations for his departure. He selected twenty-three Frenchmen, and eighteen Mohegans and Abnakis, all inured to war. The latter insisted on taking along ten of their women to cook for them, as their custom is, while they were fishing or hunting. These women had three children, so that the whole party consisted of about fifty-four persons, including the sieur de Tonty and the sieur Dautray, son of the late sieur Bourdon, procurator-general of Quebec.

On the 21st of December, I embarked with the sieur de Tonty and a party of our people on Lake Dauphin [Michigan], to go toward the divine river, called by the Indians Checagou, in order to make necessary arrangements for our voyage. The sieur de la Salle joined us there with the rest of his troop on the 4th of January, 1682, and found that Tonty had had sleighs made to put all on and carry it over the Chicago which was frozen; for though the winter in these parts is only two months long, it is notwithstanding very severe.

We had to make a portage to enter the Ilinois river, which we found also frozen; we made it on the 27th of the same month, and dragging our canoes, baggage, and provisions, about eighty leagues on the river Seignelay [Ilinois], which runs into the river Colbert [Mississippi], we traversed the great Ilinois town without finding any one there, the Indians having gone to winter thirty leagues lower down on Lake Pimiteaui [Peoria], where Fort Crévecœur stands. We found it in a good state, and La Salle left his orders here. As from this spot navigation is open at all seasons, and free from ice, we embarked in our canoes, and on the 6th of February, reached the mouth of the river Seignelay, at 38° north. The floating ice on the river Colbert, at this place, kept us till the 13th of the same month, when we set out, and six leagues lower down, found the Ozage [Missouri] river, coming from the west. It is full as large as the river Colbert into which it empties troubling it so, that from the mouth of the Ozage the water is hardly drinkable. The Indians assure us that this river is formed by many others, and that they ascend it for ten or twelve days to a mountain where it rises; that beyond this mountain is the sea where they see great ships; that on the river are a great number of large villages, of many different nations; that there are arable and prairie-lands, and abundance of cattle and beaver. Although this river is very large, the Colbert does not seem augmented by it; but it pours in so much mud, that from its mouth the water of the great river, whose bed is also slimy, is more like clear mud than river water, without changing at all till it reaches the sea, a distance of more than three hundred leagues, although it receives seven large rivers, the water of which is very beautiful, and which are almost as large as the Mississippi.

On the 14th, six leagues further, we found on the east the village of the Tamaroas, who had gone to the chase; we left there marks of our peaceful coming, and signs of our route, according to practice, in such voyages. We went slowly, because we were obliged to hunt and fish almost daily, not having been able to bring any provisions but Indian corn.

Forty leagues from Tamoroa is the river Oüabache [Ohio], where we stopped. From the mouth of this river yóu must advance forty-two leagues without stopping, because the banks are low and marshy, and full of thick foam, rushes and walnut trees. . . .

On the 14th of the same month, the sieur de la Salle took possession of this country with great ceremony. He planted a cross, and set up the king's arms, at which the Indians showed a great joy. You can talk much to Indians by signs, and those with us managed to make them-

selves a little understood in their language. I took occasion to explain
something of the truth of God, and the mysteries of our redemption,
of which they saw the arms.   During this time they showed that they
relished what I said, by raising their eyes to heaven, and kneeling as
if to adore. We also saw them rub their hands over their bodies after
rubbing them over the cross.   In fact, on our return from the sea, we
found that they had surrounded the cross with a palisade.   They finally
gave us provisions and men, to conduct us, and serve as interpreters
with the Taensa, their allies, who are eighty leagues distant from their
village. . . .

On the 22d we reached the Taensa, who dwell around a little lake
formed in the land by the river Mississippi.   They have eight villages.
The walls of their houses are made of earth mixed with straw ; the roof
is of canes, which form a dome adorned with paintings ; they have
wooden beds, and much other furniture, and even ornaments in their
temples, where they inter the bones of their chiefs.   They are dressed
in white blankets made of the bark of a tree which they spin ; their
chief is absolute, and disposes of all without consulting anybody.   He
is attended by slaves, as are all his family.   Food is brought him outside
his cabin ; drink is given him in a particular cup, with much neatness.
His wives and children are similarly treated, and the other Taensa address
him with respect and ceremony. . . .

The whole country is covered with palm-trees, laurels of two kinds,
plums, peaches, mulberry, apple, and pear trees of every kind.   There
are also five or six kinds of nut-trees, some of which bear nuts of extraordinary size.   They also gave us several kinds of dried fruit to taste ; we
found them large and good.   They have also many other kinds of fruit-
trees which I never saw in Europe ; but the season was too early to
allow us to see the fruit.   We observed vines already out of blossom.
The mind and character of this people appeared on the whole docile
and manageable, and even capable of reason.   I made them understand
all I wished about our mysteries.   They conceived pretty well the necessity of a God, the creator and director of all, but attribute this divinity
to the sun.   Religion may be greatly advanced among them, as well as
among the Akansas, both these nations being half civilized.

Our guides would go no further for fear of falling into the hands of
their enemies, for the people on one shore are generally enemies of those
on the other.   There are forty villages on the east, and thirty-four on
the west, of all of which we were told the names.

The 26th of March resuming our course, we perceived, twelve leagues lower down, a periagua or wooden canoe, to which the sieur de Tonty gave chase, till approaching the shore, we perceived a great number of Indians. The sieur de la Salle, with his usual precaution, turned to the opposite banks, and then sent the calumet of peace by the sieur de Tonty. Some of the chief men crossed the river to come to us as good friends. They were fishermen of the Nachié tribe (Natchez), enemies of the Taensa. . . .

At last, after a navigation of about forty leagues, we arrived, on the sixth of April, at a point where the river divides into three channels. The sieur de la Salle divided his party the next day into three bands, to go and explore them. He took the western, the sieur Dautray the southern, the sieur Tonty, whom I accompanied, the middle one. These three channels are beautiful and deep. The water is brackish ; after advancing two leagues it became perfectly salt, and advancing on, we discovered the open sea, so that on the ninth of April, with all possible solemnity, we performed the ceremony of planting the cross and raising the arms of France. After we had chanted the hymn of the church, " Vexilla Regis," and the " Te Deum," the sieur de la Salle, in the name of his majesty, took possession of that river, of all rivers that enter it, and of all the country watered by them. An authentic act was drawn up, signed by all of us there, and amid a volley from all our muskets, a leaden plate inscribed with the arms of France, and the names of those who had just made the discovery, was deposited in the earth. The sieur de la Salle, who always carried an astrolabe, took the latitude of the mouth. Although he kept to himself the exact point, we have learned that the river falls into the gulf of Mexico, between 27° and 28° north, and, as is thought, at the point where maps lay down the Rio Escondido. This mouth is about thirty leagues distant from the Rio Bravo, [Rio Grande], sixty from the Rio de Palmas, and ninety or a hundred leagues from the river Panuco [Tampico], where the nearest Spanish post on the coast is situated. We reckoned that Espiritu Santo bay [Appalachee Bay], lay northeast of the mouth. From the Ilinois' river, we always went south or southwest ; the river winds a little, pre- serves to the sea its breadth of about a quarter of a league, is every- where very deep, without banks, or any obstacle to navigation, although the contrary has been published. This river is reckoned eight hundred leagues long ; we travelled at least three hundred and fifty from the mouth of the river Seignelay. . . .

To conclude, our expedition of discovery was accomplished without having lost any of our men, French or Indian, and without anybody's being wounded, for which we were indebted to the protection of the Almighty, and the great capacity of Monsieur de la Salle.   I will say nothing here of conversions ; formerly the apostles had but to enter a country, when on the first publication of the gospel, great conversions were seen.   I am but a miserable sinner, infinitely destitute of the merits of the apostles ; but we must also acknowledge that these miraculous ways of grace are not attached to the exercise of our ministry ; God employs an ordinary and common way, following which I contented myself with announcing, as well as I could, the principal truths of Christianity to the nations I met.   The Ilinois language served me about a hundred leagues down the river, and I made the rest understand by gestures and some term in their dialect which I insensibly picked up ; but I can not say that my little efforts produced certain fruits.   With regard to these people, perhaps, some one by a secret effect of grace, has profited ; God only knows.   All we have done has been to see the state of these tribes, and to open the way to the gospel and to missionaries ; having baptized only two infants, whom I saw struggling with death, and who, in fact, died in our presence.

John Gilmary Shea, *Discovery and Exploration of the Mississippi Valley*, in B. F. French, *Historical Collections of Louisiana* (New York, 1852), Part IV. 165–184 *passim*.

PART III

CONDITIONS OF COLONIZATION

CHAPTER VI — REASONS FOR COLONIZATION

44. The Condition of England (1577)

BY WILLIAM HARRISON

Harrison, an Oxford B.A. and M.A., prepared this account for the first edition of Holinshed's *Chronicle* (1577). Furnivall calls him " one of the most often quoted and trusted authorities." — Bibliography : Channing and Hart, *Guide*, §§ 93, 110.

WE in England diuide our people commonlie into foure sorts, as gentlemen, citizens or burgesses, yeomen, which are artificers, or laborers. Of gentlemen the first and chéefe (next the king) be the prince, dukes, marquesses, earls, viscounts, and barons : and these are called gentlemen of the greater sort, or (as our common vsage of spéech is) lords and noblemen : and next vnto them be knights, esquiers, and last of all they that are simplie called gentlemen ; so that in effect our gentlemen are diuided into their conditions, whereof in this chaptter I will make particular rehearsall. . . . Who soeuer studieth the lawes of the realme, who so abideth in the vniuersitie giuing his mind to his booke, or professeth physicke and the liberall sciences, or beside his seruice in the roome of a capteine in the warres, or good counsell giuen at home, whereby his common-wealth is benefited, can liue without manuell labour, and thereto is able and will beare the port, charge and countenance of a gentleman, he shall for monie haue a cote and armes bestowed vpon him by heralds (who in the charter of the same doo of custome pretend antiquitie and seruice, and manie gaie things) and therevnto being made so good cheape be called master, which is the title that men giue to esquiers and gentlemen, and reputed for a gentleman euer after. . . .

In this place also are our merchants to be installed, as amongst the citizens (although they often change estate with gentlemen, as gentle-

men doo with them, by a mutuall conuersion of the one into the other)
whose number is so increased in these our dates, that their onelie
maintenance is the cause of the exceeding prices of forreine wares,
which otherwise when euerie nation was permitted to bring in his owne
commodities, were farre better cheape and more plentifullie to be had.
Of the want of our commodities here at home, by their great transportation of them into other countries, I speake not, sith the matter will
easilie bewraic it selfe. . . .

Yeomen are those, which by our law are called *Legales homines*, free
men borne English, and may dispend of their owne free land in yearelie
reuenue, to the summe of fortie shillings sterling, or six pounds as monie
goeth in our times. . . . This sort of people haue a certeine preheminence, and more estimation than labourers & the common sort of artificers, & these commonlie liue wealthilie, keepe good houses, and trauell
to get riches. They are also for the most part farmers to gentlemen
(in old times called *Pagani, & opponuntur militibus*, and therefore
Persius calleth himselfe *Semipaganus*) or at the leastwise artificers, &
with grasing, frequenting of markets, and keeping of seruants (not idle
seruants as the gentlemen doo, but such as get both their owne and part
of their masters liuing) do come to great welth, in somuch that manie
of them are able and doo buie the lands of vnthriftie gentlemen, and
often setting their sonnes to the schooles, to the vniuersities, and to the
Ins of the court ; or otherwise leauing them sufficient lands wherevpon
they may liue without labour, doo make them by those means to become gentlemen : these were they that in times past made all France
afraid. . . .

The fourth and last sort of people in England are daie labourers,
poore husbandmen, and some retailers (which haue no frée land) copie
holders, and all artificers, as tailers, shomakers, carpenters, brickmakers,
masons, &c. As for slaues and bondmen we haue none, naie such is
the priuilege of our countrie by the especiall grace of God, and bountie
of our princes, that if anie come hither from other realms, so soone as
they set foot on land they become so free of condition as their masters,
whereby all note of seruile bondage is vtterlie remooued from them, . . .
This fourth and last sort of people therefore haue neither voice nor
authoritie in the common wealth, but are to be ruled, and not to rule
other ; yet they are not altogither neglected, for in cities and corporat
townes, for default of yeomen they are faine to make vp their inquests
of such maner of people. And in villages they are commonlie made

churchwardens, sidemen, aleconners, now and then constables, and manie times inioie the name of hedboroughes. Unto this sort also may our great swarmes of idle seruing men be referred, of whome there runneth a prouerbe; Young seruing men old beggers, bicause seruice is none heritage. . . .

From thencefoorth also vnto our daies, and euen in this season wherein we liue, there is no restreint of anie meat, either for religions sake or publike order in England, but it is lawfull for euerie man to féed vpon what soeuer he is able to purchase, except it be vpon those daies whereon eating of flesh is especiallie forbidden by the lawes of the realme, which order is taken onelie to the end our numbers of cattell may be the better increased, & that aboundance of fish which the sea yeeldeth, more generallie receiued. Beside this there is great consideration had in making of this law for the preseruation of the nauie, and maintenance of conuenient numbers of sea faring men, both which would otherwise greatlie decaie, if some meanes were not found whereby they might be increased. But how soeuer this case standeth, white meats, milke, butter & cheese, which were neuer so deere as in my time, and woont to be accounted of as one of the chiefe states throughout the Iland, are now reputed as food appertinent onelie to the inferiour sort, whilest such as are more wealthie, doo feed vpon the flesh of all kinds of cattell accustomed to be eaten, all sorts of fish taken vpon our coasts and in our fresh riuers, and such diuersitie of wild and tame foules as are either bred in our Iland or brought ouer vnto vs from other countries of the maine. . . .

The artificer and husbandman make greatest accompt of such meat as they may soonest come by, and haue it quickliest readie, except it be in London when the companies of euery trade doo meet on their quarter daies, at which time they be nothing inferiour to the nobilitie. Their food also consisteth principallie in béefe and such meat as the butcher selleth, that is to saie, mutton, veale, lambe, porke, &c : whereof he findeth great store in the markets adioning, beside souse, brawne, bacon, fruit, pies of fruit, foules of sundrie sorts, cheese, butter, egs &c : as the other wanteth it not at home, by his owne prouision, which is at the best hand, and commonlie least charge. In feasting also this latter sort, I meane the husbandmen doo ercéed after this maner : especiallie at bridales, purifications of women, and such od méetings, where it is incredible to tell what meat is consumed & spent, ech one bringing such a dish, or so manie with him as his wife & he doo consult vpon, but

alwaies with this consideration, that the leéfer fréend shall haue the
better prouision. This also is commonlie séene at these bankets, that
the good man of the house is not charged with any thing sauing bread,
drink, sauce, houseroome and fire. But the artificers in cities and good
townes doo deale far otherwise, for albeit that some of them doo suffer
their iawes to go oft before their clawes, and diuerse of them by making
good cheere doo hinder themselues and other men : yet the wiser sort
can handle the matter well inough in these iunkettings, and therefore
their frugalitie deserueth commendation. To conclude, both the artificer and the husbandman are sufficientlie liberall, & verie fréendlie at
their tables, and when they méet, they are so merie without malice, and
plaine without inward Italian or French craft and subtiltie, that it would
doo a man good to be in companie among them. Herein onelie are
the inferiour sort somewhat to be blamed, that being thus assembled,
their talke is now and then such as sauoureth of scurrilitie and ribaldrie,
a thing naturallie incident to carters and clownes, who thinke themselues
not to be merie & welcome, if their foolish veines in this behalfe be
neuer so little restreined. This is moreouer to be added in these meetings, that if they happen to stumble vpon a péece of venison, and a cup
of wine or verie strong beere or ale (which latter they commonlie prouide against their appointed daies) they thinke their chéere so great,
and themselues to haue fared so well, as the lord Maior of London,
with whome when their bellies be full they will not often sticke to make
comparison, because that of a subiect there is no publike officer of anie
citie in Europe, that may compare in port and countenance with him
during the time of his office. . . .

An Englishman indeuoring sometime to write of our attire, made
sundrie platformes for his purpose, supposing by some of them to find
out one stedfast ground whereon to build the summe of his discourse.
But in the end (like an oratour long without exercise) when he saw what
a difficult peece of worke he had taken in hand, he gaue ouer his trauell,
and onelie drue the picture of a naked man, vnto whome he gaue a paire
of sheares in the one hand and a peece of cloth in the other, to the end
he should shape his apparell after such fashion as himselfe liked, sith he
could find no kind of garment that could please him anie while togither,
and this he called an Englishman. Certes this writer (otherwise being
a lewd popish hypocrite and vngratious priest) shewed himselfe herein
not to be altogether void of iudgement, sith the phantasticall follie of
our nation, euen from the courtier to the carter is such, that no forme

of apparell liketh vs longer than the first garment is in the wearing, if
it continue so long and be not laid aside, to receiue some other trinket
newlie deuised by the fickle headed tailors, who couet to haue seuerall
trickes in cutting, thereby to draw fond customers to more expense
of monie. For my part I can tell better how to inueigh against this
enormitie, than describe anie certeintie of our attire : sithence such is
our mutabilitie, that to daie there is none to the Spanish guise, to morrow the French toies are most fine and delectable, yer long no such
apparell as that which is after the high Alman fashion, by and by the
Turkish maner is generallie best liked of, otherwise the Morisco gowns,
the Barbarian sléeues, the mandilion worne to Collie weston ward, and
the short French breches make such a comelie vesture, that except it
were a dog in a doublet, you shall not sée anie so disguised, as are my
countrie men of England. And as these fashions are diuerse, so likewise
it is a world to see the costlinesse and the curiositie : the excesse and
the vanitie : the pompe and the brauerie : the change and the varietie :
and finallie the ficklenesse and the follie that is in all degrées : in somuch that nothing is more constant in England than inconstancie of
attire. Oh how much cost is bestowed now adaies vpon our bodies and
how little vpon our soules ! how manie sutes of apparell hath the one
and how little furniture hath the other ! how long time is asked in deck-
ing vp of the first, and how little space left wherin to feed the later ! how
curious, how nice also are a number of men and women, and how hard-
lie can the tailor please them in making it fit for their bodies ! how
manie times must it be sent backe againe to him that made it ! what
chafing, what fretting, what reprochfull language doth the poore worke-
man beare awaie ! and manie times when he dooth nothing to it at all,
yet when it is brought home againe it is verie fit and handsome ; then
must we put it on, then must the long seames of our hose be set by a plumb-
line, then we puffe, then we blow, and finallie sweat till we drop, that our
clothes may stand well vpon vs.   I will saie nothing of our heads, which
sometimes are polled, sometimes curled, or suffered to grow at length like
womans lockes, manie times cut off aboue or vnder the eares round as
by a wooddel dish : . . .

   It is not in vaine therefore in speaking of building to make a distincion
betweene the plaine and wooddie soiles : for, as in these, our houses are
commonlie strong and well timbered, so that in manie places, there are
not aboue foure, six or nine inches betweene stud and stud ; so in the
open and champaine countries they are inforced for want of stuffe to vse

no studs at all, but onelie franke posts, raisins, beames, prickepostes, groundsels, summers (or dormants) transoms, and such principals, with nere and there a girding, whervnto they fasten their splints or radels, and then cast it all ouer with thicke claie to keepe out the wind, which otherwise would annoie them. Certes this rude kind of building made the Spaniards in quéene Maries daies to woonder, but chéeflie when they saw what large diet was vsed in manie of these so homelie cottages, in so much that one of no small reputation amongst them said after this maner : These English (quoth he) haue their houses made of sticks and durt, but they fare commonlie so well as the king. Whereby it appeareth that he liked better of our good fare in such course cabins, than of their owne thin diet in their princelike habitations and palaces. In like sort as euerie countrie house is thus apparelled on the out side, so is it inwardlie diuided into sundrie roomes aboue and beneath ; and where plentie of wood is, they couer them with tiles, otherwise with straw, sedge, or réed, except some quarrie of slate be néere hand, from whence they haue for their monie so much as may suffice them.

The claie wherewith our houses are impanelled is either white, red, or blue, and of these the first dooth participat verie much with the nature of our chalke, the second is called lome, but the third eftsoones changeth colour so soone as it is wrought, notwithstanding that it looke blue when it is throwne out of the pit. Of chalke also we haue our excellent Asbestos or white lime, made in most places, wherewith being quenched we strike ouer our claie workes and stone wals, in cities, good townes, rich farmers and gentlemens houses : otherwise in steed of chalke (where it wanteth for it is so scant that in some places it is sold by the pound) they are compelled to burne a certeine kind of red stone, as in Wales, and else where other stones and shels of oisters and like fish found vpon the sea coast, which being conuerted into lime doth naturallie (as the other) abhorre and eschew water whereby it is dissolued, and neuerthelesse desire oile wherewith it is easilie mixed, as I haue seene by experience. Within their doores also such as are of abilitie doo oft make their floores and parget of fine alabaster burned, which they call plaster of Paris, whereof in some places we haue great plentie, and that verie profitable against the rage of fire. . . .

I might speake here of the great traines and troopes of seruing men also, which attend vpon the nobilitie of England in their seuerall liueries, and with differences of cognisances on their sléeues, whereby it is knowen to whome they apperteine. I could also set doune what a goodlie sight

it is to see them muster in the court, which being filled with them dooth
yéeld the contemplation of a noble varietie vnto the beholder, much like
to the shew of the pecocks taile in the full beautie, or of some medow
garnished with infinit kinds and diuersitie of pleasant floures.   But I
passe ouer the rehearsall hereof to other men, who more delite in vaine
amplification than I, and seeke to be more curious in these points than
I professe to be. . . .

   The nauie of England may be diuided into three sortes, of which the
one serueth for the warres, the other for burden, and the third for fishermen, which get their liuing by fishing on the sea.   How manie of the
first order are mainteined within the realme, it passeth my cunning to
expresse : yet sith it may be parted into the nauie roiall and common
fleete, I thinke good to speake of those that belong vnto the prince, and
so much the rather, for that their number is certeine & well knowne to
verie manie.   Certes there is no prince in Europe that hath a more
beautifull or gallant sort of ships than the quéenes maiestie of England at
this present, and those generallie are of such exceeding force, that two of
them being well appointed and furnished as they ought, will not let to encounter with three or foure of those of other countries, and either bowge
[stave in] them or put them to flight, if they may not bring them home.

   Neither are the moulds of anie forren barkes so conuenientlie made,
to brooke so well one sea as another lieng vpon the shore in anie part
of the continent as those of England.   And therefore the common report
that strangers make of our ships amongst themselues is dailie confirmed
to be true, which is, that for strength, assurance, nimblenesse and swift-
nesse of sailing, there are no vessels in the world to be compared with
ours.   And all these are committed to the regiment and safe custodie of
the admerall, . . .

   . . . In my time there are three noble vniuersities in England, to wit,
one at Oxford, the second at Cambridge, and the third in London ; of
which, the first two are the most famous, I meane Cambridge and
Oxford, for that in them the vse of the toongs, philosophie, and the
liberall sciences, besides the profound studies of the ciuill law, physicke,
and theologie, are dailie taught and had : whereas in the later, the laws
of the realme are onlie read and learned, by such as giue their minds
vnto the knowledge of the same.   In the first there are not onelie
diuerse goodlie houses builded foure square for the most part of hard
fréestone or bricke, with great numbers of lodgings and chambers in the
same for students, after a sumptuous sort, through the exceeding liber-

alitie of kings, quéenes, bishops, noblemen and ladies of the land : but also large liuings and great reuenues bestowed vpon them (the like whereof is not to be séene in anie other region, as Peter Martyr did oft affirme) to the maintenance onelie of such conuenient numbers of poore mens sonnes as the seuerall stipends bestowed vpon the said houses are able to support. . . .

In most of our colleges there are also great numbers of students, of which manie are found by the reuenues of the houses, and others by the purueiances and helpe of their rich fréends ; whereby in some one college you shall haue two hundred scholers, in others an hundred and fiftie, in diuerse a hundred and fortie, and in the rest lesse numbers ; as the capacitie of the said houses is able to receiue : so that at this present, of one sort and other, there are about thrée thousand students nourished in them both (as by a late surueie it manifestlie appeared.)   They were erected by their founders at the first, onelie for poore mens sons, whose parents were not able to bring them vp vnto learning : but now they haue the least benefit of them, by reason the rich doo so incroch vpon them. . . .

[Ralph] Holinshed, *Chronicles* (London, 1586), I, 148–200 *passim.*

---

45. Advantages of Colonization (1582)

BY SIR GEORGE PECKHAM

The author was a partner in the colonization schemes of Sir Humphrey Gilbert. — Bibliography : Winsor, *Narrative and Critical History*, III, chs. iv, v ; Channing and Hart, *Guide*, § 95.

THE second Chapter sheweth, that it is lawfull and necessarie to trade and traffique with the Sauages :   And to plant in their Countries : And diuideth planting into two sorts.

AND first for traffique, I say that the Christians may lawfully trauell into those Countries and abide there : whom the Sauages may not iustly impugne and forbidde in respect of the mutuall societie and fellowshippe betweene man and man prescribed by the Law of Nations. . . .

The first, when Christians by the good liking and willing assent of the Sauages, are admitted by them to quiet possession.

The second, when Christians being vniustly repulsed, doe seeke to attaine and mainteine the right for which they doe come. . . .

Moreouer, it shall be requisite eyther by speeche, if it be possible, either by some other certaine meanes, to signifie vnto them, that once league of friendship with all louing conuersation being admitted betweene the Christians and them : that then the Christians from thenceforth will alwayes be ready with force of Armes to assist and defend them in their iust quarrels, from all inuasions, spoyles and oppressions offered them by any Tyrants, Aduersaries, or their next borderers : and a benefite is so much the more to be esteemed, by how much the person vpon whom it is bestowed standeth in neede thereof.

For it appeareth by a relation of a Countreyman of ours, namely Dauid Ingram, (who trauelled in those countries xi. Moneths and more) That the Sauages generally for the most part, are at continuall warres with their next adioyning neighbours, and especially the Cannibals, being a cruell kinde of people whose foode is mans flesh, and haue teeth like dogges, and doe pursue them with rauenous mindes to eate their flesh, and deuoure them.

And it is not to be doubted, but that the Christians may in this case iustly and lawfully ayde the Sauages against the Cannibals. . . .

But if after these good and fayre meanes vsed, the Sauages neuerthe-lesse will not bee herewithall satisfied, but barbarously will goe about to practise violence eyther in repelling the Christians from their Ports & safe-landings, or in withstanding them afterwards to enioy the rights for which both painfully and lawfully they haue aduentured themselues thither :

Then in such a case I holde it no breach of equitie for the Christians to defend themselues, to pursue reuenge with force, and to doe whatso-euer is necessarie for the atteining of their saftie : For it is allowable by all Lawes in such distresses, to resist violence with violence : And for their more securitie to increase their strength by building of Forts for auoyding the extremitie of iniurious dealing. . . .

The third Chapter doeth shew the lawfull title which the Queenes most excellent Maiestie hath vnto those countries, which through the ayde of Almighty God are meant to be inhabited.

AND it is very euident that the planting there shal in time right amply enlarge her Maiesties Territories and Dominions, or (I might rather say) restore her to her Highnesse ancient right and interest in those Countries, into the which a noble and worthy personage, lineally descended from the blood royall, borne in Wales, named Madock ap Owen Gwyneth, departing from the coast of England, about the yeere of our Lord God 1170, arriued and there planted himselfe, and his Colonies, and afterward returned himselfe into England, leauing certaine of his people there, as appeareth in an ancient Welsh Chronicle, where he then gaue to certaine Ilands, beastes, and foules sundry Welsh names, as the Iland of Pengwin, which yet to this day beareth the same. . . .

The fourth chapter sheweth how that the trade, traffike, and planting in those countreys, is likely to proue very profitable to the whole realme in generall.

NOW to shew how the same is likely to prooue very profitable and beneficiall generally to the whole realme : it is very certaine, that the greateast iewell of this realme, and the chiefest strength and force of the same, for defence or offence in marshall matter and maner, is the multitude of ships, masters and mariners, ready to assist the most stately and royall nauy of her Maiesty, which by reason of this voyage shall haue both increase and maintenance. And it is well knowen that in sundry places of this realme ships haue beene built and set forth of late dayes, for the trade of fishing onely : yet notwithstanding the fish which is taken and brought into England by the English nauy of fishermen, will not suffice for the expense of this realme foure moneths, if there were none els brought of strangers. And the chiefest cause why our English men doe not goe so farre Westerly as the especiall fishing places doe lie, both for plenty and greatnesse of fish, is for that they haue no succour and knowen safe harbour in those parts. But if our nation were once planted there, or neere thereabouts : whereas they now fish but for two moneths in the yeere, they might then fish so long as pleased them-selues, or rather at their comming finde such plenty of fish ready taken, salted, and dried, as might be sufficient to fraught them home without long delay (God granting that salt may be found there) whereof Dauid Ingram (who trauelled in those countreys as aforesayd) sayth that there is great plenty : and withall the climate doth giue great hope, that though there were none naturally growing, yet it might as well be made there by art, as it is both at Rochel and Bayon, or elsewhere. Which being brought to passe shall increase the number of our shippes and mariners, were it but in respect of fishing onely : but much more in regard of the sundry merchandizes and commodities which are there found, and had in great abundance.

Moreouer, it is well knowen that all Sauages, as well those that dwell in the South, as those that dwell in the North, so soone as they shall begin but a little to taste of ciuility, will take maruellous delight in any garment, be it neuer so simple ; as a shirt, a blew, yellow, red or greene cotten cassocke, a cap, or such like, and will take incredible paines for such a trifle. . . .

To what end need I endeuour my selfe by arguments to proue that by this voyage our nauie and nauigation shalbe inlarged, when as there needeth none other reason then the manifest & late example of the neere neighbours to this realme, the kings of Spaine and Portugall, who since the first discouery of the Indies, haue not onely mightily inlarged their dominions, greatly inriched themselues and their subiects : but haue also by iust account trebled the number of their shippes, masters and mariners, a matter of no small moment and importance :

Besides this, it will prooue a generall benefit vnto our countrey, that through this occasion, not onely a great number of men which do now liue idlely at home, and are burthenous, chargeable & profitable to this realme, shall hereby be set on worke, but also children of twelue or fourteene yeeres of age, or vnder, may bee kept from idlenesse, in making of a thousand kindes of trifling things, which wil be good merchandize for that countrey. And moreouer, our idle women (which the Realme may well spare) shall also be imployed on plucking, drying, and sorting of feathers, in pulling, beating, and working of hempe, and in gathering of cotton, and diuers things right necessary for dying. All which things are to be found in those countreys most plentifully. And the men may imploy themselues in dragging for pearle, woorking for mines, and in matters of husbandry, and likewise in hunting the Whale for Trane [oil], and making caskes to put the same in : besides in fishing for cod, salmon, and herring, drying, salting and barrelling the same, and felling of trees, hewing and sawing of them, and such like wcrke, meete for those persons that are no men of Art or science.

Many other things may bee found to the great reliefe and good employments of no small number of the naturall Subiects of this Realme, which doe now liue here idlely to the common annoy of the whole state. Neither may I here omit the great hope and likelyhood of a passage beyond the Grand Bay into the South Seas, confirmed by sundry authours to be found leading to Cataia, by Molluccas and Spiceries, whereby may ensue as generall a benefite to the Realme, or greater then yet hath bene spoken of, without either such charges, or other inconueniences, as by the tedious tract of time and perill, which the ordinary passage to those parts at this day doeth minister. . . .

The fift chapter sheweth, that the trading and planting in those coun-
treis is likely to proue to the particular profit of all aduenturers.

I MUST, now according to my promise shew foorth some probable reasons that the aduenturers in this iourney are to take particular profit
by the same.   It is therefore conuenient that I doe diuide the aduenturers into two sorts : the noblemen and gentlemen by themselues, and
the Merchants by themselues.   For, as I doe heare, it is meant that
there shall be one societie of the noblemen and gentlemen, and another
societie of the merchants.   And yet not so diuided but that eche society
may freely and frankely trade and traffique one with the other. . . .

The sixt Chapter sheweth that the traffique and planting in those countries, shall be vnto the Sauage themselues very beneficiall and gainefull.

NOW to the end it may appeare that this voyage is not vndertaken
altogether for the peculiar commodity of our selues and our countrey (as generally other trades and iourneis be) it shall fall out in
proofe, that the Sauages shall hereby haue iust cause to blesse the
houre when this enterprise was vndertaken.

First and chiefly, in respect of the most happy and gladsome tidings
of the most glorious Gospel of our Sauiour Iesus Christ, whereby they
may be brought from falshood to trueth, from darknesse to light, from
the hie way of death, to the path of life, from superstitious idolatrie to
sincere Christianity, from the deuill to Christ, from hell to heauen.   And
if in respect of all the commodities they can yeelde vs (were they many
moe) that they should but receiue this onely benefit of Christianity, they
were more then fully recompenced. . . .

The seuenth Chapter sheweth that the planting there, is not a matter of
such charge or difficultie, as many would make it seeme to be.

NOW therefore for proofe, that the planting in these parts is a thing
that may be done without the ayde of the Princes power and
purse, contrary to the allegation of many malicious persons, who wil
neither be actors in any good action themselues, nor so much as afoord a
good word to the setting forward thereof : and that worse is, they will
take vpon them to make molehilles seeme mountaines, and flies elephants, to the end they may discourage others, that be very well or
indifferently affected to the matter, being like vnto Esops dogge, which
neither would eate Hay himselfe, nor suffer the poore hungry asse to
feede thereon :

I say and affirme that God hath prouided such meanes for the furtherance of this enterprise, as doe stand vs in stead of great treasure : for
first by reason that it hath pleased God of his great goodnesse, of long
time to hold his merciful hand ouer this realme, in preseruing the people
of the same, both from slaughter by the sword, and great death by
plague, pestilence, or otherwise, there are at this day great numbers
(God he knoweth) which liue in such penurie & want, as they could be
contented to hazard their liues, and to serue one yeere for meat, drinke
and apparell only, without wages, in hope thereby to amend their estates :
which is a matter in such like iourneyes, of no small charge to the prince.
Moreouer, things in the like iourneyes of greatest price and cost as victuall (whereof there is great plentie to be had in that countrey without
money) and powder, great artillery, or corselets are not needefull in so
plentifull and chargeable maner, as the shew of such a iourney may present : for a small quantitie of all these, to furnish the Fort only, will suffice vntill such time as diuers commodities may be found out in those
parts, which may be thought well worthy a greater charge. Also the
peculiar benefit of archers which God hath blessed this land withall before
all other nations, will stand vs in great stead amongst those naked people. . . .

To conclude, since by Christian dutie we stand bound chiefly to further all such acts as do tend to the encreasing the true Flock of Christ
by reducing into the right way those lost sheepe which are yet astray :
And that we shall therein follow the example of our right vertuous predecessors of renowmed memorie, and leaue vnto our posteritie a diuine
memoriall of so godly an enterprise : Let vs I say for the considerations
alledged, enter into iudgement with our selues, whether this action may
belong to vs or no, the rather for that this voyage through the mighty
assistance of the omnipotent God, shall take our desired effect (whereof
there is no iust cause of doubt.)   Then shal her Maiesties dominions be
enlarged, her highnesse ancient titles iustly confirmed, all odious idlenesse from this our Realme vtterly banished, diuers decayed townes
repaired, and many poore and needy persons relieued, and estates of such
as now liue in want shail be embettered, the ignorant and barbarous
idolaters taught to know Christ, the innocent defended from their bloodie
tyrannicale neighbours, the diabolicall custome of sacrificing humane
creatures abolished. . . .

Richard Hakluyt, *Voyages, Navigations, Traffiques, and Discoveries* (London,
1599), III, 167–181 *passim*.

46. How Spain may be Abased (1584)

BY RICHARD HAKLUYT

This spicy tract was written at Ralegh's request, to be laid before the Queen. Hakluyt was an enthusiast on Western geography. — Bibliography: Winsor, *Narrative and Critical History*, III, 189, 208; Channing and Hart, *Guide*, § 95.

That this voyadge will be a greate bridle to the Indies of the Kinge of Spaine, and a meane that wee may arreste at our pleasure for the space of tenne weeks or three monethes every yere one or twoo C. saile of his subjectes shippes at the fyshinge in Newfounde Land.

The cause why the Kinge of Spaine, these three or foure yeres last paste, was at suche intollerable chardges in furnishinge oute so many navies to wynne Tercera, and the other small ilandes of the Azores adjacent to the same, was the oportunitie of the places in intercepting his West Indian flete at their returne homewarde, as a matter that toucheth him indeede to the quicke. But the plantinge of twoo or three strong fortes upon some goodd havens (whereof there is greate store) betweene Florida and Cape Briton, woulde be a matter in shorte space of greater domage as well to his flete as to his westerne Indies ; for wee shoulde not onely often tymes indaunger his flete in the returne thereof, but also in fewe yeres put him in hazarde in loosinge some parte of Nova Hispania.

Touchinge the fleete, no man (that knoweth the course thereof, comynge oute betwene Cuba and the Cape of Florida, alonge the gulfe or straite of Bahama) can denye that it is caried by the currant northe and northeaste towardes the coaste which wee purpose, God willinge to inhabite ; . . . Besides the current, it is also a thinge withoute controversie, that all southerne and souht esterne windes inforce the Spanishe flete returninge home nere or upon the aforesaide coaste, and consequently will bringe them into our daunger, after wee shalbe there strongly setled and fortified. . . .

Nowe if wee (being thereto provoked by Spanishe injuries) woulde either joyne with these savages, or sende or give them armor, as the Spaniardes arme our Irishe rebells, wee shoulde trouble the Kinge of Spaine more in those partes, then he hath or can trouble us in Ireland, and holde him at suche a bay as he was never yet helde at. For if (as the aforesaide Miles Phillipps writeth) yt be true, that one negro which fledd from his cruell Spanishe master is receaved and made capitaine of multitudes of the Chichimici, and daily dothe grevously afflicte them, and hath almoste enforced them to leave and abandon their silver mynes in those quarters, what domage mighte divers hundreds of Englishe men doe them, being growen once into familiaritie with that valiaunte nation.

And this is the greatest feare that the Spaniardes have, to witt, our plantinge in those partes and joyning with those savages, their neighbours, in Florida, and on the northe side of Nova Hispania. . . .

So shall wee be able te crye quittaunce with the Kinge of Spaine if he shoulde goe aboute to make any generall arreste of our navye, or rather terrifie him from any such enterpryse, when he shall bethincke himself that his navye in Newfounde lande is no lesse in our daunger, then ours is in his domynions wheresoever. . . .

What speciall meanes may bringe Kinge Phillippe from his highe throne, and make him equall to the princes his neighboures; wherewithall is shewed his weakenes in the West Indies.

Firste, it is to be considered that his domynions and territories oute of Spaine lye farr distant from Spaine, his chefest force; and farr distante one from another; and are kepte by greate tyrannie; and *quos metuunt oderunt.* And the people kepte in subjection desire nothinge more than freedome. And like as a little passage given to water, it maketh his owne way; so give but a small meane to suche kept in tyranie, they will make their owne way to libertie; which way may easely be made. And entringe into the consideration of the way how this Phillippe may be abased, I meane firste to begynne with the West Indies, as there to laye a chefe foundation for his overthrowe. And like as the foundation of the strongest holde undermyned and removed, the mightiest and strongest walles fall flatt to the earthe; so this prince, spoiled or intercepted for a while of his treasure, occasion by lacke of the same is geven that all his territories in Europe oute of Spaine slide from him, and the Moores enter into Spaine it selfe, and the people revolte in every forrein territorie of his, and cutt the throates of the proude hatefull Spaniardes, their governours. For this Phillippe already owinge many millions, and of late yeres empaired in credite, hath by lacke of abilitie of longe tyme to pay the same, and by his shameful losse of his Spaniardes and dishonors in the Lowe Contries, and by lacke of the yerely renewe of his revenewe, he shall not be able to wage his severall garrisons kepte in his severall frontiers, territories, and places, nor to corrupte in princes courtes, nor to doe many feates. . . .

Hereunto yf wee adde our purposed westerne discoveries, and there plante and people ryally, and fortifie strongly, and there builde shippes and maineteine a navy in special porte or portes, wee may by the same either encounter the Indian fleete, or be at hande as it were to yelde freshe supplye, courage, and comforte, by men or munition, to the Chichimici and the Symerons and suche other as shalbe incited to the spoile of the mynes; which in tyme will, if it be not looked to, bringe all princes to weake estate, that Phillippe, either for relligion or other cause, dothe hate; as the aforesaide Monsieur de Aldegond, in his pithie and most earneste exhortation to all Christian kinges, princes, and potentates to beware of Kinge Phillipps ambitious growinge, dothe wisely and moste providently forwarne.

To this may be added (the realme swarming with lustie youthes that he turned to no profitable use), there may be sente bandes of them into the Base Contries in more rounde nombers then are sente as yet. Ffor if he presently prevaile there, at our doores, farewell the traficque that els wee may have there (whereof wise men can say moche). And if he settle there, then let the realme saye adewe to her quiet state and safetie.

If these enter into the due consideration of wise men, and if platformes of these thinges be sett downe and executed duelye and with spede and effecte, no doubte but the Spanishe empire falles to the grounde, and the Spanishe kinge shall be lefte bare as Aesops proude crowe; the peacocke, the perot, the pye, and the popingey, and every other birde havinge taken home from him his gorgeous fethers, he will, in shorte space, become a laughinge stocke for all the worlde; with such a mayme to the Pope and to that side, as never hapned to the sea of Rome by the practise of the late Kinge of famous memory, her Majesties father, or by all the former practises of all the Protestant princes of Germanie, or by any other advise layde downe by Monsieur de Aldegond, here after by them to be put in execution. If you touche him in the Indies, you touche the apple of his eye; for take away his treasure, which is *neruus belli*, and which he hath almoste oute of his West Indies, his olde bandes of souldiers will soone be dissolved, his purposes defeated, his power and strengthe diminished, his pride abated, and his tyranie utterly suppressed. . . .

Richard Hakluyt, *A Discourse on Western Planting*, in *Documentary History of the State of Maine* (edited by Charles Deane, Cambridge, 1877), II, 45–59 *passim*.

47. First Suggestion of Trans-continental Trade
(1602)

BY EDWARD HAYES

Hayes was of Sir Humphrey Gilbert's party in 1583. — Bibliography: Winsor,
Narrative and Critical History, III, 184–189; Channing and Hart, *Guide*, § 96.

Of a conuenient passage and trade into the
South Sea, vnder temperate regions part by
riuers, and some part ouer land, in
the continent of *America.*

I WILL adde hereunto an assured hope (grounded vpon infallible reasons) of a way to be made part ouerland, & part by riuers or lakes,
into the South seas vnto Cathay, China, and those passing rich countreys, lying in the East parts of the world : which way or passage
(supposed to be beyond the vttermost bounds of America, vnder the
frozen Zone) is neuerthelesse, held by the opinion of many learned
writers and men of iudgement now liuing, to be in these more temperate rigions ; and that the same shall neuer be made knowen, vnlesse
we plante firste ; whereby we shall learne as much by inquisition of the
naturall inhabitants, as by our owne nauigations.   I will not herein relie
vpon reports made in the French mens discoueries ; that the sea which
giueth passage vnto Cathay, extendeth from the North, neere vnto the
riuer of Canada, into 44 degrees, where the same of the Saluages is
called Tadouac.

Neither vpon the discoueries of Iaques Noel, who hauing passed
beyond the three Saults, where Iaques Cartier left to discouer, finding
the riuer of S. Laurence passable on the other side or branch ; and
afterwards, vnderstood of the inhabitants, that the same riuer did lead
into a mighty lake, which at the entrance was fresh, but beyond, was
bitter or salt ; the end whereof was vnknowen.

Omitting therefore these hopes, I will ground my opinion vpon reason
and nature, which will not faile.

For this we know alreadie, that great riuers haue beene discouered
a thousand English miles into that continent of America ; namely, that
of S. Laurence or Canada. But not regarding miles more or lesse,
most assuredly, that andother knowen riuers there doe descend from
the highest parts or mountaines, or middle of that continent, into our

M

North sea. And like as those mountains doe cast from them, streames into our North seas ; euen so the like they do into the South sea, which is on the backe of that continent.

For all mountaines haue their descents toward the seas about them, which are the lowest places and proper mansions of water : and waters (which are contained in the mountaines, as it were in cisternes) descending naturally, doe alwaies resort vnto the seas inuironing those lands : for example ; From the Alps confining Germanie, France, and Italie, the mighty riuer Danubie doth take his course East, and dischargeth into the Pontique sea : the Rhine, North, and falleth into the Germane sea ; the Rhosne, West, and goeth into the Mediterran sea : the Po, South is emptied into the Adriatick or gulfe of Venice.   other instances may be produced to like effect in Africk ; yea, at home amongst the mountaines in England.

Seeing then in nature this can not be denied, and by experience elsewhere is found to be so, I will shew how a trade may be disposed more commodiously into the South sea thorow these temperate and habitable regions, than by the frozen Zones in the supposed passages of Northwest or Northeast : where, if the very moment be omitted of the time to passe, then are we like to be frozen in the seas, or forced to Winter in extreame cold and darkenesse like vnto hell : or in the midst of Summer, we shalbe in perill to haue our ships ouerwhelmed or crusht in pieces by hideous and fearefull mountaines of yce floting vpon those seas.

Therefore foure Staple-places must be erected, when the most short and passable way is found : that is to say, two vpon the North side, at the head and fall of the riuer ; and two others on the South side, at the head and fall also of that other riuer.

Prouided, that ships may passe vp those riuers vnto the Staples, so farre as the same be nauigable into the land ; and afterwards, that boats with flat bottomes may also passe so high, and neere the heads of the riuers vnto the Staples, as possibly they can, euen with lesse than two foot water, which can not then be far from the heads ; as in the riuer of Chagre.

That necke or space of land betweene the two heads of the said riuers, if it be 100 leagues (which is not like) the commodities from the North and from the South sea brought thither, may wel be carried ouer the same vpon horses, mules or beasts of that countrey apt to labour (as the elke or buffel) or by the aid of many Saluages accustomed to burdens ; who shall stead vs greatly in these affaires.

It is moreouer to be considered, that all these countreys do yeeld (so farre as is knowen) Cedars, Pines, Firre trees and Oaks, to build, mast, and yeard ships ; wherefore we may not doubt, but that ships may be builded on the South sea.

Then as ships on the South side may goe and returne to and from Cathay, China, and other most rich regions of the East world in fiue moneths or thereabouts ; euen so the goods being carried ouer vnto the North side, ships may come thither from England to fetch the same goods, and returne by a voyage of foure or fiue moneths vsually.

So as in euery foure moneths may be returned into England the greatest riches of Cathay, China, Iapan, and the rest which will be Spices, Drugges, Muske, Pearle, Stones, Gold, Siluer, Silks, Clothes of gold, & all maner of precious things, which shall recompense the time and labour of their transportation and carriage, if it were as farre and dangerous as the Moores trade is from Fess and Marocco (ouer the burning and moueable sands, in which they perish many times and suffer commonly great distresses) vnto the riuer called Niger in Africa, and from thence, vp the said riuer manie hundred miles ; afterwards ouer-land againe, vnto the riuer Nilus ; and so vnto Cairo in Egypt, from whence they returne the way they came.

Or if it were a voyage so farre as our merchants haue made into Persia, euen to Ormus, by the way of the North, through Russia into the Caspian sea, and so foorth, with paiment of many tolles. But this passage ouer and thorow the continent of America,, as the same shall be alwaies vnder temperate and habitable climats, and a pleasant passage after it hath beene a little frequented : euen so it must fall out much shorter than it seemeth, by false description of that continent, which doth not extend so farre into the West, as by later naui- gations is found and described in more exquisit charts. Besides that, the sea extends it selfe into the land very farre in many places on the South side ; whereby our accesse vnto the South ocean, shall be by so much the shorter.

A Briefe and true Relation of the Discouerie of the North part of Virginia ; &c. Whereunto is annexed a Treatise of M. Edward Hayes, conteining im- portant inducements for the planting in those parts, a finding a passage that way to the South Sea, and China (London, 1602), 21–24.

48. The English Claims to North America (1606)

ANONYMOUS (1656)

This is a later summary of the claims under which the first English Colonies were planted, and it is printed, not as an accurate statement of fact, but as a summary of the current arguments. — Bibliography: Winsor, *Narrative and Critical History*, III, ch. i; Channing and Hart, *Guide*, §§ 92–96.

AS a part of the westward part of the fourth part of the world, called America or the West Indies was first discovered by Columbus, at the charges of Ferdinand and Isabel sovereign of Spain ; and as by virtue of that discovery their successors claim a general right and title to all the lands within that tract, and a particular, either to such land, which they shall purchase from the native proprietors of such, which are void of inhabitants, or such which they shall conquer and subdue with the sword ; and as the two first particular rights are undeniable, so they may plant and erect what colonies they please therein of their own native subjects or others. Although the third is something disputable, yet notwithstanding the general right of Spain to the above place was never yet denied or controverted by any prince or state in Europe, and no attempt made against them by any (to interrupt them in those places they had taken and kept possession of there) but only at such times, as Spain was in hostility with one or more of the nations of Europe, for as it hath been the most just custom and practice of many states, that when the commonwealth did superabound in people, rather to seek out new discoveries (than to make war with their neighbours) for the transporting and transplanting of colonies, where they might enjoy lands according to the two first particular rights, and at the public charge of the commonwealth, or the particular of some certain persons, and the discovery being made, and colonies planted, it must very easily follow they were and are to remain and to be accompted as members of their mother commonwealth : so all the lands discovered for the ends aforesaid, whether in a smaller or greater latitude, and at the charges aforesaid, and with an inclusion of the two first particular rights, are to be accompted the intentional and national right and property of the first discoverers, and that according to the law of nature, and in that the law of nations ; and whatsoever prince or state (in league and amity with that prince, state, or commonwealth) that shall intrude within the said limit, and anticipate the first discoverers, is highly guilty of the breach of civil correspondency and of the law or custom of nations civilized. And that the Dutch have both intruded and anticipated the first discoverers the English nation in these northern parts of America, is made easily to appear, and that since they cast off the yoke of Spain; for whilst they were and did acknowledge themselves subjects of Spain, they must necessarily and did acknowledge the English rights to these northern parts of America. For as the then sovereign Ferdinand and Isabel did acknowledge the same to be in our Henry VIIth of England and his successors: so the duke of Burgundy, under whom and to whom the Netherlands were subject, coming to be king of Spain, acknowledged the same, and that upon the aforesaid grounds; for as Ferdinand and Isabel employed Columbus at their own charge, and set forth a fleet of ships under his command for new discoveries; so our Henry the VIIth much about the same time employed Sebastian Cabot, sending a fleet of ships under his command upon the like design. And as Columbus discovered the western or southern parts, so Cabot (at the charge of the said king) discovered these northern parts. And ever since which the national right of the English Nation (to these parts) hath been lawfully maintained from age to age successively almost for the space of two hundred years, and that either at the public charge of the prince, or some private generous undertakers; and that by and with all fair and friendly correspondency with the natives, further discoveries, possession, and population in conveniency of time as may appear by ancient records. For king Edward the VIth employed John Cabot, the son of the said Sebastian Cabot, for this northern discovery; and upon his return, for the reward of his pains, conferred the honour of knighthood upon him, and made him pilot major. And in the reign of queen Elizabeth of famous memory that generous knight, Sir Humphry Gilbert, and after him in the same queen's reign that renowned and well knowing knight Sir Walter Ralegh, who settled the first colony in these parts of America, and that before any other of the nations of Europe, the two last kings were so careful for the maintaining the English right, that they confirmed general patents (to several of their subjects, as well of the nobility as other undertakers, for several latitudes of land, for their settling of colonies therein, and further populating these parts, and for the better effecting whereof and reducing these our wild brethren to acknowledge of Christ, and advancing the plantation called Virginia) from the maiden queen; divers of the nobility of England with several of the gentry, merchants, and others, were incorporated into a body, called the Virginia Company, and that before the name of a West India company was known in Holland, and the which has cost England more then a million of money. And as the English nation hath the best general right of all the nations in Europe to these northern parts of America, and that grounded upon the law of nature and nations; so they can shew the best evidence in their great improvements thereof almost to the world's wonder, especially in these parts called New England, lying betwixt forty and forty-eight degrees of northerly latitude.

And as by virtue of the said general right they have a particular, so they may purchase what lands they please in any part thereof, either by many or few, more, or one, always provided they give and yield an obedient acknowledgment and subordinate subjection to the general laws of their nation and mother commonwealth; and in case any shall wilfully and knowingly do otherwise, by putting themselves and lands so purchased as subjects and subject to another state, they are in a degree as guilty, as he or they, that shall in England acknowledge subjection to a foreign state.

Thus as the general and particular rights of the English to these northern parts of America are as plainly and perspicuously laid down; so upon a due examination it will be found, that the Dutch have no right at all either in the general or particular, but have intruded into and anticipated the English in their rights, and that at first by a violent usurpation and force upon the native Indians; but whether it was by particular men, or the public approbation of their state, is questionable; but of the two I rather conceive it was by particulars, my reasons being;

That in case the first ground of the grant of charter from their states to their West India company, and under whose patronage the Dutch plantation of Manhataas is now settled, be well and truly examined, it will be found, that it was only for them to subdue and conquer what they could in America, and that as from an enemy the king of Spain; for, as I am credibly informed, the present Dutch governor, in many of his public writings, terms the Dutch plantation there a conquest, or the West India company's conquest, and the which if so, it would be demanded from whom conquered.

My second reason is, that the Dutch plantations, now by them called the Netherlands, have not been commonly so called and known, until of very late years, but was better known and commonly called by them the New Virginia, as a place dependent upon or a relative to the Old Virginia. And as there is in that an acknowledgment of English right, so I conceive it to be true, which is commonly reported, that by the permission of king James they had granted from him to their states only a certain island, called therefore by them States Island, as a watery place for their West India fleets ; although as they have incroached upon, so they have given it a new Dutch name, . . . wiping out the old English names in those parts in America in their old sea-charts, and have new Dutchified them.

Thus according to my duty to my country and countrymen, and according to that portion of my weak understanding, I have briefly remonstrated the English rights to these parts of America ; although more knowing men are better able to vindicate the same. Yet nevertheless I hope it will be friendly received, it being with a real intention only of informing my countrymen, that are ignorant thereof in these parts, of their just rights thereunto, and of their great error in subjecting themselves and lands to a foreign state. And do therefore lovingly advise them, especially the English towns upon the westward parts of Long Island, or any other of the English nation, that do intend to settle down in towns and colonies, to be very cautious of making themselves guilty either of ignorant or wilful betraying the rights of their nations, by their subjecting themselves and lands to a foreign state.

John Thurloe, *Collection of State Papers* (London, 1742), V, 81–83.

———◆———

49. Why the Pilgrims left England for Holland (1607–1608)

BY WILLIAM BRADFORD

Bradford was a silk-weaver at Leyden, later Governor of Plymouth (see No. 97). — Bibliography : Winsor, *Narrative and Critical History*, III, chs. vii, viii ; Dexter, *Congregationalism as seen in its Literature ;* Channing and Hart, *Guide*, § 111.

BUT that I may come more near my intendmente ; when as by the trauell & diligence of some godly, & zealous preachers, and God's blessing on their labours, as in other places of y⁰ land, so in y⁰ North parts, many became inlightened by y⁰ word of God ; and had their ignorance & sins discouered vnto them, and begane by his grace to reforme their liues, and make conscience of their wayes. The worke of God was no sooner manifest in them, but presently they were both scoffed and scorned by y⁰ prophane multitude, and y⁰ ministers vrged with y⁰ yoak of

subscription, or els must be silenced; and yᵉ poore people were so vexed
with opparators, & pursiants, & yᵉ comissarie courts, as truly their affliction was not smale; which, notwithstanding, they bore sundrie years with
much patience, till they were occasioned (by yᵉ continuance & encrease
of these troubls, and other means which yᵉ Lord raised up in those days)
to see further into things by the light of yᵉ word of God. How not only
these base and beggerly ceremonies were unlawfull, but ᴬ ᵃˡˢᵒ that yᵉ lordly
& tiranous ᴬ ᵖᵒʷᵉʳ of yᵉ prelats ought not to be submitted vnto; which
thus, (contrary to the freedome of the gospell,) would load ᴬ & ᵇᵘʳᵈᵉⁿ mens
consciences; and by their compulsive power make a prophane mixture
of persons & things in yᵉ worship of God. And that their offices & cal-
ings; courts & cannons &c. were unlawful and Antichristian; being such
as have no warrante in yᵉ word of God but the same yᵗ were used in
poperie, & still retained. Of which a famous author thus writeth in his
Dutch comtaries. At yᵉ coming of king James into *England; The new
king* (saith he) *found their established yᵉ reformed religion, according to
yᵉ reformed religion of king Edward yᵉ 6. Retaining, or keeping still
yᵉ spirituall state of yᵉ Bishops, &c. After yᵉ ould maner, much varying
& differing from yᵉ reformed churches in Scotland, France, & yᵉ Netherlands, Embden, Geneva, &c. whose Reformation is cut, or shapen much
nerer yᵉ first Christian churches, as it was used in yᵉ Apostles times.*

So many therefore (of these proffessors) as saw yᵉ evill of these things,
(in thes parts), And whose harts yᵉ Lord had touched wᵗʰ heavenly
zeale for his trueth, they shooke of this yoake of Antichristian bondage,
And as yᵉ Lords free people, joyned them selues (by a couenant of the
Lord) into a church estate, in yᵉ felowship of yᵉ gospell, to walke in all
his wayes, made known, or to be made known unto them, (according to
their best endeauors), whatsoever it should cost them, the Lord assisting
them. And that it cost them something this ensewing historie will
declare.

These people became 2. distincte bodys or churches; & in regarde
of distance of place did congregate seuerally; for they were of sundrie
townes & vilages, some in Notingamshire, some of Lincollinshire and
some of Yorkshire, wher they border nearest togeather. In one of these
churches (besids others of note) was Mr. John Smith, a man of able
guifts, & a good preacher; who afterwards was chosen their pastor. But
these afterwards falling into some errours in yᵉ Low Countries, ther (for
yᵉ most part) buried them selues, & their names.

But in this other church (wᶜʰ must be yᵉ subjecte of our discourse) besids other worthy men, was M.ʳ Richard Clifton, a graue & reuerēd preacher; who by his paines and dilligens had done much good, and vnder God had ben a means of yᵉ conuersion of many. And also that famous and worthy man M.ʳ John Robinson, who afterwards was their pastor for many years, till yᵉ Lord tooke him away by death. Also M.ʳ William Brewster a reuerent man, who afterwards was chosen an elder of yᵉ church and liued with them till old age.

But after these things they could not long continue in any peacable condition; but were hunted, & persecuted on euery side, so as their former afflictions were but as flea-bitings in comparison of these which now came vpon them. For some were taken, & clapt vp in prison, others had their houses besett & watcht night and day, & hardly escaped their hands; and yᵉ most were faine to flie & leave their howses & habitations, and the means of their livelehood. Yet these & many other sharper things which afterward befell them, were no other then they looked for, and therefore were yᵉ better prepared to bear them by yᵉ assistance of Gods grace & spirite. Yet seeing them selues thus molested and that ther was no hope of their continuance ther, by a joynte consente they resolued to goe into yᵉ Low-countries, wher they heard was freedome of Religion for all men; as also how sundrie from London, & other parts of yᵉ land had been exiled, and persecuted for yᵉ same cause, & were gone thither, and liued at Amsterdam, & in other places of yᵉ land. So after they had continued togeither aboute a year, and kept their meetings every Saboth in one place or other, exercising the worship of God amongst them selues, notwithstanding all yᵉ dilligence & malice of their aduerssaries; they seeing they could no longer continue in yᵗ condition, they resolued to get over into Hollād as they could; Which was in yᵉ year 1607. & 1608. of which more at large in yᵉ next chap.

2. Chap.

Of their departure into Holland and
their troubls ther aboute, with
some of yᵉ many difficulties
they found and mete
with all.

Anº. 1608.

Being thus constrained to leave their native soyle and countrie, their lands & liuings, and all their friends & famillier acquaintance, it was much; and thought maruelous by many. But to goe into a cuntrie they knew not (but by hearsay), wher they must learne a new language, and get their liuings they knew not ^how^ it being a dear place, & subjecte to ye misseries of warr, it was by many thought an aduenture almost desperate, a case intolerable, & a misserie worse then death. Espetially seeing they were not aquainted with trads nor traffique (by which y^t countrie doth subsiste,) but had only been used to a plaine countrie life, & ye innocente trade of husbandrey. But these things did not dismay them (though they did some times trouble them) for their desires were sett on the ways of God, & to injoye his ordinances; but they rested on nis prouidence, & knew whom they had beleeued. Yet this was not all, for though they could not stay, yet were ye not suffered to goe, but ye ports & havens were shut against them; so as they were faine to seeke secrete means of conueance, & to bribe & fee ye mariners, & giue exterordinarie rates for their passages. And yet were they of[ ]en times betrayed (many of them), and both they, & their goods intercepted & surprised, and therby put to great trouble & charge, of which I will give an instance or tow, & omitte the rest. . . .

But y^t I be not tedious in these things, I will omitte ye rest, though I might relate many other notable passages, and troubles which they endured & underwente in these their wanderings & trauells both at land, & sea; but I hast to other things. Yet I may not omitte ye fruite that came hearby, for by these so publick troubls, in so many eminente places, their cause became famouss, & occasioned many to looke into ye same; and their godly cariage & Christian behauiour was such as left a deep impression in the minds of many. And though some few shrunk at these first conflicts, & sharp beginings (as it was no maruell,) yet many more came on with fresh courage, & greatly animated others. And in ye end, notwithstanding all these stormes of opposition, they all gatt ouer at length, some at one time & some at another, and some in one place & some in another. And mette togeather againe according to their desires, with no small rejoycing. . . .

William Bradford, *History of the Plimouth Plantation* (Fac-simile from the original manuscript, with an Introduction by John A. Doyle, London and Boston, 1896), 5–11 *passim*.

CHAPTER VII — REGULATION OF COLONIZATION

50. Supplies for the Virginia Plantation (1621)

BY THE VIRGINIA COMPANY OF LONDON

This was one of the two companies chartered in 1606, and was formed to colonize the southern part of the English possessions; its charter was annulled in 1624. — Bibliography: Winsor, *Narrative and Critical History*, VII, ch. v; Edward Eggleston, *Beginners of a Nation* (New York, 1896), 53–87; Channing and Hart, *Guide*, § 97.

AFTER oͬ very hartie Comendacōns: you shall now by this Shipp the Warwicke and the Pinace that cometh along with her, receiue those supplies that we formerly in oͬ letters by the Genge [George] and Marmaduke promised; the setting forth of wch hath beene of so exceeding and noble and laboͬˢ unto us, being but a very few on whom so great a burthen hath lien [lain], and we haue not been able to intend [care for] anything else: wherefore in that regard as also that the noble Earl of Southampton is not yet returned to London, nor those eminent persons without whose Counselle and authoritie we thinke it not fitt to proceed to resolucōn in so waightie bussinesses; yͬ letters and dispatches by the Bona Nova, and the Margrett & John must yet remaine unanswered; but by the Dutie wch about the middle of next month is to depart we hope you shall receive full sattisfaccon; wch Shipp shall bring with her store of silke worme seed and abundance of vine plants, for both wch we desire not only that generall pperations be made, but that timely notice and order be given throughout the whole colony, that every pticuler [private] man may make prouision for the receiuinge of some quantitie of them both, and that a straight charge be giuen for the pserving of vines and mulbery trees, wch we understand with others are promiscuously defrayed; and because the skill of handling them is only deriued from the Frenchmen we canot but here recomend this to yoͬ fauoͬ and regard that they may be kindly used and cherished.

We haue as by the Inuoice you shall perceiue sent them and the Dutch-men (the delay of whose most necessarie workes is with much indignation here resented) diuers provisions of victualls as also a cloth

to make them apparrell; for hose and shoes and other such matters we
desire they may be supplied by the Companies stock there, out of the
Magazine wch now comes along in the Warwicke large and abundante
in all usefull and necessarie comodities.

For as for vanities and superfluities although we find they yeeld most
profitt in Virginia; yet we haue thought it most unfitt to nourish by
such supplies that euil genius of pride and ryott [riot] wch we wish
were utterly extinguished and this oʳ care herein hath had an eie rather
to the benefitt of the plantation than the profitt of the Aduenturers;
wch shall not we hope prove preiudiciall but rather breed a willingness
and desire in the whole collony to make us a speedy and profitible
returne of the stocke now sent, (and not as hitherto euill and disgrate-
full words for o'r zeale of their welfare and nothing at all is at least less
than the principal laide out), for their relief and comfort:

For you shall understand, that (not only of the ould Magazine wch
was aboue 7,000 pounds, we canot hope to see much aboue half we
hitherto haue not receiued any one peny) but euen the new Magazine
sent last yeare by Mr. Blany is returned back with the loss of the principall it self after almost two yeares time and so many hassards born
and yet to beare; a thing so unkindly and distastefully taken here as
if the accompts had been sooner knowne we much feare that supplies
now sent had been farr short of what they now are: . . .

. . . the ould rate of 3ˢ p pound, . . . the tobacco is esteemed less worth
than that rate for although for matter of profitt it might go currant
much alike, yet thereby we should soe maintaine the collony in their
ouerweening esteeme of their darlinge Tobacco, to the ouerthrow of all
other Staple comodities, and likewise to continue the [e]vill will they
haue conceiued there and scandalous reports here spread of oppression
and exaccons from the Company, selling all theire Comodities for three
times the vallew of what they cost upon which fond and uniust surmises
they thinke it lawfull to use all maner of deceipt and falshood in their
tobacco that they put of [on] the Magazine;

Which is the next thing wherein we [urge] yoʳ care and fauoʳ being
assured from o'r Factor in Holland that except the tobacco that shall
next come thence proue to be of more pfection and goodnesse than that
was sent home last, there is no hope that it will vent [sell] at all, . . .

"The engrossinge of some of the principall Comodities in the last
Magazine is here much distasted, as a wrong to the Stocke to be
depriued of their best Comodities at a low rate; but principally to the

whole Collony who were hereby made to pay dearer and forced to take other Comodities that they needed not. . . .

By this Shipp and Pinace called the Tyger, we also send as many maids and young women as will make upp the number of fiftie, wth those twelue formerly sent in the Marmaduk, wch we hope shalbe receiued wth the same Christian pietie and charitie as they were sent from hence ; and prouidinge for them at theire first landing and disposinge of them in marriage, (wch is o^{r} cheife intent), we leaue to yor care and wisdome, to take that order as may most conduce to their good, and sattisfac̄con of the Aduenventurers, for the charges disbursed in settinge them forth, wch coming to twelue pounds and upwards, they require one hundred and fiftie [pounds] of the best leafe tobacco for each of them ; and if any of them dye there must be a proportionable addition uppon the rest ; this increase of thirty pounds weight since those sent in the Marmaduke, they have resolued to make, finding the great shrinkage and other losses, upon the tobacco from Virginia will not beare lesse, wch tobacco as it shalbe receiued, we desire may be deliuered to M^{r} Ed. Blany, who is to keepe thereof a pticular accompt.

We haue used extraordinary care and dilligence in the choise of them, and haue receiued none of whom we haue not had good testimony of theire honest life and cariadge, wch together wth their names, we send there inclosed for the sattisfaction of such as shall marry them ; for whose further encoradgement we desire you to giue publique notice that the next spring we purpose to send ouer as many youths for apprentices to those that shall now marry any of them and make us due sattisfac̄con.

This and theire owne good deserts together with yor fauo^{r} and care, will, we hope, marry them all unto honest and sufficient men, whose meanes will reach to present re-payment ; but if any of them shall unwarily or fondly bestow herself (for the liberty of marriadge we dare not infrindge) uppon such as shall not be able to giue present sattisfaction, we desire that at least as soon as abillity shalbe, they be compelled to pay the true quantity of tobacco propor̄coned, and that this debt may haue pcedence of all others to be recouered.

For the rest, wch we hope will not be many, we desire yor best furtherance for prouiding them fitting seruices till they may hapne uppon good matches, and are here perswaded by many old Planters that there will be maisters enow found there, who will readily lay down what charges shall be required, uppon assurance of repayment at their mariadges, wch as iust and reasonable we desire may be giuen them. But this and many other things in this bussiness we must referr to yor good consideracōns and fruittful endeauors in opeinge a work begun here out of piettie and tending so much to the benifitt of the Plantation shall not miscarry for any want of good will or care on yor part."

The Society of Martin's Hundred whose designes by many misfortunes, as well here as in Virginia have heen hitherto checked, do now againe go forward cherefully ; sending a supplie of people largly furnished with all necessarie prouisions : the succoring and cherishinge of them and their proceedings we in effectual man^r recomends wth yor desiringe you to be by all possible fauors aiding and assisting them, . . .

The company is by diuers waies informed that there is a great want of worthie ministers in Virginia therefore they have entertained and now send along Mr Thomas White a man of good sufficiencie for learning and recomended for integritie and uprightnes of life and of so good zeale to the Plantation that he is content to go wth that small allowance the Companie's stock is able now to aford him, and to put himself uppon such preferrment there as he shall deserue, and you shalbe able to accomodate him with, wch if it be of the places belonging to the Company we have promised him here an addicōn to the small allowance he hath now receiued ; . . .

There are two French youths now sent to Capt. Tho. Nuce, part of those ten promised him the next Springe ; this anticipation, although in a very difficult time, for want of mony, we haue yeelded unto, upon Sr John Danuers his motion, that Capt Nuce might be so much pleasured. Wee send likewise one Miles Prickett to be employed in the Companies seruice and especially in making of Salt, wch we are informed he heretofore pracktised in Virginia, he is to serue till Allhollantide in the year 1622, without any reward at all, wch is here beforehand paid him by his passage and apparrell giuen him. . . .

And so wishing a happy beginninge and prosperous successe in all yor waightie affaires we at psent betake you and the whole Colony and yor charge to the blessing of God Almightie : and rest

"Yo^r assured Louing frends. . . .

Edward D. Neill, *History of the Virginia Company of London* (Albany, 1869), 241–250 *passim*.

51. Meetings of a Colonization Company
(1622-1623)

BY THE COUNCIL FOR NEW ENGLAND

The Council for New England is a continuation of the Plymouth Company of 1606; it was organized in 1620 to colonize the northern part of the English territory. — Bibliography: Winsor, *Narrative and Critical History*, III, ch. ix; Samuel F. Haven, *History of Grants under the Great Council;* Channing and Hart, *Guide,* § 114.

Saturday the last of May 1622. *Whitehall.*

PRESENT.

The Lord Duke of Lenox.	S.ᵗ Robert Mansell.
The Earle of Arundell.	S.ᵗ Ferdinando Gorges.
The Lord Gorges.	Capt. Samuell Argall.
	D.ʳ Barnabe Goche.

First it is ordered that concerning the Complaint made of M.ʳ Weston, petition shall bee made to his Ma.ᵗⁱᵉ for y.ᵉ forfeiture of his shipp and goods to y.ᵉ presid.ᵗ and Councells use.

It is thought fitt that there shall bee an order procured from y.ᵉ Lords of his Ma.ᵗⁱᵉˢ Councell for sending for such as have in contempt of authority gone for New England this last yeare, As also to procure a furthe⌈r⌉ warning to bee given to them from further attempting, by Proclamation, and M.ʳ attorney to bee moved therein.

The patents allready granted, to bee confirmed, and order is given for patents to bee drawne for the Earle of Warwicke and his Associates, The Lord Gorges, S.ᵗ Robert Mansell, S.ᵗ Ferd. Gorges.

As concerning y.ᵉ Accompt, there are appointed to auditt them, The Lord Gorges, S.ᵗ Robert Mansell, Capt. Argall, Doctor Gauche, or any two of them

For y.ᵉ renewing y.ᵉ Patent, conferrance to be had with M.ʳ Attorney concerning the tenure, also w.ᵗʰ M.ʳ Sollicitor.

As touching y.ᵉ Governor, S.ᵗ Ferdinando Gorges is elected, the perticulars are reserved till another meeting.

For the admittance of Merchants to bee Pattentees, it is agreed, that such of the Westerne parts as are capable of the fishing trade shall bee admitted. The businesse of putting in £100,000, it is thought fitt that it were knowne what security is demanded. Also that it is rather thought convenient to these Marchants to secure y.ᵉ full sattisfaccõn and paym.ᵗˢ at delivery of y.ᵉ fish. Also to appoint y.ᵉ Lord Gorges, S.ᵗ Robert

Mansell, Sr Ferd. Gorges, Dr. Gouches and Capt. Samuel Argall, as Committees to take this to their consideraᶜᵒn and to certify their opinions.

Likewise it is thought convenient, to admitt young youths from Parishes, that have not been taynted with any villanyes or misdemen.^{rs}, to bee sent to New England, and there to bee placed out and bound Apprentices to such as shall have occasion and meanes to imploy them.

It is ordered that ye Adventurers, shall forthwith pay in their whole Adventures, otherwise to bee omitted in ye renewing of ye pattent.

The Committees aforesaid, to take ye continuance or discontinuance of ye Clerke into their consideraᶜons and therein to doe as they shall think fitt.

It is ordered that Dr Goche shall bee Treasurer.

The allowance of ye printing of ye Booke is referr'd to the Earle of Arundell.

The Resolution of undertakeing for partnershipp in ye shipp, further than their Adventure of £100 a peece, is referr'd till private conferrance, And Allowance granted to such as will willingly undertake in this kind.

Fryday ye 5th of July 1622.

. . . As also to sollicite ye Lords for procureing from his Matie a proclamation concerning ye fishermen of ye Westerne parts.   Likewise to procure some course for punishing their contempt of authority.   And that Mr Attorney bee moved herein.

It is Agreed that ye Councell meet the Morrow being ye 6th of this Instant at Sr Ferd: Gorges Lodgings for conferring about ye forme of a patent betweene 7 and 8 a clocke in ye Morneing.

The businesse of Admittance of some of the Westerne Merchts is offerred to Sr Ferd. Gorges, Sr Richard Edgecombe, Dr Barnabe Goche and Mr Drake, and other pattentees to take into their consideraᶜon ye election of six and who they shall bee.

The proposition of ye Businesse of £100,000 is respited in regard of ye Difficulty of findeing security.

Conserning ye proposition to bee made unto the Citty for takeing away of poore Children for New-England, It is thought fitt, that there should bee Letters gotten from ye Lords for the furtherance hereof to ye Citty, and that those Children be of 14 yeares of age apeece or upwards.

It is ordered that a Letter bee drawne and sent to y.ᵉ pticular pattentees for y.ᵉ sending in forthw.ᵗʰ of their moneys, or else they to bee left
out of y.ᵉ New pattent and others admitted, And an order to bee procured from y.ᵉ Lords to y.ᵉ Treãr to that effect. . . .

It is ordered and allowed that M.ʳ Secretary Calvert shall bee admitted
on [e] of y.ᵉ Councell for New England in y.ᵉ new pattent. . . .

Wednesday y.ᵉ 24.ᵗʰ of July 1622. . . .

It is order'd and agreed that the Lord Duke of Lenox have for his
devident and part of the mayne Land of New-England in America, from
y.ᵉ Middle of Sawahquatock towards Sagadahoc, and his bounds that way
to reach mid-way betweene Sawahquatock and Sagadahoc upon y.ᵉ Coast.
And to reach 30 Miles backward into y.ᵉ Mayne.   And 3 Leagues into y.ᵉ
Sea.

M.ʳ Secretary Calvert to begin his Devident from y.ᵉ Middle of Sagadehoc, and to goe close to y.ᵉ Lord Duke his bounds.

And to have further into his devident the Island called by y.ᵉ name of
Setquin.

The Earle of Arundle to have for his devident, from ye middle of
Sagadehoc, and to goe North east soe much on his side, as M.ʳ Secretary
goes on y.ᵉ other side upon y.ᵉ Coast.   And to reach [   ] Miles backward into y.ᵉ Mayne, and 3 Leagues into y.ᵉ Sea.   And to have further
into his Devident y.ᵉ island called Menehigan.

It is propounded that y.ᵉ Tenure in y.ᵉ Grand pattent is thought meet
to bee held of y.ᵉ Croune of England by y.ᵉ Sword.

And that private Planters shall hold of the Chamber of State to bee
established there, and shall have power to create their owne Tenures to
such as shall hold under them.

The Country to be called Nova Albion.

That there may bee power given in the Grand Pattent to create Titles
of Honour and precedency, soe as y.ᵉ differ in nominacõn from the titles
used here in England.

M.ʳ Ratcliffe is sent for by a Messinger of the Chamber to attend the
Earle of Arundell, to morrow by two of y.ᵉ Clock, touching timber stay'd
by his Appointment in y.ᵉ woods of Whiteby.

It is thought meet that the two great Islands lying in y.ᵉ River of Sagadehoc bee reserved for the publike plantacõn.

Further that a place bee reserved betweene the branches of the two
Rivers, for a publike Citty. . . .

N

Sondaie 29° Junij. 1623.

ATT GREENWICH.

There were presented to the Kings most excellent Matie a Plott of all the Coasts and lands of New England devided into twenty parts each part conteyning two shares, And twenty lotts conteyning the said double shares made upp in little bales of waxe, And the names of twenty Pattentees by whom these lotts were to be drawne. And for that the Lord Duke of Buckingham was then absent, his Matie was gratiously pleased to drawe the first lott in his Graces behalf. . . .

American Antiquarian Society, *Proceedings,* 1867 (Cambridge, 1867), 59–96 *passim.*

---

52. How to order a Colony (1629)

BY THE MASSACHUSETTS COMPANY

The New England Council made no permanent settlements, but in 1628 they granted lands to the " Governor and Company of the Massachusetts Bay in New England," confirmed by royal grant of 1629. — Bibliography : Winsor, *Narrative and Critical History,* III, ch. ix, and *Memorial History of Boston,* I, 87–98; Channing and Hart, *Guide,* §§ 115–117.

LOVING Friends, Wee hartylie salute you. Wee have received Letter of the 13th of September, by which wee take Notice of your safe Arrivall, blessing God for it. Wee have formerly requested Mr. Cradock, our Governor to wryte you of the Receipt thereof, and give advice how wee purposed to proceed in seting forward our Plantacon ; whose Letters, if they bee come to your Handes, (as wee hope they are) will put Lyfe into your Affaires, and encourage you to provide for the Entertainment of such as are now coming.

Since your Departure wee have for the further strengthening of our Graunt from the Councell at Plymouth, obtained a Confirmacon of it from his Majesty by his Letters-pattents vnder the broad Seale of England, by which said Letters-pattents wee are incorporated into a body pollitique, with ample Power to governe and rule all his Majesty's Subiects that reside within the Limitts of our plantacon, as by the Duplicate therof, vnder the broad Seale, which wee have delivered to Mr. Sharpe to be delivered to you, doth fully appeare.

And for that the propagating of the Gosple is the Thinge wee doo

profess aboue all to bee our Ayme in setling this Plantacon, wee have
bin carefull to make plentyfull provision of Godly Ministers, by whose
faithfull preachinge, Godly Conversacon, and exemplary Lyfe, wee trust
not only those of our owne Nation wilbe built vp in the Knowledge of
God, but also the Indians may, in God's appointed tyme, bee reduced
to the Obedyence of the Gosple of Christ : . . .   For the Manner of
exercising their Ministrie, and teaching both our owne People and the
Indians, wee leave that to themselves, hoping they will make God's
Word the Rule of their Accons, and mutually agree in the Discharge
of their Duties ; and because their Doctrine will hardly bee well
esteemed whose persons are not reverenced, wee desire that both by
your owne Example, and by comanding all others to doe the like, our
Ministers may receive due Honor. . . .

   . . . for that wee haue ordered, that the Body of the Government there
shall consist of 13 persons, wee are content the old Planters that are now
there within our Plantacon and Lymitts thereof, shall chose two of the
discreetest and juditiall Men from amongst themselves to bee of the
Government, that they may see wee are not wanting to give them fitting
Respect in that wee would haue their consent (if it may bee) in making
wholesome Constitucons for Government. Alwayes provyded, that none
shalbe chosen, or meddle in their choice but such as will live amongst
Vs and conforme themselues to our Government : . . .

   And that it may appeare as well to all the Worlde, as to the old
Planters themselues, that wee seek not to make them Slaves, as it
seemes by your Letter some of them thinke themselues to bee become
by meanes of our Patent, wee are content they shall be Partakers of such
Priviledges, as wee, from his Majesty's espetiall Grace, with great Cost,
Fauor of Personages of Note, and much Labor, have obtained ; and
that they shalbe incorporated into this Socyetie, and enioy not only
those Lands which formerly they have . . . , but such a further Proporcon, as by th' Advice and Judgment of your selfe, and the rest of the
Councell, shalbe thought fitt for them, or any of them.   And besides
it is still our Purpose, that they should have some Benefitt by the comon
Stock, . . .

   And as touching the old Planters, their earnest Desire for the present
to continue the planting of Tobacco, (a Trade by this whole Companie
generally disavowed, and vtterly disclaymed by some of the greatest
Adventurers amongst Vs, who absolutely declared themselves vnwilling
to haue Hand in this Plantacon, if Wee intended to cherish or permit

the planting thereof, or any other kinde, then for a Man's private Vse
for meere Necessitie; Wee are of opinion the old Planters will haue
small Encouragement to that Employment, for wee finde heere by late
Experience, that it doth hardly produce the Fraight and Custome,
neither is there Hope of Amendment, there being such great Quantities
made in other Places, that ere long it is like to be little worth; Nevertheless if the old Planters (for wee exclude all others) conceive that they
cannot otherwise provyde for their Livelyhood, wee leave it to the Dis-
crecon of your selfe and the Councell there, to give way for the present
to their planting it in such Manner, and with such Restriccons, as you
and the said Councell shall thinke fittinge, having an espetiall Care with
as much convenyencie as may bee, vtterly to suppress the planting of it
(except for meere Necessitie), but however, Wee absolutely forbid the
sale of it, or the Vse of it by any of our owne or particuler Men's Servants vnless vpon vrgent Occasion, for the Benefitt of Health, and taken
privately.

Mr. John Oldham came from New England not long before your
Arrivall there, by whom wee have had noe small Distraccon in our Business, . . . with whom, after long Tyme spent in sundry Treatyes, finding him a Man altogeather vnfitt for vs to deale with, wee have at last
left him to his owne Way: And as wee are informed, hee, with some
others, are provyding a Vessell, and is mynded, as soon as he can
dispatch, to come for New England, pretending to settle himselfe in
Mattachusetts-Bay; clayming a Title and Right, by a Grant from Sir
Ferdinando Gorges Sonne, which wee are well satisfyed, by good
Councell, is voyde in Lawe. . . . Now, as wee shall unwillingly doe
any Act in debarringe suche as were inhabitants before vs of that Trade,
as in Conscience they ought to enioy, soe shall we as vnwillingly permitt any to appropriate that to their own private Lucar, which we in our
religious Intencons have dedicated to the common Charge of Building
houses for God's Worshipp, and Forts to defend such as shall come
thither to inhabite. Wee feare, that as he hath bin obstinate and violent in his Opinions heere, soe hee will persist, and bee ready to drawe
a Partie to himselfe there, to the great Hinderance of the comon Quiett;
wee have therefore thought fitt to give you Notice of his Disposicon, to
the end, you may beware how you meddle with him, as also that you
may vse the best Meanes you can to settle an Agreement with the old
Planters soe as they may not harken to Mr. Oldham's dangerous though
vaine Propositions: . . .

Wee take Notice that you desire to have Frenchmen sent you that might bee experienced in making of Salt and planting of Vynes : Wee have enquired diligently for such, but cannot meete with any of that Nation ; nevertheless, God hath not left vs altogeather vnprovided of a Man able to vndertake that Worke, for that, wee have entertained Mr. Thomas Groves, . . .

In our next, wee intend to send you a particuler of such as are to haue Land allotted and sett out vnto them, that soe you may appoint vnto each Man an equal Proporcon by Lott, according to what is to be allowed in the first Devident, touching which, wee shall then giue you more large Instruccons ; . . .

For such of our Nation as sell Munition, Gunns, or other Furniture, to arme the Indians against Vs, or teach them the Vse of Armes, wee would have you to apprehend them, and send Prisoners for England, where they will not escape severe Punishment, being expressly against the Proclamacon. You have had former Caution giuen you, of taking heede of beeing too secure in trusting the Indians, which wee againe comend to your Care, and that you may bee the better able to resist both Forraigne Enemies and the Natiues, if either should assaile you, wee pray you lett all such as live under our Gouernment, both our Servants, and other Planters and their Servants, bee exercised in the Vse of Armes, and certain tymes appointed to muster them, . . .

. . . Wee also send you the particuler Names of such as are enter-tained for the Company's Service ; amongst which wee hope you will fynde many religious, discreete, and well ordered Persons, which you must sett over the rest, devyding them into Famylies, placing some with the Ministers, and others vnder such as beeing honest Men (and of their oune Calling as neere as may bee) may have Care to see them well educated in their generall Callings as Christians, and particuler accord-ing to their severall Trades, or fitness in Disposicon to learn a Trade : And whereas amongst such a Nombre, (notwithstanding our Care to purge them) there may still remaine some Libertines, wee desire you to be carefull that such (if any bee) may bee forced, by inflicting such Punishment as their Offences may deserve, . . . and above all wee pray you bee carefull that there be none in our Precincts permitted to doe any iniurie (in the least kinde) to the Heathen People, and if any offend in that way, lett them receive due Correccon ; and wee hold it fitting you publish a Proclamacon to that Effect, by leaving it fixed vnder the Company's Seale in some eminent Place, for all to take Notice, at such

Tyme, as both the Heathen themselues, as well as our People, may take Notice of it ; and for avoyding of the Hurt that may follow through our much Familiaritie with the Indians, wee conceive it fitt that they bee not permitted to come to our Plantacon but at certaine Tymes and Places to be appointed them. If any of the Saluages pretend Right of Inheritance to all or any Part of the Lands graunted in our Pattent, wee pray you endeavor to purchase their Tytle, that we may avoyde the least Scruple of Intrusion.

We haue in the former Part of our Lrē cerryfied you of the good Hopes wee haue of the Loue and vnanimus Agreement of our Ministers, they having declared themselues to be of one Judgment, to be fully agreed on the Manner how to exercise their Minestory, which wee hope wilbe by them accordingly performed ; yett because it is often found that some busy Persons (led more by their Will then any good Warrant out of God's Word) take Opportunities by moving needless Questions to stirr vp Strife, and by that Way to begett a Question, and bring Men to declare some Difference in Judgment (most commonly in Things indifferent), from which small Beginnings great Mischiefs have followed ; wee pray you and the rest of the Councell, that if any such Disputes should happen amongst you, that you suppress them, and bee carefull to maintaine Peace and Vnitie. . . .

For the better Accomodacon of Businesses wee haue devyded the Servants belonging to the Company into seuerall Famylies, as wee desire and intend they should liue togeather, . . .

Our earnest Desire is, that you take spetiall Care in settlinge these Families, that the Cheife in the Familie (at least some of them) bee grounded in Religion, wherby Morning and Evening Famylie Dutyes may bee duly performed, and a watchfull Eye held over all in each Familie, by one or more in Each Famylie to be appointed thereto, that soe Disorders may bee prevented, and illweeds nipt before they take too great a Head ; . . . And wee hartely pray you, that all be kept to Labor, as the only Meanes to reduce them to civill, yea a Godly Life, and to keepe Youth from falling into many Enormities, which by Nature wee are all too much enclyned vnto. God, who alone is able and powerfull, enable you to this greate Worke ; and graunt, that our chiefest Ayme may bee his Honor and Glory. . . .

Ebenezer Hazard, *Historical Collections* (Philadelphia, 1792), I, 256-267 *passim.*

53. An Attempt to sift Emigration (1637)

BY KING CHARLES FIRST

This Proclamation was an attempt to restrain the Puritans from emigration, but it had no great effect. — Bibliography : Winsor, *Narrative and Critical History*, III, ch. vii; Channing and Hart, *Guide*, § 118.

THE KING'S most Excellent Majesty being informed, that great numbers of his Subjects have been, and are every year transported into those parts of *America*, which have been granted by Patent to several Persons, and there settle themselves, some of them with their Families and whole Estates, among which Numbers, there are also many idle and refractory Humours, whose only or principal end is, to live as much as they can without the reach of authority.

His Majesty having taken the Premises into Consideration, is minded to restrain for the time to come, such promiscuous and disorderly departing out of the Realm, and doth therefore straightly charge and command, all and every the Officers and Ministers of his several Ports in *England*, *Wales*, and *Berwick*, that they do not hereafter permit or suffer, any Persons, being Subsidy Men [liable for taxes], or of the value of Subsidy Men, to imbarque themselves in any the said Ports or the Members thereof, for any of the said Plantations, without Licence from his Majesty's Commissioners for Plantations, first had and obtained in that behalf, nor that they admit to be imbarqued any Persons under the degree or value of Subsidy Men, without an Attestation or Certificate from two Justices of the Peace, living next the place where the Party last of all or lately then before dwelt, that he hath taken the Oaths of Supremacy and Allegiance, and like Testimony from the Minister of the Parish of his Conversation and Conformity to the Orders and Discipline of the Church of *England*.

And further his Majesty's express Will and Pleasure is, that the Officers and Ministers of his said several Ports and the Members thereof, do return to his Majesty's said Commissioners for Plantations every half Year, a particular and perfect List of the Names and Qualities of all such Persons, as shall from time to time be imbarqued in any of the said Ports for any of the said Plantations ; And of these his Majesty's Royal Commands, all the Officers and Ministers of the said Ports, and the Members thereof, are to take care, as they will answer the neglect thereof at their perils.

Given at our Court at *Whitehall*, the last day of *April*.

Thomas Rymer and Robert Sanderson, *Foedera, Conventiones, Literae et Cujus-cunque Generis Acta Publica inter Reges Angliae* (London, 1735), XX, 143.

54. Instructions for the Councill appointed for Forraigne Plantacôns (1660)

BY KING CHARLES SECOND

This was the first body charged with general supervision of all the Colonies. A later substitute, the Lords of Trade, will be described in Vol. II. — Bibliography: Winsor, *Narrative and Critical History*, III, ch. x; Channing and Hart, *Guide*, §§ 105, 125.

I. YOU shall informe yourselves by the best wayes and meanes you can of the state and condicôn of all Forraigne Plantac[i]ôns, and by what cô[m]missions or authorities they are and have bene governed and disposed of; and are to procure either from such persons as have any graunts thereof from the Crown, or from the records themselves, the copies of all such cômissions or graunts, to be transcribed and registered in a booke provided for that purpose, that you may be the better able to understand judge and administer such affaires, as by yor cômission and instruccôns are intrusted to yor care and managem^t.

2 You shall forthwith write letters to evrie of our Governo^{rs} for the time being of all our English Plantacôns and to evrie such person or persons who by any Letters Pattents from us or any of our predecesso^{rs} doe claime or exercise a right of governem^t in any of the said plantacôns; in wch lrês you are to informe them of our gratious care and provision in their behalfe both in erecting a Gen^rall Councill of Trade wherein their concernm^{ts} are mingled and provided for with the rest of our dominions and especially of this pticular Councell wch is applyed only to the inspeccôn care and conduct of Forraigne Plantacôns.

3. You are in the said letters to require the said Governo^{rs} and persons abovemecôned, to send unto you in writeing wth the advice of the Councell of evrie of the said plantacôns respectively, perticuler and exact accompt of the state of their affaires; of the nature and constitucôn of their lawes and governem^t and in what modell and frame they move and are disposed; what numbers of men; what fortifications and other strengths and defences are upon the place, and how furnished and provided for.

4. You are to order and settle such a continuall correspondencie that you may be able, as often as you are required thereunto, to give up to us an accompt of the Governm^t of each Colonie; of their complaints, their wants, their abundance; of their severall growths and cômodities

of every shipp tradeing there and its ladeing and whither consigned and
what the proceeds of that place have beene in the late yeares; that
thereby the intrinsick value and the true condicôn of each part & of the
whole may be thoroughly understood; whereby a more steady judgem^t
and ballance may be made for the better ordering and disposing of trade
& of the proceede and improvem^{ts} of the Plantacôns; that soe each
place within it selfe, and all of them being collected into one viewe and
managem^t here, may be regulated and ordered upon common and equall
ground & principles.

5. You are to applie your selves to all prudentiall meanes for the
rendering those dominions usefull to England and England helpfull to
them, and for the bringing the severall Colonies and Plantacôns, within
themselves, into a more certaine civill and uniforme of goverem^t and for
the better ordering and distributeing of publique justice among them.

6 You are to enquire diligently into the severall governm^{ts} and Councells of Colonies Plantacôns and distant Dominions, belonging to other
Princes or States, and to examine by what conduct and pollicies they
governe or benefit them; and you are to consult and provide that if
such councells be good wholsome and practicable, they may be applied
to the use of our Plantacôns; or if they tend or were designed to the
prejudice or disadvantage thereof or of any of our subjects or of trade
or cômerce, how they may be ballanced or turned back upon them.

7 You are to call to yor assistance from time to time as often as
the matter in consideracôn shall require any well experienced persons,
whether merchants, planters, seamen, artificers, &c.

8. You are to take especiall care and enquire into the strict execucôn
of the late Act of Parliament entituled An Act for the encouragem^t &
increasing of Shipping and Navigacôn, that asmuch as in you lyes none
of these good ends and purposes may be disappointed for wch the said
Act was intended and designed.

9. You are to take into yor consideracôn how our severall Plantacôns
may be best supplied with servants, that neither our Collonies, especially
such as are imediately under our cômissions, may be unprovided in so
essentiall an assistance, nor any of our good subjects may be forced or
inticed away by any unlawfull or indirect way; and that such as are
willing to be transported thither to seeke better fortunes than they can
meete with at home, may be encouraged thereunto; and how such a
course may be legally settled for the future that vagrantes and others
who remaine here noxious and unprofitable, may be soe transplanted to

the generall advantage of the publique aswell as the particuler commoditie of our Forraine Plantacôns.

10. You are most especially to take an effectuall care of the propogacôn of the Gospell in the severall Forraine Plantacôns, by provideing that there be good encouragem^t settled for the invitacôn and maintenance of lerned and orthodox ministers, and by sending strict orders and injunccôns for the regulating and reforming the debaucheries of planters and servants, whose ill example doth bring scandall upon Christianitie, and deterr such as yet are not admitted thereunto, from affecting or esteeming it.   And you are to consider how such of the Natives or such as are purchased by you from other parts to be servants or slaves may be best invited to the Christian Faith, and be made capable of being baptized thereunto ; it being the hono^r of our Crowne and of the Protestant Religion that all persons in any of our Dominions should be taught the knowledge of God, andbe made acquainted with the misteries of Salvation.

11. You are lastly required and impowered to advise order settle and dispose of all matters relating to the good governm^t improvement and management of our Forraine Plantacôns or any of them, with your utmost skill direccôn and prudence.   And in all cases wherein you shall judge that further powers and assistants shall be necessary, you are to addresse your selves to us [or] our Privy Councill for our further pleasure resolucôn and direccôns therein.

Edmund Bailey O'Callaghan, editor, *Documents relative to the Colonial History of the State of New York* (Albany, 1853), III, 34–36.

CHAPTER VIII — THE EMIGRANTS

55. Advice to Pilgrim Colonists (1620)

BY REV. JOHN ROBINSON

Pastor of the Puritan churches at Scrooby and Leyden. — Bibliography: H. M. Dexter, *Congregationalism as seen in its Literature*, 359–410; Winsor, *Narrative and Critical History*, III, 259–264, 288; Edward Eggleston, *Beginners of a Nation*, 181–186, 216–219; Channing and Hart, *Guide*, §§ 110, 111.

LOVING Christian friends, I do heartily, and in the Lord salute you, as being those with whom I am present in my best Affections, and most earnest Longings after you, though I be constrained for awhile to be bodily absent from you: I say, constrained; God knowing how willingly and much rather than otherwise, I would have born my Part with you in this first Brunt, were I not by strong Necessity held back for the present. Make Account of me in the mean Time, as a Man divided in myself, with great Pain, and (as natural Bonds set aside) having my better part with you: And although I doubt not, but in your Godly Wisdomes, you both foresee and resolve upon that which concerneth your present State and Condition, both severally and jointly; yet I thought it but my Duty to adde some further Spur of Provocation unto them who run already, if not because you need it, yet because I owe it in Love and Duty. And first, as we are daily to renew our Repentance with our God, especially for our Sins known, and generally for our unknow Trespasses: so doth the Lord call us in a singular manner, upon Occasions of such Difficulty and Danger as lieth upon you, to a both narrow Search, and careful Reformation of your Wayes in his Sight, lest he calling to Remembrance our Sins forgotten by us, or unrepented of, take Advantage against us, and in Judgement leave us to be swallowed up in one Danger or other: whereas on the contrary Sin being taken away by earnest Repentance, and the Pardon thereof from the Lord sealed up to a Man's Conscience by his Spirit, great shall be his Security and Peace in all Dangers, sweet his Comforts in all Distresses, with happy Deliverance from all Evil, whether in Life or Death. Now next after this heavenly Peace with God and our own Consciences, we are carefully to provide for Peace with all Men, what in us lieth, especially with our Associates; and for that, Watchfulness must be had that we neither at all in our selves do give, no nor easily take, Offence being given by others. *Woe be to the World for Offences;* for although it be necessary, considering the Malice of Satan, and Man's Corruption, *that Offences come,* yet, *Woe unto the Man,* or Woman either, *by whom the Offence cometh,* saith Christ, *Matt.* xviii. 7. and if Offences in the unseasonable Use of Things in themselves indifferent, be more to be feared than Death itself, as the Apostle teacheth, 1 *Cor.* ix. 15. how much more in Things simply Evil, in which neither Honour of God, nor Love of Man, is thought worthy to be regarded; neither yet is it sufficient that we keep ourselves by the Grace of God from giving of Offence, except withall we be armed against the taking of them when they are given by others; for how imperfect and lame is the Work of Grace in that Person, who wants Charity *to cover a Multitude of Offences?* as the Scripture speaks. Neither are you to be exhorted to this Grace onely upon the common Grounds of Christianity, which are, that Persons ready to take Offence, either want Charity to cover Offences, or Wisdome duly to weigh humane Frailties; or lastly, are gross though close Hypocrites, as Christ our Lord teacheth, *Matt.* vii. 1, 2, 3. as indeed in my own Experience, few or none have been found which sooner give Offence, than such as easily take it; neither have they ever proved sound and profitable Members in Societies, who have nourished this *touchy Humour.* But besides these, there are divers Motives provoking you above others to great Care and Conscience this way; as first, there are many of Strangers as to the Persons, so to the Infirmities one of another, and so stand in Need of Watchfulness this way, lest when such things fall out in Men and Women as you expected not, you be inordinately affected with them, which doth require at your hands much Wisdome and Charity for the covering and preventing of incident Offences that way. And lastly, your intended Course of Civil Community will minister continual Occasion of Offence, and will be as Fewel for that Fire, except you diligently quench it with *brotherly Forbearance:* And if taking offence causelessly or easily at Men's Doings, be so carefully to be avoided, how much more heed is to be taken, that we take not Offence at God himself? Which yet we certainly do, so oft as we murmure at his Providence in our Crosses, or bear impatiently such Afflictions, as wherewith he is pleased to visit us. Store up therefore Patience against the evil day; without which we take Offence at the Lord himself, in his holy

and just Works. A fourth Thing there is carefully to be provided for;
viz. That with your common Imployments, you join common Affections,
truly bent upon the General Good, avoiding as a deadly Plague of your
both common and special Comforts, all Retiredness of Minde for proper
Advantage; and all singularly affected every Manner of Way, let every
Man repress in himself, and the whole Body in each Person, as so many
Rebels against the common Good, all *private Respects of Mens selves*,
not sorting with the general Convenience. And as Men are careful not
to have a new House shaken with any Violence, before it be well settled,
and the Parts firmly knit; so be you, I beseech you, Brethren, much
more careful that the House of God, (which you are, and are to be) be
not shaken with unnecessary Novelties, or other Oppositions, at the first
settling thereof.

Lastly, Whereas you are to become a Body Politick, using amongst
yourselves Civil Government, and are not furnished with Persons of
special Eminency above the Rest, to be chosen by you into Office of
Government; Let your Wisdome and Godliness appear not onely in
choosing such Persons as do intirely love, and will promote the common
Good; but also in yielding unto them all due Honour and Obedience
in their lawful Administrations, not beholding in them the Ordinariness
of their Persons, but God's Ordinance for your Good: not being like the
foolish Multitude, who more honour the gay Coat, than either the virtuous Minde of the Man, or the glorious Ordinance of the Lord: but you
know better Things, and that the Image of the Lord's Power and Authority which the Magistrate beareth is honourable, in how mean Persons
soever; and this Duty you may the more willingly, and ought the more
conscionably to perform, because you are (at least for the present) to
have them for your ordinary Governours, which you yourselves shall
make choice of for that Work.

Sundry Things of Importance I could put you in Mind of, and of those
before mentioned in more Words; but I will not so far wrong your Godly
Mindes, as to think you heedless of these Things, there being also divers
amongst you, so well able both to admonish themselves and others of
what concerneth them. These few Things therefore, and the same in
few Words, I do earnestly commend unto your Care and Conscience,
joyning therewith, my daily and incessant Prayers unto the Lord, That
He who hath made the Heavens, and the Earth, and Sea, and all Rivers
of Waters, and whose Providence is over all his Works, especially over
all his dear Children for Good, would so guide and guard you in your

Wayes, as inwardly by his Spirit, so outwardly by the Hand of his Power, as that both you, and we also for and with you, may have after-matter of praising his Name all the Dayes of your and our Lives.   Fare you well in Him in whom you trust, and in whom I rest. . . .

Ebenezer Hazard, *Historical Collections* (Philadelphia, 1792), I, 96–99.

───◆───

56. A Pious Emigrant Ship (1629)

BY REV. FRANCIS HIGGINSON

Minister at Leicester, England; later pastor in Salem. — Bibliography: Winsor, *Narrative and Critical History*, III, 346; T. W. Higginson, *Life of Francis Higginson;* Channing and Hart, *Guide*, § 117.

. . . Any curious criticke that lookes for exactness of phrases ; or expert seaman that regards propriety of sea-termes, may be disappointed.

A true relation of the last voyage to New England, made the last summer, begun the 25th of April, being Saturday Anno Domini, 1629.

THE Company of New England, consisting of many worthy gentlemen in the citty of London, Dorchester, and other places, ayming at the glory of God, the propagation of the gospell of Christ, the conversion of the Indians, and the enlargement of the King's Majesty's dominions in America, and being authorised by his royal letters patents for that end, at their very great costs and charges, furnished 5 ships to go to New England, for the further settling of the English plantation that they had already begun there.

The names of the 5 shipps were as followeth.

The first is called the Talbot, a good and strong ship of 300 tunnes, and 19 pieces of ordinance, and served with 30 mariners.   This ship carried about an 100 planters, 6 goates, 5 great pieces of ordinance, with meale, oatmeale, pease, and all manner of munition and provision for the plantation for a twelve monthe.

The second the George, another strong ship also, about 300 tunnes, 20 pieces of ordinance, served with about 30 mariners ; her chiefe carriage were cattell, 12 mares, 30 kyne, and some goates : Also there gad in her 52 planters and other provision.

The third is called the Lyon's Whelpe, a neat and nimble ship of 120 tunnes, 8 pieces of ordinance, carrying in her many mariners and about 40 planters, specially from Dorcester and other places thereabouts, with provision, and 4 goats.

The 4th is called the Four Sisters, as I heare of about 300 tunns, which sayme ship carried many cattell, with passengers and provision.

The 5th is called the Mayflower, carrying passengers and provision. . . .

Monday morning (11th) blew a fayre wind from E. S. E. and the Lion's Whelpe having taken in all her provision for passengers, about 3 of the clocke in the afternoone we hoysed sayle for the Needles, and by God's guidance safely passed that narrow passage a little after 4 a clocke in the afternoone. And . . . entred into the sea. . . .

Thursday (21st) there being two ministers in the ship, Mr. Smith and myselfe, we endeavoured, together with others, to consecrate the day as a solemn fasting and humiliation to Almighty God, as a furtherance of our present worke. And it pleased God the ship was becalmed all day, so that we were freed from any encumbrance : And as sonne as we had done prayers, see and behold the goodnes of God, about 7 a clock at night the wind turned to N.E. and we had a fayre gale that night, as a manifest evidence of the Lord's hearing our prayers. I heard some of the mariners say, they thought this was the first sea-fast that ever was kept, and that they never heard of the like perfourmed at sea before.

Fryday (22d) the wind fayre, and east northerly, and for our purpose for New England. It did blow strongly and carried us on amayne with tossing waves, which did affright them that were not wonted to such sights.

Saturday (23d) the same wind blowing but more gently. Now we were comforted with the hope of my sonne Samuel's recovery of the small pockes. . . .

Wednesday (27th) the wind still N. and calme in the morning, but about noone there arose a So. wind, which encreased more and more, so that it proved to us that are landmen a sore and terrible storme ; for the wind blew mightily, the rayne fell vehemently, the sea roared and the waves tossed us horribly ; besides it was fearefull darke and the mariners mait was afraid ; and noyse on the other side with their running here and there, lowd crying one to another to pull at this and that rope. The waves powred themselves over the ship that the 2 boats were filled with water, that they were fayne to strike holes in the midst of them to let the water out. Yea by the violence of the waves the long boats roape which held it was broken, and it had like to have been washed overboard. had not the mariners with much payne and daunger recovered the same. But this lasted not many houres; after which it became a calmish day. All which while 1 lay close and warme in my cabine but farre from having list to sleepe with Jonah; my thoughts were otherwise employed as the tyme and the place required. Then I saw the truth of the scripture Psal. 107 from the 23d to the 32d. And my feare at this tyme was the lesse when I remembred what a loving friend of myne, a minister accustomed to sea stormes said to me that I might not be dismayed at such stormes, for they were ordinary at sea, and it seldome falls out that a ship perisheth at them if it have sea-roome. Which I the rather wryte that others as well as myselfe by the knowledge hereof may be encouraged and prepared against these ordinary sea-stormes. . . .

Thursday (11th) the wind at N. an easye gale and fayre morning. We saw a mountayne of ice shining as white as snow like to a great rocke or clift on shoare, it stood still and therefore we thought it to be on ground and to reach the bottome of the sea. For though there came a mighty streame from the north yet it moved not, which made us sound, and we found a banke of 40 fathom deepe whereupon we judged it to rest: and the height above was as much. . . .

Thursday (18th) wind full W. and contrary to us. This day a notorious wicked fellow that was given to swering and boasting of his formei wickednes . . . mocked at our daies of fast, railing and jesting against puritans, this fellow fell sick of the pockes and dyed. We sounded and found 38 fathom, and stayed, for a little while, to take some cod fish, and feasted ourselves merrily.

Fryday (19th) wind West still, a very fayre cleare day. About 4 a clock in the afternoone some went up to the top of the mast, and affirmed to our great comfort they saw land to the northeastward. . . .

Fryday (26th) a foggie morning, but after cleare and wind calme. We saw many scools of mackrill, infinite multitudes on every side oui ship. The sea was abundantly stored with rock weed and yellow flowers like gilly-flowers. By noon we were within 3 leagues of Capan, and as we sayled along the coast we saw every hill and dale and every island full of gay woods and high trees. The nearer we came to the shoare the more flowers in abundance, sometymes scattered abroad, sometymes joyned in sheets of 9 or 10 yards long, which we supposed to be brought from the low meadowes by the tyde. Now what with fine woods and greene trees by land, and these yellow flowers paynting the sea, made us all desirous to see our new paradise of New England, whence we saw such forerunning signals of fertilitie afarre off.   Coming neare the harbour towards night we takt about for sea-roome.

Saturday (27th) . . .

We had a westerly wind which brought us between 5 and 6 o'clock to a fyne and sweet harbour, 7 miles from the head point of Capan [Cape Ann]. . . .

(28th) The Sabbath, being the first we kept in America, and the 7th Lord's day after we parted with England.

Monday (29th) we came from Capan, to go to Naimkecke [Naum-keag, *i.e.* Salem], the wind northerly. . . . and this day, by God's blessing and their directions, we passed the curious and difficult entrance into the large spacious harbour of Naimkecke.   And as we passed along it was wonderful to behould so many islands replenished with thicke woode and high trees, and many fayre greene pastures.   And being come into the harbour we saw the George to our great comfort then being come on Tuesday which was 7 daies before us.   We rested that night with glad and thankful hearts that God had put an end to our long and tedious journey through the greatest sea in the world.

The next morning (30th) the governour came aboard to our ship, and bade us kindly welcome, and invited me and my wiffe to come on shoare, and take our lodging in his house, which we did accordingly. . . .

NOW in our passage divers things are remarkeable.

FIRST, through God's blessing our passage was short and speedy, for whereas we had 1000 leagues, that is 3000 miles English, to saile from Ould to New England, we performed the same in 6 weeks and 3 dayes.

Secondly, our passage was comfortable and easie for the most part, having ordinarily fayre and moderate wind, and being freed for the most part from stormie and rough seas, saving one night only, which we that were not used thought to be more terrible than indeed it was, and this was Wednesday at night May 27th.

Thirdly, our passage was also healthfull to our passengers, being freed from the great contagion of the scurvie and other maledictions, which in other passages to other places had taken away the lives of many. And yet we were in all reason in wonderful danger all the way, our ship being greatly crowded with passengers ; but through God's great good-ness we had none that died of the pockes but that wicked fellow that

o

scorned at fasting and prayer. There were indeed 2 little children, one of my owne and another beside ; but I do not impute it meerely to the passage ; for they were both very sickly children, and not likely to have lived long, if they had not gone to sea. And take this for a rule, if children be healthfull when they come to sea, the younger they are the better they will endure the sea, and are not troubled with sea-sicknes as older people are, as we had experience in many children that went this voyage. My wiffe indeed, in tossing weather, was something ill by vomiting, but in calme weather she recovered agayne, and is now much better for the sea sicknes. And for my owne part, whereas I have for divers yeares past been very sickly and ready to cast up whatsoever I have eaten, and was very sicke at London and Gravesend, yet from the tyme I came on shipboard to this day, I have been straungely healthfull. And now I can digest our ship diett very well, which I could not when I was at land. And indeed in this regard I have great cause to give God praise, that he hath made my coming to be a method to cure me of a wonderful weake stomacke and continual payne of melancholly wynd from the splene : Also divers children were sicke of the small pockes, but are safely recovered agayne, and 2 or 3 passengers towards the latter end of the voyage fell sicke of the scurvie, but coming to land recovered in a short tyme.

Fourthly, our passage was both pleasurable and profitable. For we received instruction and delight in behoulding the wonders of the Lord in the deepe waters, and sometimes seeing the sea round us appearing with a terrible countenance, and as it were full of high hills and deepe vallyes ; and sometimes it appeared as a most plain and even meadow. And ever and anon we saw divers kyndes of fishes sporting in the great waters, great grampuses and huge whales going by companies and puffing up water-streames. Those that love their owne chimney corner, and dare not go farre beyond their owne townes end shall neever have the honour to see these wonderfull workes of Almighty God.

Fifthly, we had a pious and christian-like passage ; for I suppose passengers shall seldom find a company of more religious, honest and kynd seamen than we had. We constantly served God morning and evening by reading and expounding a chapter, singing, and prayer. And the Sabbath was solemnely kept by adding to the former, preaching twise and catechising. And in our great need we kept 2 solemne fasts, and found a gracious effect. Let all that love and use fasting and praying take notise that it is as prevaileable by sea as by land, wheresoever it is faithfully performed. Besides the ship master and his company used every night to sett their 8 and 12 a clocke watches with singing a psalme and prayer that was not read out of a booke. This I wryte not for boasting and flattery; but for the benefit of those that have a mynd to come to New England hereafter, that if they looke for and desyre to have as prosperous a voyage as we had, they may use the same meanes to attayne the same. So letting passe our passage by sea, we will now bring our discourse to land on the shoare of New England, and I shall by God's assistance endeavour to speake nothing but the naked truth, and both acquaint you with the commodities and discommodities of the country.

Thomas Hutchinson, *A Collection of Original Papers Relative to the History of the Colony of Massachusets-Bay* (Boston, 1769), 32–46 *passim*.

————————◆————————

57. How a Settler left England (1630)

BY CAPTAIN ROGER CLAP

Clap was for twenty-one years Captain of the Castle of Boston. — Bibliography: Winsor, *Memorial History of Boston*, I, 424–428.

I THOUGHT good, my dear Children, to leave with you some Account of God's remarkable *Providences* to me, in bringing me into this Land, and placing me here among his dear Servants, and in his House, who am most unworthy of the least of his Mercies. The Scripture requireth us to tell God's wondrous Works to our Children, that they may tell them to their Children, that God may have Glory throughout all Ages. *Amen.*

I was Born in *England* in *Sallcom* in *Devonshire*, in the Year of our Lord 1609. My Father was a Man fearing God, and in good esteem among God's faithful Servants: His outward Estate was not great; I think not above *Eighty Pounds* per *Annum*. We were *Five Brethren* (of which I was the youngest) and *Two Sisters*. God was graciously pleased to breathe by his holy Spirit (I hope) in all our Hearts, if in mine; which I am not altogether without hopes of. *Four* of us *Brethren* lived at *home*: I did desire my dear Father (my dear Mother being dead) that I might live *abroad*, which he consented to: So I first went for tryal to live with a worthy Gentleman, Mr. *William Southcot*, who lived about *Three Miles* from the City of *Exon*. He was careful to keep a Godly Family. There being but a very mean Preacher in that Place, we went every Lord's-Day into the *City*, where were many famous Preachers of the Word of God. I then took such a liking unto the Revd. Mr. *John Warham*, that I did desire to live near him : So I removed (with my Father's Consent) into the *City*, and lived with one Mr. Mossiour, as famous a Family for Religion as ever I knew : He kept Seven or Eight Men, and divers Maid-Servants ; and he had a Conference upon a Question propounded once a Week in his own Family : With him I Covenanted. I never so much as heard of *New-England* until I heard of many godly Persons that were going there, and that Mr. *Warham* was to go also. My Master asked me whether I would go ? I told him were I not engaged unto him I would willingly go : He answered me, that should be no hindrance, I might go for him or for my self which I would. I then wrote to my Father who lived about *Twelve Miles* off, to Intreat his leave to go to *New-England* ; who was so much displeased at first, that he wrote me no Answer, but told my Brethren that I should not go. Having no Answer, I went and made my Request to him, and God so Inclined his Heart, that he never said me Nay : For now God sent the Reverend Mr. *Maverick*, who lived *Forty Miles* off, a Man I never saw before : He having heard of me, came to my Father's House, and my Father agreed that I should be with him and come under his Care, which I did accordingly.

Mind by what I have already expressed, That it was God that did draw me by his Providence out of my Father's Family, and weaned me from it by degrees ; It was God put it into my Heart to incline to Live abroad ; and it was God that made my Father willing. God by his Providence brought me near Mr. *Warham*, and inclined my Heart to his Ministry ; God by his Providence moved the Heart of my Master Mossiour to ask me whether I would go to *New-England* : It was God by his Providence that made me willing to leave my dear Father, and dear Brethren and Sisters, my dear Friends and Country : It was God that made my Father willing upon the first Motion I made in Person, to let me go : It was God that sent Mr. *Maverick* that pious Minister to me, who was unknown to him, to seek me out that I might come hither. So God brought me out of *Plymouth* the 20th of *March* in the Year, 1629, 30, and landed me in Health at *Nantasket*, on the 30th of May – 1630, I being then about the Age of *Twenty one* Years. *Blessed be God that brought me Here !* . . .

Capt. Roger Clap, *Memoirs* (Boston. 1731), 1–3.

58. A Godless Emigrant Ship (1679)

BY JASPAR DANKERS AND PETER SLUYTER

(TRANSLATED BY HENRY C. MURPHY, 1867)

These were two Dutch gentlemen who came over to find a site for a colony of the
"Labadist" sect, to which they belonged. — Bibliography: Long Island Historical
Society, *Memoirs*, I, Introduction; Winsor, *Narrative and Critical History*, IV,
429; Channing and Hart, *Guide*, § 102.

ALTHOUGH this is such a miserable subject, that I deliberated
long whether it were worth while to take any notice of it, yet
since one does not know when a matter can be serviceable, I will
nevertheless say something.

The persons who belonged to the ship were :

The captain, Thomas Singleton, an Englishman, and a quaker, from
London, I believe. He had his wife with him, who was quite young,
about 24 or 26 years old, and he was a person of 40 or 45. He was
not the best or most experienced seaman by a long distance. He was
proud and very assiduous or officious to please men, especially Margaret
and her man ; yet he had some amiable qualities, he was affable. He
was stingy; for when many mackerel were caught, he would not give
one to the poor sailors. He was even displeased if the sailors came
with their fish lines to fish near the place, where he was, because the
fish might come to their lines instead of his. His wife was a young,
worldly creature, who had not the least appearance of quakerism, but
entirely resembled an English lady fashioned somewhat upon the Dutch
model. She was proud, and wore much silver and gold ; and when
Margaret once spoke to him about it, he said, "I did not give it to
her." Whereupon Margaret asked, "Why did you give her money to
buy them?" To which he replied, "She wanted it."

The English mate, who afterwards became captain, was a passionate
person, inwardly still more than he showed outwardly, a great man-
pleaser where his interest was to be promoted. He was very close, but
was compelled to be much closer in order to please Margaret.

The Dutch mate, Evert, was a wicked, impious fellow, who also drank
freely. He was very proud of his knowledge and experience, which
were none of the greatest.

The boatswain, Abram, of Plymouth, was rough and wicked in his
orders, but he was a strong and able seaman. Robyn was the best.

I cannot permit myself to go further; it is too unpleasant a subject.

The passengers and crew were a wretched set. There was no rest, night or day, especially among the wives — a rabble I cannot describe. It was as if they were in the fish market or apple market, night and day, without cessation; where, indeed, some of them had obtained their living, and even in worse places. There were nine or ten of them always together. Among the men there were some persons who drank like beasts, yes, drank themselves dead drunk, as you may judge from the fact that two or three of them drank thirty-five gallons of brandy, besides wine from the time we left England or Holland. It is not to be told what miserable people Margaret and Jan were, and especially their excessive covetousness. In fine, it was a Babel. I have never in my life heard of such a disorderly ship. It was confusion without end. I have never been in a ship where there was so much vermin, which were communicated to us, and especially not a few to me, because being in the cordage at night I particularly received them. There were some bunks and clothes as full as if they had been sown. But I must forbear.

When we first came on board the ship we eat where we were, and with those we found there, but afterwards the messes were regulated, and we were placed on deck with five or six uncouth youngsters; where, nevertheless, we continued. This so exercised the other passengers, seeing us submit so willingly, that they themselves could no longer endure it, and desired us to come with them, and make a mess of eight. We had been compelled to buy our stores in England, as what we had were spoiled, or not sufficient. There was not a bit of butter or vinegar on the food during the whole voyage, except what we had purchased at Falmouth. I do not know how long it was we had nothing to eat except heads of salt fish, and those spoiled for the most part. We had to eat them till they were thrown overboard. Most of the time we had white peas, which our cook was too lazy to clean, or were boiled in stinking water, and when they were brought on the table we had to throw them away. The meat was old and tainted; the pork passable, but enormously thick, as much as six inches; and the bread was mouldy or wormy. We had a ration of beer three times a day to drink at table. The water smelt very bad, which was the fault of the captain. When we left England they called us to eat in the cabin, but it was only a change of place and nothing more. Each meal was dished up three times in the cabin, first for the eight passengers, then for the captain, mate, and wife, who sometimes did not have as good as we had, and lastly for Margaret and Mr. Jan who had prepared for them hardly any thing else except poultry and the like. But this is enough.

After we left England, I took upon myself, out of love of the thing, and because there were so few persons to work the ship, namely, ten in all, including the captain, to watch and attend the rudder, as well as to make observations in navigation ; but when I perceived the sailors, on this account, became lazy and depended upon me, I left the rudder-gang.   Nevertheless, when an English ship came near running us down in the watch off Cape Cod, causing thereby much uproar and confusion in our ship, I did my best to unfasten a rope which they could not make loose, at which the mate raved and swore, and for which he would have almost struck or killed me. When my comrade heard of it he wished me not to do any thing more, and that was my opinion. I could not, however, refrain from helping to the last, but I abandoned the watch, and so caused the mate to feel that we were not insensible, for there was nothing else to be done to him. He, nevertheless, invited us daily more than any one else.   Finally, when the voyage was completed, there was no one, either captain, or mate, or sailor, or Margaret, who said " We thank you," except our poor Robyn. We had a little package put in the ship at Falmouth, about a foot and a half square, on which the captain charged us four guilders freight, in the money of Holland. We represented to Margaret how we had managed with only one chest between us, although each passenger was entitled to have one of his own, but it was all to no purpose. Four guilders it must be. It was not that we had any difficulty in giving it, but it was only to be convinced of her unblushing avarice.   The mate's wife was the least evil-inclined, and listened most to what was said to her, which we hope will bear fruit. We have truly conducted ourselves towards all in general and each one in particular, so that not only has every one reason to be edified and convinced, but, by the grace of God, every one renders us testimony that we have edified and convinced them as well by our lives as our conversation.   Let him alone who is the author of all grace, receive therefor all the glory, to all eternity. Amen.

Journal of a Voyage to New York, in Long Island Historical Society, *Memoirs* (Brooklyn, 1867), I, 102–106.

PART IV

THE SOUTHERN COLONIES

CHAPTER IX — CONDITIONS

59. An Account of Virginia (1618)

BY WILLIAM STRACHEY

Strachey was Secretary and Recorder of the Colony. — Bibliography : Winsor, *Narrative and Critical History*, III, 156, 190–193 ; Maine Historical Society, *Collections*, III, 283–286 ; Moses Coit Tyler, *American Literature*, I, 41–45 ; Edward Eggleston, *Beginners of a Nation*, 59–72 ; Channing and Hart, *Guide*, § 97.

VIRGINIA BRITANNIA is a country in America ; yt lyeth betweene the degrees of 30 and 44 of the north latitude ; the bowndes whereof may well be thus layd : on the east runneth the great ocean, or mayne Atlantique Sea ; on the south side, Florida ; on the north, Nova Francia ; as for the west, the lymitts thereof are unknowne, only it is supposed there maye be found the discent into the South Sea, by the Spaniards called Mar del zur, so meeting with the doubtfull north-west passage, which leades into the east, to China, Cathay, Giapan, the Moluccaes, etc., now ymagined to be discovered by our countryman Hudson, and therefore, for the more certainty therof, the search anew this presente yeare, undertaken by Capt. Button, Capt. Nelson, and Capt.   : albeit, there be who affirme that if there should be a third land-locked sea, which hath no entercourse at all with the ocean (like the Mare Caspium, and Mare Mortuum in Palestina), yt lieth upon the north-west of America ; when yet againe Gemma Frisius recordeth three brethren that went this passage, and left a name unto the Streights of Anian, where the sea striketh south into Mar-del-zur, beyond America, whereby that streict is nowe called *Fretum trium fratrum* : we doe reade, likewise, of a Portugal that passed this streict, of whom Sir Martin Furbisher speaketh, that was imprisoned therefore many yeares in Lishbon, likewise Anordaneta, a frier of Mexico, came out of Mar del zur this way into Germany, whose card [map] hath ben seene by gentlemen of good credit

It is a spatious and ample tract of land; from north to south, upon a right lyne, yt maye be seven hundred myles; from east to west (in the narrowest place) supposed some three hundred myles, and in other places one thousand; a sufficient space, and ground ynough to satisfie the most covetous and wide affection of him whoe frames to himself any other end, then the only true one, of this plantation. . . .

Concerning the high-land little can we say as yet, because thereof little have we discovered; only some Indians' relations and some fewe daies' marches into the Monocan country of our owne, have instructed us thus far.

This high land, or Britannia, then, say we, is the mayne and firme continent, which extendeth, we wot not how far, beyond that cataract or fall of water, which the Indians call Paquachowng, from whence one daie's jorney into the Monocan country. Our elder planters (at their first comyng) proclaymed His Majestie king of the country at Mohominge (a neighbour village), and sett up a crosse there with His Majestie's name inscribed thereon, the said falls being one hundred and fifty myles up from the mouth of the bay, and where the current there at his head falleth, with an easye discent, three or four fathome downe into the low contry.

From the falls our men have heretofore marched (as the river led them) about forty or fifty miles, and fownd the high land woody, little champion, with rising hills, rockey and mountanous, and so all along from the north, by a sowth-west lyne, in so much as the more so-ward the further off from the bay are those mountaynes; from them fall certaine brooks, which after come to be five principall navigable rivers, these run from the nor-west into the so-est, and so into the west side of the bay, as hastinge themselves to emptye into the bay, to paye their tribute to the ocean.

The mountaines here at the head are of divers natures, for the rocks are of a constitution like milstones; some of a blue metallyne coulour, some of marble, etc.; and many pieces of scattered cristall we find, as throwne downe by water from the mountaines; for in wynter these mountaines are covered with snow, and when yt dissolveth, the waters fall with such violence that they cawse great inundacions in the narrowe vallies, which yet is scarse perceaved, being oute in the rivers. These waters wash from the rocks such glistening tinctures, that the grownd in some places seemeth as gilded, where both the rocks and the earth are so splendant to behold, that very good judgments would perhapps be

perswaded they conteyned more then probabilities. Sure it is that
some mineralls have ben there found. . . .

To the norward of the Falls, and bending to the nor-east, lieth the
skirt of this high land country, from whence the aforesaid five great
navigable rivers take their heads, which run through the low land (as
is before mencyoned) into the Chesapeack Bay; this quarter is altogither unknowen to us as yet, only herein are seated (say the Indians)
those people whom Powhatan calls the Bocootawwonaukes, who (he
saith) doe likewise melt copper and other mettalls; how true we must
leave to further discovery.

To the nor-ward againe of this, in the height of 44, lyeth the country
called Panaquid, the kingdome wherein our westerne colony, uppon the
river of Sachadehock, was sometyme planted, which is a high land, and
noe lesse fruictfull then these other parts, save only the extremity of the
winter's coldness makes yt lesse pleasant; yet did our men, in their yll
built and bleake cottages, endure one whole wynter there, without any
great losse or danger; nor is it more cold then the winter in Scotland;
and therefore, though that colonye be now discontynued, yet is not yt
the reason, but rather the death of the honorable gentleman, Sir John
Popham, knight, late lord chief justice, chief patron of the same. . . .

South Virginia is a very low, sandy soyle, without rocks, or any stones
at all; yt is thick sett with woodes of divers kindes, and in all things
resembleth North Virginia, excepted the lownesse of the land and want
of stones; yt hath divers rivers in yt, but none navigable to our knowledge; yt hath many islands, which lie into the sea before the firme
land, but the water is not deepe for shippinge betweene them and the
mayne. Yt is said to have of the same silke whereof the Chynoes
make their damaske, called by the Portugalls *sone del cherua*, in great
aboundaunce, and sondry apothecary druggs, which are nowe found
likewise as frequent in our north parte; it is a fruitfull countrey, and
not much subject to cold; in this country it was that Sir Walter Raleigh
planted his two colonies, in the islande aforesaid, called Roanoack. . . .

The sommer here is hot as in Spaine, the winter cold as in Fraunce
or England; the heate of the sommer is in June, July, and August, but
comonly the cool breeses asswage the vehemency of the heat; the
chief of winter is half December, January, February, and half March.

The temperature of this country doth well agree with the English
constitucions, being sometymes seasoned in the same, which hath appeared unto us by this, that albeyt, by many occasions, ill lodging at the

first (the poorer on the bare ground, and the best in such miserable
cotages at the best, as through which the fervent piercing heat of the
sun, which there (it is true) is the first cause, creating such sommer
fevers amongst them, found never resistaunce) hard fare, and their owne
judgments and saffeties instructing them to worke hard in the faint tyme
of sommer, (the better to be accomodated and fitted for the wynter,)
they have fallen sick, yet have they recovered agayne, by very small
meanes, without helpe of fresh diet, or comfort of wholsome phisique,
there being at the first but few phisique helpes, or skilfull surgeons, who
knew how to apply the right medecine in a new country, or to search
the quality and constitucion of the patient, and his distemper, or that
knew how to councell, when to lett blood, or not, or in necessity to use
a launce in that office at all. . . .

William Strachey, *The Historie of Travaile into Virginia Britannia* (Hakluyt Society, *Works issued, 1849*, London, 1849), 23-30 *passim*.

---

60. The Indians of the South (1618)

BY WILLIAM STRACHEY

For the author, see No. 59 above. — Bibliography of the Indians: Winsor, *Narrative and Critical History*, III, 156; Channing and Hart, *Guide*, § 80.

THEIRE habitations or townes are for the most part by the rivers, or
not far distant from fresh springs, comonly upon a rice of a hill,
that they may overlooke the river, and take every small thing into view
which sturrs upon the same. Their howses are not many in one towne,
and those that are stand dissite and scattered without forme of a street,
farr and wyde asunder.

As for their howses, who knoweth one of them knoweth them all, even
the chief kyng's house yt selfe, for they be all alike builded one to the
other. They are like garden arbours, at best like our sheppards' cotages, made yet handsomely enough, though without strength or gay-
nes[s], of such yong plants as they can pluck up, bow and make the
greene toppes meete togither, in fashion of a round roofe, which they
thatche with matts throwne over. The walls are made of barkes of
trees, but then those be principall howses, for so many barkes which goe
to the making up of a howse are long tyme of purchasing. In the midst
of the howse there is a louer, out of which the smoake issueth, the fier

being kept right under.   Every house comonly hath twoo dores, one
before and a posterne.   The doores be hung with matts, never locked
nor bolted, but only those matts be to turne upp, or lett fall at pleasure ;
and their howses are so comonly placed under covert of trees, that the
violence of fowle weather, snowe, or raine, cannot assalt them, nor the
sun in sommer annoye them ; and the roofe being covered, as I say,
the wynd is easily kept out, insomuch as they are as warme as stoves,
albeit very smoakye.   Wyndowes they have none, but the light comes in
at the doore and at the louer ; for should they have broad and open wyndowes in the quarters of their howses, they know not well how, upon
any occasion, to make them close and let in the light too, for glasse they
knowe not. . . .

By their howses they have sometymes a scæna, or high stage, raised
like a scaffold, of small spelts, reedes, or dried osiers, covered with matts,
which both gives a shadowe and is a shelter, and serves for such a covered place where men used in old tyme to sitt and talke for recreation
or pleasure, which they called præstega, and where, on a loft of hurdells,
they laye forth their corne and fish to dry.   They eate, sleepe, and dresse
their meate all under one roofe, and in one chamber, as it were.

Rownd about the house on both sides are theire bedstedes, which are
thick short posts stalkt into the ground, a foot high and somewhat more,
and for the sydes small poles layed along, with a hurdle of reeds cast
over, wherein they rowle downe a fyne white matte or twoo (as for a
bedd) when they goe to sleepe, and the which they rowle up againe in
the morning when they rise, as we doe our palletts, and upon these,
rownd about the howse, they lye, heads and points, one by the other,
especially making a fier before them in the midst of the howse, as they
doe usually every night, and some one of them by agreement maynteynes
the fier for all that night long ; . . .

About their howses they have commonly square plotts of cleered
grownd, which serve them for gardens, some one hundred, some two
hundred foote square, wherein they sowe their tobacco, pumpons, and
a fruit like unto a musk million, . . .

It is straung to see how their bodies alter with their dyett ; even as
the deare and wild beasts they seeme fatt and leane, strong and weake.
Powhatan and some others that are provident, roast their fish and flesh
upon hurdells, and reserve of the same untill the scarse tymes ; . . .

Their corne they eat in the eares greene, roasted, and sometyme bruising yt in a morter of wood with a little pestle ; they lap yt in rowlls

within the leaves of the corne, and so boyle yt for a deyntie ; they also reserve that corne late planted that will not ripe, by roasting yt in hott ashes, the which in wynter (being boyled with beanes) they esteeme for a rare dish, calling yt pausarawmena : . . .

Their drinck is, as the Turkes, cliere water ; for albeit they have grapes, and those good store, yet they have not falne upon the use of them, nor advised how to presse them into wyne.   Peares and apples they have none to make syder or perry of, nor honye to make meath, nor licoris to seeth in their water.   They call all things which have a spicy tast wassacan, which leaves a supposition that they maie have some kind of spice trees, though not perhapps such as ellswhere.

The men bestow their tymes in fishing, hunting, warres, and such manlike exercises, without the dores, scorninge to be seene in any effemynate labour, which is the cause that the women be very painfull and the men often idle. . . .

A kynd of exercise they have often amongst them much like that which boyes call bandy in English, and maye be an auncient game, as yt seem-eth in Virgil ; for when Æneas came into Italy at his marriage with Lavinia, King Latinus' daughter, yt is said the Troyans taught the Latins scipping and frisking at the ball.   Likewise they have the exercise of football, in which they only forceably encounter with the foot to carry the ball the one from the other, and spurned yt to the goale with a kind of dexterity and swift footmanship, which is the honour of yt ; but they never strike up one another's heeles, as we doe, not accompting that praiseworthie to purchase a goale by such an advantage. . . .

There is yet, in Virginia, no place discovered to be so savadge and simple, in which the inhabitaunts have not a religion and the use of bow and arrowes : all things they conceave able to doe them hurt beyond their prevention, they adore with their kind of divine worship, as the fier, water, lightning, thunder, our ordinaunce pieces, horses, etc. ; but their chief god they worship is no other, indeed, then the divell, whome they make presentments of, and shadow under the forme of an idoll, which they entitle Okeus, and whome they worship, as the Romans did their hurtfull god Vejovis, more for feare of harme then for hope of any good ; . . .

William Strachey, *The Historie of Travaile into Virginia Britannia*, in Hakluyt Society, *Works issued, 1849* (London, 1849), 70–82 *passim*.

61. Character of the First Colonists (1610)

BY GOVERNOR SIR THOMAS GATES

This is a somewhat prejudiced account, written by a man who had counselled the abandonment of the colony. — Bibliography: Winsor, *Narrative and Critical History*, III, 133–138; Edward Eggleston, *Beginners of a Nation*, 59–72, 94–97; Channing and Hart, *Guide*, § 97.

. . . NO man ought to judge of any Countrie by the fennes and marshes (such as is the place where *James* towne standeth) except we will condemne all England, for the Wilds and Hundreds of Kent and Essex. In our particular, wee haue an infallible proofe of the temper of the Countrie : for of an hundred and odd, which were seated at the *Falles*, vnder the gouernment of *Captaine Francis West*, and of an hundred to the Sea-ward on the South side of the riuer, (in the Countrie of the *Nansamunds*) vnder the charge of *Captaine Iohn Martin* ; of all these two hundred, there did not so much as one man miscarrie : when in *Iames* towne, at the same time, and in the same moneths, 100. sickned, and halfe the number died. . . .

If any man shall accuse these reports of partiall falshood, supposing them to be but Vtopian, and legendarie fables, because he cannot conceiue, that plentie and famine, a temperate climate, and distempered bodies, felicities, and miseries can be reconciled together, let him now reade with judgement, but let him not judge before he hath read.

The ground of all those miseries, was the permissiue prouidence of God, who, in the fore-mentioned violent storme, seperated the head from the bodie, all the vitall powers of regiment being exiled with *Sir Thomas Gates* in those infortunate (yet fortunate) Ilands. The broken remainder of those supplies made a great shipwrack in the continent of *Virginia*, by the tempest of dissention : euery man ouervaluing his own worth, would be a Commander : euery man vnderprising an others value, denied to be commanded. . . .

The next fountaine of woes was secure negligence, and improuidence, when euery man sharked for his present bootie, but was altogether carelesse of succeeding penurie. Now, 1 demand whether *Sicilia*, or *Sardinia*, (sometimes the barnes of *Rome*) could hope for increase without manuring ? A Colony is therefore denominated, because they should be *Coloni*, the tillers of the earth, and stewards of fertilitie : our mutinous loiterers would not sow with prouidence, and therefore they reaped the fruits of too deare-bought repentance. An incredible example of their idlenes, is the report of *Sir Thomas Gates*, who affirmeth, that after his first coming thither, he had seen some of them eat their fish raw, rather than they would go a stones cast to fetch wood and dresse it. *Dij laboribus omnia vendunt*, God sels vs all things for our labour, when *Adam* himselfe might not liue in paradice without dressing the garden.

Vnto idlenesse, you may ioyne treasons, wrought by those vnhallowed creatures that forsooke the Colony, and exposed their desolate brethren to extreame miserie. You shall know that 28. or 30. of the companie, were appointed (in the Ship called the Swallow) to truck for Corne with the *Indians*, and hauing obtained a great quantitie by trading, the most seditious of them, conspired together, persuaded some, & enforced others to this barbarous proiect. They stole away the Ship, they made a league amongst themselues to be professed pirates, with dreames of mountaines of gold, and happy robberies: thus at one instant, they wronged the hopes, and subuerted the cares of the Colony, who depended vpon their returne, fore-slowed to looke out for further prouision: they created the *Indians* our implacable enemies by some violence they had offered: they carried away the best Ship (which should haue been a refuge, in extremities) they weakened our forces, by substraction of their armes, and succours. These are that scum of men that fayling in their piracy, that beeing pinched with famine and penurie, after their wilde rouing vpon the Sea, when all their lawlesse hopes failed, some remained with other pirates, they men vpon the Sea, the others resolued to returne to England, bound themselues by mutuall oath, to agree all in one report, to discredit the land, to deplore the famyne, and to protest that this their comming awaie, proceeded from desperate necessitie: . . .

Vnto Treasons, you may ioyne couetousnesse in the Mariners, who for their priuate lucre partly imbezeled the prouisions, partly preuented our trade with the *Indians*, making the matches in the night, and forestalling our market in the day: whereby the Virginians were glutted with our trifles, and inhaunced the prices of their Corne and Victuall. That Copper which before would haue prouided a bushell, would not now obtaine so much as a pottle; *Non habet euentus fordida præda bonos*, the consequent of sordid gaine is vntimely wretchednesse.

Ioyne vnto these an other euill: there is great store of Fish in the riuer, especially of Sturgeon; but our men prouided no more of them, then for present necessitie, not barrelling vp any store against that season the Sturgeon returned to the sea. And not to dissemble their folly, they suffered fourteene nets (which was all they had) to rot and spoile, which by orderly drying and mending might haue been preserued : but being lost, all help of fishing perished. *Quanto maiora timentur dispendia, tanto promptior debet esse cautela,* fundamentall losses that cannot be repealed, ought with the greatest caution to be preuented.

The state of the Colony, by these accidents began to find a sensible declyning : which *Powhatan* (as a greedy Vulture) obseruing, and boyling with desire of reuenge, he inuited *Captaine Ratclife,* and about thirty others to trade for Corne, and vnder the colour of fairest friendship, he brought them within the compasse of his ambush, whereby they were cruelly murthered, and massacred. . . .

Cast vp this reckoning together : want of gouernment, store of idlenesse, their expectations frustrated by the Traitors, their market spoyled by the Mariners, our nets broken, the deere chased, our boats lost, our hogs killed, our trade with the *Indians* forbidden, some of our men fled, some murthered, and most by drinking of the brackish water of *Iames* fort weakened, and indaungered, famyne and sicknesse by all these meanes increased, here at home the monies came in so slowly, that the *Lo. Laware* could not be dispatched, till the Colony was worne and spent with difficulties : Aboue all, hauing neither Ruler, nor Preacher, they neither feared God nor man, which prouoked the wrath of the Lord of Hosts, and pulled downe his iudgements vpon them. *Discite iustitiam moniti.* Now, (whether it were that God in mercie to vs would weede out these ranke hemlockes ; or whether in iudgement to them he would scourge their impieties ; or whether in wisedome he would trie our patience, *Vt magna magnè desideremus,* that wee may beg great blessings earnestly) our hope is that our Sunne shall not set in a cloude, since this violent storme is dispersed, since all necessarie things are prouided, an absolute and powerful gouernment is setled, as by this insuing relation shall be described. . . .

A Trve Declaration of the Estate of the Colonie in Virginia, etc. (London, 1610), 32–43 *passim.*

CHAPTER X — VIRGINIA

62. The Founding of Virginia (1607)

BY CAPTAIN JOHN SMITH

Captain John Smith, as explorer, military man, and later President of the Colony, had the best of opportunities for seeing the foundation of Virginia, and a somewhat boastful way of relating it. — Bibliography: Winsor, *Narrative and Critical History*, III, 128–133, 153–154; notes to Edward Eggleston, *Beginners of a Nation*, 59–61; Channing and Hart, *Guide*, § 97.

A

True relation of such occurrences
and accidents of note, as hath hapned in *Virginia*, since the first planting of that Collony,
which is now resident in the South part
thereof, till the last returne.

KINDE Sir, commendations remembred, &c. you shall vnderstand that after many crosses in the downes by tempests wee arriued safely vppon the Southwest part of the great Canaries : within foure or fiue daies after we set saile for Dominica, the 26. of Aprill : the first land we made, wee fell with Cape Henry, the verie mouth of the Bay of Chissiapiacke, which at that present we little expected, hauing by a cruell storme bene put to the Northward : anchoring in this Bay twentie or thirtie went a shore with the Captain, and in comming aboard, they were assalted with certaine Indians, which charged them within Pistoll shot : in which conflict, Captaine Archer and Mathew Morton were shot : whereupon, Captaine Newport seconding them, made a shot at them, which the Indians little respected, but hauing spent their arrowes retyred without harme, and in that place was the Box opened, wherein the Counsell for Virginia was nominated : and arriuing at the place where wee are now seated, the Counsel was sworn, & the President elected, which for that yeare was Maister Edm. Maria Wingfield, where was made choice for our scituation, a verie fit place for the erectng of a great cittie, about which some contention passed betwixt Captaine Wingfield and Captaine Gosnold, notwithstanding all our prouision was brought a shore, and with as much speede as might bee wee went about our fortification

The two and twenty day of Aprill, Captain Newport and myselfe with

diuers others, to the number of twenty two persons, set forward to discouer the Riuer, some fiftie or sixtie miles, finding it in some places
broader, & in some narrower, the Countrie (for the moste part) on each
side plaine high ground, with many fresh Springes, the people in places
kindely intreating vs, daunsing and feasting vs with strawberies, Mul-
beries, Bread, Fish, and other their Countrie prouisions wherof we had
plenty : for which Captaine Newport kindely requited their least fauours,
with Bels, Pinnes, Needles, beades or Glasses, which so contented them
that his liberallitie made them follow vs from place to place, and euer
kindely to respect vs.   In the midway staying to refresh our selues in a
little Ile foure or fiue sauages came vnto vs which described vnto vs the
course of the Riuer, and after in our iourney, they often met vs, trading
with vs for such prouision as wee had, and arriuing at Arsatecke, hee
whom we supposed to bee the chiefe King of all the rest, moste kindely
entertained vs, giuing vs in a guide to go with vs up the Riuer to Powhatan, of which place their great Emperor taketh his name, where he that
they honored for King vsed vs kindely.   But to finish this discourie, we
passed on further, where within an ile we were intercepted with great
craggy stones y^e in midst of the riuer, where the water falleth so rudely,
and with such a violence, as not any boat can possibly passe, and so
broad disperseth the streame, as there is not past fiue or sixe Foote at a
low water, and to the shore scarce passage with a barge, the water floweth
foure foote, and the freshes by reason of the Rockes haue left markes of
the inundations 8. or 9. foote : The South side is plaine low ground, and
the north side high mountaines, the rockes being of a grauelly nature,
interlaced with many vains of glistring spangles.   That night we returned
to Powhatan : the next day (being Whitsunday after dinner) we returned
to the fals, leauing a mariner in pawn with the Indians for a guide of
theirs, hee that they honoured for King followed vs by the riuer.   That
afternoone we trifled in looking vpon the Rockes and riuer (furtherhe
would not goe) so there we erected a crosse, and that night taking our
man at Powhatans, Cap. Newport congratulated his kindenes with a Gown
and a Hatchet : returning to Arsetecke, and stayed there the next day to
obserue the height thereof, & so with many signes of loue we departed.
The next day the Queene of Agamatack kindely intreated vs, her people
being no lesse contented then the rest, and from thence we went to another
place (the name whereof I doe not remember) where the people shewed vs
the manner of their diuing for Mussels, in which they finde Pearles. . . .

John Smith, *A Trve Relation*, etc. (London, 1608), 1-3.

63. The Earliest Days of Virginia (1607)

BY PRESIDENT EDWARD MARIA WINGFIELD

Wingfield was first President of the Council in Virginia, a rival of Smith; he was removed after six months. — Bibliography: Winsor, *Narrative and Critical History*, III, 155; Edward Eggleston, *Beginners of a Nation*, 59–72, 94–97; Channing and Hart, *Guide*, § 97.

Here followeth what happened in James Towne, in Virginia, after Captayne Newport's departure for Engliund.

CAPTAYNE Newport, haueing allwayes his eyes and eares open to the proceedings of the Collonye, 3 or 4 dayes before his departure asked the President [Wingfield] how he thought himself settled in the gouernment : whose answere was, that no disturbance could indaunger him or the Collonye, but it must be wrought eyther by Captayne Gosnold or Mr Archer ; for the one was strong wth freinds and followers, and could if he would ; and the other was troubled wth an ambitious spirit, and would if he could.

The Captayne gaue them both knowledge of this, the President's opinion ; and moued them, with many intreaties, to be myndefull of their dutyes to His Ma^Tie and the Collonye.

June, 1607. — The 22th, Captayne Newport retorned for England ; for whose good passadge and safe retorne wee made many prayers to our Almighty God.

June the 25th, an Indian came to us from the great Poughwaton wth the word of peace ; that he desired greatly our freindshipp ; that the wyrounnces, Pasyaheigh and Tapahanagh, should be our freindes ; that wee should sowe and reape in peace, or els he would make warrs vpon them wth vs. This message fell out true ; for both those wyroaunces haue ever since remayned in peace and trade with vs. Wee rewarded the messinger wth many tryfles wch were great wonders to him.

This Powatan dwelleth 10 myles from vs, upon the River Pamaonche, wch lyeth North from vs. The Powatan in the former iornall mencōned (a dwellar by Captn. Newport's faults) ys a wyroaunce, and vnder this Great Powaton, wch before wee knew not.

July. — Th 3 of July, 7 or 8 Indians presented the President a dear from Pamaonke, a wyrouance, desiring our friendshipp. They enquired after our shipping ; wch the President said was gon to Croutoon. They fear much our shipps ; and therefore he would not haue them think it farr from us. Their wyrounce had a hatchet sent him. They wear well contented wth trifles. A little after this came a dear to the President from the Great Powatan. He and his messingers were pleased wth the like trifles. The President likewise bought diuers tymes dear of the Indyans; beavers, and other flesh; wch he alwayes caused to be equally deuided among the Collonye.

About this tyme, diuers of our men fell sick. We myssed aboue fforty before September did see us; amongst whom was the worthy and religious gent. Captn. Bartholomew Gosnold, vpon whose liefs stood a great part of the good succes and fortune of our gouernment and Collony. In his sicknes tyme, the President did easily foretel his owne deposing from his comaund; so much differed the President and the other Councellors in managing the government of the Collonye. . . .

The . . . of . . . Mr Kendall was put of from being of the Counsell, and comitted to prison; for that it did manyfestly appeare he did practize to sowe discord betweene the President and Councell.

Sicknes had not now left us vj [6] able men in our towne. God's onely mercy did now watch and warde for us: but the President hidd this our weaknes carefully from the salvages; neuer suffring them, in all his tyme, to come into our towne.

Septem. — The vjth of September, Pasyaheigh sent vs a boy that was run from vs. This was the first assurance of his peace wth vs; besides, wee found them no canyballs. . . .

The Councell demanded some larger allowance for themselues, and for some sick, their fauorites; wch the President would not yeeld vnto, wthout their warrants.

This matter was before ppounded by Captn. Martyn, but so nakedly as that he neyther knew the quantity of the stoare to be but for xiij weekes and a half, under the Cap Merchaunt's hand. He prayed them further to consider the long tyme before wee expected Captn. Newport's retorne; the incertainty of his retorne, if God did not fauo^r his voyage; the long tyme before our haruest would bee ripe; and the doubtfull peace that wee had wth the Indyans, wch they would keepe no longer then oportunity served to doe vs mischief.

It was then therefore ordered that euery meale of fish or fleshe should excuse the allowance for poridg, both against the sick and hole. The Councell, therefore, sitting againe upon this proposition, instructed in the former reasons and order, did not thinke fit to break the former order by enlarging their allowance, as will appeare by the most voyces reddy to be shewed vnder their handes. Now was the comon store of oyle, vinigar, sack, & aquavite all spent, saueing twoe gallons of each: the sack reserued for the Comunion Table, the rest for such extreamityes as might fall vpon us, wch the President had onely made knowne to Captn. Gosnold; of wch course he liked well. The vessells wear, therefore, boonged vpp. When Mr Gosnold was dead, the President did acquaint the rest of the Counsell wth the said remnant! but, Lord, how they then longed for to supp up that little remnant! for they had nowe emptied all their own bottles, and all other that they could smell out. . . .

The President, well seeing to what end their ympacience would grow, desired them earnestly & often tymes to bestow the Presidentshipp amonge themselues; that he would obey, a private man, as well as they could comand. But they refused to discharge him of the place; sayeing they mought not doe it, for that hee did his Matie good service in yt. In this meane tyme, the Indians did daily relieue us wth corne and fleshe, that, in three weekes, the President had reared vpp xx men able to worke; for, as his stoare increased, he mended the comon pott: he had laid vp, besides, prouision for 3 weekes' wheate before hand.

By this tyme, the Councell had fully plotted to depose Wingfield, ther then President; and had draune certeyne artycles in wrighting amongst themselues, and toke their oathes vpon the Evangelists to obserue them: . . .

Septem. — The 10 of September, Mr Ratcliff, Mr Smyth, and Mr Martynn, came to the President's tennt with a warrant, subscribed vnder their handes, to depose the President; sayeing they thought him very unworthy to be eyther P^esident or of the Councell, and therefore discharged him of bothe. He answered them, that they had eased him of a great deale of care and trouble; . . .

I will now write what followeth in my owne name, and giue the new President his title. I shall be the briefer being thus discharged. I was comytted to a Serieant, and sent to the pynnasse; but I was answered w^th, "If they did me wronge, they must answere it." . . .

Mr Archer, being settled in his authority, sought how to call Mr Smyth's lief in question, and had indited him vpon a chapter in Leuiticus for the death of his twoe men. He had had his tryall the same daie of his retorne, and, I believe, his hanging the same or the next daie, so speedie is our lawe there. But it pleased God to send Captn. Newport vnto us the same evening, to o^r vnspeakable comfort; whose arrivall saued Mr Smyth's leif and mine, because hee took me out of the pynnasse,

and gaue me leaue to lye in the towne.   Also by his comying was p^evented
a parliame^t, wch ye newe Counsailo^r, Mr Recorder, intended thear to summon.   Thus error begot error.

Captayne Newport, haueing landed, lodged, and refreshed his men,
ymploied some of them about a faire stoare house, others about a stove,
and his maryners aboute a church ; all wch workes they finished cheerefully and in short tyme.

January.— The 7 of January, our towne was almost quite burnt, with
all our apparell and prouision ; but Captn. Newport healed our wants,
to our great comforts, out of great plenty sent vs by the prouident and
loving care of our worthie and most worthie Councell. . . .

Edward Maria Wingfield, *A Discourse of Virginia* (edited by Charles Deane,
    Boston, 1860), 13–37 *passim.*

---

64. The Tale of Pocahontas (1613–1614)

BY RAPHE HAMOR

Hamor was Secretary of the Colony. There is no reason to doubt the substantial
truth of the story, as he tells it.— Bibliography: Winsor, *Narrative and Critical
History,* III, 139–146, 157; J. A. Doyle, *English Colonies, Virginia, Maryland, and
the Carolinas,* note to ch. vi; Edward Eggleston, *Beginners of a Nation,* 62, 63, 66–
68; Channing and Hart, *Guide,* § 97.

. . . IT CHAVNCED *Powhatans* delight and darling, his daughter
Pocahuntas, (whose fame hath euen bin spred in England
by the title of *Nonparella* of *Virginia*) in her princely progresse, if I may
so terme it, tooke some pleasure (in the absence of Captaine *Argall*) to
be among her friends at *Pataomecke,* (as it seemeth by the relation I had)
imploied thither, as shopkeepers to a *Fare,* to exchange some of her fathers
commodities for theirs, where residing some three months or longer, it
fortuned vpon occasion either of promise or profit, Captaine *Argall* to
arriue there, whom *Pocahuntas,* desirous to renue hir familiaritie with
the English, and delighting to see them, as vnknowne, fearefull perhaps to be surprised, would gladly visit as she did, of whom no sooner
had Captaine *Argall* intelligence, but he delt with an old friend, and
adopted brother of his *Iapazeus,* how and by what meanes he might procure hir captiue, assuring him, that now or neuer, was the time to pleasure him, if he entended indeede that loue which he had made profession
of, that in ransome of hir he might redeeme some of our English men

and armes, now in the possession of her Father, promising to vse her withall faire, and gentle entreaty: *Iapazeus* well assured that his brother, as he promised would vse her curteously promised his best indeuours and secresie to accomplish his desire, and thus wrought it, making his wife an instrument (which sex haue euer bin most powerfull in beguiling inticements) to effeἀ his plot which hee had thus laid, he agreed that himselfe, his wife, and *Pocahuntas*, would accompanie his brother to the water side, whether come, his wife should faine a great and longing desire to goe aboorde, and see the shippe, which being there three or foure times, before she had neuer seene, and should bee earnest with her husband to permit her : he seemed angry with her, making as he pretended so vnnecessary a request, especially being without the company of women, which denial she taking vnkindely, must faine to weepe (as who knows not that women can command teares) whereupon her husband seeming to pitty those counterfeit teares, gaue her leaue to goe aboord, so that it would please *Pochahuntas* to accompany her: now was the greatest labour to win her, guilty perhaps of her fathers wrongs, though not knowne as she supposed to goe with her, yet by her earnest perswasions, she assented : so forthwith aboord they went, the best cheere that could be made was seasonably prouided, to supper they went, merry on all hands, especially *Iapazeus* and his wife, who to express their ioy, would ere be treading vpō Capt. *Argals* foot, as who should say tis don, she is your own.   Supper ended, *Pochahuntas* was lodged in the Gunners roome, but *Iapazeus* and his wife desired to haue some conference with their brother, which was onely to acquaint him by what stratagem they had betraied his prisoner, as I haue already related : after which discourse to sleepe they went, *Pochahuntas* nothing mistrusting this policy, who neuertheless being most possessed with feare, and desire of returne, was first vp, and hastened *Iapazeus* to be gon.   Capt. *Argall* hauing secretly well rewarded him, with a small Copper kettle, and som other les valuable toies so highly by him esteemed, that doubtlesse he would haue betraied his owne father for them, permitted both him and his wife to returne, but told him, that for diuers considerations, as for that his father had then eigh of our English men, many swords, peeces, and other tooles, which he had at seuerall times by trccherons murdering our men, taken from them, which though of no vse to him, he would not redeliuer, he would reserve *Pocahuntas*, whereat she began to bef exceeding pensiue, and discontented, yet ignorant o[f] the dealing of *Iapazeus*, who in outward appearance was no les discontented that he should be the meanes of her captiuity, much a doe there was to perswade her to be patient, which with extraordinary curteous vsage, by little and little was wrought in her, and so to *Iames* towne she was brought, a messenger to her father forthwith dispatched to aduertise him, that his only daughter was in the hands & possession of the English : ther to be kept til such time as he would ransom her with our men, swords, peeces, & other tools treacherously taken from vs : the news was vnwelcome, and troublesom vnto him, partly for the loue he bare to his daughter, and partly for the loue he bare to our men his prisoners, of whom though with vs they were vnapt for any imployment) he made great vse : and those swords, and peeces of ours, (which though of no vse to him) it delighted him to view, and looke vpon.

He could not without long aduise & delibertion with his Councell, resolue vpon any thing, and it is true, we heard nothing of him till three moneths after, by perswasions of others he returned vs seauen of our men, with each of them a Musket vnseruiceable, and by them sent vs word, that whensoeuer wee pleased to deliuer his daughter, he would giue vs in satisfaction of his iniuries done to vs, and for the rest of our peeces broken and stolne from him, 500 Bushells of Corne, and be for euer friends with vs, the men and Peeces in part of payment we receiued : and returned him answere, that his daughter was very well, and kindely intreated, and so should be howsoeuer he dealt with vs : but we could not beleeue that the rest of our Arms were either lost, or stolne from him, and therefore till he returned them all, we would not by any meanes deliuer his daughter, and then it should be at his choice, whether he would establish peace, or continue enemies with vs.   This answere as it seemed, pleased him not very wel, for we heard no more from him till in March last, when with Captaine *Argalls* Shippe, and some other Vessells belonging to the Colony, Sir *Thomas Dale* with an hundred and fifty men well appointed, went vp into his owne Riuer, where his chiefest habitations were, and carried with vs his daughter, either to moue them to fight for her, if such were their courage and boldnesse,, as hath been reported, or to restore the residue of our demands, which were our peeces, swords, tooles. . . . we proceeded, and had no sooner entred the narrow of the riuer, the channell there lying within shot of the shoare, but they let their arrowes flie amongst vs in the shippe, themselues vnseene to vs, and in the forehead hurt one of our men, which might haue hazarded his life without the present help of a skilfull Chirurgion.

Being thus iustly prouoked, we presently manned our boates, went ashoare, and burned in that verie place some forty houses, and of the things we found therein, made freeboote and pillage, and as themselues afterward confest vnto vs, hurt and killed fiue or sixe of their men, with this reunge satisfying our selues, for that their presumption in shooting at vs, and so the next day proceeded higher vp the Riuer, . . . the time now come, we inquired what *Powhatan* would doe, . . . higher vp the riuer we went, and ancored neere vnto the chiefest residencie *Powhatan* had, at a towne called *Matchcot* where were assembled (which we saw) about 400 men, well appointed with their bowes and arrowes to welcome vs, here they dared vs to come a shoare, a thing which we purposed before, so a shoare we went, . . . two of *Powhatans* sonnes being very desirous to see their sister who was there present ashore with vs, came vnto vs, at the sight of whom, and her well fare, whom they suspected to be worse intreated, though they had often heard the contrary, they much reioiced, and promised that they would vndoubtedly perswade their father to redeeme her, and to conclude a firme peace foreuer with vs, and vpon this resolution the two brothers with vs retired aboarde, we hauing first dispatched two English men, Maister Iohn *Rolfe* and maister *Sparkes* to acquaint their father with the businesse in hand, the next day being kindly intreated, they returned, not at all admitted *Powhatans* presence, but spake with his brother *Apachamo*, his successor, one who hath already the commaund of all the people, who likewise promised vs his best indeauors to further our iust requests, and we because the time of the yeere being then Aprill, called vs to our businesse at home to prepare ground, and set corne for our winters prouision, vpon these termes departed, giuing them respite till haruest to resolue what was best for them to doe, with this Prouiso, that if finall agrcement were not made betwixt vs before that time, we would thither returne againe and destroy and take away all their corne, burne all the houses vpon that riuer, leaue not afishing *Weere* standing, nor a *Canoa* in any creeke therabout, and destroy and kill as many of them as we could.

Long before this time a gentleman of approued behauiour and honest cariage, maister Iohn *Rolfe* had bin in loue with *Pocahuntas* and she with him, which thing at the instant that we were in parlee with them, my selfe made knowne to Sir Thomas *Dale* by a letter from him, whereby he intreated his aduise and furtherance in his loue, if so it seemed fit to him for the good of the Plantation, and *Pocahuntas* her selfe, acquainted her brethren therewith ; which resolution Sir Thomas *Dale* wel approuing was the onely cause : hee was so milde amongst them, who otherwise would not haue departed their riuer without other conditions.

The bruite of this pretended marriage came soone to *Powhatans* knowledge, a thing acceptable to him, as appeared by his sudden consent thereunto, who some ten daies after sent an olde vncle of hirs, named *Opachisco*, to giue her as his deputy in the Church, and two of his sonnes to see the marriage solemnized, which was accordingly done about the fift of Aprill, and euer since we haue had friendly commerce and trade, not onely with *Powhatan* himselfe, but also with his subjects round about vs; so as now I see no reason why the Collonie should not thriue a pace. . . .

Raphe Hamor, *A Trve Discovrse of the Present Estate of Virginia*, etc. (reprinted, Albany, 1860), 4–11 *passim*.

---

65. The First Representative Assembly in America (1619)

BY JOHN TWINE

Twine was clerk of the Assembly, and wrote the official report. — Bibliography: Winsor, *Narrative and Critical History*, III, 142–145 ; Edward Eggleston, *Beginners of a Nation*, 70; Channing and Hart, *Guide*, § 97.

A REPORTE *of the manner of proceeding in the General assembly convented at James citty in Virginia, July 30, 1619, consisting of the Governor, the Counsell of Estate and two Burgesses elected out of eache Incorporation and Plantation, and being dissolved the 4th of August next ensuing.*

First. Sir George Yeardley, Knight Governor & Captaine general of Virginia, having sente his sumons all over the Country, as well to invite those of the Counsell of Estate that were absente as also for the election of Burgesses, there were chosen and appeared

For James citty

    Captaine William Powell,
    Ensigne William Spense.

For Charles citty

    Samuel Sharpe,
    Samuel Jordan.

For the citty of Henricus

    Thomas Dawse,
    John Polentine.

For Kiccowatan

    Captaine William Tucker,
    William Capp.

For Martin Brandon— Capt. John Martin's Pla'tation

   Mr Thomas Davis,
   Mr Robert Stacy.

For Smythe's hundred

   Captain Thomas **Graves,**
   Mr Walter Shelley.

For Martin's hundred

   Mr John Boys,
   John Jackson.

For Argall's guiffe

   Mr Pawlett,
   Mr Gourgaing.

For Flowerdieu hundred

   Ensigne Rossingham,
   Mr Jefferson.

For Captain Lawne's plantation

   Captain Christopher Lawne,
   Ensigne Washer.

For Captaine Warde's plantation

   Captaine Warde,
   Lieutenant Gibbes.

The most convenient place we could finde to sitt in was the Quire of the Churche Where Sir George Yeardley, the Governour, being sett down in his accustomed place, those of the Counsel of Estate sate nexte him on both handes, excepte onely the Secretary then appointed Speaker, who sate right before him, John Twine, clerke of the General assembly, being placed nexte the Speaker, and Thomas Pierse, the Sergeant, standing at the barre, to be ready for any Service the Assembly should comaund him. But forasmuche as men's affaires doe little prosper where God's service is neglected, all the Burgesses tooke their places in the Quire till a prayer was said by Mr. Bucke, the Minister, that it would please God to guide and sanctifie all our proceedings to his owne glory and the good of this Plantation. Prayer being ended, to the intente that as we had begun at God Almighty, so we might proceed wth awful and due respecte towards the Lieutenant, our most gratious and dread Soveraigne, all the Burgesses were intreatted to retyre themselves into the body of the Churche, wch being done, before they were fully admitted, they were called in order and by name, and so every man (none staggering at it) tooke the oathe of Supremacy, and then entred the Assembly. . . .

These obstacles removed, the Speaker, who a long time had bene extreame sickly and therefore not able to passe through long harrangues, delivered in briefe to the whole assembly the occasions of their meeting. Which done, he read unto them the comission for establishing the Counsell of Estate and the general Assembly, wherein their duties were described to the life.

Having thus prepared them, he read over unto them the greate Charter, or comission of priviledges, orders and lawes, sent by Sir George Yeardly out of Englande. Which for the more ease of the Committies, having divided into fower books, he read the former two the same fore-noon for expeditious sake, a second time over and so they were referred to the perusall of twoe Comitties, wch did reciprocally consider of either, and accordingly brought in their opinions. But some men may here objecte to what ende we should presume to referre that to the examination of the Comitties wch the Counsell and Company in England had already resolved to be perfect, and did expecte nothing but our assente thereunto? To this we answere that we did it not to the ende to correcte or controll anything therein contained, but onely in case we should finde ought not perfectly squaring wth the state of this Colony or any lawe wch did presse or binde too harde, that we might by waye of humble petition, seeke to have it redressed, especially because this great Charter is to binde us and our heyers for ever. . . .

After dinner the Governo^r and those that were not of the Comitties sate a seconde time, while the said Comitties were employed in the perusall of those twoe bookes. And whereas the Speaker had propounded fower severall objects for the Assembly to consider on : namely, first, the great charter of orders, lawes, and priviledges ; Secondly, which of the instructions given by the Counsel in England to my lo : la : warre, Captain Argall or Sir George Yeardley, might conveniently putt on the habite of lawes ; Thirdly, what lawes might issue out of the private conceipte of any of the Burgesses, or any other of the Colony ; and lastly, what petitions were fitt to be sente home for England. It pleased the Governou^r for expedition sake to have the second objecte of the fower to be examined & prepared by himselfe and the Non-Comitties. Wherin after having spente some three howers conference, the twoe Committies brought in their opinions concerning the twoe former bookes, (the second of which beginneth at these words of the Charter : And foreasmuche as our intente is to establish one equall and uniforme kinde of government over all Virginia &c.,) wch the whole Assembly, because it was late, deffered to treatt of till the next morning.

SATTURDAY, July 31.

The nexte daye, therefore, out of the opinions of the said Comitties, it was agreed, these Petitions ensuing should be framed, to be presented to the Treasurer, Counsel & Company in England. . . .

These petitions thus concluded on, those twoe Comitties broughte me a reporte what they had observed in the two latter bookes, wch was noth-ing else but that the perfection of them was suche as that they could finde nothing therein subject to exception, only the Governo^rs particular opin-ion to my selfe in private hathe bene as touching a clause in the thirde booke, that in these doubtfull times between us and the Indians, it would beehoove us not to make as lardge distances batween Plantation and Plan-tation as ten miles, but for our more strength ande security to drawe nearer together.

At the same time, there remaining no farther scruple in the mindes of the Assembly, touching the said great Charter of lawes, orders and privi-ledges, the Speaker putt the same to the question, and so it had both the general assent and the applause of the whole assembly, who, as they pro-fessed themselves in the first place most submissivily thankfull to almighty god, therefore so they commaunded the Speaker to returne (as nowe he doth) their due and humble thankes to the Treasurer, Counsell and com-pany for so many priviledges and favours as well in their owne names as in the names of the whole Colony whom they represented,

This being dispatched we fell once more debating of suche instructions given by the Counsell in England to several Governo^rs as might be con-verted into lawes, the last whereof was the Establishment of the price of Tobacco, namely, of the best at 3 d and the second at 18 d the pounde. . . .

SUNDAY, Aug. 1.

Mr. Shelley, one of the Burgesses, deceased.

MUNDAY, Aug. 2.

. . . , the Committies appointed to consider what instructions are fitt to be converted into lawes, brought in their opinions, and first of some of the general instructions.

> Here begin the lawes drawen out of the In-
> structions given by his Mat^ies Counsell
> of Virginia in England to my lo : la
> warre, Captain Argall and Sir George
> Yeardley, knight.

By this present Generall Assembly be it enacted, that no injury or oppression be wrought by the Englishe against the Indians whereby the present peace might be disturbed and antient quarrells might be revived. And farther be it ordained that the Chicohomini are not to be excepted out of this lawe ; untill either that suche order come out of Englande, or that they doe provoke us by some newe injury.

Against Idleness, Gaming, durunkenes & excesse in apparell the Assembly hath enacted as followeth :

First, in detestation of Idlenes be it enacted, that if any men be
founde to live as an Idler or renagate, though a freedman, it shalbe lawfull for that Incorporation or Plantation to wch he belongeth to appoint
him a M^r to serve for wages, till he shewe apparant signes of amendment.

Against gaming at dice & Cardes be it ordained by this present assembly that the winner or winners shall lose all his or their winninges and both
winners and loosers shall forfaicte ten shillings a man, one ten shillings
whereof to go to the discoverer, and the rest to charitable & pious uses
in the Incorporation where the faulte is comitted.

Against drunkenness be it also decreed that if any private person be
found culpable thereof, for the first time he is to be reprooved privately
by the Minister, the second time publiquely, the thirde time to lye in
boltes 12 howers in the house of the Provost Marshall & to paye his
fee, and if he still continue in that vice, to undergo suche severe punishment as the Governo^r and Counsell of Estate shall thinke fitt to be
inflicted on him.   But if any officer offende in this crime, the first time
he shall receive a reprooff from the Governour, the second time he shall
openly be reprooved in the churche by the minister, and the third time
he shall first be comitted and then degraded.   Provided it be understood that the Governo^r hath alwayes power to restore him when he
shall, in his discretion thinke fitte.

Against excesse in apparell that every man be cessed in the churche
for all publique contributions, if he be unmarried according to his owne
apparrell, if he be married according to his owne and his wives, or either
of their apparrell. . . .

Be it enacted by this present assembly that for laying a surer foundation of the conversion of the Indians to Christian Religion, eache towne,
citty, Borrough, and particular plantation do obtaine unto themselves by
just means a certaine number of the natives' children to be educated by
them in the true religion and civile course of life — of wch children the
most towardly boyes in witt & graces of nature to be brought up by them
in the first elements of litterature, so to be fitted for the Colledge intended
for them that from thence they may be sente to that worke of conversion.

As touching the business of planting corne this present Assembly doth
ordaine that yeare by yeare all & every householder and householders have
in store for every servant he or they shall keep, and also for his or their
owne persons, whether they have any Servants or no, one spare barrell of

corne, to be delivered out yearly, either upon sale or exchange as need shall require. For the neglecte of wch duty he shalbe subjecte to the censure of the Govern^r and Counsell of Estate. Provided always that the first yeare of every newe man this lawe shall not be of force.

About the plantation of Mulberry trees, be it enacted that every man as he is seatted upon his division, doe for seven years together, every yeare plante and maintaine in growte six Mulberry trees at the least, and as many more as he shall thinke conveniente and as his virtue & Industry shall move him to plante, and that all suche persons as shall neglecte the yearly planting and maintaining of that small proportion shalbe subjecte to the censure of the Governour & the Counsell of Estate.

Be it farther enacted as concerning Silke-flaxe, that those men that are upon their division or setled habitation doe this next yeare plante & dresse 100 plantes, wch being founde a comedity, may farther be increased. And whosoever do faill in the performance of this shalbe subject to this punishment of the Governour & Counsell of Estate.

For hempe also both Englishe & Indian, and for Englishe flax & Anniseeds, we do require and enjoine all householders of this Colony that have any of those seeds to make tryal thereofe the nexte season.

Moreover be it enacted by this present Assembly, that every householder do yearly plante and maintaine ten vines untill they have attained to the art and experience of dressing a Vineyard either by their owne industry or by the Instruction of some Vigneron. And that upon what penalty soever the Governo^r and Counsell of Estate shall thinke fitt to impose upon the neglecters of this acte.

Be it also enacted that all necessary tradesmen, or so many as need shall require, suche as are come over since the departure of Sir Thomas Dale, or that shall hereafter come, shall worke at their trades for any other man, each one being payde according to the quality of his trade and worke, to be estimated, if he shall not be contented, by the Governo^r and officers of the place where he worketh.

Be it further ordained by this General Assembly, and we doe by these presents enacte, that all contractes made in England between the owners of lande and their Tenants and Servantes wch they shall sende hither, may be caused to be duely performed, and that the offenders be punished as the Governour and Counsell of Estate shall thinke just and convenient.

Be it established also by this present Assembly that no crafty or advantagious means be suffered to putt in practise for the inticing awaye the Tenants or Servants of any particular plantation from the place where

they are seatted. And that it shalbe the duty of the Governo^r & Counsell of Estate most severely to punishe both the seducers and the seduced,
and to returne these latter into their former places. . . .

TUESDAY, Aug. 3, 1619.

. . . Captaine William Powell presented a Petition to the generall Assembly against one Thomas Garnett, a servant of his, not onely for extreame neglect of his business to the great loss and prejudice of the said
Captaine, and for openly and impudently abusing his house, . . . but
also for falsely accusing him to the Governo^r both of Drunkenes & Thefte,
and besides for bringing all his fellow servants to testifie on his side,
wherein they justly failled him. It was thought fitt by the general assembly (the Governour himselfe giving sentence), that he should stand
fower dayes with his eares nayled to the Pillory, viz: Wednesday, Aug.
4th, and so likewise Thursday, fryday and Satturday next following, and
every of those fower dayes should be publiquely whipped. Now, as touching the neglecte of his worke, what satisfaction ought to be made to his
M^r for that is referred to the Governour and Counsell of Estate.

The same morning the lawes abovewritten, drawen out of the instructions, were read, and one by one thoroughly examined, and then
passed once again the general consente of the whole Assembly. . . .

WEDNESDAY Aug. 4th.

This daye (by reason of extream heat, both paste and likely to ensue,
and by that meanes of the alteration of the healthes of diverse of the
general Assembly) the Governour, who himselfe also was not well, resolved
should be the last of this first session ; so in the morning the Speaker (as
he was required by the Assembly) redd over all the lawes and orders
that had formerly passed the house, to give the same yett one reviewe
more, and to see whether there were any thing to be amended or that
might be excepted againste. This being done, the third sorte of lawes
wch I am nowe coming to sett downe, were read over thoroughly discussed,
wch together wth the former, did now passe the last and finall consente of
the General Assembly.

A third sorte of lawes, suche as may issue out of
every man's private conceipte.

. . . All Ministers in the Colony shall once a year, namely, in the
moneth of Marche, bring to the Secretary of Estate a true account of all
Christenings, burials and marriages, upon paine, if they faill, to be cen-

sured for their negligence by the Governo[r] and Counsell of Estate ; likewise, where there be no ministers, that the comanders of the place doe
supply the same duty. . . .

All ministers shall duely read divine service, and exercise their ministerial function according to the Ecclesiasticall lawes and orders of the
churche of Englande, and every Sunday in the afternoon shall Catechize
suche as are not yet ripe to come to the Com.　And whosoever of them
shalbe found negligent or faulty in this kinde shalbe subject to the censure of the Governo[r] and Counsell of Estate. . . .

All persons whatsoever upon the Sabaoth daye shall frequente divine
service and sermons both forenoon and afternoon, and all suche as beare
arms shall bring their pieces, swordes, poulder and shotte.　And every
one that shall transgresse this lawe shall forfaicte three shillinges a time
to the use of the churche, all lawfull and necessary impediments excepted.
But if a servant in this case shall wilfully neglecte his M[rs] commande he
shall suffer bodily punishmente.

No maide or woman servant, either now resident in the Colonie or hereafter tò come, shall contract herselfe in marriage w[th]out either the consente
of her parents, or of her M[r] or M[ris], or of the magistrat and minister of
the place both together.　And whatsoever minister shall marry or contracte
any suche persons w[th]out some of the foresaid consentes shalbe subjecte to the severe censure of the Govern[r] and Counsell of Estate. . . .

In sume Sir George Yeardley, the Governo[r] prorogued the said General Assembly till the firste of Marche, which is to fall out this present
yeare of 1619, and in the mean season dissolved the same.

Thomas H. Wynne and W. S. Gilman, editors, *Colonial Records of Virginia*
(Richmond, 1874), 9–32 *passim*.

66.　The " Dismasking of Virginia " (1622)

BY CAPTAIN NATHANIEL BUTLER

Butler was Governor of the Somers Islands (Bermuda), and had been accused of
extortion.　This paper is therefore tinged by malice. — Bibliography : Winsor, *Narrative and Critical History*, III, 144–146; J. A. Doyle, *English in America, Virginia*,
227–228; Channing and Hart, *Guide*, § 97.

I FOUND the plantations generally seated upon meer salt marshes, full
of infectious boggs and muddy creeks and lakes, and hereby subjected to all those inconveniences and diseases which are so commonly

Q

found in the most unsound and most unhealthy parts of England, whereof every country and climate hath some.

I found the shores and sides of those parts of the main river, where our plantations are settled, every where so shallow that no boats can approach the shores; so that besides the difficulty, danger and spoil of goods in the landing of them, the poor people are forced to the continual wading and wetting themselves, and that in the prime of winter, when the ships commonly arrive, and thereby get such violent surfeits of cold upon cold as seldom leave them until they leave to live.

The new people that are yearly sent over, which arrive here for the most part very unseasonably in winter, find neither guest-house, inn, nor any the like place to shroud themselves in at their arrival; no, not so much as a stroke given towards any such charitable work, so that many of them, by want hereof, are not only seen dying under hedges, and in the woods, but being dead lye some of them for many days unregarded and unburied.

The colony was this winter in much distress of victual, so that English meal was sold at the rate of thirty shillings a bushel, their own native corn, called maize, at ten and fifteen shillings ℔ bushel, the which, howsoever it lay heavy upon the shoulders of the generality, it may be suspected not to be unaffected by some of the chief, for they only having the means in those extremities to trade with the natives for corn, do hereby engross all into their own hands, and to sell it abroad at their own prices, and I myself have heard from the mouth of a prime one among them that he would never wish that their own corn should be cheaper amongst them than eight shillings the bushel.

Their houses are generally the worst that ever I saw, the meanest cottages in England being every way equal (if not superior) with the most of the best, and besides, so improvidently and scatteringly are they seated one from another, as partly by their distance, but especially by the interposition of creeks and swamps, as they call them, they offer all advantages to their savage enemies, and are utterly deprived of all sudden recollection of themselves upon any terms whatsoever.

I found not the least piece of fortification; three pieces of ordnance only mounted at James City, and one at Flowerde Hundreds, but never a one of them serviceable, so that it is most certain that a small bark of a hundred tun may take its time to pass up the river in spite of them, and coming to an anchor before the town may beat all their houses down about their years, and so forcing them to retreat into the woods may land under the favour of their ordnance and rifle the town at pleasure.

Expecting, according to their printed books, a great forwardness of divers and sundry commodities at mine arrival, I found not any one of them so much as in any towardness of being, for the iron works were utterly wasted, and the men dead, the furnaces for glass and pots at a stay, and small hopes ; as for the rest they were had in a general derision even amongst themselves, and the pamphlets that had published their, being sent thither by hundreds, were laughed to scorn, and every base fellow boldly gave them the lye in divers particulars ; so that tobacco only was the business, and for ought that I could hear every man madded upon that little thought or looked for anything else.

I found the ancient plantations of Henrico and Charles City wholly quitted and left to the spoil of the Indians, who not only burnt the houses, said to be once the best of all others, but fell upon the poultry, hogs, cows, goats and horses, whereof they killed great numbers, to the great grief as well as ruin of the old inhabitants, who stick not to affirm that these were not only the best and healthiest parts of all others, but might also, by their natural strength of situation, have been the most easily preserved of all others.

Whereas, according to his Majesty's most gracious letters-patents, his people are as near as possibly may be to be governed after the excellent laws and customs of England, I found in the Government here not only ignorant and enforced strayings in divers particulars, but wilful and intended ones ; in so much as some who urged due conformity have in contempt been termed men of law, and were excluded from those rights which by orderly proceedings they were elected and sworn unto here.

There having been, as it is thought, not fewer than ten thousand souls transported thither, there are not, thro' the aforementioned abuses and neglects, above two thousand of them to be found alive at this present * * * many of them also in a sickly and desperate state. So that it may undoubtedly be expected that unless the confusions and private ends of some of the Company here, and the bad execution in seconding them by their agents there, be redressed with speed by some divine and supream hand, that instead of a plantation it will get the name of a slaughter-house, and so justly become both odious to ourselves and contemptible to all the world.

Abstract of the Proceedings of the Virginia Company of London, in Virginia Historical Society, *Collections*, VIII (Richmond, 1889), II, 171–173.

67. Defence of the Virginia Charter (1623)

BY THE VIRGINIA COMPANY

For the status of this Company, see No. 50 above. The document is self-explanatory. — Bibliography: Winsor, *Narrative and Critical History*, 145–146; Edward Eggleston, *Beginners of a Nation*, 66–67; Channing and Hart, *Guide*, § 97.

AT AN extraordinary court held the 12th of April, 1623, the Lord Cavendish acquainted the Company that the cause of calling this court at so unseasonable a time was to acquaint them how that Alderman Johnson, together with some others, his associates, had presented a petition to his Majesty complaining much of the misgovernment of the Companies and plantations these four last years, which, to the intent it might not make any impression in his royal breast to the prejudice of the Company, his Lordship conceived that the Company were to think of some present course to give his Majesty satisfaction by a declaration of both the estate of the colony and of the carriage of business here at home by the Company. But to the intent they might proceed herein with the greater certainty, the court sent some of the Company to Mr. Alderman Johnson, to desire him either to send or bring them a copy of the said petition which he had delivered, who sent answer by them that they had no copy of the petition, nor did know of any that did keep a copy thereof, and that the petition was not against the Company, which was likewise affirmed by some of them who were present in court and had been at the delivery of that petition, desiring the Company not to engage themselves therein until they saw the petition (professing that they intended the good of the plantation and the Company as much as any other); whereupon they were desired to declare what it was they had complained of, and who the persons were, it being said by the Lord Cavendish that if they did not find themselves agrieved with the Company they ought not to have complained unto his Majesty until they had acquainted the court with their grievances, and seen what remedy by them would have been apply'd. Whereupon Mr. Palavicnie (being one of those that was at the delivery of the petition) said that the things which they chiefly complained of were, perhaps, such as the Company had been often moved about and would give no redression.

Whereupon Sir Edward Sackvill said that although Alderman Johnson would not send a copy of the petition, yet himself and some others in the court could fully inform the Company and certainly of the substance thereof. He said, therefore, that petition was in effect a comparison of the Government in former times with the latter four years, and that in three points.

First, that in former times the Government was so mild and moderate as a multitude of adventurers were brought in, but now there was much oppression and injury offered both to adventurers and planters.

Secondly, that whereas formerly things were carried quietly both here and in the plantations, now there was nothing but contentions and dissentions, to the ruin almost and overthrow of the plantations.

Thirdly, that whereas divers excellent commodities were formerly set up, now there was nothing but smoke and tobacco; whereupon they desired his Majesty that a commission might be awarded that these things might be amended.

This being delivered upon his certain knowledge to be the substance of the petition, and confirmed by the Lord Cavendish, it was, by a general erection of hands, conceived that this petition and complaint was against the Company itself, and so that they accordingly ought to justify themselves and to defend their proceedings against these unjust and untrue informations, but yet withall for the very issue of the petition itself, the court liked very well, and, by erection of hands, ordered that a petition should be presented in the name of the Company to beseech his Majesty that the Lords of the Council might have the examinations of these things, and that their innocency or guiltiness might be clear or punished, and in the meanwhile for a true information of his Majesty, the Lord Cavendish presented to the court two several writings, the one being a declaration of the State of Virginia comparatively with what had been done in former times, which, by order of the Earl of Southampton, was drawn up by some of the Council at Christmas last, which being now read and weighed from point to point, was, with some small alterations, approved and confirmed by the court and ordered to be delivered to his Majesty as their act, being this which followeth, viz :

A Declaration of the present State of Virginia humbly presented to the King's most Excellent Majesty by the Virginia Company.

May it please Your Majesty:

In the end of December, in the year 1618, being the 12th year after the beginning of this plantation, and after the expense of four-score thousand pounds of the publick stock and upwards, besides other sums

of voluntary planters, there were remaining there in the colony about
six hundred persons — men, women, and children — and cattle about
three hundred at the most, and the Company was then left in debt
about five thousand pounds.

At this time (through God's blessing), notwithstanding the great
mortalities which, in some of these four latter years, have generally
seized upon all those parts of America, and besides the late massacre
of three hundred and fifty persons, and a great mortality thereby occasioned by being driven from their habitation and provisions, there are
remaining, as we compute, above five and twenty hundred persons, sent
with the expense only of thirty thousand pounds of the public stock
besides the charges of particular societies and planters. And the cattle,
what by new supplies and what by increase of the former provision, are
multiplied to above one thousand of beasts, and of swine an infinite
number ; and the old debt of the Company hath been discharged.

At the beginning of these four last years the only commodities of
price, and upon which only a valuation was set to maintain the trade,
were tobacco and sassafras, for in the two last years before there was no
course taken up for the setting up of any others through the poverty of
the Company.

During these 4 last years there hath been expended in setting up
of iron works (the oar whereof is there in great plenty and excellent)
above five thousand pounds, which work being brought in a manner to
perfection was greatly interrupted by the late massacre, but ordered to
be restored again with all possible diligence.

For the making of wine, it is to be known that the soil there doth
of itself produce vines in great abundance and some of a very good
sort, besides divers plantations been sent thither of the better hands of
Christendom.

There hath also been sent thither eight vigneroons procured from
Languedock, and careful order hath been taken for setting up of that
commodity, which we doubt not in a short time will show itself in great
plenty, and had not the business been interrupted by the massacre e'er
this effect had been seen, there being divers vineyards planted in the
country whereof some contained ten thousand plants.

For silk the country is full of mulberry trees of the best kind, and
general order taken for the planting of them abundantly in all places
inhabited. True it is that the silkworm seed hath, till this last year,
miscarried, to the great grief of the Company, having had large supplie?

thereof from your Majesty's store; but in September last we sent near 80 ounces with extraordinary care and provision that we doubt not but that it will prosper and yield a plentiful return, there being sent also men skilful to instruct the planters for all things belonging to bring the silk to perfection, and we have notice that the seed hath been received safe and order given for the disposing and nourishing them through the whole plantation.

There have been sent also, at the great charge of the Company, skilful men from Germany for setting up of sawing mills, and divers shipwrights from hence for making boats and ships, and others for salt works and others for other commodities, the good effect whereof we doubt not will shortly appear.

We will not here enlarge in declaring the great and assidual care which the Council and Company, with their principal officers, have from time to time taken, as well from reclaiming the colony from overmuch following tobacco (every man being now stinted to a certain proportion), as also in setting forward the other staple and rich commodities, as well by the charges and provisions aforesaid as likewise by setting upon them a competent valuation, not doubting but that whosoever will be pleased to take the pains to peruse their frequent letters, instructions and charters to that effect, together with sundry printed books made purposely and published for their help and direction (the full view whereof is prohibited to no man), will be far from censuring them for any omission. Neither may we forbear to do that justice to the Governor and Commission and other principal officers now residing in Virginia as not to testify their solicitous care and industry in putting in execution our desires and instructions, as appeareth by their proclamation and other orders to be seen.

Touching the government, it hath in these four latter years been so reformed, according to your Majesty's original directions, that the people who in former times were discontent and mutinous by reason of their inassurance of all things, through want of order and justice, live now amongst themselves in great peace and tranquility, each knowing his own and what he is mutually to receive and perform.

And to the end that worthy persons may be allured to these places of council and government, and all occasion of rapine and extortion be removed, the Council and Company have now, at their very great charge, caused to be set up a competent annual provision and revenue for maintenance of the Governor, with other magistrates and officers, and particularly the ministry, according to the degree and quality of each place.

Neither have these our cares and courses been ineffectual, but as they have settled the colony there in a great quiet and content, so have they raised here at home so great a fame of Virginia, that not only men of meaner estates, as at the first by necessity, but many persons of good sort, out of choice and good liking, have removed themselves thither, and are dayly in providing to remove.

There have been in these four last years granted forty-four patents for land to persons, who have undertaken to transport each of them at least one hundred men, whereas in the former twelve years there was not above six.

There have come in ten times more adventurers in these four last years than in almost twice that time before, so that whereas in former times there were sometimes hardly got twenty to keep the quarter-court, there are now seldom less than two hundred, and sometimes many more.

There have been employed in these four last years forty-two sail of ships of great burthen, whereas in four years before there were not above twelve.

We may not here omit one extraordinary blessing, which it hath pleased God Almighty in the four last years so as to excite the heart of well-minded people to extend their aid towards the forwarding of this glorious work, that there hath been contributed towards in presents, to the value of fifteen hundred pounds by zealous and devout persons, most of them refusing to be named, of which fruit the preceding years were altogether barren.

It cannot be denied, but 'tis to be deplored with much sorrow, that the blessing of God appearing in the increase and prosperity of the plantation drew on that bloody resolution from the infidels, and as it is conceived hath excited here at home divers troublesome opposition by persons (it seemeth little favouring Virginia's prosperity), but the one we hope will be sharply revenged, and the other must be born with patience and with constancy overcome.

To conclude, for the better securing of the plantation, besides the continual sending of multitudes of persons and shipping (whereof there were lately, about Christmas last, seventeen sail in James River, in Virginia), the Council and Company, to their great charge, have given order for the erecting of a fort in some convenient place in the same river to keep out foreign invasion till better preparation be made.

And if your Majesty, being the first founder and great supporter of this action (which will remain a constant monument of your glorious name forever), will be pleased that the four hundred young and able men desired by the Company and not denied but respited, may now at length be levied, as was petitioned, and sent to Virginia for the rooting out of those treacherous and barbarous murderers, as also for the supply of the plantation in parts yet defective, we doubt not but in a short time to yield unto your Majesty so good and real account of the fruits of our cares, endeavours, and labours as may be answerable to our duty and your princely expectation.

Abstract of the Proceedings of the Virginia Company of London, in Virginia Historical Society, *Collections*, VIII (Richmond, 1889), II, 146–151.

---

68. Appeal of a Loyal Governor (1651)

BY GOVERNOR SIR WILLIAM BERKELEY

Berkeley was Governor of Virginia from 1642 to 1652, and again from 1660 to 1677 ; a violent and headstrong man. — Bibliography : Winsor, *Narrative and Critical History*, III, 148, 157 ; Channing and Hart, *Guide*, § 98.

GENTLEMEN You perceave by the Declaration, that the men of *Westminister* have set out, which I beleeve you have all seene, how they meane to deale with you hereafter, who in the time of their wooing and courting you proposed such hard conditions to be performed on your part & on their owne nothing but a benigne acceptance of your duties to them.   Indeed methinks they might have proposed something to us which might have strengthened us to beare those heavy chaines they are making ready for us, though it were but an assurance that we shall eat the bread for which our owne Oxen plow, and with owne sweat we reape, but this assurance (it seems) were a franchise beyond the condition they have *resolv'd on the Question* we ought to be in : For the reason why they talk so *Magisterially* to us, is this, we are forsooth their worships slaves, bought with their money, and by consequence ought not to buy or sell, but with those they shall authorize, with a few trifles, to cozen us of all for which we toile and labour.

If the whole Current of their reasoning were not as ridiculous, as their actions have been Tyrannicall and bloudy; we might wonder with what browes they could sustaine such impertinent assertions : For if you look into it, the strength of their argument runs onely thus : we have laid violent hands on your Land-Lord, possess'd his Manner house where you used to pay your rents, therefor now tender your respects to the same house you once reverenced : . . .

Surely Gentlemen we are more slaves by nature, then their power can make us, if we suffer ourselves to be shaken with these paper bulletts & those on my life are the heaviest they Either can or will send us. . . . Consider with what prisons and Axes they have paid those that have served them to the hazard of their Soules : Consider yourselves how happy you are, and have been, how the Gates of Wealth and Honour are shut on no man, and that there is not here an Arbitrary hand, that dares to touch the substance of either poore or rich. But, that which I would haue you chiefly to consider with thankfulness is : That God hath separated you from the guilt of the crying bloud of our Pious Soveraigne of ever blessed memory : But mistake not Gentlemen part of it will yet staine your garments if you willingly submit to those mur-therers hands that shed it.

. . . what is it can be hoped for in a change, which we have not already ? Is it liberty ? The sun looks not on a people more free than we are from all oppression. Is it wealth ? Hundreds of examples shew us that Industry & Thrift in a short time may bring us to as high of it as the country and and our Conditions are yet capable of. Is it secu-rity to enjoy this wealth when gotten ? Without blushing I will speake it, I am confident theare lives not that person can accuse me of attempt-ing the least act against any man's property. Is it peace ? The Indians, God be blessed, round about us are subdued : we can only feare the Londoners, who would faine bring us to the same poverty, wherein the Dutch found and relieved us, would take away the liberty of our con-sciences, and tongues, and our right of giving and selling our goods to whom we please.

But, Gentlemen, by the Grace of God, we will not so tamely part with our King, and all these blessings we enjoy under him, and if they oppose us, do but follow me, I will either lead you to victory, or loose a life which I cannot more gloriously sacrifice than for my loyalty and your security.

Edward D. Neill, *Virginia Carolorum* (Albany, 1886), 212–215 *passim*.

69. Surrender of Virginia to Parliament (1652)

BY GOVERNOR RICHARD BENNET AND OTHERS

Bennet was a Governor set up by the Assembly; the transaction described below
was enforced by a Parliamentary fleet. — Bibliography : Winsor, *Narrative and Critical History*, III, 148; J. A. Doyle, *English in America*, *Virginia*, ch. viii; Channing and Hart, *Guide*, § 98.

*ARTICLES agreed on and concluded at James Cittie in Virginia for
the surrendering and settling of that plantation vnder the obedience
and goverment of the Common Wealth of England, by the commissioners
of the Councill of State, by authoritie of the Parliament of England and
by the Grand Assembly of the Governour, Councill and Burgesses
of that countrey.*

FIRST, It is agreed and cons'ted that the plantation of Virginia, and
all the inhabitants thereof, shall be and remaine in due obedience and
subjection to the common wealth of England, according to the lawes
there established, And that this submission and subscription bee acknowledged a voluntary act not forced nor constrained by a conquest
vpon the countrey, And that they shall have and enjoy such freedomes
and priviledges as belong to the free borne people of England, and that
the former government by the commissions and instructions be void
and null.

2dly. Secondly, that the Grand Assembly as formerly shall convene
and transact the affairs of Virginia, wherein nothing is to be acted or
done contrarie to the government of the common wealth of England
and the lawes there established.

3dly. That there shall be a full and totall remission and indempnitie
of all acts, words or writeings done or spoken against the parliament of
England in relation to the same.

4thly. That Virginia shall have and enioy the antient bounds and
lymitts granted by the charters of the former Kings, And that we shall
seek a new charter from the parliament to that purpose against any that
have intrencht vpon the rights thereof.

5thly. That all the pattents of land granted vnder the collony seale,
by any of the precedent Governours shall be and remaine in their full
force and strength.

6thly. That the priviledge of haveing ffiftie acres of land for every
person transported in the collony shall continue as formerly granted.

7thly. That the people of Virginia have free trade as the people of

England do enjoy in all places and with all nations according to the lawes of that common-wealth, And that Virginia shall enjoy all priviledges equall with any English plantations in America.

8thly. That Virginia shall be free from all taxes, customes and impositions whatsoever, and none to be imposed on them without consent of the Grand Assembly, And soe that neither ffortes nor castles bee erected or garrisons maintained without their consent.

9thly. That noe charge shall be required from this country in respect to this present ffleet.

10thly. That for the future settlement of the countrey in their due obedience, the engagement shall be tendred to all the inhabitants according to act of parliament made to that purpose, that all persons who shall refuse to subscribe the said engagement, shall have a yeares time if they please to remove themselves, and their estates out of Virginia, and in the mean time during the said yeare to have equall justice as formerly.

11thly. That the vse of the booke of common prayer shall be permitted for one yeare ensueinge with referrence to the consent of the major part of the parishes, Provided that those things which relate to kingshipp or that government be not vsed publiquely ; and the continuance of ministers in their places, they not misdemeaning themselves : And the payment of their accustomed dues and agreements made with them respectively shall be left as they now stand dureing this ensueing yeare.

12thly. That no man's cattell shall be questioned as the companies vnles such as have been entrusted with them or have disposed of them without order.

13thly. That all amunition, powder and arms, other then for private vse shall be delivered vp, securitie being given to make satisfaction for it.

14thly. That all goods allreadie brought hither by the Dutch or others which are now on shoar shall be free from surprizall.

15thly. That the quittrents granted vnto vs by the late Kinge for seaven yeares bee confirmed.

16thly. That the commissioners for the parliament subscribing these articles enage themselves and the honour of the parliament for the full performance thereof : And that the present Governour and the Councill and the Burgesses do likewise subscribe and engage the whole collony on their parts. . . .

William Waller Hening, *Statutes at Large* (New York, 1823), I, 363-365.

70. An Official Report on Virginia (1671)

BY GOVERNOR SIR WILLIAM BERKELEY

Berkeley (see No. 68 above) sent these answers to queries sent out by the Commissioners of Plantations in 1670. — Bibliography: Winsor, *Narrative and Critical History*, III, 164; Channing and Hart, *Guide*, § 98.

1. What councils, assemblies, and courts of judicature are within your government, and of what nature and kind?

Answer. There is a governor and sixteen counsellors, who have from his sacred majestie, a commission of *Oyer and Terminer*, who judge and determine all causes that are above fifteen pound sterling; for what is under, there are particular courts in every county, which are twenty in number. Every year, at least the assembly is called, before whom lye appeals, and this assembly is composed of two burgesses out of every county. These lay the necessary taxes, as the necessity of the war with the Indians, or their exigencies require.

2. What courts of judicature are within your government relating to the admiralty?

Answer. In twenty eight yeares there has never been one prize brought into the country; so that there is no need for a particular court for that concern.

3. Where the legislative and executive powers of your government are seated?

Answer. In the governor, councel and assembly, and officers substituted by them.

4. What statute laws and ordinances are now made and in force?

Answer. The secretary of this country every year sends to the lord chancellor, or one of the principal secretaries, what laws are yearly made; which for the most part concern only our own private exigencies; for, contrary to the laws of England, we never did, nor dare make any, only this, that no sale of land is good and legal, unless within three months after the conveyance it be recorded in the general court, or county courts.

5. What number of horse and foot are within your government, and whether they be trained bands or standing forces?

Answer. All our freemen are bound to be trained every month in their particular counties, which we suppose, and do not much mistake in the calculation, are near eight thousand horse: there are more, but it is too chargeable for poor people, as wee are, to exercise them.

6. What castles and fforts are within your government, and how situated, as also what stores and provisions they are furnished withall?

Answer. There are five fforts in the country, two in James river and one in the three rivers of York, Rappahannock and Potomeck; but God knows we have neither skill or ability to make or maintain them; for there is not, nor, as far as my enquiry can reach, ever was one ingenier in the country, so that we are at continual charge to repair unskilfull and inartificial buildings of that nature. There is not above thirty great and serviceable guns; this we yearly supply with powder and shot as far as our utmost abilities will permit us.

7. What number of priviteers do frequent your coasts and neighbouring seas; what their burthens are; the number of their men and guns, and the names of their commanders?

Answer. None to our knowledge, since the late Dutch war.

8. What is the strength of your bordering neighbours, be they Indians or others, by sea and land; what correspondence do you keep with your neighbours?

Answer. We have no Europeans seated nearer to us than St. Christophers or Mexico that we know of, except some few ffrench that are beyond New England. The Indians, our neighbours are absolutely subjected, so that there is no fear of them. As for correspondence, we have none with any European strangers; nor is there a possibility to have it with our own nation further than our traffick concerns.

9. What armes, ammunition and stores did you find upon the place, or have been sent you since, upon his majestyes account; when received; how employed; what quantity of them is there remaining, and where?

Answer. When I came into the country, I found one only ruinated ffort, with eight great guns, most unserviceable, and all dismounted but four, situated in a most unhealthy place, and where, if an enemy knew the soundings, he could keep out of danger of the best guns in Europe. His majesty, in the time of the Dutch warr, sent us thirty great guns, most of which were lost in the ship that brought them. Before, or since this, we never had one great or small gun sent us, since my coming hither; nor, I believe, in twenty years before. All that have been sent by his sacred majesty, are still in the country, with a few more we lately bought.

10. What monies have been paid or appointed to be paid by his majesty, or levied within your government for and towards the buying

of armes or making or maintaining of any ffortifications or castles, and how have the said monies been expended?

Answer. Besides those guns I mentioned, we never had any monies of his majesty towards the buying of ammunition or building of fforts. What monies can be spared out of the publick revenue, we yearly lay out in ammunition.

11. What are the boundaries and contents of the land, within your government?

Answer. As for the boundaries of our land, it was once great, ten degrees in latitude, but now it has pleased his majesty to confine us to halfe a degree. Knowingly, I speak this. Pray God it may be for his majesty's service, but I much fear the contrary.

12. What commodities are there of the production, growth and man-ufacture of your plantation; and particularly, what materials are there already growing, or may be produced for shipping in the same?

Answer. Commodities of the growth of our country, we never had any but tobacco, which in this yet is considerable, that it yields his majesty a great revenue; but of late, we have begun to make silk, and so many mulberry trees are planted, and planting, that if we had skilfull men from Naples or Sicily to teach us the art of making it perfectly, in less than half an age, we should make as much silk in an year as England did yearly expend three score years since; but now we hear it is grown to a greater excess, and more common and vulgar usage. Now, for shipping, we have admirable masts and very good oaks; but for iron ore I dare not say there is sufficient to keep one iron mill going for seven years.

13. Whether salt-petre is or may be produced within your plantation, and if so, at what rate may it be delivered in England?

Answer. Salt-petre, we know of none in the country.

14. What rivers, harbours or roads are there in or about your planta-tion and government, and of what depth and soundings are they?

Answer. Rivers, we have four, as I named before, all able, safely and severally to bear an harbour a thousand ships of the greatest burthen.

15. What number of planters, sevants and slaves; and how many parishes are there in your plantation?

Answer. We suppose, and I am very sure we do not much miscount, that there is in Virginia above forty thousand persons, men, women and children, and of which there are two thousand *black slaves,* six thousand *christian servants,* for a short time, the rest are born in the country or

have come in to settle and seat, in bettering their condition in a growing country.

16. What number of English, Scots or Irish have for these seven
yeares last past come yearly to plant and inhabite within your government; as also what *blacks* or *slaves* have been brought in within the
said time?

Answer. Yearly, we suppose there comes in, of servants, about fifteen hundred, of which, most are English, few Scotch, and fewer Irish,
and not above two or three ships of negroes in seven years.

17. What number of people have yearly died, within your plantation
and government for these seven years last past, both whites and blacks?

Answer. All new plantations are, for an age or two, unhealthy, 'till
they are thoroughly cleared of wood; but unless we had a particular
register office, for the denoting of all that died, I cannot give a particular answer to this query, only this I can say, that there is not often
unseasoned hands (as we term them) that die now, whereas heretofore
not one of five escaped the first year.

18. What number of ships do trade yearly to and from your plantation, and of what burthen are they?

Answer. English ships, near eighty come out of England and Ireland
every year for tobacco; few New England ketches; but of our own, we
never yet had more than two at one time, and those not more than
twenty tuns burthen.

19. What obstructions do you find to the improvement of the trade
and navigation of the plantations within your government?

Answer. Mighty and destructive, by that severe act of parliament
which excludes us the having any commerce with any nation in Europe
but our own, so that we cannot add to our plantation any commodity
that grows out of it, as olive trees, cotton or vines. Besides this, we
cannot procure any skilfull men for one now hopefull commodity, silk;
for it is not lawfull for us to carry a pipe stave, or a barrel of corn to any
place in Europe out of the king's dominions. If this were for his majesty's service or the good of his subjects, we should not repine, whatever
our sufferings are for it; but on my soul, it is the contrary for both.
And this is the cause why no small or great vessells are built here; for
we are most obedient to all laws, whilst the New England men break
through, and men trade to any place that their interest lead them.

20. What advantages or improvement do you observe that may be
gained to your trade or navigation?

Answer.   None, unless we had liberty to transport our pipe staves, timber and corn to other places besides the king's dominions.

21. What rates and duties are charged and payable upon any goods exported out of your plantation, whither of your own growth or manufacture, or otherwise, as also upon goods imported?

Answer.   No goods, either exported or imported, pay any the least duties here, only two shillings the hogshead on tobacco exported, which is to defray all public charges ; and this year we could not get an account of more than fifteen thousand hogsheads, out of which the king allows me a thousand yearly, with which I must maintain the part of my place, and one hundred intervening charges that cannot be put to public account. And I can knowingly affirm, that there is no government of ten years settlement, but has thrice as much allowed him.   But I am supported by my hopes, that his gracious majesty will one day consider me.

22. What revenues doe or may arise to his majesty within your government, and of what nature is it ; by whom is the same collected, and how answered and accounted to his majesty?

Answer.   There is no revenue arising to his majesty but out of the quit-rents ; and this he hath given away to a deserving servant, Col. Henry Norwood.

23. What course is taken about the instructing the people, within your government in the christian religion ; and what provision is there made for the paying of your majesty?

Answer.   The same course that is taken in England out of towns ; every man according to his ability instructing his children.   We have fforty eight parishes, and our ministers are well paid, and by my consent should be better *if they would pray oftener and preach less.*   But of all other commodities, so of this, *the worst are sent us,* and we had few that we could boast of, since the persicution in *Cromwell's* tiranny drove divers worthy men hither.   But, I thank God, *there are no free schools* nor *printing,* and I hope we shall not have these hundred years ; for *learning* has brought disobedience, and heresy, and sects into the world, and *printing* has divulged them, and libels against the best government.   God keep us from both !

William Waller Hening, *Statutes at Large* (New York, 1823), II, 511–517.

R

71. Bacon's Rebellion (1676)

ANONYMOUS, 1677

The author of this piece is possibly one Cotton, of Aquia Creek. — Bibliography: Winsor, *Narrative and Critical History*, III, 151, 164; Channing and Hart, *Guide*, § 98.

THERE is no Nation this day under the copes of Heaven can so experimentally speak the sad Effects of men of great Parts being reduc't to necessity, as *England;* but not to rake up the notorious misdemeanours of the dead, I shall endeavour to prevent the sad effects of so deplorable a Cause, by giving you an account of the remarkable Life and Death of this Gentleman of whom I am about to discourse. And because when a man has once ingag'd himself in an ill action, all men are ready to heap an innumerable aspersions upon him, of which he is no ways guilty, I shall be so just in the History of his Life as not to rob him of those commendations which his Birth and Acquisitions claim as due, and so kind both to Loyalty and the wholsom constituted Laws of our Kingdom, as not to smother any thing which would render him to blame.

This Gentleman who has of late becconed the attention of all men of understanding who are any ways desirous of Novelty, [or] care what becomes of any part of the World besides that themselves live in, had the honour to be descended of an Ancient and Honourable Family, his Name *Nathanael Bacon,* to which to the long known Title of Gentleman, by his long study [at] the Inns of Court he has since added that of Esquire. He was the Son of Mr. *Thomas Bacon* of an ancient Seat known by the denomination of *Freestone-Hall* in the County of *Suffolk,* a Gentleman of known loyalty and ability. His Father as he was able so he was willing to allow this his Son a very Gentile Competency to subsist upon, but he as it proved having a Soul too large for that allowance, could not contain himself within bounds ; which his careful Father perceiving, and also that he had a mind to Travel (having seen divers parts of the World before) consented to his inclination of going to *Virginia*, and accomodated him with a Stock for that purpose, to the value of 1800*l. Starling*, as I am credibly informed by a Merchant of very good wealth, who is now in this City, and had the fortune to carry him thither.

He began his Voyage thitherwards about Three years since, and lived for about a years space in that Continent in very good repute, his extraordinary parts like a Letter of recommendation rendring him accept-

able in all mens company, whilst his considerable Concerns in that place
were able to bear him out in the best of Society. These Accomplishments of mind and fortune rendred him so remarkable, that the worthy
Governour of that Continent thought it requisite to take him into his
Privy Council.

That Plantation which he chose to settle in is generally known by the
name of *Curles*, situate in the upper part of *James* River and the time
of his Revolt was not till the beginning of *March*, 167⅝. At which
time the *Susquo-hannan Indians* (a known Enemy to that Country)
having made an Insurrection, and kild divers of the *English*, amongst
whom it was his fortune to have a Servant slain ; in revenge of whose
death, and other dammage(s) he received from those turbulent *Susquo-
hanians*, without the Governour's consent he furiously took up Arms
against them and was so fortunate as to put them to flight, but not content therewith ; the aforesaid *Governour* hearing of his eager pursuit
after the vanquisht *Indians*, sent out a select Company of Souldiers to
command him to desist ; but he instead of listning thereunto, persisted
in his Revenge, and sent to the *Governour* to intreat his Commission,
that he might more chearfully prosecute his design ; which being denyed
him by the Messenger he sent for that purpose, he notwithstanding continued to make head with his own Servants, and other *English* then
resident in *Curles* against them. In this interim the people of *Henrica*
had returned him Burgess of their County ; and he in order thereunto
took his own Sloop and came down towards *James Town*, conducted by
thirty odd Souldiers, with part of which he came ashore to Mr. *Lau-
rences* House, to understand whether he might come in with safety or
not, but being discovered by one Parson *Clough*, and also it being perceived that he had lined the Bushes of the said Town with Souldiers, the
Governour thereupon ordered an allarm to be beaten through the whole
Town, which took so hot, that *Bacon* thinking himself not secure whilst
he remained there within reach of their Fort, immediately commanded
his men aboard, and tow'd his Sloop up the River ; which the Governour
perceiving, ordered the Ships which lay at *Sandy-point* to pursue and
take him ; and they by the industry of their Commanders succeeded so
well in the attempt, that they presently stopt his passage ; so that Mr.
Bacon finding himself pursued both before and behind, after some ca-
pitulations, quietly surrendred himself Prisoner to the Governours Commissioners, to the great satisfaction of all his Friends ; which action of
his was so obliging to the Governour, that he granted him his liberty

immediately upon Paroll, without confining him either to Prison or Chamber, and the next day, after some private discourse passed betwixt the Governour, the Privy Council, and himself, he was amply restored to all his former Honours and Dignities, and a Commission partly promised him to be General against the *Indian* Army ; but upon further enquiry into his Affairs it was not thought fit to be granted him ; whereat his ambitious mind seem'd mightily to be displeas'd ; insomuch that he gave out, that it was his intention to sell his whole concerns in *Virginia,* and to go with his whole Family to live either in *Merry-land* or the *South,* because he would avoid (as he said) the scandal of being accounted a factious person there.   But this resolution it seems was but a pretence, for afterwards he headed the same Runnagado *English* that he formerly found ready to undertake and go sharers with him in any of his Rebellions, and adding to them the assistance of his own Slaves and Servants, headed them so far till they toucht at the *Occonegies* Town, where he was treated very civilly, and by the Inhabitants informed where some of the *Susquohanno's* were inforted, whom presently he assails, and after he had vanquished them, slew about seventy of them in their Fort : But as he returned back to the *Occoneges,* he found they had fortified themselves with divers more *Indians* than they had at his first arrival ; wherefore he desired Hostages of them for their good behaviour, whilst he and his followers lay within command of their Fort.   But those treacherous *Indians* grown confident by reason of their late recruit, returned him this Answer, *That their Guns were the only Hostages he was like to have of them, and if he would have them he must fetch them.* Which was no sooner spoke, but the *Indians* sallied out of the Fort and shot one of his Sentinels, whereupon he charged them so fiercely, that the Fight continued not only all that day, but the next also, till the approach of the Evening, at which time finding his men grow faint for want of Provision, he laid hold of the opportunity, being befriended by a gloomy night, and so made an honourable retreat homewards.   *Howbeit* we may judge what respect he had gain'd in *James-Town* by this subsequent transaction.   When he was first brought hither it was frequently reported among the Commonalty that he was kept close Prisoner, which report caused the people of that Town, those of *Charles-city,* *Henrico,* and *New-Kent* Countries, being in all about the Number of eight hundred, or a thousand, to rise and march thitherwards in order to his rescue ; whereupon the Governor was forced to desire Mr. *Bacon* to go himself in Person, and by his open appearance quiet the people.

This being past, Mr. *Bacon*, about the 25*th* of *June* last, dissatisfied that he could not have a Commission granted him to go against the *Indians*, in the night time departed the Town unknown to any body, and about a week after got together between four and five hundred men of *New-Kent* County, with whom he marched to *James-Town*, and drew up in order before the House of State; and there peremptorily demanded of the Governor, *Council* and *Burgesses* (there then collected) a Commission to go against the *Indians*, which if they should refuse to grant him, he told them that neither he nor ne're a man in his Company would depart from their Doors till he had obtained his request; whereupon to prevent farther danger in so great an exigence, the Council and Burgesses by much intreaty obtain'd him a Commission Signed by the *Governor*, an Act for one thousand men to be Listed under his command to go against the *Indians*, to whom the same pay was to be granted as was allowed to them who went against the *Fort*. But *Bacon* was not satisfied with this, but afterwards earnestly importuned, and at length obtained of the *House*, to pass an Act of Indemnity to all Persons who had sided with him, and also Letters of recommendations from the Governor to his Majesty in his behalf; and moreover caused Collonel *Claybourn* and his Son Captain *Claybourn*, Lieutenant Collonel *West*, and Lieutenant Collonel *Hill*, and many others, to be degraded for ever bearing any Office, whether it were Military or Civil.

Having obtained these large Civilities of the *Governor, &c.* one would have thought that if the Principles of honesty would not have obliged him to peace and loyalty, those of gratitude should. But, alas, when men have been once flusht or entred with Vice, how hard is it for them to leave it, especially it tends towards ambition or greatness, which is the general lust of a large Soul, and the common error of vast parts, which fix their Eyes so upon the lure of greatness, that they have no time left them to consider by what indirect and unlawful means they must (if ever) attain it.

This certainly was Mr. *Bacon's* Crime, who after he had once lanched into Rebellion, nay, and upon submission had been pardoned for it, and also restored, as if he had committed no such hainous offence, to his former honour and dignities (which were considerable enough to content any reasonable mind) yet for all this he could not forbear wading into his former misdemeanors, and continued his opposition against that prudent and established Government, ordered by his Majesty of *Great Brittain* to be duely observed in that Continent.

In fine, he continued (I cannot say properly in the Fields, but) in the Woods with a considerable Army all last Summer, and maintain'd several Brushes with the Governors Party : sometime routing them, and burning all before him, to the great damage of many of his Majesties loyal Subjects there resident ; sometimes he and his Rebels were beaten by the Governor, &c. and forc't to run for shelter amongst the Woods and Swomps. In which lamentable condition that unhappy Continent has remain'd for the space of almost a Twelve-month, every one therein that were able being forc't to take up Arms for security of their own lives, and no one reckoning their Goods, Wives, or Children to be their own, since they were so dangerously expos'd to the doubtful Accidents of an uncertain War.

But the indulgent Heavens, who are alone able to compute what measure of punishments are adequate or fit for the sins or transgressions of a Nation, has in its great mercy thought fit to put a stop, at least, if not a total period and conclusion to these *Virginian* troubles, by the death of this *Nat. Bacon*, the great Molestor of the quiet of that miserable Nation ; so that now we who are here in *England*, and have any Relations or Correspondence with any of the Inhabitants of that Continent, may by the arrival of the next Ships from that Coast expect to hear that they are freed from all their dangers, quitted of all their fears, and in great hopes and expectation to live quietly under their own Vines, and enjoy the benefit of their commendable labours.

I know it is by some reported that this Mr. *Bacon* was a very hard drinker, and that he dyed by inbibing, or taking in two much Brandy. But I am informed by those who are Persons of undoubted Reputation, and had the happiness to see the same Letter which gave his Majesty an account of his death, that there was no such thing therein mentioned : he was certainly a Person indued with great natural parts, which notwithstanding his juvenile extravagances he had adorned with many elaborate acquisitions, and by the help of learning and study knew how to manage them to a Miracle, it being the general vogue of all that knew him, that he usually spoke as much sense in as few words, and delivered that sense as opportunely as any they ever kept company withal : Wherefore as I am my self a Lover of Ingenuity, though an abhorrer of disturbance or Rebellion, I think fit since Providence was pleased to let him dye a Natural death in his Bed, not to asperse him with saying he kill'd himself with drinking.

Strange News from Virginia, etc. (London, 1677), 2–8.

CHAPTER XI — MARYLAND

72. Instructions to Colonists (1633)

BY CECILIUS CALVERT, LORD BALTIMORE

Cecilius Calvert was son of George Calvert, founder of the Colony; he did not come to America himself. — Bibliography: Winsor, *Narrative and Critical History*, III, 553–562; Edward Eggleston, *Beginners of a Nation*, 262–264; Channing and Hart, *Guide*, § 100.

INSTRUCTIONS 13 Nouem: 1633 directed by the Right Hono^ble Cecilius Lo: Baltimore & Lord of the Prouinces of Mary Land and Avalon vnto his well beloued Brother Leo: Caluert Esqr his Lop^t Deputy Gouernor of his prouince of Mary Land and vnto Jerom Hawley and Thomas Cornwaleys Esq^rs his Lo^pps Comissioners for the Gouernment of the said Prouince.

1. Inpri: His Lo^pp requires his said Gouernour & Commissioners th^t in their voyage to Mary Land they be very carefull to preserue vnity & peace amongst all the passengers on Shipp-board, and that they suffer no scandall nor offence to be giuen to any of the Protestants, whereby any iust complaint may heereafter be made, by them, in Virginea or in England, and that, for that end, they cause all Acts of Romane Catholique Religion to be done as priuately as may be, and that they instruct all the Romane Catholiques to be silent vpon all occasions of discourse concerning matters of Religion; and that the said Gouernor & Comissioners treate the Protestants wth as much mildness and fauor as Justice will permitt. And this to be obserued at Land as well as at Sea.

2. That while they are aboard, they do theyre best endeauors by such instruments as they shall find fittest for it, amongst the seamen & passengers to discouer what any of them do know concerning the priuate plotts of his Lo^pps aduersaries in England, who endeauored to ouerthrow his voyage: . . .

3. That as soone as it shall please god they shall arriue vpon the coast of Virginea, they be not perswaded by the master or any other of the shipp, in any case or for any respect whatsoeuer to goe to James

Towne, or to come wth in the com̄and of the fort at Poynt-Comfort:
vnless they should be forct vnto it by some extremity, of weather,
(wch god forbidd) for the preseruation of their liues & goodes, and
that they find it altogether impossible otherwise to preserue themselues:
But that they come to an Anchor somewhere about Acomacke, so as it
be not vnder the com̄and of any fort; & to send ashoare there, to inquire
if they cann find any to take wth them, that cann giue them some good
informatione of the Bay of Chesapeacke and Pattawomeck Riuer, and
that may giue them some light of a fitt place in his Lo^pps Countrey to
sett downe on; wherein their cheife care must be to make choicc of a
place first that is probable to be healthfull and fruitfull, next that it may
be easily fortified, and thirdly that it may be convenient for trade both
wth the English and sauages.

4. That by the first opportunity after theyr arriuall in Mary Land
they cause a messenger to be dispatcht away to James Town such a one
as is conformable to the Church of England, and as they may according
to the best of their iudgments trust; and he to carry his ma^ties letter to
Sr John Haruie the Gouernor and to the rest of the Councell there,
as likewise his Lo^pps letter to S^r Jo: Haruie, and to giue him notice of
their arriuall: And to haue in charge, vpon the deliuery of the said letters to behaue himself wth much respect vnto the Gouernor, . . . and
to lett him vnderstand how much his L^opp desires to hold a good correspondency wth him and that Plantation of Virginea, wch he wilbe ready
to shew vpon all occasions and to assure him by the best words he cann,
of his Lo^pps particuler affection to his person, in respect of the many reports he hath heard of his worth, and of the ancient acquaintance and
freindshipp wch he hath vnderstood was between his Lo^pps father & him
as likewise for those kind respects he hath shewne vnto his Lo^pp by his
letters since he vnderstoode of his L^opps intention to be his neighbor in
those parts: And to present him wth a Butt of sacke from his L^opp wch his
L^opp hath giuen directions for, to be sent vnto him.

5. That they write a letter to Cap: Clayborne as soone as conveniently other more necessary occasions will giue them leaue after
their arriuall in the Countrey, to giue him notice of their arriuall and of
the Authority & charge com̄itted to them by his L^opp and to send the
said letter together wth his Lo^pps to him by some trusty messenger that is
likewise conformable vnto the Church of England, wth a message also
from them to him if it be not inserted in their letter wch is better, to invite him kindly to come vnto them, and to signify that they haue some

business of importance to speake wth him about from his L^opp wch concernes his good very much ; . . .   And that they assure him in fine that
his L^opp intends not to do him any wrong, but to shew him all the loue
and fauor that he cann, and that his L^opp gaue them directions to do so
to him in his absence ; in confidence that he will, like a good subiect
to his ma^tie conforme himself to his highness gratious letters pattents
granted to his Lo^pps whereof he may see the Duplicate if he desire it
together wth their Comission from his L^opp.   If he do refuse to come
vnto them vpon their invitation, that they lett him alone for the first
yeare, till vpon notice giuen to his L^opp of his answere and behauiour
they receiue farther directions from his L^opp ; and that they informe
themselues as well as they cann of his plantation and what his designes
are, of what strength & what Correspondency he keepes wth Virginea,
and to giue an Account of euery particular to his L^opp.

6. That when they haue made choice of the place where they intend
to settle themselues and that they haue brought their men ashoare
wth all their prouisions, they do assemble all the people together in a
fitt and decent manner and then cause his ma^ties letters pattents to be
publikely read by his L^opps Secretary John Bolles, and afterwards his
L^opps Comission to them, and that either the Gouernor or one of the
Comissioners presently after make some short declaration to the people
of his L^opps intentions wch he means to pursue in this his intended plantation, wch are first the honor of god by endeauoring the conversion of
the sauages to Christianity, secondly the augmentation of his ma^tie's Empire & Dominions in those parts of the world by reducing them vnder
the subiection of his Crowne, and thirdly by the good of such of his
Countreymen as are willing to aduenture their fortunes and themselves
in it, by endeauoring all he cann, to assist them, that they may reape
the fruites of their charges & labors according to the hopefulnes of the
thing, wth as much freedome comfort and incouragement as they cann
desire ; and wth all to assure them, that his L^opps affection & zeale is so
greate to the aduancement of this Plantacon and consequently of their
good, that he will imploy all his endeauors in it, and that he would not
haue failed to haue come himself in person along wth them this first
yeare, to haue beene partaker wth them in the honor of the first voyage
thither, but that by reasons of some vnexpected accidents, he found it
more necessary for their good, to stay in England some time longer, for
the better establishment of his and their right, then it was fitt that the
shipp should stay for him, but that by the grace of god he intends w^thout

faile to be wth them the next year : And that at this time they take occasion to minister an oath of Allegeance to his ma^{tie} vnto all and euery one vpon the place, after hauing first publikely in the presence of the people taken it themselues; letting them know that his Lo^{pp} gaue particuler directions to haue it one of the first thinges that were done, to testify to the world that none should enioy the benefitt of his ma^{ties} gratious Grant vnto his L^{opp} of that place, but such as should giue a publique assurance of their fidelity & allegeance to his ma^{tie}.

7. That they informe themselues what they cann of the present state of the old Colony of Virginea, both for matter of gouernment & and Plantacon as likewise what trades they driue both at home and abroade, who are the cheife and richest men, & haue the greatest power amongst them whether their clamors against his Lo^{pps} pattent continue and whether they increase or diminish, who they are of note that shew themselues most in it, and to find out as neere as they cann, what is the true reason of their disgust against it, or whether there be really any other reason but what, being well examined proceedes rather from spleene and malice then from any other cause; And to informe his L^{opp} exactly what they vnderstand in any of these particulers.

8. That they take all occasions to gaine and oblige any of the Councell of Virginea, that they shall vnderstand incline to haue a good correspondency wth his L^{opps} plantation, either by permission of trade to them in a reasonable proportion, wthin his L^{opps} precincts, or any other way they can, so it be cleerely vnderstood that it is by the way of courtesy and not of right.

9. That where they intend to settle the Plantacon they first make choice of a fitt place, and a competent quantity of ground for a fort wthin wch or neere vnto it a convenient house, and a church or a chappel adiacent may be built, for the seat of his L^{opp} or his Gouernor or other Comissioners for the time being in his absence, both wch his Lo^{pp} would haue them take care should in the first place be erected, in some proportion at least, as much as is necessary for present vse though not so compleate in euery part as in fine afterwards they may be and send to his L^{opp} a Platt of it and of the scituation, by the next oportunity, if it be done by that time, if not or but part of it neuertheless to send a Platt of what they intend to do in it.   That they likewise make choise of a fitt place neere vnto it to seate a towne.

10. That they cause all the Planters to build their houses in as decent and vniforme a maner as their abilities and the place will afford,

& neere adioyning one to an other, and for that purpose to cause streetes to be marked out where they intend to place the towne and to oblige euery man to buyld one by an other according to that rule and that they cause diuisions of Land to be made adioyning on the back sides of their houses and to be assigned vnto them for gardens and such vses according to the proportion of euery ones building and adventure and as the conueniency of the place will afford w^(ch) his L^(opp) referreth to their discretion, but is desirous to haue a particuler account from them what they do in it, that his Lo^(pp) may be satisfied that euery man hath iustice done vnto him.

11. That as soone as conueniently they cann they cause his L^(opps) surveyor Robert Simpson to survay out such a proportion of Land both in and about the intended towne as likewise w^(th)in the Countrey adioyning as wilbe necessary to be assigned to the present aduenturers, and that they assigne euery adventurer his proportion of Land both in and about the intended towne, as alsoe w^(th)in the Countrey adioyning, according to the proportion of his aduenture and the conditions of plantacōn propounded by his Lo^(pp) to the first aduenturers, w^(ch) his L^(opp) in convenient time will confirme vnto them by Pattent. . . .   That they cause his Lo^(pps) survayor likewise to drawe an exact mapp of as much of the countrey as they shall discouer together w^(th) the soundings of the riuers and Baye, and to send it to his L^(opp).

12. That they cause all the planters to imploy their seruants in planting of sufficient quantity of corne and other prouision of victuall and that they do not suffer them to plant any other comōdity whatsoeuer before that be done in a sufficient proportion w^(ch) they are to obserue yearely.

13. That they cause all sorts of men in the plantation to be mustered and trained in military discipline and that there be days appoynted for that purpose either weekely or monthly according to the conueniency of other occasions; w^(ch) are duly to be obserued and that they cause constant watch and ward to be kept in places necessary.

14. That they informe themselues whether there be any conuenient place w^(th)in his L^(opps) precincts for the making of Salt whether there be proper earth for the making of salt-peeter and if there be in what quantity; whether there be probability of Iron oare or any other mines and that they be carefull to find out what other comōdities may probably be made and that they giue his L^(opp) notice together w^(th) their opinions of them.

15. That In fine they bee uery carefull to do iustice to euery man w^{th}out partiality, and that they auoid any occasion of difference wth those of Virginea and to haue as litle to do wth them as they cann this first yeare that they conniue and suffer little iniuryes from them rather than to engage themselues in a publique quarrell wth them, wch may disturbe the buisness much in England in the Infancy of it.   And that they giue vnto his Lo^{pp} an exact account by their letters from time to time of their proceedings both in these instructions from Article to Article and in any other accident that shall happen worthy his Lo^{pps} notice, that therevpon his L^{opp} may giue them farther instructions what to doe and that by euery conveyance by wch they send any letters as his Lo^{pp} would not haue them to omitt any they send likewise a Duplicate of the letters wch they writt by the last conveyance before that, least they should haue failed and not be come to his Lo^{pps} hands.

The Calvert Papers (Maryland Historical Society, *Fund-Publications*, No. 28, Baltimore, 1889), 131–140 *passim.*

---

73. First Impressions of Maryland (1634)

BY FATHER ANDREW WHITE

(TRANSLATED BY N. C. BROOKS, 1847)

Written in Latin by Father White, an accomplished Jesuit. — Bibliography : Winsor, *Narrative and Critical History*, III, 353-354; Channing and Hart, *Guide*, § 100.

AT length, sailing from this, we reached what they call Point Comfort, in Virginia, on the 27th of February, full of fear lest the English inhabitants, to whom our plantation is very objectionable, should plot some evil against us.   Letters, however, which we brought from the King and the Chancellor of the Exchequer to the Governor of these regions, served to conciliate their minds, and to obtain those things which were useful to us. For the Governor of Virginia hoped, by this kindness to us, to recover the more easily from the royal treasury a great amount of money due to him.   They announced only a vague rumor, that six ships were approaching, which would reduce all things under the power of the Spanish.   For this reason all the inhabitants were under arms.   The thing afterwards proved to be in a measure true.

After a kind entertainment for eight or nine days, making sail on the

3d of March, and carried into the Chesapeake bay, we bent our course to the north, that we might reach the Potomac river. The Chesapeake bay, ten leagues broad, and four, five, six, and even seven fathoms deep, flows gently between its shores; it abounds in fish when the season of the year is favorable. A more beautiful body of water you can scarcely find. It is inferior, however, to the Potomac, to which we gave the name of St. Gregory.

Having now arrived at the wished for country, we appointed names as occasion served. And, indeed, the point which is at the south we consecrated under the title of St. Gregory; designating the northern point, we consecrated it to St. Michael, in honor of all the angels. A larger or more beautiful river I have never seen. The Thames, compared with it, can scarcely be considered a rivulet. It is not rendered impure by marshes, but on each bank of solid earth rise beautiful groves of trees, not choked up with an undergrowth of brambles and bushes, but as if laid out by the hand, in a manner so open, that you might freely drive a four horse chariot in the midst of the trees.

At the very mouth of the river we beheld the natives armed. That night fires were kindled through the whole region, and since so large a ship had never been seen by them, messengers were sent everywhere to announce " that a canoe as large as an island had brought as many men as there was trees in the woods." We proceeded, however, to the Heron islands, so called from the immense flocks of birds of this kind.

The first which presented itself we called by the name of St. Clement's, the second St. Catharine's, the third St. Cecilia's. We landed first at St. Clement's, to which access is difficult, except by fording, because of the shelving nature of the shore. Here the young women, who had landed for the purpose of washing, were nearly drowned by the upsetting of the boat — a great portion of my linen being lost — no trifling misfortune in these parts.

This island abounds in cedar, sassafras, and the herbs and flowers for making salads of every kind, with the nut of a wild tree which bears a very hard nut, in a thick shell, with a kernel very small but remarkably pleasant. However, since it was only four hundred acres in extent, it did not appear to be a sufficiently large location for a new settlement. Nevertheless, a place was sought for building a fort to prohibit foreigners from the trade of the river, and to protect our boundaries, for that is the narrowest crossing of the river.

On the day of the annunciation of the Holy Virgin Mary, on the 25th of March, in the year 1634, we offered in this island, for the first time, the sacrifice of the mass : in this region of the world it had never been celebrated before. Sacrifice being ended, having taken up on our shoulders the great cross which we had hewn from a tree, and going in procession to the place that had been designated, the Governor, commissioners, and other catholics participating in the ceremony, we erected it as a trophy to Christ the Saviour, while the litany of the holy cross was chaunted humbly on the bended knees, with great emotion of soul.

But when the Governor had understood that many sachems are subject to the chieftain of Piscataway, he resolved to visit him, that the cause of our coming being explained, and his good will being conciliated, a more easy access might be gained to the minds of the others. Therefore, having added another pinnace to ours which he had bought in Virginia, and having left the ship at anchor at St. Clement's, retracing his course, he landed at the south side of the river. And when he had found out that the savages had fled into the interior, he proceeded to a village which is also called Potomac, a name derived from the river. Here the tutor [guardian] of the king, who is a youth, is Archihu, his uncle, and holds the government of the kingdom — a grave man and prudent.

To father John Altham, who had come as the companion of the Governor (for he left me with the baggage,) he willingly gave ear while explaining, through an interpreter, certain things concerning the errors of the heathens, now and then acknowledging his own ; and when informed that we had not come thither for the purpose of war, but for the sake of benevolence, that we might imbue a rude race with the precepts of civilization, and open up a way to heaven, as well as impart to them the advantages of remote regions, he signified that we had come acceptably. The interpreter was one of the protestants of Virginia. Therefore when the father could not discuss matters further for want of time, he promised that he would return before long. "This is agreeable to my mind," said Archihu, "we will use one table ; my attendants shall go hunt for you, and all things shall be common with us."

From this we went to Piscataway, where all flew to arms. About five hundred men, equipped with bows, stood on the shore with their chieftain. Signs of peace being given them, the chief, laying aside his apprehensions, came on board the pinnace, and having understood the intentions of our minds to be benevolent, he gave us permission to settle in whatever part of his empire we might wish.

In the meantime, while the Governor was on his visit to the chieftain, the savages at St. Clement's having grown more bold, mingled familiarly with our guards, for we kept guard day and night, both that we might protect our woodcutters as well as the brigantine which with boards and beams we were constructing as a refuge from sudden attacks. It was amusing to hear them admiring every thing. In the first place, where in all the earth did so large a tree grow, from which so immense a mass of a ship could be hewn? for they conceived it cut from the single trunk of a tree, in the manner of a canoe. Our cannon struck them all with consternation, as they were much louder than their twanging bows, and loud as thunder.

The Governor had taken as companion in his visit to the chieftain, Captain Henry Fleet, a resident of Virginia, a man very much beloved by the savages, and acquainted with their language and settlements. At the first he was very friendly to us; afterwards, seduced by the evil counsels of a certain Claiborne, who entertained the most hostile disposition, he stirred up the minds of the natives against us with all the art of which he was master. In the meantime, however, while he remained as a friend among us, he pointed out to the Governor a place for a settlement, such that Europe cannot show a better for agreeableness of situation.

From St. Clement's, having proceeded about nine leagues towards the north, we entered the mouth of a river, to which we gave the name of St. George. This river, in a course from south to north, runs about twenty miles before it is freed from its salt taste — not unlike the Thames. Two bays appeared at its mouth, capable of containing three hundred ships of the largest class. One of the bays we consecrated to St. George; the other bay, more inland, to the blessed Virgin Mary. The left bank of the river was the residence of King Yoacomico. We landed on the right, and having advanced about a thousand paces from the shore, we gave the name of St. Mary's to the intended city; and that we might avoid all appearance of injury and of hostility, having paid in exchange axes, hatchets, hoes, and some yards of cloth, we bought from the King thirty miles of his territory, which part now goes by the name of Augusta Carolina.

The Susquehannoes, a tribe accustomed to wars, and particularly troublesome to King Yoacomico, in frequent incursions devastate all his land, and compel the inhabitants, through fear of danger, to seek other habitations. This is the reason why so readily we obtained a part of his kingdom ; God, by these miracles, opened a way for his law and for eternal life. Some emigrate, and others are daily relinquishing to us their houses, lands, and fallow-fields. Truly this is like a miracle, that savage men, a few days before arrayed in arms against us, so readily trust themselves like lambs to us, and surrender themselves and their property to us. The finger of God is in this ; and some great good God designs to this people. Some few have granted to them the privilege of remaining with us till the next year. But then the ground is to be given up to us, unencumbered.

The natives are of tall and comely stature, of a skin by nature somewhat tawny, which they make more hideous by daubing, for the most part, with red paint mixed with oil, to keep away the mosquitoes ; in this, intent more on their comfort than their beauty. They smear their faces also with other colors ; from the nose upwards, seagreen, downwards, reddish, or the contrary, in a manner truly disgusting and terrific. And since they are without beard almost to the end of life, they make the representation of beard with paint, a line of various colors being drawn from the tip of the lips to the ears. They encourage the growth of the hair, which is generally black, and bind it with a fillet when brought round in a fashionable style to the left ear, something which is held in estimation by them, being added by way of ornament. Some bear upon their forehead the representation of a fish in copper. They encircle their necks with glass beads strung upon a thread, after the manner of chains. These beads, however, begin to be more common with them, and less useful for traffic. . . .

Ignorance of their language renders it still doubtful for me to state what views they entertain concerning religion ; for we trust less to protestant interpreters. These few things we have learned at different times. They recognize one God of heaven, whom they call " Our God " ; nevertheless, they pay him no external worship, but by every means in their power, endeavor to appease a certain evil spirit which they call Okee, that he may not hurt them. They worship corn and fire, as I am informed, as Gods wonderfully beneficent to the human race. . . .

We have been here only one month, and so other things must be reserved for the next sail. This I can say, that the soil appears particularly fertile, and strawberries, vines, sassafras, hickory nuts, and walnuts, we tread upon every where, in the thickest woods. The soil is dark and soft, a foot in thickness, and rests upon a rich and red clay. Every where there are very high trees, except where the ground is tilled by a scanty population. An abundance of springs afford water. No animals are seen except deer, the beaver, and squirrels, which are as large as the hares of Europe. There is an infinite number of birds of various colors, as eagles, herons, swans, geese, and partridges. From which you may infer that there is not wanting to the region whatever may serve for commerce or pleasure. . . .

Rev. Father Andrew White, *A Relation of the Colony of the Lord Baron of Baltimore in Maryland* (Baltimore, 1847), 18–24 *passim*.

---

74. The Question of Kent Island (1638)

BY CLAYBOURNE, BALTIMORE, AND THE COMMISSIONERS OF PLANTATIONS

Claybourne was a contentious man who had established himself on Kent Island. Baltimore was striving for the territory included within the boundaries of his charter. The blanks are gaps in the original manuscript record. — Bibliography: Winsor, *Narrative and Critical History*, III, 522–562; Channing and Hart, *Guide*, § 100.

A. CLAYBOURNE'S PETITION

THE humble Petition of Captain William Clepborne on the behalfe of himself and Partners, —

Shewing

THAT the Pet^n by vertue of a Comission under Your Majesties hand and Signet thereunto annexed, divers years past discovered, and did then plant upon an Island in the Great Bay of Chesapeak in Virginia, by them named the Isle of Kent, which they bought of the Kings of that Country, and built houses   transported Cattell, and Settled people thereon to their very great Costs and Charges which the Lord Baltemore takeing notice of, and the great hopes for : trade of beavers and other Comodities like to ensue by the Peticoners discoverys hath Since obtained a Pattent from your Majesty Comprehending the said Island with the Limitts thereof, and Sought thereby to dispossess the Peticoners thereof and debarr them of their discovery and hopefull trade for beavers Complaint being made thereof, your Majesty was graciously pleased to signifie your Royal pleasure by a Letter under your Majesty's hand and Signett Intimating therein that was contrary to Justice and the

s

true intent of your Majesty's Grant to the said Lord, that Notwithstanding the said Patent the Peticoners should have freedom of trade
enjoy the same therein requiring the Governor and all others in Virginia
to be aiding and assisting unto them, prohibiting the Lord Baltemore
and all other pretenders vnder him to offer Them any Violence, or
to disturb or molest them in their said   and plantation, as by
your Majesty's Said Letter annexed appeareth, Since which ti
be it your Majīy's Said Royal pleasure hath been made known to Sr John
          Governor of Virginia (who Slighted the Same) as also to the
Lord Baltemore   Agents there, Yet they have in a most wilfull
and contemptuous manner disobeyed the same, and, violently Set upon
your Peticoners Pinnaces and boats   goods to trade, and Surprized them, and doe Still detain the same, By the   of which
Pinnaces and goods the Inhabitants within the said Isle were reduced
          So great famine and misery as they became utterly destitute of
any corn   Sustain themselves, which enforced them to send a
small boat   ow th   why they obeyed not your Majesty's
said Royal Letters and Command   to   the said Pinnaces
and goods to enable them to trade for corne   feed   boat
approaching near unto Some Vessell of the said Lord Baltemore
Agents, they shott among the Peticoners men and slew three of them and
hu   more, And not content with these great Injuries, the said Lord
Baltemore and his Agents, have openly defamed and unjustly accused
the Peticon^rs of   crimes to his exceeding great grief, which hath
caused him purposely   pair into this Kingdom and humbly prostrate himself and his Cause vn   Majesty's feet to be relieved
herein
     And the Peticoner having likewise discovered   lantāo
and ffactorie upon a small Island in the Mouth of a River in the bottom of
the said Bay in the Sasquesahanoughs Country at the Indians Desire. . . .
     And the Peticoner being desirous to propose a way Whereby, your
Majesty may receive to the Crown for Plantacons an Annual benefit and
the Planters be certain to enjoy the Same with the fruits of their Labour,
They doe Offer unto your Majesty 100^lb p annu vizt 50^t for the said Isle
of Kent, and fifty pound for the said Plantation in the Sasquesahanoughs
Country, . . .
     May it therefore please your Most Excellent Majesty, to grant unto
the Peticoners a Confirmation of your Majesty's said Comission
and Letter, under your Majesty's broad seal for the quiet keeping,

enjoying and governing of the said Island Plantations and people thereon as aforesaid, to send now with the said ship, and to referr the speedy Examination of the said wrongs and injuries unto whome your Majesty shall please to think fitt to certify your Majesty thereof, And that the Peticōners may chearfully proceed in soe hopefull a design without any lett or Interruption of the Lord Baltemores Agents or any other whatsoever

And as in duty bound they shall pray. &c

Att the Court at New Markett the 26ᵗʰ ffebʳy 1637 [1638] . . .

B. BALTIMORE'S PETITION

THE humble Petition of Cecill Lord Baltimore.

? March. 1638.

Most humbly Sheweth :

THAT whereas your Subject being desirous to plant a Colony of English in some part of Virginia, did humbly desire to have a part of that Territory granted to him, which was referred to the consideration of some of the Lords of the Councell, who upon hearing of the old Virginia Company and your Petitioner at severall times thought fitt to advise your Majestie to grant to your petitioner that patent of Maryland, which now he enjoyeth ; After the passing whereof, the said Company having procured a petition from Virginia against the said patent, subscribed by William Clayborne and many others, presented the same to your Majᵗⁱᵉ in May 1633, who was pleased to referr the consideration thereof to the Boord, and their Lordshipps did thereupon then heare both partys interested at large : And being desirous before they gave their judgement in the cause, that there might be a mutuall accommodation of the Controversy, did appoint that both parties should meete and make propositions and answers to each other, and present them in writing to the Boord which was accordingly done ; Whereupon their Lordships having heard and maturely considered the allegations on either part, and perticularly the pretences of Clayborne, did then thinke fitt by an Order of the 3. of July 1633, to leave your petitioner to the right of his patent, and the other party to the course of Law ; whereupon your petitioner hath proceeded in sending to that country divers Colonyes of your Majᵗⁱᵉˢ Subjects at his greate charges, who have planted themselves in severall parts thereof, to the great hazard of their persons, and to the benefitt and service of your Majᵗⁱᵉˢ subjects in Virginia as is confessed

by the Governor and Councell there. Yet notwithstanding the said
William Clayborne being not contented with the said Order, because he
well knew he had no legall right to his unjust pretences, not long after,
did conspire with the Indians to destroy two of your petitioners Brothers,
with divers Gentlemen, and others of your Maj^ties subjects, and by many
other unlawfull wayes to overthrow his plantations, . . .

May it therefore please your most Excellent Maj^tie seeing that your
petitioner's patent and right, have passed so many tryalls ; and that in
confidence thereof, and of your Majestie's Royall justice and favor, he
hath expended a great part of his eState in planting that Countrey ; that
you wilbe pleased in confirmation of the said Order of the Boord, to
leave your petitioner to his right and the said Clayborne to the Courte
of Law ; that thereby your Maj^tie may be free from the clamour of such
pretenders, and your Subject encouraged to proceed in the plantation
as he intends : And to that end that you wil be pleased to revoke the
reference made for the said Clayborne, and to give order, that no grant
shall pass to him, or to any other, of any part of your petitioners Countrey. And that you will likewise be pleased touching the examination
of the injuryes pretended to be done by your petitioners Agents in those
parts, seeing they are alledged to be done in Virginia, that your Maj^tie
wilbe pleased to direct your royall Letters to your Governor and Councell there, to examine the said complaints, and to certifie their opinions
to your Maj^tie ; that thereupon you may proceed according to Justice ;
for your Petitioner is confident that upon a true examination of the fact
where it was committed ; it will appeare that the said Clayborne and his
Servants are guilty of Piracy and murder. . . .

C. DECISION IN FAVOR OF BALTIMORE

THE Ld Comissioners for plantations their Order Vppon Capt William Cleyborne & his Partners Pet^n ag̅s̅t the Ld Baltemore.

Att White-Hall the 4th of Aprill 1638. . . .

WHEREAS a Pet^n was presented to his Ma^ty by Capt William Clayborne, on the behalfe of himselfe & Partners. Showing th^t by
uertue of a Comis^n under his Ma^tys hand & Signett, they diuers yeares
past, discouered & planted upon an Iland, in the great Bay Chesapeack
in Virginia, named by them the Ile of Kent ; Wheruppon they pretended
they had bestowed great charges, & th^t the Ld Baltemore, as they alleaged,
taking notice of the great benefitt th^t was likely to arrise to them thereby

obteyned a Pattent from his Ma^{ty} comprehending the s^d Iland, wthin the lymitts thereof.   And th^t they had likewise settled another Plant^n uppon th^e mouth of a Ryu^r in the bottome of the s^d Bay, in the Sasquesahan-oughs Country. wch the s^d Ld Baltemores Agents there, as they alleage sought to dispossesse them of, pretending likewise great iniuries & uio-lence offered to them, in their trade, & possessions in those parts, by the s^d Agents, in killing some of the s^d Capt Claybornes men, & taking their Boates contrary to the s^d Commis^n & the expresse words of a letter from his Ma^{ty} under his hand & Signett. . . .   Whereupon all parties attend-ing their L^{ps} this day, wth their Councell learned, & being fully heard, the s^d Commis^n & Letter being likewise read.   It appeared clearely to their L^{ps}, & was confessed by the s^d Clayborne himselfe then p^{r}sent. That the s^d Isle of Kent is wthin the Bownds & Lymitts of the Ld Balte-mores Pattent.   And th^t the s^d Capt Claybornes Commis^n as it likewise appeared, was only a Lycense under the Signett of Scotland, to trade wth the Indians of America in such places, where the sole Trade had not bene formerly graunted by his Ma^{ty} to any other.   W^{ch} Commis^n their L^{ps} declared did not extend, nor giue any warrant to the s^d Clayborne, or any other : nor had they any right or tytle thereby, to the s^d Island of Kent, or to plant, or trade there, or in any other parts or places, wth the Indians or Sauages wthin the precints of the Ld Baltemores Pattent. . . . Their Lo^{ps} hauing resolued & declared as aboues^d.   The Right & Tytle to the Ile of Kent & other places in question to be absolutely belonging to the Ld Baltemore, & th^t noe Plant^n or Trade wth the Indians ought to be wthin the precincts of his Pattent wthout Lycence from him. Did therfore likewise thinke fitt & declare, th^t noe Graunt from his Ma^{ty} should passe to the s^d Clayborne or any others of the s^d Ile of Kent, or any other parts or places wthin the s^d Pattent Whereof his Ma^{tys} Attorney & Soliciter gr$\overline{a}$ll are hereby prayed to take notice.   And concerning the Violences & wrongs by the s^d Clayborne & the rest complayned of in the s^d Pet^n to his Ma^t their Lo^{pps} did now allso declare, th^t they fownd noe cause att all to releiue them, butt doe leaue both sides to the ordi-nary course of Justice. . . .

Proceedings of the Council of Maryland, in *Maryland Archives* (Baltimore, 1885), III, 65–73 *passim*.

75. Puritan Commotions in Maryland (1656)

BY JOHN HAMMOND

Hammond had been expelled from the Virginia Assembly as "a scandalous person"; but, though prejudiced, he gives a credible picture of the times. — Bibliography: Winsor, *Narrative and Critical History*, III, 554; Channing and Hart, *Guide*, § 101.

HAVING for 19. yeare served *Virginia* the elder sister, I casting my eye on Mary-land the younger, grew in amoured on her beauty, resolving like Jacob when he had first served for Leah, to begin a fresh service for Rachell.

Two year and upward have I enjoyed her company with delight and profit, but was enforced by reason of her unnatural disturbances to leave her weeping for her children & would not be comforted, because they were not; yet will I never totally forsake or be beaten off from her.

Twice hath she been deflowerd by her own Inhabitants, stript, shorne and made deformed; yet such a naturall fertility and comelinesse doth she retain that she cannot but be loved, but be pitied; and although she would ever have vailed to *Virginia* as her elder, yet had not these two fatall mischiefs hapened, she would ere long have spread her self as largly, and produced as much in every respect as *Virginia* does or could doe.

Mary-land is a province not commonly knowne in England, because the name of *Virginia* includes or clouds it, it is a Country wholy belonging to that honorable Gentleman the Lord of *Baltamore*, granted him by Pattent under the broad Seal of England long since, and at his charge settled, granted for many reasons, and this for one; that *Virginia* having more land then they could . . . look after inconvenient time, first the Duch came and tooke from the English much land which they still hold, next the Swead, who intrenched neerer and had not this Pattent came and prevented it, Dutch, Swead, French & other strangers had pend up our Nation with in the bounds of *Virginia*, whereas now they have now all *Mary land*, as it were their own, it being only granted for the use of Brittaines and Irish.

It is (not an Island as is reported, but) part of that maine adjoyning to *Virginia*, only separated or parted from *Virginia*, by a river of ten miles broad, called *Patomack* river, the commodities and manner of living as in *Virginia*, the soyle somewhat more temperate (as being more

Northerly) many stately and navigable rivers are contained in it, plentifully stored with whol some springs, a rich and pleasant soile, and so
that its extraordinary goodnes hath made it rather desired then envied,
which hath been fatall to her (as beauty is often times to those that are
endued with it) and that the reader may thoroughly be informed how
she hath suffered.   I shall in brief relate, and conclude.

It is to be understood that in the time of the late King; *Virginia*
being whol for monarchy, and the last Country belonging to England
that submitted to obedience of the Common-wealth of England.   And
there was in *Virginia* a certaine people congregated into a Church,
calling themselves Independents, which daily encreasing, severall consultations were had by the state of that Coloney, how to suppresse and
extinguish them, which was daily put in execution, as first their Pastor
was banished, next their other Teachers, then many by informatiõs clapt
up in prison, then generally disarmed) wch was very harsh in such a
country where the heathen live round about them) by one Colonel
Samuel Mathews then a Counsellor in *Virginia* and since Agent for
Virginia to the then parliament, and lastly in a condition of banishment, so that they knew not in those streights how to dispose of, themselves.

Mary-land (my present subject) was courted by them as a refuge,
the Lord Proprietor and his Governor solicited to, and severall addresses
and treaties made for their admittance & entertainment into that province, their conditions were pitied, their propositions were harkened to
and agree on, which was that they should have convenient portions of
land assigned them, libertie of conscience, and priviledge to choose
their owne officers, and hold courts within themselves, all was granted
them, they had a whole Country of the richest land in the province
asigned them, & such as themselves made choyce of, the conditions
of plantations (such as were common to all adventurers) were shewed
and propounded to them, which they extreamly approved of, and nothing was in those conditions exacted from them, but appeales to the
Provincial court, quit-rents, and an oath of fidelitie to the Proprietor :
An assembly was called thoroughout the whole Country after their comming over (consisting aswell of themselves as the rest) and because
there were some few papists that first inhabited these themselves, and
others of being different judgments, an act passed that all professing
in Jesus Christ should have equall justice, priviledges and benefits in that
province, and that none on penaltie (mentioned) should disturb each

other in their several professions, nor give the urging termes, either of Round-heads, sectarie, Independent, Jesuit, Papist, &c. Intending an absolute peace and union; the Oath of Fidelitie (although none other then such as every Lord of a manner requires from his tenant) was over hauled, and this clause added to it (provided it infring not the libertie of the conscience.)

They sat downe joyfully, followed their vocations chearfully, trad increased in their province, and divers others were by this incouraged and invited over from *Virginia*.

But these people finding themselves in a capacitie not only to capitulate, but to oversway, those that had so received and relieved them.

Began to pick quarrells, first with the Papists, next with the oath, and lastly declared their aversness to all conformalitie, wholy ayming (as themselves since confessed) to deprive the Lord proprietor of all his interest in that country, and make it their own: with unworthinesse? What ingratitude? with unparalled inhumanitie was in these practices made obvious.

Amongst others that became tenants in this aforesaid distress was one *Richard Bennet* Merchant, who seated and settled amongst them, and so (not only owed obedience to that government, but) was obliged as a man received in his pretended distresse, to be a gratfull benefactor upon the setting forth of a fleet intended for the reducement of *Virginia*, the said *Bennet* and one *Claiborne* (a pestilent enemie to the wel-faire of that province and the Lord Proprietor, although he had formerly submissively acknowledged he owed his forfeited life to the said proprietor, for dealing so favorably with him for his misdemeanors, as by his treacherous letters under his hand (now in print) is manifest, and many other acts of grace conferred on him, having a commission directed to them and others (who miscarried by sea) to reduce *Virginia* (not *Mary-land*, for they were in obedience to the Commonwealth of England, and great assistance to the said fleet) although they knew *Mary-land* to be excluded and dasht out of their Commission yet because the commission mentioned the Bay of Chesapeack (in which *Mary-land* was (as well as *Virginia*) yet they were resolved to wreth and stretch their commission to the prejudice of *Mary-land* and becomming abbetters and confederats with those serpents that have been so taken in, presumed to alter the government, and take away the governours Commission, putting in others in their place, *viz.* a Papist in cheife, and one more, who misgoverning the Country, they were excluded, and the former governor restored with an addition of Commissioners of their owne creatures, and as taking power from them, untill further knowledge from England, driving herein at their own interest.

The governour (so restored) being truly informed that their proceedings were illegal; held Courts and proceeds as if no such alteration had been made, issues out Writs (according to order) In the name of the Lord proprietor, but they require and command them to do it in the name of the Keepers of the Liberties of England, according to act of Parliament, to which answer sufficient was given, that they never were in opposition to the present power, they had taken the Engagement, & for the tenure or form of writs, they were not compelled byvertue of that act to make them other wise then they always had done, for by Patent from the late K. they had power to issue out in the Proprietors name, and never had used the Kings name at all, therefore that act requiring all Writs formerly issuing out in the late Kings name, now to revolve to the Keepers of the Liberties of England, was no way binding to them, who had never used the kings name at all.

But it was not religion, it was not punctilios they stood upon, it was that sweete, that rich, that large Country they aimed at; and therefore agrees amongst themselves to frame petitions, complaints, and subscriptions from those bandetoes [bandits] to themselves (the said *Bennet* and *Claiborne*) to ease them of their pretended sufferings, and then come with arms, and againe make the Province their own, exalting themselves in all places of trust and command, totally expulsing the Governer, and all the hospitable Proprietors, Officers out of their places.

But when his Highnesse (not acquainted with these matchinations) had owned and under his hand and signet acknowledged Cap. *Will. Stone* (the former governor) Governor for the Lord *Baltamore* of his Province of *Mary-land*, he again endeavored to reasume the government, and fetched away the records from those usurpers, proclaimed peace to all not obstinate, and favorably received many submissives, who with seeming joy returned, bewailing their unworthy ingratitude & inhumanitie, blaming the unbridled ambition and base averice of those that had misled them.

The Province consists of foure Counties already inhabited, viz. St. *Maries, Calverton, An Arundal* and *Kent.* St. *Maries* and *Calverton* submitted, *An Arundall* and part of *Kent* opposed.

The Governor desirous to reclaim those opposing, takes a partie about 130. persons with him, and sailes into those parts, one *Roger*

Heamans who had a great ship under him, and who had promised to be instrumentall to the governor, to wind up those differences (being *Judas*-like, hired to joyn with those opposing Countries) and having the Governour and his vessells within reach of his Ordnance, perfidiously & contrary to his undertaking and ingagments, fires at them and enforces them to the first shore to prevent that mischief.

The next morning he sends messengers to those of *An Arundall* to treat, and messengers aboard that . . . *Heamans,* but all were detained ; and on the 25. of *March* last (being the next day and the Lords day) about 170. and odd of *Kent* and *Anne Arundall* came marching against them, *Heaman* fires a pace at them, and a small vessel of *New-England* under the command of one *John Cutts* comes neere the shore and seazes the boats, provision and amunition belonging to the Governour and his partie, and so in a nick, in a streight were they fallen upon.

The Governour being shot in many places yeilds on quarter, which was granted ; but being in hold, was threatned (notwithstanding that quarter given) to be imediatly executed, unlesse he would writ to the rest to take quarter, which upon his request they did, twentie odd were killed in this skirmish, and all the rest prisoners on quarter, who were disarmed & taken into custodie.

But these formerly distressed supplicants for admittance, being now become High and Mighty States, and supposing their Conquest unquestionable, consult with themselves (notwithstanding their quarter given) to make their Conquest more absolute, by cutting off the heads of the Province, *viz.* the Governor, the Counsel and Commanders thereof : And so make themselves a Counsel of War, and condemn them to death : Foure were presently executed, scilicet, Mr. *William Elton-head,* one of the Councel ; Capt. *William Lewis,* Mr. *John Legate* Gentleman, and *John Pedro ;* the rest at the importunity of some women, and resolutions of some of their souldiers (who would not suffer their designe to take thorough effect, as being pricked in Conscience for their ingratitudes) were saved, but were Amerced, Fined and Plundred at their pleasures : And although this was prophetiquely foreseen by diverse eminent Merchants of *London,* who Petitioned his Highnesse for prevention, and that his Highnesse sent a gracious command to *Bennet,* and all others, not to disturb the Lord *Baltamores* Officers, nor People in *Mary-land,* but recalled all Power or pretence of Power from them ; yet they still hold, and possesse (in defiance of so sacred a mandate)

the said **Province** of *Mary-land,* and sent an impious Agent home to
Parlie whilest they plundred ; but he hath long since given up his account
to the great avenger of all injuries : Although sticklers (somewhat more
powerfull, but by many degrees more brazen fac't then his spirit could
bare him forth to appear) now labour to justifie these inhumanities, disorders, contempts, and rebellions ; so that I may say with the Prophet
Jeremiah; How doth the Citty sit solitary that was full of people?
How is she become as a wildow? She that was great amongst the
Nations, and Princesse amongst the Provinces? How is she become
tributary. Thus have they brought to desolation, one of the happiest
Plantations that ever *Englishmen* set foot in, and such a Country (that
if it were again made formall) might harbor in peace and plenty all such
as *England* shall have occasion to disburthen, or desire to forsake
England.

A pious consideration of these distractions is by his Highnesse taking
notice of, and these controversies are by him referred to the Hearing,
and Report of those two Honourable and judicious Gentlemen the
Lords *Whitlock* and *Widdrington,* whose Pains and Moderation in Hearing, and mildly disputing indifferently the condition of these uproars,
gives not onely hopes of relief, but have added to their renowns. . . .

John Hammond, *Leah and Rachel; or, the Two Fruitfull Sisters Virginia,*
and Maryland, etc. (London, 1656), 20–27.

———◆———

76. "A Character of the Province of Mary-Land" (1666)

BY GEORGE ALSOP

Alsop had been an indentured servant in Maryland. This tract is one of the most
entertaining of its kind, though evidently overdrawn. — Bibliography : Winsor,
Narrative and Critical History, III, 555; Channing and Hart, *Guide,* § 101.

Of the Government and natural disposition of the People.

MARYLAND, not from the remoteness of her situation, but from
the regularity of her well-ordered Government, may (without
sin, I think) be called *Singular :* And though she is not supported
with such large Revenues as some of her Neighbours are, yet such is
her wisdom in a reserved silence, and not in pomp, to shew her well-

conditioned Estate, in relieving at a distance the proud poverty of those that wont be seen they want, as well as those which by undeniable necessities are drove upon the Rocks of pinching wants : Yet such a loathsome creature is a common and folding-handed Begger, that upon the penalty of almost a perpetual working in Imprisonment, they are not to appear, nor lurk near our vigilant and laborious dwellings. The Country hath received a general spleen and antipathy against the very name and nature of it ; and though there were no Law provided (as there is) to suppress it, I am certainly confident, there is none within the Province that would lower themselves so much below the dignity of men to beg, as long as limbs and life keep house together ; so much is a vigilant industrious care esteem'd.

He that desires to see the real Platform of a quiet and sober Government extant, Superiority with a meek and yet commanding power sitting at the Helme, steering the actions of a State quietly, through the multitude and diversity of Opinionous waves that diversly meet, let him look on *Mary-Land* with eyes admiring, and he'le then judge her, *The Miracle of this Age*.

Here the *Roman Catholick*, and the *Protestant Episcopal*, (whom the world would perswade have proclaimed open Wars irrevocably against each other) contrarywise concur in an unanimous parallel of friendship, and inseparable love intayled unto one another : All Inquisitions, Martyrdom, and Banishments are not so much as named, but unexpressably abhorr'd by each other.

The several Opinions and Sects that lodge within this Government, meet not together in mutinous contempts to disquiet the power that bears Rule, but with a reverend quietness obeys the legal commands of Authority. Here's never seen Five Monarchies in a Zealous Rebellion, opposing the Rights and Liberties of a true setled Government, or Monarchical Authority : Nor did I ever see (here in *Mary-Land*) any of those dancing Adamitical Sisters . . . ; but I conceive if some of them were there at some certain time of the year, between the Months of *January* and *February*, when the winds blow from the North-West quarter of the world, that it would both cool, and (I believe) convert the hottest of these Zealots. . . .

The Government of this Province doth continually, by all lawful means, strive to purge her Dominions, from such base corroding humors, that would predominate upon the least smile of Liberty, did not the Laws check and bridle in those unwarranted and tumultuous Opinions. And truly, where a Kingdom, State or Government, keeps or cuts down the weeds of destructive Opinions, there must certainly be a blessed Harmony of quietness. And I really believe this Land or Government of *Mary-Land* may boast, that she enjoys as much quietness from the disturbance of Rebellious Opinions, as most States or Kingdoms do in the world : For here every man lives quietly, and follows his labour and imployment desiredly ; and by the protection of the Laws, they are supported from those molestious troubles that ever attend upon the Commons of other States and Kingdoms, as well as from the Aquafortial operation of great and eating Taxes. Here's nothing to be levyed out of the Granaries of Corn ; but contrarywise, by a Law every Domestick Governor of a family is enjoyned to make or cause to be made so much Corn by a just limitation, as shall be sufficient for him and his Family : So that by this wise and *Fanus*-like providence, the thin jawed Skeliton with his starv'd Carkess is never seen walking the Woods of *Mary-Land* to affrighten Children.

Once every year within this Province is an Assembly called, and out of every respective County (by the consent of the people) there is chosen a number of men, and to them is deliver'd up the Grievances of the Country ; and they maturely debate the matters, and according to their Consciences make Laws for the general good of the people ; and where any former Law that was made, seems and is prejudicial to the good or quietness of the Land, it is repeal'd. These men that determine on these matters for the Republique, are called Burgesses, and they commonly sit in Junto about six weeks, being for the most part good ordinary Housholders of the several Counties, which do more by a plain and honest Conscience, then by artificial Syllogisms drest up in gilded Orations.

Here Suits and Tryals in Law seldome hold dispute two Terms or Courts, but according as the Equity of the Cause appears is brought to a period, the *Temples* and *Grays-Inne* are clear out of fashion here : Marriot would sooner get a paunch-devouring meal for nothing, then for his invading Counsil. Here if the Lawyer had nothing else to maintain him but his bawling, he might button up his Chops, and burn his Buchrom Bag, or else hang it upon a pin untill its Antiquity had eaten it up with durt and dust : Then with a Spade, like his Grandsire *Adam*, turn up the face of Creation, purchasing his bread by the sweat of his brows, that before was got by the motionated Water-works of his jaws. So contrary to the Genius of the people, if not to the quiet Government

of the Province, that the turbulent Spirit of continued and vexatious
Law, with all its querks and evasions, is openly and most eagerly
opposed, that might make matters either dubious, tedious, or troublesom. All other matters that would be ranging in contrary and improper
Spheres, (in short) are here by the Power moderated, lower'd, and
subdued. All villanous Outrages that are committed in other States,
are not so much as known here : A man may walk in the open Woods
as secure from being externally dissected, as in his own house or dwelling. So hateful is a Robber, that if but once imagin'd to be so, he's
kept at a distance, and shun'd as the Pestilential noysomness.

It is generally and very remarkably observed, That those whose Lives
and Conversations have had no other gloss nor glory stampt on them in
their own Country, but the stigmatization of baseness, were here (by
the common civilities and deportments of the inhabitants of this Province) brought to detest and loath their former actions. Here the Constable hath no need of a train of Holberreers, that carry more Armour
about them, then heart to guard him : Nor is he ever troubled to leave
his Feathered Nest to some friendly successor, while he is placing of his
Lanthern-horn Guard at the end of some suspicious Street. . . .
Here's no *Newgates* for pilfering Felons, nor *Ludgates* for Debtors, nor
any *Bridewels* to lash the soul . . . into a chast Repentance. For as
there is none of these Prisons in *Mary-Land*, so the merits of the Country deserves none, but if any be foully vitious, he is so reserv'd in it, that
he seldom or never becomes popular. Common Ale-houses, (whose dwellings are the only Receptacles of debauchery and baseness, and those
Schools that trains up youth, as well as Age to ruine) in this Province there
are none ; neither hath youth his swing or range in such a profuse and unbridled liberty as in other Countries ; for from an ancient Custom at the
primitive seating of the place, the Son works as well as the Servant, (an
excellent cure for untam'd Youth) so that before they eat their bread,
they are commonly taught how to earn it ; which makes them by that
time Age speaks them capable of receiving that which their Parents indul-
gency is ready to give them, and which partly is by their own laborious
industry purchased, they manage it with such a serious, grave, and
watching care, as if they had been Masters of Families, trained up in
that domestick and governing power from their Cradles. These Christian Natives of the Land, especially those of the Masculine Sex, are
generally conveniently confident, reservedly subtle, quick in apprehend-
ing, but slow in resolving ; and where they spy profit sailing towards

them with the wings of a prosperous gale, there they become much familiar. The Women differ something in this point, though not much : They are extreme bashful at the first view, but after a continuance of time hath brought them acquainted, there they become discreetly familiar, and are much more talkative than men. All Complemental Court-ships, drest up in critical Rarities, are meer strangers to them, plain wit comes nearest their Genius ; so that he that intends to Court a *Mary-Land* Girle, must have something more than the Tautologies of a long-winded speech to carry on his design, or else he may (for aught I know) fall under the contempt of her frown, and his own windy Oration.

One great part of the Inhabitants of this Province are desiredly Zealous, great pretenders to Holiness ; and where any thing appears that carries on the Frontispiece of its Effigies the stamp of Religion, though fundamentally never so imperfect, they are suddenly taken with it, and out of an eager desire to any thing that's new, not weighing the sure matter in the Ballance of Reason, are very apt to be catcht. *Quakerism* is the only Opinion that bears the Bell away : The Anabaptists have little to say here, as well as in other places, since the Ghost of *John of Leyden* haunts their Conventicles. The *Adamite, Ranter,* and *Fift-Monarchy men, Mary-Land* cannot, nay will not digest within her liberal stomach such corroding morsels : So that this Province is an utter Enemy to blasphemous and zealous Imprecations, drain'd from the Lymbeck of hellish and damnable Spirits, as well as profuse prophaness, that issues from the prodigality of none but crackt-brain Scots.

> *'Tis said the Gods lower down that Chain above.*
> *That tyes both Prince and Subject up in Love ;*
> *And if this Fiction of the Gods be true,*
> *Few,* MARY-LAND, *in this can boast but you :*
> *Live ever blest, and let those Clouds that do*
> *Eclipse most States, be alwayes Lights to you ;*
> *And dwelling so, you may for ever be*
> *The only Emblem of Tranquility.*

George Alsop, *A Character of the Province of Mary-Land,* etc. (London, 1666), 15-26.

77. The Quaker and the Nobleman (1683)

BY WILLIAM PENN AND CHARLES, LORD BALTIMORE

The beginning of this correspondence marks an early stage in a controversy which ended in the surveying of Mason and Dixon's Line in 1767. — Bibliography: Hazard, *Annals of Pennsylvania*, 586–615; Winsor, *Narrative and Critical History*, III, 488, 514; Channing and Hart, *Guide*, §§ 100, 107.

A. BALTIMORE'S PROTEST

S.ʳ   Munday the 5ᵗʰ of June 1682

I HAUE receiud yo.ʳ of the 26ᵗʰ of the last month and am Sorry it came noe sooner to my hands for I haue dispatcht some Gentlemen away to meet you at the time Appointed and therefore am no wise willing to put of this businesse of the ascertaining the bounds betwixt M.ʳ Pen and me There are many Reasons to be giuen by me for it but at present shall only offer you these two, ffirst that by a letter from his Most sacred Maiesty procured and sent by the same Penn I am Commanded to joyne with M.ʳ Penn or his Agents for the speedy settling our bounds and then M.ʳ Penns owne letter which you brought me prest very much the same thing; Secondly that M.ʳ Penn the last Shipping writt and sent in a letter to seuerall Gentlemen of note that are Certainly within my Prouince as M.ʳ Augustin Herman Capt.ⁿ Ward, Coll Wells &c hinting to them that he was confident they would come within his Gouerm.ᵗ a thing not kindly taken and to be plaine not according to the Goulden rule mentioned in M.ʳ Penns Letter to me, *Doe to thy neighbor as thou wouldst he should doe to thee* Now certainly such proceedings were not Neighbour like and when I haue the happiness to see my friend I must be plaine w.ᵗʰ him as to that point for as I desire noe more then my due soe I take it very vnkindly that some of the Inhabitants vp the Bay should be soe Posest as they haue been by th.ᵗ Letter of M.ʳ William Penns — ffor these reasons S.ʳ I must begg leaue to say I will not admitt of any further delay you well knowing th.ᵗ yo.ʳ Late sickness has bin the only hinderance hitherto. Let me therfore now presse you to send persons qualified and equally impowr'd w.ᵗʰ those persons who on my part are already gon and will be in all probability with you afore this will arriue at your hands I haueing Possitiuely ordered them to request the same from you on the behalf of

Yo.ʳ faithfull friend & Seru.ᵗ

C. B. :

B. PENN'S CONVENIENCY

My Noble Fr.ᵈ

IF vpon my arrival in this Province, I did immediately dispatch my
Secretary with two other gentlemen to Salute the Lord Baltimore &
assure him of my respects & frdshp's If so soon as I had pay'd my duty
to my Royall Patrone the Duke, I did incontinently take a long Journy
in a cold and unpleasant season, thᵗ I might personally give him the
further Pledges, of a freindly agreement & neighbourhood. And if I
did then therefore wave to press myn own Advantages, because I found
it uneasy to him ; And lastly, if in my after Correspondences, and especially as our last interview, I have declined the rigour of my plea & both
propos'd and prest some of the mildest & most healing expedients thᵗ if
possible, we might be the last Arbitrators of our own affaires without the
need of an other umpire, then the good will we ought to bear to a
mutual & lasting union, The Lord Baltimori, I would think, will be so
kinde as to lett me hope, he will pardon me if I stop here, & shall hold
myself acquitted by the endeavours I have used, wᵗʰ so much Industry
& submission, for a freindly Issue. And if there were anything below
what I have already offer'd besides Ruine to my Province, God is both
my wittness & my Judge, I should be but too apt to encline.

My Noble Fr.ᵈ I am not mov'd by the power of Ambition or Avarice ;
It is Conveniency yea necessity thᵗ bids me stand. I deal freely. I
have outrun all Councels, thᵗ I might purchase peace, tho' with loss ;
but wᵗʰ distruction, even nature & Reason forbid. What I seek be it
myn own, & so my due ; or the Lord Baltim.ʳ & such, if he please, my
Purchass, It is of thᵗ minute Consequence to him & mighty moment to
me, because to his Country the Tale or Skirt, to my Province the Mouth
or Inlett, that the disproportion of the vallue & Conveniency thᵗ it beares
to either of us, will defend, at least, indulge my greater Importunity ;
And yet while the advantage seems to be mine, It is most manefest it
will be greatly his proffitt to comply ; since it will lay his Province between two planted Countrys, And the People transporting themselves to
Pennsilvania in Ships consign'd to Maryland and thos ships yearly bringing such englesh goods as we shall want, will naturally draw our people
into his Province to furnish themselves, & to make Maryland the Mark
of englesh trade, at least for many yeares.

What shall I say, My Noble Freind, if the powerfull charmes of interest, if the Love of good Neighbourhood, if thᵗ wᶜʰ is always to be prefer'd, wᵗʰ Persons of the Lord Baltimores Loyalty, I mean Duty to the

T

King, prevale, I must yet promess myselfe an agreement in some faire & happy expedient, & lay by (wch shall be wth delight) the thoughts of an english voyage, th^t else, the state of my affaires here, & of my famely there, will of necessity obleidge me to & that^t speedely.

I shall end wth this assurance wch I have often Given, and shall most religiously observe, that I shall sincerely embrace all occasions by wch I may approve my selfe

My Noble Fr^d
Thy very Firme
& Affect. Fr^d & Neigh^r
Wm Penn

The Calvert Papers (Maryland Historical Society, *Fund-Publications*, No. 28, Baltimore, 1889), 330-331 ; 328-329.

CHAPTER XII — THE CAROLINAS

78. "A Declaration & Proposealls to all yᵗ will plant in Carrolina" (1663)

BY THE LORDS PROPRIETORS

Charles II made a grant of Carolina to various favorites as a proprietary colony: this document is their invitation to settlers. — Bibliography: Winsor, *Narrative and Critical History*, V, 290, 335-356; Channing and Hart, *Guide*, § 102.

HIS Maᵗⁱᵉ. haveing been graciously pleased, by his Charter bareing date yᵉ 24ᵗʰ of March in yᵉ 15th yeare of his reigne [1663], out of a Pious & good Intention for yᵉ propogaͨõn of yᵉ Christian faith amongst yᵉ Barbarous & Ignorant Indians, yᵉ Inlargemᵗ of his Empire & Dominions, & inriching of his Subjects: To Graunte & confirme unto us, Edward Earl of Clarending, High Chancellʳ. of England, George, Duke of Albemarle, Master of his Maᵗⁱᵉˢ. Horse & Capt. Genˡˡ. of all his Forces; Wᵐ. Lord Craven, John Lord Berkeley, Antho. Lord Ashley, Chancˡˡʳ. of his Maᵗⁱᵉˢ. Exchequʳ., Sʳ. George Carteret, Kᵗ. & Barᵗ., Vice-Chamberline of his Maᵗⁱᵉˢ. Household, Wm. Berkeley, Kᵗ. & Sʳ. John Colleton, Kᵗ. & Bart. All yᵗ. terrytory or tract of Ground wᵗʰ. yᵉ Islandes & Isletts sittuate, lyeinge & being in his Dominions in America, extending from yᵉ north end of the Island called Lucke Island, wᶜʰ. lyeth in yᵉ Southerne Verginia Sea, & wᵗʰ in 36 degrees of yᵉ Northine Lattitude & to the west as farr as yᵉ South Seas, and soe southerly as farr as yᵉ river St. Mathias, wᶜʰ. bordereth upon yᵉ Coast of Florida & wᵗʰ. in   degrees of yᵉ Northine Lattitude in pursewance of wᶜʰ. Grannte, & wᵗʰ. a cleare & good intention to make those parts usefull & advantagious to his Maᵗⁱᵉ. & his people. Wee doe hereby declare & propose to all his Maᵗⁱᵉˢ. loveing Subjects wheresoever abideing or resideing, and doe hereby ingaige inviolably to performe & make good these ensueing proposealls in such manʳ. as yᵉ first Undʳtakʳˢ. of yᵉ first Setlemᵗ. shall resonably desire.

1. If yᵉ first Collony will setle on Charles River neare Cape Feare wᶜʰ. seemes to be desired it shalbe free for them soe to doe on yᵉ Larboard side entring [south side]. If in any other part of yᵉ Terrytory,

then to choose eith^r. side, if by a riv^r., we reserveing to o^rselves 20,000 acres of Land, to be bounded & leyed out by o^r. Agents in each Setlem^t. in such places as they shall see fitt, & in such man^r. as ye Collony shall not be thereby incomoaded or weakned wch. we intend by o^r. Agents or Assignes in dew time to setle & plant, they submitting to ye Goverment of that Collony.

2. That ye first Collony may have pow^r. when desired at there owne charge to fortifie ye entrance of ye riv^r., as alsoe ye sea coast & Islands, they ingageing to be trew & faithfull to his Matie., his heires & Successo^{rs} by some oath or Ingaigem^t. of their owne frameing.

3. That ye Undertakers of y^t. Settlem^t. doe before they or any of them repaire theither to setle present to us 13 persons of those y^t intend to goe, of wch. numb^r. we shall comissionate one to be Govr. for 3 yeares from ye date of his Comission, and 6 more of ye 13 to be of his Councell, ye Maio^r. parte of wch. numb^r. ye Govern^r. or his Deputy to be one to governe for ye time afores^d. & will alsoe nominate Successo^{rs}. to ye govern^r, whoe shalbe of ye 6 Councello^{rs} afores^d. to succeed in ye Goverm^t. in case of deth or removeall, & likewayse Councell^{rs} out of ye remayneing 6 of ye 13 to succeed in case of death or removeall of any of ye Councell^{rs}. & aft^r. ye expiracon of ye first three yeares & soe successively for every 3 yeares. Upon or before ye 25th day of March, before ye expiracon of ye time of ye Governo^r in being a new presentm^t. by ye freehold^{rs} of ye Collony, or by such persons as they shall constitute to be made of ye 13 persons, 4 of wch. shall consist of those y^t. shalbe in ye Governm^t. at ye time of ye Election of ye 13 out of wch. we will upon or before ye 10th day of Aprill following, declare & Comissionate a Govern^r. & 6 Councell^{rs}., wth. there respective Success^{rs}., in case & manor as afores^d.

4. Wee shall as farr as o^r. Charter permitts us, impower ye Maio^r. parte. of ye freehold^{rs}., or there Deputyes or Assemblymen, to be by them choasen out of themselves, viz.: Two out of every tribe, devision or parish, in such mano^r as shall be agreed on to make there owne lawes by & wth ye advice & consent of ye Govern^r & Councell, soe as they be not repugnant to ye lawes of England, but as neare as may be agreing wth them in all Civill affaires wth submission to a Superintendancy of a Gen^{ll}. Councill, to be choasen out of every Gover^t. of ye Province, in man^r as shalbe agreed on for ye Comon defence of ye whole, wch. lawes shall, wthin one yeare aft^r. publication be presented to us to receave o^r. Rattification, & to be in force untill s^d. Rattification be denyed, & by us

certyfied, but if once rattifyed, to continew until repealed by ye same power or by time expired.

5. We will Grante, in as ample man^r. as ye Und^{r}takers shall desire, freedomes & libertye of contience in all religious or spirituall things, & to be kept inviolably wth. them, we haveing power in o^r. Charter soe to doe.

6. We will Grante ye full benefitt of these Imunityes to ye Und^r-takers & Setlers wch. by ye Charter is granted to us (for o^r. services to his Matie.,) in relation to freedome, of customes, of tooles, of all sorts usefull there to be exported from England for ye planters use, & of certine Groathes of ye Plantaçõns, as Wine, Oyle, reasons of all sorts, Ollives, Capers, Wax, Currants, Almondes & Silkes to be imported into any of his Maties. Dominions for 7 years for each comodity, aft^r 4 touns of every respective spetie is imported as afores^d. in one Bottome.

7. Wee will Grante to every present Und^{r}taker for his owne head, 100 acres of land, to him and his heires forever, to be held in free and comon Soccage, & for every man Sarv^t. y^t. he shall bringe or send thith^r. y^t. is fitt to bare Armes, armed wth. a good fierlocke Musket, performed boare, 12 bullets to ye pound, & wth. 20 lb. of powder & 20 lb. of Bullets, 50 acres of land, & for every woman Sarv^t. 30 Acres, & to every man Sarv^t. y^t. shall come wthin y^t. time, 10 Acres aft^r. ye expiraçõn of his time, & to every woman Sarv^t. 6 Acres aft^r. ye expiraçõn of her time. Note y^t. we intend not heareby to be obliged to give ye proportions of lands above mentioned to Mast^{rs}. & Sarv^{ts}. long^r then in ye first five yeares to comence at ye begining of ye first Setlem^t.

8. We will injoine ye Governo^r and Councill to take care y^t. there be alwayse one man armed & provided as afores^d. in ye Collony for every 50 Acres wch. we shall Grante, & y^t. there be a Supply to make up y^e numb^r. in case of deth or quitting y^e Collony by y^e owners of s^d. lands wthin 12 moneths aft^r. notice given of y^e defect.

In consideration of y^e premises we doe expect by way of acknowledgem^t. & towardes y^e charge we have beene & shal be at one $\frac{1}{2}$ penny for every acre y^t. shal be graunted as afores^d. wthin y^e time before limitted & exprest, & y^t. y^e Court houses & howses for publicke meetings be erected by y^e publicke monyes of y^e Collony on y^e landes taken up by us, but to be & continew to y^e Countryes use forever, they paying some small acknowledgem^t.

Given und^r. o^r. handes this twenty-fifth day of August, Anno D^{ni}., 1663.

William James Rivers, *A Sketch of the History of South Carolina* (Charleston, 1856), 335–337.

79. Suggestions on Granting Lands (1665)

BY THOMAS WOODWARD

Woodward was Surveyor for the Proprietors; his suggestions are shrewd and weighty. — Bibliography as in No. 78 above.

. . . I UNDERSTAND by Mr Drummond and Mr Carterett that you and the rest of the Right Honorable the Lords Proprietors of the Province of Carolina have appointed me to be Surveyor for your Countie of Albemarle Wherein ("Pray be pleased to assure your Lordships") I will endeavour to serve you faithfully, and to the uttermost of my Power promote your Interest. And though I know it befitts not me to dispute your comands but rather to operate them Cœca Obedientia yet (by your Honors permission) I cannot omit to performe another part of my dutie (so I am though unworthy) one of the counsell here to give you my opinion concerning some passages in the Instructions your Honore sent us. First for the bounds of the Countie of Albemarle fortie miles square will not comprehend the Inhabitants there already seated. And sixteen hundred square miles may be laid out by runing only on the Verges of the Rivers and Creekes where generally men seat and where (for the most part) the plantable land lies so disadvantagious to your Honores Interest, and the Inhabitants Welfare; that no reasonable line of communication will be able to unite them either for defence or Traffick. So that I conceive it will be most comodious to bound this Governmt. On the south side with the North end of Croatan Island Thence west to Morattuck, Including all the Branches thereof, Thence North as far as your Patent extends Then East to the Sea; And to prohibit all Persons for some time from seating beyond there bounds as also not yet to seat up Morattuck: Which bounds though they are greater than your Honors Instructions allow for Albemarle countie yet are they not more than will consist well with one Governmt. It being (in my opinion) very inconvenient to erect divers Governments to have Passage through one-an-others Territories or Inletts: as Maryland having no Inlet for shipping but through the Capes of Virginia. May (if any difference shall happen between those two Governments) in a high measure feel the Inconvenience And the Inhabitants of all the streams or rivers within this Government must be supplyed with Commodities from such Vessells as shall arrive through Roanokea Inlett which for ought we can perceive must always be of very small burthen. for although Capt Whitties vessell this winter at her coming in found fifteene feete water, yet her going out she had but eleaven feete and though she drew not eight foote water, struck twice or thrice notwithstanding they had Beatoned the Chanell and went out in the best of it, at full sea; so uncertaine are all those Inletts. There is another Inlett at Wococock or Wococon which hereafter may serve for an other Government betweene this and Cape Feare, if to your Honore it shall seem Convenient.

Next the Proportione of Land you have allotted with the Rent, and conditione are by most People not well resented and the very Rumor of them dis-courages many who had intentions to have removed from Virginia hether: Whilst my Lord Baltamore allowed to every Persons imported but fiftie acres; Maryland for many yeares had scarce fiftie families, though there Rent was rather easier then in Virginia; but when he allotted one hundred Acres for a Person, it soone began to People. and when he found them begin to increase, he brought it to fiftie a head againe So if your Lordships please to give large Incouragement for some time till the country be more fully Peopled, your Honore may contract for the future upon what condition you please But for the present, To thenke that any men will remove from Virginia upon harder Conditione then they can live there will prove (I feare) a vaine Imagination, It bein Land only that they come for.

I shall give you Sr Francis Bacons owne words in his Essay of Plantation

" Planting of Counties is like planting of Woods, for you must make account to loose almost Twenty years Profitt and expect your recompense in the end: for the Principall thing that hath bin the destruction of most Plantations hath bin the hastee drawing of Profit in the first yeares."

And it is my Opinion, (which I submitt to better Judgements) that it will for some time conduce more to your Lordshipe Profit to permit men to take up what tracts of Land they please at an easie rate, then to stint them to small proportions at a great rent, Provided it be according to the custome of Virginia which is fifty Pole by the river side, and one mile into the woods for every hundred acres; there being no man that will have any great desire to pay Rent (though but a farthing an acre) for more land than he hopes to gaine by. Rich men (which Albemarle stands in much need of) may perhaps take up great Tracts; but then they will endeavour to procure Tenants to helpe towards the payment of their Rent, and will at their owne charge build howseing

(which poore men cannot compasse) to invite them : Besides to have
some men of greater possessions in Land then others, will conduce more
to the well being and good Governement of the Place than any Levelling
Paritie To reduce Planters into Townes, is here almost impossible ; when
the country is Peopled and comerce increased it may more easily be
effected, by appoynting Ports and Marketts whether not only Merchants
but all Tradesmen and Artificers will resort for habitation, and in short
time lay the foundation to superstructures of Townes and Citties;
Alwayes Provided there be a course taken for procuring a coine with out
which no Towne nor Markitt can well subsist : And this can no way be
effected but by the ballance of Trade ; And therefore I doe most highly
applaude your Lordshipe designe of making Wine in this Country : for
I am confident that if the value of the drinke only within Twenty yeares
past brought into Virginia had been Imported in Silver; Virginia would
have had more money for the number of her English Inhabitants then
most if not the most opulent countrys have in Europe.　But S^r I begin
now to go beyond my last.　If my zeale to this Place (which I have many
years endeavoured and encouraged to seate) transports me to this kind
of building Castles in the Aire, I hope your Goodnesse will be pleased
to excuse me since I perceive there are some well willers to this Place
in England doe the like : I shall therefore conclude with this humble
request that you will be pleased to entertain thes Truth for a Maxim

　　Those that live upon a Place are best able to Judge of that Place
Therefore the Petition of the Generall Assemblie that was here convened will diserve your Honors serious consideration ; of which with
theire other proceedings likewise, I doubt not but our Noble Governor
will give you a true Accompt, he being by the Assembly therewith intrusted　And if in any thing (besides the Publique) I can serve your
Perticular Interest Command . . .

William L. Saunders, editor, *Colonial Records of North Carolina* (Raleigh,
　　1886), I, 99-101.

————

80.　The Fundamental Constitutions Altered (1682)

BY THE LORDS PROPRIETORS

The so-called " Fundamental Constitutions " were a scheme of feudal government,
drawn up by the philosopher Locke in 1669 for the Proprietors, but not adapted to
the times or the conditions of a colony of freemen.　The document is omitted, since

ít never really went into effect; this piece summarizes parts of it. — Bibliography: Winsor, *Narrative and Critical History*, V, 290–292 ; Channing and Hart, *Guide*, § 102.

WEE having been prevailed upon at the request of severall eminent worthy Persons who have a mind to become settlers in our Province of Carolina, to make review of our fundamentall Constitutions, & to make therein some additions & alterations, wee have now sent them to you signed & sealed anew, & as they are to be for the future, & these additions & alterations being for the greater Liberty, security & Quiet of the people, wee doe not doubt but you will acquiesce in them, which is the reason that wee have done it without proposeing of it first unto you. The additions & alterations we have made are as followeth :

In the first place, our fundamentall Constitutions, bearing date the first of March, 1669, hath appointed y^t. ye eldest man of the then Lords Proprietors shall be Palatine, & soe on untill they are all deceased, & the next eldest, & soe on, shall have their choyce of the severall great offices, but since that time some of the then Lords Proprietors having sold their Proprietorships, & in our Constitutions of the first of March, 1669, there being no Provison made who those who by succession or bying are or shall become Proprietors shall succeed to be Palatine, or have their choyce of the other great offices, nor how ye inconveniencies shall be avoided that may possibly happen to the Inhabitants of your Province, by leaveing those Proprietors that have bought out others, & are younger than others that have bought or succeeded to be proprietors in a capacity (out of avarice or perverseness) to make leases or fraudilent conveyances of their Proprietorships to men elder than the other Proprietors that have bought or are succeeded to be Proprietors, thereby to defraud them of the proffitts of ye Palatin's Place or the government, by which means Little men & of unjust Principalls may get into ye Governm^t., & the administration of the offices of greatest trust, w^h can neither be for ye ease nor safety of the Inhabitants of our Province, of which we have a most tender regard — to obviate those inconveniences have thought fitt by our Constitutions to apoint that he that hath been longest a proprietor of those that have bought or succeed, shall after the death of those who were Proprietors in 1669, succeed to be Palatine, & have the choice of the other seaven great offices, untill after the yeare 1700, when the Power of disposeing of Proprietorships ends, & takes away the forementioned inconvenience.

The next alteration is, that whereas in the fformer constitutions the assistants of the Colledges were chosen into the Grand Councill by the Grand Councill, by these constitutions he that hath been longest an assistant of any of the Colledges, & of the same degree & choice of him who is dead or removed, shall succeed to be of the Grand Councill, w^h wee judge to be more equall & lesse dependent than ye former way.

The next is, whereas by the former Constitutions nothing was to be proposed in the Parliament that had not first passed the Grand Councill, w^h. is the Senate of Carolina, & yett a negative reserved in the Palatine's Court upon all votes & orders of the Grand Councill, wee have in these our constitutions, left the Senate or Grand Councill at liberty to propose to the Parliament all such things as they shall, upon mature consideration, thinke fitting for the good of the people.

And whereas it is not impossible that even the Grand Councill or Senate of Carolina, that we have taken such care to have equally constituted for the good & quiet of the inhabitants of Carolina, may become corrupt & forgett their duty, & not take sufficient care to remedy inconveniences by proposing fitting Laws to be passed by the Parliament, wee have thought fitt to apoint that if the major part of the grand Juryes of the Countyes shall present a thing necessary to be passed into a law, & that if the Grand Councill do not in convenient time propose it to the Parli^mt., that then it shall be lawfull for any of the chambers to take cognizance of it, & propose it to ye house.

The next considerable alteration is, that whereas by the former constitutions all men whatsoever possessing Land in Carolina were obliged to pay a rent to ye Lords Proprietors after the yeare 1689, to comply with the desires of severall eminent wealthy men, who have an intention to become settlers in Carolina, & others that are already settled that have no mind to be Incombered with rent, wee have in these constitutions left a Liberty to the Lords Propri^tors to remitt it by an agreement under their hands & seals, all which alterations & additions being for the good & ease of the Inhabitants of our Province, wee doe not doubt but you will take kindly from us, nor doe wee pretend at any time hereafter to have power to alter any thing in our fundamentall Constitutions that restrains the liberty of the people, or inlarges the power of ye Proprietors, unlesse the Inhabitants of our Province shall by their Representatives first consent unto it. Wee rest, . . .

William James Rivers, *A Sketch of the History of South Carolina* (Charleston, 1856), 395-396.

81. An Account of the Province of Carolina (1682)

BY SAMUEL WILSON

Wilson was Secretary to the Proprietors.   As the Carolinas had been settled only about twenty-four years in 1689, most of the material upon them goes into Vol. II of this series. — Bibliography: Winsor, *Narrative and Critical History*, V, 340.

CAROLINA, is that part of *Florida*, which lies between *twenty nine* and *thirty six* degrees, and *thirty Minutes* of *Northern Latitude:* On the *East* it is washed with the *Atlantick Ocean*, and is bounded on the *West* by *Mare Pacificum* (or the South Sea) [Pacific Ocean] and within these bounds is contained the most healthy Fertile and pleasant part of *Florida*, which is so much commended by the Spanish Authors.

This *Province* of *Carolina*, was in the Year 1663. Granted by *Letters Pattents* in Propriety of his most Gracious *Majesty*, unto the Right Honourable *Edward Earl of Clarendon*, *George* Duke of *Albemarle*, *William* Earl of *Craven*, *John* Lord *Berkely*, *Anthony* Lord *Ashly*, now Earl of *Shaftsbury*, Sir *George Carteret*, and Sir *John Colleton*, Knights and Barronets, Sir *William Berkeley* Knight, by which Letters Pattents the Laws of *England* are to be of force in *Carolina :* but the *Lords Proprietors* have power with the consent of the Inhabitants to make By-Laws for the better Government of the said *Province :* So that no Money can be raised or Law made, without the consent of the Inhabitants or their Representatives.   They have also power to appoint and impower Governours, and other Magistrates to Grant Liberty of Conscience, make Constitutions, *&c*. With many other great Priviledges, as by the said Letters Pattents will more largely appear.   And the said Lords Proprietors have there setled a Constitution of Government, whereby is granted Liberty of Conscience, and wherein all possible care is taken for the equal Administration of Justice, and for the lasting Security of the Inhabitants both in their Persons and Estates.

By the care and endeavours of the said Lords Proprietors, and at their very great charge, two Colonys have been setled in this *Province*, the one at *Albemarle* in the most Northerly part, the other at *Ashly* River, which is in the Latitude of thirty two Degrees odd Minutes.   *Albemarle* bordering upon *Virginia*, and only exceeding it in Health, Fertility, and Mildness of the Winter, is in the Growths, Productions, and other things much of the same nature with it : Wherefore I shall not trouble the Reader with a perticular Description of that part ; but apply my self principally to discourse of the Collony at *Ashly-River*, which being many Degrees more Southward than *Virginia*, differs much from it in the Nature of its Clymate and Productions.

Ashly-River was first setled in *April* 1670. the Lords Proprietors having at their sole charge, set out three Vessels, with a considerable number of able Men ; eighteen Months Victuals, with Cloths, Tools, Ammunition, and what else was thought necessary for a new Settlement, and continued at this charge to supply the Collony for divers years after, until the Inhabitants were able by their own Industry to live of themselves ; in which condition they have been for divers years past, and are arrived to a very great Degree of Plenty of all sorts of Provisions. Insomuch, that most sorts are already cheaper there, than in any other of the English Collonys, and they are plentifully enough supplied with all things from *England* or other Parts. *Ashly-River*, about seven Miles in from the Sea, divides it self into two Branches ; the Southermost retaining the name of *Ashly-River*, the North Branch is called *Cooper-River*. In May, 1680. the Lords Proprietors sent their Orders to the Government there, appointing the Port-Town for these two Rivers to be Built on the Poynt of Land that divides them, and to be called *Charles* Town, since which time about an hundred Houses are there Built, and more are Building daily by the Persons of all sorts that come there to Inhabit, from the more Northern English Collonys, and the Sugar Islands, *England* and *Ireland ;* and many Persons who went to *Carolina* Servants, being Industrious since they came out of their times with their Masters, at whose charge they were Transported, have gotten good Stocks of Cattle, and Servants of their own ; have here also Built Houses, and exercise their Trades : And many that went thither in that condition, are now worth several Hundreds of Pounds, and live in a very plentiful condition, and their Estates still encreasing. And Land is become of that value near the Town, that it is sold for twenty Shillings *per* Acre, though pillaged of all its valuable Timber, and not cleared of the rest, and Land that is clear'd and fitted for Planting, and Fenced, is let for ten Shillings *per annum* the Acre, though twenty miles distant from the Town, and six men will in six weeks time, Fall, Clear, Fence in, and fit for Planting, six Acres of Land.

At this Town, in *November*, 1680. There Rode at one time sixteen Sail of Vessels (some of which were upwards of 200 Tuns) that came from divers parts of the Kings Dominions to trade there, which great concourse of shipping, will undoubtebly in a short time make it a considerable Town.

Samuel Wilson, *An Account of the Province of Carolina, in America* (London, 1682), 5–8.

CHAPTER XIII — SOUTHERN COLONIAL LIFE

82. "Newes from Virginia" (1610)

BY ROBERT RICH

The original is in stanzas of eight verses, here set in four lines to save space.—
Bibliography: Winsor, *Narrative and Critical History*, III, 81, 155; Alexander
Brown, *Genesis of the United States*, I, 420–426, II, 980; Edward Eggleston, *Beginners of a Nation*, 59–72.

READER, — how to stile thee I knowe not, perhaps Learned, perhaps unlearned; happily captious, happily envious; indeed, what or how to tearme thee I know not, only as I began I will proceede.

Reader, thou dost peradventure imagine that I am mercenarie in this busines, and write for money (as your moderne Poets use) hired by some of those ever to be admired adventurers to flatter the world. No, I disclaime it. I have knowne the voyage, past the danger, seene that honorable work of Virginia, and I thanke God am arrivd here to tell thee what I have seene, don, and past. If thou wilt believe me, so; if not, so too; for I cannot force thee but to thy owne liking. I am a soldier, blunt and plaine, and so is the phrase of my newes; and I protest it is true. If thou aske why I put it in verse, I prethee knowe it was only to feede mine owne humour. I must confesse that, had I not debard myselfe of that large scope which to the writing of prose is allowed, I should have much easd myselfe, and given thee better content. But I intreat thee to take this as it is, and before many daies expire, I will promise thee the same worke more at large.

I did feare prevention by some of your writers, if they should have gotten but some part of the newes by the tayle, and therefore, though it be rude, let it passe with thy liking, and in so doing I shall like well of thee; but, how ever, I have not long to stay. If thou wilt be unnaturall to thy countryman, thou maist, — I must not loose my patrymonie, I am for Virginia againe, and so I will bid thee hartily farewell with an honest verse, —

> As I came hether to see my native land,
> To waft me backe lend me thy gentle hand.

Thy loving Country-man,

R. R.

NEWES FROM VIRGINIA

It is no idle fabulous tale, nor is it fayned newes:
For *Truth* herselfe is heere arriv'd, because you should not muse.
With her both Gates and Newport come, to tell Report doth lye,
Which did devulge unto the world, that they at sea did dye.

Tis true that eleaven monthes and more, these gallant worthy wights
Was in the shippe *Sea-venture* nam'd depriv'd Virginia's sight.
And bravely did they glyde the maine, till Neptune gan to frowne,
As if a courser prowdly backt would throwe his ryder downe.

The seas did rage, the windes did blowe, distressed were they then;
Their ship did leake, her tacklings breake, in daunger were her men.
But heaven was pylotte in this storme, and to an iland nere,
Bermoothawes call'd, conducted then, which did abate their feare.

But yet these worthies forced were, opprest with weather againe,
To runne their ship betweene two rockes, where she doth still remaine.
And then on shoare the iland came, inhabited by hogges,
Some foule and tortoyses there were, they only had one dogge.

To kill these swyne, to yeild them foode that little had to eate,
Their store was spent, and all things scant, alas! they wanted meate.
A thousand hogges that dogge did kill, their hunger to sustaine,
And with such foode did in that ile two and forty weekes remaine.

And there two gallant pynases did build of seader-tree;
The brave *Deliverance* one was call'd, of seaventy tonne was shee.
The other *Patience* had to name, her burthen thirty tonne;
Two only of their men which there pale death did overcome.

And for the losse of these two soules, which were accounted deere,
A sonne and daughter then was borne, and were baptized there.
The two and forty weekes being past, they hoyst sayle and away;
Their ships with hogs well freighted were, their harts with mickle joy.

And so unto Virginia came, where these brave souldiers finde
The English-men opprest with greife and discontent in minde.
They seem'd distracted and forlorne, for those two worthyes losse,
Yet at their home returne they joyd, among'st them some were crosse.

And in the mid'st of discontent came noble Delaware;
He heard the greifes on either part, and sett them free from care.
He comforts them and cheeres their hearts, that they abound with joy;
He feedes them full and feedes their soules with Gods word every day.

A discreet counsell he creates of men of worthy fame,
That noble Gates leiftenant was the admirall had to name.
The worthy Sir George Somers knight, and others of commaund;
Maister Georg Pearcy, which is brother unto Northumberland.

Sir Fardinando Wayneman knight, and others of good fame,
That noble lord his company, which to Virginia came,
And landed there; his number was one hundred seaventy; then
Ad to the rest, and they make full foure hundred able men.

Where they unto their labour fall as men that meane to thrive;
Let's pray that heaven may blesse them all, and keep them long alive.
Those men that vagrants liv'd with us, have there deserved well;
Their governour writes in their praise, as divers letters tel.

And to th' adventurers thus he writes be not dismayd at all,
For scandall cannot doe us wrong God will not let us fall.
Let England knowe our willingnesse, for that our worke is goode;
Wee hope to plant a nation, where none before hath stood.

To glorifie the lord tis done, and to no other end;
He that would crosse so good a worke, to God can be no friend.
There is no feare of hunger here for corne much store here growes,
Much fish the gallant rivers yeild, tis truth without suppose.

Great store of fowle, of venison, of grapes and mulberries,
Of chestnuts, walnuts, and such like, of fruits and strawberries,
There is indeed no want at all, but some, condiciond ill,
That wish the worke should not goe on, with words doe seeme to kill.

And for an instance of their store, the noble Delaware
Hath for the present hither sent, to testifie his care
In mannaging so good a worke, two gallant ships, by name
The *Blessing* and the *Hercules* well fraught, and in the same

Two ships, are these commodities, furres, sturgeon, caviare,
Blacke walnut-tree, and some deale boords, with such they laden are;
Some pearle, some wainscot and clapbords, with some sassafras wood,
And iron promist, for tis true their mynes are very good.

Then, maugre scandall, false report, or any opposition,
Th' adventurers doe thus devulge to men of good condition,
That he that wants shall have reliefe, be he of honest minde,
Apparel, coyne, or any thing, to such they will be kinde.

To such as to Virginia do purpose to repaire;
And when that they shall thither come, each man shall have his share.
Day wages for the laborer, and for his more content,
A house and garden plot shall have; besides, t'is further ment

That every man shall have a part, and not thereof denaid,
Of generall profit, as if that he twelve pounds ten shillings paid;
And he that in Virginia shall copper coyne receive,
For hyer or commodities, and will the country leave

Upon delivery of such coyne unto the Governour,
Shall by exchange at his returne be by their treasurer
Paid him in London at first sight, no man shall cause to grieve,
For, tis their generall will and wish that every man should live.

The number of adventurers, that are for this plantation,
Are full eight hundred worthy men, some noble, all of fashion.
Good, discreete, their worke is good, and as they have begun,
May Heaven assist them in their worke, and thus our newes is done.

R. Rich, *Newes from Virginia* (edited by J. O. Halliwell, London, 1865), 8–22.

———◆———

83. "Restraint of the Disordered Trading of Tobacco" (1620)

BY KING JAMES FIRST

King James, "the wisest fool in Christendom," besides this proclamation wrote an elaborate attack on tobacco, called *A Counter-Blast to Tobacco* (1604). — Bibliography: J. A. Doyle, *English in America, Virginia*, 221–235; Edward Eggleston, *Beginners of a Nation*, 73–98; Channing and Hart, *Guide*, § 97.

WHEREAS We,
      Out of the dislike we had of the use of Tobacco, tending to a generall and new Corruption both of Men's Bodies and Manners, and yet nevertheles houlding it of the two more tollerable that the same should be ymported amongest many other Vanities and Superfluities which came beyond the Seas, then permitted to be planted here within this Realm, thereby to abuse and misimploy the Soile of this fruitfull Kingdome;

Did, by our Proclamation, dated the *thirtieth Day of December nowe last past*, straightly charg and commaund, all, and everie Person and Persons, of what Degree or Condition soever, that they, or any of them, by themselves their Servantes, Workemen or Laborers, should not, from and after the *Second Day of February then next following*, presume to sowe set or plant or cause to be sowen set or planted, within this our Realme of England, and the Dominion of Wales, any sort or kinde of Tobacco whatsoever, and that they or any of them shold not maintaine or conteynue any old Stockes or Plantes of Tobacco formerly sowen or planted, but shold forthwith utterly destroy and roote up the same :

And whereas we have taken in into our Roiall Consideration, as well the great Waste and Consumption of the Wealth of our Kingdomes, as the endangering and impairing of the Health of our Subjectes, by the inordinate Liberty and Abuse of Tobacco, being a Weed of no necessarie Use, and but of late Yeares brought into our Dominions, and being credibly informed that divers Tobacconists, and other mean Persons, taking upon them to trade and adventure into the Partes beyond the Seas of Tobacco, to the intent to forestall and ingross the said Comodity upon unmerchantlike Condition, doe transport much Gould, Bullion and Coyne out of our Kingdomes, and do barter and vent the Staple Comodities of our Realme at under Values, to the intent to buy Tobacco, to the Discreditt of our native Marchandizes, and extream enhansing of the Rates and Prizes of Tobacco, and the great Disturbance and Decay of the Trade of the orderly and good Merchants ;

We, taking the Premises into our Princely Consideration, and being desirous to put a Remedy to the said Inconveniences, which we have long endevoured, though with less effect than we expected, have resolved to make some further Redress by restraining the disordered Traffique in that Comodity, and reduceing it into the Handes of able Persons that may manage the same without Inconvenience, whereby the general Abuse may be taken away, and the necessarie Use, if any be, may be preserved ;

Wee doe therefore, not only by these Presents, straitly charg and commaund, that our said Proclamation restraineing the Planting of Tobacco be in everie respect observed and performed, according to the tenor thereof, upon the Penalties therein contained, but also that no Person or Persons whatsoever, Englishmen, Denizens or Strangers, other then such as shal be authorized and appointed thereunto by Letters Patents under our Great Seal of England, doe import or cause to be imported into this our Realme of England or Domynion of Wales, or any part of them, or either of them, any Tobacco of what nature kinde or sorte soever after the *Tenth Day of July next ensueing the Date hereof*, from any the Partes beyond the Seas upon paine of Forfeiture to Us of all such Tobacco soe to be imported contrarie to the true meaneing of theis Presents, and upon such further Paines and Penalties as by the Lawes and Statutes of this Realme, or by the Severity or Censure of our Court of Starrchamber may be inflicted upon the Offendors for Contempt of this our Royall Comaunde : . . .

U

And, for the better Execution of this our Pleasure, we do hereby commaund all and singuler Customers, Comptrollers, Searchers, Waiters, and other Officers attending in all and everie the Portes, Creekes, or Places of lading or unlading, for the takeing collecting or receiving of any our Customes, Subsidies or other Dutyes, to take notice of this our Pleasure ; and we do hereby comaund and give Power and Authoritie unto them, and everie or any of them from tyme to tyme, as well to search any Shipp or other Vessell or Bottom riding or lying within any Port, Haven or Creeke within their several Charg and Place of Attendance for all Tobacco imported contrarie to the Intent of this our Proclamation, and the same being found to seize and take to our use, as also to take notice of the Names, and apprehend the Bringers and Buyers of the same to th' End they may receive condign Punishment for their Offences upon Pain that everie of the said Officers, which shall be found negligent, remisse or corrupt therein, shall loose his Place and Entertainment, and undergo such Paines and Penalties as by our Lawes, or the Censure of our said Court of Starchamber maie be inflicted upon them for the same,

And likewise we do hereby will ordaine and appoint, that it shall and may be lawfull to and for such Person and Persons, as shall be so as aforesaid authorized and appointed, by Letters Patents under our Great Seal to import Tobacco, by hymself or themselves, or his or their Deputy or Deputies with a lawfull Officer, to enter into any suspected Places at lawfull and convenient tymes, and there search, discover and fynd out any Tobacco imported, uttered, sould or vented, not marked or sealed as aforesaid contrarie to the true meaning hereof, and all such Tobacco soe found to seize, take away and dispose of, and the Owners thereof, or in whose Custodie the same shall be found, to informe and complaine of, to the end they may receave Punishment according to our Pleasure before herein declared.

And further, we do by theis Presents will and require all and singuler Majors, Sherriffes, Justices of Peace, Bailiffes, Constables, Headboroughes, Customers, Comptrollers, Searchers, Waiters, and all other our Officers and Ministers whatsoever, that they and everie of them, in their severall Places and Offices, be diligent and attendant in the Execution of this our Proclamation, and also aiding and assisting unto such Person and Persons, and his and their Deputies and Assignes, as we shall so as aforesaid authorize and appoint to import Tobacco, as well in any Search for Discoverie of any Act or Actes to be performed contrarie to the Intent of theis Presents, as otherwise in the doing or executeing of any Matter or Thing for the Accomplishment of this our Roiall Comaund.

And lastly our Will and Pleasure is, and we do hereby charg and comaund our Attorney Generall for the tyme being, to informe against such Persons in our Court of Starchamber from tyme to tyme, whose Contempt and Disobedience against this our Roiall Comaund, shall meritt the Censure of that Court. . . .

Thomas Rymer and Robert Sanderson, *Fœdera, Conventiones, Literæ, et Cujuscunque Generis Acta Publica, inter Reges Angliæ* (London, 1727), XVII, 233-235 *passim*.

---

84. Toleration in Maryland (1649)

BY THE MARYLAND ASSEMBLY

One of the vexed questions in colonial history is the real purpose and effect of this wise and humane statute. — Bibliography : Winsor, *Narrative and Critical History*, III, 560-561; Edward Eggleston, *Beginners of a Nation*, 258-265.

. . . FFORASMUCH as in a well governed and Xpian Comon Wealth matters concerning Religion and the honor of God ought in the first place to bee taken, into serious consideracōn and endeavoured to bee settled. Be it therefore ordered and enacted by the Right Ho^{ble} Cecilius Lord Baron of Baltemore absolute Lord and Proprietary of this Province with the advise and consent of this Generall Assembly. That whatsoever Ꝑson or Ꝑsons within this Province and the Islands thereunto belonging shall from henceforth blaspheme God, that is Curse him, or deny our Saviour Jesus Christ to bee the sonne of God, or shall deny the holy Trinity the ffather sonne and holy Ghost, or the Godhead of any of the said Three Ꝑsons of the Trinity or the Vnity of the Godhead, or shall use or utter any reproachfull Speeches, words or language concerning the said Holy Trinity, or any of the said three Ꝑsons thereof, shalbe punished with death and confiscatōn or forfeiture of all his or her lands and goods to the Lord Proprietary and his heires, And bee it also Enacted by the Authority and with the advise and assent aforesaid. That whatsoever Ꝑson or Ꝑsons shall from henceforth use or utter any reproachfull words or Speeches concerning the blessed Virgin Mary the Mother of our Saviour or the Holy Apostles or Evangelists or any of them shall in such case for the first offence forfeit to the said Lord Proprietary and his heirs Lords and Proprietaries of this Province the sume of ffive pound Sterling or the value thereof to be Levyed on the goods and chattells of every such Ꝑson soe offending, but in case such

Offender or Offenders, shall not then have goods and chattells sufficient
for the satisfyeing of such forfeiture, or that the same bee not otherwise
speedily satisfyed that then such Offender or Offenders shalbe publiquely
whipt and bee ymprisoned during the pleasure of the Lord Proprietary
or the Leive‍ᵗ or chiefe Governor of this Province for the time being.
And that every such Offender or Offenders for every second offence shall
forfeit tenne pound sterling or the value thereof to bee levyed as aforesaid, or in case such offender or Offenders shall not then haue goods and
chattells within this Province sufficient for that purpose then to bee publiquely and severely whipt and imprisoned as before is expressed. And
that every ꝑson or ꝑsons before mentioned offending herein the third
time, shall for such third Offence forfeit all his lands and Goods and bee
for ever banished and expelled out of this Province. And be it also
further Enacted by the same authority advise and assent that whatsoever ꝑson or ꝑsons shall from henceforth vppon any occasion of Offence
or otherwise in a reproachful manner or Way declare call or denominate
any ꝑson or ꝑsons whatsoever inhabiting residing traffiqueing trading or
comerceing within this Province or within any the Ports, Harbors, Creeks
or Havens to the same belonging an heritick, Scismatick, Idolator, puritan, Independant, Prespiterian popish prest, Jesuite, Jesuited papist, Lutheran, Calvenist, Anabaptist, Brownist, Antinomian, Barrowist, Roundhead,
Seꝑatist, or any other name or terme in a reproachfull manner relating to
matter of Religion shall for every such Offence forfeit and loose the som̄e
or [sic] tenne shillings sterling or the value thereof to bee levyed on the
goods and chattells of every such Offender and Offenders, the one half
thereof to be forfeited and paid unto the person and persons of whom
such reproachfull words are or shalbe spoken or vttered, and the other
half thereof to the Lord Proprietary and his heires Lords and Proprietaries of this Province, But if such ꝑson or ꝑsons who shall at any time vtter
or speake any such reproachfull words or Language shall not have Goods
or Chattells sufficient and overt within this Province to bee taken to satisfie the penalty aforesaid or that the same bee not otherwise speedily
satisfyed, that then the ꝑson or persons soe offending shalbe publickly
whipt, and shall suffer imprisonm͏ᵗ without baile or maineprise vntill hee
shee or they respectively shall satisfy the party soe offended or greived
by such reproachfull Language by asking him or her respectively for-
givenes publiquely for such his Offence before the Magistrate or cheife
Officer or Officers of the towne or place where such Offence shalbe
given. And be it further likewise Enacted by the Authority and con-

sent aforesaid That every person and persons within this Province that
shall at any time hereafter p̄phane the Sabbath or Lords day called Sunday by frequent swearing, drunkennes or by any uncivill or disorderly
recreacōn, or by working on that day when absolute necessity doth not
require it shall for every such first offence forfeit 2ˢ 6ᵈ sterling or the
value thereof, and for the second offence 5ˢ sterling or the value thereof,
and for the third offence and soe for every time he shall offend in like
manner afterwards 10ˢ sterling or the value thereof.   And in case such
offender and offenders shall not have sufficient goods or chattells within
this Province to satisfy any of the said Penalties respectively hereby
imposed for prophaning the Sabbath or Lords day called Sunday as
aforesaid, That in Every such case the p̄tie soe offending shall for the
first and second offence in that kinde be imprisoned till hee, or shee
shall publickly in open Court before the cheife Commander Judge or
Magistrate, of that County Towne or precinct where such offence shalbe
committed acknowledg the Scandall and offence he hath in that respect
given against God and the good and civill Governmᵗ of this Province And
for the third offence and for every time after shall also bee publickly
whipt.   And whereas the inforceing of the conscience in matters of
Religion hath frequently fallen out to be of dangerous Consequence in
those commonwealthes where it hath been practised, And for the more
quiett and peaceable governemᵗ of this Province, and the better to p̄serve
mutuall Love and amity amongst the Inhabitants thereof.   Be it Therefore also by the Lo : Proprietary with the advise and consent of this
Assembly Ordeyned & enacted (except as in this p̄sent Act is before
Declared and sett forth) that noe person or P̄sons whatsoever within
this Province, or the Islands, Ports, Harbors, Creekes, or havens thereunto belonging professing to beleive in Jesus Christ, shall from henceforth bee any waies troubled, Molested or discountenanced for or in
respect of his or her religion nor in the free exercise thereof within this
Province or the Islands thereunto belonging nor any way compelled to
the beleife or exercise of any other Religion against his or her consent,
soe as they be not unfaithfull to the Lord Proprietary, or molest or conspire against the civill Governemᵗ established or to bee established in
this Province vnder him on his heires.   And that all & every P̄son and
P̄sons that shall presume Contrary to this Act and the true intent and
meaning thereof directly or indirectly either in person or estate willfully
to wrong disturbe trouble or molest any person whatsoever within this
Province professing to beleive in Jesus Christ for or in respect of his

or her religion or the free exercise thereof within this Province other than is provided for in this Act that such p͂son or p͂sons soe offend-ing, shalbe compelled to pay trebble damages to the party soe wronged or molested, and for every such offence shall also forfeit 20ˢ ster-ling in money or the value thereof, half thereof for the vse of the Lo : Proprietary, and his heires Lords and Proprietaries of this Province and the other half for the vse of the party soe wronged or molested as aforesaid, Or if the p͂tie soe offending as aforesaid shall refuse or bee vnable to recompense the party soe wronged, or to satisfy such ffyne or forfeiture, then such Offender shalbe severely punished by publick whip-ping & imprisonmᵗ during the pleasure of the Lord Proprietary, or his Leivetenāt or cheife Governor of this Province for the tyme being with-out baile or maineprise   And bee it further alsoe Enacted by the author-ity and consent aforesaid That the Sheriff or other Officer or Officers from time to time to bee appointed & authorized for that purpose, of the County Towne or precinct where every particular offence in this p͂sent Act conteyned shall happen at any time to be cōmitted and where-vppon there is hereby a fforfeiture ffyne or penalty imposed shall from time to time distraine and seise the goods and estate of every such p͂son soe offending as aforesaid against this p͂sent Act or any p͂t thereof, and sell the same or any part thereof for the full satisfaccōn of such for-feiture, ffine, or penalty as aforesaid, Restoring vnto the p͂tie soe offend-ing the Remainder or overplus of the said goods or estate after such satisfaccōn soe made as aforesaid

The ffreemen haue assented. Tho : Hatton
Enacted by the Governor Willm Stone

Archives of Maryland (edited by William Hand Browne, Baltimore, 1883), I, 244–247.

———————◆———————

85. Religion in Virginia (1661)

BY R. G.

This "advisive narrative" was presented to the Bishop of London, September 2, 1661. — Bibliography: Winsor, *Narrative and Critical History*, III, 157.

TO shew the unhappy State of the Church in *Virginia*, and the true Remedy of it, I shall first give a brief Description of the Manner of our Peoples scatter'd Habitations there ; next shew the sad unhappy consequents of such their scatter'd Living both in reference to them-

selves and the poor Heathen that are about them, and by the way briefly
set down the cause of scattering their Habitations, then proceed to propound the Remedy, and means of procuring it ; next assert the Benefits
of it in reference both to themselves, and the Heathen ; set down the
cause why this Remedy hath not been hitherto compass'd ; and lastly,
till it can be procured, give directions for the present supply of their
Churches.

That part of *Virginia* which hath at present craved your Lordships
Assistance to preserve the Christian Religion, and to promote the
Building Gods Church among them, by supplying them with sufficient
Ministers of the Gospel, is bounded on the North by the great River
Patomek, on the South by the River *Chawan*, including also the Land
inhabited on the East side of *Chesipiack Bay*, called *Accomack*, and
contains about half as much Land as *England;* it is divided into several
Counties and those Counties contain in all about Fifty Parishes, the Families whereof are dispersedly and scatteringly seated upon the sides of
Rivers ; some of which running very far into the Country, bear the
English Plantations above a hundred Miles, and being very broad, cause
the Inhabitants of either side to be listed in several Parishes. Every
such Parish is extended many Miles in length upon the Rivers side, and
usually not above a mile in Breadth backward from the River, which is
the common stated breadth of every Plantation belonging to each particular Proprietor, of which Plantations, some extend themselves half a
mile, some a mile, some two miles, some three miles, and upward upon
the sides of those Rivers, many of them are parted from each other by
small Rivers and Creeks, which small Rivers and Creeks are seated after
the manner of the great Rivers. The families of such Parishes being
seated after this manner, at such distances from each other, many of
them are very remote from the House of God, though placed in the
middest of them. Many Parishes as yet want both Churches and Gleabes,
and I think not above a fifth part of them are supplyed with Ministers,
where there are Ministers the people meet together Weekly, but once
upon the Lords day, and sometimes not at all, being hindred by Extremities of Wind and Weather : and divers of the more remote Families
being discouraged, by the length or tediousnesse of the way, through
extremities of heat in Summer, frost and Snow in Winter, and tempestu-
ous weather in both, do very seldome repair thither.

By which brief Description of their manner of seating themselves in
that Wildernesse, Your Lordship may easily apprehend that their very

manner of Planting themselves, hath caused them hitherto to rob God in a great measure of that publick Worship and Service, which as a Homage due to his great name, he requires to be constantly paid to him, at the times appointed for it, in the publick Congregations of his people in his House of Prayer. . . .

But though this be the saddest Consequent of their dispersed manner of Planting themselves (for what Misery can be greater than to live under the Curse of God?) yet this hath a very sad Train of Attendants which are likewise consequents of their scatter'd Planting. For, hence is the great want of Christian Neighbourhood, of brotherly admonition, of holy Examples of religious Persons, of the Comfort of theirs, and their Ministers Administrations in Sicknesse, and Distresses, of the Benefit of Christian and Civil Conference and Commerce.

And hence it is, that the most faithfull and vigilant Pastors, assisted by the most carefull Church-wardens cannot possibly take notice of the Vices that reign in their Families, of the spiritual defects in their Conversations, or if they have notice of them, and provide Spiritual Remedies in their publick Ministery, it is a hazard if they that are most concerned in them be present at the application of them : and if they should spend time in visiting their remote and far distant habitations, they would have little or none left for their necessary Studies, and to provide necessary spiritual food for the rest of their Flocks. And hence it is that through the licentious lives of many of them, the Christian Religion is like still to be dishonoured, and the Name of God to be blasphemed among the Heathen, who are near them, and oft among them, and consequently their Conversion hindred.

Lastly, their almost general want of Schooles, for the education of their Children, is another consequent of their scattered planting, of most sad consideration, most of all bewailed of Parents there, and therefore the arguments drawn from thence, most likely to prevail with them chearfully to embrace the Remedy. This want of Schooles, as it renders a very numerous generation of Christians Children born in *Virginia* (who naturally are of beautifull and comely Persons, and generally of more ingenious Spirits then these in *England*) unserviceable for any great Employments either in Church or State, so likewise it obstructs the hopefullest way they have, for the Conversion of the Heathen, which is, by winning the Heathen to bring in their Children to be taught and instructed in our Schooles, together with the Children of the Christians. For as it is the Beauty and Glory of Christian Graces, shining in the lives of

Christians, which must make the Heathen that are men, in love with the Christian Religion ; so it is that love, which can only perswade them to bring in their Children to be taught and instructed in it : But as it is unlikely that such love should be wrought in them by the Glory of Christian Graces appearing in the Christians lives ; who (as now planted) are for the most part destitute of the ordinary means of Grace : so granting that this might be, yet it is very unlikely that any rationall Heathen should be perswaded to commit their Children to the teaching and education of such Christians, whom they shall perceive to want Schooles of learning (the means of both) for their own.

It were easie to adde to these a heap of evill consequents of their scattered Planting, which hinder their Temporal, as well as Spirituall happinesse. But I forbear, it being a task unsuitable for my Profession, and for that I know the Remedy to be the same for both, and the removing the one will be the removing of the other.

Onely for conclusion of this part, discovering *Virginia's* Disease and Misery, Your Lordship may be pleased to represent to your thoughts the Evills of the fore-mentioned consequents of their scattered Planting in reference to the poor Heathen ; the effecting whose conversion, should be the great and designed by all, who would be subservient to the Providence of God, in Transporting our Colonies thither.

The Heathen enter frequently into some of the remote dispers'd habitations of the Christians, the premises considered, what can they see which should make them in love with their Religion ? They see their Families disordered, their Children untaught, the publick Worship and Service of the great God they own, neglected ; neglected upon that very day, which they heare call'd the Lords Day, and to be by the Christians peculiarly set a part for it; yea so farre neglected, that some of the Heathen have complained it was the worst of the seven to them, because the servants of the Christians Plantations nearest to them, being then left at liberty, oft spent that day in visiting their *Indian* Towns, to the disquiet of the Heathen, but certainly to the great Scandall of the Christian Religion, and little hopes have the poor Heathen of redresse, whilst they see that Day so far neglected by the Christians, that in many Parishes they see no publick holy Assemblies of our people, no Ministers provided for the holy Ministrations of such Assemblies, no Churches erected and consecrated for such publique Sacred Ministrations ; or such in such desolate Places, and so remote from many of their habitations that an ingenuous Christian would blush to tell a Heathen, that They are the houses of the Christians great God, that made the Heaven and the Earth of nothing, in which he is honoured, worshipp'd, prayed unto, and his heavenly will taught from his holy Word: for if a sober discreet Heathen (and there are many such) should reply, Why hath not every Parish one of them, and Ministers belonging to them? why are they not better built? why will not all the Christians of a Parish bestow as much cost in building the house of their great God, as one particular Christian among them bestows upon his own house? what defence could an ingenuous Christian make, which should not at once both shame himself and the Christians he would defend? . . .

R. G., *Virginia's Cure: or an Advisive Narrative concerning Virginia* (London, 1662), 1–7 *passim.*

---

86. "Proposals for the Carrying on of the Negro's Christianity" (1681)

BY REV. MORGAN GODWYN

Godwyn was one of the few clergymen of his day to try to ameliorate the condition of the slaves. He published also *The Negro's & Indian's Advocate.* He had been in both Virginia and Barbadoes. — Bibliography: J. A. Doyle, *English in America, Virginia,* 356; E. D. Neill, *English Colonization of America,* 330.

BEFORE we enter upon this Debate, to prevent all troublesome Clamors and Objections against it, upon the score of *Interest,* this Position should first be laid down, and as a Principle fixt and Eternal, and from which a true Christian cannot recede, be resolved on, (*viz.*) That no Interest how great or (otherwise) just soever, may be admitted to stand in Competition with *Christianity.* . . .

And here also in this Consideration, we are especially to avoid Splitting upon this Solecism, both in Policy and Discretion, and against which, *Ecclus* hath so wisely cautioned us, ch. 37, *v.* 11. [*Not to ask Counsel for Religion of one that hath no Religion, nor of Justice of him that hath no Justice*] *nor of a Coward about Matters of War, nor of a Merchant concerning Exchange, nor of a Buyer concerning selling* &c. *for such will counsel for themselves, ver.* 8. So likewise for a *Christian* not to be guided or led by *Self-ended* Men, Enemies to his Profession, in these Debates and Proposals made for the Advancement of it. Such being only like to raise *Obstructions,* as hitherto they have always done;

and (as lately) to render that for impossible, which has not the least difficulty in it, where a right Method is used for effecting it.

No more are we to proceed herein, by the sole Advice of Persons *unacquainted* with the true State and Condition of the places where this Settlement or Conversion is to be wrought. . . .

These things being agreed on, we must then fall to consider of the People amongst whom we are to take our lot, and thereto to have an especial regard : As, whether they be *Slaves*, subject to the *English*, such as most of the *Negro's* there are ; or *free People* living of themselves, either amongst, or distant from the *English;* such as most of the *Indians* on the Continent (in *Virginia*, &c.) are. Or lastly, whether this is to be performed by way of further Setling and Establishment, even amongst the *English* themselves, which also is no less necessary. . . .

Now concerning the *Negro's*, whom I should think fit to be first taken in hand (as being the easiest Task, would their Owners be perswaded to consent thereto ; & the most absolutely necessary, this neglect being the most scandalous, and withal, the most impossible to be defended or excused :) The first and great step will be to procure (what I but just mentioned) their *Owners consent*, as being to be supposed *averse* thereto : not altogether, as is here believed, out of *Interest* (it being already secured to them by Laws of their own ;) but by reason of the trouble, and the fancied *needlessness* of the Work ; and to prevent all danger from their Slaves being furnisht with knowledge, consequent, they conceive thereto. However, because they pretend the other (and something there may be in that too,) to take off that *pretence*, it will be requisite,

1. That a Law be enacted to confirm such Laws of theirs, as are or shall be hereafter made to *secure their just Interest* in their Slaves ; That they may thereby be continued in their present State of *Servitude*, notwithstanding their being afterward *baptised*.

2. That all *unjust* Interests, and *ungodly* Advantages arising from their Slaves *Sunday-labour* and *Polygamie* (neither of them sufferable among *Christians*) be upon severest Penalties prohibited ; and this as well to the *unbaptised*, as to the rest. . . .

These *pretences* being thus fairly removed, if any *Aversion* still remains (as 'tis feared there will, and that for the truest Reasons above mentioned,) they must afterwards be invited thereto by good *Sermons* & *Books*, Preacht and Writ upon this Subject, and by discoursing with them in *private*. As also by the Example of the *Ministers* themselves in their *Families*. And lastly, (and which will do more then all the rest) by *Encouragments* from the *Government*. . . .

Another way, and which 'tis possible might prove most effectual, would be to get this impiety decryed here in *England*, where our *Planters* have an extraordinary *Ambition* to be *thought well of*, and thereby to *shame* them into *better Principles*. . . .

Now for the *Planter's* late Objections against this Work, as I have heard them represented (and I believe they are the best they had), . . .

1. They object their *Negro's* want of *English;* Whereas 'tis certain that there are some thousands of them, who understand *English*, no worse than our own People. *Let them begin with those.*

2. That it would make them *less governable;* the contrary to which is experimentally known amongst their Neighbours, both *French* & *Spaniards* in those parts. Now 'twould be too great a blemish to the *Reformation*, to suppose that *Popery* only makes its Converts better, but *Protestancy* worse; as this Allegation being admitted, it must be granted. And to prevent any fond conceit in them of Libertie, (an especial Branch of the same *Article*,) if there be any such danger, let two or three of each great *Family* be first *baptised;* whereby the rest seeing them continued as they were, that Opinion would soon vanish : . . .

3. As for their pretended Aversion to Christianity, the contrary thereto is known of most of them. And tho it is to be confessed that some are more careless and indifferent (having bin taught by the *English* to be *needless for them*) yet for the *general* they are observed to be rather *ambitious* of it. Nor, I dare affirm, can any single *Instance* of such *aversion* in any one of them, be produced.

4. As to their (alike pretended) *Stupidity*, there is as little truth therein : divers of them being known and confessed by their *Owners*, to be extraordinary *Ingenious*, and even to exceed many of the *English*. And for the rest, they are much the same with other People, destitute of the means of knowledge, and wanting *Education*.

5. One thing more there remains to be added, of which, tho they may be most afraid, yet they carefully keep it to themselves, and that is the possibility of their Slaves Expectation, not of *Freedom*, but of more *merciful Vsage* from them. . . .

§ IX. Yet now after this, if *difficulties* shall still be urged, (as no doubt but there will) and this Work upon that *stale pretence* must be further neglected and deferred ; I shall in opposition thereto, be bold to make some few demands : As, what those *difficulties* should be, which are so much greater, it seems, than those our *Ancestors* encountered with, even in *Pagan* Regions, and happily overcame ?   Whether we ever *tryed* how *difficult* the Work was, thereby to satisfie our selves, whether (indeed) it be such as it is apprehended (or, at least, *pretended*?) And whether such a trial would not justify us more, than thus, without trying, to conclude it *Impossible ?* . . .

In short, there is nothing upon Earth *more fecible* than this Design, were it but *heartily undertaken*, and, as I have said, *a right Method used for the effecting* of it. . . .

M. G. [Morgan Godwyn], *A Supplement to the Negro's & Indian's Advocate* (London, 1681), 5–12 *passim.*

87. Life of a Southern Planter (1681–1686)

BY COLONEL WILLIAM FITZHUGH

These extracts give a lively picture of the life of a busy and prosperous tobacco-planter, merchant, and lawyer, and throw light on the course of trade between the colony and the mother country. — Bibliography: Winsor, *Narrative and Critical History*, III, 161.

SIR: . . . I have no new matter to add only I would have you be very careful of my flax, hemp and hayseed, two bushels of each of which I have sent for because we have now resolved a cessation of making Tob° next year.   We are also going to make Towns, if you can meet with any tradesmen that will come in and live at the Town, they may have large privileges and immunitys.   I would have you to bring me in a good Housewife.   I do not intend or mean to be brought in as the ordinary servants are, but to pay her passage and agree to give her fifty shillings or three pound a year during the space of five years, upon which terms I suppose good Servants may be had, because they have their passage clear and as much wages as they can have there.   I would have a good one or none : I look upon the generality of wenches you usually bring in not worth the keeping.   I expect to hear from you by all conveniences for I assure you I let slip none to tell you, I am &c.   I would have you bring me two large Paper books, one to contain about fourteen or fifteen Quire of Paper the other about ten Quire and one other small one. . . .

Sir: Both yours I have received by Capt. Paine am glad of yours, sorry you came to no better market. I hope this year Tob° will rise by reason there's but small crops made throughout this country and Maryland too. I have got ready the Tob° I owe you which when your brother comes or any one by your order may receive ; we now look out every day for his arrival by whom I intend to ship thirty or fourty hh^{ds}, crops are so small and debts comes in so badly that I cannot send so much as I thought by twenty hh^{ds}, but what I do send is pretty good. What friends I can advise shall assuredly secure you. Mr. Scarlet has promised me to consign you twenty hh^{ds} and I believe shall get you some more this year. . . . I have ventured on a bargain of 20 £ Sterling for two negroes of Mr. Vincent Goddard for which I have drawn bills of Exchange upon you, which please give due exceptance. . . .

Sir: By Mr. Lucum and Mr. Lymes, bearing date 31st May and 2d June, I have given you an account of eleven hh^{ds} Tob° consigned to you together with several bills of Exchange to the value of £ 31 Sterling, besides Mr. Lucum's bills of Exchange for what value I know not yet, which according to my order receive of him. I desire your care in sending me in those things I sent for and do now send for, which are for my own particular use, therefore I desire you to take care in the goodness of them and what my money comes to more than I have given you advice of, please to send me it in Linnen, of which let gentish holland be finest except one piece of kenting and let there be two pieces of white Dimmety and one piece of colored. I refer the sorting the linnen to yourself, being mindfull of blue Linnen in the Parcel. If you could possibly procure me a Bricklayer or Carpenter or both, it would do me a great kindness and save me a great deal of money in my present building, and I should be willing to advance something extraordinary for the procuration of them or either of them. If you send in any tradesmen be sure send in their tools with them. Sir, my small acquaintance begs my excuse for not giving you an account of news Stirring. Although I have sent none yet I hope to receive some from you, together with the present transactions of affairs in England ; if the market gives any encouragement you may be sure to hear more from me for the future. . . .

I cannot miss this opportunity to beg my Excuse for parting so rudely without taking leave, I am sure some of the Company were equally concerned in the Bacchanalian Banquet and those that were not, cannot deny an Excuse to the great absurdity of Solacisms committed by

Bacchanals who have Priviledge by Bacchus himself the first Institutor of the Order. . . .

Absolute necessity of business calls me abroad so often that I am glad when I can have some leisure at home, I am taking of some and assure your self that you be one of the first whom when I get time I intend to visit.

Necessity as 'tis the mother of Invention, so it is the more so of Industry, which has so far been cherished here that there's little of any wool left in our parts not wrought up either in stockings and therefore no hopes of the purchase of any here. . . .

. . . S^r your promise to assist me in the purchase of those Negroes I requested you to buy for me, only desire farther advice and more particular directions which I shall now do.   I desired you in my former to buy me five or six, whereof three or four to be boys, a man and woman or men and women, the boys from eight to seventeen or eighteen, the rest as young as you can procure them, for price I cannot direct therein because boys according to there age and growth are valued in price, therefore S^r shall refer that wholly to yourself and doubt not your care therein and if you please to hire a messenger to come either way with them or to come immediately and give me notice thereof.   I shall gladly pay the Messenger and readily come down myself to make payment for the same. . . .

. . . what remains I will hereafter take care honestly to pay but hope you will make me some abatement for your Dumb Negro that you sold me ; had she been a new Negro, I must have blamed my fate not you ; but one that you had two years, I must conclude you knew her qualities which is bad at work worse at talking and took the opportunity of the Softness of my Messenger to quit your hands of her.   I will freely give you the £ 3, 5, o, overplus of £ 20 that he gave for her to take her again and will get her convey'd to your hands or hope if my offer be not acceptable you will make me some abatement of so bad a bargain. . . .

This is the first opportunity since I had left the honour of your good company to assure you that I am not unprovided with Arguments (if the Assembly requires it) to prove that the Laws of England are in force here, except where the Acts of Assembly have otherwise provided, by reason of the constitution of the place and people.   The Gentleman the bearer is my neighbour Doct^r Bancks whose health we drank at Maj^r Beverley's, he is come to wait upon the Govenour to get a grant of the high Sheriff's place whose predecessor Mr. Thos. Bunbury was a great sufferer by his untimely death in the said Office, and he as his sucessor has been a considerable sufferer thereby, as he is able truly to inform you and I dare say would esteem it an infinite obligation if your Hounour would be pleased to introduce him into the Govenour's knowledge and second his Endeavours. . . .

Instructions for Mr. Jnᵒ Withers his proceedings in his York journey June 5th, 1682. . . .

Eighthly. To purchase what likely Negroes you can either 1, 2, 3, 4, 5 or 6 what boys and men you possibly can, as few women as may be, but be sure not above two, to purchase neither man nor woman above thirty years old, not to exceed £20 for the price of a man unless he be extraordinary likely, to buy Mr. Walters' boy alone for £20 if you can or to give £54 for the three at most, what under you can, if you cannot purchase him alone. To proceed to £34 for Maj'r Peyton's two boys if you can't get them under or can't hear of a better purchase to do for me as for yourself in choosing and purchasing.

Ninthly, To pass Haverton's bills away in the purchase of Negroes if you Can.

Tenthly, To pass George Boyce his two bills in the Purchase of Negroes or any other swap to advantage nay though with loss.

Eleventhly, To pass Corbett's bills of £6 for anything to my best advantage though at halves or for any truck. . . .

. . . this conveniency give me this opportunity of returning you thanks for your favours especially your last which was accompanied with a generous promise of lending me the second and third part of Rushworth's Historical Collections and his tryal of the Earle of Strafford which I earnestly desire you will please send me by this bearer who will take great care of them and safely convey them to my hand. . . .

. . . Sʳ I have a great mind to try if Olives would not thrive well in the Streights, as far in the Northern Latitude as we are here, some of which sort you might procure in London : Therefore I will desire you to procure for me some of them, with directions how to manage them. And I hope you will furnish yourself with other rareties both for your own and your friends use, . . .

I have occasion for two pair of small Andirons for Chamber Chimneys, one pair of brass ones, with fire shovel and tongs, and one pair of iron ones well glazed ; with fire shovel, and tongs, also two indifferent large Iron backs for Chimneys wᶜʰ I would have you send me by the first ships. . . .

By a Stranger who had once occasion to buy some books of you, I had a relation of your living and thriving; therefore take this first conveniency of congratulating you and together w^t you, of a respectfull obedient and loving remembrance of all friends and relations there and desire not only by you to hear how they all do but intreat you to desire them to write to me than nothing would be more welcome or acceptable especially from my mother, brothers and Sister, uncles and Cousins and as many of them as are living and would be so kind to write. I have a long time in a strange land, struggled hard with fortune's adverse hand, but thank God in the end by God Almighty's blessing upon my mean endeavours (having no friend or relative to lend a supporting hand) have overcome, and I praise God live very contentedly and well and should be heartily glad of that communication, which this Distance admits of, by letters to hear from you and all friends there. . . .

With the Same Content and Satisfaction as wearied travellers take up their In, or weather Beaten Voyagers their desired Port After a long tedious and stormy voyage, so did I the most welcome joyfull and glad news of your health, welfare and prosperity, . . .

God Almighty hath been pleased to bless me with a very good wife and five pledges of our conjugall affection, three of which he has been pleased to call into the Arms of his Mercy, and lent me two, a hopefull boy and girle, . . . And as he has been pleased to dispense these, his choicest of blessings he hath likewise added a plentifull Dispensation of his favours in giving me a competent subsistence to support myself and them comfortably and handsomely. . . .

. . . for my Sister if she cannot otherwise better herself, I should be heartily glad of her good company, with an Assurance she shall never want as long as I have it to supply her. And if her inclination be to come I would desire and entreat you, that she come out handsomely & gentelely & well cloathed, with a maid to wait on her & both their passage paid there, . . .

. . . As first the Plantation where I now live contains a thousand acres, at least 700 acres of it being rich thicket, the remainder good hearty plantable land, without any waste either by marshes or great swamps the commodiousness, conveniency & pleasantness yourself well knows, upon it there is three quarters well furnished with all necessary houses; grounds and fencing, together with a choice crew of negro's at each plantation, most of them this Country born, the remainder as likely as most in Virginia, there being twenty-nine in

x

all, with stocks of cattle & hogs at each quarter, upon the same land, is my oun Dwelling house furnished with all accomodations for a comfortable & gentile living, as a very good dwelling house with rooms in it, four of the best of them hung & nine of them plentifully furnished with all things necessary & convenient, & all houses for use furnished with brick chimneys, four good Cellars, a Dairy, Dovecot, Stable, Barn, Henhouse, Kitchen & all other conveniencys & all in a manner new, a large Orchard, of about 2500 Aple trees most grafted, well fenced with a Locust fence, which is as durable as most brick walls, a Garden, a hundred foot square, well pailed in, a Yeard wherein is most of the foresaid necessary houses, pallizado'd in with locust Punchens, which is as good as if it were walled in & more lasting than any of our bricks, together with a good Stock of Cattle, hogs, horses, mares, sheep, &c, & necessary servants belonging to it, for the supply and support thereof.   About a mile & half distance a good water Grist miln, whose tole I find sufficient to find my own family with wheat & Indian corn for our necessitys & occasions up the River in this country three tracts of land more, one of them contains 21996 acres, another 500 acres, & one other 1000 acres, all good convenient & commodius Seats, & wch in few years will yield a considerable annual Income.   A stock of Tob^{o} with the crops and good debts lying out of about 25000$^{o'b}$ besides sufficient of almost all sorts of goods, to supply the familys & the Quarter's occasion for two if not three years.   Thus I have given you some particulars, which I thus deduce the yearly crops of Corn & Tob^{o} together with the surplusage of meat more than will serve the family's use, will amount annually to 60 000^{lb} Tob^{o} W^{ch} at 10 shilings p C^{os} 300£ p annum, & the negroes increase being all young & a considerable parcel of breeders will keep that stock good forever.   The stock of Tob^{o} managed with an inland trade will yearly yield 60000^{lb} Tob^{o} without hazard or risque, which will be both clear without charge of house keeping or disbursements for servants clothing.   The Orchard in a very few years will yield a large supply to plentifull house keeping or if better husbanded yield at least 10000^{lb} Tob^{o} annual income. . . .

Virginia Magazine of History and Biography (Richmond, Va.), I, 30–396 *passim.*

88. The Cultivation of Tobacco (1686)

BY REV. JOHN CLAYTON

Clayton was rector of Wakefield in Yorkshire: these extracts are from a report made to the Royal Society, May 12, 1688. — Bibliography: see No. 83 above; Channing and Hart, *Guide*, § 98.

. . . THE soil in general is sandy : I had designed, and I think it might be worth a critical Remark, to observe, the difference of Soils seem appropriated to the several Sorts of Tobacco : For there is not only the two distinct Sorts of sweet-scented and Aranoko Tobacco, but of each of these be several Sorts much different, the Seeds whereof are known by distinct Names, they having given them the Names of those Gentlemen most famed for such Sort of Tobacco, as of *Prior* Seed, &c.   Nay, the same Sort of Seed in different Earths, will produce Tobacco much different as to Goodness. The richer the Ground, the better it is for Aranoko Tobacco, whose Scent is not much minded, their only Aim being to have it specious, large, and to procure it a bright Kite's Foot Colour. . . .   The World knows little of the Efficacy of its Oil, which has wonderful Effects in the curing of old inveterate Sores, and scrophulous Swellings, and some, otherwise applied and qualified.   The Goodness of Tobacco I look on primarily consists in the Volatility of its Nitre : And hence the sandy Grounds that are most impregnated therewith, and whose nitrous Salt is most volatile, for such Grounds are quickliest spent, yield Tobacco's that have the richest Scent and that shortly become a pleasant Smoak ; whereas, in Tobacco that grows on stiff Ground, the Salts seem more fix'd, and locked up in the Oyl, so that whilst new, 'tis very heady and strong, and requires some time for its Salts to free themselves, and become volatile ; which it manifests, by its having an urinous Smell.   The same Reason satisfies, why Tobacco that grows on low Lands as far as the Salts, tho' the Plant be never overflowed with salt Water, yet the Ground that feeds the Plant being impregnated with salt Water, that Tobacco smoaks not pleasantly, and will scarcely keep Fire ; but do all that a Man can, will oft go out, and gives much trouble in frequent lighting the Pipe, 'till after it has been kept some considerable Time : . . .   I have observed, that that which is called Pine-wood Land, tho' it be a sandy Soil, even the sweet-scented Tobacco that grows thereon is large and porous, agreeable to Aranoko Tobacco, and smokes as coarsely as Aranoko : Wherefore 'tis, that I believe the Microscope might make nota-

ble Discoveries towards the Knowledge of good Tobacco: For the
closer the Composition of the Leaf, the better the Tobacco ; and therefore the Planters and Merchants brag of the Substance of their Tobacco ;
which Word, did they always take it in a true Sense, for the Solidness,
and not mistake it for the Thickness, it would be more consonant to a
true Observation : For as I said of the Pine-wood Tobacco, some of it
is thick and not solid, and differs from the best Tobacco, as Buff does
from tanned Leather ; so that if the Tobacco be sound and not rotten,
you may give a great guess at the Goodness of Tobacco, when you weigh
the Hogsheads, before you see them ; For if an equal Care be taken in the
packing of them, the best Tobacco will weigh the heaviest, and pack
the closest. Now I said, that the sweet-scented Tobacco most in vogue,
which was most famed for its Scent, was that which grew on sandy Land ;
which is true, if you would smoak it whilst new, or whilst only two or
three Years old ; but if you keep the stiff Land Tobacco, which is generally a Tobacco of great Substance five or six Years, it will much excel :
. . . Having proceeded thus far to speak of Tobacco, I shall add one
or two things more. The Planters differ in their Judgments about the
time of planting, or pitching their Crops : Some are for pitching their
Crops very early, others late, without any Distinction of the nature of
the Soils ; and 'tis from the different Effects that they find, in that, sometimes early, sometimes the late planting succeeds : But they have not
the reason to judge of the Cause, to consider the Accidents of the Year,
and the difference of the Soils. . . . they plant them as we do Cab-
bages, raising Hills to set every Plant in, about the bigness of a common
Mole-hill : observing this on the Plantation where I lived, that it was stiff
Ground, I advised them to plant their Crops as early as possible ; . . .
There are various Accidents and Distempers, whereunto Tobacco is liable, as the Worm, the Fly, firing to turn, as they call them, Frenchmen,
and the like. . . . Tobacco-seed is very small, and by consequence so
is the young Plant at first, that if gloomy Weather happen at that time, it
breeds a small Fly, which consumes the Plume of the Plant ; now it being
early in the Year when they sow the Seed, *viz.* about the fourteenth of
January, they cover the Ground, to secure, as well as they can, their tendei
Plants, from the niping Frosts, that may happen in the Nights ; they cover
them only with a few Oak-leaves, or the like, for Straw they find apt to harbour and breed this Fly : . . . What they call firing is this : When Plants
are of small Substance, as when there has been a very wet and cold Season,
and very hot Weather suddenly ensues, the Leaves turn brown, and dry

to Dust: . . . *French-men* they call those Plants whose Leaves do not spread and grow large, but rather spire upwards, and grow tall; these Plants they don't tend, being not worthy their Labour. . . . The Country of it self is one entire Wood, consisting of large Timber Trees of several sorts, free from Thickets or Under-Wood, the small Shrubs growing only on Lands that have been clear'd, or in Swamps; and thus it is for several hundreds of Miles, even as far as has yet been discovered. . . .

. . . but to return to the parts of *Virginia* inhabited by the *English*, which in general is a very fertile Soil, far surpassing *England*, . . . And yet in truth 'tis only the barrenest Parts that they have cultivated, by tilling and planting only the High-Lands, leaving the richer Vales unstirr'd, because they understand not any thing of Draining. So that the richest Meadow-Lands, which is one third of the Country, is Boggy, Marsh, and Swamp, whereof they make little Advantage, but lose in them abundance of their Cattle, especially at the first of the Spring, when the Cattle are weak, and venture too far after young Grass. Whereas vast Improvements might be made thereof; for the generality of *Virginia* is a sandy Land with a shallow Soil: so that after they have clear'd a fresh piece of Ground out of the Woods, it will not bear Tobacco past two or three Years, unless Cow-pened; . . . Therefore every three or four Years they must be for clearing a new piece of Ground out of Woods, which requires much Labour and Toil, it being so thick grown all over with massy Timber. Thus their Plantations run over vast Tracts of Ground, each ambitious of engrossing as much as they can, that they may be sure to have enough to plant, and for their Stocks and Herds of Cattle to range and to feed in; that Plantations of 1000, 2000, or 3000 Acres are common, whereby the Country is thinly inhabited; the Living solitary and unsociable; Trading confused and dispersed; besides other Inconveniences: Whereas they might improve 200 or 300 Acres to more Advantage, and would make the Country much more healthy; for those that have 3000 Acres, have scarce cleared 600 Acres thereof, which is peculiarly term'd the Plantation, being surrounded with the 2400 Acres of Wood: So that there can be no free or even Motion of the Air, . . . The Gentlewoman where I lived, was a very acute ingenious Lady, who one Day discoursing the Overseer of her Servants, about pitching the ensuing year's Crop; the Overseer was naming one place where he designed to plant 30000 Plants, another place for 15000, another for 10000, and so forth, the whole Crop designed to be about 100000 Plants: Having observed the Year before he had done the like, and scattered his Crop up and down the Plantation, at

Places a Mile, or a Mile and a half asunder, which was very inconvenient, and whereby they lost much time. I interposed, and asked, why they did not plant all their Crop together? The Fellow smiled as it were at my Ignorance, and said, there was very good Reason for it. I replied, that was it I enquired after. He returned, the Plantation had been an old planted Plantation, and being but a small Plot of Ground, was almost worn out, so that they had not Ground all together that would bring forth Tobacco. I told him then they had better Ground than ever yet they had planted, and more than their hands could manage. He smil'd again, and asked me, where? I then named such a Swamp. He then said scornfully, he thought what a Planter I was; that I understood better how to make a Sermon, than managing Tobacco. I replied with some warmness, tho' I hoped so, that was Impertinence, and no Answer. He then said, that the Tobacco there would drown, and the Roots rot. I replied, that the whole Country would drown if the Rivers were stopt, but it might be laid as dry as any Land on the Plantation. . . . Now you must know they top their Tobacco, that is, take away the little top-bud, when the Plant has put forth as many Leaves as they think the richness of the Ground will bring to a Substance; but generally when it has shot forth four or six Leaves. And when the top-bud is gone, it puts forth no more Leaves, but Side-branches, which they call Suckers, which they are careful ever to take away, that they may not impoverish the Leaves. I have been more tedious in the Particulars, the fullier to evince how resolute they are and conceitedly bent to follow their old Practice and Custom, rather than to receive Directions from others, tho' plain, easie and advantageous. . . .

Peter Force, compiler, *Tracts and Other Papers* (Washington, 1844), III, No. xii, 15–23.

––––◆––––

89. " Concerning the College of William and Mary " (1692)

BY HENRY HARTWELL, JAMES BLAIR, AND EDWARD CHILTON (1727)

James Blair, the principal writer of this selection, was chiefly instrumental in the founding of the College of William and Mary, and was its first president. — Bibliography: J. A. Doyle, *English in America, Virginia*, 357–364; Channing and Hart, *Guiae*, § 99.

IN THE Year 1691, Colonel *Nicholson* being Lieutenant Governor, the General Assembly considering the bad Circumstances of the Country for want of Education for their Youth, went upon a Proposition of a Col-

lege, to which they gave the Name of *William* and *Mary*. They propos'd
that in this College there should be three Schools, *viz.* A Grammar School,
for teaching the *Latin* and *Greek* Tongues : A Philosophical School, for
Philosophy and Mathematicks : and A Divinity School, for the Oriental
Tongues and Divinity ; for it was one part of their Design that this College should be a Seminary for the breeding of good Ministers, with which
they were but very indifferently supply'd from abroad : They appointed
what Masters should be in each of these Schools, and what Salaries they
should have.   For the Government and Visitation of this College, they
appointed a College-Senate, which should consist of 18, or any other Number not exceeding 20, who were then the Lieutenant-Governor, four
Gentlemen of the Council, four of the Clergy, and the rest nam'd out of
the House of Burgesses, with Power to them to continue themselves by
Election of a Successor in the room of any one that should dye, or remove
out of the Country.   They petition'd the King that he would make these
Men Trustees for founding and building this College, and governing it by
such Rules and Statutes, as they, or the major Part of them, should from
Time to Time appoint.   Accordingly, the King pass'd his Charter under
the Great Seal of *England* for such a College, and contributed very
bountifully, both to the Building and Endowment of it.   Toward the
Building he gave near 2000 *l.* in ready Cash, out of the Bank of Quit-
Rents, in which Governor *Nicholson* left at that Time about 4500 *l.* And
towards the Endowment the King gave the neat Produce of the Penny *per*
Pound in *Virginia* and *Maryland*, worth 200 *l. per Annum*, (mention'd
pag. 60) and the Surveyor General's Place, worth about 50 *l. per Annum*,
and the Choice of 10000 Acres of Land in *Panmuckey Neck*, and 10000
more on the South-side of the *Black-water-swamp*, which were Tracts of
Land till that Time prohibited to be taken up.   The General Assembly
also gave the College a Duty on Skins and Furrs, worth better than 100 *l.*
a Year, and they got Subscriptions in *Virginia* in Governor *Nicholson's*
Time for about 2500 *l.* towards the Building.   With these Beginnings
the Trustees of the College went to work, but their good Governor, who
had been the greatest Encourager in that Country of this Design, (on
which he has laid out 350 *l.* of his own Money) being at that time
remov'd from them, and another put in his Place that was of a quite
different Spirit and Temper, they found their Business go on very heavily,
and such Difficulties in every thing, that presently upon change of the
Governor they had as many Enemies as ever they had had Friends ; such
an universal Influence and Sway has a Person of that Character in all

Affairs of that Country. The Gentlemen of the Council, who had been the forwardest to subscribe, were the backwardest to pay ; then every one was for finding Shifts to evade and elude their Subscriptions ; and the meaner People were so influenc'd by their Countenance and Example, (Men being easily perswaded to keep their Money) that there was not one Penny got of new Subscriptions, nor paid of the old 2500 *l.* but about 500 *l.* Nor durst they put the Matter to the Hazard of a Law-Suit, where this new Governor and his Favourites were to be their Judges. Thus it was with the Funds for Building : And they fared little better with the Funds for Endowments ; for notwithstanding the first Choice they are to have of the Land by the Charter, Patents were granted to others for vast Tracts of Land, and every one was ready to oppose the College in taking up the Land ; their Survey was violently stop'd, their Chain broke, and to this Day they can never get to the Possession of the Land. But the Trustees of the College being encourag'd with a Gracious Letter the King writ to the Governor to encourage the College, and to remove all the Obstructions of it, went to work, and carry'd up one Half of the design'd Quadrangle of the Building, advancing Money out of their own Pockets, where the Donations fell short. They founded their Grammar-School, which is in a very thriving Way ; and having the clear Right and Title to the Land, would not be baffled in that Point, but have struggled with the greatest Man in the Government, next the Governor, *i.e.* Mr. Secretary *Wormley*, who pretends to have a Grant *in furturo* for no less than 13000 Acres of the best Land in *Panmuckey Neck*. The Cause is not yet decided, only Mr. Secretary has again stop'd the Chain, which it is not likely he would do, if he did not know that he should be supported in it. The Collectors of the Penny *per* Pound likewise are very remiss in laying their Accompts before the Governors of the College, according to the Instructions of the Commissioners of the Customs, so that illegal Trade is carry'd on, and some of these Gentlemen refuse to give any Account upon Oath. This is the present State of the College. It is honestly and zealously carry'd on by the Trustees, but is in Danger of being ruin'd by the Backwardness of the Government. . . .

Hartwell, Blair, and Chilton, *The Present State of Virginia, and the College* (London, 1727), 67-71.

PART V

NEW ENGLAND

CHAPTER XIV — CONDITIONS

90. "A Description of New-England" (1614)

BY CAPTAIN JOHN SMITH

For Smith's character and opportunities, see No. 62 above. — Bibliography: Winsor, *Narrative and Critical History*, III, 211; Edward Eggleston, *Beginners of a Nation*, 61–64; Channing and Hart, *Guide*, § 109.

IN the moneth of Aprill, 1614. with two Ships from *London*, of a few Marchants, I chanced to arriue in *New-England*, a parte of *Ameryca*, at the Ile of *Monahiggan*, in 43½ of Northerly latitude : our plot was there to take Whales and make tryalls of a Myne of Gold and Copper. If those failed, Fish and Furres was then our refuge, to make our selues sauers howsoeuer : we found this Whale-fishing a costly conclusion : we saw many, and spent much time in chasing them ; but could not kill any : They beeing a kinde of Iubartes, and not the Whale that yeeldes Finnes and Oyle as wee expected. For our Golde, it was rather the Masters deuice to get a voyage that proiected it, then any knowledge hee had at all of any such matter. Fish & Furres was now our guard : & by our late arriual, and long lingring about the Whale, the prime of both those seasons were past ere wee perceiued it ; we thinking that their seasons serued at all times : but wee found it otherwise ; for, by the midst of Iune, the fishing failed. Yet in Iuly and August some was taken, but not sufficient to defray so great a charge as our stay required. Of dry fish we made about 40000. of Cor fish about 7000. Whilest the sailers fished, my selfe with eight or nine others of them might best bee spared ; Ranging the coast in a small boat, wee got for trifles neer 1100 Beuer skinnes, 100 Martins, and neer as many Otters; and the most of them within the distance of twenty leagues. We ranged the Coast both East and West much furder ; but Eastwards our commodities were not esteemed, they were so neare the French who affords them better :

313

and right against vs in the Main was a Ship of Sir *Frances Popphames*, that had there such acquaintance, hauing many yeares vsed onely that porte, that the most parte there was had by him.   And 40 leagues westwards were two French Ships, that had made there a great voyage by trade, during the time wee tryed those conclusions, not knowing the Coast, nor Saluages habitation.   With these Furres, the Traine, and Corfish I returned for *England* in the Bark : where within six monthes after our departure from the *Downes*, we safe arriued back.   The best of this fish was solde for fiue pound the hundreth, the rest by ill vsage betwixt three pound and fifty shillings.   The other Ship staied to fit herselfe for *Spaine* with the dry fish which was sould, by the Sailers reporte that returned, at forty ryalls the quintall, each hundred weighing two quintalls and a halfe.

New England is that part of *America* in the Ocean Sea opposite to *Noua Albyon* in the South Sea ; discouered by the most memorable Sir *Francis Drake* in his voyage about the worlde.   In regarde whereto this is stiled *New England,* beeing in the same latitude.   *New France,* off it, is Northward : Southwardes is *Virginia,* and all the adioyning Continent, with *New Granado, New Spain, New Andolosia* and the *West Indies.*   Now because I haue beene so oft asked such strange questions, of the goodnesse and greatnesse of those spatious Tracts of land, how they can bee thus long vnknown, or not possessed by the *Spaniard,* and many such like demands ; I intreat your pardons, if I chance to be too plaine, or tedious in relating my knowledge for plaine mens satisfaction. . . .

That part wee call *New England* is betwixt the degrees of 41. and 45 : but that parte this discourse speaketh of, stretcheth but from *Pennobscot* to *Cape Cod,* some 75 leagues by a right line distant each from other : within which bounds I haue seene at least 40. seuerall habitations vpon the Sea Coast, and sounded about 25 excellent good Harbours ; In many whereof there is ancorage for 500. sayle of ships of any burthen ; in some of them for 5000 : And more then 200 Iles ouergrowne with good timber, of diuers sorts of wood, which doe make so many harbours as requireth a longer time then I had, to be well discouered. . . .

And surely by reason of those sandy cliffes and cliffes of rocks, both which we saw so planted with Gardens and Corne fields, and so well inhabited with a goodly, strong and well proportioned people, besides the greatnesse of the Timber growing on them, the greatnesse of the fish and the moderate temper of the ayre (for of twentie fiue, not any was sicke, but two that were many yeares diseased before they went, notwithstanding our bad lodging and accidentall diet) who can but approoue this a most excellent place, both for health & fertility? And of all the foure parts of the world that I haue yet seene not inhabited, could I haue but meanes to transport a Colonie, I would rather liue here then any where : and if it did not maintaine it selfe, were wee but once indifferently well fitted, let vs starue.

The maine Staple, from hence to bee extracted for the present to produce the rest, is fish ; which howeuer it may seeme a mean and a base commoditie : yet who who will but truely take the pains and con-sider the sequell, I thinke will allow it well worth the labour. . . .

First, the ground is so fertill, that questionless it is capable of pro-ducing any Grain, Fruits, or Seeds you will sow or plant, growing in the Regions afore named : But it may be, not euery kinde to that perfection of delicacy ; or some tender plants may miscarie, because the Summer is not so hot, and the winter is more colde in those parts wee haue yet tryed neere the Sea side, then we finde in the same height in *Europe* or *Asia*; Yet I made a Garden vpon the top of a Rockie Ile in 43.½, 4 leagues from the Main, in May, that grew so well, as it serued vs for sallets in Iune and Iuly. All sorts of cattell may here be bred and fed in the Iles, or *Peninsulaes*, securely for nothing. In the *Interim* till they encrease if need be (obseruing the seasons) I durst vndertake to haue corne enough from the Saluages for 300 men, for a few trifles ; and if they should bee vntoward (as it is most certaine they are) thirty or forty good men will be sufficient to bring them all in subiection, and make this prouision ; if they vnderstand what they doe : 200 whereof may nine monethes in the yeare be imployed in making marchandable fish, till the rest prouide other necessaries, fit to furnish vs with other commodities. . . .

Now, young boyes and girles Saluages, or any other, be they neuer such idlers, may turne, carry, and return fish, without either shame, or any great paine : hee is very idle that is past twelue yeares of age and cannot doe so much : and she is very olde, that cannot spin a thred to make engines to catch them. . . .

But, to returne a little more to the particulars of this Countrey, which I intermingle thus with my proiects and reasons, not being so sufficiently yet acquainted in those parts, to write fully the estate of the Sea, the Ayre, the Land, the Fruites, the Rocks, the People, the Gouernment,

Religion, Territories, and Limitations, Friends, and Foes: but, as I gathered from the niggardly relations in a broken language to my vnderstanding, during the time I ranged those Countries &c. The most Northern part I was at, was the Bay of *Pennobscot*, which is East and West, North and South, more then ten leagues; but such were my occasions, I was constrained to be satisfied of them I found in the Bay, that the Riuer ranne farre vp into the Land, and was well inhabited with many people, but they were from their habitations, either fishing among the Iles, or hunting the Lakes and Woods, for Deer and Beuers. The Bay is full of great Ilands, of one, two, six, eight, or ten miles in length, which diuides it into many faire and excellent good harbours. On the East of it, are the *Tarrantines*, their mortall enemies, where inhabit the *French*, as they report that liue with those people, as one nation or family. And Northwest of *Pennobscot* is *Mecaddacut*, at the foot of a high mountaine, a kinde of fortresse against the *Tarrantines* adioyning to the high mountaines of *Pennobscot*, against whose feet doth beat the Sea: But ouer all the Land, Iles, or other impediments, you may well see them sixteene or eighteene leagues from their situation. *Segocket* is the next; then *Nufconcus, Pemmaquid*, and *Sagadahock*. Vp this Riuer where was the Westerne plantation are *Aumuckcawgen, Kinnebeck*, and diuers others, where there is planted some corne fields. Along this Riuer 40 or 50 miles, I saw nothing but great high cliffes of barren Rocks, ouergrowne with wood: but where the Saluages dwelt there the ground is exceeding fat & fertill. Westward of this Riuer, is the Countrey of *Aucocisco*, in the bottome of a large deepe Bay, full of many great Iles, which diuides it into many good harbours. *Sowocotuck* is the next, in the edge of a large sandy Bay, which hath many Rocks and Iles, but few good harbours, but for Barks, I yet know. But all this Coast to *Pennobscot*, and as farre I could see Eastward of it is nothing but such high craggy Cliffy Rocks & stony Iles that I wondered such great trees could growe vpon so hard foundations. It is a Countrie rather to affright, then delight one. And how to describe a more plaine spectacle of desolation or more barren I knowe not. Yet the Sea there is the strangest fish-pond I euer saw; and those barren Iles so furnished with good woods, springs, fruits, fish, and foule, that it makes mee thinke though the Coast be rockie, and thus affrightable; the Vallies, Plaines, and and interior parts, may well (notwithstanding) be verie fertile. But there is no kingdome so fertile hath not some part barren: and *New England* is great enough, to make many Kingdomes and Countries, were it all inhabited.   As you passe the Coast still West-ward, *Accominticus* and *Passataquack* are two conuenient harbors for small barks ; and a good Countrie, within their craggie cliffs.   *Angoam* is the next ; This place might content a right curious iudgement : but there are many sands at the entrance of the harbor : and the worst is, it is inbayed too farre from the deepe Sea.   Heere are many rising hilles, and on their tops and descents many corne fields, and delightfull groues. On the East, is an Ile of two or three leagues in length ; the one halfe, plaine morish grasse fit for pasture, with many faire high groues of mul-berrie trees gardens : and there is also Okes, Pines, and other woods to make this place an excellent habitation, beeing a good and safe harbor.

Naimkeck though it be more rockie ground (for *Angoam* is sandie) not much inferior ; neither for the harbor, nor any thing I could per-ceiue, but the multitude of people.   From hence doth stretch into the sea the faire headland *Tragabigzanda*, fronted with three Iles called the three *Turks heads* : to the North of this, doth enter a great Bay, where wee founde some habitations and corne fields : they report a great Riuer, and at least thirtie habitations, doo possesse this Countrie.   But because the *French* had got their Trade, I had no leasure to discouer it. The Iles of *Mattahunts* are on the West side of this Bay, where are many Iles, and questionlesse good harbors : and then the Countrie of the *Massachusets*, which is the Paradise of all those parts : for, heere are many Iles all planted with corne ; groues, mulberries, saluage gardens, and good harbors : the Coast is for the most part, high clayie sandie cliffs.   The Sea Coast as you passe, shewes you all along large corne fields, and great troupes of well proportioned people : but the *French* hauing remained heere neere six weekes, left nothing, for vs to take occasion to examine the inhabitants relations, *viz*, if there be neer three thousand people vpon these Iles ; and that the Riuer doth pearce many daies iourneies the intralles of that Countrey.   We found the people in those parts verie kinde ; but in their furie no lesse valiant.   For, vpon a quarrell wee had with one of them, hee onely with three others crossed the harbor of *Quonahassit* to certaine rocks whereby wee must passe ; and there let flie their arrowes for our shot, till we were out of danger.

Then come you to *Accomack*, an excellent good harbor, good land ; and no want of any thing, but industrious people.   After much kind-nesse, vpon a small occasion, wee fought also with fortie or fiftie of those : though some were hurt, and some slaine ; yet within an houre after they became friendes.   *Cape Cod* is the next presents it selfe :

which is onely a headland of high hils of sand, ouergrowne with shrubbie pines, hurts, and such trash; but an excellent harbor for all weathers. This *Cape* is made by the maine Sea on the one side, and a great Bay on the other in forme of a sickle: on it doth inhabit the people of *Pawmet:* and in the bottome of the Bay, the people of *Chawum*. Towards the South and Southwest of this *Cape*, is found a long and dangerous shoale of sands and rocks. But so farre as I incircled it, I found thirtie fadom water aboard the shore, and a strong current: which makes mee thinke there is a Channell about this shoale; where is the best and greatest fish to be had, Winter and Summer, in all that Countrie. But, the Saluages say there is no Channell, but that the shoales beginne from the maine at *Pawmet*, to the Ile of *Nausit;* and so extends beyond their knowledge into the Sea. The next to this is *Capawack*, and those abounding Countries of copper, corne, people, and mineralls; which I went to discouer this last yeare: but because I miscarried by the way, I will leaue them, till God please I haue better acquaintance with them. . . .

Captain John Smith, *A Description of New England* (London, 1616), 1–27 *passim*.

———————◆———————

91. An Account of the New England Indians (1642)

BY THOMAS LECHFORD

Thomas Lechford, the first Boston lawyer. — Bibliography: Winsor, *Narrative and Critical History*, III, 350; Channing and Hart, *Guide*, § 118.

THEY are of body tall, proper, and straight. . . . Seldome they are abroad in extremity of Winter, but keep in their *wigwams*, till necessity drives them forth; and then they wrap themselves in skins, or some of our English coorse cloth: and for the Winter they have boots, or a kind of laced tawed-leather stockins. They are naturally proud, and idle, given much to singing, dancing, and playes; they are governed by *Sachems*, Kings; and *Saggamores*, petie Lords; by an absolute tyrannie. Their women are of comely feature, industrious, and doe most of the labour in planting, and carrying of burdens; their husbands hold them in great slavery, yet never knowing other, it is the lesse grievous to them. They say, *Englishman* much foole, for spoiling good working creatures, meaning women: And when they see any of our *English* women sewing with their needles, or working coifes, or such things, they will cry out,

Lazie *squaes!* but they are much the kinder to their wives, by the example of the *English*. Their children, they will not part with upon any
terms, to be taught. They are of complexion swarthy and tawny ; their
children are borne white, but they bedawbe them with oyle, and colours,
presently. They have all black haire, that I saw.

In times of mourning, they paint their faces with black lead, black,
all about the eye-brows, and part of their cheeks. In time of rejoycing,
they paint red, with a kind of vermilion. They cut their haire of divers
formes, according to their Nation or people, so that you may know a
people by their cut ; and ever they have a long lock on one side of their
heads, and weare feathers of Peacocks, and such like, and red cloath, or
ribbands at their locks ; beads of *wampompeag* about their necks, and a
girdle of the same, wrought with blew and white *wampom*, after the
manner of chequer work, two fingers broad, about their loynes : Some
of their chiefe men goe so, and pendants of *wampom*, and such toyes in
their ears. And their women, some of the chiefe, have faire bracelets,
and chaines of *wampom*. Men and women, of them, come confidently
among the *English*. Since the *Pequid* war, they are kept in very good
subjection, and held to strict points of Justice, so that the *English* may
travail safely among them. But the *French* in the East, and the *Dutch*
in the South, sell them guns, powder and shot. They have *Powahes*, or
Priests, which are Witches, and a kind of Chirurgions, but some of them,
notwithstanding, are faine to be beholding to the *English* Chirurgions.
They will have their times of *powaheing*, which they will, of late, have
called Prayers, according to the *English* word. The *Powahe* labours
himselfe in his incantations, to extreame sweating and wearinesse, even
to extasie. The *Powahes* cannot work their witchcrafts, if any of the
English be by ; neither can any of their incantations lay hold on, or doe
any harme to the *English*, as I have been credibly informed. The
Powahe is next the King, or *Sachem*, and commonly when he dyes, the
Powahe marryes the *Squa Sachem*, that is, the queene. They have marriages among them ; they have many wives ; they say, they commit
much filthinesse among themselves. But for every marriage, the *Sagga-
more* hath a fadome of *wampom*, which is about seven or eight shillings
value. Some of them will diligently attend to any thing they can understand by any of our Religion, and are very willing to teach their language to
any *English*. They live much the better, and peaceably, for the *English;*
and themselves know it, or at least their *Sachems*, and *Saggamores* know
so much, for before they did nothing but spoile and destroy one another.

They live in *Wigwams*, or houses made of mats like little hutts, the fire in the midst of the house.   They cut downe a tree with axes and hatchets, bought of the *English*, *Dutch*, or *French*, & bring in the butt-end into the *wigwam*, upon the hearth, and so burne it by degrees.   They live upon parched corne, (of late, they grinde at our *English* mills), Venison, Bevers, Otters, Oysters, Clammes, Lobsters, and other fish, Groundnuts, Akornes, they boyle all together in a kettle.   Their riches are their *wampom*, bolles, trayes, kettles, and spoones, bever, furres, and canoos. He is a *Sachem*, whose wife hath her cleane spoons in a chest, for some chief *English* men, when they come on guest wise to the *wigwam*.   They lye upon a mat, with a stone, or a piece of wood under their heads; they will give the best entertainment they can make to any *English* comming amongst them.   They will not taste sweet things, nor alter their habit willingly; onely they are taken with tobacco, wine, and strong waters; and I have seen some of them in *English*, or *French* cloathes. Their ordinary weapons are bowes and arrowes, and long staves, or halfe pykes, with pieces of swords, daggers, or knives in the ends of them: They have Captaines, and are very good at a short mark, and nimble of foot to run away.   Their manner of fighting is, most commonly, all in one fyle.   They are many in number, and worship *Kitan*, their good god, or *Hobbamocco*, their evill god; but more feare *Hobbamocco*, because he doth them most harme.   Some of their Kings names are *Canonicus*, *Meantinomy*, *Owshamequin*, *Cushamequin*, *Webbacowitts*, and *Squa Sachem* his wife: She is the Queene, and he is *Powahe*, and King, in right of his wife.   Among some of these Nations, their policie is to have two Kings at a time; but, I thinke, of one family; the one aged for counsell, the other younger for action.   Their Kings succeed by inheritance.

Master *Henry Dunster*, Schoolmaster of *Cambridge*, deserves commendations above many; he hath the plat-forme and way of conversion of the Natives, indifferent right, and much studies the same, wherein yet he wants not opposition, as some other also have met with: He will, without doubt, prove an instrument of much good in the Countrey, being a good Scholar, and having skil in the Tongues; He will make it good, that the way to instruct the *Indians*, must be in their *owne* language, not *English;* and that their language may be perfected.

Thomas Lechford, *Plain Dealing: or, Nevvs from New-England* (London, 1642), 49-53.

92. A Typical Indian Treaty (1645)

BY THE COMMISSIONERS OF THE UNITED COLONIES OF NEW ENG-
LAND, WITH PESSECUS, AUMSEQUEN, AND OTHERS

This document will serve as an example of the written agreements made with Indian
tribes. — Bibliography: Winsor, *Narrative and Critical History*, III, 354, 373, and
Memorial History of Boston, I, 299–301; Channing and Hart, *Guide*, § 124.

A TREATY and agreement betwixt the Comission's for the vnited Colonies of New England
on the one part And Pessecus Mexanno eldest of Ca-
nownacus sonns Jannemo (al's) Nenegelett and Wipe-
tamock and others Sagamores of the Narrohiggansets
and Nyantick Indians on the other þt made & concluded at Bostone in the Massachusetts the xxvij'h
of the sixt month 1645. . . .

Pessecus and Mexanno w'h other captaines & Counsellors of the Narrohiggansets and one Deputie for the Nyanticks being come to Bostone, and
joyntly affirmeing they had comission to treate and conclude not onely for
the Narrohiggansets but for the Nyantick Indians, and engageing themselues one for another were after a larg debate and conferrence about
former greevances betwixt themselues and Vncas, and a due consideracõn
of former Treaties and agreements w'h the English convinced and acknowledged that they had broken their Couenants and had thereby not
onely endamnaged Vncas but had brought much charge and trouble
vpon all the English Colonies w'eh they confest were just they should
satisfy.

It was agreed betwixt the Comission's of the vnited Colonies and the
foremencõned Sagamores and Nyantick Deputie That the said Narrohigganset and Nyantick Sagamores should pay or cause to be payd at
Boston tɔ the Massachusets Comission's the full sum̅ of two thousand
fathome of good white wampom or a third part of good black wampem
peage in foure payments namely fiue hundred fathome w'hin twenty dayes,
fiue hundred fathome w'hin foure months, fiue hundred fathome at or
before next planting tyme, and fiue hundred w'hin two yeares next after
the date of these presents w'eh two thousand fathome the Comission's
accept for satisfaccõn of former charges expended.

The foresaid Sagamores and Deputie (on the behalf of the Narrohiggansets and Nyantick Indians hereby þmise and couenant that they

Y

will vpon demaund and proofe satisfy and restore vnto Vncas the
Mohegan Sagamore all such Captiues whether men weomen or children
and all such Canowes as they or any of their men haue taken, or as many
of their owne Canowes in the roome of them full as good as they were
wᵗh full satisfacc͂on for all such Corne as they or any of their men haue
spoyled or destroyed of his or his mens since last planting tyme   And
yᵉ English Comissionʳs hereby þmise that Vncas shall do the like to
them. . . .

The said Narrohiggansett and Nyantick Sagamores and deputies do
hereby þmise and couenant to keepe and mayntaine a firme & þpetuall
peace both wᵗh all the English vnited Colonies and their Successors and
wᵗh Vncas the Mohegan Sachem and his men wᵗh Vssamequin, Pomham,
Sokakonooco, Cutchamakin, Shoanan, Passaco͂naway, and all other Indian
Sagamores and their companies, who are in frendship wᵗh or subject to
any of the English hereby engageing themselues that they will not at
any tyme hereafter, disturbe the peace of the Countrey, by any assaults,
hostile attempts, invasions or other injuries, to any of the vnited Colonies
or their Successors or to the aforesaid Indians either in their þsons,
buildings cattell or goods directly or indirectly, nor will they confederate wᵗh any other against them,   And if they know of any Indians
or others that conspire or intend hurt either against the said English
or any Indian subject to or in frendship wᵗh them, they will wᵗhout
delay acquaint & giue notice thereof to the English Comissionʳs or some
of them.

And if any questions or differences shall at any tyme hereafter arise or
grow betwixt them and Vncas or any Indians before menc͂oned, they will
according to former engagements (wᶜh they hereby confirme and ratyfy)
first acquaint the English & craue their judgments and advice therein,
and will not attempt or begin any warr or hostile invasion till they haue
liberty and allowance from the Comissionʳs of the vnited Colonies so to
doe.

The said Narrohigganset and Nyantick Sagamores and deputie do
hereby þmise that they will forthwᵗh deliuer and restore all such Indian
fugitiues or captiues wᶜh haue at any tyme fled from any of the English,
and are now liueing or abideing wᵗh or amongst them, or giue due satis-
facc͂on for them to the Comissionʳs for the Massachusets,   And further
that they will (wᵗhout more delayes) pay or cause to be payd An yearely
tribute a month before Indian haruest euery yeare after this at Boston to
the English Colonies for all such Pecotts as liue amongst them according

to the former treatie and agreement made at Hartford 1638 namely one fathome of white wampam for euery Peacott man, and half a fathome for eich Peacott youth, and one hand length wampom for eich Peacott manchild   And if Weekwash Cooke refuse to pay this tribute for any peacotts w^{t}h him the Narrohigganset Sagamores þmise to assist the English against him.   And they further couenant that ye will resigne and yeild vp the whole Peacott Countrey and euery þt of it to the English Colonies, as due to them by conquest

The said Narrohigganset and Nyantick Sagamores and Deputy do hereby þmise and couenant, that w^{t}hin fourteene dayes they will bring and deliuer to the Massachusetts Commission^{r}s on the behalf of all the Colonies foure of their children . . . to be kept (as pledges or hostages) by the English till both the foremencõned two thousand fathome of wampom be payd at the tymes aboue expressed, and the differences betwixt themselues and Vncas be heard and ordered, and till these Articles of agreement be vnderwritten at Boston by Janemo, and Wypetock. . . .

The Comission^{r}s for the vnited Colonies do hereby þmise and agree, That at the charg of the vnited Colonies the foure Indians now left as pledges shalbe þuided for, and that the foure children to be brought and deliûed as hostages, shalbe kept and mayntained at the same charg, that they will require Vncas and his men w^{t}h all the other Indian Sagamores before named to forbeare all acts of hostility against the Narrohigganset & Nyantick Indians for the future. . . .

It is fully agreed by and betwixt the said þties that if any hostile attempt be made while this treaty is in hand or before notice of this agreement (to stay former p^{r}paracõns and direccons) can be giuen, such attempts and the consequents thereof shall on neither þt be accounted a vyolacõn of this Treaty nor a breach of the peace here made and concluded

The Narrohigganset and Nyantick Sagamores and Deputie hereby agree and couenant to and w^{t}h the Commission^{r}s of the vnited Colonies, that hencforward they will neither giue graunt, sell or in any manner alienate any part of their Countrey nor any þcell of land therein either to any of the English or others w^{t}hout consent or allowance of the said Comissione^{r}s.

Lastly they þmise that if any Peacott or other be found and discoûed amongst them who hath in tyme of peace murthered any of the English, he or they shalbe deliuered to just punishment.   In witnes whereof the parties aboue named haue interchaungably subscribed these p'sents the day and yeare aboue written.

The marke	the marke of
of PESSECUS	
the mark of	MEEKESANNO
AUMSEQUEN the	
Nyantick Deputy	the marke of
ABDAS marke	
the marke of POMMUSH	
CUTCHAMEKINS marke	WITTOWASH

[Each of above with characteristic totem mark.]

Records of the Colony of New Plymouth in New England (edited by David Pulsifer, Boston, 1859), IX, 45–48 *passim.*

93. Puritan Principles of Government (1559)

BY REVEREND JOHN CALVIN

(TRANSLATED BY JOHN ALLEN, 1813)

Calvin, the great Genevan divine and statesman, in his system of theology included a study of government, from which this extract is taken. It was much quoted by the New England ministers and statesmen. — Bibliography: Edward Eggleston, *Beginners of a Nation,* 134–140, 346–349; H. M. Dexter, *Congregationalism, as seen in its Literature;* Channing and Hart, *Guide,* § 110.

HAVING already stated that man is the subject of two kinds of government, and having sufficiently discussed that which is situated in the soul, or the inner man, and relates to eternal life ; we are, in this chapter, to say something of the other kind, which relates to civil justice, and the regulation of the external conduct. For, though the nature of this argument seems to have no connection with the spiritual doctrine of faith which I have undertaken to discuss, the sequel will shew that I have sufficient reason for connecting them together, and, indeed, that necessity obliges me to it : . . .

III. . . . Nor let any one think it strange that I now refer to human polity the charge of the due maintenance of religion, which I may appear to have placed beyond the jurisdiction of men. For I do not allow men to make laws respecting religion and the worship of God now, any more than I did before ; though I approve of civil government, which provides

that the true religion which is contained in the law of God, be not violated, and polluted by public blasphemies, with impunity.   But the per-
spicuity of order will assist the readers to attain a clearer understanding
of what sentiments ought to be entertained respecting the whole system
of civil administration, if we enter on a discussion of each branch of it.
These are three : The Magistrate, who is the guardian and conservator
of the laws : The Laws, according to which he governs : The People, who
are governed by the laws, and obey the magistrate.   Let us, therefore,
examine, first, the function of a magistrate, whether it be a legitimate
calling and approved by God, the nature of the duty, and the extent of
the power : secondly, by what laws christian government ought to be
regulated : and lastly, what advantage the people derive from the laws,
and what obedience they owe to the magistrate.

IV. The Lord hath not only testified that the function of magistrates
has his approbation and acceptance, but hath eminently commended it
to us, by dignifying it with the most honourable titles. . . . This is
just as if it had been affirmed, that the authority possessed by kings and
other governors over all things upon earth is not a consequence of the
perverseness of men, but of the providence and holy ordinance of God ;
who hath been pleased to regulate human affairs in this manner ; forasmuch as he is present, and also presides among them, in making laws
and in executing equitable judgments. . . .

VI. This consideration ought continually to occupy the magistrates
themselves, since it is calculated to furnish them with a powerful stimu-
lus, by which they may be excited to their duty, and to afford them
peculiar consolation, by which the difficulties of their office, which certainly are many and arduous, may be alleviated.   For what an ardent
pursuit of integrity, prudence, clemency, moderation, and innocence
ought they to prescribe to themselves, who are conscious of having been
constituted ministers of the divine justice ! . . . And this admonition
is entitled to have considerable weight with them : for if they fail in their
duty, they not only injure men by criminally distressing them, but even
offend God by polluting his sacred judgments. On the other hand, it opens
a source of peculiar consolation to them to reflect, that they are not employed in profane things, or occupations unsuitable to a servant of God, but
in a most sacred function, inasmuch as they execute a divine commission.

VII. Those who are not restrained by so many testimonies of Scripture, but still dare to stigmatise this sacred ministry as a thing incom-
patible with religion and Christian piety, do they not offer an insult to

God himself, who cannot but be involved in the reproach cast upon his ministry? And in fact they do not reject magistrates, but they reject God, " that he should not reign over them." . . .

VIII. And for private men, who have no authority to deliberate on the regulation of any public affairs, it would surely be a vain occupation to dispute which would be the best form of government in the place where they live. Besides, this could not be simply determined, as an abstract question, without great impropriety, since the principle to guide the decision must depend on circumstances. And even if we compare the different forms together, without their circumstances, their advantages are so nearly equal, that it will not be easy to discover of which the utility preponderates. The forms of civil government are considered to be of three kinds: Monarchy, which is the dominion of one person, whether called a king, or a duke, or any other title: Aristocracy, or the dominion of the principal persons of a nation: and Democracy, or popular government, in which the power resides in the people at large. It is true that the transition is easy from monarchy to despotism; it is not much more difficult from aristocracy to oligarchy, or the faction of a few; but it is most easy of all from democracy to sedition. Indeed, if these three forms of government, which are stated by philosophers, be considered in themselves, I shall by no means deny, that either aristocracy or a mixture of aristocracy and democracy far excels all others; and that indeed not of itself, but because it very rarely happens that kings regulate themselves so that their will is never at variance with justice and rectitude; or in the next place, that they are endued with such penetration and prudence, as in all cases to discover what is best. The vice or imperfection of men therefore renders it safer and more tolerable for the government to be in the hands of many, that they may afford each other mutual assistance and admonition, and that if any one arrogate to himself more than is right, the many may act as censors and masters to restrain his ambition. . . . And to this object the magistrates likewise ought to apply their greatest diligence, that they suffer not the liberty, of which they are constituted guardians, to be in any respect diminished, much less to be violated: if they are inactive and unconcerned about this, they are perfidious to their office, and traitors to their country. But if those, to whom the will of God has assigned another form of government, transfer this to themselves so as to be tempted to desire a revolution, the very thought will be not only foolish and useless, but altogether criminal. . . .

X. But here, it seems, arises an important and difficult question. If by the law all Christians are forbidden to kill, and the prophet predicts respecting the Church, that "they shall not hurt nor destroy in all my holy mountain, saith the Lord"; how can it be compatible with piety for magistrates to shed blood? But if we understand, that in the infliction of punishments, the magistrate does not act at all from himself, but merely executes the judgments of God, we shall not be embarrassed with this scruple. . . .

XI. Now as it is sometimes necessary for kings and nations to take up arms for the infliction of such public vengeance, the same reason will lead us to infer the lawfulness of wars which are undertaken for this end. For if they have been entrusted with power to preserve the tranquillity of their own territories, to suppress the seditious tumults of disturbers, to succour the victims of oppression, and to punish crimes; can they exert this power for a better purpose, than to repel the violence of him, who disturbs both the private repose of individuals and the general tranquillity of the nation; who excites insurrections, and perpetrates acts of oppression, cruelty, and every species of crime? . . .

XIII. In the last place, I think it necessary to add, that tributes and taxes are the legitimate revenues of princes; which indeed they ought principally to employ in sustaining the public expenses of their office, but which they may likewise use for the support of their domestic splendour, which is closely connected with the dignity of the government that they hold. . . .

XIV. From the magistracy we next proceed to the laws, which are the strong nerves of civil polity, or, according to an appellation which Cicero has borrowed from Plato, the *souls of states*, without which magistracy cannot subsist, as on the other hand without magistrates laws are of no force. No observation therefore can be more correct than this, that the law is a silent magistrate, and the magistrate a speaking law. . . .

XVII. It now remains for us, as we proposed, in the last place, to examine, what advantage the common society of Christians derives from laws, judgments, and magistrates: with which is connected another question; what honour private persons ought to render to magistrates, and how far their obedience ought to extend. . . . But if it be in vain that he is given to us by the Lord for our protection, unless it be lawful for us to avail ourselves of such an advantage, it clearly follows that we may appeal to him, and apply for his aid, without any violation of piety. . . .

XVIII. Let such persons therefore understand, that judicial processes are lawful to those who use them rightly : . . .

XXI. . . . It is certainly incumbent on Christians, in all cases, to prefer a concession of their right to an entrance on a lawsuit; from which they can scarcely come out without a mind exasperated and inflamed with enmity to their brother. But when one sees that, without any breach of charity, he may defend his property, the loss of which would be a serious injury to him; if he do it, he commits no offence against that sentence of Paul. In a word, as we have observed at the beginning, charity will give every one the best counsel; for whatever litigations are undertaken without charity, or are carried to a degree inconsistent with it, we conclude them beyond all controversy to be unjust and wicked.

XXII. The first duty of subjects towards their magistrates is to entertain the most honourable sentiments of their function, which they know to be a jurisdiction delegated to them from God, and on that account to esteem and reverence them as God's ministers and vicegerents. For there are some persons to be found, who shew themselves very obedient to their magistrates, and have not the least wish that there were no magistrates for them to obey, because they know them to be so necessary to the public good ; but who, nevertheless, consider the magistrates themselves as no other than necessary evils. But something more than this is required of us by Peter, when he commands us to " honour the king " ; and by Solomon when he says, " Fear thou the Lord and the king " : for Peter, under the term *honour*, comprehends a sincere and candid esteem ; and Solomon, by connecting the king with the Lord, attributes to him a kind of sacred veneration and dignity. It is also a remarkable commendation of magistrates which is given by Paul, when he says, that we " must needs be subject, not only for wrath, but also for conscience sake " : by which he means, that subjects ought to be induced to submit to princes and governors, not merely from a dread of their power, as persons are accustomed to yield to an armed enemy, who they know will immediately take vengeance upon them if they resist ; but because the obedience which is rendered to princes and magistrates is rendered to God, from whom they have received their authority. I am not speaking of the persons, as if the mask of dignity ought to palliate or excuse folly, ignorance, or cruelty, and conduct the most nefarious and flagitious, and so to acquire for vices the praise due to virtues : but I affirm that the station itself is worthy of honour and reverence : so that, whoever our governors are, they ought to possess our esteem and veneration on account of the office which they fill.

XXIII. Hence follows another duty, that, with minds disposed to honour and reverence magistrates, subjects approve their obedience to them, in submitting to their edicts, in paying taxes, in discharging public duties and bearing burdens which relate to the common defence, and in fulfilling all their other commands. . . . For as it is impossible to resist the magistrate without, at the same time, resisting God himself; though an unarmed magistrate may seem to be despised with impunity, yet God is armed to inflict exemplary vengeance on the contempt offered to himself. Under this obedience I also include the moderation which private persons ought to prescribe to themselves in relation to public affairs, that they do not, without being called upon, intermeddle with affairs of state, or rashly intrude themselves into the office of magistrates, or undertake any thing of a public nature. If there be any thing in the public administration which requires to be corrected, let them not raise any tumults, or take the business into their own hands, which ought to be all bound in this respect, but let them refer it to the cognizance of the magistrate, who is alone authorised to regulate the concerns of the public. I mean, that they ought to attempt nothing without being commanded: for when they have the command of a governor, then they also are invested with public authority. For, as we are accustomed to call the counsellors of a prince *his eyes and ears:* so they may not unaptly be called *his hands* whom he has commissioned to execute any of his commands. . . .

XXV. But, if we direct our attention to the word of God, it will carry us much further; even to submit to the government, not only of those princes who discharge their duty to us with becoming integrity and fidelity, but of all who possess the sovereignty, even though they perform none of the duties of their function. For though the Lord testifies that the magistrate is an eminent gift of his liberality to preserve the safety of men, and prescribes to magistrates themselves the extent of their duty; yet he, at the same time, declares, that whatever be their characters, they have their government only from him; that those who govern for the public good are true specimens and mirrors of his benificence; and that those who rule in an unjust and tyrannical manner are raised up by him to punish the iniquity of the people; that all equally possess that sacred majesty which he hath invested with legitimate authority. . . .

XXIX. . . . But it will be said, that rulers owe mutual duties to their subjects. That I have already confessed. But he who infers from this that obedience ought to be rendered to none but just rulers, is a very bad reasoner. For husbands owe mutual duties to their wives, and parents to their children. Now, if husbands and parents violate their obligations, if parents conduct themselves with discouraging severity and fastidious moroseness towards their children, whom they are forbidden to provoke to wrath : if husbands despise and vex their wives, whom they are commanded to love and to spare as the weaker vessels ; does it follow that children should be less obedient to their parents ; or wives to their husbands? They are still subject, even to those who are wicked and unkind. . . .

XXXII. But in the obedience which we have shewn to be due to the authority of governors, it is always necessary to make one exception, and that is entitled to our first attention, that it do not seduce us from obedience to him, to whose will the desires of all kings ought to be subject, to whose decrees all their commands ought to yield, to whose majesty all their sceptres ought to submit. . . .

John Calvin, *Institutes of the Christian Religion* (London, 1813), III, 515–551 *passim.*

———————◆———————

94. A Defence of Theocracy (1638)

BY REVEREND JOHN DAVENPORT

Davenport was an English clergyman who had got the ill-will of King James I by reproving him for swearing. He came to New Haven in 1639, and was one of the chief men of the colony of New Haven till 1667. — Bibliography : New Haven Historical Society, *Papers*, II, 234; Winsor, *Narrative and Critical History*, III, 332, 352.

Q. *WHETHER a new Plantation, where all or the most considerable part of free Planters profess their purpose and desire of securing to themselves and to their posterity, the pure and peaceable enjoyment of Christ's Ordinances; Whether, I say, such Planters are bound in laying the Foundations of Church and Civil State, to take order, that all the free Burgesses be such as are in fellowship of the Church or Churches which are, or may be gathered according to Christ; and that those free Burgesses have the only power of chusing from among themselves Civil Magistrates, and men to be intrusted with transacting all publick Affairs of Importance, according to the rules and directions of Scripture?*

I hold the Affirmative part of this Question upon this ground, that this course will most conduce to the good of both States ; and by consequence to the *common welfare of all*, whereunto all men are bound principally to attend in laying the *Foundation of a Common-wealth*, lest Posterity rue the first Miscarriages, when it will be too late to redress them.   They that are skilful in Architecture observe, *that the breaking or yielding of a stone in the groundwork of a Building but the breadth of the back of a knife, will make a cleft of more then half a foot in the Fabrick aloft: So important* (saith mine Author) *are fundamental Errours*.   The Lord awaken us to look to it in time, and send us his Light and Truth to lead us into the safest wayes in these beginnings.

The Question being thus stated, I now proceed with Gods help to prove the Affirmative part : and thus I argue, to prove that *the Form of Government which is described in the true stating of the Question is the best, and by consequence, that men that are free to chuse (as in new Plantations they are) ought to establish it in a Christian Common-wealth.*

Theocratic, *or to make the Lord God our Governour, is the best Form of Government in a Christian Common-wealth, and which men that are free to chuse (as in new Plantations they are) ought to establish. The Form of Government described in the true stating of the Question is* Theocratic, *or that wherein we make the Lord God our Governour. Therefore that Form of Government which is described in the true stating of the Question, is the best Form of Government in a Christian Common-wealth, and which men that are free to chuse (as in new Plantations they are) ought to establish.*   The Proposition is clear of it self.   The Assumption I prove thus :

That Form of Government where 1. *The people that have the power of chusing their Governors are in Covenant with God* 2. *Wherein the men chosen by them are godly men, and fitted with a spirit of Government:* 3. *In which the Laws they rule by are the Laws of God:* 4. *Wherein Laws are executed, Inheritances allotted, and civil differences are composed, according to Gods appointment:* 5. *In which men of God are consulted with in all hard cases, and in matters of Religion,* is the Form which was received and established among the people of *Israel* whil'st the Lord God was their Governour, as the places of Scripture alledged shew ; and is the very same with that which we plead for, as will appear to him that shall examine the true stating of the Question. The Conclusion follows necessarily.

That Form of Government which giveth unto Christ his due preheminence, is the best Form of Government in a Christian Common-wealth, and which men that are free to chuse (as in new Plantations they are) ought to establish. The Form of Government described in the true stating of the Question, is that which giveth unto Christ his due preheminence. Therefore the Form of Government which is described in the true stating of the Question, is the best Form of Government in a Christian Common-wealth, and which men that are free to chuse (as in new Plantations they are) ought to establish.

The Proposition is proved out of two places of Scripture, *Col.* I. 15. to 19, with *Eph.* I. 21, 22. From which Texts it doth appear, that it is a prehemi[ne]nce due to Christ, that all things, and all Governments in the world, should serve to Christs ends, for the welfare of the Church whereof he is the Head. For 1. In relation to God, he hath this by Right of Primogeniture, as he is *the first-born, and so Heir of all things, higher then the Kings of the earth.* 2. In relation to the World, it is said, *All things were made by him, and for him, and do consist in h[i]m,* and therefore it is a preheminence due to him, that they all serve him. 3. In relation to the Church, it is said, *He hath made all things subject under his feet, and hath given him over all things to be Head of the Church, that in all things he might have the preheminence.* And indeed that he upholdeth the Creatures, and the Order that is in them, it is for his Churches sake; when that is once compleat, the world shall soon be at an end. And if you reade the stories of the great Monarchies that have been, and judge of them by Scripture-light, you will finde they stood or fell, according as God purposed to make use of them about some service to be done about his Church. So that the onely considerable part for which the world standeth at this day, is the Church: and therefore it is a Preheminence due to Christ, that his Headship over the Church should be exalted and acknowledged, and served by all. In which respect also the Title of *The first-born* is given to the Members of the Church, and they are called *The first-fruits of his Creatures,* to shew both their preheminence above others, and that they are fittest to serve to Gods ends.

The Assumption (*That the Form of Government described in the true stating of the Question, doth give unto Christ his due preheminence*) will easily be granted by those that shall consider what Civil Magistrates and Rulers in the Common wealth those are, who are fittest to serve to Christ's ends for the good and welfare of his Church; which will be evident from two places of Scripture : First, in *Psa.* 2. 10, 11, 12 you have a description of those that are fitted to order Civil Affairs in their Magistracy to Christ's ends ; they are such as are not onely wise and learned in matters of Religion, but also do reduce their knowledge into practice : they *Worship the Lord in fear;* and not only so, but *Kiss the Son,* which was a solemn & outward *Profession of love* and *of Subjection* and *of Religious Worship,* and so fitly serveth to express their joyning themselves to the Church of Christ. Secondly, in *Isa.* 49. 23. it is promised to the Church, that *Kings and Queens shall be their nursing-fathers and nursing-mothers,* and therefore it is added, *They shall worship with their faces to the earth, and lick up the dust of thy feet;* which is a proverbial expression of their voluntary humbling of themselves to Christ in his Ordinances, (taken from the manner of the *Persians,* in declaring their Subjection to their Emperour, which the Apostle calls *a voluntary submission to the Gospel,* which is the spirit of the Members of the Churches of Christ. And for this Reason it is, that the Lord, when he moulded a Communion among his own People, wherein all Civil Administrations should serve to holy ends, he described the men to whom that Trust should be committed, by certain Properties, which also qualified them for fellowship in Church-Ordinances, as *Men of ability and power over their own affections;* secondly, *fearing God, Truly Religious, Men of Courage, hating Covetousness, men of Wisdom, men of understanding,* and *men known* or approved of *among the people of God, & chosen by the Lord from among their Brethren,* & not a stranger, which is no Brother : the most of which concurre to describe Church-members in a Church rightly gathered and ordered, who are also in respect of their union with Christ, and fellowship together, called *Brethren* frequently in the New Testament, wherein the equity of that Rule is established to us. Object. *Christ will have his due Preheminence, though the Civil Rulers oppose him, and persecute the Churches, as in* Rome : *Therefore it is not necessary that this course be taken in Civil Affairs to establish Christs Preheminence.* Ans. The Question is of a Christian Commonwealth that should willingly subject themselves to Christ, not of a Heathen State that shall perforce be subdued unto Christ. It is concerning what Gods people being free should chuse, not what his enemies are compell'd unto. . . .

John Davenport, *A Discourse about Civil Government in a New Plantation* (1673), 14–17.

95. A Dutch Opinion of New England Character (1646)

BY GOVERNOR WILLIAM KEIFT

Keift was a bankrupt Amsterdam merchant, sent out as Director General of the Dutch West India Company at New Amsterdam, but recalled in disgrace in 1647. — Bibliography: Winsor, *Narrative and Critical History*, III, 441; see also No. 93 above.

To the most noble and worthy Comissioners of the federated English met togeither at the Red Mounte, or Newhaven in New Netherlands Wm. Keift Director and the Senate of New Netherland doe send many salutations.

YOURS dated the 5th September old style we receaued the 21. new style by your messenger to which we thincke sufficient to giue this short answere.

That the Inhabitants of Hartford haue deceiued you with false accusations as were easy to be euidenced by us if it were now seasonable to produce our allegations which we can proue to be true by diuerse attestations as well of your owne Country men, as ours, togeither with other authenticke writinge, but that we may not seeme to be willing to evade you with vaine words, we shall at this time present you a few particulars, out of soe great an heap, as by the claw you may iudge of the talants of the lyon, and therefore passinge by their vsurpinge of our jurisdiccon, and of our proper grounde against possession solemnly taken by vs, and our protestacons formerly made, we doe say, that the bloude of our Country men wrongfully shed by the inhabitants of Hartford, and the sellinge of our domesticke beasts by them, doe sufficiently testify the equity of their proceedings and therefore your prejudgement supported by this Oath Creto Coxtius, as if you should say Amen, Amen, seemes wonderful to vs, and done contrary to the modesty requisite in such an Assemblie, who should allwaies keepe one eare for the other party.

Soe far as concernes the Barbarian handmaide although it be apprehended by some that she is no slaue but a free woeman, because she was neither taken in war nor bought with price, but was in former time placed with me by her parents for education, yet we will not suffer her to be wrongfully detayned, but whither he shall pay the damadge to her Mr. or she shalbe restored to him we will not suffer him that desires her for his wife to marry her, vntill she be lawfully baptised.   Concern-

ing the breaking in of our Agent vpon the watch at Hartford we truely
conceiue that watches are appointed for the defence of townes against
the violence of enemies, and not for the hinderinge of freinds returne to
their owne houses, and therefore least mischeifes happen, it were good
to committ such a trust to skilfull men, and not to ignorant boyes who
when they once finde themselues loaden with armes, thincke they may
alsoe lawfully cry out, *etiam nos poma natamus.*

Certainely when we heare the Inhabitants of Hartford complayninge
of vs, we seeme to heare Esops wolfe complayninge of the lamb, or the
admonition of the younge man who cryed out to his mother chideinge
with her neighboures, oh mother revile her, least she first take vp that
practise against you : But being taught by precedent passages we received
such an answere to our Protest from the inhabitants of Newhaven as we
expected, the Eagle allwaies despiseth the Beetle fly, yet notwithstand-
inge we doe vndauntedly continue in our purpose of pursueinge our
owne right by just armes and righteous meanes, and doe hope without
scruple to execute the expresse comands of our superiours.

To conclude we protest against all you Comissioners mett at the Red
Mounte as against breakers of the comon league, and alsoe infringers
of the speciall right of the Lords, the States our superiours, in that ye
have dared without expresse Comission to hould your generall meeting
within the limits of New Netherlande, these things are spoken from the
Duty of our place, in other respects we are yours. . . .

Ebenezer Hazard, *Historical Collections* (Philadelphia, 1794), II, 68-70.

———————◆———————

6. John Cotton, an Ideal Puritan (1652)

BY REVEREND JOHN NORTON

Norton was a highly educated man, minister at Ipswich, and afterward at the
"First Church" in Boston. — Bibliography: Winsor, *Narrative and Critical History*,
III, 357-358.

HIS Birth-place, *Derby*, we shall not detain the Reader at, though
a Scituation in respect of the purity, and frequent Agitation of
the air, attempered (in the judgment of the Orator) for the breeding
of better Wits.   Creatures are in their kind subservient ; but, tis God,
(not the air) who puts Wisdom into the inward parts, and giveth understanding to the heart.   As the wise man and the Fool die, so are they

both ordinarily born in the same place. The glory of every good and perfect gift reserved for the Father of Lights. . . .

This care in the Parents was quickly above expectation encouraged in the First-Fruits of their young Sons proficiency, more and more increasing great hopes concerning him throughout the whole time of his minority, wherein he was trained up in the Grammar-School of *Derby*, Three ingredients *Aristotle* requires to compleat a man : An innate excellency of Wit, Instruction, and Government : The two last we have by nature, in them man is Instrumental : The first we have by nature more immediately from God. . . .

About thirteen years of age he was admitted into *Trinity*-Colledge in *Cambridge*, . . . 'Tis not Youth, but Licentiousness in Youth, that unfits for an Academical state ; such as *Philostratus* long since complained of, who stain an *Athenian* life with wicked manners. . . .

From *Trinity* he was removed to *Emanuel*, that happy Seminary both of Piety and Learning. The occasion I cannot now learn : howsoever it may call to minde that Maxim of the Herbalists, *Plantæ translatio est plantæ perfectio ;* The transplantation of a plant, is the perfection of a plant. In that Society the Lord gave him favor, so that in due time he was honored with a Fellowship amongst them, after a diligent and strict Examen according to the statutes of that House. . . . This providence is here remarkable concerning him ; That whereas his Father (whose Calling was towards the Law) had not many Clients that made use of his Advice in Law-matters before, it pleased God after his Son's going to *Cambridge* to bless him with great Practice, so that he was very able to keep him there, and to allow him liberal maintenance : Insomuch that this blessed man hath been heard to say, *God kept me in the University.* . . .

That which first made him famous in Cambridge, was his Funeral Oration for Doctor *Some*, Master of Peter-house ; so accurately performed, in respect of Invention, Elegancy, Purity of Style, Ornamens of Rhetorick, Elocution, and Oratorious beauty of the whole, as that he was thenceforth looked at as another *Xenephon*, or *Musa Attica* throughout the University. . . .

Unto this earthen vessel thus filled with heavenly treasure, *Boston* in *Lincolnshire* made their address, saying, *Come and help us !* And in that Candlestick the Father of spirits placeth this burning and shining light : To whom he removed from *Cambridge* about the 28. year of his age. . . .

. . . the God of the Spirits of all flesh, stirreth up many of his Faithful ones to leave that pleasant Land, their Estates, their Kindred, their
Fathers houses, and sail over the Atlantick-Ocean unto this vast Jeshi-
mon. Amongst whom this choice-Servant of God, with many others
graciously fitted for such a Work, are sent over to set up the worship
of Christ in this desert. . . .

. . . His flight was not like that of *Pliny's* Mice, that forsake a house
foreseeing the ruine of it; or of Mercenaries, who flie from duty in time
of danger: but Providence Divine shutting up the door of service in
England, and on the other hand opening it in *New-England*, he was
guided both by the word and eye of the Lord. . . .

Thus this Infant and small Commonwealth being now capacitated
both in respect of Civil and Church-estate, to walk with God according
to the prescript of his Word; it was the good hand of the Lord unto
his servants who had afflicted their souls to seek of him a right way for
themselves, their little ones, and their substance, to send unto them
(amongst many others) this man of understanding, that might be unto
them as eyes in this wilderness. . . .

In order whereunto the Court considering, That that people of God,
all the members of which Republick were Church-members, were to
be governed conformably to the Law of God, desired Mr. *Cotton* to
draw an Abstract of the Judicial Laws delivered from God by *Moses*,
so far forth as they were of moral (*i.e.* of perpetual and universal)
equity. Which he did, advising them to persist in their purpose of
establishing a *Theocraty* (*i.e.* Gods Government) over Gods people. . . .

. . . He was a general Scholar, studious to know all things, the want
whereof might in one of his profession be denominated Ignorance; and
piously ignorant of those things, the nescience whereof made him more
learned. One man is not born to all things. No calling (besides Divine
requisites) calleth for more Abilities, or a larger measure of humane
knowledge then the Ministery; deservedly therefore is his praise great
in all the Churches, that he not only gave himself thereunto, but exceeded
many that had done virtuously therein. The greater part of the *Encu-*
clopaideia he excelled in. Those Arts which the University requireth
such a proficiency from her graduates in, he both digested and refined
by his more accurate knowledge of them. He was a good *Hebrician*,
in Greek a Critick, and could with great facility both speak and write
Latine in a pure and elegant Ciceronian Stile, a good Historian, no
stranger to the Fathers, Councils, or School-men: Abundantly exercised

z

in Commentators of all sorts. His Library was great, his reading and learning answerable, himself a living and better Library. Though he was a constant Student, yet he had all his Learning out of his Books. He was a man of much Communion with God, and acquaintance with his own heart, observing the daily passages of his life. He had a deep fight into the Mystery of Gods grace, and mans corruption, and large apprehensions of these things. . . .

He began the Sabbath at evening; therefore then performed Family-duty after supper, being larger then ordinary in Exposition, after which he Catechised his children and servants, and then returned into his Study. The morning following, Family-worship being ended, he retired into his Study, until the Bell called him away. Upon his return from Meeting, he returned again into his Study (the place of his labour and prayer) unto his private devotion : where (having a small repast carried him up for his dinner) he continued till the tolling of the bell. The publick service being over, he withdrew for a space to his prementioned Oratory for his sacred addresses unto God, as in the forenoon; then came down, repeated the Sermon in the family, prayed, after supper sung a Psalm, and towards bed-time betaking himself again to his Study, he closed the day with prayer. Thus he spent the Sabbath continually.

In his Study, he neither sate down unto, nor arose from his meditations without prayer : whilst his eyes were upon his book, his expectation was from God. He had learned to study, because he had learned to pray : An able Student, a Gospel-Student, because unable to study without Jesus Christ. . . .

A mans wisdom maketh his face to shine. He had a happy, a quick, comprehensive, and benign Understanding, as having received the manifestation of the Spirit, for the service and profit of others. . . .

He was a man of an ingenuous and pious candor, rejoicing (as opportunity served) to take notice of, and testifie unto the gifts of God in his brethen; thereby drawing the hearts of them to him, and of others to them; both to their encouragement, and the edification of many. He did not think himself a loser by putting honor upon his Fellow-Elders, but was willing they should communicate with him in the esteem and love of the people. He was not only a son of peace, enjoying the continual feast of a good conscience with serenity and tranquillity of affections at home; but also a Peace-maker, qualified by the graces forementioned to be a choice Instrument in the hand of the Prince of Peace, amongst the Churches. . . .

As concerning any Tenet wherein he may seem singular, Remember, he was a man, and therefore to be heard and read with judgment, and haply sometimes with favour. *Hierom* makes a difference between reading the writings of the Apostles, and the Tractates of other Authors: They (saith he) always spake the truth; These, as men, in some things erre. Let him but receive with some proportion to the measure that he gave, and he will be found no debtor upon that account: No man did more placidly bear a Dissentient. . . .

John Norton, *Abel being Dead yet Speaketh; or, the Life & Death of . . . Mr. John Cotton* (London, 1658), 6-41 *passim*.

CHAPTER XV — PLYMOUTH

97. Why the Pilgrims left Holland (1620)

BY GOVERNOR WILLIAM BRADFORD

For Bradford, see No. 49 above. — Bibliography: Winsor, *Narrative and Critical History*, III, 285-287; H. M. Dexter, *Congregationalism, as seen in its Literature*, 390-391; Channing and Hart, *Guide*, § 111.

AFTER they had liued in this citie about some .11. or .12. years (which is yᵉ more obseruable being yᵉ whole time of yᵗ famose truce between that state & yᵉ Spaniards) And sundrie of them were taken away by death ; & many others begane to be well striken in years (the graue mistris Experience haueing taught them many things) Those prudent gouernours, with sundrie of ye sagest members begane both deeply to apprehend their present dangers, & wisely to foresee yᵉ future ; & thinke of timly remedy. In yᵉ agitation of their thoughts, and much discours of things hear aboute ; at length they began to incline to this conclusion, of remoouall to some other place. Not out of any new-fanglednes, or other such like giddie humor, by which men are oftentimes transported to their great hurt, & danger. But for sundrie weightie, & solid reasons ; some of yᵉ cheefe of which, I will hear breefly touch. And first they saw, & found by Experience, the hardnes of yᵉ place, & cuntrie to be such ; as few in comparison would come to them ; and fewer that would bide it out, and continew with them. for many yᵗ came to them, and many more yᵗ desired to be with them ; could not endure yᵗ great labor, and hard fare, with other Inconueniences, which they vnderwent, & were contented with. But though they loued their persons, approued their cause, and honoured their sufferings ; yet they left them, as it weer weeping, as Orpah did her mother in law Naomie ; or as those Romans did Cato in Vtica, who desired to be excused, & borne with, though they could not all be Catoes. for many, though they desired to Injoye yᵉ ordinances of God in their puritie, and yᵉ libertie of the Gospell with them. Yet (alass) they admitted of bondage, with danger of conscience ; rather then to Indure these hardships, yea some preferred, & chose yᵉ prisons in England, rather then this libertie in

Holland, with these afflictions. But it was thought that If a better, and easier place of liuing could be had ; It would draw many, & take away these discouragments. Yea their pastor would often say, that many of those w° both wrote, & preached now against them, If they were in a place, wher they might haue libertie, and liue comfortably, they would then practise as they did.

2^ly. They saw, that though ye people generally, bore all these difficulties very cherfully, & with a resolute courage, being in ye best, & strength of their years ; yet old age began to steale on many of them (and their great, & continuall labours, with other crosses, and sorrows, hastened it before ye time) so as it was not only probably thought, but apparently seen, that within a few years more, they would be in danger to scatter (by necessities pressing them) or sinke vnder their burdens, or both. And therfore according to ye deuine prouerb, y^t a wise man seeth ye plague when it cometh, & hideth him selfe. pro. 22. 3. so they like skillfull & beaten souldiers were fearfull, either to be intrapped, or surrounded by their enimies ; so as they should neither be able to fight, nor flie. And therfor thought it better to dislodge betimes, to some place of better aduantage, & less danger, If any such could be found.

Thirdly, as necessitie was a taskmaster ouer them, so they were forced to be such, not only to their seruants (but in a sorte), to their dearest children ; the which as it did not a little wound ye tender harts of many a louing father, & mother ; so it produced likwise sundrie sad, and sorowful effects. For many of their children, that were of best dispositions, and gracious Inclinations (haueing lernde to bear ye yoake in their youth) and willing to bear parte of their parents burden, were (often times) so oppressed with their heuie labours ; that though their minds were free and willing, yet their bodies bowed vnder ye waight of ye same, and became decreped in their early youth ; the vigor of nature being consumed in ye very budd as it were. But that which was more lamentable, and of all sorowes most heauie to be borne ; was that many of their children, by these occasions (and ye great licentiousnes of youth in y^t countrie) and ye manifold Temptations of the place, were drawne away by euill examples into extrauagante, & dangerous courses, getting ye raines off their neks, & departing from their parents. some became souldjers, others tooke vpon them farr viages by Sea ; and other some worse courses, tending to dissolutnes, & the danger of their soules ; to ye great greefe of their parents, and dishonour of God. so that they saw their posteritie would be in danger to degenerate, & be corrupted.

Lastly (and which was not least) a great hope, & Inward zeall they had of laying some good foundation (or at least to make some way thervnto) for y⁰ propagating, & aduancing y⁰ Gospell of y⁰ kingdom of Christ in those remote parts of y⁰ world ; yea though they should be, but euen as stepping-stones, vnto others for y⁰ performing of so great a work.

These, & some other like reasons, moued them to vndertake this resolution of their remouall ; the which they afterward prosecuted with so great difficulties, as by the sequell will appeare.

The place they had thoughts on, was some of those vast, and vnpeopled countries of America, which are frutfull, & fitt for habitation ; being deuoyd of all ciuill Inhabitants ; wher ther are only saluage, & brutish men, which range vp, and downe, litle otherwise then y⁰ wild beasts of the same. This proposition being made publike, and coming to y⁰ scaning of all ; It raised many variable opinions amongst men, and caused many fears, & doubts amongst them selues. some from their reasons, and hops conceiued ; laboured to stirr vp & Incourage the rest to vndertake, & prosecute y⁰ same ; others againe out of their fears, objected against it, & sought to diuerte from it ; aledging many things, and those neither vnreasonable, nor vnprobable. As that it was a great designe, and sub-jecte to many vnconceiuable perills, & dangers as (besids the the casulties of y⁰ seas (which none can be freed from) the length of y⁰ vioage was such, as y⁰ weake bodys of women, and other persons worne out with age, & trauille (as many of them were) could neuer be able to endure. And yet if they should, the miseries of y⁰ land, which they should be exposed vnto, would be to hard to be borne ; and lickly some, or all of them togeither, to consume, & vtterly to ruinate them. for ther they should be liable to famine, and nakednes, & y⁰ wante in a maner of all things. The chang of aire, diate, & drinking of water, would Infecte their bodies with sore sickneses, and greeuous diseases. And also those which should escape, or ouercome these difficulties, should yett be in continuall dangers of y⁰ saluage people ; who are cruell, barbarous, & most trecherous, being most furious in their rage, and merciles wher they ouercome ; not being contente only to kill, & take away life, but delight to tormente men in y⁰ most bloodie mañer that may be ; fleaing some aliue with y⁰ shells of fishes, cutting of y⁰ members, & Ioynts of others by peesmeale ; and broiling on y⁰ coles eate y⁰ collops of their flesh in their sight whilst they liue, with other cruelties horrible to be related. And surely It could not be thought but y⁰ very hearing of these things, could not but moue ye very bowels of men to grate within them, and make ye weake to quake, & tremble. It was furder objected, that it would require greater sumes of money to furnish such a voiage (and to fitt them with necessaries) then their consumed estats would amounte too ; and yett they must as well looke to be seconded with supplies, as presently to be trasported. Also many presidents of ill success, & lamentable misseries befalne others, in the like designes, were easie to be found, and not forgotten to be aledged. Besids their owne experience, in their former troubles, & hardships, in their remouall into Holand ; and how hard a thing it was for them to liue in that strange place, though it was a neighbour countrie, & a ciuill and rich comone wealth.

It was answered, that all great, & honourable actions, are accompanied with great difficulties ; and must be, both enterprised, and ouercome with answerable courages. It was granted ye dangers were great, but not desperate ; the difficulties were many, but not Inuincible. For though their were many of them likly, yet they were not cartaine ; It might be sundrie of ye things feared, might neuer befale; others by prouidente care & ye vse of good means (might in a great measure be preuented ; and all of them (through ye help of God) by fortitude, and patience, might either be borne, or ouercome. True it was that such atempts were not to be made, and vndertaken without good ground, & reason ; not rashly, or lightly as many haue done for curiositie, or hope of gaine, &c But their condition was not ordinarie ; their ends were good & honourable ; their calling lawfull, & vrgente ; and therfore they might expecte ye blessing of God in their proceding. yea though they should loose their liues in this action, yet might they haue comforte in the same, and their endeauors would be honourable. They liued hear but as men in exile, & in a poore condition; and as great miseries might possiblie befale them in this place ; for ye .12. years of truce were now out, & ther was nothing but beating of drumes, and preparing for warr, the euents wherof are allway vncertaine ; ye Spaniard might prooue as cruell, as The saluages of America ; and ye famine, and pestelence, as sore hear as ther ; & their libertie less to looke out for remedie. After many other perticuler things answered, & aledged on both sids, It was fully concluded by ye major parte, to put this designe in execution ; and to prosecute it by the best means they could.

William Bradford, *History of the Plimoth Plantation* (Fac-simile from the original manuscript, with an Introduction by John A. Doyle, London and Boston, 1896), 15-18.

98. The Germ of Popular Government (1620)

BY GOVERNOR WILLIAM BRADFORD

For Bradford, see No. 49 above. — Bibliography: Winsor, *Narrative and Critical History*, III, 289–290; J. A. Doyle, *English in America*, *Puritan Colonies*, I, ch. ii.

THIS day, before we came to harbour, observing some not well affected to unity and concord, but gave some appearance of faction, it was thought good there should be an association and agreement, that we should combine together in one body, and to submit to such government and governors as we should by common consent agree to make and choose, and set our hands to this that follows, word for word.[1] . . .

IN ye name of God Amen. We whose names are vnderwriten, the loyall subjeċts of our dread Soueraigne Lord King James by yᵗ grace of God, of great Britaine, Franc, & Ireland king, defender of ye faith, &c.

Haueing vndertaken, for ye glorie of God, and advancemente of ye christian faith and honour of our king & countrie, a voyage to plant ye first colonie in ye Northene parts of Virginia. Doe by these presents solemnly & mutualy in ye presence of God, and one of another, couenant, & combine our selues togeather into a Ciuill body politick; for our better ordering, and preseruation & furtherance of ye ends aforesaid; and by Vertue hearof to enacte, constitute, and frame such just & equall lawes, ordinances, Acts, constitutions, & offices, from time to time, as shall be thought most meete & conuenient for ye generall good of ye Colonie: vnto which we promise all due submission and obedience. In witnes wherof we haue herevnder subscribed our names at Cap-Codd ye. 11. of Nouember, in ye year of ye raigne of our soueraigne Lord King Iames of England, France, & Ireland ye eighteenth and of Scotland ye fiftie fourth. Anᵒ: Dom. 1620.[2]

---

[1] Alexander Young, *Chronicles of the Pilgrim Fathers* (Boston, 1841), 120.
[2] William Bradford, *History of the Plimoth Plantation* (Fac-simile from the original manuscript, with an Introduction by John A. Doyle, London and Boston, 1896), 54.

99. The First Landing at Plymouth (1620)

BY GOVERNOR WILLIAM BRADFORD

For Bradford, see No. 49 above. — Bibliography: Winsor, *Narrative and Critical History*, III, 285–289; Channing and Hart, *Guide*, § 112.

. . . BUT to omite other things (that I may be breefe) after longe beating at sea, they fell with that land which is called Cape Cod; the which being made, & certainly knowne to be it they were not a little Ioyfull. After some deliberation had amongst them selues, & with ye m^r of ye ship; they tacked aboute, and resolued to stande for ye southward (ye wind & weather being faire) to finde some place, aboute Hudsons riuer for their habitation. But after they had sailed y^t course aboute halfe ye day, they fell amongst deangerous shoulds, and roring breakers, and they were so farr Intangled ther with, as they conceiued them selues in great danger, & ye wind shrinking vpon them withall, they resolued to bear vp againe for the cape; and thought them selues hapy to gett out of those dangers, before night ouertooke them, as by gods good prouidence they did; And ye next day they gott into ye cape-harbor wher they ridd in saftie. A word or too by ye way of this cape, It was thus first named by Capten Gosnole, & his company, An°: 1602. And after by Capten Smith was caled Cape Iames, but it retains ye former name amongst sea-men. Also y^t pointe which first shewed those dangerous shoulds vnto them, they called pointe care, & Tuckers Terrour; but ye French, & Dutch to this day call it malabarr, by reason of those perilous shoulds, and ye losses they haue suffered their.

Being thus ariued in a good harbor, and brought safe to land, they fell vpon their knees & blessed ye God of heauen, who had brought them ouer ye vast, & furious Ocean, and deliuered them from all ye periles, & miseries therof againe to set their feete on ye firme and stable earth, their proper elemente. And no maruell if they were thus Ioyefull, seeing wise Seneca was so affected with sailing a few miles on ye coast of his owne Italy; as he affirmed, that he had rather remaine twentie years on his way by land, then pass by sea to any place in a short time; so tedious, & dreadfull was ye same vnto him.

But hear I cannot but stay, and make a pause, and stand half amazed at this poore peoples presente condition; and so I thinke will the reader too, when he well considers ye same. Being thus passed ye vast Ocean, and a sea of troubles before in their preparation (as may be remembred by y^t which wente before) they had now no freinds to wellcome them, nor Inns to entertaine, or refresh their weatherbeaten bodys, no houses, or much less townes to repaire too, to seeke for succoure ; It is recorded in scripture as a mercie to ye apostle & his shipwraked company, y^t the barbarians shewed them no smale kindnes in refreshing them, but these sauage barbarians, when they mette with them (as after will appeare) were readier to fill their sids full of arrows then otherwise. And for ye season it was winter, and they that know ye winters of y^t cuntrie, know them to be sharp & violent, & subjecte to cruell & feirce stormes, deangerous to trauill to known places, much more to serch an vnknown coast. Besids what could they see, but a hidious & desolate wildernes, full of wild beasts, & willd men, and what multituds ther might be of them they knew not ; nether could they (as it were) goe vp to ye tope of pisgah, to vew from this willdernes, a more goodly cuntrie to feed their hops ; for which way so euer they turnd their eys (saue vpward to ye heavens) they could haue little solace or content, in respecte of any outward objects, for sumer being done, all things stand vpon them with a wetherbeaten face; an ye whole countrie (full of woods & thickets) represented a wild & sauage heiw ; If they looked behind them, ther was ye mighty Ocean which they had passed, and was now as a maine barr, & goulfe, to seperate them from all ye ciuill parts of ye world. If it be said they had a ship to sucour them, it is trew ; but what heard they daly from ye m^r & company? but y^t with speede they should looke out a place (with their shallop) wher they would be, at some near distance ; for ye season was shuch, as he would not stirr from thence, till a safe harbor was discouered by them, wher they would be, and he might goe without danger ; and that victells consumed apace, but he must & would keepe sufficient for them selues, & their returne ; yea it was muttered by some, that if they gott not a place in time, they would turne them, & their goods a shore, & leaue them. Let it be also considered what weake hopes of supply, & succoure, they left behinde them ; y^t might bear vp their minds in this sade condition, and trialls they were vnder ; and they could not but be uery smale ; It is true indeed, ye affections & loue of their brethren at Leyden was cordiall & entire towards them, but they had litle power to help them, or them selues ; and how ye case stoode betwene them, & ye marchants, at their coming away hath allready been declared. What could now sustaine them, but ye Spirite of God & his grace? may not, & ought not the children of these fathers rightly say, our faithers were *English men which came ouer this great Ocean, and*

were ready to perish in this willdernes, but they cried vnto ye Lord, and
he heard their voyce, and looked on their aduersitie, &c. Let them ther-
fore praise ye Lord, because he is good; & his mercies endure for euer.
yea, let them which haue been redeemed of ye Lord, shew how he hath
deliuered them, from ye hand of ye oppressour. when they wandered in
ye deserte willdernes out of ye way, and found no citie to dwell in, both
hungrie, & thirstie, their sowle was ouerwhelmed in them. let them
confess before ye Lord his louing kindnes, and his wonderfull works before
ye sons of men.

The .10. Chap.

Showing how they sought out a place of habitation ; and what befell them
theraboute.

Being thus arriued at Cap-Cod y^e .11. of Nouember, and necessitie
calling them to looke out a place for habitation, (as well as the maisters
& mariners Importunitie), They hauing brought a large shalop with them
out of England, stowed in quarters in ye ship, they now gott her out, &
sett their carpenters to worke to trime her vp, but being much brused
& shatered in ye shipe wth foule weather, they saw she would be longe in
mending. Whervpon a few of them tendered them selues, to goe by
land and discouere those nearest places, whilst ye shallop was in mending, and ye rather because as they wente into y^t harbor ther seemed to
be an opening some .2. or .3. leagues of, which ye maister Iudged to be a
riuer   It was conceiued ther might be some danger in ye attempte, yet
seeing them resolute they were permited to goe ; being .16. of them
well armed vnder ye conduct of Captein Standish, having shuch Instructions giuen them as was thought meete. . . .   After some houres saill-
ing, it begane to snow, & raine, & about ye midle of ye afternoone, y^e
wind Increased, & ye sea became very rough ; and they broake their
rudder, & it was as much as .2. men could doe to steere her with a
cupple of oares. But their pillott bad them be of good cheere for he
saw ye harbor, but ye storme Increasing, & night drawing on, they bore
what saile they could to gett in, while they could see ; but herwith they
broake their mast in .3. peeces & their saill fell ouer bord, in a very
grown sea, so as they had like to haue been cast away ; yet by gods
mercie they recouered them selues, & hauing ye floud with them struck
into ye harbore. But when it came too, ye pillott was deceiued in y^e
place, and said ye Lord be mercifull vnto them, for his eys neuer saw

y^t place before ; & he, & the m^r mate would haue rune her a shore, in a coue full of breakers before ye winde   But a lusty seaman which steered, bad those which rowed if they were men, about with her, or ells they were all cast away; the which they did with speed, so he bid them be of good cheere, & row lustly for ther was a faire sound before them, & he doubted not, but they should find one place or other, wher they might ride in saftie.   And though it was *very darke*, and rained sore ; yet in ye end they gott vnder ye lee of a smalle Iland and remained ther all *y^t night* in saftie.   But they knew not this to be an Iland till morning, but were deuided in their minds, some would keepe ye boate for fear they might be amongst ye Indians ; others were so weake and could, they could not endure, but got a shore, & with much adoe got fire (all things being so wett) and ye rest were glad to come to them, for after midnight ye wind shifted to the north-west, & it frose hard.   But though this had been a day, & night of much trouble, & danger vnto them ; yet god gaue them a *morning* of comforte & refreshinge (as vsually he doth to his children) for ye next day was a faire sunshinīge day, and they found them sellues to be on an Iland secure from ye Indeans ; wher they might drie their stufe, fixe their peeces, & rest them selues, and gaue god thanks for his mercies, in their manifould deliuerances.   And this being the *last day of ye weeke*, they prepared ther to keepe y^e *Sabath;* on *munday* they sounded ye harbor, and founde it fitt for shipping ; and marched into ye land, & found diuerse cornfeilds, & litle runing brooks, a place as they supposed) fitt for situation, at least it was ye best they could find, and ye season, & their presente necessitie made them glad to accepte of it.   So they returned to their shipp againe with this news to ye rest of their people, which did much comforte their harts.

On y^e *.15. of Desem^r:* they wayed anchor to goe to ye place they had discouered, & came within *.2.* leagues of it, but were faine to bear vp againe, but y^e *.16. day* ye winde came faire, and they arriued safe in this harbor. And after wards tooke better veiw of ye place, and resolued wher to pitch their dwelling ; and y^e *.25. day* begane to erecte ye first house, for comōne vse to receiue them, and their goods.

William Bradford, *History of the Plimoth Plantation* (Fac-simile from the original manuscript, with an Introduction by John A. Doyle, London and Boston, 1896), 46–53 *passim*.

100. Life in a Pilgrim Commonwealth (1620–1623)

BY GOVERNOR WILLIAM BRADFORD

Bradford (see No. 49 above) was at once a colonist, a statesman, and an historian; his work is of the highest value, as a conscious account of the beginning of America. — Bibliography: Winsor, *Narrative and Critical History*, III, 285–294; Edward Eggleston, *Beginners of a Nation*, Book II, ch. iii; J. A. Doyle, *English in America, Puritan Colonies*, I, ch. ii.

. . . AFTER this they chose, or rather confirmed Mr John Caruer (a man godly & well approued amongst them) their Gouernour for that year. And after they had prouided a place for their goods, or comone store, (which were long in vnlading for want of boats, foulnes of ye winter weather, and sicknes of diuerce) and begune some small cottages for their habitation; as time would admitte they mette and consulted of lawes, & orders, both for their ciuill, & military Gouermente, as ye necessitie of their condition did require, still adding thervnto as vrgent occasion in seuerall times, and as cases did require.

In these hard & difficulte beginings they found some discontents & murmurings arise amongst some, and mutinous speeches & carriags in other; but they were soone quelled, & ouercome, by ye wisdome, patience, and Just & equall carrage of things, by ye Gou^r and better part wch claue faithfully togeather in ye maine. But that which was most sadd, & lamentable, was, that in .2. or .3. moneths time halfe of their company dyed, espetialy in Jan: & February, being ye depth of winter, and wanting houses & other comforts; being Infected with ye Scuruie and other diseases, which this long vioage & their Inacomodate condition had brought vpon them; so as ther dyed some times .2. or .3. of a day, in ye foresaid time; that of .100. & odd persons scarce .50. remained: and of these in ye time of most distres ther was but .6. or .7. sound persons; who to their great comendations, be it spoken, spared no pains, night nor day, but with abundance of toyle and hazard of their owne health, fetched them wood made them fires, drest them meat, made their beads, washed ther lothsome cloaths, cloathed & vncloathed them   In a word did all ye homly, & necessarie offices for them, wch dainty & quesie stomacks cannot endure to hear named and all this willingly & cherfully, without any grudging In ye least, shewing herein their true loue vnto their freinds & bretheren; A rare example & worthy to be remembred. tow of these .7. were Mr William Brewster ther reuerend Elder, & Myles Standish ther Captein & military comander, (vnto whom my selfe, &

many others were much beholden in our low, & sicke condition) and yet the Lord so vpheld these persons, as in this generall calamity they were not at all Infected either with sicknes, or lamnes. And what I haue said of these, I may say of many others who dyed in this generall vissitation & others yet liuing ; that whilst they had health, yea or any strength continuing they were not wanting to any that had need of them ; And I doute not but their recompence is with ye Lord. . . .

All this while ye Indians came skulking about them, and would sometimes show them selues aloofe of, but when any aproached near them, they would rune away; and once they stoale away their tools wher they had been at worke & were gone to diner. But about y^e *.16. of march* a certaine Indian came bouldly amongst them, and spoke to them in broken English which they could well vnderstand, but maruelled at it ; at length they vnderstood by discourse with him, that he was not of these parts, but belonged to ye eastrene parts where some English-ships came to fhish, with whom he was aquainted, & could name sundrie of them by their names, amongst whom he had gott his language   He became proftable to them In aquainting them with many things concerning ye state of ye cuntry in ye East-parts wher he liued which was afterwards profitable vnto them ; as also of ye people hear, of their names, number & strength, of their situation & distance from this place, and who was cheefe amongst them.   His name was *Samasett*; he tould them also of another Indian whos name was *Squanto*, a natiue of this place, who had been in England & could speake better English then him selfe.   Being after some time of entertainmente, & gifts dismist, a while after he came againe, & .5. more with him, & they brought againe all ye tooles that were stolen away before, and made way for ye coming of their great Sachem, called *Massasoyt*.   Who about *.4. or .5. days after* came with the cheefe of his freinds, & other attendance with the aforesaid *Squanto*.   With whom after frendly entertainment, & some gifts giuen him, they made a peace with him (which hath now continued this .24. years) In these terms.   1. That neither he nor any of his, should Injurie or doe hurte, to any of their peopl,

2. That if any of his, did any hurte to any of theirs ; he should send ye offender, that they might punish him.

3. That if any thing were taken away from any of theirs, he should cause it to be restored ; and they should doe ye like to his.

4. If any did vnjustly warr against him, they would aide him ; If any did warr against them, he should aide them.

5. He should send to his neigbours confederats, to certifie them of this, that they might not wrong them, but might be likewise comprised in yᵉ conditions of peace.

6. That when ther men came to them, they should leaue their bows & arrows behind them. . . .

May .12. was yᵉ first mariage in this place; which acording to yᵉ laudable custome of yᵉ Low-cuntries, in which they had liued, was thought most requisite to be performed, by the magestrate; as being a ciuill thing, vpon which many questions aboute Inheritances doe depende, with other things most proper to their cognizans; and most consonante to yᵉ Scriptures. Ruth. 4. And no-wher found in yᵉ Gospell to be layed on yᵉ ministers as a part of their office. This decree or law about mariage „ was publisht by yᵉ Stats of yᵉ Low-countries Anº: 1590 That those of „ any religion (after lawfull, and open publication coming before yᵉ magis-„ trats, in yᵉ Town, or stat-house, were to b[e] orderly (by them) maried „ one, to another. Petets Hist. fol: 1029. And this practiss hath continued amongst, not only them, but hath been followed by all yᵉ famous churches of christ in these parts to this time. Anº: 1646. . . .

They begane now to gather in yᵉ small haruest they had; and to fitte vp their houses and dwellings, against winter, being all well recouered in health & strenght; and had all things in good plenty, for as some were thus Imployed in affairs abroad; others were excersised in fishing, aboute codd, & bass, & other fish of which yᵉʸ tooke good store, of which euery family had their portion; all yᵉ somer ther was no wante; and now begane to come in store of foule, as winter aproached, of which this place did abound when they came first, (but afterward decreased by degrees), and besids water foule, ther was great store of wild Turkies, of which they tooke many, besids venison &c. Besids they had aboute a peck a meale a weeke to a person, or now since haruest, Indean corne to yᵗ proportion. Which made many afterwards write so largly of their plenty hear to their freinds in England, which were not fained, but true reports. . . .

After yᵉ departure of this ship (which stayed not aboue .14. days) the Gouer & his assistante haueing disposed these late comers into seuerall families, as yᵉʸ best could; tooke an exacte acconte of all their prouissions in store, and proportioned yᵉ same to yᵉ number of persons; and found that it would not hould out aboue .6. months, at halfe alowance, and hardly that; and they could not well giue less this winter time till fish came In againe. So they were presently put to half alowance, one as well as an other, which begane to be hard, but they bore it patiently vnder hope of supply. . . .

But this made them ye more carefully to looke to them selues so as they agreed to Inclose their dwellings with a good strong pale, and make flankers in conuenient places with gates to shute which were euery night locked; and a watch kept, and when neede required ther was also warding on ye day time. And ye company was by ye captaine and ye Gou^r aduise, deuided into .4. Squadrons, and euery one had ther quarter apoynted them, vnto which they were to repaire vpon any suddane alarme. And if ther should be any crie of fire, a company were appointed for a gard, with muskets, whilst others quenched ye same, to preuent Indean treachery. This was accomplished very cherfully, and ye towne Impayled round by ye begining of march, In which eury family had a pretty garden plote secured. And herewith I shall end this year. Only I shall remember one passage more, rather of mirth, then of waight. One ye day called Chrismas-day, ye Gou^r caled them out to worke, (as was vsed) but ye most of this new-company excused them selues, and said it wente against their consciences to work on y^t day. So ye Gou^r tould them that if they made it mater of conscience, he would spare them, till they were better Informed; so he led-away ye rest and left them; but when they came home at noone, from their worke, he found them in ye streete at play openly; some pitching ye barr, & some at stoole-ball, and such like Sports. So he went to them, and tooke away their Implements, and tould them, that was against his conscience, that they should play, & others worke; if they made ye keeping of it mater of deuotion, let them kepe their houses, but ther should be no gameing, or reuelling in ye streets. Since which time nothing hath been atempted that way, at least openly. . . .

All this whille no supply was heard of, neither knew they when they might expecte any. So they begane to thinke how they might raise as much corne as they could, and obtaine a beter crope then they had done; that they might not still thus languish in miserie. At length, after much debate of things, The Gou^r (with ye aduise of ye cheefest amongest them) gaue way that they should set corne euery man for his owne perticuler, and in that regard trust to them selues; in all other things to goe on in ye generall way as before. And so assigned to euery family a parcell of land, according to the proportion of their number, for that end, only for present vse (but made no deuission for Inheritance), and rainged all boys, & youth vnder some familie. This had very good success; for

it made all hands very Industrious, so as much more corne was planted,
then other waise would haue bene; by any means yᵉ Gouᵗ or any other
could vse, and saued him a great deall of trouble, and gaue farr better
contente; the women now wente willingly into yᵉ feild, and tooke their
litle ons with them to set corne; which before would aledg weaknes and
Inabilitie; whom to haue compelled would have bene thoug[ht] great
tiranie, and oppression.

The experience that was had in this comone course, and condi[ti]on,
tried sundrie years, and that amongst godly, and sober men; may well
euince, they vanitie of that conceite, of Platos, & other ancients, applauded
by some of later times. That yᵉ taking away of propertie, and bringing in
comunitie, into, a comone wealth; would make them happy, and florish-
ing; as if they were wiser then God for this comunitie, (so farr as it
was) was found to breed much confusion, & discontent, and retard much
Imploymēt, that would haue been to their benefite, and comforte. for
yᵉ yong-men that were most able and fitte for labour, & seruice; did
repine that they should spend their time, & streingth to worke for other
mens wiues, and children, with out any recompence.   The strong, or man
of parts, had no more in deuission of victails, & cloaths, then he that was
weake, and not able to doe a quarter yᵉ other could, this was thought
Injuestice.   The aged and grauer men to be ranked, and equalised, in
labours, and victails, cloaths &c., with yᵉ meaner, & yonger sorte, thought
it some Indignite, & disrespect vnto them.   And for mens wiues to be commanded, to doe seruise for other men, as dresing ther meate, washing
their cloaths &c. they deem[ed] it a kind of Slauerie, neither could many
husbands well brooke it.   Vpon yᵉ poynte all being to haue alike, and
all to doe alike, they thought them selues in yᵉ like condition, and one
as good as another; and so if it did not cut of, those relations, that god
hath set amongest men; yet it did at least much diminish, and take of,
yᵉ mutuall respects, that should be preserued amongst them.   And would
have bene worse if they had been men of another condition. let none
objecte this is mens corruption; and nothing to yᵉ course it selfe; I
answer seeing all men haue this coruption in them, God in his wisdome
saw another course fiter for them. . . .

With yᵉ former letter write by Mʳ Sherley, there were sente sundrie
objections concerning which he thus writeth. These are the cheefe
objections which they That are now returned make against you, and the
countrie; I pray you consider them, and answer them by the first con-
ueniencie. These objections were made by some of those that came

2 A

ouer on their perticuler and were returned home, as is before mentioned and were of yͤ same suite with those yͭ this other letter mentions.

I shall here set them them downe, with yͤ answers then made vnto them, and sent ouer at yͤ returne of this ship : Which did so confound yͤ objecters ; As some confessed their falte, and others deneyed what they had said, and eate their words, & some others of them, haue since come ouer againe, and haue liued to conuince them selues sufficiently, both in their owne, & other mens Judgments.

1. obj was diuersitie aboute Religion. Ans : we know no such matter, for here was neuer any controuersie, or opposition, either publicke, or priuate (to our knowledg) since we came.

2. ob : Neglecte of familie duties, one yͤ Lords day

Ans. We allow no such thing, but blame it in our selues, & others ; and they that thus reporte it, should haue shewed their christian loue, the more if they had in loue, tould yͤ offenders of it ; rather then thus to reproach them behind their baks. But (to say no more) we wish them selues had giuen better example.

3. ob : Wante of both the sacrements.

Ans. The more is our greefe, that our pastor is kept from vs, by whom we might Injoye them ; for we vsed to haue the Lords Supper, euery Saboth, and baptisme as often as ther was occasion, of children to baptise.

4. ob : Children not catachised, nor taught to read.

Ans : neither is true ; for diuerse take pains with their owne as they can, Indeede we haue no com̄one schoole for want of a fit person, or hithertoo means to maintaine one ; though we desire now to begine

5. ob. Many of yͤ perticuler members of yͤ plantation, will not work for yͤ generall.

Ans : this allso is not wholy true ; for though some doe it not willingly, & other not honestly, yet all doe it ; and he that doth worst gets his owne foode, & some thing besids. But we will not excuse them, but labour to reforme them yͤ best we cane ; or else to quitte yͤ plantation of them.

6. ob : The water is not wholsome.

Ans : If they mean, not so wholsome as yͤ good beere, and wine in London (which they so dearly loue) we will not dispute with them, but els for water it is as good as any in yͤ world, (for ought we knowe) and it is wholsome enough to vs, that can be contente therwith.

7. ob : The ground is barren, and doth bear no grasse.

Ans : It is hear (as in all places) some better, & some worse ; and if they well consider their woods in England, they shall not find such grasse in them, as in their feelds, & meadows. The catle find grasse for they are as fatt as need be ; we wish we had but one for euery hundred, that here is grase to keep. Indeed this objection (as some other) are ridiculous to all here which see, and know yᵉ contrary.

8. ob : The fish will not take salt to keepe sweete.

Ans : This is as true, as that which was written, that ther is scarce a foule to be seene, or a fish to be taken. Things likly to be true? in a cuntrie, wher so many sayle of ships come yearly a fishing ; they might as well say, ther can no aile, or beere in London, be kept from sowering.

9. ob : Many of them are theeuish, and steale on from an other.

Ans : Would London had been free from that crime ; then we shoulɾ not haue been trobled with these here ; It is well knowne sundrie haue smarted well for it, and so are yᵉ rest like to doe, if they be taken.

10. ob : The cuntrie is anoyed with foxes, and woules.

Ans : So are many other good cuntries tow ; but poyson, Traps, and other such means will help to destroy them.

11. ob : The Dutch are planted nere Hudsons Bay, and are likly to ouer throw the trade.

Ans : They will come and plante in these parts, also, If we, and others doe not, but goe home and leaue it to them. We rather commend them, then condemne them for it.

12. ob : The people are much anoyed with muskeetoes.

Ans : They are too delicate, and vnfitte to begine new-plantations, and collonies that cannot enduer yᵉ biting of a muskeeto ; we would wish such to keepe at home, till at least they be muskeeto proofe. yet this place is as free as any ; and experience teacheth that yᵉ more yᵉ land is tild, and yᵉ woods cut downe, the fewer ther will be, and in the end scarse any at all. . . .

William Bradford, *History of the Plimoth Plantation* (Fac-simile from the original manuscript, with an Introduction by John A. Doyle, London and Boston, 1896), 54–113 *passim*.

101. Conditions of Life in Plymouth (1621)

BY GOVERNOR EDWARD WINSLOW

Next to Bradford, Winslow was the leading man in the colony. — Bibliography as in No. 100 above.

ALTHOUGH I received no letter from you by this ship, yet forasmuch as I know you expect the performance of my promise, which was, to write unto you truly and faithfully of all things, I have therefore at this time sent unto you accordingly, referring you for further satisfaction to our more large Relations.

You shall understand that in this little time that a few of us have been here, we have built seven dwelling-houses and four for the use of the plantation, and have made preparation for divers others. We set the last spring some twenty acres of Indian corn, and sowed some six acres of barley and pease; and according to the manner of the Indians, we manured our ground with herrings, or rather shads, which we have in great abundance, and take with great ease at our doors. Our corn did prove well; and, God be praised, we had a good increase of Indian corn, and our barley indifferent good, but our pease not worth the gathering, for we feared they were too late sown. They came up very well, and blossomed; but the sun parched them in the blossom.

Our harvest being gotten in, our governor sent four men on fowling, that so we might, after a special manner, rejoice together after we had gathered the fruit of our labors. They four in one day killed as much fowl as, with a little help beside, served the company almost a week. At which time, amongst other recreations, we exercised our arms, many of the Indians coming amongst us, and among the rest their greatest king, Massasoyt, with some ninety men, whom for three days we entertained and feasted; and they went out and killed five deer, which they brought to the plantation, and bestowed on our governor, and upon the captain and others. And although it be not always so plentiful as it was at this time with us, yet by the goodness of God we are so far from want, that we often wish you partakers of our plenty.

We have found the Indians very faithful in their covenant of peace with us, very loving, and ready to pleasure us. We often go to them, and they come to us. Some of us have been fifty miles by land in the country with them, the occasions and relations whereof you shall understand by our general and more full declaration of such things as are worth the noting. Yea, it hath pleased God so to possess the Indians with a fear of us and love unto us, that not only the greatest king amongst them, called Massasoyt, but also all the princes and peoples round about us, have either made suit unto us, or been glad of any occasion to make peace with us; so that seven of them at once have sent their messengers to us to that end. Yea, an isle at sea, which we never saw, hath also, together with the former, yielded willingly to be under the protection and subject to our sovereign lord King James. So that there is now great peace amongst the Indians themselves, which was not formerly, neither would have been but for us; and we, for our parts, walk as peaceably and safely in the wood as in the highways in England. We entertain them familiarly in our houses, and they as friendly bestowing their venison on us. They are a people without any religion or knowledge of any God, yet very trusty, quick of apprehension, ripe-witted, just. . . .

For the temper of the air here, it agreeth well with that in England; and if there be any difference at all, this is somewhat hotter in summer. Some think it to be colder in winter; but I cannot out of experience so say. The air is very clear, and not foggy, as hath been reported. I never in my life remember a more seasonable year than we have here enjoyed; and if we have once but kine, horses, and sheep, I make no question but men might live as contented here as in any part of the world. For fish and fowl, we have great abundance. Fresh cod in the summer is but coarse meat with us. Our bay is full of lobsters all the summer, and affordeth variety of other fish. In September we can take a hogshead of eels in a night, with small labor, and can dig them out of their beds all the winter. We have muscles and othus [others?] at our doors. Oysters we have none near, but we can have them brought by the Indians when we will. All the spring-time the earth sendeth forth naturally very good sallet herbs. Here are grapes, white and red, and very sweet and strong also; strawberries, gooseberries, raspas, &c.; plums of three sorts, white black, and red, being almost as good as a damson; abundance of roses, white, red and damask; single, but very sweet indeed. The country wanteth only industrious men to employ; for it would grieve your hearts if, as I, you had seen so many miles together by goodly rivers uninhabited; and withal, to consider those parts of the world wherein you live to be even greatly burthened with abundance of people. These things I thought good to let you understand. being the truth of things as near as I could experimentally take knowledge of, and that you might on our behalf give God thanks, who hath dealt so favorably with us.

Our supply of men from you came the 9th of November, 1621, putting in at Cape Cod, some eight or ten leagues from us. The Indians that dwell thereabout were they who were owners of the corn which we found in caves, for which we have given them full content, and are in great league with them. They sent us word there was a ship near unto them, but thought it to be a Frenchman; and indeed for ourselves we expected not a friend so soon. But when we perceived that she made for our bay, the governor commanded a great piece to be shot off, to call home such as were abroad at work. Whereupon every man, yea boy, that could handle a gun, were ready, with full resolution that, if she were an enemy, we would stand in our just defence, not fearing them. But God provided better for us than we supposed. These came all in health, not any being sick by the way, otherwise than by sea-sickness, and so continue at this time, by the blessing of God. . . .

When it pleaseth God we are settled and fitted for the fishing business and other trading, I doubt not but by the blessing of God the gain will give content to all. In the mean time, that we have gotten we have sent by this ship; and though it be not much, yet it will witness for us that we have not been idle, considering the smallness of our number all this summer. We hope the merchants will accept of it, and be encouraged to furnish us with things needful for further employment, which will also encourage us to put forth ourselves to the uttermost.

Now because I expect your coming unto us, with other of our friends, whose company we much desire, I thought good to advertise you of a few things needful. Be careful to have a very good bread-room to put your biscuits in. Let your cask for beer and water be iron-bound, for the first tire, if not more. Let not your meat be dry-salted; none can better do it than the sailors. Let your meal be so hard trod in your cask that you shall need an adz or hatchet to work it out with. Trust not too much on us for corn at this time, for by reason of this last company that came, depending wholly upon us, we shall have little enough till harvest. Be careful to come by some of your meal to spend by the way; it will much refresh you. Build your cabins as open as you can, and bring good store of clothes and bedding with you. Bring every man a musket or fowling-piece. Let your piece be long in the barrel, and fear not the weight of it, for most of our shooting is from stands. Bring juice of lemons, and take it fasting; it is of good use. For hot

waters, aniseed water is the best; but use it sparingly. If you bring
any thing for comfort in the country, butter or sallet oil, or both, is very
good. Our Indian corn, even the coarsest, maketh as pleasant meat as
rice; therefore spare that, unless to spend by the way. Bring paper
and linseed oil for your windows, with cotton yarn for your lamps. Let
your shot be most for big fowls, and bring store of powder and shot. I
forbear further to write for the present, hoping to see you by the next
return. So I take my leave, commending you to the Lord for a safe
conduct unto us, resting in him,

Your loving friend,

E. W.

Plymouth, in New England, this 11th of December, 1621.

Edward Winslow, *Relation or Iournall,* etc. (London, 1622), in Alexander
Young, *Chronicles of the Pilgrim Fathers* (Boston, 1841), 230–238 *passim.*

———◆———

102. Suggestions on the Government of Plymouth (1625)

BY ROGER WHITE

White was minister at Leyden to the English Puritans who remained there.—
Bibliography as in No. 99 above.

*To his very loving friend, Mr. William Bradford, Governor of Plymouth
in New England, there be, &c.*

MY LOVING AND KIND FRIEND, AND BROTHER IN THE LORD,

M Y own and my wife's true love and hearty salutations to yourself
and yours and all the rest of our loving friends with you; hoping
in the Lord of your good healths, which I beseech him long to continue
for the glory of his name and good of his people. Concerning your kind
letter to the church, it was read publicly; whereunto (by the church) I
send you here enclosed an answer. Concerning my brother Robinson's
sickness and death and our practice, I wrote you at large, some five or
six months since; but lest it should miscarry, I have now written to
Mr. Brewster thereof, to whom I refer you.

Now concerning your course of choosing your governors yearly, and
in special of their choosing yourself year after year, as I conceive they

still do, and Mr. Allerton your assistant; howsoever I think it the best way that can be, so long as it please the Lord to continue your lives, and so good governors offer you, yet, considering man's mortality, whose breath is in his nostrils, and the evils of the times wherein we live, in which it is ordinarily seen that worse follow them that are good, I think it would be a safer course, for after time, the government was sometime removed from one to another; so the assistant one year might be governor next, and a new assistant chosen in his place, either of such as have or have not been in office; sometimes one, sometimes another, as it shall seem most fit to the corporation. My reasons are, 1st, because other officers that come after you, will look (especially if they be ambitiously minded) for the same privileges and continuance you have had; and if he have it not, will take great offence, as though unworthy of the place, and so greatly disgraced, whom to continue, might be very dangerous, and hazard (at least) the overthrow of all; men not looking so much at the reasons why others were so long continued as at the custom. 2dly, because others that are unexperienced in government might learn by experience; and so there might be fit and able men continually, when it pleaseth the Lord to take any away. 3dly, by this means, you may establish the things begun, or done before; for the governor this year, that was assistant last, will in likelihood rather ratify and confirm and go on with that he had a hand in the beginning of, when he was assistant, than otherwise, or persuade the new to it; whereas new governors, especially when there are factions, will many times overthrow that which is done by the former, and so scarcely any thing goeth forward for the general good; neither, that I see, can this be any prejudice to the corporation; for the new may always have the counsel and advice of the old for their direction, though they be out of office. These things I make bold to put to your godly wisdom and discretion, entreating you to pardon my boldness therein, and so leaving it to your discretion to make use of as you see it fitting, not having written the least inkling hereof to any other.

Now I entreat you, at your best leisure to write to me, how you think it will in likelihood go with your civil and church estate; whether there be hope of the continuance of both, or either; or whether you fear any alteration to be attempted in either. The reason of this my request is, the fear of some amongst us, (the which, if that hinder not, I think will come unto you,) occasioned partly by your letter to your father-in-law, Mr. May, wherein you write of the troubles you have had with

some, who it is like (having the times and friends on their sides) will
work you what mischiefs they can; and that they may do much, many
here do fear; and partly by reason of this king's proclamation, dated
the 13th of May last, in which he saith that his full resolution is, — to
the end that there may be one uniform course of government in and
through all his whole monarchy, — that the government of Virginia shall
immediately depend on himself, and not be committed to any company
or corporation, &c., so that some conceive he will have both the same
civil and ecclesiastical government that is in England, which occasioneth
their fear.   I desire you to write your thoughts of these things, for the
satisfying of others; for my own part and some others, we durst rely
upon you for that, who, we persuade ourselves, would not be thus
earnest for our pastor and church to come to you, if you feared the
danger of being suppressed.   Thus desiring you to pardon my boldness,
and remember us in your prayers, I for this time and ever, commit you
and all your affairs to the Almighty, and rest

Your assured loving friend
And brother in the Lord,
ROGER WHITE.

Leyden, December 1, *anno* 1625.

P. S. The church would entreat you to continue your writing to them,
which is very comfortable.

Alexander Young, *Chronicles of the Pilgrim Fathers* (Boston, 1841), 483-486.

---

103. "Of the Revells of New Canaan" (1628)

BY THOMAS MORTON (1637)

Morton, a former London attorney, was the head of a disorderly settlement at
Merry-Mount near Boston, and scandalized the Plymouth people. — Bibliography:
Winsor, *Narrative and Critical History*, III, 283; C. F. Adams, *Three Episodes of
Massachusetts History*, I, 162-182.

THE Inhabitants of Pasonagessit (having translated the name of
their habitation from that ancient Salvage name to Ma-reMount;
and being resolved to have the new name confirmed for a memorial to
after ages) did devise amongst themselves to have it performed in a
solemne manner with Revels, & merriment after the old English cus-

tome : prepared to sett up a Maypole upon the festivall day of Philip and Iacob ; & therefore brewed a barrell of excellent beare, & provided a case of bottles to be spent, with other good cheare, for all commers of that day. And because they would have it in a compleat forme, they had prepared a song fitting to the time and present occasion. And upon Mayday they brought the Maypole to the place appointed, with drumes, gunnes, pistols, and other fitting instruments, for that purpose ; and there erected it with the help of Salvages, that came thether of purpose to see the manner of our Revels. A goodly pine tree of 80. foote long, was reared up, with a peare of buckshorns nayled one, some-what neare unto the top of it : where it stood as a faire sea marke for directions ; how to finde out the way to mine Hoste of Ma-reMount.

And because it should more fully appeare to what end it was placed there, they had a poem in readines made, which was fixed to the May-pole, to shew the new name confirmed upon that plantation ; which allthough it were made according to the occurrents of the time, it being Enigmattically composed) pusselled the Seperatists most pittifully to expound it, . . .

The setting up of this Maypole was a lamentable spectacle to the precise seperatists : that lived at new Plimmouth. They termed it an Idoll ; yea they called it the Calfe of Horeb : and stood at defiance with the place, naming it Mount Dagon ; threatning to make it a woe-full mount and not a merry mount. . . .

There was likewise a merry song made, which (to make their Revells more fashionable) was sung with a Corus, every man bearing his part ; which they performed in a daunce, hand in hand about the Maypole, whiles one of the Company sung, and filled out the good liquor like ᵹammedes and Iupiter.

THE SONGE

DRinke and be merry, merry, merry boyes,
    Let all your delight be in Hymens ioyes,
Iô to Hymen now the day is come,
About the merry Maypole take a Roome.
    Make greene garlons, bring bottles out;
    And fill sweet Nectar, freely about,
    Vncover thy head, and feare no harme,
    For hers good liquor to keepe it warme.
Then drinke and be merry, &c.
Iô to Hymen, &c.
    Nectar is a thing assign'd,
    By the Deities owne minde,

> To cure the hart opprest with greife,
> And of good liquors is the cheife,
> Then drinke, &c.
> Iô to Hymen, &c.
>> Give to the Mellancolly man,
>> A cup or two of't now and than;
>> This physick' will soone revive his bloud,
>> And make him be of a merrier moode.
> Then drinke &c.
> Iô to Hymen &c.
>> Give to the Nymphe thats free from scorne,
>> No Irish; stuff nor Scotch over worne,
>> Lasses in beaver coats come away,
>> Yee shall be welcome to us night and day.
> To drinke and be merry &c.
> Iô to Hymen, &c.

This harmles mirth made by younge men (that lived in hope to have wifes brought over to them, that would save them a laboure to make a voyage to fetch any over) was much distasted, of the precise Seperatists : that keepe much a doe, about the tyth of Muit [mint] and Cummin ; troubling their braines more then reason would require about things that are indifferent : and from that time sought occasion against my honest Host of Ma-reMount to overthrow his ondertakings, and to destroy his plantation quite and cleane. . . .

Thomas Morton, *New English Canaan* (Amsterdam, 1637), 132–136 *passim*.

———————◆———————

104. Impending Annexation by Massachusetts (1690)

BY THE GENERAL COURT OF NEW PLYMOUTH

The legislature of Plymouth accepted annexation without much opposition in 1691. — Bibliography: Winsor, *Narrative and Critical History*, III, 282–294; Channing and Hart, *Guide*, §§ 113, 127, 128.

THIS Gen^ll Court having information from England that the colony of Plimouth had been joyned to the government of New Yorke, but the same was prevented by the Reverend Mr Mather, who gave an accompt to Govern^r Sclater how little service it would be

to their ma^{ties}, and how great dissatisfaction & inconvenience it would
be to the people ; we are also informed that after that we were like to
be annexed to Boston, but the same hindered by Mr Wiswall for the
present ; being also informed there is a possibillity that we may obtain
a charter for our selves if we speedily address to their ma^{ties} imploy a
suitable person to manage & rayse sufficient moneys to cary the same
an end ; this Court thinking it their duty to informe the several inhabitants in the severall towns in this colony thereof, that they may not
hereafter say they had no notice, and that they may make use of the
present oppertunity as they may sē it like to be for their benifit, — it
is therefore ordered, that the magistrates or deputies in each town forthwith order the constables to warn the inhabitants of the towns to assemble, and give notice to them of the occasion, and that they there have
the information above mentioned, that they may consider thereof, and
draw up their minds therein, and that the same be signified to ye adjournment of this Court ; and in particular that it be known whether it
be their minds we should sit still & fall into the hands of those that can
catch us, without using means to procure that which may be for our
good, or prevent that which may be our inconvenience, or if they will
act, then to know what instruments they would improve, and what
money they can rayse ; and must also know that if a pattent can be
procured, it will not take up less than 500^{ld} sterling, which will take
nere 700^{ld} of our money. . . .

It is ordered and agreed, that the honour^d Govr, in behalf of the
colony, return their hearty thanks to the Honorable Sr Henry Ashurst,
& the Reverend Mr Increase Mather, & ye Reverend Mr Ichabod Wiswall, for their care & service for ye good of this colony.   And thō the
colony labour under many inconveniences, being small in number, low
in estate, & great publique charges, by reason whereof are not capable
to manifest their thankfullness sutable to the obligations that we have
and may be layed under, yet doe desire the Hon^rable Sr Henry Ashurst
to accept 50 guineas, and the Reverend Mr Mather & Mr Wiswall 25^{ld}
a peece, and to desire & impower the Hon^rable Sr Henry Ashurst that
he would be pleased to use his care & endeavour to procure a charter
from the King for a distinct goveřment for this colony, wth such regulations & enlargements as his majesty shall be pleased to graunt, and to
send such power and instructions as are necessary ; and that Sr Henry
be pleased to advise with s^d Mr Mather & Mr Wiswall as he hath oppertunity and seeth cause in any thing that may relate to us, and that the

said Mr Mather and Mr Wiswall be wrote unto, to give such informations to Sr Henry as they think may be any ways advantageous for us.

And in particular that we may be sufficiently impowered & required to sẽ that the gospel be preached in the severall towns, & that care be taken for the maintainance of them that dispence the same.

It is alsoe ordered, that 100^{ll} sterling, besides, be sent unto Sr Henry Ashurst, towards the charge of procuring a charter as aforesaid, & if he shall find it is like to be obtained, that he would please to informe us thereof, and w^t is like to be the farther charge, that we may take care therein as may be necessary.

Agred on by this Court, that the Govern^r, in behalf of the colony, send an address to their ma^{ties} for a new charter for governm^t; and that the Govr send to Sr Henry Ashurst a copy of our charter, and such other letters & papers as may be of use, and such other informations as may be necessary.

Ordered by the Court, &c., that whatsoever town or p̃ticular p̃sons shall adventure to disburse any moneys for or towards the procuring us a patent from their ma^{ties} for this colony, according to this Courts address, ordered to be made to their said ma^{ties} for the enjoyment of our ancient civill & religious liberties, shall be reimbursed the same according to a just and equall proportion thereof, if God please to favour us to be in a due capacity for the same. . . .

Records of the Colony of New Plymouth in New England (edited by N. B. Shurtleff, Boston, 1856), VI, 259–261 *passim*.

CHAPTER XVI — EARLY MASSACHUSETTS

105. The Settlement of Massachusetts (1628–1630)

BY CAPTAIN EDWARD JOHNSON (1654)

Captain Johnson, founder of Woburn, is a typical Puritan farmer-colonist, pious, brave, and fond of recording the deeds of his time. The *Wonder-working Providence* was published anonymously. — Bibliography : Winsor, *Narrative and Critical History*, III, ch. ix ; Tyler, *American Literature*, I, 137–146 ; J. A. Doyle, *English in America, Puritan Colonies*, I, ch. iii ; Edward Eggleston, *Beginners of a Nation*, Book II, ch. iv ; Channing and Hart, *Guide*, §§ 115–117.

WHEN *England* began to decline in Religion, like luke-warme *Laodicea*, and instead of purging out Popery, a farther compliance was sought not onely in vaine Idolatrous Ceremonies, but also in prophaning the Sabbath, and by Proclamation throughout their Parish churches, exasperating lewd and prophane persons to celebrate a Sabbath like the Heathen to *Venus, Baccus* and *Ceres ;* in so much that the multitude of irreligious lascivious and popish affected persons spred the whole land like *Grashoppers,* in this very time Christ the glorious King of his Churches, raises an Army out of our *English* Nation, for freeing his people from their long servitude under usurping Prelacy ; and because every corner of *England* was filled with the fury of malignant adversaries, Christ creates a New *England* to muster up the first of his Forces in ; Whose low condition, little number, and remotenesse of place made these adversaries triumph, despising this day of small things, but in this hight of their pride the *Lord Christ* brought sudden, and unexpected destruction upon them.   Thus have you a touch of the time when this worke began.

Christ Jesus intending to manifest his Kingly Office toward his Churches more fully then ever yet the Sons of men saw, . . . stirres up his servants as the Heralds of a King to make this Proclamation for Voluntiers as followeth.

Oh yes ! oh yes ! oh yes !   *All you the people of Christ that are here Oppressed, Imprisoned and scurrilously derided, gather your selves together, your Wifes and little ones, and answer to your severall Names as*

366

you shall be shipped for his service, in the Westerne World, and more
especially for planting the united Collonies of new England ; *Where you*
are to attend the service of the King of Kings, upon the divulging of this
Proclamation by his Herralds at Armes. Many (although otherwise
willing for this service) began to object as followeth :

Can it possible be the mind of Christ, (who formerly inabled so
many Souldiers of his to keepe their station unto the death here) that
now so many brave Souldiers disciplined by Christ himselfe the Captaine
of our salvation, should turne their backs to the disheartning of their
Fellow-Souldiers, and losse of further opportunity in gaining a greater
number of Subjects to Christs Kingdome?

Notwithstanding this Objection, It was further proclaimed as fol-
oweth : What Creature, wilt not know that Christ thy King crusheth
with a rod of Iron, the Pome and Pride of man, and must he like man
cast and contrive to take his enemies at advantage?   No, of purpose
hee causeth such instruments to retreate as he hath made strong for
himselfe : that so his adversaries glorying in the pride of their power,
insulting over the little remnant remaining, Christ causeth them to be
cast downe suddenly forever, and wee find in stories reported, Earths
Princes have passed their Armies at need over Seas and deepe Torrents.
Could *Casar* so suddenly fetch over fresh forces from *Europe* to *Asia*,
Pompy to foyle?   How much more shall Christ who createth all power,
call over this 900. league Ocean at his pleasure, such instruments as he
thinks meete to make use of in this place, from whence you are now to
depart, but further that you may not delay the Voyage intended, for your
full satisfaction, know this is the place where the Lord will create a new
Heaven, and a new Earth in, new Churches, and a new Common-wealth
together ; . . .

THis *Proclamation* being audibly published through the Ile of Great
Brittaine by sundry Herraulds, which *Christ* had prepared for that end :
the rumour ran through Cities, Townes and Villages ; when those that
were opposites heard it, some cried one thing, and some another, . . .
Amidst this great hurry the sincere servants of *Christ* humbly seeke the
Lords assistance in days of Humiliation, taking up some serious cogitations, how to begin this worthy worke, upon which it was thought meete
a patterne should be procured, comprised after the manner of a Cor-
poration-company or Brotherhood, with as large liberty for government
of this Association, as could be got under the Broad Seale of *England*,
which accordingly was done by advise of one Mr. *White* an honest

Counsellor at Law, as also furthered by the honoured Mr. *Richard Belinham*, and under the name of many worthy personages, as Governour, Dep. Gov. Assistant and Freemen, &c. Granted, Ingrossed and Sealed as holding of the manner of East *Greenwitch*, yeelding by way of homage the sixth part of all such Ore of Gold or Silver, as might for after time be found within the Limits of the said Grant bounded on the North, with the most Northerly part of the pleasant River of *Merimech*, one mile beyond, and on the South with the most Southern part of that oft frequented River commonly called *Charles*, one mile beyond, with power to rule and govern in all those parts both by Sea and Land ; To elect and set up all sorts of Officers, as well Superior and Inferior ; to point out their power and places, to defend and maintaine the said Land, and Inhabitants thereof with all their lawfull liberties (against all such as at any time should Invade, Molest or Disturbe the same) as well by offensive as defensive War, as also to constitute and ordaine Lawes, &c. Thus these Souldiers of *Jesus Christ* prepared to advance his Kingly Government, much like *Samuel*, when he went to annoynt *David*, . . .

. . . let us leave our *English* Nation in way of preparation for this Voyage intended, and tell of the marvelous doings of *Christ* preparing for his peoples arrivall in the Western World, . . .

. . . this was the first working providence of *Christ* to stir up our *English* Nation, to plant these parts in hope of a rich Trade for Beverskins, and this made some of our Countrymen make their abode in these parts, whom this Army of *Christ* at their comming over found as fit helps to further their designe in planting the Churches of *Christ;* Who by a more admirable act of his Providence not long after prepared for his peoples arrivall as followeth.

The Summer after the blazing Starre (whose motion in the Heavens was from *East* to *West*, poynting out to the sons of men the progresse of the glorious Gospell of *Christ*, the glorious King of his Churches) even about the yeare 1618. a little before the removeall of that Church of *Christ* from *Holland* to *Plimoth* in New *England*, as the ancient *Indians* report, there befell a great mortality among them [the Indians], the greatest that ever the memory of Father to Sonne tooke notice of, chiefly desolating those places, where the *English* afterward planted . . .

. . . But by this meanes *Christ* (whose great and glorious workes the Earth throughout are altogether for the benefit of his Churches and chosen) not onely made roome for his people to plant ; but also tamed the hard and cruell hearts of these barbarous *Indians*, insomuch that halfe a handfull of his people landing not long after in *Plimoth*-Planta-tion, found little resistance, of whom the Author purposes not to speake particularly, . . .

NOw it will be time to returne againe to *England*, to speake further of the people that wee left in way of preparation ; who in the yeare 1628. sent forth some store of servants to provide against the wants of a Desart Wildernesse, amongst whom came over a mixt multitude, insomuch that very little appeared of the following worke, onely the much honoured Mr. *John Indicat*, came over with them to governe, a fit instrument to begin this Wildernesse-worke, of courage bold undanted, yet sociable, and of a chearfull spirit, loving and austere, applying himselfe to either as occasion served. . . .

The place picked out by this People to settle themselves in, was in the bosome of the out-stretched arme of *Cape Anne*, now called *Gloster*, but at the place of their abode they began to build a Town, which is called *Salem*, after some little space of time having made tryall of the Sordid spirits of the Neighbouring *Indians*, the most bold among them began to gather to divers places, which they began to take up for their owne, those that were sent over servants, having itching desires after novelties, found a reddier way to make an end of their Masters provi-sion, then they could finde meanes to get more ; They that came over their own men had but little left to feed on, and most began to repent when their strong Beere and full cups ran as small as water in a large Land, but little Corne, and the poore *Indians* so far from relieving them, that they were forced to lengthen out their owne food with Acorns, and that which added to their present distracted thoughts, the Ditch betweene *England* and their now place of abode was so wide, that they could not leap over with a lope-staffe, yet some delighting their Eye with the rarity of things present, and feeding their fancies with new discoveries at the Springs approach, they made shift to rub out the Winters cold by the Fire-side, having fuell enough growing at their very doores, turning down many a drop of the Bottell, and burning Tobacco with all the ease they could, discoursing betweene one while and another, of the great progresse they would make after the Summers-Sun had changed the Earths white furr'd Gowne into a greene Mantell. . . .

THis year 1629. came over three godly Ministers of *Christ Jesus*, intending to shew his power in his peoples lowest condition as his man-ner is, thereby to strengthen their Faith in following difficulties, and now although the number of the faithfull people of Christ were but few,

2 B

yet their longing desires to gather into a Church was very great ; . . .
Wherefore they Elected and Ordained one Mr. *Higgingson* to be
Tracher of this first Church of *Christ*, set up in those parts, a man
indued with grace apt to teach, and mighty in the Scriptures, Learned
in the Tongues, able to convince gain-sayers, aptly applying the word to
his hearers, who departed this life not long after, of whom it may be
said.

The Reverend Mr. Higgingson, *first Pastor of the Church of Christ at*
Salem *in* New England.

WHat Golden gaine made Higginson *remove,*
    From fertill Soyle to Wildernesse of Rocks;
'Twas Christs rich Pearle stir'd up thee toile to love,
    For him to feed in Wildernesse his flocks.
First Teacher, he here Sheepe and Lambs together,
    First crownd shall be, hee in the Heavens of all,
Christs Pastors here, but yet Christ folke had rather,
    Him here retaine, blest he whom Christ hath call'd.

ANd now behold the severall Regiments of these Souldiers of *Christ*,
as they are shipped for his service in the *Western* World, part thereof
being come to the Towne and Port of *Southhamptan* in *England*, where
they were to be shipped, that they might prosecute this designe to the
full, one Ship called the *Eagle*, they wholy purchase, and many more
they hire, filling them with the seede of man and beast to sow this yet
untilled Wildernesse withall, making sale of such Land as they possesse,
to the great admiration of their Friends and Acquaintance, . . .

BUt to goe on with the Story, the 12 of *July* or thereabout 1630.
these Souldiers of *Christ* first set foote one this *Westerne* end of the
World ; where arriveing in safety, both Men, Women and Children. On
the North-side of *Charles* River, they landed neare a small Island, called
Noddells Island, where one Mr. *Samuel Mavereck* then living, a man of
a very loving and curteous behaviour, very ready to entertaine strangers,
yet an enemy to the Reformation in hand, being strong for the Lordly
Prelaticall power one this Island, he had built a small Fort with the helpe
of one Mr. *David Tompson*, placing therein foure Murtherers to protect
him from the *Indians*. About one mile distant upon the River ran a
small creeke, taking its Name from Major Gen. *Edward Gibbons*, who
dwelt there for some yeares after ; One the South side of the River one

a point of Land called *Blaxtons* point, planted Mr. *William Blaxton*, of whom we have formerly spoken : to the South-East of him, neare an Island called *Tompsons* Island lived some few Planters more, these persons were the first Planters of those parts, having some small Trading with the *Indians* for *Beaver*-Skins, which moved them to make their aboade in those parts, whom these first Troopes of *Christs* Army, found as fit helpes to further their worke.   At their arrivall those small number of Christians gathered at *Salem*, greatly rejoycing and the more, because they saw so many that came chiefly for promoting the great Work of *Christ* in hand, the Lady *Arrabella* and some other godly Women aboad at *Salem*, but their Husbands continued at *Charles* Town, both for the settling the civill Government, and gathering another Church of *Christ*. The first Court was holden aboard the *Arrabella* the 23. of *August*. When the much honoured *John Wintrope* Esq. was chosen Governour for the remainder of that yeare, 1630.   Also the worthy *Thomus Dudly* Esq. was chosen Deputy Governour, and Mr. *Simon Brodestreet* Secretary, the people after their long Voyage were many of them troubled with the *Scurvy*, and some of them died : the first station they tooke up was at *Charles* Towne, where they pitched some Tents of Cloath, other built them small Huts, in which they lodged their Wifes and Children.   The first beginning of this worke seemed very dolorous ; . . .

[Edward Johnson], *A History of New-England*, or *Wonder-working Providence of Sions Saviour* (London, 1654), 1–38 *passim*.

---

106. The Agreement at Cambridge, England (1629)

BY SIR RICHARD SALTONSTALL AND OTHERS

The signers were twelve of the most influential members of the Massachusetts Company in England. Saltonstall was for a year a resident Assistant. — Bibliography: Winsor, *Narrative and Critical History*, III, 348.

UPON due consideration of the state of the plantation now in hand for New England, wherein wee (whose names are hereunto subscribed) have engaged ourselves : and having weighed the greatnes of the worke in regard of the consequence, God's glory and the churches good : As also in regard of the difficultyes and discouragements which in all probabilityes must be forecast upon the execution of this businesse ·

Considering withall that this whole adventure growes upon the joynt confidence we have in each others fidelity and resolution herein, so as no man of us would have adventured it without assurance of the rest: Now, for the better encouragement of ourselves and others that shall joyne with us in this action, and to the end that every man may without scruple dispose of his estate and afayres as may best fitt his preparation for this voyage, it is fully and faithfully agreed amongst us, and every of us doth hereby freely and sincerely promise and bind himselfe in the word of a christian and in the presence of God who is the searcher of all hearts, that we will so really endeavour the execution of this worke, as by God's assistance we will be ready in our persons, and with such of our severall familyes as are to go with us, and such provision as we are able conveniently to furnish ourselves withall, to embarke for the said plantation by the first of March next, at such port or ports of this land as shall be agreed upon by the Companie, to the end to passe the seas (under God's protection) to inhabite and continue in New England. Provided always, that before the last of September next the whole government together with the patent for the said plantation be first by an order of court legally transferred and established to remain with us and others which shall inhabite upon the said plantation. And provided also that if any shall be hindered by such just and inevitable lett or other cause to be allowed by 3 parts of foure of these whose names are hereunto subscribed, then such persons for such tymes and during such letts to be discharged of this bond. And we do further promise every one for himselfe, that shall fayle to be ready through his own default by the day appointed, to pay for every day's default the sum of 3*l.* to the use of the rest of the Companie who shall be ready by the same day and time.

     This was done by order of court the 29th of August, 1629.

Richard Saltonstall	Isaack Johnson
Tho : Dudley	John Humfrey
William Vassall	Tho : Sharp
Nicko : West	Increase Nowell.

John Winthrop
Will : Pinchon
Kellam Browne
William Colbron.

Thomas Hutchinson, *A Collection of Original Papers Relative to the History of the Colony of Massachusets-Bay* (Boston, 1769), 25–26.

107. Organization of Representative Government in Massachusetts Bay (1631–1639)

BY GOVERNOR JOHN WINTHROP

Winthrop is the greatest of the Puritan historians, and is also the most striking Puritan statesman. As a man of wealth, of family, of public spirit, and of great abilities, he became the leading figure in New England affairs. His carefully kept contemporary journal is an invaluable source for the history of all the New England colonies. — Bibliography: Winsor, *Narrative and Critical History*, III, 354 ; J. A. Doyle, *English in America, Puritan Colonies*, I, ch. iii ; Channing and Hart, *Guide*, §§ 117, 118.

[1631. April 12.]

AT a court holden at Boston, (upon information to the governour, that they of Salem had called Mr. Williams to the office of a teacher,) a letter was written from the court to Mr. Endecott to this effect : That whereas Mr. Williams had refused to join with the congregation at Boston, because they would not make a public declaration of their repentance for having communion with the churches of England, while they lived there ; and, besides, had declared his opinion, that the magistrate might not punish the breach of the Sabbath, nor any other offence, as it was a breach of the first table ; therefore, they marvelled they would choose him without advising with the council ; and withal desiring him, that they would forbear to proceed till they had conferred about it. . . .

[May 17.] A general court at Boston. The former governour was chosen again, and all the freemen of the commons were sworn to this government. At noon, Cheeseborough's house was burnt down, all the people being present. . . .

June 14.] . . . At this court one Philip Ratcliff, a servant of Mr. Cradock, being convict, ore tenus, of most foul, scandalous invectives against our churches and government, was censured to be whipped, lose his ears, and be banished the plantation, which was presently exe-cuted. . . .

[1632/3. February 17.] The governour and assistants called before them, at Boston, divers of Watertown; the pastor and elder by letter, and the others by warrant. The occasion was, for that a warrant being sent to Watertown for levying of £ 8, part of a rate of £ 60, ordered for the fortifying of the new town, the pastor and elder, etc., assembled the people and delivered their opinions, that it was not safe to pay moneys after that sort, for fear of bringing themselves and posterity into bondage.

Being come before the governour and council, after much debate, they acknowledged their fault, confessing freely, that they were in an error, and made a retractation and submission under their hands, and were enjoined to read it in the assembly the next Lord's day. The ground of their error was, for that they took this government to be no other but as of a mayor and aldermen, who have not power to make laws or raise taxations without the people; but understanding that this government was rather in the nature of a parliament, and that no assistant could be chosen but by the freemen, who had power likewise to remove the assistants and put in others, and therefore at every general court (which was to be held once every year) they had free liberty to consider and propound anything concerning the same, and to declare their grievances, without being subject to question, or, etc., they were fully satisfied; and so their submission was accepted, and their offence pardoned. . . .

May 8.]   A general court at Boston. Whereas it was (at our first coming) agreed, that the freemen should choose the assistants, and they the governour, the whole court agreed now, that the governour and assistants should all be new chosen every year by the general court, (the governour to be always chosen out of the assistants;) and accordingly the old governour, John Winthrop, was chosen; accordingly all the rest as before, and Mr. Humfrey and Mr. Coddington also, because they were daily expected. . . .

Every town chose two men to be at the next court, to advise with the governour and assistants about the raising of a public stock, so as what they should agree upon should bind all, etc.

This court was begun and ended with speeches for the, etc., as formerly. . . .

[1633. November.]   . . . The scarcity of workmen had caused them to raise their wages to an excessive rate, so as a carpenter would have three shillings the day, a laborer two shillings and sixpence, etc.; and accordingly those who had commodities to sell advanced their prices sometime double to that they cost in England, so as it grew to a general complaint, which the court, taking knowledge of, as also of some further evils, which were springing out of the excessive rates of wages, they made an order, that carpenters, masons, etc., should take but two shillings the day, and laborers but eighteen pence, and that no commodity should be sold at above four pence in the shilling more than it cost for ready money in England; oil, wine, etc., and cheese, in regard of the hazard of bringing, etc., [excepted]. . . .

[1634. April 1.] . . . Notice being sent out of the general court to be held the 14th day of the third month, called May, the freemen deputed two of each town to meet and consider of such matters as they were to take order in at the same general court; who, having met, desired a sight of the patent, and, conceiving thereby that all their laws should be made at the general court, repaired to the governour to advise with him about it, and about the abrogating of some orders formerly made, as for killing of swine in corn, etc. He told them, that, when the patent was granted, the number of freemen was supposed to be (as in like corporations) so few, as they might well join in making laws; but now they were grown to so great a body, as it was not possible for them to make or execute laws, but they must choose others for that purpose: and that howsoever it would be necessary hereafter to have a select company to intend that work, yet for the present they were not furnished with a sufficient number of men qualified for such a business, neither could the commonwealth bear the loss of time of so many as must intend it. Yet this they might do at present, viz., they might, at the general court, make an order, that, once in the year, a certain number should be appointed (upon summons from the governour) to revise all laws, etc., and to reform what they found amiss therein; but not to make any new laws, but prefer their grievances to the court of assistants; and that no assessment should be laid upon the country without the consent of such a committee, nor any lands disposed of. . . .

[May 14.] At the general court, Mr. Cotton preached, and delivered this doctrine, that a magistrate ought not to be turned into the condition of a private man without just cause, and to be publicly convict, no more than the magistrates may not turn a private man out of his freehold, etc., without like public trial, etc. This falling in question in the court, and the opinion of the rest of the ministers being asked, it was referred to further consideration.

The court chose a new governour, viz., Thomas Dudley, Esq., the former deputy; and Mr. Ludlow was chosen deputy; and John Haines, Esq., an assistant, and all the rest of the assistants chosen again.

At this court it was ordered, that four general courts should be kept every year, and that the whole body of the freemen should be present only at the court of election of magistrates, etc., and that, at the other three, every town should send their deputies, who should assist in making laws, disposing lands, etc. Many good orders were made this court. It held three days, and all things were carried very peaceably, notwithstanding that some of the assistants were questioned by the freemen for some errors in their government, and some fines imposed, but remitted again before the court brake up. The court was kept in the meeting-house at Boston, and the new governour and the assistants *were together entertained* at the house of the old governour, as before. . . .

September 4.] The general court began at Newtown, and continued a week, and then was adjourned fourteen days. Many things were there agitated and concluded, as fortifying in Castle Island, Dorchester, and Charlestown; also against tobacco, and costly apparel, and immodest fashions; and committees appointed for setting out the bounds of towns; with divers other matters, which do appear upon record. But the main business, which spent the most time, and caused the adjourning of the court, was about the removal of Newtown. . . .

Upon these and other arguments the court being divided, it was put to vote; and, of the deputies, fifteen were for their departure, and ten against it. The governour and two assistants were for it, and the deputy and all the rest of the assistants were against it, (except the secretary, who gave no vote;) whereupon no record was entered, because there were not six assistants in the vote, as the patent requires. Upon this grew a great difference between the governour and assistants, and the deputies. They would not yield the assistants a negative voice, and the others (considering how dangerous it might be to the commonwealth, if they should not keep that strength to balance the greater number of the deputies) thought it safe to stand upon it. So, when they could proceed no farther, the whole court agreed to keep a day of humiliation to seek the Lord, which accordingly was done, in all the congregations, the 18th day of this month; and the 24th the court met again. Before they began, Mr. Cotton preached, (being desired by all the court, upon Mr. Hooker's instant excuse of his unfitness for that occasion). He took his text out of Hag. ii, 4, etc., out of which he laid down the nature or strength (as he termed it) of the magistracy, ministry, and people, viz., — the strength of the magistracy to be their authority; of the people, their liberty; and of the ministry, their purity; and showed how all of these had a negative voice, etc., and that yet the ultimate resolution, etc., ought to be in the whole body of the people, etc., with answer to all objections, and a declaration of the people's duty and right to maintain their true liberties against any unjust violence, etc., which gave great satisfaction to the company. And it pleased the Lord so to assist him, and to bless his own ordinance, that the affairs of the court went on cheerfully ; and although all were not satisfied about the negative voice to be left to the magistrates, yet no man moved aught about it, and the congregation of Newtown came and accepted of such enlargement as had formerly been offered them by Boston and Watertown ; and so the fear of their removal to Connecticut was removed. . . .

[September 18.]   At this court were many laws made against tobacco, and immodest fashions, and costly apparel, etc., as appears by the Records ; and £ 600 raised towards fortifications and other charges. . . .

[December 19.]   All the ministers, except Mr. Ward of Ipswich, met at Boston, being requested by the governour and assistants, to consider of these two cases : 1. What we ought to do, if a general governour should be sent out of England? 2. Whether it be lawful for us to carry the cross in our banners? — In the first case, they all agreed, that, if a general governour were sent, we ought not to accept him, but defend our lawful possessions, (if we were able ;) otherwise to avoid or protract. . . .

[1635. March 4.]   . . . At this court, one of the deputies was questioned for denying the magistracy among us, affirming that the power of the governour was but ministerial, etc.   He had also much opposed the magistrates, and slighted them, and used many weak arguments against the negative voice, as himself acknowledged upon record.   He was adjudged by all the court to be disabled for three years from bearing any public office. . . .

[May 6.]   A general court was held at Newtown, where John Haynes, Esq., was chosen governour, Richard Bellingham, Esq., deputy governour, and Mr. Hough and Mr. Dummer chosen assistants to the former ; and Mr. Ludlow, the late deputy, left out of the magistracy.   The reason was, partly, because the people would exercise their absolute power, etc., and partly upon some speeches of the deputy, who protested against the election of the governour as void, for that the deputies of the several towns had agreed upon the election before they came, etc.   But this was generally discussed, and the election adjudged good.

Mr. Endecott was also left out, and called into question about the defacing the cross in the ensign. . . .

[October 6.]   . . . Here came also one Mr. Henry Vane, son and heir to Sir Henry Vane, comptroller of the king's house, who, being a young gentleman of excellent parts, and had been employed by his father (when he was ambassador) in foreign affairs ; yet, being called to the obedience of the gospel, forsook the honors and preferments of the

court, to enjoy the ordinances of Christ in their purity here.   His
father, being very averse to this way, (as no way savoring the power of
religion,) would hardly have consented to his coming hither, but that,
acquainting the king with his son's disposition and desire, he commanded
him to send him hither, and gave him license for three years' stay
here. . . .

[1635/36 Jan. 18.]   Mr. Vane and Mr. Peter, finding some distraction
in the commonwealth, arising from some difference in judgment, and
withal some alienation of affection among the magistrates and some
other persons of quality, and that hereby factions began to grow among
the people, some adhering more to the old governour, Mr. Winthrop,
and others to the late governour, Mr. Dudley, — the former carrying
matters with more lenity, and the latter with more severity, — they procured a meeting, at Boston, of the governour, deputy, Mr. Cotton, Mr.
Hooker, Mr. Wilson, and there was present Mr. Winthrop, Mr. Dudley,
and themselves ; . . .

Whereupon the governour, Mr. Haynes, spake . . . to which Mr.
Winthrop answered, that his speeches and carriage had been in part
mistaken ; but withal professed, that it was his judgment, that in the
infancy of plantation, justice should be administered with more lenity
than in a settled state, because people were then more apt to transgress,
partly of ignorance of new laws and orders, partly through oppression
of business and other straits ; but, if it might be made clear to him,
that it was an error, he would be ready to take up a stricter course.
Then the ministers were desired to consider of the question by the next
morning, and to set down a rule in the case.   The next morning, they
delivered their several reasons, which all sorted to this conclusion, that
strict discipline, both in criminal offences and in martial affairs, was
more needful in plantations than in a settled state, as tending to the
honor and safety of the gospel.   Whereupon Mr. Winthrop acknowledged that he was convinced, that he had failed in over much lenity and
remissness, and would endeavor (by God's assistance) to take a more
strict course hereafter.   Whereupon there was a renewal of love amongst
them. . . .

[1637. May 17.]   Our court of elections was at Newtown.   So soon
as the court was set, being about one of the clock, a petition was preferred by those of Boston.   The governour would have read it, but the
deputy said it was out of order ; it was a court for elections, and those
must first be despatched, and then their petitions should be heard.

Divers others also opposed that course, as an ill precedent, etc.; and the petition, being about pretence of liberty, etc., (though intended chiefly for revoking the sentence given against Mr. Wheelwright,) would have spent all the day in debate, etc.; but yet the governour and those of that party would not proceed to election, except the petition was read. Much time was already spent about this debate, and the people crying out for election, it was moved by the deputy, that the people should divide themselves, and the greater number must carry it. And so it was done, and the greater number by many were for election. But the governour and that side kept their place still, and would not proceed. Whereupon the deputy told him, that, if he would not go to election, he and the rest of that side would proceed. Upon that, he came from his company, and they went to election; and Mr. Winthrop was chosen governour, Mr. Dudley deputy, and Mr. Endecott of the standing council; and Mr. Israel Stoughton and Mr. Richard Saltonstall were called in to be assistants; and Mr. Vane, Mr. Coddington, and Mr. Dummer, (being all of that faction,) were left quite out.

There was great danger of a tumult that day; for those of that side grew into fierce speeches, and some laid hands on others; but seeing themselves too weak, they grew quiet. They expected a great advantage that day, because the remote towns were allowed to come in by proxy; but it fell out, that there were enough beside. But if it had been otherwise, they must have put in their deputies, as other towns had done, for all matters beside elections. Boston, having deferred to choose deputies till the election was passed, went home that night, and the next morning they sent Mr. Vane, the late governour, and Mr. Coddington, and Mr. Hoffe, for their deputies; but the court, being grieved at it, found a means to send them home again, for that two of the freemen of Boston had not notice of the election. So they went all home, and the next morning they returned the same gentlemen again upon a new choice; and the court not finding how they might reject them, they were admitted. . . .

[1639. May 22.] The court of elections was; at which time there was a small eclipse of the sun. Mr. Winthrop was chosen governour again, though some laboring had been, by some of the elders and others to have changed, not out of any dislike of him, (for they all loved and esteemed him,) but out of their fear lest it might make way for having a governour for life, which some had propounded as most agreeable to God's institution and the practice of all well ordered states. But neither

the governour nor any other attempted the thing; though some jealousies arose which were increased by two occasions. The first was, there
being want of assistants, the governour and other magistrates thought
fit (in the warrant for the court) to propound three, amongst which
Mr. Downing, the governour's brother-in-law, was one, which they conceived to be done to strengthen his party, and therefore, though he
were known to be a very able man, etc., and one who had done many
good offices for the country for these ten years, yet the people would
not choose him. Another occasion of their jealousy was, the court,
finding the number of deputies to be much increased by the addition
of new plantations, thought fit, for the ease both of the country and
the court, to reduce all towns to two deputies. This occasioned some
to fear, that the magistrates intended to make themselves stronger, and
the deputies weaker, and so, in time, to bring all power into the hands
of the magistrates; so as the people in some towns were much displeased with their deputies for yielding to such an order. Whereupon,
at the next session, it was propounded to have the number of deputies,
restored; and allegations were made, that it was an infringement of
their liberty; so as, after much debate, and such reasons given for
diminishing the number of deputies, and clearly proved that their liberty
consisted not in the number, but in the thing, divers of the deputies,
who came with intent to reverse the last order, were, by force of reason,
brought to uphold it; so that, when it was put to the vote, the last
order for two deputies only was confirmed. Yet, the next day, a petition
was brought to the court from the freemen of Roxbury, to have the third
deputy restored. Whereupon the reasons of the court's proceedings were
set down in writing, and all objections answered, and sent to such towns
as were unsatisfied with this advice, that, if any could take away those
reasons, or bring us better for what they did desire, we should be ready,
at the next court, to repeal the said order.

The hands of some of the elders (learned and godly men) were to
this petition, though suddenly drawn in, and without due consideration,
for the lawfulness of it may well be questioned: for when the people
have chosen men to be their rulers, and to make their laws, and bound
themselves by oath to submit thereto, now to combine together (a lesser
part of them) in a public petition to have any order repealed, which is
not repugnant to the law of God, savors of resisting an ordinance of
God; for the people, having deputed others, have no power to make
or alter laws, but are to be subject; and if any such order seem unlaw

ful or inconvenient, they were better prefer some reasons, etc., to the court, with manifestation of their desire to move them to a review, than peremptorily to petition to have it repealed, which amounts to a plain reproof of those whom God hath set over them, and putting dishonor upon them, against the tenor of the fifth commandment.

There fell out at this court another occasion of increasing the people's jealousy of their magistrates, viz.: One of the elders, being present with those of his church, when they were to prepare their votes for the election, declared his judgment, that a governour ought to be for his life, alleging for his authority the practice of all the best commonwealths in Europe, and especially that of Israel by God's own ordinance. But this was opposed by some other of the elders with much zeal, and so notice was taken of it by the people, not as a matter of dispute, but as if there had been some plot to put it in practice, ... And here may be observed, how strictly the people would seem to stick to their patent, where they think it makes for their advantage, but are content to decline it, where it will not warrant such liberties as they have taken up without warrant from thence, as appears in their strife for three deputies, etc., when as the patent allows them none at all, but only by inference, etc., voting by proxies, etc. . . .

The people had long desired a body of laws, and thought their condition very unsafe, while so much power rested in the discretion of magistrates. Divers attempts had been made at former courts, and the matter referred to some of the magistrates and some of the elders; but still it came to no effect; for, being committed to the care of many, whatsoever was done by some, was still disliked or neglected by others. At last it was referred to Mr. Cotton and Mr. Nathaniel Warde, etc., and each of them framed a model, which were presented to this general court, and by them committed to the governour and deputy and some others to consider of, and so prepare it for the court in the 3d month next. Two great reasons there were, which caused most of the magistrates and some of the elders not to be very forward in this matter. One was, want of sufficient experience of the nature and disposition of the people, considered with the condition of the country and other circumstances, which made them conceive, that such laws would be fittest for us, which should arise pro re nata upon occasions, etc., and so the laws of England and other states grew, and therefore the fundamental laws of England are called customs, consuetudines. 2. For that it would professedly transgress the limits of our charter, which provide, we shall made no laws repugnant to the laws of England, and that we were assured we must do. But to raise up laws by practice and custom had been no transgression; as in our church discipline, and in matters of marriage, to make a law, that marriages should not be solemnized by ministers, is repugnant to the laws of England; but to bring it to a custom by practice for the magistrates to perform it, is no law made repugnant, etc. At length (to satisfy the people) it proceeded, and the two models were digested with divers alterations and additions, and abbreviated and sent to every town, (12,) to be considered of first by the magistrates and elders, and then to be published by the constables to all the people, that if any man should think fit, that any thing therein ought to be altered, he might acquaint some of the deputies therewith against the next court. . . .

John Winthrop, *The History of New England from 1630 to 1649* (edited by James Savage, Boston, 1853), I, 63–389 *passim*.

108. The Trial of a Woman Antinomian (1637)

ANONYMOUS

Mrs. Hutchinson was an able and well-educated woman, who disagreed in doctrine with the heads of the colony, and was banished for her heresy. This account is preferred to the parallel narrative of Winthrop, who was one of the judges. — Bibliography: Winsor, *Narrative and Critical History*, III, 349; C. F. Adams, *Three Episodes of Massachusetts History*, I, 363–509; J. A. Doyle, *English in America, Puritan Colonies*, I, ch. iv; Edward Eggleston, *Beginners of a Nation*, 329–349; Channing and Hart, *Guide*, § 119. — The italic headings do not appear in Thomas Hutchinson's text.

THE Examination of Mrs. Ann Hutchinson at the court at Newtown.

Mr. Winthrop, governor. MRS. Hutchinson, you are called here as one of those that have troubled the peace of the commonwealth and the churches here; you are known to be a woman that hath had a great share in the promoting and divulging of those opinions that are causes of this trouble, and to be nearly joined not only in affinity and affection with some of those the court had taken notice of and passed censure upon, but you have spoken divers things as we have been informed very prejudicial to the honour of the churches and ministers thereof, and you have maintained a meeting and an assembly in your house that hath been condemned by the general assembly as a thing not tolerable nor comely in the sight of God nor fitting for your sex, and notwithstanding that was cried down you have continued the same, therefore we have thought good to send for you to understand how things are, that if you be in an erroneous way we may reduce you that so you may become a profitable member here among us, otherwise if you be obstinate in your course that then the court may take such course that you may trouble us no further, therefore I would entreat you to express whether you do not assent and hold in practice to those opinions and factions that have been handled in court already, that is to say, whether you do not justify Mr. Wheelright's sermon and the petition.

Mrs. Hutchinson. I am called here to answer before you but I hear no things laid to my charge.

Gov. I have told you some already and more I can tell you. (*Mrs. H.*) Name one Sir.

Gov. Have I not named some already?

Mrs. H. What have I said or done?

Gov. Why for your doings, this you did harbour and countenance those that are parties in this faction that you have heard of. (*Mrs. H.*) That's matter of conscience, Sir.

Gov. Your conscience you must keep or it must be kept for you.

Mrs. H. Must not I then entertain the saints because I must keep my conscience. . . .

Gov. You have joined with them in the faction.

Mrs. H. In what faction have I joined with them?

Gov. In presenting the petition.

Mrs. H. Suppose I had set my hand to the petition what then? (*Gov.*) You saw that case tried before.

Mrs. H. But I had not my hand to the petition.

Gov. You have councelled them. (*Mrs. H.*) Wherein?

Gov. Why in entertaining them.

Mrs. H. What breach of law is that Sir?

Gov. Why dishonouring of parents.

Mrs. H. But put the case Sir that I do fear the Lord and my parents, may not I entertain them that fear the Lord because my parents will not give me leave?

Gov. If they be the fathers of the commonwealth, and they of another religion, if you entertain them then you dishonour your parents and are justly punishable. . . .

Gov. Why do you keep such a meeting at your house as you do every week upon a set day?

Mrs. H. It is lawful for me so to do, as it is all your practices and can you find a warrant for yourself and condemn me for the same thing? The ground of my taking it up was, when I first came to this land because I did not go to such meetings as those were, it was presently reported that I did not allow of such meetings but held them unlawful and therefore in that regard they said I was proud and did despise all ordinances, upon that a friend came unto me and told me of it and I to prevent such aspersions took it up, but it was in practice before I came therefore I was not the first. . . .

Mrs. H. I conceive their lyes a clear rule in Titus, that the elder women should instruct the younger and then I must have a time wherein I must do it.

Gov. All this I grant you, I grant you a time for it, but what is this to the purpose that you Mrs. Hutchinson must call a company together from their callings to come to be taught of you?

Mrs. H. Will it please you to answer me this and to give me a rule for then I will willingly submit to any truth. If any come to my house to be instructed in the ways of God what rule have I to put them away? . . .

Mrs. H. . . . Do you think it not lawful for me to teach women and why do you call me to teach the court?

Gov. We do not call you to teach the court but to lay open yourself.

Mrs. H. I desire you that you would then set me down a rule by which I may put them away that come unto me and so have peace in so doing.

Gov. You must shew your rule to receive them.

Mrs. H. I have done it.

Gov. I deny it because I have brought more arguments than you have.

Mrs. H. I say, to me it is a rule.

Mr. Endicot. You say there are some rules unto you. I think there is a contradiction in your own words. What rule for your practice do you bring, only a custom in Boston.

Mrs. H. No Sir that was no rule to me but if you look upon the rule in Titus it is a rule to me. If you convince me that it is no rule I shall yield.

Gov. You know that there is no rule that crosses another, but this rule crosses that in the Corinthians. But you must take it in this sense that elder women must instruct the younger about their business and to love their husbands and not to make them to clash.

Mrs. H. I do not conceive but that it is meant for some publick times. . . .

Gov. Well, we see how it is we must therefore put it away from you or restrain you from maintai[n]ing this course.

Mrs. H. If you have a rule for it from God's word you may.

Gov. We are your judges, and not you ours and we must compel you to it. . . .

Dep. gov. I would go a little higher with Mrs. Hutchinson. About three years ago we were all in peace. Mrs. Hutchinson from that time she came hath made a disturbance, and some that came over with her in the ship did inform me what she was as soon as she was landed. I being then in place dealt with the pastor and teacher of Boston and desired them to enquire of her, and then I was satisfied that she held nothing different from us, but within half a year after, she had vented divers of her strange opinions and had made parties in the country, and at length it comes that Mr. Cotton and Mr. Vane were of her judgment, but Mr. Cotton hath cleared himself that he was not of that mind, but now it appears by this woman's meeting that Mrs. Hutchinson hath so forestalled the minds of many by their resort to her meeting that now she hath a potent party in the country. Now if all these things have endangered us as from that foundation and if she in particular hath disparaged all our ministers in the land that they have preached a covenant of works, and only Mr. Cotton a covenant of grace, why this is not to be suffered, and therefore being driven to the foundation and it being found that Mrs. Hutchinson is she that hath depraved all the ministers and hath been the cause of what is fallen out, why we must take away the foundation and the building will fall.

Mrs. H. I pray Sir prove it that I said they preached nothing but a covenant of works.

Dep. Gov. Nothing but a covenant of works, why a Jesuit may preach truth sometimes.

Mrs. H. Did I ever say they preached a covenant of works then?

Dep. Gov. If they do not preach a covenant of grace clearly, then they preach a covenant of works.

Mrs. H. No Sir, one may preach a covenant of grace more clearly than another, so I said.

D. Gov. We are not upon that now but upon position.

2 C

Mrs. H.   Prove this then Sir that you say I said.

D. Gov.   When they do preach a covenant of works do they preach truth?

Mrs. H.   Yes Sir, but when they preach a covenant of works for salvation, that is not truth. . . .

D. Gov.   Likewise I will prove this that you said the gospel in the letter and words holds forth nothing but a covenant of works and that all that do not hold as you do are in a covenant of works.

Mrs. H.   I deny this for if I should so say I should speak against my own judgment.

Mr. Endicot.   I desire to speak seeing Mrs. Hutchinson seems to lay something against them that are to witness against her.

Gover.   Only I would add this.   It is well discerned to the court that Mrs. Hutchinson can tell when to speak and when to hold her tongue.   Upon the answering of a question which we desire her to tell her thoughts of she desires to be pardoned.

Mrs. H.   It is one thing for me to come before a public magistracy and there to speak what they would have me to speak and another when a man comes to me in a way of friendship privately there is difference in that. . . .

Dep. Gov.   I called these witnesses and you deny them.   You see they have proved this and you deny this, but it is clear.   You said they preached a covenant of works and that they were not able ministers of the new testament; now there are two other things that you did affirm which were that the scriptures in the letter of them held forth nothing but a covenant of works and likewise that those that were under a covenant of works cannot be saved.

Mrs. H.   Prove that I said so.   (*Gov.*) Did you say so?

Mrs. H.   No Sir it is your conclusion. . . .

Gov.   What say you to this, though nothing be directly proved yet you hear it may be.

Mrs. H.   I acknowledge using the words of the apostle to the Corinthians unto him, that they that were ministers of the letter and not the spirit did preach a covenant of works.   Upon his saying there was no such scripture, then I fetched the bible and shewed him this place 2 Cor. iii. 6.   He said that was the letter of the law.   No said I it is the letter of the gospel.

Gov.   You have spoken this more than once then.

Mrs. H.   Then upon further discourse about proving a good estate and holding it out by the manifestation of the spirit he did acknowledge that to be the nearest way, but yet said he, will you not acknowledge that which we hold forth to be a way too wherein we may have hope ; no truly if that be a way it is a way to hell.

Gov. Mrs. Hutchinson, the court you see hath laboured to bring you to acknowledge the error of your way that so you might be reduced, the time now grows late, we shall therefore give you a little more time to consider of it and therefore desire that you attend the court again in the morning. . . .

Thomas Hutchinson, *History of the Province of Massachusets-Bay* (London, 1768), II, Appendix, 482-497 *passim*.

———◆———

109. Demand for the Return of the Massachusetts Charter (1638)

BY THE LORDS COMMISSIONERS FOR FOREIGN PLANTATIONS

This demand is a part of the general struggle between the king and the English Puritans. The Civil War broke out in England before the quashing of the charter could be carried out. — Bibliography : Winsor, *Narrative and Critical History*, III, 342-346; Channing and Hart, *Guide*, § 127.

A Coppie of a Letter sent by the appointment of the Lords of the Council to Mr. Winthrop, for the Patent of this Plantation to be sent to them.

At Whitehall April 4th 1638.   Present,

Lord Archbishop of Canterbury	Earle of Holland
Lord Keeper	Lord Cottington
Lord Treasurer	Mr. Treasurer
Lord Privy Seale	Mr. Controuler
Earle Marshall	Mr. Secretary Cooke
Earle of Dorset	Mr. Secretary Windebank

THIS day the Lords Commissioners for foreign Plantations, taking into consideration that the petitions and complaints of his Majestys subjects, planters and traders in New-England grow more frequent than heretofore for want of a settled and orderly government in those parts, and calling to mind that they had formerly given order about two or three years since to Mr. Cradock a member of that plantation, to cause the grant or letters patent of that plantation (alleadged by him to be there remaining in the hands of Mr. Winthrop) to be sent over hither, and that notwithstanding the same, the said letters patent were not as yet brought over : And their Lordships being now informed by Mr. Attorney General that a Quo Warranto had been by him brought according to former order against the said patent, and the same was proceeded to judgment against so many as had appeared, and that they which had not appeared, were outlawed.

Their lordships well approving of Mr. Attorney's care and proceeding therein did now resolve and order, that Mr. Meawtis clerk of the council attendant upon the said commissioners for foreign plantations should in a letter from himselfe to Mr. Winthrop inclose and convey this order unto him.   And their Lordships hereby in his Majestys name, and according to his express will and pleasure strictly require and enjoine the said Winthrop or any other in whose power and custody the said letters patent are, that they fail not to transmit the said patent hither by the returne of the ship in which the order is conveyed to them, it being resolved that in case of any further neglect or contempt by them shewed therein, their lordships will cause a strict course to be taken against them, and will move his Majesty to reassume into his hands the whole plantation.

Thomas Hutchinson, *A Collection of Original Papers Relative to the History of the Colony of Massachusets-Bay* (Boston, 1769), 105–106.

———◆———

110. "A Note of what things I misliked in the Country " (1641)

BY THOMAS LECHFORD

The first lawyer in the colony (see No. 91 above); he was not kindly received, and his notes are rather prejudiced. — Bibliography: Winsor, *Narrative and Critical History*, III, 351–353; Channing and Hart, *Guide*, § 118.

I doubt,

1. WHETHER so much time should be spent in the publique Ordinances, on the Sabbath day, because that thereby some necessary duties of the Sabbath must needs be hindered, as visitation of the sick, and poore, and family.

2. Whether matters of offence should be publiquely handled, either before the whole Church, or strangers.

3. Whether so much time should be spent in particular catechizing those that are admitted to the communion of the Church, either men or women; or that they should make long speeches; or when they come publiquely to be admitted, any should speak contradictorily, or in recommendation of any, unlesse before the Elders, upon just occasion.

4. Whether the censures of the Church should be ordered, in publique, before all the Church, or strangers, other then the denunciation of the censures, and pronunciation of the solutions.

5. Whether any of our *Nation* that is not extremely ignorant or scandalous, should bee kept from the Communion, or his children from *Baptisme*.

6. That many thousands of this Countrey have forgotten the very principles of Religion, which they were daily taught in *England*, by set forms and Scriptures read, as the Psalmes, first and second Lesson, the ten Commandments, the Creeds, and publique catechizings. And although conceived Prayer be good and holy, and so publike explications and applications of the Word, and also necessary both in and out of season: yet for the most part it may be feared they dull, amaze, confound, discourage the weake and ignorant, (which are the most of men) when they are in ordinary performed too tediously, or with the neglect of the Word read, and other premeditated formes inculcated, and may tend to more ignorance and inconvenience, then many good men are aware of.

7. I doubt there hath been, and is much neglect of endeavours, to teach, civilize, and convert the *Indian Nation*, that are about the Plantations.

8. Whether by the received principles, it bee *possible* to teach, civilize, or convert them, or when they are converted, to maintain Gods worship among them.

9. That electorie courses will not long be safe here, either in Church or Common-wealth.

10. That the civill government is not so equally administred, nor can be, divers orders or by-laws considered.

11. That unlesse these things be wisely and in time prevented, many of your usefullest men will remove and scatter from you.

At *Boston* July 5. 1641.

Thomas Lechford, *Plain Dealing or News from New England* (edited by J. H. Trumbull, Boston, 1867), 129-131.

111. A Demand for a Share in the Government (1646)

BY ROBERT CHILD AND OTHERS

These were influential Presbyterians, who were by law excluded from the suffrage because not members of the established Congregational churches. — Bibliography: Winsor, *Narrative and Critical History*, III, 354; Channing and Hart, *Guide*, § 118.

TO the worshipful the Governor, the Deputy Governor, and the rest of the Assistants of the Massachusets Bay in New England, together with the Deputyes of the Generall Court now assembled at Boston.

The Remonstrance and humble Petition of us whose names are under-written, in behalfe of ourselves and divers others within this jurisdiction, humbly sheweth, . . .

1. Whereas this place hath been planted by the incouragement, next under God, of letters patents given and granted by his Majesty of England to the inhabitants thereof, with many privileges and immunities, viz. Incorporation into a company, liberty of choosing governors, setling government, making lawes not repugnant to the lawes of England, power of administring the oath of allegiance to all, &c. as by the said letters patents more largely appeareth. Notwithstanding, we cannot, according to our judgments, discerne a setled forme of government according to the lawes of England, which may seeme strange to our countrymen, yea to the whole world, especially considering we are English. Neither do we understand and perceyve our owne lawes or libertyes, or any body of lawes here so established, as that thereby there may be a sure and comfortable enjoyment of our lives, libertyes, and estates, according to our due and naturall rights, as freeborne subjects of the English nation, By which, many inconveniences flow into plantations, Viz. jealousies of introducing arbitrary government, which manny are prone to beleeve, construing the procrastination of such setled lawes to proceed from an overgreedy spirit of arbitrary power (which it may be is their weaknes) such proceedings being detestable to our English nation, and to all good men, and at present the chief cause of the intestine warre in our deare country: Further, it gives cause to many to thinke themselves hardly dealt with, others too much favored, and the scale of justice too much bowed and unequally balanced: From whence also proceedeth feares and jealousies of illegall committments,

unjust imprisonments, taxes, rates, customes, levyes of ungrounded and undoing assessments, unjustifiable presses, undue fynes, unmeasurable expences and charges, of unconceyvable dangers through a negative or destructive vote unduly placed, and not well regulated, in a word, of a non certainty of all things we enjoy, whether lives, liberties, or estates; and also of undue oaths, being subject to exposition, according to the well of him or them that gives them, and not according to a due and unbowed rule of law, which is the true interpreter of all oathes to all men, whether judge or judged.

Wherefore our humble desire and request is, that you would be pleased to consider of our present condition and upon what foundation we stand, and unanimously concurr to establish the fundamentall and wholesome lawes of our native country, and such as others are no wayes repugnant to them, unto which all of us are most accustomed; and we suppose them best agreeable to our English tempers, and yourselves obliged thereunto by the generall charter and your oathes of allegiance. . . .

2. Whereas there are many thousands in these plantations, of the English nation, freeborne, quiett and peaceable men, righteous in their dealings, forward with hand, heart and purse, to advance the publick good, knowne friends to the honorable and victorious Houses of Parliament, lovers of their nation, &c. who are debarred from all civill imployments (without any just cause that we know) not being permitted to bear the least office (though it cannot be denied but some are well qualifyed) no not so much as to have any vote in choosing magistrates, captains or other civill and military officers; notwithstanding they have here expended their youth, borne the burthen of the day, wasted much of their estates for the subsistence of these poore plantations, paid all assessments, taxes, rates, at least equall, if not exceeding others, yea when the late warre was denounced against the Narrowganset Indians, without their consent, their goods were seized on for the service, themselves and servants especially forced and impressed to serve in that warre, to the hazarding of all things most dear and near unto them, whence issue forth many great inconveniences, secret discontents, murmurings, rents in the plantations, discouragements in their callings, unsettlednes in their minds, strife, contention, and the Lord only knows to what a flame in time it may kindle; also jealousies of too much unwarranted power and dominion on the one side, and of perpetual slavry and bondage on the other, and which is intollerable, even by those who ought to love and respect them as brethren.

We therefore desire that civill liberty and freedom be forthwith granted to all truely English, equall to the rest of their countrymen, as in all plantations is accustomed to be done, and as all freeborne enjoy in our native country ; (we hoping here in some things to enjoy greater liberties than elsewhere, counting it no small losse of liberty to be as it were banished from our native home, and enforced to lay our bones in a strange wildernes) without imposing any oathes or covenant on them, . . . Further, that none of the English nation, who at this time are too forward to be gone, and very backward to come hither, be banished, unles they break the known lawes of England in so high a measure, as to deserve so high a punishment ; and that those few that come over may settle here without having two magistrates hands, which sometimes not being possible to obtain, hath procured a kind of banishment to some, who might have been serviceable to this place, as they have been to the state of England, &c.   And we likewise desire that no greater punishments be inflicted upon offenders than are allowed and sett by the laws of our native country.

3. Whereas there are diverse sober, righteous and godly men, eminent for knowledge and other gracious gifts of the holy spirit, no wayes scandalous in their lives and conversation, members of the church of England (in all ages famous for piety and learning) not dissenting from the latest and best reformation of England, Scotland, &c. yet they and their posterity are deteined from the seales of the covenant of free grace, because, as it is supposed, they will not take these churches covenants, for which as yet they see no light in Gods word ; neither can they clearly perceive what they are, every church having their covenant differing from anothers, at least in words. . . .

We therefore humbly intreat you, in whose hands it is to help and whose judicious eyes discern these great inconveniences, for the glory of God and the comfort of your brethren and countrymen, to give liberty to the members of the church of England, not scandalous in their lives and conversations (as members of these churches) to be taken into your congregation and to enjoy with you all those liberties and ordinances Christ hath purchased for them. . . .

Thomas Hutchinson, *A Collection of Original Papers Relative to the History of the Colony of Massachusets-Bay* (Boston, 1769), 188-194 *passim*.

112. The Simple Cobbler of Agawam against Toleration (1647)

BY REVEREND NATHANIEL WARD

Ward was minister of Agawam (Ipswich); he had been excommunicated by Archbishop Laud.   He was discontented at the predominance of Boston. — Bibliography : Winsor, *Narrative and Critical History*, III, 356 ; Tyler, *American Literature*, 227–241 ; J. A. Doyle, *English in America, Puritan Colonies*, II, ch. i ; Channing and Hart, *Guide*, § 118.

. . . FIRST, such as have given or taken any unfriendly reports of us *New-English*, should doe well to recollect themselves.   Wee have beene reputed a Colluvies of wild Opinionists, swarmed into a remote wildernes to find elbow-roome for our phanatick Doctrines and practises : I trust our diligence past, and constant sedulity agains such persons and courses, will plead better things for us.   I dare take upon me, to bee the Herauld of *New-England* so farre, as to proclaime to the world, in the name of our Colony, that all Familists, Antinomians, Anabaptists, and other Enthusiasts shall have free Liberty to keepe away from us, and such as will come to be gone as fast as they can, the sooner the better.

Secondly, I dare averre, that God doth no where in his word tolerate Christian States, to give Tolerations to such adversaries of his Truth, if they have power in their hands to suppresse them. . . .

Not to tolerate things meerly indifferent to weak consciences, argues a conscience too strong : pressed uniformity in these, causes much disunity : To tolerate more then indifferents, is not to deale indifferently with God : He that doth it, takes his Scepter out of his hand, and bids him stand by.   Who hath to doe to institute Religion but God.   The power of all Religion and Ordinances, lies in their purity : their purity in their simplicity : then are mixtures pernicious.   I lived in a City, where a Papist preached in one Church, a Lutheran in another, a Calvinist in a third ; a Lutheran one part of the day, a Calvinist the other, in the same Pulpit : the Religion of that place was but motly and meagre, their affections Leopard-like. . . .

That State is wise, that will improve all paines and patience rather to compose, then tolerate differences in Religion.   There is no divine Truth, but hath much Cœlestiall fire in it from the Spirit of Truth : nor no irreligious untruth, without its proportion of Antifire from the spirit of Error to contradict it : the zeale of the one, the virulency of the other, must necessarily kindle Combustions.   Fiery diseases seated in the spirit, imbroile the whole frame of the body : others more externall and coole, are lesse dangerous. They which divide in Religion, divide in God ; they who divide in him, divide beyond *Genus Generalissimum*, where there is no reconciliation, without atonement; that is, without uniting in him, who is One, and in his Truth, which is also one.

Wise are those men who will be perswaded rather to live within the pale of Truth where they may bee quiet, than in the purlieves, where they are sure to be hunted ever & anon, do Authority what it can. Every singular Opinion, hath a singular opinion of it self; and he that holds it a singular opinion of himself, & a simple opinion of all contra sentients : he that confutes them, must confute at three at once, or else he does nothing; which will not be done without more stir than the peace of the State or Church can indure.

And prudent are those Christians, that will rather give what may be given, then hazard all by yeelding nothing. To sell all peace of Coun-try, to buy some peace of conscience unseasonably, is more avarice than thrift, imprudence than patience : they deal not equally, that set any Truth of God at such a rate ; but they deal wisely that will stay till the Market is fallen.

My prognosticks deceive me not a little, if once within three seaven years, peace prove not such a penny-worth at most Marts in Christen-dome, that hee that would not lay down his money, his lust, his opinion, his will, I had almost said the best flower of his Crowne for it, while he might have had it ; will tell his own heart, he plaid the very ill husband.

Concerning Tolerations I may further assert.

That Persecution of true Religion, and Toleration of false, are the *Jannes* and *Jambres* to the Kingdome of Christ, whereof the last is farre the worst. *Augustines* tongue had not owed his mouth one penny-rent though he had never spake word more in it, but this, *Nullum malum pejus libertate errandi.*

Frederick Duke of *Saxon*, spake not one foote beyond the mark when he said. He had rather the Earth should swallow him up quick, then he should give a toleration to any opinion against any truth of God.

He that is willing to tolerate any Religion, or discrepant way of Reli-gion, besides his own, unless it be in matters meerly indifferent, either doubts of his own, or is not sincere in it.

He that is willing to tolerate any unsound Opinion, that his own may also be tolerated, though never so sound, will for a need hang Gods Bible at the Devills girdle.

Every Toleration of false Religions, or Opinions hath as many Errours and sins in it, as all the false Religions and Opinions it tolerats, and one sound one more.

That State that will give Liberty of Conscience in matters of Religion, must give Liberty of Conscience and Conversation in their Morall Laws, or else the Fiddle will be out of tune, and some of the strings crack.

He that will rather make an irreligious quarell with other Religions then try the Truth of his own by valuable Arguments, and peaceable Sufferings ; either his Religion, or himselfe is irreligous.

Experience will teach Churches and Christians, that it is farre better to live in a State united, though a little Corrupt, then in a State, whereof some Part is incorrupt, and all the rest divided.

I am not altogether ignorant of the eight Rules given by Orthodox divines about giving Tolerations, yet with their favour I dare affirme,

That there is no Rule given by God for any State to give an affirmative Toleration to any false Religion, or Opinion whatsoever; they must connive in some Cases, but may not concede in any.

That the State of *England* (so farre as my Intelligence serves) might in time have prevented with ease and may yet without any great difficultie deny both Toleration, and irregular connivences *salva Republica*.

That if the State of *England* shall either willingly Tolerate, or weakly connive at such Courses, the Church of that Kingdome will sooner become the Devils dancing-Schoole, then Gods Temple : The Civill State a Beare-garden, then an Exchange : The whole Realme a Pais base then an *England*. And what pity it is, that that Country which hath been the Staple of Truth to all Christendome, should now become the Aviary of Errors to the whole world, let every fearing heart judge.

I take Liberty of Conscience to be nothing but a freedome from sinne, and error. *Conscientia in tantum libera, in quantum ab errore liberata.* And Liberty of Errour nothing but a Prison for Conscience. Then small will be the kindnesse of a State to build such Prisons for their Subjects.

The Scripture saith, there is nothing makes free but Truth, and Truth faith, there is no Truth but one : If the States of the World would make it their summ-operous Care to preserve this One Truth in its purity and Authority it would ease you of all other Politicall cares.   I am sure Sathan makes it his grand, if not only taske, to adulterate Truth ; Falshood is his sole Scepter, whereby he first ruffled, and ever since ruined the World.

If Truth be but One, me thinks all the Opinionists in *England* should not be all in that One Truth, some of them I doubt are out. He that can extract an unity out of such a disparity, or contract such a disparity into an unity; had need be a better Artist, then ever was *Drebell*.

If two Centers (as we may suppose) be in one Circle, and lines drawn from both to all the points of the Compasse, they will certainly crosse one another, and probably cut through the Centers themselves.

There is talk of an universall Toleration, I would talke as loud as I could against it, did I know what more apt and reasonable Sacrifice *England* could offer to God for his late performing all his heavenly Truths then an universall Toleration of all hellish Errors, or how they shall make an universall Reformation, but by making Christs Academy the Divills University, where any man may commence Heretique *per saltum;* where he that is *filius Diabolicus*, or *simpliciter pessimus*, may have his grace to goe to Hell *cum Publico Privilegio;* and carry as many after him, as he can. . . .

It is said, Though a man have light enough himselfe to see the Truth, yet if he hath not enough to enlighten others, he is bound to tolerate them, I will engage my self, that all the Devills in *Britanie* shall sell themselves to their shirts, to purchase a Lease of this Position for three of their Lives, under the Seale of the Parliament.

It is said, That Men ought to have Liberty of their Conscience, and that it is persecution to debarre them of it: I can rather stand amazed then reply to this: it is an astonishment to think that the braines of men should be parboyl'd in such impious ignorance; Let all the wits under the Heavens lay their heads together and finde an Assertion worse then this (one excepted) I will petition to be chosen the universall Ideot of the world.

It is said, That Civill Magistrates ought not to meddle with Ecclesiasticall matters.

I would answer to this so well as I could, did I not know that some papers lately brought out of *New-England*, are going to the Presse, wherein the Opinions of the Elders there in a late Synod, concerning this point are manifested, which I suppose will give clearer satisfaction then I can.

The true English of all this their false Latine, is nothing but a generall Toleration of all Opinions; which motion if it be like to take, it were very requisite, that the City would repaire *Pauls* with all the speed they can, for an English *Pantheon*, and bestow it upon the Sectaries, freely to assemble in, then there may be some hope that *London* will be quiet in time. . . .

Theodore de la Guard [Nathaniel Ward], *The Simple Cobler of Aggavvamm in America* (London, 1647), 3–12 *passim.*

CHAPTER XVII — RHODE ISLAND

113. Settlement in Rhode Island (1646)

BY SAMUEL GORTON

Gorton was a contentious and troublesome man; his neighbors disliked him and tried to have him expelled by the agency of Massachusetts. This extract seems to give a truthful, though one-sided, account of the controversy. The full page is reprinted as an example of the pedantic style of the time. — Bibliography: Winsor, *Narrative and Critical History*, III, 354–364; J. A. Doyle, *English in America, Puritan Colonies*, I, ch. vi; Channing and Hart, *Guide*, § 120.

SIMPLICITIES DEFENCE

against

SEVEN-HEADED POLICY.

OR

Innocency Vindicated, being unjustly **Accused,**
and sorely Censured, by that
Seven-headed Church-Government
United in

NEW-ENGLAND:

OR

That Servant so Imperious in his Masters Absence
Revived, and now thus re-acting in Nevv-England.

OR

The combate of the United Colonies, not onely
against some of the Natives and Subjects, but against the
Authority also of the Kingdme of *England,* with their execution of
Laws, in the name and Authority of the servant, (or of themselves)
and not in the Name and Authority of the Lord, or
fountain of the Government.
Wherein is declared an Act of a great people and
Country of the *Indians* in those parts, both Princes and

People (unanimously) in their voluntary Submission and
Subjection unto the Protection and Government of Old England (from
the Fame they hear thereof) together with the true manner and forme
of it, as it appears under their own hands and seals, being stirred up, and provoked thereto, by the
Combate and courses above-said.
Throughout which Treatise is secretly intermin-
gled, that great Opposition, which is in the goings forth of
those two grand Spirits, that are, and ever have been, extant
in the World (through the sons of men) from the beginning and foundation thereof.

Imprimatur, Aug. 3ᵈ. 1646. Diligently perused, approved, and Licensed
to the Presse, according to Order by publike Authority.

LONDON,

Printed by *John Macock,* and are to be sold by LUKE FAVVNE, at his
shop in *Pauls Church-yard,* at the sign of the *Parrot.*   1646.

. . .   WHEREAS we removed our selves and families out of our
native Country, about ten or twelve years ago by the leave
of this State, only to injoy the liberty of our consciences, in respect of our
faith towards God, and for no other end, not scrupling any Civill Ordinance, for the education, ordering, or government of any Civil State.

Landing by the providence of God at *Boston* in the *Massachusets*
Bay, we found our Countrymen at great variance in point of Religion,
prosecuting it very hotly in their publique Courts unto fines and banishments, occasioning men thereby much to vent and bring forth themselves ; and we understanding that they had formerly banished one
Master *Roger Williams,* a man of good report both for life and doctrine
(even amongst themselves) for dissenting from them in some points
about their Church Government, and that in the extremity of winter,
forcing him to betake himselfe into the vast wilderness to sit down
amongst the Indians, in a place by their own confessions, out of all their
Jurisdictions : And at that time of our arrivall at *Boston,* they were
proceeding against one Master *John Wheelwright,* a man of like life
and conversation, whom they also banished for differing with them in
point of Doctrine, the summ whereof consisted in this, *That sanctifica-*

tion is not the first evidence unto a Christian of his salvation; and many others manifesting their thoughts about such points then controverted amongst them, were also imprisoned, fined, banished, disarmed, and cast out from amongst them.

And we plainly perceiving that the scope of their doctrine was bent onely to maintain that outward forme of worship which they had erected to themselves, tending only to the outward carriage of one man toward another, leaving those principles of Divinity, wherein we had been instructed in our native Country, tending to faith towards God in Christ : and we finding no ground nor warrant for such an order in the Church (to bind mens consciences unto) as they had established amongst them ; our consciences could not close with them in such their practices, which they perceiving, denied us the common benefit of the Country, even so much as a place to reside in, and plant upon, for the maintenance and preservation of our selves, our wives and little ones ; as also proceeded against us, as they had done to others ; yea with more severity, unto confinements, imprisonments, chains, fines, whippings, and banishment out of all their Jurisdictions, to wander in the wildernesse in extremity of winter, yea when the snow was up to the knee, and rivers to wade through up unto the midle, and not so much as one of the Indians to be found in that extremity of weather to afford us either fire, or any harbor, such as themselves had ; being removed into swamps and thickets, where they were not to be found ; in which condition, in the continuation of the weather, we lay diverse nights together, having no victuals, but what we took on our backs, and our drink as the snow afforded unto us, whereupon we were constrained with the hazard of our lives to betake our selves into a part of the Country called the *Nanhyganset* Bay, buying severall parcels of Land of the Indians there inhabiting ; and sat down in, and neer the place where Master *Roger Williams* was where we built houses, and bestowed our labors to raise up means to maintain our wives and little ones (which our Countrymen out of their zeal had deprived us of, and taken away from us) quietly possessing them for the space of seven or eight years (some of us) no man interrupting us, but both the *Massachusets*, and also *Plymouth* confessed us to be out of the confines of their Patents ; but when they perceived those parts to be a refuge for such as were oppressed and grieved amongst themselves, who repaired unto us for shelter, then they went about to bring those parts to be under their Jurisdictions, by all possible pretences, and stretching their line for that purpose, thinking to get some colour for their proceedings ; yet fell they short of our Plantations fourteen or fifteen miles, as did evidently appear, and was by themselves acknowledged, and when they saw they could not accomplish their ends by that project, they then insinuated themselves into the minds of three il-affected persons amongst us, that they should acknowledge themselves to be subjects unto them, and to depend upon them for protection and government, . . .

Now when the *Massachusets* had gained these men to be instruments in this manner to effect their end, then did they institute them as officers to execute their warrants amongst us in those parts, upon any complaint these above named subjects should make unto them upon the grounds above mentioned, who presently sent a Warrant unto us, to command our appearance at their Courts, under the hand of the Governor and divers of the assistants in the *Massachusets*, threatning to use violence a gainst us in case we obeyed not. . . .

This Warrant being delivered unto us by their new made officer *William Arnold*, in the name of the *Massachusets*, we took into serious consideration, having former experience abundantly of their unkind and inhumane dealing with us, yea towards our wives and children, when our selves were sometimes in banishments, and sometimes in prison, and irons (by them) before. We thought it meet (for the preservation of our peace, together with that Compassion we had of our wives and little ones) to leave our houses, and the rest of our labors, lying neer unto those their pretended subjects (whom we saw maliciously bent) and to remove our selves and families further off, from the *Massachusets*, and such their coadjutours, being then amongst us : For we saw that they did not only endeavor to take away our livelyhood, but intended to take away our lives also, in case they could find a way to satisfie the Country in doing of such an act and execution : For we had never accusation brought in against us, but what rose from the Magistrates and the Ministers ; for we walked so, as to do no man wrong, only justified the cause of our Religion, as we had learned and received the principles thereof before we went amongst them ; as also the laws and government of this Kingdome of *England* unto which we ever willingly acknowledged our selves to be loyall subjects, and therefore could not suffer our selves to be intrenched upon by our fellow subjects, further then the laws of our King and State doth allow.

. . . But we removing our selves, as abovesaid, into another part of the *Nanhyganset* Bay, further from the *Massachusets*, and where none of the *English,* nor other Nations had any thing to do, but only Indians, the true natives, of whom we bought a parcell of land called *Shaw-omet* (as is abovesaid) not only of *Myantonomy,* chiefe Sachim, or prince of those parts of the Country; but also with the free consent of the Inhabitants of the place. . . .

[Samuel Gorton], *Simplicities Defence against Seven-Headed Policy* (London, 1646), 2–9 *passim.*

---

114. Objections to the New Charter (1651)

BY WILLIAM ARNOLD

Arnold represents the opposition to Williams; he was one of the residents of Pawtuxet, who were trying to get under the jurisdiction of Massachusetts. — Bibliography: Samuel G. Arnold, *History of Rhode Island,* I, 237–239; Winsor, *Narrative and Critical History,* III, 376–380; Channing and Hart, *Guide,* § 120.

. . . I THOUGHT it my dutie to give intelligence unto the much honoured court of that which I understand is now working here in these partes. So that if it be the will of God, an evill may be prevented before it come to too greate a head, viz.

Whereas Mr. Coddington have gotten a charter of Roade Iland and Conimacucke Iland to himselfe, he have thereby broken the force of their charter that went under the name of Providence, because he have gotten away the greater parte of that colonie.

Now these company of the Gortonists that live at Showomut, and that company of Providence are gathering of 200£. to send Mr. Roger Williams unto the Parlyament to get them a charter of these partes, they of Showomut have given 100£. already, and there be some men of Providence that have given 10£. and 20£. a man to helpe it forward with speede, they say heere is a faire inlett, and I heare they have said, that if the Parlyament doe take displeasure against Massachusitt, or the rest of the colonies, as they have done against Barbadas and other places, then this will serve for an inroade to lett in forces to over-runne the whole country.

It is greate petie and very unfitt that such a company as these are, they all stand professed enemies against all the united colonies, that they should get a charter for so smale a quantity of land as lyeth in and about Providence, Showomut, Pautuxit and Coicett, all which now Roade Iland is taken out from it, it is but a strape of land lying in betweene

2 D

the colonies of Massachusits, Plymouth and Conitaquot, by which meanes, if they should get them a charter, off it there may come some mischiefe and trouble upon the whole country if their project be not prevented in time, for under the pretence of liberty of conscience about these partes there comes to lieve all the scume the runne awayes of the country, which in tyme for want of better order may bring a heavy burthen upon the land, &c. This I humbly commend unto the serious consideration of the much honored court, and rest your humble servant to command.

William Arnold.

They are making hast to send Mr. Williams away.

We that lieve heere neere them and doe know the place and hear their wordes and doe take notice of their proceeding doe know more and can speake more of what evill may come to the country by their meanes, then the court do yet consider off: We humblie desire God their purpose may be frusterated for the country's peace.

I humblie desire my name may be conceled lest they hearing of what I have herein written they will be enraged against me and so will revenge themselves upon me.

Some of them of Showomut that cryeth out much against them which putteth people to death for witches; for say they there be no other witches upon earth nor devils, but your own pastors and ministers and such as they are, &c. . . .

Thomas Hutchinson, *A Collection of Original Papers Relative to the History of the Colony of Massachusets-Bay* (Boston, 1769), 237–238.

---

115. Toleration in Rhode Island (1670)

BY REVEREND ROGER WILLIAMS

Roger Williams was distinguished as a divine, as the founder of Providence, as one of the Antinomians, and as the apostle of religious liberty in New England. He wrote much and well, in his own crabbed style. — Bibliography: Narragansett Club, *Publications*, I, Introduction; Winsor, *Narrative and Critical History*, III, 368–384; Edward Eggleston, *Beginners of a Nation*, 307–314; J. A. Doyle, *English in America, Puritan Colonies*, I, chs. vi, viii; Channing and Hart, *Guide*, §§ 120, 124. See No. 108 above.

Providence, 22 June, 1670, (Ut Vulgo.)

MY honoured deare and antient friend. My due respects and earnest desires to God for your eternall peace, &c.

I crave your leave and patience to present you with some few considerations occasioned by the late transactions between your colony and ours. The last yeare you were pleased, in one of your lines to me, to tell me that you longed to see my face once more before you died : I embraced your love, though I feared my old lame bones, and yours, had arrested travelling in this world, and therefore I was and am ready to lay hold on all occasions of writing as I do at present.

The occasion I confesse is sorrowful, because I see yourselves, with others, embarqued in a resolution to invade and despoil your poor countrimen, in a wildernes, and your antient friends of our temporal and soul liberties. . . .

Sir I am not out of hopes but that while your aged eyes and mine are yet in their orbes, and not yet sunck doune into their holes of rottennes, we shall leave our friends and countrimen, our children and relations and this land in peace behind us. To this end Sir please you with a calme and steadie and a christian hand, to hold the ballance and to weigh these few considerations in much love and due respect presented.

First, when I was unkindly and unchristianly, as I believe, driven from my house and land and wife and children (in the midst of New-England winter, now about 35 yeaors past) at Salem, that ever honoured Governour Mr. Winthrop privately wrote to me to steer my course to Nahigonset-Bay and Indians for many high and heavenly and publike ends, incouraging me from the freenes of the place from any English claims or pattents. I took his prudent motion as an hint and voice from God and waving all other thoughts and motions, I steered my course from Salem (though in winter snow which I feel yet) unto these parts, wherein I may say *Peniel*, that is, I have seene the face of God.

2. I first pitch't, and begun to build and plant at *Secunk*, now Rehoboth, but I received a letter from my antient friend Mr. Winslow, then Governour of Plymmouth, professing his oune and others love and respect to me, yet lovingly advising me, since I was fallen into the edge of their bounds and they were loth to displease the Bay, to remove but to the other side of the water and then he said I had the country free before me and might be as free as themselves and wee should be loving neighbour's togeather. These were the joynt understandings of these two eminently wise and christian Governours and others, in their day, togeather with their councell and advice as to the freedome and vacancie of this place, which in this respect and many other Providences of the most holy and only wise, I called *Providence*.

3. Sometime after Plymmouth great Sachim (Ousamaquin) upon occasion affirming that Providence was his land and therefore Plymmouth's land and some resenting it, the then prudent and godly Governour Mr. Bradford and others of his godly councell, answered that if after due examination it should be found true what the barbarian said, yet having, to my loss of a harvest that yeare, been now (though by their gentle advice) as good as banished from Plymmouth as from the Massachusetts; and I had quietly and patiently departed from them, at their motion, to the place where now I was, I should not be molested and tost up and down againe while they had breath in their bodies; and surely betweene those my friends of the Bay and Plymmouth, I was sorely tost for one fourteen weekes, in a bitter winter season, not knowing what bread or bed did meane; beside the yearly losse of no small matter in my trading with English and natives, being debarred from Boston, the chiefe mart and port of New England. God knows that many thousand pounds cannot repay the very temporary losses I have sustained. It lies upon the Massachusetts and me, yea and other colonies joining with them to examine, with feare and trembling before the eyes of flaming fire, the true cause of all my sorrows and sufferings. It pleased the Father of spirits to touch many hearts, dear to him, with some relentings; amongst which that great and pious soule Mr. *Winslow* melted, and kindly visited me at Providence and put a piece of gold into the hands of my wife for our supply.

4. When the next yeare after my banishment the Lord drew the bow of the Pequot warr against the country, in which, Sir, the Lord made yourselfe, with others, a blessed instrument of peace to all New England. I had my share of service to the whole land in that Pequot busines, inferiour to very few that acted, . . .

5 *Consid*. Upon frequent exceptions against Providence men that we had no authoritie for civill government, I went purposely to England and upon my report and petition, the Parliament granted us a charter of government for these parts, so judged vacant on all hands. And upon this the country about us was more friendly, and wrote to us and treated us as an authorised colony; only the differences of our consciences much obstructed. The bounds of this our first charter I (having ocular knowledge of persons, places and transactions) did honestly and conscientiously, as in the holy presence of God, draw up from Pawcatuck river, which I then believed and still doe is free from all English claims and conquests. . . .

6. Some time after the Pequt war and our charter from the Parliament, the government of Massachusetts wrote to myselfe (then chief
officer in this Colony) of their receaving of a pattent from the Parliament
for these vacant lands, as an addition to the Massachusetts, &c. and
thereupon requiring me to exercise no more authorite, &c. for, they
wrote, their charter was granted some few weeks before ours.   I returned
what I beleived righteous and waighty to the hands of my true friend,
Mr. *Winthrop*, the first mover of my coming into these parts, and to that
answer of mine I never received the least reply ; only it is certain that
at Mr. Gorton's complaint against the Massachusetts, the Lord High
Admiral, President, said openly, in a full meeting of the commissioners,
that he knew no other charter for these parts than what Mr. Williams
had obtained, and he was sure that charter, which the Massachusetts
Englishmen pretended, had never past the table. . . .

8. But the Kings Majestie sending his commissioners, among other
his royall purposes, to reconcile the differences of, and to settle the
bounds betweene the colonies, yourselves know how the King himself
therefore hath given a decision to this controversie.   Accordingly the
Kings Majesties aforesaid commissioners at Rode —— (where, as a
commissioner for this colony, I tranacted with them as did also commissioners from Plymmouth) they composed a controversie betweene
Plymmouth and us and settled the bounds betweene us in which we
rest. . . .

10. Alas, Sir, in calme midnight thoughts, what are these leaves and
flowers, and smoke and shadows, and dreams of earthly nothings, about
which we poore fools and children, as David saith, disquiet ourselves in
vain?   Alas, what is all the scuffling of this world for but, *come will
you smoke it?*   What are all the contentions and wars of this world
about, generally, but for greater dishes and bowls of porridge, of which,
if we believe God's spirit in scripture, Esau and Jacob were types? . . .

. . . Besides Sir the matter with us is not about these children's toys
of land, meadows, cattell, government, &c.   But here all over this colonie,
a great number of weake and distressed soules, scattered are flying hither
from Old and New England, the Most High and only wise hath in his
infinite wisdom provided this country and this corner as a shelter for
the poor and persecuted, according to their several perswasions. . . .

Thus Sir, the Kings Majestie . . . hath vouchsafed his royall promise
under his hand and broad seal that no person in this Colony shall be
molested or questioned for the matters of his conscience to God, so he

be loyall and keep the civil peace. Sir. we must part with lands and lives before we part with such a jewell. . . .

Some of yours, as I heard lately, told tales to the Archbishop of Canterbury, viz. that we are a prophane people and do not keep the Sabbath, but some doe plough, &c. But (1) you told him not how we suffer freely all other perswasions, yea the common prayer, which yourselves will not suffer. If you say you will, you confesse you must suffer more, as we doe.

2. You know this is but a colour to your design for, first, you know that all Engand : It selfe (after the formalitie and superstition of morning and evening prayer) play away their Sabbath. . . .

6. I have offered and doe by these presents to discusse by disputation writing or printing, among other points of differences these three positions ; first that forced worship stincks in Gods nostrils. 2d that it denies Christ Jesus yet to be come, and makes the church yet national, figurative and ceremonial. 3d That in these flames about religion, as his Majestie his father and grandfather have yielded, there is no other prudent, christian way of preserving peace in the world but by permission of differing consciences. . . .

. . . I know you are both of you hot, I fear myself also, if both desire, in a loving and calm spirit, to enjoy your rights I promise you, with God's help, to help you to them in a fair and sweet and easie way : — My receit will not please you all. If it should so please God to frowne upon us that you should not like it, I can but humbly mourne and say with the Prophet that which must perish, must perish. And as to myself, in endeavouring after yor temporall and spirituall peace, I humbly desire to say, if I perish, I perish — It is but a shadow vanished, a bubble broke, a dreame finish't eternitie will pay for all. . . .

Massachusetts Historical Society, *Collections* (Boston, 1792), I, 275–283 *passim*.

116. Rhode Island in 1680

BY GOVERNOR PELEG SANDFORD

This is one of the series of answers to circular inquiries sent out from England (compare No. 70 above and No. 156 below). — Bibliography: see Nos. 113-115 above; Channing and Hart, *Guide*, §§ 120, 124, 128.

WHEREAS wee the Governor and Councill of his Majesties Colloney of Rhoade Island and Providence Plantations receaved from your Lordships the Right Honorable, the Lords of his Majesties most Honorable Privy Councill, appointed a committee for Trade and Forreign Plantations certain heads of inquiery, subscribed by the honorable secretary William Blathwayt, in obedience to your Lordships commands requiring an answer thereunto; wee the Governor and Councill aforesaid accordinge to the best of our understandinge make answer as followeth, vizt.

To the first wee humbly answer that the Councells and Assemblies are stated accordinge to his Majesties appointment in his gratious letters Pattents, and our Courts of judicature are two in the yeare certain appointed accordinge to Charter, and are carried on by Judges and Jurors, accordinge to Law and Charter.

To the second, concerninge the court of Admiralty wee answer that wee have made provision to act accordinge to the Lawes of England as neare as the constitution of our place will bear havinge but little occasion thereofe.

To the third wee answer that accordinge to our Charter the Legislative power is seated in our Generall Assemblies, and the executive power of the government is in our Courts of Trialls settled accordinge to Charter.

To the fourth wee answer that our Lawes are made accordinge to the Charter not repugnant but agreable to the Lawes of England.

To the fifth we answer, that as for Horse wee have but few, but the chief of our Militia consists of ten companys of foote, being Trayned Bands under one Generall Commander, and their arms are firelockes.

To the sixth, wee answer that in the late Indian warres wee fortified ourselves against the Indians as necessity required, but as for fortification against a Forreign enemie, as yet wee have had no occasion but have made as good provision as at present wee are capacitated to doe.

To the seventh wee answer, that our coast is little frequented and not at all at this time with privateers or pirates.

To the eighth wee answer, as with respect to other Nations, that the French being seated at Canada and up the Bay of Funde are a very considerable number, as wee judge about two thousand, but as for the Indians, they are generally cut off by the late warr, that were inhabitinge our Colloney.

To the 9th wee answer, that as for Forreighners and Indians, we have no commerce with, but as for our neighbouringe English, wee have and shall endeavor to keepe a good correspondency with them.

To the 10th wee answer as to the Boundaryes of our Land within our Patent that our Charter doth declare the same viz — (extracts the bounds from the charter, and adds, "the greatest part of it uncultivated, and is about a degree as we conceave.")

To the 11th wee answer that the principal town for trade in our Colloney is the Towne of Newport, that the generality of our buildinge is of timber and generally small.

To the 12th, That wee have nine towns or divisions within our Colloney.

To the 13th, That wee have several good Harbors in the Colloney of very good depth and soundinge, navigable for any shippinge.

To the 14th, That the principall matters that are exported amongst us, is Horses and provisions, and the goods chiefly imported is a small quantity of Barbadoes goods for supply of our familyes.

To the 15th, That as for Salt Peter we know of none in this Colloney.

To the 16th, Wee answer that wee have severall men that deale in buyinge and sellinge although they cannot properly be called Merchants, and for Planters wee conceave there are about five hundred and about five hundred men besides.

To the 17th, that we have had few or none either of English, Scots, Irish or Forreighners, onely a few blakes imported.

To the 18th, That there may be of Whites and Blakes about two hundred borne in a yeare.

To the 19th, That for marriages we have about fifty in a yeare.

To the 20th, That for burrials this seaven yeares last past accordinge to computation amounts to foure hundred fifty and five.

To the 21st, That as for Merchants wee have none, but the most of car Colloney live comfortably by improvinge the wildernesse.

To the 22d, That wee have no shippinge belonginge to our Colloney but only a few sloopes.

To the 23d, that the great obstruction concerninge trade is the want of Merchants and Men of considerable Estates amongst us.

To the 24th, wee answer that a fishinge trade might prove very beneficiall provided accordinge to the former artickle there were men of considerable Estates amongst us and willing to propagate it.

To the 25th, That as for goodes exported and imported, which is very little, there is no Custome imposed.

To the 26th, wee answer that those people that goe under the denomination of Baptists and Quakers are the most that publiquely congregate together, but there are others of divers persuasions and principles all which together with them injoy their liberties accordinge to his Majesties gratious Charter to them granted, wherein all people in our Colloney are to enjoy their liberty of conscience provided their liberty extend not to licentiousnesse, but as for Papists, wee know of none amongst us.

To the 27th, That we leave every Man to walke as God shall persuade their hartes, and doe actively and passively yield obedience to the Civill Magistrate and doe not actively disturb the Civill peace and live peaceably in the Corporation as our Charter requires, and have liberty to frequent any meetings of worship for their better Instruction and information, but as for beggars and vagabonds wee have none amongst us; and as for lame and impotent persons there is a due course taken. This may further humbly informe your Lordships that our predecessors about forty years since left their native countrey and comfortable settlements there because they could not in their private opinions conform to the Lithurge, formes and ceremonies of the Church of England, and transported themselves and familyes over the Ocean seas to dwell in this remote wildernesse, that they might injoy their liberty in their opinions, which upon application to his gratious Majesty after his happy restouration did of his bountifull goodnesse graunt us a Charter full of liberty of conscience, provided that the pretence of liberty extend not to licentiousnesse, in which said Charter there is liberty for any persons that will at their charges build Churches and maintaine such as are called Ministers without the least molestation as well as others. . . .

Samuel Greene Arnold, *History of the State of Rhode Island and Providence Plantations* (New York, 1859), I, 488–491.

CHAPTER XVIII—CONNECTICUT AND NEW HAVEN

117. The English in the Connecticut (1633)

BY WILLIAM BRADFORD

For the Dutch claims, see No. 153 below; for Bradford, see No. 49 above. — Bibliography: Winsor, *Narrative and Critical History*, III, 368–375; J. A. Doyle, *English in America, Puritan Colonies*, I, ch. v; Channing and Hart, *Guide*, §§ 121, 122.

. . . HAUING had formerly conuerse and fam[i]liarity with ye Dutch (as is before remembred,) they seeing them seated here in a barren quarter, tould them of a riuer called by them ye fresh riuer, but now is known by ye name of Conightecute-River, which they often comended vnto them for a fine place both for plantation, and trade, and wished them to make vse of it. But their hands being full otherwise, they let it pass But afterwards ther coming a company of banishte Indeans Into these parts, that were driuene out from thence by the potencie of ye Pequents, which vsurped vpon them, and driue them from thence They often sollisited them to goe thither and they should haue much trad, espetially if they would keep a house ther; and hauing now good store of comodities, and allso need to looke out wher they [c]ould aduantage them selues to help them out of their great Ingagments, they now began to send that way to discouer ye same, and trade with ye natiues, they found it to be a fine place but had no great store of trade, but ye Indeans excused ye same in regard of ye season, and the fear ye Indans were in of their enemise, So the[y] tried diuerce times, not with out profite, But saw ye most certainty would be by keeping a house ther, to receiue ye trad when it came down out of ye Inland These Indeans not seeing them very forward to build ther, solisited them of ye Massachusets in like sorte, (for their end was to be restored to their countrie againe,) but they in ye Bay being but latly come, were not fitte for ye same, but some of their cheefe made a motion to joyne wth the partners here, to trad Joyntly with them in y^t riuer, the

which they were willing to Imbrace, and so they should haue builte, and
put in equall stock togeather, a time of meeting was appointed at
ye Massachusets, and some of ye cheefe here, was appointed to treat
with them, and went accordingly; but they cast many fears, of deanger,
& loss and the like; which was perceiued to be the maine obstacles,
though they alledged they were not prouided of trading goods; but
those hear offered at presente to put in sufficente for Both, prouided
they would become Ingaged for ye halfe, and prepare against ye nexte
year. They conffessed more could not be offered, but thanked them,
and tould them they had no mind to it. They then answered, they
hoped it would be no offence vnto them, If them sellues wente on without them, If they saw it meete; they said there was no reason they
should, and thus this treaty broake of, and those here tooke conueniente
time to make a begining ther, and were ye first English that both discouered that place, and built in ye same. Though they were litle better
then thrust out of it afterward as may appeare

But ye dutch (begane now to repente) and hearing of their purpose,
& preparation Indeoured to preuente them; and gott in a litle before
them, and made a slight forte, and planted 2 peeces of ordnance,
thretening to stopp their passage   But they hauing made a smale frame
of a house ready, and haueing a great new-barke they stowed their
frame in her hold, & bords to couer & finishe it, hauing nayles, & all
other prouisions fitting for their vse (this they did ye rather, that they
might haue a presente defence against ye Indeans) who weare much
offended that they brought home & restored ye right Sachem of ye place
(called Natawanute) so as they were to Incounter with a double danger in this attempte, both ye dutch, and ye Indeans   When they came
vp ye riuer, the dutch demanded what they Intended, and whither they
would goe, they answered vp ye riuer to trade (now their order was to
goe, and seat a boue them) they bid them strike, & stay, or els they
would shoote them, (& stood by ther ordnance ready fitted) they
answered they had comission from ye Gou^r. of Plimoth to goe vp ye riuer
to such a place, and if they did shoote, they must obey their order, and
proceede they would not molest them, but would goe one   So they
passed along, and though the dutch threatened them hard, yet they
shoot not, coming to their place, they clapt vp their house quickly
and landed their prouissions, and left ye companie appoynted, and sent
the barke home, and afterwards palisadoed their house aboute, and
fortified them selues better, the Dutch sent word home to ye Monhatas

what was done, and in proces of time, they sent a band of aboute .70. men in warrlike maner with collours displayed, to assaulte them, but seeing them strengthened, & that it would cost blood, they came to parley, and returned in peace.   And this was their enterance ther ; who deserued to haue held it, and not by freinds to haue been thrust out as in a sorte they were, as will after appere   They did yᵉ dutch no wrong, for they took not a foote of any land they bought, but went to yᵉ place aboue them, and bought that tracte of land which belonged to these Indeans which they carried with them, and their friends, with whom yᵉ dutch had nothing to doe.   But of these matters more in another place . . .

William Bradford, *History of the Plimouth Plantation* (Fac-simile from the original manuscript, with an Introduction by John A. Doyle, London and Boston, 1896), 196–197.

---

118. The Founding of Connecticut (1636)

BY JOHN WINTHROP

For Winthrop, see No. 107 above. — Bibliography: Winsor, *Narrative and Critical History*, III, 369–371; Channing and Hart, *Guide*, § 121.

[1632. August 14.]
. . . THE Braintree company, (which had begun to sit down at Mount Wollaston,) by order of court, removed to Newtown   These were Mr. Hooker's company. . . .

[1634. September 4.] . . . But the main business, which spent the most time, and caused the adjourning of the court, was about the removal of Newtown.   They had leave, the last general court, to look out some place for enlargement or removal, with promise of having it confirmed to them, if it were not prejudicial to any other plantation ; and now they moved, that they might have leave to remove to Connecticut.   This matter was debated divers days, and many reasons alleged pro and con.   Their principal reasons for their removal were, 1.   Their want of accommodation for their cattle, so as they were not able to maintain their ministers, nor could receive any more of their friends to help them ; and here it was alleged by Mr. Hooker, as a fundamental error, that towns were set so near each to other.

2. The fruitfulness and commodiousness of Connecticut, and the danger of having it possessed by others, Dutch or English.

3. The strong bent of their spirits to remove thither.

Against these it was said, 1. That, in point of conscience, they ought not to depart from us, being knit to us in one body, and bound by oath to seek the welfare of this commonwealth.

2. That, in point of state and civil policy, we ought not to give them leave to depart.   1. Being we were now weak and in danger to be assailed.   2. The departure of Mr. Hooker would not only draw many from us, but also divert other friends that would come to us.   3. We should expose them to evident peril, both from the Dutch (who made claim to the same river, and had already built a fort there) and from the Indians, and also from our own state at home, who would not endure they should sit down without a patent in any place which our king lays claim unto.

3. They might be accommodated at home by some enlargement which other towns offered.

4. They might remove to Merimack, or any other place within our patent. . . .

. . . the 24th the court met again.   Before they began, Mr. Cotton preached, . . .   And it pleased the Lord so to assist him, and to bless his own ordinance, that the affairs of the court went on cheerfully ; and although all were not satisfied about the negative voice to be left to the magistrates, yet no man moved aught about it, and the congregation of Newtown came and accepted of such enlargement as had formerly been offered them by Boston and Watertown ; and so the fear of their removal to Connecticut was removed. . . .

[1635. May.]   Also, Watertown and Roxbury had leave to remove whither they pleased, so as they continued under this government.   The occasion of their desire to remove was, for that all towns in the bay began to be much straitened by their own nearness to one another, and their cattle being so much increased. . . .

[1636. May. 31.]   Mr. Hooker, pastor of the church of Newtown, and the most of his congregation, went to Connecticut.   His wife was carried in a horse litter ; and they drove one hundred and sixty cattle, and fed of their milk by the way. . . .

John Winthrop, *The History of New England from 1630 to 1649* (edited by James Savage, Boston, 1853), I, 104–223 *passim*.

119. The Foundation of New Haven (1637)

BY CAPTAIN EDWARD JOHNSON (1654)

For Johnson, see No. 105 above. — Bibliography : Winsor, *Narrative and Critical History*, III, 371–373 ; Channing and Hart, *Guide*, § 122.

THE Lord Christ having now in his great mercy taken out of the way these mountains that seemed in the eye of Man to block up his Churches further proceedings, they had now leisure to welcome the living stones that the Lord was pleased to adde unto this building, and with thankfull acknowledgment to give him of his owne for his mercyes multitude, whose was the work in planting, not onely more Churches, but another Colony also ; for the honoured Mr, *Eaton* being accompanied with many worthy persons of note, whom the Lord had furnished with store of substance for this wildernesse-work, although they would willingly have made their abode under the government of the Mattachusets ; yet could they finde no place upon the Sea-coasts for their settling : the Lord intending to enlarge his peoples border, caused them, after much search, to take up a place somewhat more southwardly, neare the shalles of *Cape-cod*, where they had very flatt water ; yet being entred in, they found a commodious harbour for shipping, and a fit place to erect a Towne, which they built in very little time, with very faire houses, and compleat streets ; but in a little time they overstockt it with Chattell, although many of them did follow merchandizing, and Maritime affairs, but their remotenesse from the Mattachusets Bay, where the chiefe traffique lay, hindred them much. Here did these godly and sincere servants of Christ, according to the rule of the Word, gather into Church Estate, and called to the office of a Pastor the reverend, judicious, and godly Mr, *John Davenport*. . . .

This Church and Town soon procur'd some Sisters to take part with her, and among them they erected a godly and peaceable Government, and called their frontier towne *New-haven*, of which the Government is denominated, being inhabited by many men eminent in gifts for the populating thereof, and managing of affaires both by Sea and Land ; they have had some shipping built there, but by the sad losse of Mr : *Lambertons* ship and goods also, they were much disheartned, but the much honoured Mr. *Eaton* remaines with them to this very day. . . .

This government of *New-haven*, although the younger Sister of the foure yet was she as beautifull as any of this broode of travellers, &

most minding the end of her coming hither, to keep close to the rule
of Christ both in Doctrine and Discipline; and it were to be wished
her elder Sister would follow her example, to nurture up all her children
accordingly: here is not to be forgotten the honoured Mr *Hopkins*,
who came over about this time a man of zeale and courage for the
truths of Christ, assisting this blessed work, both in person and estate;
for the which the Author cannot forget him, being oft in commission for
the good of all the united Colonyes. . . .

[Edward Johnson], *A History of New-England*, or *Wonder-working Providence of Sions Saviour* (London, 1654), 122–124 *passim*.

———◆———

120. The First Popular Written Constitution (1639)

BY "A GEN^RALL CORT AT HARTEFORD"

These so-called "Fundamental Orders" are the first example in history of a frame
of government drawn up by a popular assembly for its own commonwealth. No contemporary account of its history has been found. — Bibliography: Winsor, *Narrative and Critical History*, III, 371; Channing and Hart, *Guide*, § 121.

FORASMUCH as it hath pleased the Allmighty God by the wise disposition of his diuyne p^ruidence so to Order and dispose of things
that we the Inhabitants and Residents of Windsor, Harteford and Wethersfield are now cohabiting and dwelling in and vppon the River of Conect-
ecotte and the Lands thereunto adioyneing; And well knowing where a
people are gathered togather the word of God requires that to mayntayne
the peace and vnion of such a people there should be an orderly and decent
Gouerment established according to God, to order and dispose of the
affayres of the people at all seasons as occation shall require; doe therefore assotiate and conioyne our selues to be as one Publike State or
Comonwelth; and doe, for our selues and our Successors and such as
shall be adioyned to vs att any tyme hereafter, enter into Combination
and Confederation togather, to mayntayne and p^rsearue the liberty and
purity of the gospell of our Lord Jesus wch we now p^rfesse, as also the
disciplyne of the Churches, wch according to the truth of the said gospell
is now practised amongst vs; As also in o^r Ciuell Affaires to be guided
and gouerned according to such Lawes, Rules, Orders and decrees as
shall be made, ordered & decreed, as followeth : —

   1. It is Ordered, sentenced and decreed, that there shall be yerely

two generall Assemblies or Courts, the on the second thursday in Aprill, the other the second thursday in September, following ; the first shall be called the Courte of Election, wherein shall be yerely Chosen frō tyme to tyme soe many Magestrats and other publike Officers as shall be found requisitte : Whereof one to be chosen Gouernour for the yeare ensueing and vntill another be chosen, and noe other Magestrate to be chosen for more then one yeare ; p^ruided allwayes there be six chosen besids the Gouernour ; wch being chosen and sworne according to an Oath recorded for that purpose shall haue power to administer iustice according to the Lawes here established, and for want thereof according to the rule of the word of God ; wch choise shall be made by all that are admitted freemen and haue taken the Oath of Fidellity, and doe cohabitte wthin this Jurisdiction, (hauing beene admitted Inhabitants by the maior p^rt of the Towne wherein they liue,) or the mayor p^rte of such as shall be then p^rsent.

2. It is Ordered, sentensed and decreed, that the Election of the aforesaid Magestrats shall be on this manner : euery p^rson p^rsent and quallified for choyse shall bring in (to the p^rsons deputed to receaue thē) one single pap^r wth the name of him written in yt whom he desires to haue Gouernour, and he that hath the greatest nūber of papers shall be Gouernor for that yeare. And the rest of the Magestrats or publike Officers to be chosen in this manner : The Secretary for the tyme being shall first read the names of all that are to be put to choise and then shall seuerally nominate them distinctly, and euery one that would haue the p^rson nominated to be chosen shall bring in one single paper written vppon, and he that would not haue him chosen shall bring in a blanke : and euery one that hath more written papers then blanks shall be a Magestrat for that yeare ; wch papers shall be receaued and told by one or more that shall be then chosen by the court and sworne to be faythfull therein ; but in case there should not be six chosen as aforesaid, besids the Gouernor, out of those wch are nominated, then he or they wch haue the most written pap^rs shall be a Magestrate or Magestrats for the ensueing yeare, to make vp the foresaid nūber.

3. It is Ordered, sentenced and decreed, that the Secretary shall not nominate any p^rson, nor shall any p^rson be chosen newly into the Magestracy wch was not p^rpownded in some Generall Courte before, to be nominated the next Election ; and to that end yt shall be lawfull for ech of the Townes aforesaid by their deputyes to nominate any two whō they conceaue fitte to be put to Election ; and the Courte may ad so many more as they iudge requisitt.

4. It is Ordered, sentenced and decreed that noe p^rson be chosen Gouernor aboue once in two yeares, and that the Gouernor be alwayes a m̄eber of some approved congregation, and formerly of the Magestracy w^thin this Jurisdiction; and all the Magestrats Freemen of this Com̄onwelth: and that no Magestrate or other publike officer shall execute any p^rte of his or their Office before they are seuerally sworne, wch shall be done in the face of the Courte if they be p^rsent, and in case of absence by some deputed for that purpose.

5. It is Ordered, sentenced and decreed, that to the aforesaid Courte of Election the seu^rall Townes shall send their deputyes, and when the Elections are ended they may p^rceed in any publike searuice as at other Courts. Also the other Generall Courte in September shall be for makeing of lawes, and any other publike occation, wch conserns the good of the Com̄onwelth.

6. It is Ordered, sentenced and decreed, that the Gou^rnor shall, ether by himselfe or by the secretary, send out sum̄ons to the Constables of eu^r Towne for the cauleing of these two standing Courts, on month at lest before their seu^rall tymes: And also if the Gou^rnor and the gretest p^rte of the Magestrats see cause vppon any spetiall occation to call a generall Courte, they may giue order to the secretary soe to doe w^thin fowerteene dayes warneing: and if vrgent necessity so require, vppon a shorter notice, giueing sufficient grownds for yt to the deputyes when they meete, or els be questioned for the same; And if the Gou^rnor and Mayor p^rte of Magestrats shall ether neglect or refuse to call the two Generall standing Courts or ether of th̄e, as also at other tymes when the occasions of the Com̄onwelth require, the Freemen thereof, or the Mayor p^rte of them, shall petition to them soe to doe: if then yt be ether denyed or neglected the said Freemen or the Mayor p^rte of them shall haue power to giue order to the Constables of the seuerall Townes to doe the same, and so may meete togather, and chuse to themselues a Moderator, and may p^rceed to do any Acte of power, wch any other Generall Courte may.

7. It is Ordered, sentenced and decreed that after there are warrants giuen out for any of the said Generall Courts, the Constable or Constables of ech Towne shall forthw^th give notice distinctly to the inhabitants of the same, in some Publike Assembly or by goeing or sending frō howse to howse, that at a place and tyme by him or them lymited and sett, they meet and assemble th̄e selues togather to elect and chuse certen deputyes to be att the Generall Courte then following to agitate

2 E

the afayres of the comonwelth; wch said Deputyes shall be chosen by all that are admitted Inhabitants in the seu^rall Townes and haue taken the oath of fidellity; p^ruided that non be chosen a Deputy for any Generall Courte wch is not a Freeman of this Comonwelth.

The foresaid deputyes shall be chosen in manner following: euery p^rson that is p^rsent and quallified as before exp^rssed, shall bring the names of such, written in seu^rall papers, as they desire to haue chosen for that Imployment, and these 3 or 4, more or lesse, being the nūber agreed on to be chosen for that tyme, that haue greatest nūber of papers written for thē shall be deputyes for that Courte; whose names shall be endorsed on the backe side of the warrant and returned into the Courte, wth the Constable or Constables hand vnto the same.

8. It is Ordered, sentenced and decreed, that Wyndsor, Hartford and Wethersfield shall haue power, ech Towne, to send fower of their freemen as deputyes to euery Generall Courte; and whatsoeuer other Townes shall be hereafter added to this Jurisdiction, they shall send so many deputyes as the Courte shall judge meete, a resonable p^rportion to the nūber of Freemen that are in the said Townes being to be attended therein; wch deputyes shall have the power of the whole Towne to giue their voats and alowance to all such lawes and orders as may be for the publike good, and unto wch the said Townes are to be bownd.

9. It is ordered and decreed, that the deputyes thus chosen shall haue power and liberty to appoynt a tyme and a place of meeting togather before any Generall Courte to aduise and consult of all such things as may concerne the good of the publike, as also to examine their owne Elections, whether according to the order, and if they or the gretest p^rte of them find any election to be illegall they may seclud such for p^rsent frō their meeting, and returne the same and their resons to the Courte; and if yt proue true, the Courte may fyne the p^rty or p^rtyes so intruding and the Towne, if they see cause, and giue out a warrant to goe to a newe election in a legall way, ether in p^rte or in whole. Also the said deputyes shall haue power to fyne any that shall be disorderly at their meetings, or for not coming in due tyme or place according to appoyntment; and they may returne the said fynes into the Court if yt be refused to be paid, and the Tresurer to take notice of yt, and to estreete or levy the same as he doth other fynes.

10. It is Ordered, sentenced and decreed, that euery Generall Courte, except such as through neglecte of the Gou^rnor and the greatest p^rte of

Magestrats the Freemen themselves doe call, shall consist of the Gouernor, or some one chosen to moderate the Court, and 4 other Magestrats at lest, wth the mayor p^rte of the deputyes of the seuerall Townes legally chosen ; and in case the Freemen or mayor p^rte of the, through neglect or refusall of the Gouernor and mayor p^rte of the magestrats, shall call a Courte, y^t shall consist of the mayor p^rte of Freemen that are p^rsent or their deputyes, wth a Moderator chosen by the : In wch said Generall Courts shall consist the supreme power of the Comonwelth, and they only shall haue power to make lawes or repeale the, to graunt leuyes, to admitt of Freemen, dispose of lands vndisposed of, to seuerall Townes or p^rsons, and also shall haue power to call ether Courte or Magestrate or any other p^rson whatsoeuer into question for any misdemeanour, and may for just causes displace or deale otherwise according to the nature of the offence ; and also may deale in any other matter that concerns the good of this comon welth, excepte election of Magestrats, wch shall be done by the whole boddy of Freemen.

In wch Courte the Gouernour or Moderator shall haue power to order the Courte to giue liberty of spech, and silence vnceasonable and disorderly speakeings, to put all things to voate, and in case the voate be equall to haue the casting voice. But non of these Courts shall be adiorned or dissolued w^thout the consent of the maior p^rte of the Court.

11. It is ordered, sentenced and decreed, that when any Generall Courte vppon the occations of the Comonwelth haue agreed vppon any sume or somes of mony to be leuyed vppon the seuerall Townes w^thin this Jurisdiction, that a Comittee be chosen to sett out and appoynt w^t shall be the p^rportion of euery Towne to pay of the said leuy, p^rvided the Comittees be made vp of an equall nuber out of each Towne.

14th January, 1638 [1638/9], the 11 Orders abouesaid are voted.

J. Hammond Trumbull, compiler, *The Public Records of the Colony of Connecticut, 1636-1665* (Hartford, 1850), 20-25.

121. Remonstrance against Consolidation (1663)

BY THE GENERAL COURT OF NEW HAVEN

The Connecticut agents in 1662 received a charter including the colony of New Haven under their boundaries ; it was carried out, notwithstanding this protest. — Bibliography : Winsor, *Narrative and Critical History*, III, 373 ; Channing and Hart, *Guide*, § 122.

GENTLEMEN,

THE professed grounds and ends of your and our coming into these parts are not unknown, being plainly expressed in the prologue to that solemn confederation entered into by the four colonies of New-England, printed and published to the world, viz. to advance the kingdom of our LORD JESUS CHRIST, and to enjoy the liberties of the gospel in purity with peace, for which we left our dear native country, and were willing to undergo the difficulties we have since met with, in this wilderness, yet fresh in our remembrance ; being the only ends we still pursue, having hitherto found by experience so much of the presence of God with us, and of his goodness and compassion towards us in so doing, for these many years. . . . And whereas, in the pursuance of the said ends, and upon other religious and civil considerations, as the security of the interest of each colony, within itself in ways of righteousness and peace, and . . . from the Indians and other enemies, they did judge it to be their bounden duty, for mutual strength and helpfulness, for the future, in all their said concernments to enter into a consociation among themselves, thereupon fully agreed and concluded by and between the parties or jurisdictions, in divers and sundry articles, and at last ratified as a perpetual confederation by their several subscriptions : Whereunto we conceived ourselves bound to adhere, until with satisfaction to our judgments and consciences, we see our duty, with the unanimous consent of the confederates, orderly to recede, leaving the issue unto the most wise and righteous God. As for the patent, upon your petition, granted to you by his majesty, as Connecticut colony, so far, and in that sense we object not against it, much less against his majesty's act in so doing, the same being a real encouragement to other of his subjects to obtain the like favor, upon their humble petition to his royal highness, in the protection of their persons and purchased rights and interests, is also a ground of hope to us. But if the line of your patent doth circumscribe this colony by your contrivement, without our cognizance, or consent, or regard to the said confed-

eration on your parts, we have, and must still testify against it, as not
consistent (in our judgment) with brotherly love, righteousness and
peace : And that this colony (for so long time a confederate jurisdiction,
distinct from yours and the other colonies) is taken in under the administration of the said patent, in your hands, and so its former being
dissolved, and distinction ceasing, there being no one line or letter in
the patent, expressing his majesty's pleasure that way. Although it is
your sense of it, yet we cannot so apprehend ; of which we having
already given our grounds at large in writing, we shall not need to say
much more ; nor have we met with any argumentative or rational convictions from you, nor do we yet see cause to be of another mind.

As for your proceedings upon pretence of the patent towards us, or
rather against us, in taking in sundry of the inhabitants of this colony
under your protection and government, who, as you say, offered themselves, from which a good conscience, and the obligation under which
most of them stood to this colony, should have restrained them, without the consent of the body of this colony first had, and in concurrence
with them, upon mature deliberation and conviction of duty yet wanting, we cannot but again testify against as disorderly in them, and which
admission, on your parts, we conceive, your christian prudence might
have easily suspended, for prevention of that great offence to the consciences of your confederate brethren, and those sad consequences
which have followed, disturbing the peace of our towns, destroying our
comforts, hazard of our lives and liberties, by their frequent threats and
unsufferable provocations, hath been, and is, with us, matter of complaint, both to God and man ; especially when we consider, that thus
you admitted them and put power into their hands, before you had
made any overture to us, or had any treaty with us, about so weighty
a business, as if you were in haste to make us miserable, as indeed, in
these things, we are at this day.

And seeing upon the answer returned to your propositions made by
you afterwards, of joining with you in your government, finding ourselves already so dismembered, and the weighty grounds and reasons
we then presented to you, we could not prevail so far with you, as to
procure a respite of your further proceedings, until Mr. Winthrop's
return from England, . . . we saw it then high time and necessary
(fearing these beginnings) to appeal unto his majesty, and so we did,
concluding according to the law of appeals, in all cases and among all
nations, that the same, upon your allegiance to his majesty, would have

obliged you to forbear all further process in this business; for our own parts resolving (notwithstanding all that we had formerly suffered) to sit down patient under the same, waiting upon God for the issue of our said appeal. But seeing that, notwithstanding all that we had presented to you by word and writing — notwithstanding our appeal to his majesty — notwithstanding all that we have suffered, (by means of that power you have set up, viz. a constable at Stamford,) of which informations have been given you, yet you have gone further, to place a constable at Guilford, in like manner, over a party there, to the further disturbance of our peace and quiet, a narrative whereof, and of the provocations and wrongs we have met with at Stamford, we have received, attested to us by divers witnesses, honest men. We cannot but, on behalf of our appeal to his majesty, whose honour is highly concerned therein, and of our just rights, but (as men exceedingly afflicted and grieved) testify in the sight of God, angels, and men, against these things. Our end therein being not to provoke or further any offence, but rather as a discharge of duty, on our parts, as brethren and christian confederates, to call upon you, to take some effectual course to ease and right us, in a due redress of the grievances you have caused by these proceedings; and that after you had complimented us with large offers of patent privileges, with desire of a treaty with us for union of our colonies; and you know, as your good words were kindly accepted, so your motion was fairly answered by our committee. That in regard we were under an appeal to his majesty, that being limited by our freemen, not to conclude any thing for altering our distinct colony state and government, without their consent, and without the approbation of the other confederate colonies, they were not in present capacity so to treat; but did little suspect such a design on foot against us, the effect whereof quickly appeared at Guilford, before mentioned.

But we shall say no more at this time, only tell you, whatever we suffer by your means, we pray the Lord would help us to choose it, rather than to sin against our consciences, hoping the righteous God will, in due time, look upon our affliction, and incline his majesty's heart to favour our righteous cause.

Subscribed in the name, and by order of
the general court of New-Haven colony.
Per JAMES BISHOP, Secretary.

Benjamin Trumbull, *A Complete History of Connecticut* (New Haven, 1818), I, Appendix, 517–520 *passim*.

122. The Struggle with Andros (1689)

BY "THE GOVERNOR AND COMPANY" OF CONNECTICUT

This spirited account is really a brief history of the colony from 1662 to 1689. — Bibliography: J. G. Palfrey, *New England*, III, 537–545, 596; Winsor, *Narrative and Critical History*, III, 362; Channing and Hart, *Guide*, § 128.

TO the King's most excellent Majesty:
    The Humble Addresse of your Majestie's dutifull & loyall subjects, yᵉ Governʳ and Company of your Majestie's Colony of Conecticot in New England.

Great Sʳ.   Great was that day when yᵉ Lord who sitteth upon yᵉ floods and sitteth King forever did divide his and your adversaries from one another like yᵉ waters of Jordan forced to stand upon an heap, and did begin to magnifie you like Joshua in yᵉ sight of all Israel, by those great actions that were so much for yᵉ honour of God and yᵉ great deliverance of yᵉ English dominions from popery and slavery, and all this separated from those sorrowes that usually attend yᵉ introducing of a peaceable settlement in any troubled state; all which doth affect vs with a sense of our duty to return yᵉ highest praises unto yᵉ King of Kings and Lord of Hosts, and blesse Him who hath delighted in you to set you on yᵉ throne of His Israell, and to say, Because yᵉ Lord loved Israell forever therefore hath he made you King, to do Justice and Judgement; and also humble and hearty acknowledgements for that great zeal that by your Majesty hath been expressed, in those hazards you have put your Royall Person to, and in yᵉ expense of so great treasure in yᵉ defense of yᵉ Protestant interest: In yᵉ consideration of all which, we your Majestie's dutifull and loyall subjects of your sᵈ Colony, are incouraged humbly to intimate that we with much favour obtained a Charter of King Charles yᵉ 2d of happy memory, bearing date Aprill 23, 1662, in yᵉ 14th year of his reign, granted to the Governʳ and Company of his Majestie's Colony of Conecticot, yᵉ advantages and priveledges whereof made us indeed a very happy people; and by yᵉ blessing of God upon our endeavours we have made a considerable improvement of your dominions here, which with yᵉ defense of ourselves from yᵉ force of both forraign & intestine enemies has cost vs much expence of treasure & blood; yet in yᵉ 2d year of yᵉ reign of his Late Majesty King James yᵉ 2d we had a Quo Warranto served upon us by Edw: Randolph, requiring our appearance before his Majesties Courts in England; and

althô yᵉ time of our appearance was elapsed before yᵉ serving yᵉ sᵈ Quo
Warranto, yet we humbly petitioned his Majesty for his favour and
yᵉ continuance of our charter with yᵉ priveledges thereof; but we
received no other favour but a 2d Quo Warranto ; and we well observing that yᵉ charter of London and other considerable cities in England
were condemned, and that yᵉ charter of yᵉ Massachusets had vndergon
yᵉ like fate, plainly saw what we might expect : yet we not judging it
good or lawfull to be active in surrendering what had cost us so dear,
nor to be altogether silent, we improved an attourney to appear on our
behalf and to present our humble Addresse to his Majesty to entreat his
fauour. But quickly upon it (as Sʳ Edmond Andros informed us) he
was impowered by his Majesty to receive yᵉ surrender of our charter,
if we saw meet so to do, and also to take us under his government.
Also Col : Tho : Dongan, his Majesties governʳ of New Yorke, laboured
to gain us over to his government. We withstood all these motions and
in our reiterated Adresses we petitioned his Majesty to continue vs in
yᵉ full and free enjoyment of our liberties and properties, civill and
sacred according to our charter : we also petitioned that if his Majesty
should not see meet to continue vs as we were but was resolved to
annex vs to some other governmᵗ, we then desired that (inasmuch as
Boston had been our old correspondents and a people whose principles
and manners we had been acquainted with), we might be annexed
rather to Sʳ Edmund Androsse his government then to Col. Dongan's ;
which choice of ours was taken for a resignation of our Government,
tho that was never intended by us for such, nor had it yᵉ formalityes in
law to make it a resignation as we humbly conceive. Yet Sʳ Edm :
Andros was commissionated by his Majesty to take us vnder his government. Pursuant to which, about yᵉ end of October, 1687, he with a
company of Gentlemen and Granadeers to yᵉ number of sixty or upwards
came to Hartford (yᵉ chief seat of this Government) caused his commission to be read and declared our government to be dissolved, and
put into comῖission both civill and military officers thro out our Colony
as he pleased when he passed thrô yᵉ principall parts thereof. Yᵉ good
people of yᵉ colony, tho they were vnder a great sense of yᵉ injuries
they sustained hereby, yet chose rather to be silent and patient then
to oppose, being indeed surprised into an involuntary submission to an
arbitrary power ; but when yᵉ government we were thus put vnder seemed
to us to be determined, and we being in dayly hazard of those many
inconveniences that will arise from a people in want of government,

being also in continuall danger of our lives by reason of yᵉ natives being
at war with us, with whom we had just fears of our neighbouring French
to joyn, not receiving any orders or directions what methods to take for
our security, we were necessitated to put ourselves into some form of
government; and there being none so familiar to us as that of our
charter, nor what we could make so effectuall for yᵉ gaining yᵉ vniversall
complyance of yᵉ people, and having never received any intimation of
an enrollment of that which was interpreted a resignation of our charter,
we have presumed by yᵉ consent of yᵉ major part of yᵉ freemen assembled
for that end, May 9th, 1689, to resume our government according to
yᵉ rules of our charter, and this to continue till farther order.   Yet as
we have thus presumed to dispose ourselves not waiting orders from
your Majesty, we humbly submit ourselves herein, intreating your Majesties most gracious pardon, and that what our urgent necessityes have
put vs vpon may no wayes interrupt your Majesties grace and favour
towards us your most humble and dutifull subjects, but that in your
clemency you would be pleased to grant us such directions as to your
princely wisdome may seam meet, with such ratifications and confirma-
tions of our charter, in yᵉ full and free enjoymᵗ of all our properties,
priveledges and liberties both civill and sacred as therein granted to us
by your Royall predecessor, King Charles yᵉ 2ᵈ, which may yet farther
ensure it an inheritance to us and our posterities after vs, with what
farther grace and favour your Royall and enlarged heart may be moved
to confer upon us, which we trust we shall not forget nor be unprofitable
under, but as we have this day, with yᵉ greatest expressions of joy, proclaimed your Majesty and Royall Consort, King and Queen of England,
France and Ireland, with yᵉ dominions thereto belonging, so we shall
ever pray that God would grant your Majesties long to live and pros-
perously to reigne over all your dominions, and that great and happy
worke you have begun may be prospered here and graciously rewarded
with a crowne of glory hereafter.

                                                ROBᵗ TREAT, Govʳ.
p order of the Generall Court of Conecticut, signed,
⊤
                                                JOHN ALLYN, Secʳy.

J. Hammond Trumbull, compiler, *The Public Records of the Colony of Connecticut, 1678–1689* (Hartford, 1859), Appendix, 463–466.

CHAPTER XIX — NEW HAMPSHIRE AND MAINE

123. The Indian Grant (1638)

BY SAGAMORE WEHANOWNOWITT AND OTHERS

This document is typical of Indian cessions made in all the colonies. An earlier grant of New Hampshire, dated 1636, is now known to have been a forgery. — Bibliography: Winsor, *Narrative and Critical History*, III, 366; Channing and Hart, *Guide*, § 123.

KNOW all men by these presents that I Wehanownowit Sagamore of piskatoquacke for good considerations me therevnto mouing and for certen commoditys which I have received have graunted and sould unto John Whelewright of piscatoquake, Samuel Hutchinson and Augustus Stor of Boston Edward Calcord and Darby Field of piscatoquake and John Compton of Roxbury, and Nicholas Needome of Mount Walliston, all the right title and interest in all such lands, woods, meadows, rivers, brookes, springs, as of right belongs unto me from Merimack river to the patents of piscatoquake bounded with the South East side of piscatoquake patents and so to goe into the Country north-West thirty miles as far as the easte line, to have and to hold the same to them and their heires for ever. onely the ground wch is broken up is excepted. and that it shall be lawfull for the said Sagamore to hunt and fish and foul in the said limits. In Witness whereof I have hereunto set my hand the 3d day of April. 1638

Signed and possession given
These being present

James Cornall
James ¶ his mrke
His — *W C* — mrke
William Cole
His   mrke
Lawrence Cowpland

WEHANOWNOWITT   his mrke

Know all men by these presents yt. I Wehanownowitt Sagamore of Pusscataquke for a certaine some of money to mee in hand payd and other Mercantable comodities which I have recd as likewise for other good causes and considerations mee yr into specially mouing haue graunted bargained alienated and sould unto John Wheelewright of Piscataqua and Augustine Storr of Bostone all those Lands woods Medowes Marshes rivers brooks springs with all the appurtenantes emoluments pfitts comodyts there unto belonging lying and situate within three miles on the Northerne side of ye. river Meremake extending thirty miles along by the river from the sea side and from the sayd river side to Pisscataqua Patents thirty miles up into the countrey North West, and soe from the ffalls of Piscataqua to Oyster river thirty miles square eury way, to have and to hould the same to them and yr heyres for ever, only the ground wh is broaken up is excepted and it shall bee lawfull for ye sayd Sagamore to hunt fish and foule in the sayd lymits.   In witnesse wrof I have here unto sett my hand and seale the third day of Aprill 1638

WEHANOWNOWITT   his mrke.

TUMMADOCKYON   his mrke.
the sagamores son

Signed sealed and delivered, and possession
        given In the presence of
    Sameb ‡ his mrk
    Aspamabough ↑ his mrke.
Edward Calcord
Nicholas Needham
William Ffurbur
                          [Endorsed]
Know all men by these prsents that I Watchanowet doe fully consent to the grant within written and do yield up all my right in the said purchased lands to the prtys w'in written

In witnesse whereof I have hereunto set my hand the tenth day of April. 1639.

I doe likewise grant unto them for goode consideration all the meadows and grounds extending for the space of one English mile on the East side of oyster river.   April. 10. 1639.

    These being prsent
Jo : Underhill   his mrke.
Darby Ffield § his mrke

                                    WATCHANOWET

New-Hampshire Historical Society, *Collections* (Concord, 1824), I, 147-149.

124. Condition of the Northern Provinces (1665)

BY COMMISSIONERS MAVERICK, CARR, AND CARTWRIGHT

This report was made by the commissioners appointed to visit New England with a view to curbing the independent policy of the colonies, and it is therefore somewhat prejudiced. — Bibliography : J. A. Doyle, *English in America, Puritan Colonies*, II, ch. ii ; Channing and Hart, *Guide*, § 127.

NEW HAMPSHIRE is the name of a Province granted to Capt Robert Mason about the yeare 1635 and was to begin on the Sea Coast 3 Miles easterly of Merimack River and reaches to Piscatoquay, and 60 miles of that Breath up into the Country, but now it us usurped by the Mattachusets who pretend that it is within their Bounds, and that the People Petitioned to be within their Protection, it is true that difference of Opinion made a Division amongst them, and a few who were for Congregationall Churches did Petition for their Assistance by which occasion partly by force, partly by Composition they haue engrossed the whole and named it Norfolke /

When the Mattachusets Charter was first granted the Mouths only of the two Rivers Charles and Merimack were knowne to them, for they durst not travaile farre up into the Country, presently after there was an house erected 3 large Miles north from Merimack which was for 17 yeares called and knowne to be the bounds of the Matachusetts, and in that time was this Pattent graunted to Capt Mason /

Mr Wheelewright was banished out of the Jurisdictiõ of the Mattachusetts and was permitted to inhabite immediatly beyond that bound house, as himselfe gaue Testimony before the Commissioners.

Mr Mason had a Pattent for some Land about Cape Anne before the Mattachusetts had their first Pattent, whereupon Capt Mason and Mr Cradock, who was the first Governour of the Mattachusetts, and lived in London agreed that the Matachusetts should haue that Land which was graunted to Capt Mason about Cape Anne, and Capt Mason should haue that Land which was beyond Merimack River and graunted to the Matachusets / This agreement was sent to Mr Henry Jocelin to get recorded at Boston, but before he could haue leisure to goe thither he heard that Capt Mason was dead, and therefore went not, of this he made Affidavit before the Commissrs who forbore to doe any thing about the Limitts of this Province till this might more fully be proved, though the Generality of the People Petitioned to be taken from under the Matachusets Tyranny, as themselues styled it /

The Matachusetts since they had, the Governement of this Province, haue graunted and divided the Land into severall Tounshipps, which are very large and thinn, three of which are seated upon Piscatoway River, which is a very good Harbour, and very capable of Fortification, here are excellent Masts gotten, and here dry Docks might be made, and upon this River are aboue 20 Saw Mills, and here great Store of Pipe Staues are made, and great store of good timber Spoyled. /

MAINE /

The Province of Mayn begins at the Easterne side of Piscatoway and reacheth to Kenebec River it was so named and granted to Sr Ferdinando Gorges by King Charles the first, but was usurped also by the Matta-chusets under Pretence that it was within the Limitts of their Charter, and that the People Petitioned to be under their Governement and they named it Yorkshire, One Gentleman who refused to submitt to the Matta-chusetts, and suffered great Losses by them, shewed the Commissioners a Warr^t which the Mattachusets made to haue him brought to Bostom aliue or dead, and now demands justice against them. This Province upon Petition of the Inhabitants and the differences betwixt Mr Gorges Commissioners and the Mattachusetts, his Maties Commissioners tooke into his Maties Protection and Governement, and appointed Justices of the Peace to governe them, untill his Maties pleasure be further knowne /

The Inhabitants afterwards Petitioned his Majesty that they might alwaies continue under his Maties immediate Governement, and that Sr Robert Carre might continue there their Governour under his Matie which Petition was lost at Sea /

In this Province also an Indian Sachim who liues neare to the great Lake from whence flowes Merimack River Petitioned his Matie to take him under his Protection which is also lost /

In this Province there are but few Tounes, and those much scattered as generally they are all throughout New England, They are rather farmes than Townes but in this Province there is a Bay called Casko Bay in which are very many Islands, 2 Out lets to the Sea, many good Har-bours, and great store of fish and Oysters, Crabs and Lobsters, In this Province as in all the rest there are great store of wild Ducks Geese and Deere in their Seasons, Strawberries Resburies Goosberries, Barberies, and severall sorts of Bilberries, Severall sorts of Oakes and Pines, Chestnut Trees, and Walnut Trees, sometimes for 4 or 5 Miles togeather, the more Northerly the Country is, the better the Timber is accounted /

KENEBECK /

On the North East side of Kenebeck River, which is the bounds of the Province of Mayne, upon Shipscot River, and upon Pemaquid 8 or 10 miles Asunder are 3 small Plantations belonging to his Royall highnesse the biggest of which hath not aboue 30 houses in it, and those very meane ones too. and spread over 8 Miles of ground at least. The People for the most part are fishermen, and never had any Governement amongst them, and most of them are such as haue fled thither from other places to avoyd Justice, Some here are of Opinion, that as many Men may share in a Woman, as they doe in a Boate, and some haue done so, The Commiss^{rs} for necessity sake haue appointed the best whome they could find in each place to be a Justice of the Peace, and haue ordered three of those Justices of the Peace in the Province of Mayne, who liue next to them to joyne with them in holding of Sessions till further order be taken /

In these parts are the best white Oakes for shipp timber all the Lands graunted to his Royall High^{s} in these Northerne parts of New England except these 3 Plantations are also graunted to Sr Thomas Temple in the Pattent of Nova Scotia / . . .

Documentary History of the State of Maine (Maine Historical Society, *Collections*, Portland, 1889), IV, 296–299.

---

125. "The People in the Province of Main" (1675)

BY JOHN JOSSELYN

Josselyn was an Englishman of good family, fond of natural history and of outdoor life, but rather malicious in his comments on the people. For early settlements in Maine, see No. 37 above. — Bibliography: Winsor, *Narrative and Critical History*, III, 360–366; Channing and Hart, *Guide*, § 123.

. . . THE Province of *Main*, (or the Countrey of the *Troquoes*) heretofore called *Laconia* or *New-Summersetshire*, is a Colony belonging to the Grandson of Sir *Ferdinando Gorges* of *Ashton Phillips* in the County of *Sommerset*, the said Sir *Ferdinando Gorges* did expend in planting several parts of *New-England* above Twenty thousand pounds *sterling;* and when he was between three and four score years of age did personally engage in our Royal Martyrs service ; and particularly in the Seige of *Bristow*, and was plundered and imprisoned several times, by reason whereof he was discountenanced by the pretended Commissioners for forraign plantations, and his Province incroached upon by the *Massachusets* Colony, who assumed the Government thereof. His Majestie that now Reigneth sent over his Commissioners to reduce them within their bounds, and to put Mr. *Gorges* again into possession. But there falling out a contest about it, the Commissioners settled it in the Kings name (until the business should be determined before his Majestie) and gave Commissions to the Judge of their Courts, and the Justices to Govern and Act according to the Laws of *England*, & by such Laws of their own as were not repugnant to them : But as soon as the Commissioners were returned for *England*, the *Massachusets* enter the province in a hostile manner with a Troop of Horse and Foot and turn'd the Judge and his Assistants off the Bench, Imprisoned the Major or Commander of the Militia, threatned the Judge, and some others that were faithful to Mr. *Gorges* interests. I could discover many other foul proceedings, but for some reasons which might be given, I conceive it not convenient to make report thereof to vulgar ears ; & *quae supra nos nihil ad nos.* Onely this I could wish, that there might be some consideration of the great losses, charge and labour, which hath been sustained by the Judge, and some others for above thirty years in upholding the rights of Mr. *Gorge* and his Sacred Majesties Dominion against a many stubborn and elusive people.

Anno Dom. 1623. Mr. *Robert Gorge*, Sir *Ferdinando Gorges* brother had for his good service granted him by Patent from the Council of *Plimouth* all that part of the Land commonly called *Massachusiack*, situated on the North-side of the Bay of *Massachusets*.

Not long after this Sir *Ferdinando Gorges* had granted to him by Patent from the middest of *Merrimack*-River to the great River *Sagadehock*, then called *Laconia*.

In 1635. Capt. *William Gorge*, Sir *Ferdinando's* Nephew, was sent over Governour of the Province of *Main*, then called *New-Summersetshire*.

Sir *Ferdinando Gorge* received a Charter-Royal from King *Charles* the first the third of *April* in the Fifttenth of his Raign, granting to him all that part and portion of *New-England*, lying and being between the River of *Pascataway*, that is, beginning at the entrance of *Pascatawayharbour*, and so to pass up the same into the River of *Newichawanoe* or

Neqhechewanck, and through the same unto the farthest head thereof aforesaid, North-eastward along the Sea-coasts, for Sixty miles to *Saga-dehoc-*River to *Kenebeck,* even as far as the head thereof, and up into the main land North-westward for the space of one hundred and twenty miles. . . .

Towns there are not many in this province. *Kittery* situated not far from *Pascataway* is the most populous.

Next to that Eastward is seated by a River near the Sea *Gorgiana,* a Majoraltie, and the Metropolitan of the province.

Further to the Eastward is the Town of *Wells.*

Cape-Porpus Eastward of that, where there is a Town by the Sea side of the same name, the houses scatteringly built, all these Towns have store of salt and fresh marsh with arable land, and are well stockt with Cattle.

About eight or nine mile to the East-ward of *Cape-Porpus,* is *Winter harbour,* a noted place for Fishers, here they have many stages.

Saco adjoyns to this, and both make one scattering Town of large extent, well stored with Cattle, arable land and marshes, and a Saw-mill.

Six mile to the Eastward of *Saco* & forty mile from *Gorgiana* is seated the Town of *Black point,* consisting of about fifty dwelling houses, and a Magazine or *Doganne,* scatteringly built, they have store of neat and horses, of sheep near upon Seven or Eight hundred, much arable and marsh salt and fresh, and a Corn-mill. . . .

The mountains and hills that are to be taken notice of, are first *Acomenticus* hills, between *Kettery* and *Gorgiana,* the high hills of *Ossapey* to the West-ward of *Saco* River, where the princely *Pilhanaw* Ayries, the white mountains, to the North-ward of *Black-point,* the highest *Terrasse* in *New-England,* you have the description of it in my Treatise of the rarities of *New-England.* . . .

The people in the province of *Main* may be divided into Magistrates, Husbandmen, or Planters, and fishermen ; of the Magistrates some be Royalists, the rest perverse Spirits, the like are the planters and fishers, of which some be planters and fishers both, others meer fishers.

Handicrafts-men there are but few, the Tumelor or Cooper, Smiths and Carpenters are best welcome amongst them, shop-keepers there are none, being supplied by the *Massachusets* Merchants with all things they stand in need of, keeping here and there fair Magazines stored with *English* goods, but they set excessive prices on them, if they do not gain *Cent per Cent*, they cry out that they are losers, hence *English* shooes are sold for Eight and Nine shillings a pair, worsted stockins of Three shillings six pence a pair, for Seven and Eight shillings a pair, Douglass that is sold in *England* for one or two and twenty pence an ell, for four shillings a yard, Serges of two shillings or three shillings a yard, for Six and Seven shillings a yard, and so all sorts of Commodities both for planters and fishermen, as Cables, Cordage, Anchors, Lines, Hooks, Nets, Canvas for Sails, &c. Bisket twenty five shillings a hundred, Salt at an excessive rate, pickled-herrin for winter bait Four and five pound a barrel. . . .

The planters are or should be restless pains takers, providing for their Cattle, planting and sowing of Corn, fencing their grounds, cutting and bringing home fuel, cleaving of claw-board and pipe-staves, fishing for fresh water fish and fowling takes up most of their time, if not all ; the diligent hand maketh rich, but if they be of a droanish disposition as some are, they become wretchedly poor and miserable, scarce able to free themselves and family from importunate famine, especially in the winter for want of bread.

They have a custom of taking Tobacco, sleeping at noon, sitting long at meals sometimes four times in a day, and now and then drinking a dram of the bottle extraodinarily : the smoaking of Tobacco, if moderately used refresheth the weary much, and so doth sleep. . . .

Their Servants which are for the most part *English*, when they are out of their time, will not work under half a Crown a day, although it be for to make hay, and for less I do not see how they can, by reason of the dearness of clothing. If they hire them by the year, they pay them Fourteen or Fifteen pound, yea Twenty pound at the years end in Corn, Cattle and fish. . . .

The fishermen take yearly upon the coasts many hundred kentals of Cod, hake, haddock, polluck, &c. which they split, salt and dry at their stages, making three voyages in a year. When they share their fish (which is at the end of every voyage) they separate the best from the worst, the first they call Merchantable fish, being sound, full grown fish and well made up, which is known when it is clear like a Lanthorn horn and without spots ; the second sort they call refuse fish, that is such as is salt burnt, spotted, rotten, and carelesly ordered : these they put off to the *Massachusets* Merchants. . . .

To every Shallop belong four fishermen, a Master or Steersman, a Midship-man, and a Foremast-man, and a shore man who washes it out of

2 F

the salt, and dries it upon hurdles pitcht upon stakes breast high and
tends their Cookery; these often get in one voyage Eight or Nine pound
a man for their shares, but it doth some of them little good, for the
Merchant to increase his gains by putting off his Commodity in the
midst of their voyages, and at the end thereof comes in with a walking
Tavern, a Bark laden with the Legitimate bloud of the rich grape, which
they bring from *Phial, Madera, Canaries*, with *Brandy, Rhum*, the *Barbadoes strong-water*, and *Tobacco*, coming ashore he gives them a
Taster or two, which so charms them, that for no perswasions that their
imployers can use will they go out to Sea, although fair and seasonable
weather, for two or three days, nay sometimes a whole week till
they are wearied with drinking, taking ashore two or three Hogsheads
of *Wine* and *Rhum* to drink off when the Merchant is gone. If a man
of quality chance to come where they are roystering and gulling in
Wine with a dear felicity, he must be sociable and *Roly-poly* with
them, taking off their liberal cups as freely, or else be gone, which is
best for him. . . . When the day of payment comes, they may justly
complain of their costly sin of drunkenness, for their shares will do
no more than pay the reckoning; if they save a Kental or two to buy
shooes and stockins, shirts and wastcoats with, 'tis well, otherwayes
they must enter into the Merchants books for such things as they
stand in need off, becoming thereby the Merchants slaves, & when
it riseth to a big sum are constrained to mortgage their plantation
if they have any, the Merchant when the time is expired is sure to
seize upon their plantation and stock of Cattle, turning them out of
house and home, poor Creatures, to look out for a new habitation in
some remote place where they begin the world again. The lavish
planters have the same fate, partaking with them in the like bad husbandry, of these the Merchant buys Beef, Pork, Pease, Wheat and *Indian*
Corn, and sells it again many times to the fishermen. Of the same nature
are the people in the Dukes province, who not long before I left the
Countrey petitioned the Governour and Magistrates in the *Massachusets*
to take them into their Government, Birds of a feather will ralley
together. . . .

John Josselyn, *An Account of Two Voyages to New-England* (London, 1675),
197–213 *passim*.

126. Request to be Joined to Massachusetts (1690)

BY NATHANIEL WEARE

Weare had at one time been agent for New Hampshire in England. — Bibliography: Jeremy Belknap, *New Hampshire*, I, 191, 194; Winsor, *Narrative and Critical History*, III, 367; Channing and Hart, *Guide*, § 123.

. . . THE many revolutions and chainges that *has* happened abroad *is* very wonderfull and almost amazinge : Besides, what has hapned amonge and upon ourselves is very awfull, and thinges loke very darke, the consideration thereof is so oppressive, that [I] cannot but seke for some ease, and I know no beter way (as to man) then to communicat some things to your honour, from whose prudent direction, I may receive mutch sasiffaction, and shall therefore crave the boldness to ofer a few lynes to your consideration not to medell with thynges further off.   I shall, as brief as I may, ofer you what has happned in this prouince of New-Hampshire, and more pertiquerly in the towne of Hampton.   Sir, it is no new thynge to tell you how that him that was both gouernor in your collony and also in our prouince was seazed and the occashon thereof, whereupon, wee had only the Justices and Inferiouer oficers left, the superior commanders being layd aside, that great questions arose whether Justeces retayned theire power, or any Captain, or other oficer, deringve his authorety from him so seazesed.   My opinion I shall altogether wave in that mater : But so it was that it was for the most part concluded of, that we had no gouerners nor authority in this prouince, so as to answer the ends of gouernment, and to command and doe in the defence of theire majestys subjects against the comon enemy, therefore many asayes was maid in this provance to make some gouernment till theire majestys should take further order, but all proued ineffectuall. At first there was in the seuerall Towns in the Prouince persons chosen to manage the affairs of Gouernment in this juncture of time, but that was for some reasons laid aside, afterward there was in the town of Hampton 3 persons chosen in the towne of Hampton to meet with the Comiss : [Commissioners] of the other towns, if they see cause to apoint any to debate and conclude of what was necessary at this time to be done in relation to some orderly way of Gouernment, and to make their returne to the seuerall Towns for approbation or otherwise.   But the inhabitants of Portsmouth met and made choice of some persons to meet with the Commissioners of the other Towns to Debate and con-

sider of what was to be done in order to the settlement of some Gouernment, till their Majestys should give order in the matter. What they
did, they ingaged themselves certainly to comply with. The inhabitants
of the town of Hampton, began to be very jealous of their friends and
neighbours, that they would bring them under seuerall inconveniences in
comanding from them their men, and mony as they pleased, and so
were very hard to be brought to any thing; but after seuerall meetings
and debates, did chose 6 persons as Comissioners, with power according to the other towns, (viz.) Portsmouth, Dover and Exeter, and after
debats, jointly and fully, euery man then present agreed to such a
method as was then drawne up. Then the seuerall towns was to nominate and chose meet persons for the end aforesaid; but whereas the
Inhabitance of the towne of Hampton meet on warning for that end,
the major part by far of the said towne semed to bee ferful and suspicious of theyer neighbour townes [that] they did not intend to doe as
was pretended, but to bring them under to theyer disadvantage, which I
thought was very ill so to think, yet they would give som instance of
som former acts don, which notwithstanding, I seposed they were too
uncharitable.

And so they made a voat they would not chose any person according
to the direction of the Committee meet, and so all proued inefectuall.
After some time, the apprehention of the necessity of some orderly way
of gouernment and therby to be in the beter method to defend themselves against the comon enemy, semed to inforse them to another
asay for the obtayning thereof, and so the inhabitance of Portsmouth,
drew up and signed, so many as did, a pettition, as I am informed, (for
I never saw it,) to the honorable the gouernor and councill of the
Matathusetts Collony to take this prouince into theire care and protection, and gouernment as formerly; and so the other townes, Dover and
Exeter, complyed with it, how generally I know not, and so brought to
Hampton on Wensday, the 26th of February last part [past], when the
soldiers were there warned to appeare for consernes specified in said
order, but no intemation given for the end of signinge to the petition,
so that seuerall children and servants made up the number of names,
when theyer parrants and masters, its said, did know nothinge of the
maters, and I doubt too true. It was quickly after by William Vaughan,
Esq. and Capt. John Pickeringe brought into the prouince, declareing to
bee excepted [accepted] by the said gouernor and councell, with orders
given forth to meet on such a day for chusinge of selectmen and con-

stables and other towne oficers, according to former usage and custom
as appears by order given to Justice Greene bearinge date the 4th of
March, 1689–90. Coppes I sepose your selfe have. What was done on
that day, I need not tell. Yourselfe knows very well. But this I shall
insert — that chusinge of major, treasurer, and recorder was not accordinge to former usage and custom. It was prest by some to have it
voated whether they would in this towne of Hampton acquies and comply with the pettition and the returne, or words to that efect, which
yourselfe was pleased to say all would bee knoct on the head at one
blow. Now how comfortable it will, bee for about 50 persons to prescribe the method and way of gouernment for about 200, I shall leave to
your honour to consider. For my owne part, its well knowne, I am
for gouernment, and so are severall others whose names are not to the
pettition and hath a great esteme of, and good will to, the Matathusetts
gouernment and to those worthy persons that doth administer the
same. And with very littell alteration, I doubt not but many more
would have, if they might have their hands to the pettition ; but to have
hands in the several towns to the same pettition to bee under the gouernment of the Mattathusetts collony as formerly, when we are so dif-
ferently sarcomstanced as som of us know wee have been, is hard ; to
draw such a pettition, and when such a pettition is draune, subscribed as
it is and excepted [accepted] of, for the subscribers to act contrary to
the same is very strange. Formerly, not to medell with the custom and
usage of the gentlemen of Pascataway, wee, at Hampton, had the choice
of our magistrats and publike oficers, as yourselfe knows ; And how the
assistance or magistrats at Portsmouth can grant any warrants or exersise the administration of gouernment over Hampton that never chose
them, I know not ; so that upon the whole the gouernment of the Matathusetts cannot, I suppose, exersise nor apoint any gouernors over us till
they have authority so to doe from the crowne of England, or wee, or
the major part in the seuerall towns doe pray for it, which at present is
not in Hampton as it plainly appears : So that to bee subjected to a
gouernment in the prouince and principally at Portsmouth, which have
bin so much spoken against by so meny in Hampton will be very teadious
to them : And the chusinge of milletery oficers as hath bin, to give all
due respects to thare persons, I shall not say of excedentell quallefica-
tions so well knowne to yourselfe, but only say that ffranzey leaders may
happen to have mad followers ; so that to have a gouernment so imposed, what will I feare follow but destractions, hartburnings, disobedi-

ance to the seposed comanders, publike diclerations, remonstrenses set forth that may reach as far as England, and so make way for a person to be deputed by the crowne of England, that may, under the collor of Commission, exersise his owne will, not to speak of declerations of userpations still continued in the collony.   Some have thought forthwith publekly to declare themselves to the gouevernors in said collony that all may be heald as quietly and as sillently as it may bee, and I doubt not, your wisdome will be exersised in this matter, and that wee may have peace and vnety with you, and that at lentth we may have a happy peaseable settlement: And that the God of peace would by all means geve us peace and truth, is the desier and prayer of your very humble servant,

NATH^LL. WEARE.

New-Hampshire Historical Society, *Collections* (Concord, 1824), I, 135–140.

CHAPTER XX — NEW ENGLAND'S DEVELOPMENT

127. The Pequot War (1635)

BY CAPTAIN JOHN UNDERHILL

John Underhill was the black sheep of Massachusetts, — a good soldier, but a disorderly character, as James Russell Lowell delightfully describes him in *New England Two Centuries Ago.* — Bibliography : Winsor, *Narrative and Critical History*, III, 348–349; Tyler, *American Literature*, I, 151, note ; Channing and Hart, *Guide*, § 121.

. . . THE *Pequeats* having slaine one Captaine *Norton*, and Captaine *Stone*, with seven more of their company, order was given us to visit them, sayling along the *Nahanticot* shore with five vessels, the Indians spying of us came running in multitudes along the water side, crying, what cheere Englishmen, what cheere, what doe you come for? They not thinking we intended warre went on cheerefully untill they come to Pequeat riuer. We thinking it the best way did forbeare to answer them ; first, that we might the better bee able to runne through the worke. Secondly, that by delaying of them, we might drive them in securitie, to the end wee might have the more advantage of them : but they seeing wee would make no answer, kept on their course, and cryed, what Englishman, what cheere, what cheere, are you hoggerie, will you cram us? That is, are you angry, will you kill us, and doe you come to fight. That night the *Nahanticot* Indians, and the *Pequeats*, made fire on both sides of the River, fearing we would land in the night. They made most dolefull, and wofull cryes all the night, (so that wee could scarce rest) hollowing one to another, and giving the word from place to place, to gather their forces together, fearing the English were come to warre against them.

The next morning they sent early aboard an Ambassadour, a grave Senior, a man of good understanding, portly, cariage grave, and majesticall in his expressions ; he demanded of us what the end of our comming was, to which we answered, that the Governours of the *Bay* sent us to demand the heads of those persons that had slaine Captaine *Norton*, and Captaine *Stone*, and the rest of their company, and that it was not the custome of the English to suffer murtherers to live, and therefore if they desired their owne peace and welfare, they will peaceably answer our expectation, and give us the heads of the murderers.

They being a witty and ingenious Nation, their Ambassadour laboured to excuse the matter, and answered, we know not that any of ours have slaine any English : true it is, saith he, we have slaine such a number of men, but consider the ground of it ; . . . we distinguish not betweene the *Dutch* and *English*, but tooke them to be one Nation, and therefore we doe not conceive that we wronged you, for they slew our king ; and thinking these Captaines to be of the same Nation and people, as those that slew him, made us set upon this course of revenge.

Our answer was, they were able to distinguish betweene *Dutch* and *English*, having had sufficient experience of both Nations, and therefore seeing you have slaine the king of *Englands* subjects, we come to demand an account of their blood, for we our selves are lyable to account for them. . . .

But wee seeing their drift was to get our Armes, we rather chose to beat up the Drum and bid them battell, marching into a champion field we displayed our colours, but none would come neere us, but standing remotely off did laugh at us for our patience, wee suddenly set upon our march, and gave fire to as many as we could come neere, firing their Wigwams, spoyling their corne, and many other necessaries that they had buried in the ground we raked up, which the souldiers had for bootie. Thus we spent the day burning and spoyling the Countrey, towards night imbarqued our selves the next morning, landing on the *Nahanticot* shore, where we were served in like nature, no *Indians* would come neere us, but runne from us, as the Deere from the dogges ; but having burnt and spoyled what we could light on, wee imbarqued our men, and set sayle for the *Bay*, having ended this exploit came off, having one man wounded in the legge ; but certaine numbers of theirs slaine, and many wounded ; this was the substance of the first yeares service : now followeth the service performed in the second yeare.

This insolent Nation, seeing wee had used so much Lenitie towards them, and themselves not able to make good use of our patience, set upon a course of greater insolencie then before, and slew all they found in their way : they came neere *Seabrooke* fort, and made many proud challenges, and dared them out to fight. . . .

The *Conetticot* Plantation understanding the insolencie of the enemie to bee so great, sent downe a certaine number of souldiers under the conduct of Captaine *Iohn Mason* for to strengthen the Fort. The enemy lying hovering about the Fort, continually tooke notice of the

supplies that were come, and forbore drawing neere it as before : and
Letters were immediatly sent to the *Bay*, to that Right worshipfull
Gentleman, Master *Henry Vane*, for a speedy supply to strengthen the
Fort. For assuredly without supply suddenly came in reason all would
be lost, and fall into the hands of the enemy ; This was the trouble and
perplexity that lay upon the spirits of the poore garrisons. Upon serious
consideration the Governour and Councell sent forth my selfe with 20.
armed souldiers to supply the necessitie of those distressed persons, and
to take the government of that place for the space of three moneths :
reliefe being come, Captaine *Iohn Mason* with the rest of his company
returned to the Plantation againe : we sometimes fell out with a matter of twentie souldiers to see whether we could discover the enemy or
no ; they seeing us (lying in ambush) gave us leave to passe by them,
considering we were too hot for them to meddle with us ; our men
being compleatly armed, with Corslets, Muskets, bandileeres, rests, and
swords (as they themselves related afterward), did much daunt them ;
thus we spent a matter of six weeks before we could have any thing to
doe with them, perswading our selves that all things had beene well.
But they seeing there was no advantage more to be had against the Fort,
they enterprized a new action, and fell upon *Water towne*, now called
Wethersfield with two hundred *Indians* ; before they came to attempt
the place, they put into a certaine River, an obscure small river running
into the maine, where they incamped, and refreshed themselves, and
fitted themselves for their service, and by breake of day attempted their
enterprise, and slew nine men, women and children, having finished their
action, they suddenly returned againe, bringing with them two maids
captives, having put poles in their Conoos, as we put Masts in our boats,
and upon them hung our English mens and womens shirts and smocks,
in stead of sayles, and in way of bravado came along in sight of us as
we stood upon *Seybrooke* Fort, and seeing them passe along in such a
triumphant manner, wee much fearing they had enterprised some desperate action upon the *English*, wee gave fire with a peece of Ordnance,
and shotte among their Conooes. And though they were a mile from us,
yet the bullet grazed not above twentie yards over the Conooe, where the
poore maids were ; it was a speciall providence of God it did not hit
them, for then should we have beene deprived of the sweet observation
of Gods providence in their deliverance : we were not able to make
out after them, being destitute of meanes, Boats, and the like. . . .

I told you before, that when the *Pequeats* heard and saw *Seabrooke*

Fort was supplied, they forbore to visit us : But the old Serpent according to his first malice stirred them up against the Church of Christ, and
in such a furious manner, as our people were so farre disturbed, and
affrighted with their boldnesse that they scarce durst rest in their beds :
threatning persons and cattell to take them, as indeed they did : so insolent were these wicked imps growne, that like the divell their commander, they runne up and downe as roaring Lyons, compassing all
corners of the Countrey for a prey, seeking whom they might devoure :
It being death to them for to rest without some wicked imployment or
other, they still plotted how they might wickedly attempt some bloody
enterprise upon our poore native Countrey-men. . . .

Having imbarqued our souldiers, wee weighed ankor at *Seabrooke*
Fort, and set sayle for the *Narraganset Bay*, deluding the *Pequeats*
thereby, for they expected us to fall into *Pequeat* River; but crossing their expectation, bred in them a securitie : wee landed our men in
the *Narraganset Bay*, and marched over land above two dayes journey
before wee came to *Pequeat*; quartering the last nights march within
two miles of the place, wee set forth about one of the clocke in the
morning, having sufficient intelligence that they knew nothing of our
comming : Drawing neere to the Fort yeelded up our selves to God, and
intreated his assistance in so waightie an enterprize. We set on our
march to surround the Fort, Captaine *Iohn Mason*, approching to the
West end, where it had an entrance to passe into it, my selfe marching
to the Southside, surrounding the Fort, placing the *Indians*, for wee had
about three hundred of them without, side of our souldiers in a ring
battalia, giving a volley of shotte upon the Fort, so remarkable it
appeared to us, as wee could not but admire at the providence of God
in it, that souldiers so unexpert in the use of their armes, should give so
compleat a volley, as though the finger of God had touched both match
and flint : which volley being given at breake of day, and themselves
fast asleepe for the most part, bred in them such a terrour, that they
brake forth into a most dolefull cry, so as if God had not fitted the
hearts of men for the service, it would have bred in them a commisera-
tion towards them : but every man being bereaved of pitty fell upon
the worke without compassion, considering the bloud they had shed of
our native Countrey-men, and how barbarously they had dealt with them,
and slaine first and last about thirty persons. Having given fire, wee
approached neere to the entrance which they had stopped full, with
armes of trees, or brakes : my selfe approching to the entrance found

the worke too heavie for mee, to draw out all those which were strongly forced in. We gave order to one Master *Hedge*, and some other souldiers to pull out those brakes, having this done, and laid them betweene me and the entrance, and without order themselves, proceeded first on the South end of the Fort : but remarkable it was to many of us ; men that runne before they are sent, most commonly have an ill reward. Worthy Reader, let mee intreate you to have a more charitable opinion of me (though unworthy to be better thought of) then is reported in the other Booke : you may remember there is a passage unjustly laid upon mee, that when wee should come to the entrance, I should put forth this question : shall we enter? others should answer againe ; What came we hither for else? It is well knowne to many, it was never my practise in time of my command, when we are in garrison, much to consult with a private souldier, or to aske his advise in point of Warre, much lesse in a matter of so great a moment as that was, which experience had often taught mee, was not a time to put forth such a question, and therefore pardon him that hath given the wrong information : having our swords in our right hand, our Carbins or Muskets in our left hand, we approched the Fort. Master *Hedge* being shot thorow both armes, and more wounded ; though it bee not commendable for a man to make mention of any thing that might tend to his owne honour ; yet because I would have the providence of God observed, and his Name magnified, as well for my selfe as others, I dare not omit, but let the world know, that deliverance was given to us that command, as well as to private souldiers. Captaine *Mason* and my selfe entring into the Wigwams, hee was shot, and received many Arrowes against his head-peece, God preserved him from any wounds ; my selfe received a shotte in the left hippe, through a sufficient Buffe coate, that if I had not beene supplyed with such a garment, the Arrow would have pierced through me ; another I received betweene necke and shoulders, hanging in the linnen of my Head-peece, others of our souldiers were shot some through the shoulders, some in the face, some in the head, some in the legs : Captaine *Mason* and my selfe losing each of us a man, and had neere twentie wounded : most couragiously these *Pequeats* behaved themselves : but seeing the Fort was to hotte for us, wee devised a way how wee might save our selves and prejudice them, Captaine *Mason* entring into a Wigwam, brought out a fire-brand, after hee had wounded many in the house, then hee set fire on the West-side where he entred, my selfe set fire on the South end with a traine of Powder, the fires of both meeting in the center of the Fort blazed most terribly, and burnt all in the space of halfe an houre; many couragious fellowes were unwilling to come out, and fought most desperately through the Palisadoes, so as they were scorched and burnt with the very flame, and were deprived of their armes, in regard the fire burnt their very bowstrings, and so perished valiantly : mercy they did deserve for their valour, could we have had opportunitie to have bestowed it ; many were burnt in the Fort, both men, women, and children, others forced out, and came in troopes to the *Indians*, twentie, and thirtie at a time, which our souldiers received and entertained with the point of the sword ; downe fell men, women, and children, those that scaped us, fell into the hands of the *Indians*, that were in the reere of us ; it is reported by themselves, that there were about foure hundred soules in this Fort, and not above five of them escaped out of our hands.　Great and dolefull was the bloudy sight to the view of young souldiers that never had beene in Warre, to see so many soules lie gasping on the ground so thicke in some places, that you could hardly passe along.　It may bee demanded, why should you be so furious (as some have said) should not Christians have more mercy and compassion?　But I would referre you to *Davids* warre, when a people is growne to such a height of bloud, and sinne against God and man, and all confederates in the action, there hee hath no respect to persons, but harrowes them, and sawes them, and puts them to the sword, and the most terriblest death that may bee : sometimes the Scripture declareth women and children must perish with their parents ; some time the case alters : but we will not dispute it now.　We had sufficient light from the word of God for our proceedings. . . .

Captaine Iohn Underhill, *Newes from America* (London, 1638), 9–40 *passim*.

---

128. Reasons for the Surrender of the New England Charter (1635)

BY THE COUNCIL FOR NEW ENGLAND

For the foundation of this Council, see No. 51 above.　Bibliography: Winsor. *Narrative and Critical History*, III, 340–342; J. A. Doyle, *English in America, Puritan Colonies*, I, 144; Channing and Hart, *Guide*, § 114.

FORASMUCH as we have found by a long experience, that the faithful endeavours of some of us, that have sought the Advancement of the Plantation of New England, have not been without frequent and inevitable troubles as companions to our undertakings from our first discovery of that Coast to this present, by great Charges and necessary Expences; but also depriving us of divers of our near Friends and faithful Servants employed in that work abroad, whilst ourselves at home were assaulted with sharp litigious questions before the Lords of his Majesty's most honorable Privy Council, by the Virginia Company, and that in the very infancy thereof; who, finding they could not prevail in that way, they failed not to prosecute the same in the House of Parliament, presenting our said Plantation to be a grievance to the Commonwealth, and for such pretended it unto King James, of blessed memory; who, although his Justice and Royal Nature could not so relish it, but was otherwise pleased to give His gracious encouragement for prosecution thereof, yet such was the times as the affections of the multitude was thereby disheartened; and so much the more by how much it pleased God, about that time, to bereave us of the most noble and principal Props thereof, as the Duke of Lenox, Marquess Hamilton, and many other strong stayes to this weak building; then followed the Claim of the French Ambassador, taking advantage of the divisions made of the Sea Coast between ourselves, to whom we made a just and satisfactory Answer as it seems, for that he rested contented therewith, and since that we heard no more thereof.

Nevertheless these crosses did draw upon us such a disheartened Weakness, as there only remained a Carcass, in a manner breathless, 'till the end of the last parliament, when there were certain that desired a Patent of some lands in the Massachusetts-Bay to plant upon, who presented the names of honest and religious men, easily obtained their first desires; but those being once gotten, they used other means to advance themselves, and step beyond their first Proportions to a second Grant surruptitiously gotten of other lands, also justly passed unto Captain Robert Gorges, and others long before, who being made governor of these parts, went in person and took an absolute Seisure and actual Possession of that country by a settled Plantation he made in the Massachusetts-Bay, which afterwards he left to the charge and custody of his servants and certain other Undertakers and Tenants belonging unto some of us, who were thrust out by these Intruders that had exorbitantly bounded their Grant from east to west through all that main land from sea to sea, being near about three thousand miles in length, withal riding over the heads of those Lords and others that had their Portions assigned unto them in His late Majesty's presence, and with his Highness's appro-

bation, by Lot upon the south coast from east to west some eighty and
one hundred leagues long; but herewith not yet content, they laboured
and obtained unknown to us, a Confirmation of all this from his Majesty,
and unwitting thereof, by which means they did not only enlarge their
first extents to the west limits spoken of, but wholly excluded themselves
from the public government of the council authorised for those affairs,
and made themselves a free people, and for such Hold of themselves at
present, whereby they did rend in pieces the first foundation of the
Building, and so framed vnto themselves both new laws and new con-
ceipts of matter of Religion and forms of Ecclesiastical and Temporal
Orders and government, punishing divers that would not approue thereof,
some by whipping, and others by burning their Houses over their heads,
and some by banishing, and for the like, and all this partly under other
pretences, though indeed for no other cause, save only to make themselves absolute masters of the Country, and unconscionable in their new
Laws, so as these Complaints posting first unto ourselves that had no
sufficient means to redress, or give satisfaction to the persons aggrieved,
they were at last of Necessity Petitioners to his Majesty, who, pitying
their cases, referred them to the lords to examine the truths thereof and
to consider of the means of Reformation; who, calling some of us to
give account by what authority, or by whose means, these people were
sent over, and conceiving us to be guilty thereof, we were called for from
our houses, far remote in the country, at unseasonable times, to our great
charge and trouble: but, as innocence is confident, so we easily made it
appear that we had no share in the evils committed, and wholly dis-
claimed the having any hand therein, humbly referring to their Lordships
to do what might best sort with their wisdoms; who found matters in so
desperate a case, as that they saw a necessity for his Majesty to take the
whole busines into his own hands, if otherwise we could not undertake to
rectify what was brought to ruin; but finding it a task too great for us
to perform, we rather chose to resign all into his Majesty's Hands to do
therein as he pleased, to whom we conceived it did principally belong,
to have care of a business of so high consequence as now it is found to
be.   After all these troubles, and upon those considerations it is now
resolved, that the patent shall be surrendered unto his Majesty, with
reservation of all such lawful Rights as any is or hath been seized with,
either before or since the Patent granted to those of the Bay of the
Massachusetts, and that it may please his Royal Majesty to pass particular
grants unto us of such proportions of lands as we have mutually agreed

upon and are recorded before in this book ; that so we having his Majesty's Grants of the same under a settled government, may the more chearfully proceed in the planting of our several provinces, and with a better courage and assurance prosecute the same to a full settling of the state of those countries, and a dutiful obedience to all such as shall come unto us, to his Majesty's laws and ordinances there to be established and put in execution by such his Majesty's Lieutenants or Governors as shall be employed for those services, to the Glory of Allmighty God, the Honour of his Majesty, and public Good of his faithful Subjects.

And thus much we have thought fit to have recorded, and in convenient time published, that Posterity may know the reasons and necessities moving us to quit ourselves of these Inconveniences and dangers that might have fallen upon the Plantations for want of power to reform the same.

Ebenezer Hazard, *Historical Collections* (Philadelphia, 1792), I, 390–392.

<hr>

129. Proceedings of the First American Federation (1643)

BY THE COMMISSIONERS FOR THE UNITED COLONIES OF NEW ENGLAND

The United Colonies of New England (commonly called the New England Confederation) was made up of Massachusetts, Connecticut, New Haven, and Plymouth. The Confederation lasted from 1643 to 1684. — Bibliography: Winsor, *Narrative and Critical History*, III, 354, and *Memorial History of Boston*, I, 299; Frothingham, *Rise of the Republic*, foot-notes; Channing and Hart, *Guide*, § 124.

THE Articles of Confederacōn agreed at Bostone the xix'h of May last being now read M' Edward Winslow & M' William Collyer Comissioners for the Jurisdiccōn of New Plymouth deliuered in an Order of their Gen'all Court Dated the xxix'h of August 1643 by w'h it appeares that the said Articles of the xix'h of May weere read approued and confirmed by the said Gen'all Court & by all their Towneships and they the s'd M' Winslow & M' Collyer were both authorized to ratifie them by their subscriptions and chosen & sent as Comissioners for that Jurisdiccōn w'h full power to treate and conclud in all matters concerneing warr and peace according to y' tenor and true meaneing of the said Articles of Confederacōn for this p'sent meetinge . . .

John Winthrop Esꝗ was chosen President for this meeting according to the vijᵗh Article in the Confederacõn.

Vpon a motion made by the Comissioners for New Hauen Jurisdiccõn It was graunted and ordered That the Towne of Milford may be receiued into Combinacõn and as a member of the Jursdiccõn of New Hauen, if New Hauen and Milford agree vpon the termes & condicõns among themselues The like liberty was also granted in regard of the Towne of Southhampton

The Comissioners were informed that Vncus Sagamore of the Munhegen Indians haueing in warr taken Miantinomy Sagamore of the Narrohiggunsets prisoner, had brought him to be kept at Hartford till he might receiue aduice from the English how to þ'ceed against him for sondry treacherous attempts against his life besides this last suddaine Invasion wᵗhout denounceing warr, and when Vncus was unþvided to wᵗhstand the great force Miantinomo brought against him : . . .

These thinges being duely weighed & considered the Comissioners apparently see that Vncus cannot be safe while Myantenomo liues but that either be secret treachery or open force his life wilbe still in danger. Wherefore they thinke he may justly put such a false & blood-thirsty enemie to death, but in his owne Jurisdiccõn, not in the English plantz- cõns, And adviseing that in the manner of his death all m̄cy and moderacõn be shewed, contrary to the practise of the Indians who exercise tortures & cruelty. And Vncus haueing hitherto shewed himself a frend to the English, and in this craueing their advice, if the Nanohiggansetts Indians or others shall vnjustly assault Vncus for this execucõn, vpon notice and request the English þmise to assist and þtect him, as farr as they may ag :ᵗ such vyolence.

The Comissioners do think it fitt to aduise euery gen'all Court that they would see that euery man may keepe by him a good gunn & sword one pound of pouder wᵗh foure poundes of shott wᵗh match or flints sutable, to be ready vpon all occasions, and to be carefully viewed foure tymes a yeare at least, And that ouer and aboue this euery generall Court do see that they keep a stock of pouder shott & match euer by them. . . .

It is thought fitt and ordered That there be one and the same measure throughout all yᵉ Plantacons wᵗhin these vnited Colonies, wᶜh is agreed to be Winchester measure vizᵗ eight gallons to yᵉ bushell.

It is judged meete by the Comissioners yᵗ there be trayneings at least six tymes euery yeare in each plantacõn wᵗhin this Confederacõn.

The þporcõns of men to be sent for by any of the Jurisdiccõns in

case of any p^rsent danger, vntill the Comissioners may meete according
to the fourth Article in the Confederacõn : is for the Massachusets one
hundred and fifty men Plymouth thirty Conneetacutt thirty and New
Hauen twenty fiue And according to this pporcõn are all numbers to
be ordered in case of any warr that may fall out vntill the next meeting
of the Comissioners in Septemb^r 1644

Whereas complaints haue beene made against Samuell Gorton & his
Company, and some of them weighty & of great conseqence, And
whereas the said Gorton and the rest haue beene formerly sent for, and
now lately by the generall Court of the Massachusets wth a safe conduct
both for the comeing and returne, that they might giue answere and
satisfaccon, wherein they haue doun wrong. If yet they shall stub-
bornely refuse The Comissioners for the vnited Colonies think fitt that
the Majestrats in the Massachusets pceed against them according to
what they shall fynd just : and the rest of the Jurisdiccõns will approue
and concurr in what shalbe so warrantably doun, . . .

Vpon informacõn and complaynt made by Mr Eaton and Mr Gregson
to the Comissioners of sondry injuries and outrages they haue receiued
both from the Dutch and Sweads both at Delaware Bay and elswhere
the pticulers wth their proofes being duly considered. It was agreed
and ordered That a l're [letter] be written to the Sweadish Gou'nor
expressing the pticulers and requireing satisfaction wch l're is to be vnderwritten by John Winthrop Esq̃ as Gou'n^r of the Massachusetts and President of the Comissioners for the vnited Colonies of New England. . . .

This ensuing pposicõn of A gen'all Contribucõn for the mayntenance
of poore Schollers at the Colledg at Cambridge being p^rsented to the
Comission^rs by Mr Shepard pastor to the Church at Cambridg was read
and fully approoued by them & agreed to be comended to the seu'all
gen'all Courts as a matter worthy of due consideracõn and entertaine-
ment for advance of learneing and wch we hope wilbe chearfully
embraced.

To the Honored Commission^rs.

Those whom God hath called to attend the welfare of Religious
Comon weales haue beene prompt to extend their care for the good of
publike Schooles by meanes of wch the Comon wealth may be furnished
wth knowing and vnderstanding men in all callings the Churches wth an
able ministery in all places and wthout wch it is easy to see how both
these estates may decline and degenerate into grosse ignorance, & con-

2 G

sequently into great and vniu'sall þphanesse.   May it please yᵘ therefore among other thinges of Cõmon Concernement and publike benefitt
to take into yoʳ consideracõn some way of comfortable mayntenance for
that Schoole of the Prophets that now is : . . .   If therefore it were
commended by you at least to the freedome of euery famyly (wᶜh is
able and willing to giue) throughout the plantacõns to giue yearely but
the fourth part of a bushell of Corne, or somethinge equivolent therevnto.   And for this end if euery minister were desired to stirr up the
hearts of the people once in the fittest season in the yeare to be freely
enlarged therein and one or two faythfull and fitt men appoynted in
each towne to receiue and seasonably to send in what shalbe thus giuen
by them : It is conceiued that as no man would feele any greevance
hereby, so it would be a blessed meanes of comfortable þuision for the
dyett of diuers such students as may stand in neede of some support,
& be thought meete and worthy to be continued a fitt season therein. . . .

It is ordered that no þson wᵗhin any of the vnited Colonies shall directly or indirectly sell to any Indians either pouder shott bulletts guñs
swords daggers arrow heads or any amunition vnder the penalty of twenty
for one . . .

There being a question þpounded of what esteeme and force a verdict or sentence of any one Court wᵗhin the Colonies ought to be of in
the Court of another Jurisdiccõn the Comission's well weighing the same,
thought fitt to commend it to the seu'all gen'all Courts, that euery such
verdict or sentence may haue a due respect in any other Court through
the Colonies where occation may be to make use of it and that it be
accounted good euidence for the plaintiffe vntill either better euidence
or some other just cause appeare to alter or make the same voyde, and
that in such case the yssuing of the cause in question be respited for
some convenient tyme, that the Court may be aduised wᵗh, where the
verdict or sentence first passed. . . .

Whereas a peticõn was deliu'ed to the Comission's desireing the
mending of some places in the way from the Bay to Coneetacutt It
was agreed that it be left to Mʳ Hopkins President, to take care for the
þuideing some man or men to fynd & lay out the best way to the Bay,
& the charge to be borne by the whole. . . .

. . . The Comission's þpounded to and receiued from the Elders now
pʳsent at Hartford as followeth :

Whether the Elders may not be intreated seriously to consider some
confession of doctrine and discipline wᵗh solid groundes to be approoued

by the Churches, & published by consent (till further light) for the con-
firmeing yᵉ weake among our selues, & stoping the mouths of adu'saries
abroad.

Wee who are here pʳsent in all thankfullnes acknowledg yoʳ Christian
and Religious care to further the good of our Churches and posterytie,
and do readly entertaine the motion : and shall use our best dilligence
& indeavour to acquaint the rest of our breethren wᵗh yt, and shall study
to answere yoʳ desires & expectacõn assoone as God shall giue a fitt
season. . . .

Records of the Colony of New Plymouth in New England (edited by David
Pulsifer, Boston, 1859), IX, 9–28 *passim*.

———◆———

130. New England's Opinion of Itself (1651)

BY REVEREND PETER BULKELEY

Bulkeley was minister at Woodhill, England, and then at Concord, Massachusetts,
of which place he was one of the founders. — Bibliography : C. H. Walcott, *Concord
in the Colonial Period;* Tyler, *American Literature*, I, 216–218.

. . . AND for our selves here, the people of *New-England*, we
should in a speciall manner labour to shine forth in holinesse above other people ; we have that plenty and abundance of ordinances and meanes of grace, as few people enjoy the like ; wee are as a
City set upon an hill, in the open view of all the earth, the eyes of the
world are upon us, because we professe our selves to be a people in Covenant with God, and therefore not onely the Lord our God, with whom
we have made Covenant, but heaven and earth, Angels and men, that
are witnesses of our profession, will cry shame upon us, if wee walke
contrary to the Covenant which wee have professed and promised to
walk in ; If we open the mouthes of men against our profession, by
reason of the scandalousnesse of our lives, wee (of all men) shall have
the greater sinne.

To conclude, Let us study so to walk, that this may be our excellency
and dignity among the Nations of the world, among which we live :
That they may be constrained to say of us, onely this people is wise, an
holy and blessed people ; that all that see us, may see and know that
the name of the Lord is called upon us ; and that we are the seed which

the Lord hath blessed, *Deut.* 28. 10. *Esay* 61. 9. There is no people but will strive to excell in some thing; what can we excell in, if not in holinesse? If we look to number, we are the fewest; If to strength, we are the weakest; If to wealth and riches, we are the poorest of all the people of God through the whole world, we cannot excell (nor so much as equall) other people in tnese things; and if we come short in grace and holinesse too, we are the most despicable people under heaven; our worldly dignitie is gone, if we lose the glory of grace too, then is the glory wholly departed from our *Israel,* and we are become vile; strive we therefore herein to excell, and suffer not this crown to be taken away from us: Be we an holy people, so shall we be honourable before God, and precious in the eyes of his Saints. . . .

Peter Bulkeley, *The Gospel-Covenant* (London, 1651) 431 [wrongly numbered 425]–432.

---

131. The First Nullification of a Federal Act (1653)

BY THE GENERAL COURT OF MASSACHUSETTS

This extract is the culmination of a long quarrel in the New England Confederation, over the right of the other three colonies to require Massachusetts to join in a war. — Bibliography as in No. 129 above.

. . . WHETHER the Comissioners of the vnited Collonies haue power by articles of agreement to determine the Justice of an offenciue or vindictiue warr and to engage the Collonies therin;

The Answare of the Committies to the question
　　first more pticularly from the Articles

The whole power of Gou'ment and Jurisdiction is in the 3^d and sixt Articles refered to euery Collonie whoe sawe not meet to divest themselues of theire authoritie to Invest the Comissioners with any pte therof being altogether vnsafe and vnnessesary to attaine the end of the Confeaderation;

The 9. and 10^h Articles constituteth the Comissioners Judges of the Justice of a defenciue warr

The 4^h and 5^t settle Rules for Leagues Aides and number in a defenciue warr and deuisions of spoiles; but noe where prouide for the determination of the Justice of an offenciue warr which therfore is refered wholly to the Determination of the Supreame Power of the

seuerall Confeaderate Jurisdictions; whoe would haue otherwise prouided in the case

The sixt Article which att first view seemes to Inable the Comissioners
will euidently euince the Contrary for the Confederation being betwixt
the Collonies the 4th and fift 9 and 10ᵗʰ Articles prouid Rules in seuerall Cases according to which the Confeaderates haue bound themselues
to Acte; And the sixt Article onely orders and appoints whoe and in
what mannor the said Rules and agreements should bee executed viz.
by Comissioners Improued to acte in cases specif[y]ed and regulated,
for theire number mannor of proceeding times and places of meeting
in the sixt and seauenth Articles; And that by nessesitie; because the
supreame power of the seuerall Jurisdictions Could not assemble they were
enforced to Substitute deligates to order such things as were of pʳsent
and vrgent Nessesitie or meerly prudenciall or polliticall or of Inferior
nature and that according to *themselues* [the Rules] prescribed by the
Confeaderates But such things are [as] require the Choise Actes of Authoritie; or in theire nature of Morrall Consideration and may admite of more
time of Deliberation; as an offenciue warr; The Wisdome of the Coun-
trivers of the Confederacy did not Judg meete to Refere to Comissioners and therfore haue not prouided any Rules in such cases in these
Consernments as they did in all cases of an Inferior nature;

More Generally The Comissioners of the vnited Collonies are not soe
far*e* as wee can deserne Inuested with power to Conclude an offenciue
warr to engage the Collonies to which they belonge to put the same in
execution further then they are enabled by Comission or Instructions
vnder the seale of theire Collonie; much lesse can it stand with the
Jurisdiction and Right of Gouʳment reserued to euer[y] Collonie; for
six Comissioners of the other Collonies to put forth any Acte of power
in a vindictiue warr wherby they shall comaund the Collonie decenting
to assist them in the same; neither can it bee the meaning of the
seuerall Collonies whoe are soe tender of theire power in Gouʳning theire
owne that they should put theire power out of theire owne hands in the
most waighty points; A bondage hardly to bee borne by the most Sub-
jectiue people; And cannot bee conceiued soe free a people as the
vnited Collonies should submite vnto;

It can bee noe lesse then a contradiction to affeirme the Supreame
power; which wee take to bee the Generall Courts of euery Jurisdiction
Can bee comaunded by others an absurditie in pollicye; That an Intire
Gouʳment and Jurisdiction should prostitute itselfe to the Comaund of

Strangers; A Scandall in Religion that a generall court of Christians should bee oblidged to acte and engage vpon the faith of six Delligates against theire Consience all which must bee admited In case wee acknowlidg ourselues bound to vndertake an offenciue warr vpon the bare determination of the Comissioners whoe can not nor euer did challenge Authoritie ouer vs or expecte Subjection from vs . . .

Records of the Colony of New Plymouth in New England (edited by David Pulsifer, Boston, 1859), X, 74–76.

———◆———

132. An Exculpatory Address to King Charles II (1661)

BY GOVERNOR JOHN ENDICOTT

Endicott came over to Massachusetts as agent of the Company, and settled at Salem; he was Governor from 1628 to 1630, and also much of the time from 1644 to 1665. — Bibliography: Winsor, *Narrative and Critical History*, III, 358–359; Channing and Hart, *Guide*, § 125.

To the High and Mighty Prince CHARLES *the Second, by the Grace of God, King of Great-Britain, France and Ireland, Defender of the Faith, &c.*

MOST GRACIOUS and DREAD SOVEREIGN,

MAY it please your Majesty in the Day wherein you happily say, you now know that you are King over your British Israel, to cast an Eye upon your poor Mephibosheth, now, and by reason of Lameness in Respect of Distance, not until now appearing in your Presence; we mean upon New England Kneeling, with the rest of your Subjects, before your Majesty as her restored King: We forget not our Ineptness as to these approaches; We at present own such Impotency as renders us unable to excuse our Impotency of speaking unto our Lord the King, yet contemplating such a King who hath also seen Aduersity, That he knoweth the Heart of Exiles, who hath himself been an Exile; the Aspect of Majesty thus extraordinarily circumstanced influenced and animated the exanimated Outcasts (yet outcasts, as we hope, for the Truth) to make this Address unto their Prince, hoping to find Grace in your Sight, we present this Script the Transcript of our loyal Hearts into your Royal Hands; Wherein we craue Leaue

To supplicate your Majesty for your gracious Protection of us in the continuance both of our Civil Privileges according to (and of our Religious Liberties) the Grantees known End of suing for the Patent confirmed upon this Plantation by your Royal Father; this, this, viz. our Liberty to walk in the Faith of the Gospel with all good conscience according to the order of the Gospel (unto which the former in these Ends of the Earth is but subservient) was the cause of our transporting ourselves with our Wives our little ones and our Substance from that pleasant Land ouer the Atlantick Ocean into the vast and wast Wilderness, chusing rather the pure Scripture Worship, with a good Conscience, in this poor remote Wilderness, amongst the Heathen, than the Pleasures of England, with Submission to the Impositions of the then so disposed and so far prevailing Hierarchy; which we could not do without an evil Conscience; For which cause we are at this Day in a Land which lately was not sown; wherein we haue conflicted with the Sufferings thereof much longer than Jacob was in Syria. Our Witness is in Heaven that we left not our Country upon any Dissatisfaction as to the Constitution of the Civil State. Our Lot, after the Example of the good old Non-Conformists, hath been only to act a passive Part throughout these late Vicissitudes and successiue Overturnings of State: Our Separation from our Brethren in this Desert hath been and is a sufficient Bringing to mind the Afflictions of Joseph, but Providettial Exemption of us hereby from the late Wars and Temptations of either party we account as a Favour from God: the former cloaths us with Sack Cloth, the latter with Innocence. What Reception Courtesy and Equanimity those Gentlemen and others adherers to the Royal Interest, who in their aduerse Changes visited these parts, were entertained with amongst us according to the means of our condition, we appeal to their own Report.

Touching complaints put in against us, our humble Request only is, That for the Interim wherin we are as dumb by Reason of Absence, your Majesty would permit nothing to make an Impression upon your Royal Heart against us untill we haue both opportunity and leaue to answer for ourselves; Few will be nocent, said that Impleader, if it be enough to deny; few will be innocent, replied the then Emperor, if it be enough to accuse.

Concerning the Quakers, open and capital Blasphemers, open Seducers from the glorious Trinity, the Lords Christ our Lord Jesus Christ &c. the blessed Gospel and from the holy Scripture as the Rule of Life, open Enemies to Government itself as established in the hands of any but Men of their own Principles, malignant and assiduous Promoters of Doctrines directly tending to subvert both our Churches and State ; after all other means for a long Time used in vain we were at last constrained for our own Safety to pass a Sentence of Banishment against them upon Pain of Death ; such was their dangerous impetuous and desperate Turbulency, both to Religion and the Estate Civil and Ecclesiastical, as that how unwillingly soeuer, could it haue been avoided, the Magistrate at last in conscience both to God and Man judged himself called, for the Defence of all, to keep the Passage with the Point of the Sword held towards them. This could do no Harm to him that would be warned thereby ; their wittingly rushing themselves thereupon was their own act, and we with all Humility conceive a crime, bringing their Blood upon their own Head. The Quakers died not because of their other Crimes, how capital soeuer, but upon their superadded presumptuous, and incorrigible contempt of authority, breaking in upon us notwithstanding their Sentence of Banishment made known to them : had they not been restrained, so far as appeared, there was too much cause to fear that we ourselues must quickly haue died, or worse ; and such was their Insolency that they would not be restrained but by Death : Nay, had they at last but promised to depart the Jurisdiction, and not to return without Leaue from Authority we should haue been glad of such an opportunity to haue said They should not dye.

Let not the King hear Mens Words ; your Servants are true Men, Fearers of God and of the King, not given to change, zealous of Government and order, orthodox and peaceable in Israel ; we are not seditious as to the Interest of Cæsar, nor Schismaticks as to the matters of Religion ; We distinguish between Churches and their Impurities, between a living man, though not without Sickness or Infirmity, or no man ; Irregularities either in ourselves or others we desire to be amended. We could not live without the public Worship of God ; we were not permitted the Use of publick Worship without such a yoke of Subscription and Conformity as we could consent unto without Sin : that we might therefore enjoy Divine Worship without the human Mixtures, without offence either to God, Man, or our own Consciences, wee with Leave, but not without tears, departed from our Country, Kindred and Fathers Houses into this Patmos ; in relation whereunto we do not say our Garments were become old by Reason of the very long Journey, but that ourselves, who came away in our Strength, are by Reason of very long absence many of us become grey-headed, and some of us stooping for age. The Omission of the prementioned Injunctions, together with the Walking of our Churches as to the point of order the Congregational Way is all wherein we differ from our orthodox Bretheren.

SIR,

Wee ly not before your Sacred Majesty; the Lord God of Gods, the Lord God of Gods, he knoweth, and Israel he shall know, if it were in Rebellion or Schism that we wittingly left our Dwellings in our own, or continue our Dwellings in this strange Land, save us not this Day.

ROYAL SIR,

If according to this our humble Petition and good hope, the God of the Spirits of all Flesh, the Father of Mercies who comforteth the Abject, shall make the permission of the Bereavement of that or all for which we haue and do suffer the Loss of all Precious, so precious in our Sight as that your Royal Heart shall be inclined to shew unto us the Kindness of the Lord in your Highness's Protection of us in those Liberties for which we hither came and which we haue hitherto here enjoyed; upon Hezekiah's speaking comfortably to us as to Sons, this Orphan shall not continue fatherless, but grow up as a revived Infant under its nursing Father; these Churches shall be comforted; a Door of Hope opened by so signal a Pledge of the Lengthening of their Tranquillity that these poor and naked Gentiles, not a few of whom are come, and coming in, shall still see their wonted Teachers with the Incouragement of a more plentifull Increase of the Kingdom of Christ amongst them, and the Blessing of your poor afflicted, (and yet we hope) a People trusting in God, shall come upon the Head and Heart of that great King who was some Time an Exile as we are.

With the religious Stipulation of our Prayers, we prostrate at your Royal Feet, beg Pardon for this our Boldness, craving finally that our Names may be enrolled amongst,

Your Majestys most humble Subjects and Supplicants
JOHN ENDICOTT, Governor; in the Name and by Order of the General Court of the Massachusetts.

Ebenezer Hazard, *Historical Collections* (Philadelphia, 1794), II, 579-582.

133. The Causes and Results of King Philip's War (1675)

BY EDWARD RANDOLPH

Randolph was sent over by the king as a special agent of investigation : his reports are among the most valuable documents on the period, though he was much prejudiced against New England. — Bibliography : Winsor, *Narrative and Critical History*, III, 360–361; Palfrey, *New England*, III, chs. iv, v; Channing and Hart, *Guide*, § 126.

. . . EIGHTH Enquiry. What hath been the originall cause of the present warre with the natives. What are the advantages or disadvantages arising thereby and will probably be the End?

Various are the reports and conjectures of the causes of the present Indian warre. Some impute it to an imprudent zeal in the magistrates of Boston to christianize those heathen before they were civilized and injoyning them the strict observation of their lawes, which, to a people so rude and licentious, hath proved even intollerable, and that the more, for that while the magistrates, for their profit, put the lawes severely in execution against the Indians, the people, on the other side, for lucre and gain, intice and provoke the Indians to the breach thereof, especially to drunkennesse, to which those people are so generally addicted that they will strip themselves to their skin to have their fill of rume and brandy, the Massachusets having made a law that every Indian drunke should pay 10s. or be whipped, according to the discretion of the magistrate. Many of these poor people willingly offered their backs to the lash to save their money; whereupon, the magistrates finding much trouble and no profit to arise to the government by whipping, did change that punishment into 10 days worke for such as could not or would not pay the fine of 10s. which did highly incense the Indians.

Some beleeve there have been vagrant and jesuiticall priests, who have made it their businesse, for some yeares past, to goe from Sachim to Sachim, to exasperate the Indians against the English and to bring them into a confederacy, and that they were promised supplies from France and other parts to extirpate the English nation out of the continent of America. Others impute the cause to some injuries offered to the Sachim Philip ; for he being possessed of a tract of land called Mount Hope, a very fertile, pleasant and rich soyle, some English had a mind to dispossesse him thereof, who never wanting one pretence or other to attain their end, complained of injuries done by Philip and his Indians to their stock and cattle, whereupon Philip was often summoned before the magistrate, sometimes imprisoned, and never released but upon parting with a considerable part of his land.

But the government of the Massachusets (to give it in their own words) do declare these are the great evills for which God hath given the heathen commission to rise against them : The wofull breach of the 5th commandment, in contempt of their authority, which is a sin highly provoking to the Lord : For men wearing long hayre and perewigs made of womens hayre ; for women wearing borders of hayre and for cutting, curling and laying out the hayre, and disguising themselves by following strange fashions in their apparell : For profanesse in the people not frequenting their meetings, and others going away before the blessing be pronounced : For suffering the Quakers to live amongst them and to set up their threshholds by Gods thresholds, contrary to their old lawes and resolutions.

With many such reasons, but whatever be the cause, the English have contributed much to their misfortunes, for they first taught the Indians the use of armes, and admitted them to be present at all their musters and trainings, and shewed them how to handle, mend and fix their muskets, and have been furnished with all sorts of armes by permission of the government, so that the Indians are become excellent firemen.   And at Natick there was a gathered church of praying Indians, who were exercised as trained bands, under officers of their owne ; these have been the most barbarous and cruel enemies to the English of any others. Capt. Tom, their leader, being lately taken and hanged at Boston, with one other of their chiefs.

That notwithstanding the ancient law of the country, made in the year 1633, that no person should sell any armes or ammunition to any Indian upon penalty of 10*l.* for every gun, 5*l.* for a pound of powder, and 40*s.* for a pound of shot, yet the government of the Massachusets in the year 1657, upon designe to monopolize the whole Indian trade did publish and declare that the trade of furrs and peltry with the Indians in their jurisdiction did solely and properly belong to their commonwealth and not to every indifferent person, and did enact that no person should trade with the Indians for any sort of peltry, except such as were authorized by that court, under the penalty of 100*l.* for every offence, giving liberty to all such as should have licence from them to sell, unto any Indian, guns, swords, powder and shot, paying to the treasurer 3*d.* for each gun and for each dozen of swords ; 6*d.* for a pound of powder and for every ten pounds of shot, by which means the Indians have been abundantly furnished with great store of armes and ammunition to the utter ruin and undoing of many families in the neighbouring colonies to inrich some few of their relations and church members.

No advantage but many disadvantages have arisen to the English by the warre, for about 600 men have been slaine, and 12 captains, most of them brave and stout persons and of loyal principles, whilest the church members had liberty to stay at home and not hazard their persons in the wildernesse.

The losse to the English in the severall colonies, in their habitations and stock, is reckoned to amount to 150,000*l.* there having been about 1200 houses burned, 8000 head of cattle, great and small, killed, and many thousand bushels of wheat, pease and other grain burned (of which the Massachusets colony hath not been damnifyed one third part, the great losse falling upon New Plymouth and Connecticot colonies) and upward of 3000 Indians men women and children destroyed, who if well managed would have been very serviceable to the English, which makes all manner of labour dear.

The warre at present is near an end. In Plymouth colony the Indians surrender themselves to Gov. Winslow, upon mercy, and bring in all their armes, are wholly at his disposall, except life and transportation; but for all such as have been notoriously cruell to women and children, so soon as discovered they are to be executed in the sight of their fellow Indians.

The government of Boston have concluded a peace upon these terms.

1. That there be henceforward a firme peace between the Indians and English.

2. That after publication of the articles of peace by the generall court, if any English shall willfully kill an Indian, upon due proof, he shall dye, and if an Indian kill an Englishman and escape, the Indians are to produce him, and he to passe tryall by the English lawes.

That the Indians shall not conceal any known enemies to the English, but shall discover them and bring them to the English.

That upon all occasions the Indians are to ayd and assist the English against their enemies, and to be under English command.

That all Indians have liberty to sit down at their former habitations without let. . . .

Thomas Hutchinson, *A Collection of Original Papers Relative to the History of the Colony of Massachusets-Bay* (Boston, 1769), 490–494.

134. The Death of King Philip (1676)

BY RICHARD HUTCHINSON

This piece, signed "R. H.," is almost certainly by Richard Hutchinson, grandson of Mrs. Ann Hutchinson (see No. 106 above). — Bibliography: see No. 133 above; J. A. Doyle, *English in America, Puritan Colonies*, II, 177.

. . . KING *Philip*, who hath been a pestilent Ringleader, that had once three hundred Men (Barbarously inclined) as I told you in my last, was reduced to ten, but now is killed, in this Manner. He being hid in a *Swamp* on Mount Hope Neck, with his little Party, one of his *Indians* being discontented with him made an Escape from him, and came to Rhode-Island, and informed Capt. *Church* a Plimouth Captain of a Company that was in Search after this said King *Philip*, (the Captain being at this Time on the said Island, refreshing his Men with Necessary Provisions) but understanding where King *Philip* was, and that he intended very speedily to remove far off, to provide his Winter-quarter, retaining still the same Barbarous Spirit and Purposes, without the least Appearance of Reluctancy or Offers of Mediation, towards his Surrender to Mercy; whereupon the said Captain and his Company with some *Rhode-Island* Men went in Pursuit and Search after him, taking an *Indian* Guide with them, and beset a *Swamp* where they heard he was, which was very miry, and the Ground so loose, that our Men sunk to the Middle in their Attempts to come at this sculking Company; but all in vain, the Passage was too difficult.

While we were thus beset with Difficulties in this Attempt, the Providence of God wonderfully appeared, for by Chance the *Indian* Guide and the *Plimouth* Man, being together, the Guide espied an *Indian* and bids the *Plimouth*-man shoot, whose Gun went not off, only flashed in the Pan; with that the Indian looked about, and was going to shoot, but the Plimouth-man prevented him, and shot the Enemy through the Body, dead, with a Brace of Bullets; and approaching the Place where he lay, upon Search, it appeared to be King *Philip*, to their no small Amazement and great Joy. This seasonable Prey was soon divided, they cut off his Head and Hands, and conveyed them to *Rhode-Island*, and quartered his Body, and hung it upon four Trees. One Indian more of King *Philip's* Company they then killed, and some of the Rest they wounded but the *Swamp* being so thick and miry, they made their Escape. . . .

The Warr in New-England Visibly Ended. (London, 1677.) Reprinted in Samuel G. Drake, *The Old Indian Chronicle* (Boston, 1867), 290-292.

135. The Loss of the Massachusetts Charter (1684)

BY REVEREND PRESIDENT INCREASE MATHER

Increase Mather was minister at the Old North Church of Boston for many years, and was also President of Harvard College; he conducted the diplomatic relations of the Massachusetts colony during the struggle over the charter. — Bibliography: Winsor, *Narrative and Critical History*, III, 362, and *Memorial History of Boston*, I, ch. x; Tyler, *American Literature*, II, 67–73; Channing and Hart, *Guide*, § 127.

. . . AS for your Enquiry, *By what means they came to be deprived of their Charters, Rights and Liberties* ; please to understand, that in the year 1683, a *Quo Warranto* was issued out against them, and with the notification thereof by the then King's Order there was a Declaration published, enjoining those few particular Persons mentioned in the *Quo Warranto*, to make their defence at their own perticular Charge, without any help by a publick Stock: By this it was easie to see that some Persons were resolv'd to have the Charters condemned, *quo jure quaque injuria:* Nevertheless, the Governor and Company appointed an Attorney to appear, and answer to the *Quo Warranto*, in the Court of King's Bench.

The Prosecutors not being able to make any thing of it there, a new Suit was Commenced by a *Scire facias*, in the High Court of Chancery.

But tho they had not sufficient time given them to make their Defence, yet Judgment was entred against them for Default in not appearing ; when it was impossible, considering the remote distance of *New England* from *Westminster-hall*, that they should appear in the time allowed.

Thus illegally was the Charter of the *Massachusets* Colony wrested from them : . . .

It hath indeed been objected, that in *New England* they did many Years a go Transgress *the Act of Navigation*. But the Tra[n]sgression of some few particular Persons ought not to be charged as the fault of the Government there, who did in the Year 1663, make a Law that the Act of Navigation should be Strictly observed, and their Governours are Sworn to see that Law Executed, and have to the uttermost of their power been careful therein.

Many other Things have been suggested against *New England*, the most of which having no footsteps of Truth in them, but being the Malicious Inventions of the *Tobijahs* and *Sanballats* of the Age, are not worth mentioning.

Not but the People there being but Men, have had their failings as well as other Men in all places of the World. The only thing (so far as I can learn) which can with any Coluor of Truth be justly reflected on them as a great fault, is that in some matters relating to Conscience and difference of opinion, they have been more rigid and severe than the Primitive Christians or the Gospel doth allow of.

Yet this is to be said in their behalf, that things are reported worse than indeed they were, and that now many Leading Men, and the generality of the People are of a more moderate Temper. . . .

[Increase Mather], *A Brief Relation of the State of New England* (London, 1689), 6–8 *passim*.

136. The Revolution against Andros (1689)

BY DEPUTY-GOVERNOR THOMAS DANFORTH

Danforth was leader of the popular party, and for eighteen years Treasurer of Harvard College. — Bibliography: Winsor, *Narrative and Critical History*, III, 362; Palfrey, *New England*, III, 570–582; Channing and Hart, *Guide*, § 128.

. . . YOUR loveing lines were with much joy received and read by me, for which I humbly bless God, and return yourselfe many thanks. By reason of the great expectation of your sudden arrivall (with other of your friends) I did willingly omitt writeing unto you by the last opportunity, but now, considering the times are among those things reserved by God to his own dispose, I shall adventure the riske of a few lines, committing yourselfe and my endeavours herein to the good providence of God.

Its now 14 weeks since the revolution of the government here, the manner whereof, before these can reach you, will spread farr and neare ; future consequences wee are ignorant of, yet wee know that, at present, wee are eased of those great oppressions that wee groaned under, by the exercise of an arbitrary and illegall commission, some briefe account whereof is contained in the declaration published the same day, a coppie whereof I herewith send you. The busines was acted by the soldiers that came armed into Boston from all parts, to the great amazement of all beholders, being greatly animated by the Prince's declarations, which about that time came into the country, and heightened by the oppressions of the governor, judges, and the most wicked extortion of their debauched

officers. The ancient magistrates and elders, although they had strenu-
ously advised to further waiting for orders from England, and discouraged any attempts of that nature so farr as they had opportunity, yet
were they now compelled to assist with their presence and councells for
the prevention of bloodshed, which had most certainly been the issue
if prudent counsells had not been given to both parties. A coppie of
that paper sent Sir Edm. Andross I have herewith sent you, upon which
he forthwith came and surrendered himselfe. The same day, about 30
more of the principall persons of that knot were secured, whereof some
were quickly released, and some yet remaine under restraint, Eight of
whom, viz. Mr. Dudley, Sir Edmund, Mr. Randolph, Mr. West, Mr.
Palmer, Mr Graiham, Mr. Sherlock, Mr Farwell, the representatives
of the people, at their last sessions, voted unbailable. Mr. Dudley in
a peculiar manner is the object of the peoples displeasure, even thorow
out all the colonies where he hath sat judge, they deeply resent his
correspondency with that wicked man Mr. Randolph for the overturning
the government, and the manner of his procuring his presidentship, his
extream covetousnes, getting to himself so many bags of money, to
the ruinating of trade, and since Sir Edmund's arrivall here, hath been
his great instrument in the oppression of the people, choosing rather
to do that base drudgerie then to displease, and thereby endanger the
losse of his honor and gaine. These and such like things have made
him vile in the eyes of all generally both good and bad, so that the
governor and councill, though they have done their uttermost to procure
his inlargement, yet cant prevaile, but the people will have him in the
jaile, and when he hath been by their order turned out, by force and
tumult they fetch him in againe, and both he and the rest of them there
remaine till released by orders from England. I am deeply sensible
that we have a wolfe by the ears. This one thing being circumstanced
with much difficulty, the people will not permit any inlargement, they
having accused them of treason against their king and country ; and
those restrained, they, threaten at a high rate for being denyed an
habeas corpus. I do therefore earnestly entreat of you to procure the
best advice you can in this matter that, if possible, the good intents of
the people and their loyalty to the crown of England may not turn to
their prejudice. The example of England, the declarations put forth by
the Prince of Orange, now our King, the alteration of the government
in England making the arbitrary commission of Sir Edmund null and
void in the law ; these considerations, in conjunction with the great

oppressions they lay under, were so far prevalent in the minds of all, that although some could not advise to the enterprise, yet are hopefull that we shall not be greatly blamed, but shall have a pardon granted for any error the law will charge us with in this matter. The exercise of Sir Edmund's commission, so contrarie to the magna charta, is surely enough to call him to account by his superiours, and also Mr. Dudley that led the van in that tragedy; and for others of them, may we be quit of them, as we hope for no good from them, so we are farr from desiring to revenge our selves upon them, let what they have met with be a warning to others how they essay to oppress their Majesties good subjects any more in that kind. I crave an answer hereunto by the first opportunity.

I must also yet a little further acquaint you that sundry of those gentlemen and merchants that were very active in this matter on the day of the revolution yet, since, missing of what they expected the people universally crying up their charter priviledges and urging the old governor and magistrates to reassume the former government all which they were designed to oppose but had hopes to advance their private interests of which finding themselves now disappointed, are greatly dis-contented and speake highly against the representatives of the people and present government and, as we are informed, sundry of them, mostly factors and strangers, have drawn a petition to the lords of the committee for forreign plantations, pretending loyalty and advance of revenue to the crown, and highly inveighing against the government and people, whereas, in truth, they are the transgressors of those acts for trade and navigation, and those whom they complain against are generally unconcerned in either, and so uncapable to do the thing they accuse them of. If any thing of this nature be presented, let me intreat you sedulously to divert the mischief intended and send me a coppie thereof by the first opportunity.

Capt. George, commander of the Rose frigott, was also the same day with the rest of that knott seized, reports being spread by sundry of his men, that he intended for France, there to waite on the late King James, and before his departure to shew his spleen against Boston, so that the people were afraid of being murdered and burnt up in their beds, the lieutenant also a known papist. The sails of the frigott are brought on shore and secured till the government here receive their Majesty's order, for which deed its hoped we shall not receive blame. We do crave that the circumstances of our case and condition in all respects may be con-

2 H

sidered.　Nature hath taught us selfe preservation : God commands, it as being the rule of charity towards our neighbour : Our great remotenes from England denys us the opportunity of direction and order from thence for the regulating ourselves in all imergencies, nor have we meanes to know the laws and customes of our nation : These things are our great disadvantage : We have alwayes endeavoured to approve ourselves loyall to the crown of England, and are well assured that none of our worst enemyes dare to tax us in that matter, and we have also laboured to attend the directions of our charter, under the security whereof were laid by our fathers the foundation of this his Majesties colony, and we are not without hopes but that before you do receive these lines we shall receive from their royall Majesties the confirmation of our charter, with such addition of privileges as may advance the revenue of the crown, and be an encouragement to their Majesties subjects here.　In mean time we shall pray for the long and happie reign of their Majesties, and God's blessing to be on his people in all their three kingdoms.

Committing yourselfe and all your pious endeavours for the felicity of this part of God's church to the protection and blessing of God Almighty.　Dear Sir,

I am your friend and servant,

Tho. Danforth.

Thomas Hutchinson, *A Collection of Original Papers Relative to the History of the Colony of Massachusets-Bay* (Boston, 1769), 567–571.

CHAPTER XXI — NEW ENGLAND LIFE

137. Founding of the First American College
(1636)

ANONYMOUS (1641)

This quaint account of Harvard College is the most interesting of several contemporary narratives. — Bibliography: Josiah Quincy, *History of Harvard University*, I, ch. i; Tyler, *American Literature*, I, 99-100; W. R. Thayer, *Historical Sketch of Harvard University*.

2. In respect of the Colledge, and the proceedings of *Learning* therein.

1. AFTER God had carried us safe to *New-England*, and wee had builded our houses, provided necessaries for our liveli-hood, rear'd convenient places for Gods worship, and setled the Civill Government: One of the next things we longed for, and looked after was to advance *Learning* and perpetuate it to Posterity; dreading to leave an illiterate Ministery to the Churches, when our present Ministers shall lie in the Dust. And as wee were thinking and consulting how to effect this great Work; it pleased God to stir up the heart of one Mr. *Harvard* (a godly Gentleman and a lover of Learning, there living amongst us) to give the one halfe of his Estate (it being in all about 1700. l.) towards the erecting of a Colledge, and all his Library: after him another gave 300. l. others after them cast in more, and the publique hand of the State added the rest: the Colledge was, by common consent, appointed to be at *Cambridge*, (a place very pleasant and accommodate and is called (according to the name of the first founder) *Harvard Colledge.*

The Edifice is very faire and comely within and without, having in it a spacious Hall; (where they daily meet at Common Lectures) Exercises, [Commons, Lectures, and Exercises] and a large Library with some Bookes to it, the gifts of diverse of our friends, their Chambers and studies also, fitted for, and possessed by the Students, and all other roomes of Office necessary and convenient, with all needfull Offices thereto belonging: And by the side of the Colledge a faire *Grammar*

Schoole, for the training up of young Schollars, and fitting of them for *Academicall Learning*, that still as they are judged ripe, they may be received into the Colledge of this Schoole : Master *Corlet* is the Mr. who hath very well approved himselfe for his abilities, dexterity and painfulnesse, in teaching and education of the youth under him.

Over the Colledge is master *Dunster* placed, as President, a learned conscionable and industrious man, who hath so trained up his Pupills in the tongues and Arts, and so seasoned them with the principles of Divinity and Christianity, that we have to our great comfort, (and in truth) beyond our hopes, beheld their progresse in Learning and godlinesse also ; the former of these hath appeared in their publique declamations in *Latine* and *Greeke*, and Disputations Logicall and Philosophicall, which they have beene wonted (besides their ordinary Exercises in the Colledge-Hall) in the audience of the Magistrates, Ministers, and other Schollars, for the probation of their growth in Learning, upon set dayes, constantly once every moneth to make and uphold : The latter hath been manifested in sundry of them, by the savoury breathings of their Spirits in their godly conversation. Insomuch that we are confident, if these early blossomes may be cherished and warmed with the influence of the friends of Learning, and lovers of this pious worke, they will by the help of God, come to happy maturity in a short time.

Over the Colledge are twelve Overseers chosen by the generall Court, six of them are of the Magistrates, the other six of the Ministers, who are to promote the best good of it, and (having a power of influence into all persons in it) are to see that every one be diligent and proficient in his proper place.

2. *Rules, and Precepts that are observed in the Colledge.*

1. WHen any Schollar is able to understand *Tully*, or such like classicall Latine Author *extempore*, and make and speake true Latine in Verse and Prose, *suo ut aiunt Marte* ; And decline perfectly the Paradigim's of *Nounes* and *Verbes* in the *Greek* tongue : Let him then and not before be capable of admission into the Colledge.

2. Let every Student be plainly instructed ; and earnestly pressed to consider well, the maine end of his life and studies is, *to know God and Iesus Christ which is eternall life*, Joh. **17**. **3**. and therefore to lay

Christ in the bottome, as the only foundation of all sound knowledge and Learning.

And seeing the Lord only giveth wisedome,   Let every one seriously set himselfe by prayer in secret to seeke it of him *Prov* 2, 3.

3. Every one shall so exercise himselfe in reading the Scriptures twice a day, that he shall be ready to give such an account of his proficiency therein, both in *Theoretticall* observations of the Language, and *Logick*, and in *Practicall* and spirituall truths, as his Tutor shall require, according to his ability ; seeing *the entrance of the word giveth light, it giveth understanding to the simple,* Psalm, 119. 130.

4. That they eshewing all profanation of Gods Name, Attributes, Word, Ordinances, and times of Worship, doe studie with good conscience, carefully to retaine God, and the love of his truth in their mindes, else let them know, that (nothwithstanding their Learning) God may give them up *to strong delusions,* and in the end *to a reprobate minde,* 2 Thes. 2. 11, 12.   Rom. 1. 28.

5. That they studiously redeeme the time ; observe the generall houres appointed for all the Students, and the speciall houres for their owne *Classis* : and then diligently attend the Lectures, without any disturbance by word or gesture.   And if in any thing they doubt, they shall enquire, as of their fellowes, so, (in case of *Non satisfaction*) modestly of their Tutors.

6. None shall under any pretence whatsoever, frequent the company and society of such men as lead an unfit, and dissolute life.

Nor shall any without his Tutors leave, or (in his absence) the call of Parents or Guardians, goe abroad to other Townes.

7. Every Schollar shall be present in his Tutors chamber at the 7th. houre in the morning, immediately after the sound of the Bell, at his opening the Scripture and prayer, so also at the 5th. houre at night, and then give account of his owne private reading, as aforesaid in Particular the third, and constantly attend Lectures in the Hall at the houres appointed ?   But if any (without necessary impediment) shall absent himself from prayer or Lectures, he shall bee lyable to Admonition, if he offend above once a weeke.

8. If any Schollar shall be found to transgresse any of the Lawes of God, or the Schoole, after twice Admonition, he shall be lyable, if not *adultus,* to correction, if *adultus,* his name shall be given up to the Overseers of the Colledge, that he may bee admonished at the publick monethly Act.

3. *The times and order of their Studies, unlesse experience shall shew cause to alter.*

THe second and third day of the weeke, read Lectures, as followeth. To the first yeare at 8th. of the clock in the morning *Logick*, the first three quarters, *Physicks* the last quarter.

To the second yeare, at the 9th. houre, *Ethicks* and *Politicks*, at convenient distances of time.

To the third yeare at the 10th. *Arithmetick* and *Geometry*, the three first quarters, *Astronomy* the last.

Afternoone,

The first yeare disputes at the second houre.
The 2d. yeare at the 3d. houre.
The 3d. yeare at the 4th. every one in his Art.

The 4th. day reads Greeke.

To the first yeare the *Etymologie* and *Syntax* at the eigth houre.
To the 2d. at the 9th. houre, *Prosodia* and *Dialects.*

Afternoone.

The first yeare at 2d houre practice the precepts of *Grammar* in such Authors as have variety of words.

The 2d. yeare at 3d. houre practice in *Poësy, Nonnus, Duport,* or the like.

The 3d. yeare perfect their *Theory* before noone, and exercise *Style, Composition, Imitation, Epitome,* both in Prose and Verse, afternoone.

The fift day reads Hebrew, and the Easterne Tongues.

Grammar to the first yeare houre the 8th.
To the 2d. *Chaldee* at the 9th. houre.
To the 3d. *Syriack* at the 10th. houre.

Afternoone.

The first yeare practice in the Bible at the 2d. houre.
The 2d. in *Ezra* and *Danel* at the 3d. houre.
The 3d. at the 4th. houre in *Trestius* New Testament

The 6th. day reads Rhetorick to all at the 8th. houre.

Declamations at the 9th.   So ordered that every Scholler may declaime once a moneth.   The rest of the day *vacat Rhetoricis studiis.*

The 7th. day reads Divinity Catecheticall at the 8th. houre, Common places at the 9th. houre.

Afternoone.

The first houre reads history in the Winter,
The nature of plants in the Summer.
The summe of **every** Lecture shall be examined, before the new Lecture be read.

Every Schollar, that on proofe is found able to read the Originalls of the *Old* and *New Testament* in to the Latine tongue, and to resolve them *Logically*; withall being of godly life and conversation ; And at any publick Act hath the Approbation of the Overseers and Master of the Colledge, is fit to be dignified with his first Degree.

Every Schollar that giveth up in writing a *System*, or *Synopsis*, or summe of *Logick*, Naturall and Morall *Phylosophy*, *Arithmetick*, *Geometry* and *Astronomy* : and is ready to defend his *Theses* or positions : withall skilled in the Originalls as abovesaid : and of godly life & conversation : and so approved by the Overseers and Master of the Colledge, at any publique *Act*, is fit to be dignified with his 2d. Degree.

4. *The manner of the late Commencement, expressed in a Letter sent over from the Governour, and diverse of the Ministers, their own words these.*

*T*He Students of the first Classis that have beene these foure yeeres *trained up in* University-Learning (*for their ripening in the knowledge of the Tongues, and Arts) and are appr[o]ved for their manners as they have kept their publick Acts in former yeares, our selves being present, at them ; so have they lately kept two solemne Acts for their Commencement, when the Governour, Magistrates, and the Ministers from all parts, with all sorts of Schollars, and others in great numbers were present, and did heare their Exercises ; which were Latine and Greeke Orations, and Declamations, and Hebrew Analasis, Grammaticall, Logicall & Rhetoricall of the Psalms : And their Answers and Disputations in Logicall, Ethicall, Physicall, and Metaphysicall Questions* ;

and so were found worthy of the first degree, (commonly called Batche-lour) pro more Academiarum in Anglia : Being first presented by the President to the Magistrates and Ministers, and by him, upon their Approbation, solemnly admitted unto the same degree, and a Booke of Arts delivered into each of their hands, and power given them to read Lectures in the Hall upon any of the Arts, when they shall be thereunto called, and a liberty of studying in the Library.

All things in the Colledge are at present, like to proceed even as wee can wish, may it but please the Lord to goe on with his blessing in Christ, and stir up the hearts of his faithfull, and able Servants in our owne Native Country, and here, (as he hath graciously begun) to advance this Honourable and most hopefull worke. The beginnings whereof and progresse hitherto (generally) doe fill our hearts with comfort, and raise them up to much more expectation, of the Lords goodnesse for here-after, for the good of posterity, and the Churches of Christ Iesus. . . .

Nevv Englands First Fruits (London, 1643), 12–17.

---

138. A Sheaf of Sacred Song (1640)

BY RICHARD MATHER, JOHN ELIOT, AND THOMAS WELDE

These three ministers were appointed to prepare a metrical version of the Psalms for the churches, usually called the "Bay Psalm Book." This was the first printed book in the English colonies, and is exceedingly rare. — Bibliography : Winsor, *Narrative and Critical History*, III, 350; Tyler, *American Literature*, I, 274–277; Channing and Hart, *Guide*, § 118.

IF therefore the verses are not alwayes so smooth and elegant as some may desire or expect; let them consider that Gods Altar needs not our pollishings : Ex. 20. for wee have respected rather a plaine transla-tion, then to smooth our verses with the sweetnes of any paraphrase, and soe have attended Conscience rather then Elegance, fidelity rather then poetry, in translating the hebrew words into english language, and Davids poetry into english meetre ; that soe we may sing in Sion the Lords songs of prayse according to his owne will; untill hee take us from hence, and wipe away all our teares, & bid us enter into our masters ioye to sing eternall Halleluiahs.

PSALME 18.

To the chiefe Musician, a *psalme* of Dauid, the servant of the Lord, who spake the words of this
Song, in the day that the Lord deliuered him
from the hands of all his enemies, & from the
hand of Saule. and hee Sayde,

I L'e dearely love thee, Lord, my strength:
The Lord is my rock, and my towre,
and my deliverer, my God,
I'le trust in him *who is* my powre,
My shield, & my salvationes-horne,
3 my high-fort; Who is prayse worthy,
I on the Lord will call, so shall
I bee kept from mine enemye.
4 Deaths sorrowes mee encompassed,
mee fear'd the floods of ungodlie,
5 Hells pangs beset me round about,
the snares of death prevented mee.
6 I in my streights, cal'd on the Lord,
and to my God cry'd: he did heare
from his temple my voyce, my crye,
before him came, unto his eare.
7 Then th' earth shooke, & quak't, & moūtaines
roots mov'd, & were stird at his ire,
8 Vp from his nostrils went a smoak,
and from his mouth devouring fire:
By it the coales inkindled were.
9 Likewise the heavens he downe-bow'd,
and he descended, & there was
under his feet a gloomy cloud.
10 And he on cherub rode, and flew;
yea he flew on the wings of winde.
11 His secret place hee darknes made
his covert that him round confinde,
Dark waters, & thick clouds of skies.
12 From brightnes, that before him was,
his thickned clouds did passe away,
hayl-stones and coales of fire did passe.
13 Also Iehovah thundered,
within the heavens, the most high
likewise his angry-voyce did give,
hayl-stones, and coales of fire *did fly.*
14 Yea he did out his arrows send,
and bruising he them scattered,
and lightnings hee did multiply,
likewise he them discomfited.

15 The waters channels then were seene,
    and the foundationes of the world
appear'd ; at thy rebuke, at blast,
    of the breath of thy nostrils Lord.

.   .   .   .   .   .

PSALME 24.

A psalme of david.

THe earth Iehovahs is,
    and the fulnesse of it :
the habitable world, & they
    that there upon doe sit.
2 Because upon the seas,
    he hath it firmly layd :
and it upon the water-floods
    most sollidly hath stayd.
3 The mountaine of the Lord,
    who shall thereto ascend?
and in his place of holynes,
    who is it that shall stand?
4 The cleane in hands, & pure
    in heart ; to vanity
who hath not lifted up his soule,
    nor sworne deceitfully.
5 From God he shall receive
    a benediction,
and righteousnes from the strong-God
    of his salvation.
6 This is the progenie
    of them that seek thy face :
of them that doe inquire for him :
    of Iacob 'tis the race.   Selah.
7 Yee gates lift-up your heads,
    and doors everlasting,
be yee lift up : & there into
    shall come the glorious-King.
8 Who is this glorious King?
    Iehovah, puissant,
and valiant, Iehovah is
    in battel valiant.
9 Yee gates lift-up your heads,
    and doors everlasting,
doe yee lift-up : & there into
    shall come the glorious-King.

10 Who is this glorious-King?
    loe, it is Iehovah
    of warlike armies, hee the King
    of glory is; Selah.

PSALME 29.

A psalme of David.

VNto the Lord doe yee ascribe
    (o Sonnes of the mighty)
unto the Lord doe yee ascribe
    glory & potency.
2 Vnto the Lord doe yee ascribe
    his names glorious renowne,
  in beauty of his holynes
    unto the Lord bow downe.
3 The mighty voyce of Iehovah
    upon the waters is:
  the God of glory thundereth,
    God on great waters is.
4 Iehovahs voyce is powerfull,
    Gods voyce is glorious,
5 Gods voyce breaks Cedars: yea God breaks
    Cedars of Lebanus.
6 He makes them like a calfe to skip:
    the mountaine Lebanon,
  and like to a young Vnicorne
    the hill of Syrion.
7 Gods voyce divides the flames of fire.
8   Iehovahs voyce doth make
  the desart shake: the Lord doth cause
    the Cadesh-desart shake.
9 The Lords voyce makes the hindes to calve,
    and makes the forrest bare:
  and in his temple every one
    his glory doth declare.
10 The Lord sate on the flouds: the Lord
    for ever sits as King.
11 God to his folk gives strength: the Lord
    his folk with peace blessing.

PSALME 63.

A psalme of David, when he was in the
wilderness of Iudah.

O GOD, thou art my God, early
    I will for thee inquire:

my soule thirsteth for thee, my flesh
   for thee hath strong desire,
In land whereas no water is
   that thirsty is & dry.
2 To see, as I saw in thine house
   thy strength & thy glory.
3 Because thy loving kindenes doth
   abundantly excell
ev'n life it selfe: wherefore my lips
   forth shall thy prayses tell.
4 Thus will I blessing give to thee
   whilst that alive am I:
and in thy name I will lift up
   these hands of mine on high.
5 My soule as with marrow & fat
   shall satisfied bee:
my mouth also with joyfull lips
   shall prayse give unto thee.
6 When as that I remembrance have
   of thee my bed upon,
and on thee in the night watches
   have meditation.
7 Because that thou hast been to me
   he that to me help brings;
thereforc will I sing joyfully
   in shaddow of thy wings.
8 My soule out of an ardent love
   doth follow after thee:
also thy right hand it is that
   which hath upholden mee.
9 But as for those that seek my soule
   to bring it to an end,
they shall into the lower parts
   of the earth downe descend.
10 By the hand of the sword also
   they shall be made to fall:
and they be for a portion
   unto the Foxes shall.
11 But the King shall rejoyce in God,
   all that by him doe sweare
shall glory, but stopped shall be
   their mouths that lyars are.

The Whole Booke of Psalmes faithfully translated into English Metre (1640).

139. A Puritan's Will and Inventory (1648)

BY THOMAS NOWELL, HENRY CLARKE, AND OTHERS

This piece is selected to show the degree of comfort enjoyed by new settlers. Alice Morse Earle in several books describes the home-life of the colonists. Similar documents may be found through Channing and Hart, *Guide*, §§ 118–123.

The last Will and Testament of THOMAS NOWELL.

I THOMAS Nowell, of Wyndsor on Conecticutt, being righte in vnderstanding and of perfect memory, in regard of my age and weaknes desiringe to sett my howse in order, as my last Will and Testament and a token of my loue and respect, doe bequeath vnto Robert Willson my kinsman, one steere and one cowe; and vnto Isable Phelps my kinswoman, one cowe. And in case my wife shall after my decease marry againe, then it is my will and Testament that at the time of marriage forespecefied, the said Elizabeth, ouer and aboue my foresaid gifts, shall pay to the said Robert and Isable each of them, ten pownds a peece Item, as a token of my loue, I bequeath vnto my wife Elizabeth all the rest of my estate in goods, debts or dues of what kinde soeuer, to her full and finall dispose as shee shall see best; as allso I bequeath vnto her my dwelling howse, with all my lands thereto p^rtaininge in Wyndsor aforesaid, for and during the tearme of her life. And after her decease, as a token of my loue, I bequeath my said howse and land vnto Christopher Nowell, son of Edward Nowell, of Wakefield, in Yorkshire in England, deceased, to him and his heires for euer. And to this my last Will and Testament, wittnes my hand, subscribed this present November 3^d, Anno Domini, 1648.

Wittnes, Isable Phelps,   Thomas Nowell.
　　　　Bray Rosseter.

An Inventory of the Estate of Thomas Nowell, late of Wyndsor deceased, prized by vs whose names are heere vnderwritten, Febr. 22th, 1648.

	£	s.	d.
Imp^r: The dwelling howse, barne, outhowses, with the homelott, orchyard, with an addition of meadow adioining,	75.	00.	00
Item, 13 akers of meadow, 3*l*. 10*s*. p^r acre,	45.	10.	00
Item, 66 akers of vpland, with some additions,	03.	00.	00
In the Parlour; Item, one standing bed, with its furniture,	17.	00.	00
Item, one trundle bed, with its furniture,	10.	00.	00
Item, one couerlitt, 4 p^r of sheets, 3 p^r pillow beers,	06.	12.	00
Item, 3 table cloaths, 15 table napkins,	02.	18.	00

	£.	s.	d.
Item, 14 yards ½ of new linnen, with some cotton cloath,	02.	03.	06
Item, more new cloath, 5 yards ½,	00.	13.	09
Item, a cubberd, a table, a chaire, a small box, 3 stooles,	02.	10.	00
Item, 2 truncks, one chest, 1l. 6s.; Item, 15 cushions, 2l. 6s.,	03.	12.	00
Item, 2 Bibles, and some other bookes,	00.	14.	00
Item, a pr of gold waights,	00.	03.	00
Item, his wearing apparrell, 11l. 11s.; Item, 2 carpetts, 2l.,	13.	11.	00
Item, in mony and plate,	34.	00.	00
Item, a pewter flagon, 2 platters, 3 saltes, 2 pintes,	01.	00.	00
Item, a pr. of andirons, tongs and other things,	00.	13.	00
Item, 33 yards of kersy, 11l. 4s.; Item, 5 yards ½ of searge, 1l. 15s.	12.	19.	00
In the Kittchin; Item, in Pewter,	04.	00.	00
Item, in Brass,	04.	03.	04
Item, one iron pott, one fryinge pann,	00.	12.	00
Item, 2 peeces, a pr of bandleers,	01.	06.	00
Item, one broiling iron, one cleaver, 1 spittle iron, 2 spitts, one smooth-ing iron, one gridiron,	00.	18.	06
Item, 2 pr of andirons, fire shouell and tongs,	00.	18.	00
Item, 2 chaffing dishes, potthookes and hanging,	00.	05.	06
Item, one chaire, one pr of bellowes, 7s.; Item, 2 linnen wheeles, 6s.,	00.	13.	00
In the sellar; Item, 2 beare barrills, one butter churne, 2 Runletts,	00.	13.	00
Item, one case of bottles, one salting trough,	00.	08.	00
Item, in Porke, 2l. 10s.; Item, in tubbs and other lumber, 1l.,	03.	10.	00
In the Parlour Loft; Item, one bed with its furniture,	05.	00.	00
Item, 7 bush: rye, 3 bush: maulte, 20 bush: pease,	04.	13.	00
Item, 22 bush: wheat,	04.	08.	00
Item, 2 sacks, 2 baggs, 1 hogshd., some old tooles,	00.	18.	06
Item, yearne, linnen and cotton,	01.	14.	00
Item, 12 yards of okam cloath,	00.	18.	00
In the Kitchin Lofts and Garritts; Item, 10 bush: Indian corne,	01.	05.	00
Item, in Bacon,	01.	00.	00
Item, 1 saddle, 1 cloakbag, 1 pillion, 1 sidesaddle and pillion cloath,	02.	06.	00
Item, 2 horse collars, and other geares,	00.	12.	00
Item, 3 pillowes, one blankitt,	01.	00.	00
Item, 3 hogshds, 2 sythes, flax, and other lumber,	02.	00.	00
In the yardes and outhowses; Item, 2 horses, one colte,	27.	00.	00
Item, 2 oxen, 2 steares,	23.	00.	00
Item, 3 cowes, one heifer, one young bull,	18.	05.	00
Item, 3 swyne,	02.	00.	00
Item, waine, wheeles, expinns, cops and pin,	01.	10.	00
Item, 2 yoakes with theire irons, 2 chaines, 2 pr yoake crooks,	01.	00.	00
Item, one plow, one harrow, one grynding stone,	01.	05.	00
Item, 4 stocks of Bees,	03.	00.	00
Item, (more abroad) 2 cowes, one steare,	15.	00.	00
Item, one iron crow, a saw, beetle and wedges, with some other things,	01.	10.	00

Henry Clarke,   Totall sum is, 368.   11.   01
David Willton,
John Moore.

J. Hammond Trumbull, compiler, *The Public Records of the Colony of Connecticut, 1636–1665* (Hartford, 1850), 506–508.

140. The Justification of a Condemned Quakeress (1659)

BY MARY DYER

Mary Dyer, wife of the Secretary of Rhode Island, insisted on coming to Boston, where she was condemned to death, reprieved, and banished; but she again returned, and was executed in 1660. — Bibliography: Winsor, *Narrative and Critical History*, III, 358–359, 503–505; Palfrey, *New England*, II, 474–480; J. A. Doyle, *English in America, Puritan Colonies*, II, ch. ii; Channing and Hart, *Guide*, § 125.

To the General Court now in *Boston.*

WHEREAS *I am by many charged with the guiltinesse of my own Blood ; if you mean in my coming to* Boston, *I am therein clear, and justified by the Lord, in whose Will I came, who will require my Blood of you be sure ; who have made a Law to take away the Lives of the Innocent Servants of God, if they come among you, who are called by you,* Cursed Quakers ; *although I say, and am a living Witnesse for them and the Lord, that he hath blessed them, and sent them unto you : therefore be not found fighters against God, but let my Counsel and Request be accepted with you,   To repeal all such Laws, that the Truth and Servants of the Lord may have free passage among you, and you kept from shedding Innocent Blood, which I know there are many among you would not do, if they knew it so to be : nor can the Enemy that stirreth you up thus to destroy this holy Seed, in any measure countervail the great Dammage that you will by thus doing procure : Therefore, seeing the Lord hath not hid it from me, it lyeth upon me, in love to your Souls, thus to perswade you : I have no self-ends, the Lord knoweth, for if my Life were freely granted by you, it would not avail me, nor could I expect it of you, so long as I should daily hear or see the Sufferings of these People, my dear Brethren, and Seed, with whom my Life is bound up, as I have done these two years ; and now it is like to encrease, even unto death, for no evil doing, but coming among you : Was ever the like Laws heard of among a People that profess Christ come in the flesh ? And have such no other weapons but such Laws, to fight against* Spiritual Wickedness *withall, as you call it ? Wo is me for you ! of whom take you Counsel? search with the Light of Christ in ye, and it will shew you of whom, as it hath done me and many more, who have been disobedient and deceived, as now you are ; which Light as you come into, and obeying what is made manifest to you therein, you will not repent, that you were kept from shed-*

ding Blood, though it were from a Woman: It's not mine own Life I seek, (for I chuse rather to suffer with the People of God, than to enjoy the Pleasures of Egypt) but the Life of the Seed, which I know the Lord hath blessed; and therefore seeks the Enemy thus vehemently the Life thereof to destroy, as in all Ages he ever did: Oh hearken not unto him I beseech you, for the Seeds sake, which is one in all, and is dear in the sight of God; which they that touch, touch the Apple of his Eye, and cannot escape his Wrath, whereof I having felt, cannot but perswade all men that I have to do withal, especially you who name the Name of Christ, to depart from such Iniquity, as shedding Blood even of the Saints of the Most High; Therefore let my Request have as much acceptance with you (if you be Christians) as Esther had with Ahasueras, (whose relation is short of that that's between Christians) and my Request is the same that hers was; and he said not, that he had made a Law, and it would be dishonourable for him to revoke it, but when he understood that these People were so prized by her, and so nearly concerned her, (as in truth these are to me) as you may see what he did for her; Therfore I leave these Lines with you, appealing to the faithful and true Witnesse of God, which is One in all Consciences, before whom we must all appear; with whom I shall eternally rest, in everlasting Joy and Peace, whether you will hear or forbear: with Him is my Reward, with whom to live is my Joy, and to dye is my Gain, though I had not had your forty eight hours warning, for the preparation to the Death of Mary Dyar.

And know this also, That if through the Enmity you shall declare your selves worse than Ahasuerus, and confirm your Law, though it were but by taking away the Life of one of us, That the Lord will overthrow both your Law and you, by his Righteous Judgements and Plagues powred justly upon you, who now whilst you are Warned thereof, and tenderly sought unto, may avoid the one by removing the other: If you neither hear nor obey the Lord nor his Servants, yet will he send more of his Servants among you, so that your end shall be frustrated, that think to restrain them, you call Cursed Quakers, from coming among you by any thing you can do to them; yea verily, he hath a Seed here among you, for whom we have suffered all this while, and yet suffer; whom the Lord of the Harvest will send forth more Labourers to gather (out of the mouths of the Devourers of all sorts) into his Fold, where he will lead them into fresh Pastures, even the paths of Righteousness for his Names sake: Oh! let none of you put this good day far from you, which verily in the Light of the Lord I see approaching, even to many in and about Boston, which is *the bitterest and darkest Professing place, and so to continue so long as you have done, that ever I heard of; let the time past therefore suffice, for such a Profession as brings forth such Fruits as these Lawes are.   In Love and in the Spirit of Meekness I again beseech you, for I have no Enmity to the Persons of any; but you shall know, That God will not be mocked, but what you sow, that shall ye reap from him, that will render to every one according to the deeds done in the body, whether good or evil; Even so be it, saith*

Mary Dyar.

[Edward Burrough], *A Declaration of the Sad and Great Persecution and Martyrdom of the People of God, called Quakers, in New-England, for the Worshipping of God* (London, [1660]), 25–27.

---

141. The Trial of a Quaker (1661)

ANONYMOUS

Bibliography as in No. 140 above.

ANNO 1661.   At the said next General-Court, *Wenlock Christison* was again brought to the Bar.

The Governour asked him, *What he had to say for himself, why he should not die?*

Wenlock. I have done nothing worthy of Death; if I had, I refuse not to die.

Governour. *Thou art come in among us in Rebellion, which is as the Sin of Witchcraft, and ought to be punished.*

Wenlock. I came not in among you in Rebellion, but in Obedience to the God of Heaven; not in Contempt to any of you, but in Love to your Souls and Bodies; and that you shall know one Day, when you and all Men must give an Account of your Deeds done in the Body.   Take heed, for you cannot escape the righteous Judgments of God.

Major-General *Adderton.   You pronounce Woes and Judgments, and those that are gone before you pronounced Woes and Judgments; but the Judgments of the Lord God are not come upon us yet.*

Wenlock. Be not proud, neither let your Spirits be lifted up; God doth but wait till the Measure of your Iniquity be filled up, and that you have seen your ungodly Race, then will the Wrath of God come upon you to the uttermost; And as for thy part, it hangs over thy Head,

2 I

and is near to be poured down upon thee, and shall come as a Thief in the Night suddenly, when thou thinkest not of it. By what Law will ye put me to Death?

Court. *We have a Law, and by our Law you are to die.*

Wenlock. So said the *Jews* of Christ, *We have a Law, and by our Law he ought to die.* Who empowered you to make that Law?

Court. *We have a* Patent, *and are* Patentees, *judge whether we have not Power to make Laws?*

Wenlock. How! Have you Power to make Laws repugnant to the Laws of *England?*

Governour. *Nay.*

Wenlock. Then you are gone beyond your Bounds, and have forfeited your *Patent*, and this is more than you can answer. Are you Subjects to the King, yea, or nay?

Secretary *Rawson. What will you infer from that, what Good will that do you?*

Wenlock. If you are, say so; for in your Petition to the King, you desire that he will protect you, and that you may be worthy to kneel among his loyal Subjects.

Court. *Yes.*

Wenlock. So am I, and for any thing I know, am as good as you, if not better; for if the King did but know your Hearts, as God knows them, he would see, that your Hearts are as rotten towards him, as they are towards God. Therefore seeing that you and I are Subjects to the King, I demand to be tried by the Laws of my own Nation.

Court. *You shall be tried by a Bench and a Jury.*

Wenlock. That is not the Law, but the Manner of it; for if you will be as good as your Word, you must set me at Liberty, for I never heard or read of any Law that was in *England* to hang *Quakers.*

Governour. *There is a Law to hang* Jesuits.

Wenlock. If you put me to Death, it is not because I go under the name of a *Jesuit*, but a *Quaker*, therefore I do appeal to the Laws of my own Nation.

Court. *You are in our Hand, and have broken our Laws, and we will try you.*

Wenlock. Your Will is your Law, and what you have Power to do, that you will do: And seeing that the Jury must go forth on my Life, this I have to say to you in the Fear of the Living God: Jury, take heed what you do, for you swear by the Living God, *That you will true*

Trial make, and just Verdict give, according to the Evidence. Jury, look for your Evidence : What have I done to deserve Death? Keep your Hands out of innocent Blood.

A Juryman. *It is good Counsel.*

The Jury went out, but having received their Lesson, soon returned, and brought in their Verdict *Guilty.*

Wenlock. I deny all Guilt, for my Conscience is clear in the Sight of God.

Governour. *The Jury hath condemned thee.*

Wenlock. The Lord doth justify me, who art thou that condemnest?

Then the Court proceeded to vote as to the Sentence of Death, to which several of them, *viz. Richard Russel* and others, would not consent, the Innocence and Stedfastness of the Man having prevailed upon them in his Favour. There happened also a Circumstance during this Trial, which could not but affect Men of any Tenderness or Consideration, which was, that a Letter was sent to the Court from *Edward Wharton,* signifying, *That whereas they had banished him on pain of Death, yet he was at Home in his own House in* Salem, and therefore proposing, *That they would take off their wicked Sentence from him, that he might go about his Occasions out of their Jurisdiction.* This Circumstance, however affecting to others, did only enrage *Endicot* the Governour, who was very much displeased, and in much Anger cried out, *I could find in my Heart to go Home.*

Wenlock. It were better for thee to be at Home than here, for thou art about a bloody piece of Work.

Governour. *You that will not consent, record it. I thank God, I am not afraid to give Judgment.* Wenlock Christison, *hearken to your Sentence: You must return unto the Place from whence you came, and from thence to the Place of Execution, and there you must be hanged until you be* dead, dead, dead, *upon the* 13th *Day of* June, *being the Fifth-day of the Week.*

Wenlock. The Will of the Lord be done : In whose Will I came amongst you, and in his Counsel I stand, feeling his Eternal Power, that will uphold me unto the last Gasp, I do not question it. Known be it unto you all, That if you have Power to take my Life from me, my Soul shall enter into Everlasting Rest and Peace with God, where you yourselves shall never come : And if you have Power to take my Life from me, the which I do question, I believe you shall never more take *Quakers*

Lives from them: [Note my Words] Do not think to weary out the Living God by taking away the Lives of his Servants: What do you gain by it? For the last Man you put to Death, here are *five* come in his Room. And if you have Power to take my Life from me, God can raise up the same Principle of Life in *ten* of his Servants, and send them among you in my Room, that you may have Torment upon Torment, which is your Portion: *For there is no Peace to the Wicked*, saith my God.

Governour. *Take him away.* . . .

Joseph Besse, *A Collection of the Sufferings of the People called Quakers* (London, 1753), II, 222–223.

---

142. The Wrongs of the Quakers (1660)

BY EDWARD BURROUGH

Burrough was an English Quaker, who took up the case of his brethren in Massachusetts, and got the ear of the king: orders were sent to Massachusetts to desist from the persecution. — Bibliography as in No. 140 above.

. . . 2. TWELVE Strangers in that Country, but free-born of this Nation, received twenty three Whippings, the most of them being with a Whip *of three Cords*, with *Knots at the ends*, and laid on with as much strength as they could be by the Arm of their Executioner, the stripes amounting to *Three hundred and seventy*.

3. Eighteen Inhabitants of the Country, being free-born *English*, received twenty three Whippings, the stripes amounting to two hundred and fifty.

4. Sixty four Imprisonments of the Lords People, for their obedience to his Will, amounting to five hundred and nineteen weeks, much of it being *very cold weather*, and the Inhabitants kept in Prison *in harvest time*, which was very much to their losse; besides many more Imprisoned, of which time we cannot give a just account.

5. Two beaten with Pitched Ropes, the blows amounting to an hundred thirty nine, by which one of them was brought near unto death, much of his body being beat like unto a jelly, and one of their own Doctors, a Member of their Church, who saw him, said, *It would be a Miracle if ever he recovered, he expecting the flesh should rot off the*

bones; who afterwards was banished upon pain of death. There are many Witnesses of this there.

6. Also, an Innocent man, an Inhabitant of *Boston*, they banished from his Wife and Children, and put to seek a habitation in the Winter; and in case he returned again, he was to be kept Prisoner during his life: and for returning again, he was put in Prison, and hath been now a Prisoner above a year.

7. Twenty five Banishments, upon the penalties of being whipt, or having their Ears cut; or branded in the Hand, if they returned.

8. Fines laid upon the Inhabitants for meeting together, and edifying one another, as the Saints ever did; and for refusing to swear, it being contrary to Christ's Command, amounting to about a Thousand pound, besides what they have done since, that we have not heard of; many Families, in which there are many Children, are almost ruined, by these unmerciful proceedings.

9. Five kept *Fifteen dayes* (in all) *without food*, and *Fifty eight* dayes shut up close by the Jaylor, and had none that he knew of; and from some of them he stopt up the windows, hindring them from convenient air.

10. One laid Neck and Heels in Irons for *sixteen hours*.

11. One very deeply burnt in the right hand *with the letter* H. after he had been whipt with above *Thirty stripes*.

12. One chained the most part of Twenty dayes to a Logg of wood in an open Prison in the Winter-time.

13. Five Appeals to *England*, denied at *Boston*.

14. Three had their right Ears cut by the Hangman in the Prison, the Door being barred, and not a Friend suffered to be present while it was doing, though some much desired it.

15. One of the Inhabitants of *Salem*, who since is banished upon pain of Death, *had one half of his House and Land seized on while he was in Prison*, a month before he knew of it.

16. At a General Court in *Boston*, they made an Order, That those who had not wherewithal to answer the Fines that were laid upon them (for their Consciences) should be sold for Bond-men, and Bond-women to Barbados, Virginia, or any of the English Plantations.

17. Eighteen of the People of God were at several times banished upon pain of Death, six of them were their own Inhabitants, two of which being very aged people, and well known among their Neighbours to be of honest Conversations, being Banished from their Houses and

Families, and put upon Travelling and other hardships, soon ended their dayes; whose Death we can do no lesse than charge upon the Rulers of *Boston*, they being the occasion of it.

18. Also three of the Servants of the Lord 𝔱𝔥𝔢𝔶 𝔭𝔲𝔱 𝔱𝔬 𝔇𝔢𝔞𝔱𝔥, all of them for obedience to the Truth, in the Testimony of it against the wicked Rulers and Laws at *Boston*.

19. And since they have banished four more, *upon pain of Death*; and twenty four of the Inhabitants of *Salem* were presented, and more Fines called for, and their Goods seized on, to the value of Forty pounds, for meeting together in the fear of God, and some for *refusing to swear*.

These things (O King) from time to time have we patiently suffered, and not for the transgression of any Just or Righteous Law, either pertaining to the Worship of God, or the Civil Government of *England*, but simply and barely for our Consciences to God, of which we can more at large give Thee (or whom thou mayest order) a full Account (if Thou wilt let us have admission to Thee, who are *Banished upon pain of Death*, and have had *our Ears cut*, who are, some of us, in *England* attending upon Thee) both of the *Causes of our Sufferings*, and *the Manner* of their disorderly and illegal Proceeding against us; Who begun 𝔴𝔦𝔱𝔥 𝔍𝔪𝔪𝔬𝔡𝔢𝔰𝔱𝔶, went on 𝔦𝔫 𝔍𝔫𝔥𝔲𝔪𝔞𝔫𝔦𝔱𝔶 and ℭ𝔯𝔲𝔢𝔩𝔱𝔶, and were not satisfied until 𝔱𝔥𝔢𝔶 𝔥𝔞𝔡 𝔱𝔥𝔢 𝔅𝔩𝔬𝔬𝔡 𝔬𝔣 𝔱𝔥𝔯𝔢𝔢 𝔬𝔣 𝔱𝔥𝔢 𝔐𝔞𝔯𝔱𝔶𝔯𝔰 𝔬𝔣 JESUS: Revenge for all which we do not seek, but lay them before Thee, considering Thou hast been well acquainted with Sufferings, and so mayest the better consider them that suffer, and mayest for the future restrain the Violence of these Rulers of *New-England*, having Power in Thy hands; they being but the Children of the Family, of which Thou art Chief Ruler; Who have in divers of their Proceedings 𝔣𝔬𝔯𝔣𝔢𝔦𝔱𝔢𝔡 𝔱𝔥𝔢𝔦𝔯 𝔓𝔞𝔱𝔢𝔫𝔱; as upon a strict Inquiry in many particulars will appear.

And this, O King, we are assured of, that in time to come it will not repent Thee, if by a *Close Rebuke* Thou stoppest the 𝔅𝔩𝔬𝔬𝔡𝔶 𝔓𝔯𝔬𝔠𝔢𝔢𝔡𝔦𝔫𝔤𝔰 of these 𝔅𝔩𝔬𝔬𝔡𝔶 𝔓𝔢𝔯𝔰𝔢𝔱𝔲𝔱𝔬𝔯𝔰; for in so doing, Thou wilt engage the hearts of many honest People unto Thee, both there and here; and for such Works of Mercy, the Blessing is obtained, and shewing it, is the way to prosper. . . .

[Edward Burrough], *A Declaration of the Sad and Great Persecution and Martyrdom of the . . . Quakers, in New-England*, etc. (London, [1660]), 17-20.

143. The Penalty for not Going to Church (1666)

BY THE COUNTY COURT OF MIDDLESEX

This extract is typical of the proceedings of the "county courts," which were modelled on the English Courts of Quarter Sessions; they tried for petty crimes, and also had executive powers. On church-going, see Alice Morse Earle, *The Sabbath in Puritan New-England;* Edward Eggleston, *The Beginners of a Nation,* 132–140.

At a county court held at Cambridge, on adjournment,
Aprill 17. 1666.

THOMAS GOOLD, Thomas Osburne and John George being presented by the grand jury of this county for absenting themselves from the publick worship of God on the Lords dayes for one whole yeare now past, alledged respectively as followeth, viz.

Thomas Osburne answered, that the reason of his non-attendance was, that the Lord hath discovered unto him from his word and spirit of truth that the society, wherewith he is now in communion, is more agreeable to the will of God, asserted that they were a church and attended the worship of God together, and do judge themselves bound so to do, the ground whereof he said he gave in the generall court.

Thomas Goold answered, that as for coming to publique worship they did meet in publique worship according to the rule of Christ, the grounds whereof they had given to the court of assistants, asserted that they were a publique meeting, according to the order of Christ Jesus gathered together.

John George answered, that he did attend the publique meetings on the Lord's dayes where he was a member; asserted that they were a church according to the order of Christ in the gospell, and with them he walked and held communion in the publique worship of God on the Lord's dayes.

Whereas at the general court in October last, and at the court of assistants in September last endeavours were used for their conviction. The order of the generall court declaring the said Goold and company to be no orderly church assembly and that they stand convicted of high presumption against the Lord and his holy appoyntments was openly read to them and is on file with the records of this court.

The court sentenced the said Thomas Goold, Thomas Osburne and John George, for their absenting themselves from the publique worship of God on the Lords dayes, to pay foure pounds fine, each of them, to the county order. And whereas by their owne confessions they stand convicted of persisting in their schismaticall assembling themselves together, to the great dishonour of God and our profession of his holy name, contrary to the act of the generall court of October last prohibiting them therein on penalty of imprisonment, this court doth order their giving bond respectively in 20*l.* each of them, for their appearance to answer their contempt at the next court of assistants.

The abovenamed Thomas Goold, John George, and Thomas Osburne made their appeale to the next court of assistants, and refusing to put in security according to law were committed to prison.

Thomas Hutchinson, *A Collection of Original Papers Relative to the History of the Colony of Massachusets-Bay* (Boston, 1769), 399–401.

---

144. The True Blue Laws of Connecticut (1672)

FROM THE RECORDS OF THE GENERAL COURT

In 1781 Rev. Samuel Peters published a *General History of Connecticut,* in which he presented what purported to be a code of laws, including such provisions as the following: "No woman shall kiss her child on the Sabbath or fasting-day"; "When it appears that an accused has confederates, and he refuses to discover them, he may be racked." It has long since been shown that this code is a fabrication. The true character of the Connecticut legislation, and of New England legislation in general, may be shown by extracts from the genuine code printed in 1673. It is very like the codes of Massachusetts and other colonies. — Bibliography: Winsor, *Narrative and Critical History,* III, 371–373; Channing and Hart, *Guide,* § 122.

FORASMUCH *as the free Fruition of such Liberties, as Humanity, Civility and Christianity call for, as due to every man, in his place and proportion, without Impeachment and Infringement hath ever been, and ever will be the Tranquility and Stability of Churches and Common wealths; and the denyal or deprival thereof, the disturbance, if not ruine of both:*

It is therefore Ordered by this Court and Authority thereof; That no mans life shall be taken away, no mans honour or good Name, shall be stayned, no mans person shall be Arrested, Restrained, Banished, Dismembred, nor any wayes punished; no man shall be deprived of his Wife or Children; no mans Goods or Estate shall be taken away from him, nor any wayes indamaged under colour of Law, or countenance of Authority, unless it be by the vertue or equity of some express Law of

this Colony warranting the same, established by the General Court, and
sufficiently published; or in case of the defects of a Law in any particular case by some clear and plain Rule of the word of God, in which the
whole Court shall concurre. . . .

ARRESTS.

IT is Ordered by the Authority of this Court; That no person shall be
Arrested or Imprisoned for any Debt or Fine, if the Law can finde
any competent means of satisfaction otherwise from his Estate, and if
not, his person may be Arrested and Imprisoned, where he shall be kept
at his own charge, not the Plaintiffs, till satisfaction be made; unless the
Court that hath cognizance of the cause, or some Superiour Court shall
otherwise determine: Provided nevertheless, no mans person shall be
kept in Prison for Debt, but when there appears some Estate which he
will not produce: in which case any Court, Assistant or Commissioner
may administer an Oath to the party, or any others suspected to be privy
in concealing his Estate: And if no Estate appear, he shall satisfie his
Debt by service, if the Creditor require it, in which case, he shall not be
disposed of in service to any but of the English Nation. . . .

Capital Laws.

IF any Man or Woman after legal conviction shall Have or Worship
any other God but the Lord God, he shal be put to death. *Deu.*
13. 6. 17, 21. *Ex.* 22. 2.

2. If any person within this Colony shall Blaspheme the Name of God
the Father, Son or Holy Ghost, with direct, express, presumptuous or
high-handed Blasphemy, or shall Curse in the like manner, he shall be
put to death, *Levit.* 24. 15, 16.

3. If any Man or Woman be a Witch, that is, hath or consulteth with
a Familiar Spirit, they shall be put to death, *Exo.* 22. 18. *Lev.* 20. 27.
Deu. 18. 10. 11.

4. If any person shall commit any wilful Murther, committed upon
Malice, Hatred or Cruelty, not in a mans just and necessary defence,
nor by casualty against his will, he shall be put to death. *Exod.* 21. 12,
13, 14. *Numb.* 35. 30, 31.

5. If any person shall slay another through guile, either by Poysoning,
or other such Devilish practises, he shall be put to death, *Exod.* 21.
14. . . .

10 If any Man stealeth a Man or Man kinde, and selleth him, or if he be found in his hand, he shall be put to death, *Exod.* 21. 16.

11. If any person rise up by False Witness wittingly and of purpose to take away any mans life, he or she shall be put to death, *Deut.* 19. 16, 18, 19. . . .

14. If any Childe or Children above *sixteen years old*, and of sufficient understanding, shall Curse or Smite their natural Father or Mother, he or they shall be put to death, unless it can be sufficiently testified, that the Parents have been very unchristianly negligent in the education of such Children, or so provoked them by extream and cruel correction, that they have been forced thereunto to preserve themselves from death or maiming, *Exod.* 21. 17. *Levit*, 20. 9. Exod, 21. 15.

15. If any man have a stubborn or rebellious Son, of sufficient understanding and years, *viz. sixteen years of age*, which will not obey the voice of his Father, or the voice of his Mother, and that when they have chastened him, he will not hearken unto them ; then may his Father or Mother, being his natural Parents lay hold on him, and bring him to the Magistrates assembled in Court, and testifie unto them, that their Son is Stubborn and Rebellious, and will not obey their voice and chastisement, but lives in sundry notorious Crimes, such a Son shall be put to death, *Deut.* 21. 20. 21. . . .

CHILDREN.

FOrasmuch *as the good Education of Children is of singular behoof and benefit to any Colony, and whereas many Parents and Masters are too indulgent and negligent of their duty in that kinde ;*

It is therefore Ordered by the Authority of this Court; That the Selectmen of every Town in this Jurisdiction, in their several precincts and quarters shall have a vigilant eye over their Brethren and Neighbours, to see that none of them shall suffer so much Barbarisme in any of their Families, as not to endeavour by themselves, or others, to teach their Children and Apprentices so much learning as may enable them perfectly to reade the English Tongue, and knowledge of the Capital Laws, upon penalty of *twenty shillings* neglect therein : Also that all Masters of Families do once a week at least, Catechise their Children and Servants in the Grounds and Principles of Religion ; and if any be unable to do so much, that then at the least they procure such Children and Apprentices to learn some short Orthodox Catechisme without book, that they may be able to answer to the Questions that shall be propounded

to them out of such Catechisme, by their Parents or Masters, or any of
the Select-men, when they shall call them to an accompt of what they
have learned in that kinde. . . .

CRUELTY.

IT is Ordered by the Authority of this Court ; That no man shall exercise any Cruelty towards any Bruit Creature, which are usually kept
for the use of man, upon pain of such punishment as in the judgement
of the Court the nature of the offence shall deserve. . . .

ECCLESIASTICAL.

. . . It is therefore Ordered by the Authority of this Court, That if
any Christian so called, within this Colony, shall contemptuously behave
himself towards the Word preached, or the messengers thereof, called to
Dispense the same in any Congregation, when he doth Faithfully execute
his service and Office therein, according to the Will and Word of God ;
either by Interrupting him in his Preaching, or by charging him falsly
with an Errour, which he hath not taught, in the open face of the Church ;
or like a Son of *Korah* cast upon his true Doctrine or himself, any reproach to the dishonour of the Lord Jesus who hath sent him, and to
the disparagement of that his holy Ordinance and makeing Gods wayes
contemptible and rediculous : That every such person or persons (whatsoever Censure the Church may pass) shall for the first scandall be convented and reproved openly by the Magistrate in some publick Assembly,
and bound to their good behaviour.   And if a Second time they break
forth into the like contemptuous carriages, they shall either pay *five*
pounds to the publick, or stand two hours openly upon a block or stool
four foot high upon a publick meeting day, with a paper fixed on his
Breast written with Capital Letters, AN OPEN AND OBSTINATE
CONTEMNER OF GODS HOLY ORDINANCES, that others may
fear and be ashamed of breaking out into the like wickedness.
    It is further Ordered ; That wheresoever the Ministry of the Word is
established according to the order of the Gospel throughout this Colony,
every person shall duely resort and attend thereunto respectively upon
the Lords day, and upon such publick Fast dayes, and dayes of thanksgiving, as are to be generally kept by the appointment of Authority.
And if any person within this Jurisdiction, shall without just and necessary cause, withdraw himself from hearing the publick Ministry of the

Word, after due means of conviction used, he shall forfeit for his absence from every such meeting *five shillings ;* all such offences to be heard and determined by any one Magistrate or more from time to time ; provided all breaches of this Law be complained of, and prosecuted to effect within one moneth after the same. . . .

HERETICKS.

*T*His Court being sensible of the danger persons are in of being poysoned in their Judgements and Principles by Heretick, whether *Quakers, Ranters, Adamites, or such like :*

Do see cause to Order ; That no persons in this Colony shall give any unnecessary entertainment unto any Quaker, Ranter, Adamite, or other notorious Heretick, upon penalty of *five pounds* for every such persons entertainment, to be paid by him that shall so entertain them : And *five pounds per Week* shall be paid by each Town that shall suffer their entertainment as aforesaid.

It is also Ordered by the Authority of this Court ; That it shall be in the power of the Governour, Deputy Governour or Assistants to order, that all such Hereticks as aforesaid be committed to Prison, or sent out of this Colony ; and no person shall unnecessarily fall into discourse with any such Heretick, upon the penalty of *twenty shillings.*

And it is further Ordered ; That no person within this Colony shall keep any Quaker-books or Manuscripts containing their Errours (except the Governour, Magistrates and Elders) upon penalty of *ten shillings per time* for every person that shall keep any such Books after the publication hereof, and shall not deliver such Books to the Magistrate or Minister. . . .

LYING.

*W*Hereas truth in words as well as in actions is required of all men, especially of Christians, who are the professed Servants of *the God of Truth, and whereas lying is contrary to Truth, and some sorts of Lyes are not only sinful as all Lyes are, but also pernicious to the publick Weal, and injurious to particular persons.*

It is therefore Ordered by the Authority of this Court ; That every person of the age of discretion, which is accounted *Fourteen years,* who shall wittingly and willingly make, or publish any Lye, which may be pernicious to the publick Weal, or tending to the damage or injury of any perticular person to deceive and abuse the people with false News or reports, and the same duly proved in any Court or before any one Magistrate, who hath hereby power granted to hear and determine all offences against this Law; Such persons shall be Fined for the first Offence *Ten Shillings*, or if the party be unable to pay the same, then to sit in the Stocks so long as the said Court or Magistrate shall appoint, in some open place not exceeding *Three Hours*, . . .

OPPRESSION.

WHereas Oppression is a mischievous Evil the Nature of man is prone unto, and that men may not Oppress and Wrong their Neighbours by taking excessive Wages for Work, or unreasonable Prizes for such necessary Merchandize or Commodities as shall pass from Man to Man;

It is Ordered by the Authority of this Court; That if any person or persons shall offend in any of the said Cases, he shall be punished by Fine or Imprisonment according to the quality of the Offence, as the Court to which he is presented upon lawful Tryal and Conviction shall determine. . . .

Prophanation of the Sabbath.

WHereas the Sanctification of the Sabbath is a matter of great concernment to the Weal of a People, and the Prophanation thereof is that as brings down the judgements of God upon that Place or People that suffer the same;

It is therefore Ordered by this Court; That if any person shall Prophane the Sabbath, by unnecessary Travail, or Playing thereon in the time of publick Worship, or before or after, or shall keep out of the Meeting house during the time of publick Worship unnecessarily, there being convenient room in the House, he shall Pay *five shillings* for every such offence, or sit in the Stocks one hour, any one Assistant or Commissioner to hear and determine any such case; And the Constables in the several Plantations are hereby required to make search after all Offenders against this Law, and to make return of those they shall finde transgressing to the next Assistant or Commissioner. . . .

SCHOOLS.

IT being one chief Project of Satan to keep men from the knowledge of the Scriptures, as in former times, keeping them in an unknown Tongue, so in these latter times, by perswading them from the use of

Tongues, so that at least the true sense and meaning of the Original might be clouded with false Glosses of Saint seeming deceivers; and that Learning might not be buried in the Graves of our fore-fathers in Church and Colony, the Lord assisting our endeavours:

It is therefore Ordered by this Court and the Authority thereof; That every Township within this Jurisdiction, after the Lord hath increased them to the number of *Fifty* Householders, shall then forthwith appoint one within their Town to teach all such Children as shall resort to him, to Write and Reade, whose Wages shall be paid either by the Parents or Masters of such Children, or by the Inhabitants in General by way of supply, as the major part of those who Order the Prudentials of the Town shall appoint: Provided that those who send their Children, be not oppressed by paying much more then they can have them taught for in other Towns.

And it is further Ordered; That in every County Town there shall be set up and kept a Grammar School, for the use of the County, the Master thereof being able to instruct Youths so far as they may be fitted for the Colledge. . . .

The Laws of Connecticut (reprinted from the original edition of 1673 by George Brinley, Hartford, 1865), 1–63 *passim.*

———◆———

145.　A Cynical View of New-Englanders (1674)

BY JOHN JOSSELYN

For Josselyn, see No. 125 above. — Bibliography: Winsor, *Narrative and Critical History*, III, 360; Channing and Hart, *Guide*, § 118.

. . . EVERY Town sends two Burgesses to their great and solemn general Court.

For being drunk, they either whip or impose a fine of Five shillings; so for swearing and cursing, or boring through the tongue with a hot Iron.

For kissing a woman in the street, though in way of civil salute, whipping or a fine. . . .

Scolds they gag and set them at their doors for certain hours, for all comers and goers by to gaze at.

Stealing is punished with restoring four fould, if able; if not, they are sold for some years, and so are poor debtors.

If you desire a further inspection to their Laws, I must refer you to them being in print, too many for to be inserted into this Relation.

The Governments of their Churches are Independent and Presbyterial, every Church (for so they call their particular Congregations) have one Pastor, one Teacher, Ruling Elders and Deacons.

They that are members of their Churches have the Sacraments administred to them, the rest that are out of the pale as they phrase it, are denyed it.   Many hundred Souls there be amongst them grown up to men & womens estate that were never Christened.

They judge every man and woman to pay Five shillings *per* day, who comes not to their Assemblies, and impose fines of forty shillings and fifty shillings on such as meet together to worship God.

Quakers they whip, banish, and hang if they return again.

Anabaptists they imprison, fine and weary out.

The Government both Civil and Ecclesiastical is in the hands of the thorow-pac'd Independents and rigid Presbyterians.

The grose *Goddons*, or great masters, as also some of their Merchants are damnable rich ; generally all of their judgement, inexplicably covetous and proud, they receive your gifts but as an homage or tribute due to their transcendency, which is a fault their Clergie are also guilty of, whose living is upon the bounty of their hearers.   On Sundays in the afternoon when Sermon is ended the people in the Galleries come down and march two a breast up one Ile and down the other, until they come before the desk, for Pulpit they have none : before the desk is a long pue where the Elders and Deacons sit, one of them with a mony box in his hand, into which the people as they pass put their offering, some a shilling, some two shillings, half a Crown, five shillings according to their ability and good will, after this they conclude with a Psalm ; but this by the way.

The chiefest objects of discipline, Religion, and morality they want, some are of a *Linsie-woolsie* disposition, of several professions in Religion, all like *Æthiopians* white in the Teeth, only full of ludification and injurious dealing, and cruelty the extreamest of all vices.   The chiefest cause of *Noah's* floud, Prov. 27. 26.   *Agni erant ad vestitum tuum*, is a frequent Text among them, no trading for a stranger with them, but with a *Græcian* faith, which is not to part with your ware without ready money, for they are generally in their payments recusant and slow, great Syndies, or censors, or controllers of other mens manners, and savagely factious amongst themselves. . . .

But mistake me not to general speeches, none but the guilty take exceptions, there are many sincere and religious people amongst them, descryed by their charity and humility (the true Characters of Christianity) by their Zenodochie or hospitality, by their hearty submission to their Soveraign the King of *England*, by their diligent and honest labour in their callings, amongst these we may account the Royalists, who are lookt upon with an evil eye, and tongue, boulted or punished if they chance to lash out; the tame *Indian* (for so they call those that are born in the Countrey) are pretty honest too, and may in good time be known for honest Kings men.

They have store of Children, and are well accomodated with Servants; many hands make light work, many hands make a full fraught, but many mouths eat up all, as some old planters have experimented; of these some are *English*, others *Negroes*: of the *English* there are can eat till they sweat, and work till they freeze; & of the females that are like Mrs. *Winters* paddocks, very tender fingerd in cold weather.

There are none that beg in the Countrey, but there be Witches too many, . . . amongst the Quakers, and others that produce many strange apparitions if you will believe report, of a *Shallop* at Sea man'd with women; of a Ship, and a great red Horse standing by the main-mast, the Ship being in a small *Cove* to the East-ward vanished of a suddain. Of a Witch that appeared aboard of a Ship twenty leagues to Sea to a Mariner who took up the Carpenters broad Axe and cleft her head with it, the Witch dying of the wound at home, with such like bugbears and *Terriculamentaes*. . . .

John Josselyn, *An Account of Two Voyages to New-England* (London, 1675), 178–182 *passim*.

————◆————

146. Two Dutchmen in Boston (1680)

BY JASPAR DANKERS AND PETER SLUYTER

(TRANSLATED BY HENRY C. MURPHY, 1867)

For Dankers and Sluyter, see No. 58 above. For New England life in 1680, see bibliography in Channing and Hart, *Guide*, §§ 127–130.

I680. . . . *24th, Monday.* We walked with our captain into the town, for his house stood a little one side of it, and the first house he took us to was a tavern. From there, he conducted us to the governor, who dwelt in only a common house, and that not the most costly.   He is an old man, quiet and grave.   He was dressed in black silk, but not sumptuously.   *Paddechal* explained the reasons of our visit.   The governor inquired who we were, and where from, and where we going.   Paddechal told him we were Hollanders, and had come on with him from New York, in order to depart from here, for England.   He asked further our names, which we wrote down for him.   He then presented us a small cup of wine, and with that we finished.   We went then to the house of one John Taylor, to whom William Van Cleif had recommended us ; but we did not find him.   We wanted to obtain a place where we could be at home, and especially to ascertain if there were no Dutchmen.   They told us of a silversmith, who was a Dutchman, and at whose house the Dutch usually went to lodge. . . .   We were better off at his house, for although his wife was an Englishwoman, she was quite a good housekeeper. . . .

28*th, Friday*.   One of the best ministers in the place being very sick, a day of fasting and prayer was observed in a church near by our house. We went into the church where, in the first place, a minister made a prayer in the pulpit, of full two hours in length ; after which an old minister delivered a sermon an hour long, and after that a prayer was made, and some verses sung out of the psalms.   In the afternoon, three or four hours were consumed with nothing except prayers, three ministers relieving each other alternately ; when one was tired, another went up into the pulpit.   There was no more devotion than in other churches, and even less than at New York ; no respect, no reverence ; in a word, nothing but the name of independents ; and that was all. . . .

7*th, Sunday*.   We heard preaching in three churches, by persons who seemed to possess zeal, but no just knowledge of Christianity.   The auditors were very worldly and inattentive.   The best of the ministers whom we have yet heard, is a very old man, named John Eliot, who has charge of the instruction of the Indians in the Christian religion. . . .

8*th, Monday*.   We went accordingly, about eight o' clock in the morning, to Roxbury, which is three-quarters of an hour from the city, . . . We found it justly called *Rocksbury*, for it was very rocky, and had hills entirely of rocks.   Returning to his house we spoke to him [Mr. Eliot], and he received us politely.   Although he could speak neither Dutch nor French, and we spoke but little English, and were unable to express ourselves in it always, we managed, by means of Latin and English, to understand each other.   He was seventy-seven years old, and had been

2 K

forty-eight years in these parts. He had learned very well the language of the Indians, who lived about there. We asked him for an Indian Bible. He said in the late Indian war, all the Bibles and Testaments were carried away, and burnt or destroyed, so that he had not been able to save any for himself; but a new edition was in press, which he hoped would be much better than the first one, though that was not to be despised. We inquired whether any part of the old or new edition could be obtained by purchase, and whether there was any grammar of that language in English. Thereupon he went and brought us the Old Testament, and also the New Testament, made up with some sheets of the new edition, so that we had the Old and New Testaments complete. He also brought us two or three small specimens of the grammar. We asked him what we should pay him for them; but he desired nothing. We presented him our *Declaration* in Latin, and informed him about the persons and conditions of the church, whose declaration it was, and about Madam Schurman and others, with which he was delighted, and could not restrain himself from praising God, the Lord, that had raised up men, and reformers, and begun the reformation in Holland. He deplored the decline of the church in New England, and especially in Boston, so that he did not know what would be the final result. . . .

9*th, Tuesday.* We started out to go to Cambridge, lying to the northeast of Boston, in order to see their college, and printing office. We left about six o'clock in the morning, and were set across the river at Charlestown. We followed a road which we supposed was the right one, but went full half an hour out of the way, and would have gone still further, had not a negro who met us, and of whom we inquired. disabused us of our mistake. We went back to the right road, which is a very pleasant one. We reached Cambridge, about eight o'clock. It is not a large village, and the houses stand very much apart. The college building is the most conspicuous among them. We went to it, expecting to see something curious, as it is the only college, or would-be academy of the Protestants in all America, but we found ourselves mistaken. In approaching the house, we neither heard nor saw any thing mentionable; but, going to the other side of the building, we heard noise enough in an upper room, to lead my comrade to suppose they were engaged in disputation. We entered, and went up stairs, when a person met us, and requested us to walk in, which we did. We found there, eight or ten young fellows, sitting around, smoking tobacco, with the smoke of which the room was so full, that you could hardly see; and the whole house smelt so strong of it, that when I was going up stairs, I said, this is certainly a tavern. We excused ourselves, that we could speak English only a little, but understood Dutch or French, which they did not. However, we spoke as well as we could. We inquired how many professors there were, and they replied not one, that there was no money to support one. We asked how many students there were. They said at first, thirty, and then came down to twenty ; I afterwards understood there are probably not ten. They could hardly speak a word of Latin, so that my comrade could not converse with them. They took us to the library where there was nothing particular. We looked over it a little. They presented us with a glass of wine. This is all we ascertained there. The minister of the place goes there morning and evening to make prayer, and has charge over them. The students have tutors or masters. Our visit was soon over, and we left them to go and look at the land about there. We found the place beautifully situated on a large plain, more than eight miles square, with a fine stream in the middle of it, capable of bearing heavily laden vessels. As regards the fertility of the soil, we consider the poorest in New York, superior to the best here. As we were tired, we took a mouthful to eat, and left. We passed by the printing office, but there was nobody in it ; the paper sash however being broken, we looked in ; and saw two presses with six or eight cases of type. There is not much work done there. Our printing office is well worth two of it, and even more. We went back to Charlestown, where, after waiting a little, we crossed over about three o'clock. We found our skipper, John Foy, at the house, and gave him our names, and the money for our passage, six pounds each. He wished to give us a bill of it, but we told him it was unnecessary, as we were people of good confidence. I spoke to my comrade, and we went out with him, and presented him with a glass of wine. His mate came to him there, who looked more like a merchant than a seaman, a young man and no sailor. We inquired how long our departure would be delayed, and, as we understood him, it would be the last of the coming week. That was annoying to us. Indeed, we have found the English the same everywhere, doing nothing but lying and cheating, when it serves their interest. . . .

12th, *Friday*. We went in the afternoon to Mr. John Taylor's, to ascertain whether he had any good wine, and to purchase some for our voyage, and also some brandy. On arriving at his house, we found him a little cool ; indeed, not as he was formerly. We inquired for what we wanted, and he said he had good Madeira wine, but he believed he had no brandy, though he thought he could assist us in procuring it. We also inquired how we could obtain the history and laws of this place. At last it came out. He said we must be pleased to excuse him if he did not give us admission to his house; he durst not do it, in consequence of there being a certain evil report in the city concerning us; they had been to warn him not to have too much communication with us, if he wished to avoid censure; they said we certainly were Jesuits, who had come here for no good, for we were quiet and modest, and an entirely different sort of people from themselves; that we could speak several languages, were cunning and subtle of mind and judgment, had come there without carrying on any traffic or any other business, except only to see the place and country; that this seemed fabulous as it was unusual in these parts; certainly it could be for no good purpose. As regards the voyage to Europe, we could have made it as well from New York as from Boston, as opportunities were offered there. This suspicion seemed to have gained more strength because the fire at Boston over a year ago was caused by a Frenchman. Although he had been arrested, they could not prove it against him; but in the course of the investigation, they discovered he had been counterfeiting coin and had profited thereby, which was a crime as infamous as the other. He had no trade or profession; he was condemned; both of his ears were cut off; and he was ordered to leave the country. . . .

23d, Thursday. . . . They are all *Independents* in matters of religion, if it can be called religion; many of them perhaps more for the purposes of enjoying the benefit of its privileges than for any regard to truth and godliness. I observed that while the English flag or color has a red ground with a small white field in the uppermost corner where there is a red cross, they have here dispensed with this cross in their colors, and preserved the rest. They baptize no children except those of the members of the congregation. All their religion consists in observing Sunday, by not working or going into the taverns on that day; but the houses are worse than the taverns. No stranger or traveler can therefore be entertained on a Sunday, which begins at sunset on Saturday, and continues until the same time on Sunday. At these two hours you see all their countenances change. Saturday evening the constable goes round into all the taverns of the city for the purpose of stopping all noise and debauchery, which frequently causes him to stop his search, before his search causes the debauchery to stop. There is a penalty for cursing and swearing, such as they please to impose, the witnesses thereof being at liberty to insist upon it. Nevertheless, you discover little difference between this and other places. Drinking and fighting occur there not less than elsewhere ; and as to truth and true godliness, you must not expect more of them than of others. When we were there, four ministers' sons were learning the silversmith's trade. . . .

As to Boston particularly, it lies in latitude 42° 20' on a very fine bay. The city is quite large, constituting about twelve companies. It has three churches, or meeting houses, as they call them. All the houses are made of thin, small cedar shingles, nailed against frames, and then filled in with brick and other stuff; and so are their churches. For this reason these towns are so liable to fires, as have already happened several times ; and the wonder to me is, that the whole city has not been burnt down, so light and dry are the materials. There is a large dock in front of it constructed of wooden piers, where the large ships go to be careened and rigged ; the smaller vessels all come up to the city. On the left hand side across the river, lies Charlestown, a considerable place, where there is some shipping. Upon the point of the bay, on the left hand, there is a block-house, along which a piece of water runs, called the Milk ditch. The whole place has been an island, but it is now joined to the main land by a low road to Roxbury. In front of the town there are many small islands, between which you pass in sailing in and out. . . .

Journal of a Voyage to New York in 1679-80, in Long Island Historical Society, *Memoirs* (Brooklyn, 1867), I, 377-395 *passim.*

————————

147. A Story of Indian Captivity (1677-1678)

BY QUINTIN STOCKWELL

This is one of many narratives by captives. Stockwell eventually got back to New England. — Bibliography : Winsor, *Narrative and Critical History,* I, ch. v, and III, 360; Channing and Hart, *Guide,* § 126.

' IN the year 1677. *September* 19. between Sun-set and dark, the *Indians* came upon us ; I and another Man, being together, we ran away at the out-cry the *Indians* made, shouting and shooting at some other of the *English* that were hard by. We took a *Swamp* that was at hand for our refuge, the Enemy espying us so near them, ran after us, and

shot many Guns at us, three Guns were discharged upon me, the Enemy
being within three Rod of me, besides many other, before that.   Being
in this Swamp that was miry, I slumpt in, and fell down, whereupon one
of the Enemy stept to me, with his Hatchet lift up to knock me on the
head, supposing that I had been wounded, and so unfit for any other
travel.   I (as it hapned) had a Pistol by me, which though uncharged,
I presented to the *Indian*, who presently stept back ; and told me, if I
would yield, I should have no hurt, he said (which was not true) that
they had destroyed all *Hatfield*, and that the Woods were full of *Indi*ans,
whereupon I yielded my self, and so fell into the Enemies hands, and
by three of them was led away unto the place, whence first I began to
make my flight, where two other *Indians* came running to us, and the
one lifting up the Butt end of his Gun, to knock me on the head, the
other with his hand put by the blow, and said, I was his Friend.   I was
now by my own House which the *Indians* burnt the last year, and I
was about to build up again, and there I had some hopes to escape from
them ; there was an Horse just by, which they bid me take, I did so,
but made no attempt to escape thereby, because the Enemy was near,
and the Beast was slow and dull, then was I in hopes they would send
me to take my own Horses, which they did, but they were so frighted
that I could not come near to them, and so fell still into the Enemies
hands, who now took me, and bound me, and led me away, and soon
was I brought into the Company of Captives, that were that day brought
away from *Hatfield*, which were about a mile off ; and here methoughts
was matter of joy and sorrow both, to see the Company : some Company in this condition being some refreshing, though little help any
wayes ; then were we pinioned and led away in the night over the
Mountains, in dark and hideous wayes, about four miles further, before
we took up our place for rest, which was in a dismal place of Wood on
the East side of that Mountain.   We were kept bound all that night.
The *Indians* kept waking and we had little mind to sleep in this nights
travel, the *Indians* dispersed, and as they went made strange noises, as
of Wolves and Owles, and other Wild Beasts, to the end that they might
not lose one another ; and if followed they might not be discovered by
the *English*.

'About the break of Day, we Marched again and got over the great
River at *Pecomptuck* River mouth, and there rested about two hours.
There the *Indians* marked out upon Trays the number of their Captives
and Slain as their manner is.   Here was I again in great danger ; A

quarrel arose about me, whose Captive I was, for three took me. I thought I must be killed to end the controversie, so when they put it to me, whose I was, I said three *Indians* took me, so they agreed to have all a share in me : and I had now three Masters, and he was my chief Master who laid hands on me first, and thus was I fallen into the hands of the very worst of all the Company; as *Ashpelon* the *Indian* Captain told me; which Captain was all along very kind to me, and a great comfort to the *English*. In this place they gave us some Victuals, which they had brought from the *English*. This morning also they sent ten Men forth to Town to bring away what they could find, some Provision, some Corn out of the Meadow they brought to us upon Horses which they had there taken. From hence we went up about the Falls, where we crost that River again; and whilst I was going, I fell right down lame of my old Wounds that I had in the War, and whilest I was think-- ing I should therefore be killed by the *Indians*, and what Death I should die, my pain was suddenly gone, and I was much encouraged again. We had about eleven Horses in that Company, which the *Indians* made to carry Burthens, and to carry Women. It was afternoon when we now crossed that River, We travelled up that River till night, and then took up our Lodging in a dismal place, and were staked down and spread out on our backs; and so we lay all night, yea so we lay many nights. They told me their Law was, that we should lie so nine nights, and by that time, it was thought we should be out of our knowledge. The manner of staking down was thus; our Arms and Legs stretched out were staked fast down, and a Cord about our necks, so that we could stir no wayes. The first night of staking down, being much tired, I slept as comfortably as ever; the next day we went up the River, and crossed it, and at night lay in *Squakheag Meadows*; our Provision was soon spent; and while we lay in those *Meadows* the *Indians* went an Hunt- ing, and the *English Army* came out after us: then the *Indians* moved again, dividing themselves and the Captives into many Companies, that the *English* might not follow their tract. At night having crossed the River, we met again at the place appointed. The next day we crost the River again on *Squakheag* side, and there we took up our quarters for a long time, I suppose this might be about thirty miles above *Squak- heag*, and here were the *Indians* quite out of all fear of the *English*; but in great fear of the *Mohawks*; here they built a long *Wigwam*. Here they had a great Dance (as they call it) and concluded to burn three of us, and had got Bark to do it with, and as I understood afterwards, I was one that was to be burnt. Sergeant *Plimpton* an other, and *Benjamin Wait* his Wife the third : though I knew not which was to be burnt, yet I perceived some were designed thereunto, so much I understood of their Language : that night I could not sleep for fear of next dayes work, the *Indians* being weary with that Dance, lay down to sleep, and slept soundly. The *English* were all loose, then I went out and brought in Wood, and mended the fire, and made a noise on purpose, but none awaked, I thought if any of the *English* would wake, we might kill them all sleeping, I removed out of the way all the Guns and Hatchets : but my heart failing me, I put all things where they were again. The next day when we were to be burnt, our Master and some others spake for us, and the Evil was prevented in this place : And hereabouts we lay three Weeks together. Here I had a Shirt brought to me, to make, and one *Indian* said it should be made this way, a second another way, a third his way. I told them I would make it that way that my chief Master said ; Whereupon one *Indian* struck me on the face with his Fist. I suddenly rose up in anger ready to strike again, upon this hapned a great Hubbub, and the *Indians* and *English* came about me ; I was fain to humble my self to my Master, so that matter was put up. Before I came to this place, my three Masters were gone a hunting, I was left with an other *Indian*, all the Company being upon a March, I was left with this *Indian*, who fell sick, so that I was fain to carry his Gun and Hatchet, and had opportunity, and had thought to have dispatched him, and run away ; but did not, for that the *English* Captives had promised the contrary to one another, because if one should run away, that would provoke the *Indians*, and indanger the rest that could not run away. Whilest we were here, *Benjamin Stebbins* going with some *Indians* to *Wachuset Hills*, made his escape from them, and when the news of his escape came ; we were all presently called in and Bound ; one of the *Indians* a Captain among them, and alwayes our great Friend, met me coming in, and told me *Stebbins* was run away ; and the *Indians* spake of burning us ; some of only burning and biting off our Fingers by and by. He said there would be a Court, and all would speak their minds, but he would speak last, and would say, that the *Indian* that let *Stebbins* run away was only in fault, and so no hurt should be done us, fear not : so it proved accordingly. Whilest we lingered hereabout, Provision grew scarce, one Bears Foot must serve five of us a whole day ; we began to eat Horse-flesh, and eat up seven in all : three were left alive and were not killed. Whilest we had been here, some of the *Indians* had been down and fallen upon *Hadley*, and were taken by the *English*, agreed with, and let go again ; . . . then we parted into two Companies ; some went one way and some went another way ; and we went over a mighty Mountain, we were eight dayes a going over it, and travelled very hard, and every day we had either Snow or Rain : We noted that on this Mountain all the Water run *Northward*. . . . All the *Indians* went a Hunting but could get nothing : divers dayes they *Powow'd* but got nothing, then they desired the *English* to Pray, and confessed they could do nothing ; they would have us Pray, and see what the *English-man's God* could do. I Prayed, so did Sergeant *Plimpton*, in another place. The *Indians* reverently attended, Morning and Night ; next day they got Bears : then they would needs have us desire a Blessing, return Thanks at Meals : after a while they grew : weary of it, and the *Sachim* did forbid us . . . as soon as it was light I and *Samuel Russel* vvent before on the Ice, upon a River, they said I must go vvhere I could on foot, else I should frieze. *Samuel Russel* slipt into the River vvith one Foot, the *Indians* called him back and dried his Stockins, and then sent us avvay ; and an *Indian* vvith us to Pilot us ; and vve vvent four or five miles before they overtook us : I was then pretty well spent ; *Samuel Russel* was (he said) faint, and wondred how I could live, for he had (he said) ten meals to my one : then I was laid on the Sled, and they ran away with me on the Ice, the rest and *Samuel Russel* came softly after. *Samuel Russel* I never saw more, nor know what became of him : they got but half way, and we got through to *Shamblee* about midnight. Six miles of *Shamblee* (a *French* Town) the River was open, and when I came to travail in that part of the Ice, I soon tired ; and two *Indians* run away to Town, and one only was left : he would carry me a few rods, and then I would go as many, and that trade we drave, and so were long a going six miles. This *Indian* now was kind, and told me that if he did not carry me I would die, and so I should have done sure enough : And he said, I must tell the *English* how he helped me. When we came to the first House there was no Inhabitant : the *Indian* spent, both discouraged ; he said we must now both die, at last he left me alone, and got to another House, and thence came some *French* and *Indians*, and brought me in : the *French* were kind, and put my hands and feet in cold Water, and gave me a Dram of Brandey, and a little hasty pudding and Milk ; when I tasted Victuals I was hungry, and could not have forborn it, but that I could not get it ; now and then they would give me a little as they thought

best for me ; I lay by the fire with the *Indians* that night, but could not
sleep for pain : next morning the *Indians* and *French* fell out about me,
because the *French* as the *Indian* said, loved the *English* better than
the *Indians*. The *French* presently turned the *Indians* out of doors,
and kept me, they were very kind and careful, and gave me a little
something now and then ; while I was here all the Men in that Town
came to see me : . . . it being *Christmas* time, they brought Cakes and
other Provisions with them, and gave to me, so that I had no want : the
Indians tried to cure me, but could not, then I asked for the Chirur-
geon, at which one of the *Indians* in anger, struck me on the face with
his Fist, a *Frenchman* being by, the *French-man* spake to him, I knew
not what he said, and went his way. By and by came the Captain of
the place into the *Wigwam* with about twelve armed Men, and asked
where the *Indian* was that struck the *English-man*, and took him and
told him he should go to the Bilboes, and then be hanged : . . . I spake
to the Captain by an Interpreter, and told him I desired him to set the
Indian free, and told him what he had done for me, he told me he was
a Rogue, and should be hanged ; then I spake more privately, alledging
this Reason, because all the *English Captives* were not come in, if he
were hanged, it might fare the worse with them ; then the Captain said,
that was to be considered : then he set him at liberty, upon this condition, that he should never strike me more, and every day bring me to
his House to eat Victuals. I perceived that the common People did not
like what the *Indians* had done and did to the *English*. . . . The next
day the Chirurgion came again, and dressed me ; and so he did all the
while I was among the *French*. *I* came in at *Christmass*, and went
thence *May* 2*d*. Being thus in the Captain's house, *I* was kept there
till *Ben. Waite* came : & my *Indian* Master being in want of Money,
pawned me to the Captain for 14. *Beavers*, or the worth of them, at
such a day ; if he did not pay he must lose his Pawn, or else sell me
for twenty one Beavers, but he could not get Beaver, and so *I* was
sold. . . .

Increase Mather, *An Essay for the Recording of Illustrious Providences*
     (Boston, 1684), 39–57 *passim*.

148. Career of a Self-made Man, Sir William Phipps (1656–1690)

BY REVEREND COTTON MATHER

Cotton Mather, most voluminous of colonial writers, was for many years minister at the North Church in Boston. The *Magnalia* is the most important book published in colonial times; further extracts will appear in Volume II. — Bibliography: J. A. Doyle, *English in America, Puritan Colonies,* II, 254–258 ; Tyler, *American Literature,* II, 73–83; Barrett Wendell, *Cotton Mather.*

. . . I SHALL now inform him, that this our PHIPS was Born *Feb.* 2. *A. Dom.* 1650. at a despicable Plantation on the River of *Kennebeck,* and almost the furthest Village of the Eastern Settlement of *New-England.* And as the *Father* of that Man, which was as great a Blessing as *England* had in the Age of that Man, was a *Smith,* so a *Gun-Smith,* namly, *James Phips,* once of *Bristol,* had the Honour of being the *Father* to him, whom we shall p·e.ently see, made by the God of Heaven as great a Blessing to *New-England,* as that County could have had, if they themselves had pleased. His fruitful *Mother,* yet living, had no less than *Twenty-Six* Children, whereof *Twenty-One* were Sons ; but Equivalent to them all was *WILLIAM,* one of the youngest, whom his *Father* dying, left young with his *Mother,* and with her he lived, *keeping of Sheep in the Wilderness,* until he was Eighteen Years Old ; at which time he began to feel some further Dispositions of Mind from that *Providence* of God which *took him from the Sheepfolds, from following the Ewes great with Young, and brought him to feed his People.* Reader, enquire no further who was his *Father?* Thou shalt anon see, that he was, as the *Italians* express it, *A Son to his own Labours!*

His Friends earnestly solicited him to settle among them in a Plantation of the *East*; but he had an Unaccountable *Impulse* upon his Mind, perswading him, as he would privately hint unto some of them, *That he was Born to greater Matters.* To come at those *greater Matters,* his first Contrivance was to bind himself an Apprentice unto a *Ship-Carpenter* for Four Years ; in which time he became a Master of the *Trade,* that once in a Vessel of more than *Forty Thousand Tuns,* repaired the Ruins of the Earth ; *Noah*'s, I mean ; he then betook himself an Hundred and Fifty Miles further a Field, even to *Boston,* the Chief Town of *New-England*; which being a Place of the most Business and Resort in those Parts of the World, he expected there more Commodiously to pursue the *Spes Majorum & Meliorum, Hopes* which had inspir'd him.

At *Boston,* where it was that he now learn'd, first of all, to *Read* and *Write,* he followed his Trade for about a Year; and by a laudable Deportment, so recommended himself, that he Married a Young Gentlewoman of good Repute, who was the Widow of one Mr. *John Hull,* a well-bred Merchant, but the Daughter of one Captain *Roger Spencer,* a Person of good Fashion, who having suffer'd much damage in his Estate, by some unkind and unjust Actions, which he bore with such Patience, that for fear of thereby injuring the Publick, he would not seek Satisfaction, *Posterity* might afterward see the Reward of his *Patience,* in what Providence hath now done for one of his own *Posterity.* Within a little while after his Marriage, he indented with several Persons in *Boston,* to Build them a Ship at *Sheeps-coat* River, Two or Three Leagues Eastward of *Kennebeck*; where having Lanched the Ship, he also provided a *Lading* of Lumber to bring with him, which would have been to the Advantage of all Concern'd. But just as the Ship was hardly finished, the Barbarous *Indians* on that River, broke forth into an Open and Cruel War upon the *English*; and the miserable People, surprized by so sudden a storm of Blood, had no Refuge from the Infidels, but the *Ship* now finishing in the Harbour. Whereupon he left his intended *Lading* behind him, and instead thereof, carried with him his old Neighbours and their Families, free of all Charges, to *Boston*; so the *first Action* that he did, after he was his own Man, was to *save his Father's House,* with the Rest of the Neighbourhood, from Ruin; but the Disappointment which befel him from the Loss of his other *Lading,* plunged his Affairs into greater Embarasments with such as had employ'd him.

But he was hitherto no more than beginning to make *Scaffolds* for further and higher *Actions!* He would frequently tell the Gentlewoman his Wife, That he should yet be *Captain of a King's Ship*; That he should come to have the *Command of better Men* than he was now accounted himself; and, That he should be Owner of a *Fair Brick-House* in the *Green-Lane* of *North-Boston*; and, That, it may be, this would not be all that the Providence of God would bring him to. She entertained these Passages with a sufficient Incredulity; but he had so *serious* and *positive* an Expectation of them, that it is not easie to say, what was the *Original* thereof. He was of an Enterprizing *Genius,* and naturally disdained *Littleness*: But his Disposition for *Business* was of the *Dutch* Mould, where, with a little shew of *Wit,* there is as much *Wisdom* demonstrated, as can be shewn by any Nation. His Talent lay not in the *Airs* that serve chiefly for the pleasant and sudden Turns of *Conversation* ; but he might say, as *Themistocles, Though he could not play upon a Fiddle, yet he knew how to make a little City become a Great One.* He would *prudently* contrive a weighty Undertaking, and then patiently pursue it unto the End. He was of an Inclination, cutting rather like a *Hatchet,* than like a *Razor* ; he would propose very Considerable Matters to himself, and then so *cut through* them, that no Difficulties could put by the *Edge* of his Resolutions. Being thus of the *True Temper,* for doing of *Great Things,* he betakes himself to the *Sea,* the Right *Scene* for such Things ; and upon Advice of a *Spanish Wreck* about the *Bahama's,* he took a Voyage thither ; but with little more success, than what just served him a little to furnish him for a Voyage to *England* ; whither he went in a Vessel, not much unlike that which the *Dutchmen* stamped on their *First Coin,* with these Words about it, *Incertum quo Fata ferant.* Having first informed himself that there was another *Spanish Wreck,* wherein was lost a mighty Treasure, hitherto undiscovered, he had a strong Impression upon his Mind that *He* must be the Discoverer ; and he made such Representations of his Design at *White-Hall,* that by the Year 1683. he became the Captain of *a King's Ship,* and arrived at *New England* Commander of the *Algier-Rose,* a Frigot of Eighteen Guns, and Ninety-Five Men. . . .

. . . Now with a small Company of other Men he sailed from thence to *Hispaniola,* where by the Policy of his Address, he fished out of a very old *Spaniard,* (or *Portuguese*) a little Advice about the true Spot where lay the *Wreck* which he had been hitherto seeking, as unprosperously, as the *Chymists* have their *Aurisick Stone :* That it was upon a *Reef of Shoals,* a few Leagues to the Northward of *Port de la Plata,* upon *Hispaniola,* a Port so call'd, it seems, from the Landing of some of the *Shipwreck'd* Company, with a Boat full of Plate, saved out of their Sinking Frigot : Nevertheless, when he had searched very narrowly the Spot, whereof the old *Spaniard* had advised him, he had not hitherto exactly lit upon it. Such *Thorns* did vex his Affairs while he was in the *Rose-Frigot* ; but none of all these things could retund the Edge of his Expectations to find the *Wreck* ; with such Expectations he return'd then into *England,* that he might there better furnish himself to Prosecute a *New Discovery* ; for though he judged he might, by proceeding a little further, have come at the right *Spot,* yet he found his present Company too ill a Crew to be confided in.

So *proper* was his Behaviour, that the best Noble Men in the Kingdom now admitted him into their Conversation ; but yet he was opposed by powerful Enemies, that Clogg'd his Affairs with such Demurrages, and such *Disappointments*, as would have wholly Discouraged his Designs, if his Patience had not been *Invincible*. *He who can wait hath what he desireth.* This his Indefatigable *Patience*, with a proportionable *Diligence*, at length overcame the Difficulties that had been thrown in his way; and prevailing with the Duke of *Albemarle*, and some other Persons of Quality, to fit him out, he set Sail for the *Fishing-Ground*, which had been so well *baited* half an Hundred Years before : . . . Nevertheless, as they were upon the Return, one of the Men looking over the side of the *Periaga*, into the calm Water, he spied a *Sea Feather*, growing, as he judged, out of a Rock ; whereupon they bad one of their *Indians* to Dive and fetch this *Feather*, that they might however carry home *something* with them, and make, at least, as fair a Triumph as *Caligula's*. The *Diver* bringing up the *Feather*, brought therewithal a surprizing Story, That he perceived a Number of *Great Guns* in the *Watry World* where he had found his *Feather* ; the *Report* of which *Great Guns* exceedingly astonished the whole Company ; and at once turned their *Despondencies* for their ill success into *Assurances*, that they had now lit upon the *true Spot* of Ground which they had been looking for ; and they were further confirmed in these *Assurances*, when upon further Diving, the *Indian* fetcht up a *Sow*, as they stil'd it, or a Lump of Silver, worth perhaps Two or Three Hundred Pounds. . . . and they so prospered in this *New Fishery*, that in a little while they had, without the loss of any Man's Life, brought up *Thirty Two Tuns* of Silver ; for it was now come to measuring of Silver by *Tuns*. . . .

But there was one extraordinary Distress which Captain *Phips* now found himself plunged into : For his Men were come out with him upon Seamens Wages, at so much *per* Month ; and when they saw such vast Litters of Silver *Sows* and *Pigs*, as they call them, come on Board them at the Captain's Call, they knew not how to bear it, that they should not *share* all among themselves, and be gone to lead *a short Life and a merry*, in a Climate where the Arrest of those that had hired them should not reach them. . . . Captain *Phips* now coming up to *London* in the Year 1687. with near *Three Hundred Thousand Pounds Sterling* aboard him, did acquit himself with such an Exemplary Honesty, that partly by his fulfilling his Assurances to the Seamen, and partly by his exact and punctual Care to have his Employers defrauded of nothing that might consciensiously belong unto them, he had less than *Sixteen Thousand Pounds* left unto himself : As an acknowledgment of which

Honesty in him, the Duke of *Albemarle* made unto his Wife, whom he never saw, a Present of a *Golden Cup*, near a Thousand Pound in value. The Character of an *Honest Man* he had so merited in the whole Course of his Life, and especially in this last act of it, that this, in Conjunction with his other serviceable Qualities, procured him the Favours of the Greatest Persons in the Nation; and *he that had been so diligent in his Business, must now stand before Kings, and not stand before mean Men.* . . . Accordingly the King, in Consideration of the Service done by him, in bringing such a Treasure into the Nation, conferr'd upon him the Honour of *Knighthood*; and if we now reckon him, *A Knight of the Golden Fleece*, the Stile might pretend unto some Circumstances that would justifie it.   Or call him, if you please, *The Knight of Honesty*; for it was *Honesty* with *Industry* that raised him; . . .

. . . Indeed, when King *James* offered, as he did, unto Sir *William Phips* an Opportunity to Ask what he pleased of him, Sir *William* Generously prayed for nothing but *this*, *That* New-England *might have its lost Priviledges Restored*. The King then Replied, *Any Thing but that!* Whereupon he set himself to Consider what was the *next Thing* that he might ask for the Service, not of himself, but of his *Country*. The Result of his Consideration was, That by Petition to the King, he Obtained, with expence of some Hundreds of *Guinea's*, a *Patent*, which constituted him *The High Sheriff of that Country*; hoping, by his Deputies in that Office, to supply the Country still with Consciencious Juries, which was the only Method that the *New-Englanders* had left them to secure any thing that was Dear unto them.   Furnished with this *Patent*, after he had, in Company with Sir *John Narborough*, made a Second Visit unto the *Wreck*, (not so advantageous as the former for a Reason already mentioned) in his way he Returned unto *New-England*, in the Summer of the Year 1688. able, after Five Years Absence, to Entertain his Lady with some Accomplishment of his Predictions; and then Built himself a *Fair Brick House* in the very *place* which we foretold, the Reader can tell how many *Sections* ago. . . .

Accordingly on *March* 23. 1690. after he had in the Congregation of *North-Boston* given himself up, *first unto the Lord, and then unto his People*, he was *Baptized*, and so received into the *Communion* of the Faithful there. . . .

Cotton Mather, *Magnalia Christi Americana* (London, 1702), Book II, 38–47 *passim.*

149. The Family Life of a Puritan Gentleman (1692)

BY CHIEF JUSTICE SAMUEL SEWALL

Sewall, "the Puritan Pepys," was a distinguished Massachusetts man: for a time a minister, later a judge; a man of wealth. His diary is a curiously minute picture of the times. The dates are omitted from these extracts. — Bibliography: Tyler, *American Literature*, II, 99–103; Samuel Sewall, *Letter-Book*.

. . . GO to Hog-Island with Joshua Gee and sell him 3 white oaks for thirty shillings; I am to cart them to the Water side.

I ride to Newton to see Sam., dine with Mr. Hobart, his wife, Mrs. Prentice, and 2 or 3 Cambridge Scholars; bring home some Chestnuts in the Burs to set. First went to George Bearstow's and the widow Gates's. Rains at night Oct. 1.

Mr. Willard and I visit loansom Mr. Torrey; we meet my Unkle entring Crane's Plain in his way to Boston; He turns back with us and accompanies to Weymouth. Mrs. Fisk is very dangerously ill. Got home rather before seven aclock very well, blessed be God. Mr. Torrey took our visit very kindly. Din'd in his Kitchin Chamber. He made Mr. Willard crave a Blessing and return Thanks, which He perform'd excellently. To morrow will be a moneth since Mrs. Torrey died, Sept. 10th 1692. Mr. Torrey seems to be of opinion that the Court of Oyer and Terminer should go on, regulating any thing that may have been amiss, when certainly found to be so. Fine rain after our getting home.

The Court of Oyer and Terminer is opened at Boston to trie a French Malatta for shooting dead an English youth.

Went to the Funeral of Mrs. Sarah Oliver, widow, aged 72. years; buried in the new burying place; a very good, modest, humble, plain, liberal Matron. Bearers, Sam. Sewall, Major Jn° Walley, Capt. Joshua Scottow, Capt. James Hill, Capt. Jacob Eliot, Capt. Theophilus Frary. Scarvs and Gloves.

Read Mr. Willard's Epistle to Mr. Mather's book, as to Cases of Conscience touching Witchcraft.

Set two Chestnuts at Mr. Bromfield's Orchard, and three at our own, hoping they may come up in the Spring.

Went to Cambridge and visited Mr. Danforth, and discoursed with Him about the Witchcraft; thinks there cañot be a procedure in the Court except there be some better consent of Ministers and People.

Told me of the woman's coming into his house last Sabbath-day sen-night at Even.

Went to Salem and visited my sick Brother, who has had a Fever all this moneth ; Is very desirous to live, and makes vows to serve God better, if his life be spared : was much affected at my coming in.

At night, Mr. Cook, Oakes and Wiswall arrive, got to their houses almost before any body knew it ; have been 8 week and 5 days from Plimouth. Went and saw my Landlord and Landlady Jennings ; their Son in Jamaica has a Plantation spoiled by a Mountain thrown upon it by the late Earthquake.

A Bill is sent in about calling a Fast, and Convocation of Ministers, that may be led in the right way as to the Witchcrafts. The season and mañer of doing it, is such, that the Court of Oyer and Terminer count themselves thereby dismissed. 29 Nos. and 33 yeas to the Bill. Capt. Bradstreet and Lieut. True, Wᵐ Huchins and several other interested persons there, in the affirmative.

Mr. Cotton Mather preaches from James, I. 4.

Lieut. Governour coming over the Causey is, by reason of the high Tide, so wet, that is fain to go to bed till sends for dry cloaths to Dorchester ; In the Afternoon, as had done several times before, desired to have the advice of the Governour and Council as to the sitting of the Court of Oyer and Terminer next week ; said should move it no more ; great silence, as if should say do not go. . . .

Joseph threw a knop of Brass and hit his Sister Betty on the forhead so as to make it bleed and swell ; upon which, and for his playing at Prayer-time, and eating when Return Thanks, I whipd him pretty smartly. When I first went in (call'd by his Grandmother) he sought to shadow and hide himself from me behind the head of the Cradle : which gave me the sorrowfull remembrance of Adam's carriage. . . .

I drove a Treenail in the Governour's Briganteen ; and invited his Excellency to drink a Glass of Brandy, which was pleas'd to doe with Capt. Greenough, Mr. Jackson Elliston, and his little Son. Saith tis the first time has been in the House since my Father's days, who was one of his Owners to the Wreck.

Mr. Dudley at our Meetinghouse P.M. Uproar in North Meeting House by Cry of Fire, in first Prayer, Afternoon Exercise.

Mr. Joseph Eliot, of Guilford, visited, supped and prayed with us, went not away till half an hour after nine at night.

I prayd that God would pardon all my Sinfull Wanderings, and direct

2 L

me for the future.   That God would bless the Assembly in their debates, and that would chuse and assist our Judges, &c., and save New England as to Enemies and Witchcrafts, and vindicate the late Judges, consisting with his Justice and Holiness, &c., with Fasting.   Cousin Anne Quinsy visited me in the Evening, and told me of her children's wellfare.   Now about, Mercy Short grows ill again, as formerly.

Mr. Mather sent for to her.   Bill for Courts pass'd.

Mrs. Brown, wife of Major W.ᵐ Brown, is buried this day; is much lamented in Salem.   Died on Monday about Sunset.   Mr. Bartholomew died about the same time.   Extraordinary foggy and dark wether almost all this week.

Sam. comes to see us from Newton.   Give him 16ᵈ, a Groat having engraven, *Salvum fac Regem Domine*, which he construed to me, &c. . . .

Major General tells me, that last night about 7 aclock, he saw 5. or 7 Balls of Fire that mov'd and mingled each with other, so that he could not tell them; made a great Light, but streamed not.   Twas our privat Meeting; I saw nothing of it.   Order comes out for a Fast.   I carry one to Mr. Willard.   Mrs. Willard talks to me very sharply about Capt. Alden's not being at the Lord's Supper last Sabbath-day. . . .

After this went to Nevison's and took a very good Repast provided for us by the Select-Men; by which time 'twas past Sunset.   Got home well about 7 aclock, in the dark, over the Neck alone.   *Laus Deo.*

I went to Newton to see Sam.   Mrs. Hobart is not well, has been very sick: went out about 11. and came in about 5.   Staid more than two hours there.

Serj.ᵗ Solomon Rainsford is buried.   W.ᵐ Gilbert and he died the last week.

A very extraordinary Storm by reason of the falling and driving of the Snow.   Few Women could get to Meeting.   Our two Maids and my self there.   A child named Alexander was baptized in the Afternoon. Major General not abroad in the Afternoon.   Gov.ʳ Bradstreet very sick.

Mr. Elisha Cook, Mr. Isaac Addington and I saw and heard Simon Bradstreet Esqr. sign, seal and publish a Codicil now añexed to his Will, written by said Addington at said Bradstreets direction, and read to him several times.   Signd and seald it sitting up in his Bed.   After told us that if his Estate should exceed Two hundred pounds more than was mentioned in the Will, would have his Executors distribute it accord- ing to the direction of his Overseers, and Wife, I think.   Said, the reason why would sell the little farm. was because 'twas a ruinous thing, and yielded but 8£ *per* añum in Country-pay. Call'd for Ale and made us drink.

Went in with Mr. Cotton Mather to Mr. Bradstreets, and heard him pray.

A very sunshiny, hot, thawing day. Note. Just as we came out of the Meetinghouse at Noon, Savil Simson's Chimny fell on fire, and blaz'd out much, which made many people stand gazing at it a pretty while, being so near the Meetinghouse.

Three Williams baptized ; Elisabeth Wisendunk and Abigail Winslow taken into Church, and Elisabeth Monk (formerly Woodmancy) Restored, having made a satisfactory Confession. . . .

Joseph puts his Grandmother and Mother in great fear by swallowing a Bullet which for a while stuck in his Throat : He had quite got it down, before I knew what the matter was. This day in the Afternoon One of Mr. Holyoke's Twins falls into the Well and is drownd, no body but a Negro being at home ; was a very lovely Boy of about 4 years old. Satterday, March 11, about Sunset He is buried. When I come home from the funeral, my wife shows me the Bullet Joseph swallowed. . . .

Benjamin Hallawell, late captive in Algier, and his Infant daughter, Mary, were baptized. When I first saw him in London, I could hardly persuade myself that he could live over the Sea, and now I see him and his daughter baptized. Lord let it be a Token that Thou wilt revive thy work in the midst of the years. In London, twas some discouragement to me to think how hardly 'twould come off for the father to pay me for the English Money I had disbursed for the Redemption of a dead Son : but God has given him a new life. . . .

Our kitchin chimney fell on fire about noon, and blaz'd out sorely at top, appeared to be very foul : the fire fell on the shingles so that they begun to burn in several places, being very dry : but by the good Providence of God, no harm done. Mr. Fisk was with us, and we sat merrily to dinner on the Westfield Pork that was snatch'd from the fire on this Occasion. Mother was exceedingly frighted ; and is ready to think we are called to remove. This very morning had as 'twere concluded not to build this Summer ; . . .

Carried my daughter Hañah to Salem in Company of Mr. Hathorne and Sam. Wakefield ; got thether about 8. at night.

Carried her to Rowley, Wᵐ Longfellow rid before her ; I staid Lecture at Ipswich, where unexpectedly heard Mr. Edward Tomson preach a very good Sermon from Felix's procrastination.

Rid home, having much adoe to pacify my dear daughter, she weeping and pleading to go with me.

Jnᵒ Barnard raises the Roof of the brick House, no hurt done, through God's goodness.

This day, Mrs Hunt, Mr. Torrey's Sister, is buried. Alass! that it should be so.

The Ship at Bull's Wharf of Four Hundred Tuns, named the Lere-Frigot was Lanched. Yesterday's Storm hindered her being Lanched then. Mr. Eyre's child buried this Afternoon.

I ride to Newton to see Sam and Joseph.

Our House is covered and defended against the wether.

The first Snow falls. . . .

Diary of Samuel Sewall, Vol. I, in Massachusetts Historical Society, *Collections* (Boston, 1878), Fifth Series, V, 366–385 *passim*.

PART VI

MIDDLE COLONIES

CHAPTER XXII — CONDITIONS

150. Services of a Trading Company (1629)

BY THE DIRECTORS OF THE WEST INDIA COMPANY

(TRANSLATED BY E. B. O'CALLAGHAN, 1856)

The Dutch West India Company was chartered in 1621, and the colony of New Netherland was its work. It much resembled the English East India Company in the combination of naval and commercial functions. — Bibliography: Winsor, *Narrative and Critical History*, IV, 410–416; Brodhead, *History of the State of New York*, I, 134–137; Channing and Hart, *Guide*, § 104; see also No. 153 below.

High and Mighty Lords,

ALTHOUGH we are confident that you, High and Mighty, can in your usual wisdom, and will, pursuant to your special regard and favor for us, consider that the security and welfare of our beloved Fatherland is most intimately connected with the preservation and prosperity of our Company, yet we have deemed it our duty to lay, with all submission, before you, High and Mighty, in a summary manner, the principal points which, in these parts, ought to be taken into consideration.

First: it is to be considered with what longing the Company has been expected, for many years, by all good Patriots at home, and all good wishers of our state abroad; and how slowly it has been brought to maturity, against numerous contradictions and countermines on the part of others.

Secondly: that you, High and Mighty, have, of your own motion and unasked, incorporated your subjects, and promised, in the form of a mutual contract and reciprocal connection, to afford them every help in case of war, and to maintain, in their integrity, all their contracts with foreigners.

Thirdly : that thereupon, the Capital of this Company was wholly sub-scribed and sufficiently paid in, through the several efforts of the Directors appointed thereunto by you, High and Mighty, by such as you your-selves consider have most at heart the maintenance of the true Reformed religion and the liberties of our beloved Fatherland ; so that many have contributed abundantly thereunto even out of their poverty.

Fourthly : that by means of this Company, even from its very incipi-ency, a great number of ships were partly purchased and partly char-tered, which otherwise must have lain idle in consequence of the dullness of trade.

Fifthly : that by means of the same, many large and small vessels, and especially, very fine and fast sailing yachts have been built, to the great increase of Navigation.

Sixthly : that the number of our vessels has, from time to time, so much increased, that we have at present over one hundred full rigged ships, of various burthens, at sea, mostly fitted for war.

Seventhly : that we have employed, from time to time, in said ships, a great number of seamen and soldiers, so that we had last year 9,000 men, and now, at present, full 15,000 in our service ; whereby the people were wonderfully benefited ; many experienced pilots formed, and so many educated, that the country can always find fit persons to be employed on board its ships as chief and subordinate officers.

Eighthly : that we have victualled the aforesaid ships, some for 12, some for 15, and even many for 18 months and more.

Ninthly : that we have provided our ships so well with heavy guns, that we had, last year, on board our marine, full 264 metal pieces, amongst which were many demi-carthouns ; and nearly 1400 heavy swivels, which number is much increased this year, so that we have at present over 400 metal pieces on board of our ships, and over 2000 swivels, besides pedereros to the number of far beyond 600.

And finally : that we have provided them with a great quantity of powder, mostly manufactured in this country, so that we have expended, this year, on board our ships, over one hundred thousand pounds of powder.   From all which it must at once be seen, what trade our equip-ments have created in this country ; how many people we have employed, and with what a remarkable force we have increased Your High Mighti-nesses' navy, of which Your High Mightinesses can make use in time of need, as the Company's aid, without boasting, was particularly well timed in the last public difficulties.

It is now to be further considered what wealth these, our ships, have brought into this country.

First : omitting what has been imported these previous years in course of trade in gold, elephants' teeth, pepper, hides, peltries, timber, salt and such like ; the silver, coined and in bars, received in the beginning of this year, in consequence of the capture of the fleet from New Spain, amounted to so great a treasure, that never did any fleet bring such a prize to this, or any other country.

Secondly : we have now, during some consecutive years, plundered the enemy and enriched this country with many large parcels of Indigo, so that over 4000 cases have been received at the close of the last, and the beginning of this year.

Thirdly : a large quantity of Sugar, so that we have brought in, this year alone, three thousand chests.

Fourthly : a wonderful large quantity of Raw hides, and have taken 36ᵐ principally this year from the enemy.

Fifthly : the handsomest lot of Cochineal that was ever brought into this country.

Sixthly : a considerable quantity of Tobacco, which is now an important article of commerce.

And finally, a vast amount of wealth in all sorts of precious stones, silk and silk goods, musk, amber, all sorts of drugs, Brazil and Log Wood and other wares, too numerous to mention here ; so that we have already brought several millions into this country.   All which wares, sold and distributed among the good inhabitants, were consumed here and conveyed elsewhere, and therefore enriched your High Mightinesses' subjects, and increased the revenue.

The damage done thereby to our enemies, is easily estimated. We have, moreover, captured some even of the King of Spain's galeons, hitherto considered invincible, besides some other of his men of War, exclusive of more than two hundred ships and barks which we have taken from his subjects, and partly appropriated to our own use, and partly destroyed.

Our ships and fleets also reduced, and for a time kept possession of, the rich and mighty city of St. Salvador, in Brazil ; sacked Porto Rico ; pointed out the way to seize its exceedingly enclosed harbors, and have destroyed the castle of Margrita.

By all which acts have we not only drained the King of Spain's treasury, but also further pursued him at considerable expense.

We say, exhausted his treasury —

First, by depriving him of so much silver, which was as blood from one of the arteries of his heart.

Secondly, by &c.

> Your High Mightinesses'
> Humble Servants,
> The Deputies of the Chartered West India
> Company at the Assembly of the XIX. . . .

E. B. O'Callaghan, editor, *Documents Relative to the Colonial History of the State of New-York* (Albany, 1856), I, 40–42.

---

151. A Dutch Trader (1632–1633)

BY DAVID PIETERSZ. DE VRIES (1655)

(TRANSLATED BY HENRY C. MURPHY, 1857)

De Vries was a Master Artilleryman in the army in Holland, a bold seaman, and associated with several patroons in making settlements in New Netherland. — Bibliography: Winsor, *Narrative and Critical History*, IV, 418–419; New York Historical Society, *Collections*, New Series, I, 245–249; Channing and Hart, *Guide*, § 104.

ANNO 1632. The 12th of February we again entered into an agreement to equip a ship and yacht for the whale fishery, in which much profit had not been realized ; because we had had such a losing voyage, and no returns from the whale fishery, and saw no prospect of any. But Samuel Godyn encouraged us to make another attempt. He said the Greenland Company had two bad voyages with Willen Van Muyen, and afterwards became a thrifty company. It was therefore again resolved to undertake a voyage for the whale fishery, and that I myself should go as patroon, and as commander of the ship and yacht, and should endeavour to be there in December, in order to conduct the whale fishing during the winter, as the whales come in the winter and remain till March.

Before sailing out the Texel, we understood that our little fort had been destroyed by the Indians, the people killed, — two and thirty men, — who were outside the fort working the land. . . .

The 1st of August, with a good north-east wind, weighed anchor, and made sail with my ship and yacht, and the ship New Netherland.

The 2d, passed Land's End, and laid our course for the Canary Islands.

The 13th, we saw Madeira on our larboard, and at the same time a Turk came towards us, but as soon as he observed that we were stout ships, he hauled off from us, and we sailed for him. The evening growing dark, I fired a shot for my yacht to come by me. . . .

The 14th, towards evening, we saw the Isle of Palms on our lee, and set our course from thence to Barbadoes.

The 4th of September, we came in sight of Barbadoes, and the next day, towards evening, arrived at the Island of St. Vincent. . . .

On the 8th, we weighed anchor, and passed by the islands of Martinique, Dominica, Guadaloupe, Montserrat, Redonde, and Nevis, arrived the 20th [10th] before St. Christopher, where we found some English ships, and obtained a supply of water.

The 11th, weighed anchor, in order to sail to St. Martin. Half-way between St. Martin and St. Christopher, we met a French ship with a large sloop in company; he screamed at us, as if he sought to commit some hostility towards us, but I kept my course, heeding him not. . . .

The 29th, weighed anchor with my yacht to get under sail, . . . By evening I arrived before the Island of Nevis. I went ashore to the governor, an Englishman, named Littleton. He requested me to take aboard some captive Portuguese, and to put them, on my way to St. Christophers, on board an English ship called Captain Stone's; which I could not refuse him, if I had them only three or four hours in the ship. . . .

The 14th [of November], in the thirty-second degree of latitude, the Bermudas to the east of us, encountered a severe storm from the north-west; the water turned round as if it were an hurricane; . . .

The 2d [of December], threw the lead in fourteen fathoms, sandy bottom, and smelt the land, which gave a sweet perfume, as the wind came from the north-west, which blew off land, and caused these sweet odours. This comes from the Indians setting fire, at this time of year, to the woods and thickets, in order to hunt; and the land is full of sweet-smelling herbs, as sassafras, which has a sweet smell. . . .

The 5th, the wind south-west, we weighed anchor, and sailed into the South bay, and lay, with our yacht, in four fathoms water, and saw immediately a whale near the ship. Thought this would be royal work — the whales so numerous — and the land so fine for cultivation.

The 6th, we went with the boat into the river, well manned, in order to see if we could speak with any Indians, but coming by our *house*, which was destroyed, found it well beset with palisades in place of breastworks, but it was almost burnt up. Found lying here and there the skulls and bones of our people, and the heads of the horses and cows which they had brought with them, but perceiving no Indians, the business being undone, came on board the boat, and let the gunner fire a shot in order to see if we could find any trace of them the next day. . . .

The 5th [of January, 1633], we weighed anchor in the morning, and sailed before the little fort named Fort Nassau, where formerly some families of the West India Company had dwelt. Some Indians had assembled there to barter furs, but I desired to trade for their Turkish beans, because we had no goods to exchange for peltries, and our stores had been given away at Swanendael for the purpose of making the peace, so that there were not more than two pieces of cloth left of our goods, and two kettles, for which we wanted corn. . . .

The 5th of March, determined to make a voyage to the English in Virginia, . . . Although there had never been any one there from this quarter, I said, as I had escaped the danger in the South river, I would be the first one of our nation to venture to the English in Virginia, from these parts, as the distance is not more than thirty miles from the South river or Cape Hinloopen. . . .

The 11th, went ashore, where the governor stood upon the beach, with some halberdeers and musketeers, to welcome us. On my setting foot upon the land, he came up to me, and bid me heartily welcome. He inquired of me where I came from. I answered him, from the South Bay of New Netherland. He asked how far it was from their bay. I said thirty miles. He then proceeded with me to his house, where he bid me welcome with a Venice glass of sack, and then brought out his chart, and showed me that the South Bay was called by them My Lord Delaware's Bay, who had encountered foul weather there some years ago, and, finding the place full of shoals, thought it was not navigable. They had, therefore, never looked after it since, but it was their King's land, and not New Netherland. I answered him that there was a fine river there, that for ten years no Englishman had been there, and that we for many years had had a fort there, called Fort Nassau. It was strange to him, that he should have such neighbours, and have never heard of them. He had, indeed, heard that we had a fort in the fortieth degree of latitude, at Hudson's river as they called it, and that a sloop was sent there last September, with seven or eight men, to see whether there was a river there, who had not returned, and whether they had perished at sea or not, he did not know. . . .

. . . I remained at dinner with the governor, and as we sat at the meal, Captain Stone asked why the governor had an interpreter for me, as I could speak English; at least, I had spoken English to them in the West Indies. The governor said he did not know that, and inquired whether I could also speak French. I said "Yes." Whether I understood Italian. I answered in the affirmative. Whether I had been in Italy, and in Africa, and in the East Indies. I said I had. He was astonished that I had begun so early to command. Finally, there sat at the table an Englishman, who had been in the East Indies at the same time that I was there, and who asked me who commanded the English in the East Indies when I was there. I gave him the name; and when I could see him, I looked at him well, and he at me. Then this commander said that mountains could not, but men who go and see the world can, meet each other. Besides, the commander had assisted me with provision while I was there. This commander was named Sir John Harvey. . . .

The 16th [of April], weighed anchor, and ran over to Staten Island, all along the shore of which runs a great sand-bank, entirely flat. It is necessary to sound the southeast side, and it will not do to come nearer than from three to four and a half fathoms with a large ship. Arrived at noon before Fort Amsterdam, and found a Company's ship there, called the Soutbergh, with a prize taken on the way, laden with sugar. She had brought a new governor, Wouter Van Twiller of Newkirk. He had been a clerk in the West India Department at Amsterdam. They had left Holland after us. I went ashore to the fort, out of which he came to welcome me, and inquired of me also, how the whale-fishery succeeded. I answered him that I had a sample; but that they were foolish who undertook the whale-fishery here at such great expense, when they could have readily ascertained with one, two, or three sloops in New Netherland, whether it was good fishing or not. . . .

The 18th, arrived here an Englishman, who came from New England to trade in the river, . . . This Englishman invited the governor to come and see him. I went with him, in company with a number of the officers, who became intoxicated, and got into such high words, that the Englishman could not understand how it was that there should be such unruliness among the officers of the Company, and that a governor should have no more control over them; he was not accustomed to it among his countrymen. The Englishman remained six or seven days lying before the fort, and then said he wished to go up the river, and that the land was theirs. This we denied, declaring that they had never made any settlement there. . . .

The 24th, the Englishman weighed anchor and sailed up the river to Fort Orange, where this Jacob Eelkes had formerly resided as commander for the private Company; when governor Wouter Van Twiller assembled all his forces before his door, had a cask of wine brought out, filled a bumper, and cried out for those who loved the Prince of Orange and him, to do the same as he did, and protect him from the outrage of the Englishman, who was already out of sight sailing up the river. The people all began to laugh at him; for they understood well how to drink dry the cask of wine, as it was just the thing they wanted, even if there had been six casks, and did not wish to trouble the Englishman, saying they were friends. As I sat at the table with him at noon, I told him that he had committed great folly, as the Englishman had no commission to navigate there, but a paper of the custom-house that he had paid so much duty, and might sail with so many passengers to New England, and not to New Netherland. I said, if it were my matter, I would have helped him away from the fort with *beans* from the eight-pounders, and not permitted him to sail up the river, — would rather have held him back by the tail, as he said he was a man from England. I told him as the English committed some excesses against us in the East Indies, we should take hold of them; that I had no good opinion of that nation, for they were so proud a nature, that they thought everything belonged to them; were it an affair of mine, I would send the ship Soutberg after him, and make him haul down the river, and drive him from it until he brought another commission than a custom-house license; that he was only making sport of him. . . .

When we had made everything ready, and were about to take our leave of the governor, he then came to annoy me anew. He did not want me to go with my boat to embark until his boat had first boarded our ship, in order to search her. I opposed it, and told him that she was not to be searched. I was bound home, and if he wished to write any letters, he could do so, and send them after I had gone to my boat. He immediately sent twelve musketeers after me, in order that we should not depart. My boat's crew asked whether they should row away in the boat. I said I would let them do so, and had they my

courage they would. They immediately did so, and the musketeers
were ridiculed with shouts and jeers by all the bystanders, who cried out
that they should have stopped the Englishman with shot and muskets,
from sailing past the fort, and not our own patrons of the country, who
sought to promote its interests. . . .

The bay inside of Sandy Hook is a large one, where fifty to sixty
ships can lie, well protected from the winds of the sea. Sandy Hook
stretches a full half-mile from the hills, forming a flat sandy beach, about
eight or nine paces wide, and is covered with small blue-plum trees,
which there grow wild.

The 15th June, we weighed anchor, and made sail for *patria*. . . .

David Pietersz. de Vries, *Voyages from Holland to America*, in New York
   Historical Society, *Collections* (New York, 1857), Second Series, II₁,
   Pt. 1, 16–43 *passim*.

---

152. The Iroquois (1644)

BY REVEREND JOHN MEGAPOLENSIS

(TRANSLATED BY EBENEZER HAZARD (?), 1792)

The author was a minister of the Dutch church at Rensselaerwyck, and an early
missionary to the Indians whom he describes. — Bibliography : Winsor, *Narrative
and Critical History*, IV, 420–421; Brodhead, *History of the State of New York*, I,
343, 374–376; see also Nos. 40, 60, 91 above.

. . . THE principal Nation of all the Savages and Indians here-
     abouts with which we are connected, are the *Mahakuaas*
[Mohawks], who have laid all the other Indians near us under Contribution. This Nation has a very heavy Language, and I find great Difficulty in learning it so as to speak and preach to them fluently : there
are no Christians who understand the Language thoroughly ; those who
have lived here long can hold a kind of Conversation, just sufficient to
carry on Trade, but they do not understand the Idiom of the Language.
I am making a Vocabulary of the *Mahakuaa* Language, and when I am
among them I ask them how Things are called ; then, as they are very
dumb, I cannot sometimes get an Explanation of what I want. . . .

The Indians in this Country are of much the same Stature with us
Dutchmen ; some of them have very good Features, and their Bodies
and Limbs are well proportioned ; they all have black Eyes, but their

Skin is tawney : . . .   In Winter they hang loosely about them a Deer's, or Bear's, or Panther's Skin, or they take some Beaver and Otter Skins, or Wild-Cat's, Raccoons, Martin's, Otters, Mink's, Squirrel or several Kinds of Skins, which are Plenty in this Country, and sew some of them upon others, until it is a square Piece, and that is then a Garment for them, or they buy of us Dutchmen two and an half Ells of Duffils, and that they hang loosely on them, just as it was torn off, without any sewing, and as they go away they look very much at themselves, and think they are very fine.   They make themselves Stockings and Shoes of Deer Skin, or they take the Leaves of their Corn, and plat them together and use them for Shoes. . . . the Women let their Hair grow very long, and tie it, and let it hang down their Backs : some of the Men wear their Hair on one Side of the Head, and some on both Sides, and a long Lock of Hair Hanging down : on the top of their Heads they have a Streak of Hair from the Forehead to the Neck, about the Breadth of three Fingers, and this they shorten till it is about two or three Fingers long, and it stands right on End like Hogs Bristles ; on both Sides of this Streak they cut the Hair short off, except the aforesaid Locks, and they also leave on the bare Places here and there small Locks, such as are in Sweeping-Brushes, and they are very fine.   They likewise paint their Faces, red, blue, &c. and then they look like the Devil himself. . . .
. . . The Women are obliged to prepare the Land, to mow, to plant, and do every Thing ; the Men do nothing except hunting, fishing, and going to War against their Enemies : they treat their Enemies with great Cruelty in Time of War, for they first bite off the Nails of the Fingers of their Captives, and cut off some Joints, and sometimes the whole of the Fingers ; after that the Captives are obliged to sing and dance before them . . . , and finally they roast them before a slow Fire for some Days, and eat them : . . .   Though they are very cruel to their Enemies, they are very friendly to us : we are under no Apprehensions from them ; we go with them into the Woods ; we meet with one another sometimes one or two miles from any Houses, and are no more uneasy about it than if we met with Christians : they sleep by us too in our Chambers ; I have had eight at once, who laid and slept upon the Floor near my Bed, for it is their custom to sleep only on the bare Ground, and to have only a Stone or a Bit of Wood under their Heads, they go to Bed very soon after they have supped, but rise early in the Morning ; they get up before Day Break.   They are very slovenly and dirty ; they neither wash their Face nor Hands, but let all the Dirt remain upon their tawney

Skin, and look as dirty as Hogs. Their bread is Indian Corn beaten to Pieces between two Stones, of which they make a Cake and bake it in the Ashes; they eat with it Venison, Turkies, Hares, Bears, Wild Cats, their own Dogs, &c. . . . They make their Houses of the Bark of Trees, very close and warm, and place their Fire in the middle of them: they also make of the Peeling and Bark of Trees *Canoes*, or small Boats, which will carry four, five and six Persons: in like Manner they hollow out Trees, and use them for Boats; some of them are very large. I have sometimes sailed with ten, twelve and fourteen Persons in one of these hollowed Trees; . . . The Arms used by the Indians in War were formerly a Bow and Arrow with a Stone Axe and Mallet, but now they get from our People Guns, Swords, Iron Axes and Mallets. Their Money consists of certain little Bones, made of the Shells of Cockles which are found on the Beach; a Hole is made through the middle of the little Bones; and they are strung upon Thread, or they make of them Belts as broad as a Hand or broader, which they hang on their Necks and on their Bodies; they have also several Holes in their Ears, and there they hang some; and they value these little Bones as highly as many Christians do Gold, Silver and Pearls, but they have no Value for our Money, and esteem it no better than Iron. I once shewed one of their Chiefs a Rixdollar, he asked how much it was worth among the Christians, and when I told him he laughed exceedingly at us, saying we were Fools to value a Piece of Iron so highly, and if he had such Money he would throw it into the River. . . .

They are entire Strangers to all Religion, but they have a *Tharonhi-jouaagon*, (which others also call *Athzoockkuatoriaho*) i.e. a *Genius* which they put in the Place of God, but they do not worship or present Offerings to him: they worship and present Offerings to the Devil whom they call *Otskon* or *Aireskuoni*. . . . They have otherwise no Religion: when we pray they laugh at us; some of them despise it entirely, and some when we tell them what we do when we pray, stand astonished. When we have a Sermon, sometimes ten or twelve of them, more or less, will attend, each having a long Tobacco Pipe, made by himself, in his Mouth, and will stand a while and look, and afterwards ask me what I was doing and what I wanted, that I stood there alone and made so many Words, and none of the rest might speak? I tell them I admonished the Christians, that they must not steal, . . . get drunk, or commit Murder, and that they too ought not to do these Things, and that I intend after a while to preach to them, . . . They say I do well in

teaching the Christians, but immediately add *Diatennon jawij Assyreoni hagiouisk,* that is, why do so many Christians do these Things. They call us *Assyreoni,* that is, Cloth-Makers, or *Charistooni,* that is, Iron-Workers, because our People first brought Cloth and Iron among them. . . .

The Government among them consists of the oldest, the most sensible, the best-speaking and most warlike Men; these commonly resolve, and the young and war-like Men carry into Execution; but if the common People do not approve of the Resolution, is left entirely to the Judgment of the Mob. The Chiefs are generally the poorest among them, for instead of their receiving from the common People as among Christians, they are obliged to give to them; especially when any one is killed in War, they give great Presents to the next of Kin to the deceased, and if they take any Prisoners they present them to that Family whereof one has been killed, and the Prisoner is adopted by the Family into the Place of the Person who was killed. There is no Punishment here for Murder and other Villainies, but every one is his own Avenger: The Friends of the deceased revenge themselves upon the Murderer until Peace is made by Presents to the next of Kin. But although they are so cruel, and have no Laws or Punishments, yet there are not half so many Villainies or Murders committed amongst them as amongst Christians, so that I sometimes think with astonishment upon the Murders committed in the Netherlands, notwithstanding their severe Laws and heavy Penalties. These Indians, though they live without Laws, or Fear of Punishment, do not kill People, unless they are in a great Passion, or fighting, wherefore we go along with them, or meet them in the Woods, without Fear.

Ebenezer Hazard, *Historical Collections* (Philadelphia, 1792), I, 520–526 passim.

CHAPTER XXIII — NEW YORK

153. Founding of New Amsterdam (1623–1628)

BY NICOLAS JEAN DE WASSENAER

(ANONYMOUS TRANSLATION)

Wassenaer was a Dutch historian: this extract is from a general history, and is one of the few contemporary narratives from the European side. — Bibliography: Winsor, *Narrative and Critical History*, IV, 424–428; Brodhead, *History of the State of New York*, I, chs. v, vi.

NUMEROUS voyages realize so much profit for adventurers that they discover other countries, which they afterwards settle and plant. Virginia, a country lying in 42½ degrees, is one of these. It was first peopled by the French; afterwards by the English, and is to-day a flourishing colony. The Lords States General observing the great abundance of their people as well as their desire to plant other lands, allowed the West India company to settle that same country. Many from the United Colonies did formerly and do still trade there; . . .

Those who come from the interior, yea thirty days journey, declare there is considerable water every where and that the upper country is marshy; they make mention of great freshets which lay waste their lands; so that what many say may be true, that Hudson's Bay runs through to the South Sea, and is navigable, except when obstructed by the ice to the northward. . . .

We treated in our preceding discourse of the discovery of some rivers in Virginia; the studious reader will learn how affairs proceeded. The West India Company being chartered to navigate these rivers, did not neglect so to do, but equipped in the spring [of 1623] a vessel of 130 lasts, called the *New Netherland* whereof Cornelis Jacobs of Hoorn was skipper, with 30 families, mostly Walloons, to plant a colony there. They sailed in the beginning of March, and directing their course by the Canary Islands, steered towards the wild coast, and gained the westwind which luckily (took) them in the beginning of May into the river called, first Rio de Montagnes, now the river Mauritius, lying in 40½ degrees.

He found a Frenchman lying in the mouth of the river, who would erect the arms of the King of France there; but the Hollanders would not permit him, opposing it by commission from the Lords States General and the directors of the West India Company; and in order not to be frustrated therein, with the assistance of those of the *Mackerel* which lay above, they caused a yacht of 2 guns to be manned, and convoyed the Frenchman out of the river, who would do the same thing in the south river, but he was also prevented by the settlers there.

This being done, the ship sailed up to the Maykans, 44 miles, near which they built and completed a fort named " Orange " with 4 bastions, on an island, by them called Castle Island. . . .

Respecting these colonies, they have already a prosperous beginning; and the hope is that they will not fall through provided they be zealously sustained, not only in that place but in the South river. For their increase and prosperous advancement, it is highly necessary that those sent out be first of all well provided with means both of support and defence, and that being freemen, they be settled there on a free tenure; that all they work for and gain be their's to dispose of and to sell it according to their pleasure; that whoever is placed over them as commander act as their father not as their executioner, leading them with a gentle hand; for whoever rules them as a friend and associate will be beloved by them, as he who will order them as a superior will subvert and nullify every thing; yea, they will excite against him the neighbouring provinces to which they will fly. 'Tis better to rule by love and friendship than by force. . . .

As the country is well adapted for agriculture and the raising of every thing that is produced here, the aforesaid Lords resolved to take advantage of the circumstances, and to provide the place with many necessaries, through the Honble. Pieter Evertsen Hulst, who undertook to ship thither, at his risk, whatever was requisite, to wit; one hundred and three head of cattle; stallions, mares, steers and cows, for breeding and multiplying, besides all the hogs and sheep that might be thought expedient to send thither; and to distribute these in two ships of one hundred and forty lasts, in such a manner that they should be well foddered and attended to. . . .

In company with these, goes a fast sailing vessel at the risk of the directors. In these aforesaid vessels also go six complete families with some freemen, so that forty five new comers or inhabitants are taken out, to remain there. The natives of New Netherland are very well disposed so long as no injury is done them. But if any wrong be committed against them they think it long till they be revenged. . . .

They are a wicked, bad people, very fierce in arms. Their dogs are small. When the Honble. Lambrecht van Twenhuyzen, once a skipper, had given them a big dog, and it was presented to them on ship-board, they were very much afraid of it ; calling it, also, a Sachem of dogs, being the biggest. The dog, tied with a rope on board, was very furious against them, they being clad like beasts with skins, for he thought they were game ; but when they gave him some of their bread made of Indian corn, which grows there, he learned to distinguish them, that they were men. . . .

The Colony was planted at this time, on the Manhates where a Fort was staked out by Master Kryn Frederycke an engineer. It will be of large dimensions. . . .

The government over the people of New Netherland continued on the 19th of August of this year in the aforesaid Minuict, successor to Verhulst, who went thither from Holland on 9th January, Anno, 1626, and took up his residence in the midst of a nation called Manhates, building a fort there, to be called Amsterdam, having four points and faced outside entirely with stone, as the walls of sand fall down, and are now more compact. The population consists of two hundred and seventy souls, including men, women, and children. They remained as yet without the Fort, in no fear, as the natives live peaceably with them. They are situate three miles from the Sea, on the river by us called Mauritius, by others, Rio de Montagne. . . .

After the Right Honble Lords Directors of the Privileged West India Company in the United Netherlands, had provided for the defence of New Netherland and put everything there in good order, they taking into consideration the advantages of said place, the favorable nature of the air, and soil, and that considerable trade and goods and many commodities may be obtained from thence, sent some persons, of their own accord, thither with all sorts of cattle and implements necessary for agriculture, so that in the year 1628 there already resided on the island of the Manhattes, two hundred and seventy souls, men, women, and children, under Governor Minuit, Verhulst's successor, living there in peace with the natives. But as the land, in many places being full of weeds and wild productions, could not be properly cultivated in consequence of the scantiness of the population, the said Lords Directors of the West India Company, the better to people their lands, & to bring

the country to produce more abundantly, resolved to grant divers privileges, freedoms, and exemptions to all patroons, masters or individuals
who should plant any colonies and cattle in New Netherland, and they
accordingly have constituted and published in print (certain) exemptions,
to afford better encouragement and infuse greater zeal into whomsoever
should be inclined to reside and plant his colonie in New Netherland.

The Description and First Settlement of New Netherland, from Wassenaer's
   Historie van Europa, in *Collectanea Adamantæa*, XXVII (Edinburgh,
   1888), II, 7–42 *passim*.

————◆————

154. "Of the Reasons and Causes why and how New Netherland is so decayed" (1650)

BY JUNKER ADRIAEN VAN DER DONCK AND TEN OTHERS

(TRANSLATED BY HENRY C. MURPHY, 1849)

Van der Donck, previously an advocate in Holland, later sheriff of Rensselaerwyck,
became the leader of the movement for a more liberal government in the Dutch colony. — Bibliography: Winsor, *Narrative and Critical History*, IV, 419–420; New
York Historical Society, *Collections*, New Series, I, 126–128.

AS we shall speak of the reasons and causes which have brought
   New Netherland into the ruinous condition in which it is now
found to be, we deem it necessary to state the very first difficulties, and
for this purpose regard it as we see and find it, in our daily experience.
As far as our understanding goes, to describe it in one word, (and none
better presents itself,) it is *bad government*, with its attendants and consequences, that is the true and only *foundation stone* of the decay and
ruin of New Netherland. This government from which so much abuse
proceeds, is two fold, that is ; in the Fatherland by the Managers, and
in this country. We shall first briefly and in some order point out the
mistakes in Fatherland, and afterwards proceed to show how abuses
have grown up and obtained strength here.

The Managers of the Company adopted a wrong course at first, and
as we think had more regard for their own interest than for the welfare
of the country, trusting rather to evil than just counsels. This is proven
by the unnecessary expenses incurred from time to time, the heavy
accounts of New Netherland, the registering of manors — in which
business most of the Managers themselves engaged, and in reference
to which they have regulated the trade, — and finally the not peopling

the country. It seems as if from the first, the Company have sought to stock this land with their own *employés*, which was a great mistake, for when their time was out they returned home, taking nothing with them, except a little in their purses and a bad name for the country, in regard to its means of sustenance and in other respects. In the meantime there was no profit, but on the contrary heavy monthly expenditures, as the accounts of New Netherland will show. . . .

Had the first exemptions been truly observed, according to their intention, and had they not been carried out with particular views, certainly the friends of New Netherland would have exerted themselves more to take people there and make settlements. The other conditions which were introduced have always discouraged individuals and kept them down, so that those who were acquainted with the business dare not attempt it. It is very true that the Company have brought over some persons, but they have not continued to do so, and it therefore has done little good. It was not begun properly ; for it was merely accidental, and was not intended. . . .

Trade, without which, when it is legitimate, no country is prosperous, is by their acts so decayed, that the like is nowhere else. It is more suited for slaves than freemen, in consequence of the restrictions upon it and the annoyances which accompany the exercise of the right of inspection. We approve of inspection, however, so far as relates to contraband.

This contraband trade has ruined the country, though it is now excluded from every part of it by orders given by the Managers to their officers. These orders should be executed without partiality, which is not always the case. . . . let us proceed to examine how their officers and Directors have conducted themselves from time to time, having played with the managers as well as with the people, as a cat does with a mouse. It would be possible to relate their management from the beginning, but as most of us were not here then and therefore not eye witnesses, and as a long time has passed whereby it has partly escaped recollection, and as in our view it was not so bad then as afterwards when the land was made free and freemen began to increase, we will pass by the beginning and let Mr. Lubbert van Dincklaghen, Vice Director of New Netherland, describe the government of Director Wouter Van Twiller of which he is known to have information, and will only speak of the last two miserable and impoverished administrations. We would speak well of the government under Director Kieft who is now no more, but the evil of it lives after him ; and of that under Director Stuyvesant which still stands, if indeed that may be called standing, which lies completely under foot.

The Directors here, though far from their masters, were close by their profit. They have always known how to manage their own matters with little loss, and under pretext of the public business. They have also conducted themselves just as if they were the sovereigns of the country. As they desired to have it, so always has it been ; and as they willed so was it done. " The Managers," they say, " are masters in Fatherland, but we are masters in this land." As they understand it so it is, there is no appeal. And it has not been difficult for them hitherto to maintain this doctrine in practice ; for the people were few and for the most part very simple and uninformed, and besides, had transactions with the Directors every day. As there were some intelligent men among them, *who could go upon their own feet,* them it was sought to oblige. They could not understand at first the arts of the Directors which were always subtle and dark, inasmuch as they were very frequently successful and for a long time quite advantageous. Director Kieft said himself and let it be said also by others, that he was sovereign in this country, the same as the Prince in Netherland. This was told him several times here and he never made any particular objection to it. The refusing to allow appeals, and other similar acts, prove clearly that in regard to us it is just as they say and not otherwise. The present Director does the same, and in the denial of appeal, *he is at home.* He asserts the maxim, " the Prince is above the law," and applies it so boldly to his own person that he is even ashamed of it himself. . . .

Casting our eyes upon the government of Director Kieft, the church first meets us, and we will therefore speak of the public property ecclesiastical and civil. . . .

. . . the Director then resolved to build a church, and at the place where it suited him; but he was in want of money and was at a loss how to obtain it. It happened about this time that the minister, Everadus Bogardus, gave his daughter in marriage ; and the occasion of the wedding the Director considered a good opportunity for his purpose. So after the fourth or fifth round of drinking, he set about the business, and he himself showing a liberal example let the wedding-guests subscribe what they were willing to give towards the church. All then with light heads subscribed largely, competing with one another ; and although some well repented it when they got home, they were nevertheless compelled to pay, — nothing could avail to prevent it. The church was then, contrary to every consideration of propriety, placed in the fort. . . .

We must now speak of the property belonging to the church, and, to do the truth no violence, we do not know that there has ever been any, or that the church has any income except what is given to it. There has never been any exertion made either by the Company or by the Director to obtain or provide any.

The bowl has been going round a long time for the purpose of erecting a common school and it has been built with words, but as yet the first stone is not laid. Some materials only are provided. The money nevertheless, given for the purpose has all found its way out and is mostly spent ; so that it falls short and no permanent benefit has as yet been derived from it. . . .

. . . According to the proclamations during the administration of Director Kieft, if we rightly consider and examine them all, we cannot learn or discover that any thing, — we say *any thing* large or small, — worth relating, was done, built or made, which concerned or belonged to the commonalty, the church excepted, whereof we have heretofore spoken. Yea, it has gone on so badly and negligently that nothing has ever been designed, understood or done that gave appearance of content to the people, even externally, but on the contrary, what came from the commonalty has even been mixed up with the effects of the Company, and even the company's property and means have been every where neglected, in order to make friends, to secure witnesses and to avoid accusers about the management of the war. The negroes, also, who came from Tamandare were sold for pork and peas, from the proceeds of which something wonderful was to be performed, but they just dripped through the fingers. There are, also, various other negroes in this country, some of whom have been made free for their long service, but their children have remained slaves, though it is contrary to the laws of every people that any one born of a Christian mother should be a slave and be compelled to remain in servitude. . . . But to proceed now to the administration of Director Stuyvesant, and to see how affairs have been conducted up to the time of our departure. Mr. Stuyvesant has most all the time from his first arrival up to our leaving, been busy building, laying masonry, making, breaking, repairing and the like, but generally in matters of the Company and with little profit to it ; for upon some things more was spent than they were worth ; . . .

The fort under which we shelter ourselves, and from which as it seems all authority proceeds, lies like a mole-heap or a tottering wall, on which there is not one gun carriage or one piece of cannon in a suitable frame or on a good platform. . . .

His [Stuyvesant's] first arrival — for what passed on the voyage is not for us to speak of, — was like a peacock, with great state and pomp. The declaration of His Honor, that he wished to stay here only three years, with other haughty expressions, caused some to think that he would not be a father. The appellation of *Lord General*, and similar titles, were never before known here. Almost every day he caused proclamations of various import to be published, which were for the most part never observed, and have long since been a dead letter, except the wine excise, as that yielded a profit. . . . At one time, after leaving the house of the minister, where the consistory had been sitting and had risen, it happened that Arnoldus Van Herdenbergh related the proceedings relative to the estate of Zeger Teunisz, and how he himself, as curator, had appealed from the sentence; whereupon the Director, who had been sitting there with them as an elder, interrupted him and replied, "It may during my administration be contemplated to appeal, but if any one should do it, I will *make him a foot shorter*, and send the pieces to Holland, and let him appeal in that way." . . .

In our opinion this country will never flourish under the government of the Honorable Company, but will pass away and come to an end of itself, unless the Honorable Company be reformed; and therefore it would be more profitable for them, and better for the country, that they should be rid thereof, and their effects transported hence.

To speak specifically. Care ought to be taken of the public property, as well ecclesiastical as civil, which, in beginnings, can be illy dispensed with. It is doubtful whether Divine Worship will not have to cease altogether in consequence of the departure of the minister, and the inability of the Company. There should be a public school, provided with at least two good masters, so that first of all in so wild a country, where there are many loose people, the youth be well taught and brought up, not only in reading and writing, but also in the knowledge and fear of the Lord. As it is now, the school is kept very irregularly, one and another keeping it according to his pleasure and as long as he thinks proper. There ought also to be an alms house, and an orphan asylum, and other similar institutions. The minister who now goes home, can give a much fuller explanation thereof. The country must also be provided with godly, honorable and intelligent rulers who are not very indigent, or indeed, are not too covetous. . . .

. . . We hope Their High Mightinesses will pardon our presumption and our plainness of style, composition and method. In conclusion we commit Their High Mightinesses, their persons, deliberations and measures at home and abroad, together with all the friends of New Netherland, to the merciful guidance and protection of the HIGHEST, whom we supplicate for Their High Mightinesses' present and eternal welfare. Amen. . . .

The Representation of New Netherland (1650), in New York Historical Society, *Collections* (New York, 1849), Second Series, II, 288–320 *passim*.

155. Why the Dutch Surrendered New York (1665)

BY MICHAEL TEN HOVE

(TRANSLATED BY E. B. O'CALLAGHAN, 1858)

Ten Hove was Secretary of the Dutch West India Company: this piece is an answer to Governor Stuyvesant's attempt to throw upon the Company the responsibility for the easy conquest of the Dutch colony by the English. — Bibliography: Winsor, *Narrative and Critical History*, III, 414–415; Channing and Hart, *Guide*, § 104.

To the Honorable Mighty Lords, their High Mightinesses' Deputies for the Affairs of the West India Company.

. . . FIRST taking up the Want of provisions : The Company wil. once more, in good faith, plead ignorance of there having been an insufficient supply of provisions, since it cannot imagine that, in a country so productive as New Netherland, any scarcity should exist in a year of such abundance as that of 1664, when, according to the declaration of the Director-General, made in his letter written to the Company on the 10th of June, 1664 (L^a A.), even the distant lands in and around the Esopus which could be mowed and sown in the year 1663, only at great peril and cost, on account of the war, were as productive and wore as promising an appearance as if they had been plowed and sown in the fall ; and the spring planting of the year 1664 having been blessed by God with a fructifying and abundant rain, a good and blessed harvest was expected. . . .

. . . further, that there is not the least foundation for what he sets forth both generally and particularly in his Defence, viz. : that he had not timely notice of the designs which the English, and especially the aforesaid frigates might have had against New Netherland, and that the Company had, on the contrary, as he gives out, informed him, from this place, that the English had no intention to use violence against New Netherland. For, it is true and certain that, in order that he might victual the place and fort of New Amsterdam and keep it victualed, the aforesaid Stuyvesant was warned time enough from here and from New England, of the apparent difficulties between this State and the English, and, more particularly, of the equipment and approach of the aforesaid frigates ; . . .

Under all circumstances, the aforesaid Director had so magnified in divers letters the actions of the New Englanders, their power and progress, and wrote especially that he entertained apprehensions for New Amsterdam, so that, in his letter of the 10th November, 1663 (L[a] F.), he was evidently fearful of the loss of everything that people possessed. It behoved him, therefore, even had he expected no new force from Old England, to have kept the place supplied with all necessaries, saying in his letter of the last of February, 1664 (L[a] G.), that the English on Long Island were aiming at the whole country, which was not strange, since the President of the rebellious troop had notified him to that effect, particularly stating that the Duke of York was sending some frigates to reduce New Netherland, as appears by the voucher (L[a] H.) And lastly, the aforesaid Director was, in all the Company's despatches, expressly charged and commanded to be on his guard, so that, as already stated, he cannot plead that he had not received any warning. . . .

Secondly. Herewith falls the excuse he makes, that the farmers were constrained by the English not to convey any grain into the fort, and that the said English had everywhere cut off the communication, so that grain could not be conveyed across the river ; for, having been warned in time, they ought not to have waited the arrival of the frigates, but have employed the interval between the 4th of August, when the aforesaid letter was written to the Company, and the arrival of the frigates to provide themselves with grain, and not delayed, as he has done, until the enemy was at the door. . . .

Finally, the aforesaid Stuyvesant says : That the scarcity of provisions was caused, among other things, by the arrival of the ship *Gideon* with between three and four hundred Negroes. Truly, also, a flimsy excuse. For, besides the number not being so large, one-fourth of them had been delivered to the officer of the city's Colonie on the South river, who took his departure with them for the South river three days after the arrival of the frigates, because he saw the shape things were taking in New Netherland and around the government; and the remainder were sold shortly after, so that he had not to provide for them. . . .

Want of ammunition being represented as the second fundamental cause of the surrender of the aforesaid fort, city and Province of New Netherland, the abovenamed Company will also, in good faith, plead ignorance of that want; yea, will, on the contrary, assert that it is informed for certain that, if there had not been a sufficient supply in store, a very considerable quantity of gunpowder would be found among the Burghers, and particularly at Fort Orange and the Colonie Renslaers Wyck among the traders; . . .

. . . The third point of his defence — the Unwillingness of the Burghers to defend the city — since all the world sufficiently knows what zeal they had exhibited to protect their property; working with all their might at the defence of the place, until the want of provisions and ammunition was instilled into their minds by the government, and the enemy's strength represented to be much greater than it was in fact, and, moreover, security for their private property had been given by the English, in case of surrender; and finally, until the two frigates passed the fort unobstructed, when their courage began to fail and the idea of surrender gained ground, on perceiving the intention of the government after it had permitted the aforesaid frigates to pass freely the fort unimpeded; although, under all circumstances, it is sufficiently shown in the Observations aforesaid, that the unwillingness of the Burghers to fight, cannot be any excuse for him, inasmuch as it was his duty to defend the fort. Such being his apprehension also, he endeavors to defend himself by saying, that the fort was declared untenable and, at any event, even were it maintained, that the whole Province could not be preserved thereby. . . . For, as regards the first and second, concerning the condition of the fort and the rampart and wall, 'tis indeed true that the fort was at first constructed to resist the incursions of the Barbarians; but 'tis also true, that it was afterwards so strengthened by a rampart and an earthen wall, that, if kept in good condition, it need not fear any assault from European arms. . . . Thirdly, he alleges that the fort was encompassed round about by houses. Truly a poor reason and still weaker, that he could not, on account of the damage to the Burghers, resolve on pulling them down, as the Company in its Observations hath demonstrated, ought to have been done. For, here was no longer any question of profit or loss to the Burghers who had abandoned the defence of the city. The defence of the fort only must be looked to, even though all the houses had to be pulled down; for, the fort, and consequently occupation, once lost, the State and Company lost everything. But 'tis here again to be regretted that the Company was served by men who preferred to save their own property, which they had gained in the Company's employ, than to observe their oath and honor. . . .

The fourth point was : that they had no hope of relief. This is spread out so broad, as if, for this reason alone, the place ought not to be defended. On this point the Company will merely persist in what is stated in its Observations, and accordingly submit, that it could not know what the aforesaid Director also might say if no relief should arrive. In all cases, he was not at liberty to surrender such a place without striking a blow, especially so long as it was not really attacked ; for, as regards relief, they did not know what help would arrive from Fatherland, because the Company's last letters had assured them of immediate assistance or a settlement of the Boundary. Consequently, the one or the other being to happen, he ought not to have adopted so rash a resolution. Besides, the Company has as much cause for positively asserting that the English, on seeing the Director putting himself in a posture of defence and having the courage to repel them, would not have attacked the place, as the Director for saying that no relief was at hand. And for the preceding reasons, the Company will pass over the long detail which the Director makes in his aforesaid writing of other events in the foregoing years, as both irrelevant and immaterial, and once more conclude on this point : That he ought to have waited until he saw the enemy commence the attack before he resolved on the surrender of the place for want of assistance. . . .

. . . In truth, whether this becomes a Director-General or not, the Company need not add any more; it only says, that 'tis an action that never can be palliated in a Director-General, to stand between the gabions looking at two hostile frigates passing the fort and the mouths of 20 pieces of cannon, several of them demi-cartoons, and not give an order to prevent them, but, on the contrary, lend an ear to Clergymen and other craven-hearted people, pretending that he was wishing to order fire, yet will allow himself to be led in from the rampart between the Clergymen, and then, for the first time, give himself any trouble

after the frigates have passed, when, for the first time, he will march
forth to prevent a landing. The excuse he gives, that it was resolved
not to commence the first act of hostility, is a very poor one ; for, the
English had committed all acts of hostility, carrying off the city's cattle
and the boat in which the slaves were, taking one of the soldiers who
was with them, prisoner after he had been wounded, capturing Claes
Verbraeck's sloop, afterwards taking Isaac de Foreest prisoner, forbid-
ding the farmers furnishing supplies, firing shot at the *St. Jacob's* boat,
and lastly, summoning the city and fort, in order to save the shedding
of blood, and committing many other acts, too many to be here related ;
so that there was no difficulty to answer them in the same manner. . . .

The Company now believing that it has fulfilled your Honble Mightinesses' intention, will only again say, in conclusion, that the sole cause
and reason for the loss of the aforesaid place, were these : The Authorities (*Regenten*), and the chief officer, being very deeply interested in
lands, bouweries and buildings, were unwilling to offer any opposition,
first, at the time of the English encroachments, in order thereby not
to afford any pretext for firing and destroying their properties ; and,
having always paid more attention to their particular affairs than to the
Company's interests, New Amsterdam was found, on the arrival of the
English frigates, as if an enemy was never to be expected. And, finally,
that the Director, first following the example of heedless interested
parties, gave himself no other concern than about the prosperity of his
bouweries, and, when the pinch came, allowed himself to be rode over
by Clergymen, women and cowards, in order to surrender to the English
what he could defend with reputation, for the sake of thus saving their
private properties. And the Company will further leave to your Honble
Mightinesses' good and prudent wisdom, what more ought to be done in
this case. . . .

Reply of the West India Company to the Answer of the Honble Peter Stuyve-
sant (1666), in *Documents Relative to the Colonial History of the State of*
New-York (edited by E. B. O'Callaghan, Albany, 1858), II, 491–503 *passim*

156. Condition of New York in 1687

BY GOVERNOR THOMAS DONGAN

Dongan had been a colonel in the English army, and later governor of Tangier; he was sent out by King James II because he was a Catholic. — Bibliography: Winsor, *Narrative and Critical History*, III, 415; Brodhead, *History of the State of New York*, II, ch. viii; Channing and Hart, *Guide*, § 105.

. . . I SEND a Map by Mr. Spragg whereby your Lop^{ps} may see the several Governm^{ts} &c how they lye where the Beaver hunting is & where it will be necessary to erect our Country Forts for the securing of beaver trade & keeping the Indians in community with us.

Alsoe it points out where theres a great river discovered by one Lassel a Frenchman from Canada who thereupon went into France & as its reported brought two or three vessels with people to settle there which (if true) will prove not only very inconvenient to us but to the Spanish alsoe (the river running all along from our lakes by the back of Virginia & Carolina into the Bay Mexico) & its believed Nova Mexico can not be far from the mountain adjoining to it that place being in 36d North Latitude if your Lop^{ps} thought it fit I could send a sloop or two from this place to discover that river. . . .

The Correspondence wee hold with our neighbors is very amicable & good wee on all occasions doing to each other all the offices of Friendship & Service wee cann; which has soe much endeared them to us that they desire nothing more than to be a part of this Goverm^t those of Connecticut choosing far rather to come under this Goverm^t than that of Boston for the reason afore mentioned and the Jerseys wishing the like as having once been a part of us.   And seeing that in this separation they are not soe easy nor safe, as they might expect to bee, were they re-united to us . . .

The principal towns within the Goverm^t are New York Albany & Kingston at Esopus   All the rest are country villages the buildings in New-York & Albany are generally of stone & brick.   In the country the houses are mostly new built, having two or three rooms on a floor The Dutch are great improvers of land New York and Albany live wholly upon trade with the Indians England and the West Indies.   The returns for England are generally Beaver Peltry Oile & Tobacco when we can have it.   To the West Indies we send Flower, Bread Pease pork & sometimes horses; the return from thence for the most part is rumm which pays the King a considerable excise & some molasses which serves the people to make drink & pays noe custom   There are about nine or ten three mast vessels of about 80 or 100 tons burthen two or three ketches & Barks of about 40 Tun : and about twenty sloops of about twenty or five & twenty Tun belonging to the Goverm^t   All of which trade for England Holland & the West Indies except six or seven sloops that use the river trade to Albany & that way. . . .

I believe for these 7 years last past, there has not come over into this province twenty English Scotch or Irish familys.   But on the contrarv on Long Island the people encrease soe fast that they complain for want of land & many remove from thence into the neighboring province. But of French there have been since my coming here several familys come both from St. Christophers & England & a great many more are expected as alsoe from Holland are come several Dutch familys which is another great argument of the necessity of adding to this Goverm^t the Neighboring English Colonys, that a more equal ballance may be kept between his Mat^{ys} naturall born subjects and foreigners which latter are the most prevailing part of this Government . . .

Every Town ought to have a Minister New York has first a Chaplain belonging to the Fort of the Church of England ; Secondly, a Dutch Calvinist, thirdly a French Calvinist, fourthly a Dutch Lutheran — Here bee not many of the Church of England ; few Roman Catholicks ; abundance of Quakers preachers men & Women especially ; Singing Quakers, Ranting Quakers, Sabbatarians ; Antisabbatarians ; Some Anabaptists some Independents ; some Jews ; in short of all sorts of opinions there are some, and the most part of none at all

The Great Church which serves both the English & the Dutch is within the Fort which is found to bee very inconvenient therefore I desire that there may bee an order for their building an other ground already being layd out for that purpose & they wanting not money in store wherewithall to build it

The most prevailing opinion is that of the Dutch Calvinists

It is the endeavor of all Psons here to bring up their children and servants in that opinion which themselves, profess, but this I observe that they take no care of the conversion of their Slaves.

Every Town and County are obliged to maintain their own poor, which makes them bee soe careful that noe Vagabonds, Beggers, nor Idle Persons are suffered to live here

But as for the Kings natural-born subjects that live on long-Island

& other parts of the Government I find it a hard task to make them
pay their Ministers.

THO. DONGAN.

E. B. O'Callaghan, *The Documentary History of the State of New-York*
(Albany, 1850), I, 101–117 *passim.*

———◆———

157. Leisler's Rebellion (1689–1691)

BY "A GENTLEMAN OF THE CITY OF NEW-YORK" (1698)

This is one of several contemporary narratives of this epoch. Leisler, formerly a
fur-trader, in 1689 a merchant, put himself at the head of the adherents of William
of Orange, with the result set forth in this extract. — Bibliography: Winsor, *Narrative and Critical History,* V, 240–241; Channing and Hart, *Guide,* § 105.

I CANNOT but admire to hear that some Gentlemen still have a good
Opinion of the late *D*isorders committed by Capt. *Jacob Leysler,*
and his Accomplices, in *New York,* as if they had been for His
Majesties Service, and the *S*ecurity of that Province ; and that such
Monstrous Falshoods do find Credit, . . .

It was about the beginning of *April,* 1689. when the first Reports
arrived at New-York, that the Prince of *Orange,* now his present
Majesty, was arrived in *England* with considerable Forces, and that the
late King *James* was fled into *France,* and that it was expected War
would be soon proclaimed between *England* and *France.*

The Leiut. Governour, *Francis Nicholson,* and the Council, being
Protestants, resolved thereupon to suspend all *Roman Catholicks* from
Command and Places of Trust in the Government, . . .

And because but three Members of the Council were residing in
New-York, . . . It was Resolved by the said Lieut. Governor and
Council, to call and conveen to their Assistance all the Justices of the
Peace, and other civil Magistrates, and the Commission Officers in the
*P*rovince, for to consult and advise with them what might be proper for
the Preservation of the Peace, and the Safety of said Province in that
Conjuncture, till Orders should arrive from *England.*

Whereupon the said Justices, Magistrates and Officers were accordingly convened, and stiled by the Name of *The General Convention for
the Province of* New-York ; and all matters of Government were carried on and managed by the major Vote of that Convention.

And in the first place it was by them agreed and ordered, Forth-with to fortifie the City of New-York. . . .

But against Expectation, it soon happened, that on the last day of said Moneth of *May*, Capt. *Leysler* having a Vessel with some Wines in the Road, for which he refused to pay the Duty, did in a Seditious manner stir up the meanest sort of the Inhabitants (affirming *That King* James *being fled the Kingdom, all manner of Government was fallen in this Province*) to rise in Arms, and forcibly possess themselves of the Fort and Stores, which accordingly was effected whilest the Lieut. Governour and Council, with the Convention, were met at the City Hall to consult what might be proper for the common Good and Safety ; where a party of Armed Men came from the Fort, and forced the Lieut. Governour to deliver them the Keys ; and seized also in his Chamber a Chest with *Seven Hundred Seventy Three Pounds, Twelve Shillings* in Money of the Government. And though Coll. *Bayard*, with some others appointed by the Convention, used all endeavours to prevent those Disorders, all proved vain ; for most of those that appeared in Arms were Drunk, and cryed out, *They disown'd all manner of Government.* Whereupon, by Capt. *Leysler's* perswasion, they proclaimed him to be their Commander, there being then no other Commission Officer amongst them.

Capt. *Leysler* being in this manner possest of the Fort, took some *P*ersons to his Assistance, which he call'd, *The Committee of Safety.* And the Lieut. Governour, *Francis Nicollson* being in this manner forced out of his Command, for the safety of his Person, which was daily threatned, with-drew out of the Province. . . .

The said Capt. *Leysler* finding almost every man of Sence, *R*eputation or Estate in the place to oppose and discourage his Irregularities, caused frequent false Alarms to be made, and sent several parties of his armed Men out of the Fort, drag'd into nasty Goals within said Fort several of the principal Magistrates, Officers and Gentlemen, and others, that would not own his Power to be lawful, which he kept in close Prison during Will and Pleasure, without any Process, or allowing them to Bail. And he further publish't several times, by beat of Drums, *That all those who would not come into the Fort and sign their hands,* and so thereby to own his Power to be lawful, *should be deemed and esteemed as Enemies to his Majesty and the Country, and be by him treated accordingly.* By which means many of the Inhabitants, tho' they abhor'd his Actions, only to escape a nasty Goal, and to secure their Estates, were by fear and compulsion drove to comply, submit and sign to whatever he commanded. . . .

Upon the 10th of *December* following returned the said Mr. *John Riggs* from *England*, with Letters from his Majesty and the Lords, in answer to the Letters sent by the Lieut. Governour and Council above recited, Directed, *To Our Trusty and Well-beloved* Francis Nicholson, *Esq; Our Lieutenant Governour and Commander in chief of Our Province of* New-York *in* America, *and in his absence To such as for the time being, take care for the Preservation of the Peace, and administring the Laws in Our said Province*. . . .

Soon after the Receipt of said Letters said Capt. *Leysler* stiled himself *Lieutenant Governour*, appointed a Council, and presumed further to call a select Number of his own Party, who called themselves *The General Assembly of the Province*, and by their advice and assistance raised several Taxes and great Sums of Money from their Majesties good Subjects within this *P*rovince. Which Taxes, together with that 773*l.* 12*s.* in Money, which he had seized from the Government, and the whole *R*evenue, he applyed to his own use, and to maintain said Disorders, allowing his private men 18*d. per Day*, and to others proportionably.

On the 20th of *January* following Coll. *Bayard* and Mr *Nicolls* had the ill fortune to fall into his hands, and were in a barbarous manner, by a party in Arms, drag'd into the Fort, and there put into a Nasty place, without any manner of Process, or being allowed to bayl, . . .

None in the Province, but those of his Faction, had any safety in their Estates ; for said Capt. *Leysler*, at will and pleasure, sent to those who disapproved of his Actions, to furnish him with Money, Provisions, and what else he wanted, and upon denyal, sent armed men out of the Fort, and forcibly broke open several Houses, Shops, Cellars, Vessels, and other places, where they expected to be supplyed, and without any the least payment or satisfaction, carried their Plunder to the Fort ; . . .

In this Calamity, Misery and Confusion was this Province, by those Disorders, enthrawled near the space of two years, until the arrival of his Majesties Forces, under the command of Major *Ingoldsby*, who, with several Gentlemen of the Council, arrived about the last day of *January*, 169⁰. which said Gentlemen of the Council, for the Preservation of the Peace, sent and offered to said *Leysler*, That he might stay and continue his Command in the Fort, only desiring for themselves and the Kings Forces quietly to quarter and refresh themselves in the City, till Governour *Slaughter* should arrive ; but . . . the said *Leysler* pro-

ceeded to make War against them and the Kings Forces, and fired a
vast Number of great and small Shot in the City, whereby several of
his Majesties Subjects were killed and wounded as they passed in the
streets upon their lawful Occasions, tho' no Opposition was made on the
other side.

At this height of Extremity was it when Governour *Slaughter* arrived
on the 19th of *March*, 1691. who having publish't his Commission from
the City Hall, with great signs of Joy, by firing all the Artillary within
and round the City, sent thrice to demand the surrender of the Fort
from Capt. *Leysler* and his Accomplices, which was thrice denyed, but
upon great Threatnings, the following Day surrendered to Governor
Slaughter, who forth-with caused the said Capt. *Leysler*, with some of
the chief Malefactors to be bound over to answer their Crimes at the
next Supream Court of Judicature, where the said *Leysler* and his pretended Secretary *Miliborn* did appear, but refused to plead to the In-
dictment of the grand Jury, or to own the Jurisdiction of that Court;
and so after several hearings, as Mutes, were found guilty of High
Treason and Murder, and executed accordingly. . . .

A Letter from a Gentleman of the City of New-York (New York, 1698), 3-13
passim.

CHAPTER XXIV — PENNSYLVANIA AND DELAWARE

158. Authorization for a Swedish Colony (1624)

BY KING GUSTAVUS ADOLPHUS

(TRANSLATED BY BERTHOLD FERNOW, 1877)

Usselinx (Ussling), a dissatisfied Dutch merchant, procured this document from the King of Sweden. The company thus authorized made settlements on the Delaware. — Bibliography : Winsor, *Narrative and Critical History*, IV, 488–489; Vincent, *Delaware*, ch. viii; Channing and Hart, *Guide*, § 107.

WE, Gustavus Adolphus, by the Grace of God King of Sweden, Gothland and the Wendes, Grand Duke of Finland, Duke of Esthonia and Dalecarlia, Lord of Ingermanland, etc., etc.

Know ye, that by a petition the honest and prudent William Ussling has humbly shown and proved to Us, how a General Trading Company here from Our Kingdom of Sweden to Asia, Africa, America and Magellanica could be established for the considerable improvement of Our and the Crown's revenues and the great advantage and benefit of Our subjects, besides, that the said Ussling has also promised to Us and engaged himself, that he will organize this Company using the utmost of his diligence and power, while he cherishes the certain hope, that with God's gracious blessing and help it shall have a good beginning and progress as well as a favorable result and end. Such being the proposition, which he made, We have taken it into consideration and find it to be founded and based upon so good reasons, that We cannot disapprove of it nor do We see, but what it is sure, that if God will give success, it shall tend to the honor of His Holy Name, to Our and the State's welfare and the advancement and advantage of Our subjects. We have therefore graciously received and with pleasure approved of it and consented that the said Company be organized and established. And that it may be done so much easier and better and capital and a management may be got so much quicker, We have given to the said Ussling power and permission now and in future to raise, inscribe and accept in this Our Kingdom of Sweden and its dependent provinces all those, who wish and desire to participate in the said Society or Company, not doubting, that Our faithful subjects, considering the advantages which they can have thereby both for themselves as well as their descendants in future, shall let themselves be found willing each according to his power and means to contribute something to and take a share in the said undertaking, which is with especial well-meaning directed and organized for the common welfare and everybody's advantage. We also command herewith to all Our Governors, Lords-Lieutenants, Bailiffs, Crown-farmers, Mayors and Councillors as well as to all Our other officers, whom the abovementioned Ussling shall ask for assistance and encouragement, that they receive him in friendship (*honom handen räckie*) and as far as their positions require and admit, give him for the promotion of this work, what is needed, aid and help him, while he and everybody in his place here shall communicate more detailed information and advice about it.

Given and signed in Our Royal Palace at Stockholm, the 21st of December 1624.

GUSTAVUS ADOLPHUS.

Documents Relative to the Colonial History of the State of New York (edited by Berthold Fernow, Albany, 1877), XII, 1–2.

---

159. The Swedish Colony (1645)

BY ANDREAS HUDDE

(TRANSLATED BY BERTHOLD FERNOW, 1877)

Hudde was a commissioner sent by Governor Kieft, of New Netherland, to assert the Dutch claim to the region occupied by the Swedes. — Bibliography: Winsor, *Narrative and Critical History*, IV, 495–497; Vincent, *Delaware*, ch. xv; Channing and Hart, *Guide*, § 107.

WHAT regards the garrisons of the Swedes on the South-River of New-Netherland is as follows :

At the entrance of this River three leagues up from its mouth, on the east shore, is a fort called Elsenburgh, usually garrisoned by 12 men and one lieutenant, 4 guns, iron and brass, of 12 pounds iron (balls), 1 mortar (*pots-hooft*). This Fort is an earthwork and was ordered to be erected there by the aforesaid Johan Prints, shortly after his arrival in that river. By means of this fort, the abovementioned Printz holds the river locked for himself, so that all vessels, no matter to whom they belong or whence they come, are compelled to anchor there. This is the case even with those of the Hon. Company, for it frequently happened that yachts belonging to the Hon. Company coming from the Manhattans, which without anchoring wanted to go up to their place of destination and have been damaged by shot with great danger of losing some of their crew. They were then obliged to go up about 6 leagues from there in small boats to the aforesaid Printz for his consent to proceed farther, no distinction being made, whether they were English or Dutch and regardless of their commission.

About 3 leagues farther up the river is another fort, called Kristina, on the west side on a kil called the Minquase Kil, so named because it runs very near to the Minquase land. This fort lies a good half league in the Kil and is surrounded by marshy ground, except on the N. W side, where it can be approached by land, and on the S. W. side, where the Kil runs. It is tolerably strong, but requires strengthening. This fort has no permanent garrison, but is pretty well provided and is the principal place of trade, where the Commissary also resides. Here too is the magazine for all the goods. This is the first fort built by the Swedes under command of one Peter Minwit in the year 1638, notwithstanding the Company had on the river sufficient garrisons, fortifications, men and ammunition of war, which it had had 14 years before this garrisoning by the Swedes. This Peter Minwit had served the Hon. Company as Director in this country.

About 2 leagues farther up on the same side begin some plantations, continuing about 1 league, but there are only few houses and these scattering. They extend as far as Tinnekonck, which is an island, and back from the river are surrounded by creeks and copses. Governor Johan Printz has his residence here. It had a sufficiently strong fort, made of hemlock beams laid one upon the other, but this fort with another standing near by was burned on the 5th December 1645. Farther on, on the same side, to the Schuylkil, which is about 2 leagues, there are no plantations, nor any practicable, as there is nothing but thicket and this on low lands.

As regards the Schuylkil, that is, the Hon. Company's purchased and possessed lands, he has destroyed the Hon. Company's timber and has built a fort at that place, on a very convenient island at the edge of the Kil. It is covered on the west side by another Kil, and on the south, southeast and east side by copses and low lands. It lies about a gunshot in the Kil, on the south-side of it.   Fine corn has been raised on this island.   No damage can be done to the river by this fort, but the Kil can be controlled by it.   The Kil is the only remaining avenue for the commerce with the Minquase, without which trade this river is of little value.

A little farther, beyond this fort, runs a Kil extending to the forest (which place is called Kinsessing by the Indians).   It has been a steady and permanent place of trade for our people with the Minquase, but has now been taken possession of by the Swedes with a blockhouse.   Half a league farther through the woods, Governor Printz has built a mill on the Kil, which empties into the sea a little south of Matinnekonck, and a blockhouse beyond the Kil, right on the path of the Minquase.   This place is called by the Indians Kakarikonck.   Thus there is no place open, to attract the said Minquase.   In a like manner he has almost the monopoly of the trade with the River-Indians, as most of them go hunting this way and cannot get through, without passing this place.

Regarding his force : It consists at the most of 80 to 90 men, freemen as well as servants, with whom he has to garrison all his posts.   The fortifications and garrisons of the Hon. Company are omitted here, as they are sufficiently known. . . .

Documents Relative to the Colonial History of the State of New York (edited by Berthold Fernow, Albany, 1877), XII, 28–30.

---

160. New England Settlers on the Delaware (1654)

BY THE GENERAL COURT OF NEW HAVEN COLONY

For the New Haven colony, see No. 119 above. — Bibliography : Winsor, *Narrative and Critical History*, IV, 495; Vincent, *Delaware*, ch. xviii; Channing and Hart, *Guide*, § 107.

A PETITION was p^{r}sented by Thomas Munson and Coop^r of Newhauen, on behalfe of a company of persons intending a remoue to Delaware Bay, wherein they propound, that for the inlargment of the kingdome of Christ, the spreading of the gospell, and the good of posteritie therein, that they may liue vnder the wings of Christ, they would afford some incourragment to help forward so publique a worke.

   1. That two magistrats, M^r. Samuell Eaton and Mr. Francis Newman,

may haue libertie from this court to goe in person at first, and in case
they see not themselues called to lay out so much of their estate as is like
to be disbursed in such an vndertakeing, that then it would please the
court that out of the jurisdiction they may be honnourably provided for,
as men that are willing to lay out themselues for the publique good.

2. In case that there be an vndertakeing, they that goe may at first
goe vnder the protection of this jurisdiction, and that in case of any
affront the jurisdiction will ingage to assist, till by the blessing of God
they may be able of themselues to set vp a Common wealth according to
the fundamentalls for gouerm^t laid at Newhauen.

3. That seeing our numbers are yet small, aboute or betwixt 50 and
sixty, wee desire the court to consider what number they thinke may be
a competent number, that wee may serue Gods þvidence and yet not let
the worke fall for want of too great a number.

4. That two great gunns and powder and what belongs to them might
be granted.

5. Seeing that most that haue purposes to goe doe onely for publique
respects vndertake, and not for any need at present, and therevpon doe
leaue their houses and land w^{t}hout that improvement that they themselues did make, they desire that for some time, as the court shall
thinke meete, they may be freed from rates and publique charges.

6. Seeing that they whose hearts God stirs vp to vndertake at first,
are men for the generall of no great estates, and some cannot goe w^{t}hout
help, wee desire that a some of money may be raised in this jurisdiction,
w^{c}h may be imployed, either to buy a small vessell that may attend the
service, or otherwise, as shall be thought meete. Now that w^{c}h occasions this last is not onely the sense of the great expence and charge at
first, and the present need that some haue now, but also wee haue heard
from sundrie, that generally men are willing to help on the worke, either
by þsons or estats. Thus beging pardon for our bouldness, and humbly
desire to committ all yor consultations vnto the direction of the God of
wisdome, and so remaine,

Neuhauen the 30th Yo^{r}s to be commanded,
of the 11th moneth, 1654.   John Cooper,
                                          Thomas Munson,
                                          in ye behalfe of the rest.

    To wch the Court returned,
    That hauing read and considered a papr of some propositions presented
by Thomas Munson and John Cooper of Newhauen, in the name and

behalfe of sundrie þsons of this jurisdiction and elswhere, appearing as vndertaker for the first planting of Delaware, in order to yᵉ publique good of this jurisdiction and the inlargment and further advancment of the kingdome of Christ in these parts, doe returne in answer as followeth.

1. That they are willing so farr to deny themselues for the furtherance of that worke in order to the ends propounded, as to grant libertie to one or both of those magistrats mentioned to goe alonge wᵗh them, who, wᵗh such other fitt þsons as this court shall see meete to joyne wᵗh them, may be impowered for mannaging of all matters of civill gouerment there, according to such comission as shall be giuen them by this court.

2. That they will either take the proprietie of all the purchased lands into their owne hands, or leaue it to such as shall vndertake the planting of it, provided that it be and remaine a part or member of this juris-dictiō. And for their incouragment they purpose when God shall so inlarge the English plantations in Delaware as that they shall grow the greater part of the jurisdiction, that then due consideration shall be taken for the ease and conveniency of both parts, as that the gouernor may be one yeare in one part and the next yeare in another, and the dept. gouernor to be in that part where the gouernor is not, and that genʳll courts for makeing lawes may be ordinarily but once a yeare, and where the gouernor resids ; and if God much increase plantations in Delaware and deminish them in these parts, then possibly they may see cause that the gouernor may be constantly there and the deputie gouernor here, but that the lesser part of the jurisdiction be protected and eased by the greater part, both in rates and otherwise, wᶜh they conceive will be both acceptable to God and, (as appeares by the conclusions of the comis-sionʳs, anno 1651,) most satisfying to the rest of the Vnited Colonies.

3. That for the matters of charge propounded for incouragment to be giuen or lent, to help on their first beginnings, they will propound the things to the seuerall þticuler plantations and promove the buisnes for procuring something that way, and shall returne their answer wᵗh all convenient speede. . . .

Records of the Colony or Jurisdiction of New Haven, 1653–1665 (edited by C. J. Hoadly, Hartford, 1858), 128–131.

161. The Infant Colony of Pennsylvania (1683)

BY GOVERNOR WILLIAM PENN

Penn was a Quaker of great wealth and high social position, the friend and favorite of King James II. He was the most thorough-going and systematic of all the founders of American colonies. — Bibliography: Winsor, *Narrative and Critical History*, III, 495-496; Channing and Hart, *Guide*, § 107. See also No. 77 above.

27. THE first planters in these parts were the Dutch, and soon after them the Swedes and Finns. The Dutch applied themselves to traffic, the Swedes and Finns to husbandry. There were some disputes between them for some years; the Dutch looking upon them as intruders upon their purchase and possession, which was finally ended in the surrender made by John Rizeing, the Swedish governor, to Peter Stuyvesant, governor for the States of Holland, anno 1655.

28. The Dutch inhabit mostly those parts of the province that lie upon or near the bay, and the Swedes the freshes of the river Delaware. There is no need of giving any description of them, who are better known there than here; but they are a plain, strong, industrious people, yet have made no great progress in culture, or propagation of fruit-trees; as if they desired rather to have enough than plenty or traffic. But I presume the Indians made them the more careless by furnishing them with the means of profit, to wit, skins and furs for rum and such strong liquors. They kindly received me as well as the English, who were few before the people concerned with me came among them. I must needs commend their respect to authority, and kind behaviour to the English. They do not degenerate from the old friendship between both kingdoms. As they are people proper and strong of body, so they have fine children, and almost every house full : rare to find one of them without three or four boys and as many girls; some six, seven, and eight sons. And I must do them that right, I see few young men more sober and laborious.

29. The Dutch have a meeting-place for religious worship at New-castle; and the Swedes three; one at Christina, one at Tenecum, and one at Wicoco, within half a mile of this town.

30. There rests that I speak of the condition we are in, and what settlement we have made; in which I will be as short as I can; for I fear, and not without reason, that I have tried your patience with this long story. The country lieth bounded on the east by the river and bay of Delaware and Eastern Sea. It hath the advantage of many creeks, or

rivers rather, than run into the main river or bay, some navigable for great ships, some for small craft. Those of most eminency are Christina, Brandywine, Skilpot, and Sculkil, any one of which has room to lay up the royal navy of England, there being from four to eight fathom water.

31. The lesser creeks or rivers, yet convenient for sloops and ketches of good burthen, are Lewis, Mespillion, Cedar, Dover, Cranbrook, Feversham, and Georges below; and Chichester, Chester, Toacawny, Pammapecka, Portquessin, Neshimenck, and Pennberry in the freshes: many lesser, that admit boats and shallops. Our people are mostly settled upon the upper rivers, which are pleasant and sweet, and generally bounded with good land. The planted part of the province and territories is cast into six counties: Philadelphia, Buckingham, Chester, Newcastle, Kent, and Sussex, containing about four thousand souls. Two general assemblies have been held, and with such concord and despatch that they sat but three weeks, and at least seventy laws were passed without one dissent in any material thing. But of this more hereafter, being yet raw and new in our gear. However, I cannot forget their singular respect to me in this infancy of things, who, by their own private expenses, so early considered mine for the public, as to present me with an impost upon certain goods imported and exported, which, after my acknowledgment of their affection, I did as freely remit to the province and the traders to it. And for the well-government of the said counties, courts of justice are established in every county, with proper officers, as justices, sheriffs, clerks, constables; which courts are held every two months. But, to prevent lawsuits, there are three peacemakers chosen by every county court, in the nature of common arbitrators, to hear and end differences between man and man. And spring and fall there is an orphans' court in each county, to inspect and regulate the affairs of orphans and widows.

32. Philadelphia: the expectation of those who are concerned in this province is at last laid out, to the great content of those here who are any ways interested therein. The situation is a neck of land, and lieth between two navigable rivers, Delaware and Sculkill, whereby it hath two fronts upon the water, each a mile, and two from river to river. Delaware is a glorious river; but the Sculkill, being an hundred miles boatable above the falls and its course north-east toward the fountain of Susquehannah, (that tends to the heart of the province, and both sides our own,) it is like to be a great part of the settlement of this age. I

say little of the town itself, because a platform will be shown you by my agent, in which those who are purchasers of me, will find their names and interests.   But this I will say, for the good providence of God, that of all the many places I have seen in the world, I remember not one better seated ; so that it seems to me to have been appointed for a town, whether we regard the rivers, or the conveniency of the coves, docks, and springs, the loftiness and soundness of the land, and the air, held by the people of those parts to be very good.   It is advanced within less than a year, to about fourscore houses and cottages, such as they are, where merchants and handicrafts are following their vocations as fast as they can ; while the countrymen are close at their farms. Some of them got a little winter corn in the ground last season ; and the generality have had a handsome summer-crop, and are preparing for their winter corn.   They reaped their barley this year, in the month called May, the wheat in the month following ; so that there is time in these parts for another crop of divers things before the winter season. We are daily in hopes of shipping to add to our number ; for, blessed be God ! here is both room and accommodation for them : the stories of our necessity being either the fear of our friends, or the scarecrows of our enemies ; for the greatest hardship we have suffered hath been salt meat, which, by fowl in winter and fish in summer, together with some poultry, lamb, mutton, veal, and plenty of venison, the best part of the year, hath been made very passable.   I bless God I am fully satisfied with the country and entertainment I got in it ; for I find that particu- lar content, which hath always attended me, where God in his provi- dence hath made it my place and service to reside.   You cannot imagine my station can be at present free of more than ordinary busi- ness ; and, as such, I may say it is a troublesome work.   But the method things are putting in will facilitate the charge, and give an easier motion to the administration of affairs.   However, as it is some men's duty to plough, some to sow, some to water, and some to reap, so it is the wisdom as well as the duty of a man to yield to the mind of providence, and cheerfully as well as carefully embrace and follow the guidance of it.

33.   For your particular concern I might entirely refer you to the letters of the president of the society ; but this I will venture to say, your provincial settlement, both within and without the town, for situa- tion and soil, are without exception.   Your city lot is a whole street, and one side of a street, from river to river, containing near one hundred

acres not easily valued; which is, besides your four hundred acres in the city-liberties, part of your twenty thousand acres in the country. Your tannery hath plenty of bark. The saw-mill for timber and the place of the glass-house are so conveniently posted for water-carriage, the city lot for a dock, and the whalery for a sound and fruitful bank, and the town Lewis by it to help your people, that by God's blessing the affairs of the society will naturally grow in their reputation and profit. I am sure I have not turned my back upon any offer that tended to its prosperity; and though I am ill at projects, I have sometimes put in for a share with her officers to countenance and advance her interest. You are already informed what is fit for you further to do. Whatsoever tends to the promotion of wine and to the manufacture of linen in these parts, I cannot but wish you to promote; and the French people are most likely in both respects to answer that design. To that end I would advise you to send for some thousands of plants out of France, with some able vinerons, and people of the other vocation. But because I believe you have been entertained with this and some other profitable subjects by your president, Nicholas Moore, I shall add no more, but to assure you that I am heartily inclined to advance your just interest, and that you will always find me your kind and cordial friend,

WILLIAM PENN.

Phila. 16th of 6th month, (August,) 1683.

Samuel M. Janney, *The Life of William Penn* (Philadelphia, 1852), 246–249.

---

162. Treaty-making with the Indians (1683)

BY GOVERNOR WILLIAM PENN

For bibliography, see No. 161 above. On the Indians, see Nos. 60, 91, 152 above.

23.   EVERY king hath his council; and that consists of all the old and wise men of his nation, which perhaps is two hundred people. Nothing of moment is undertaken, be it war, peace, selling of land, or traffic, without advising with them, and, which is more, with the young men too. It is admirable to consider how powerful the kings are, and yet how they move by the breath of their people. I have had occasion to be in council with them upon treaties for land,

and to adjust the terms of trade. Their order is thus: The king sits in the middle of an half-moon, and has his council, the old and wise, on each hand. Behind them, or at a little distance, sit the younger fry in the same figure. Having consulted and resolved their business, the king ordered one of them to speak to me. He stood up, came to me, and in the name of the king saluted me, then took me by the hand, and told me that he was ordered by his king to speak to me, and that now it was not he but the king who spoke, because what he should say was the king's mind. He first prayed me to excuse them, that they had not complied with me the last time. He feared there might be some fault in the interpreter, being neither Indian nor English. Besides, it was the Indian custom to deliberate and take up much time in council before they resolved; and that, if the young people and owners of the land had been as ready as he, I had not met with so much delay. Having thus introduced his matter, he fell to the bounds of the land they had agreed to dispose of, and the price; which now is little and dear, that which would have bought twenty miles not buying now two. During the time that this person spoke, not a man of them was observed to whisper or smile — the old grave, the young reverent, in their deportment. They speak little, but fervently, and with elegance. I have never seen more natural sagacity, considering them without the help (I was going to say the spoil) of tradition: and he will deserve the name of wise who outwits them in any treaty about a thing they understand. When the purchase was agreed, great promises passed between us of kindness and good neighbourhood, and that the English and Indians must live in love as long as the sun gave light; which done, another made a speech to the Indians, in the name of all the sachamakers or kings; first, to tell them what was done; next, to charge and command them to love the Christians, and particularly to live in peace with me and the people under my government; that many governors had been in the river; but that no governor had come himself to live and stay here before: and having now such an one, who had treated them well, they should never do him or his any wrong; at every sentence of which they shouted, and said Amen in their way. . . .

25. We have agreed, that in all differences between us, six of each side shall end the matter. Do not abuse them, but *let them have justice, and you win them.* . . .

Samuel M. Janney, *The Life of William Penn* (Philadelphia, 1852), 244–246 *passim.*

163. Germans in Pennsylvania (1684)

BY FRANCIS DANIEL PASTORIUS (1700)

(TRANSLATED BY LEWIS H. WEISS, 1850)

Pastorius was a German advocate, a man of excellent education. As agent of the Frankfort Land Company he founded Germantown, near Philadelphia. — Bibliography: Winsor, *Narrative and Critical History*, III, 502; Channing and Hart, *Guide*, § 108.

. . . THE German Society commissioned myself, Francis Daniel Pastorius, as their licensed agent, to go to Pennsylvania and to superintend the purchase and survey of their lands.

I set out from Frankford on the Mayne, went to London, where I made the purchase, and then embarked for America.

Under the protection of the Almighty, I arrived safely at Philadelphia, and I was enabled to send my report home to Germany, on the 7th of March, 1684. . . .

Our first lot in the city is of the following dimensions. It has one hundred feet front, and is four hundred feet deep. Next to it is to be a street; adjoining it lies the second lot of the same size as No. 1. Then another street. Lot No. 3 joins this street, its size being the same as the other two. On these lots, we can build two dwellings at each end, making in all, twelve buildings with proper yards and gardens, and all of them fronting on the streets.

For the first few years, little or no profit can reasonably be expected to accrue from these lots, on account of the great scarcity of money in this province, and also that as yet, this country has no goods or productions of any kind to trade with, or export to Europe.

Our Governor, William Penn, intends to establish and encourage the growing and manufactory of woollens ; to introduce the cultivation of the vine, for which this country is peculiarly well adapted, so that our Company had better send us a quantity of wine-barrels and vats of various sorts, also all kinds of farming and gardening implements. *Item*, several iron boilers of various sizes, and copper and brass kettles. *Item*, an iron stove, several blankets and mattrasses, also a few pieces of *Barchet* and white linens, which might be sold in our trading-house here, to good advantage.

On the 16th of November last, a fair had been held at Philadelphia, but we only sold about ten dollars worth at our trading-house, owing altogether to the scarcity of money, as has been already mentioned. . . .

The Governor, William Penn, laid out the city of Philadelphia, between the two rivers Dellavarra and Scolkill, naming it with the pious wish and desire, that its inhabitants might dwell together in brotherly love and unity.

The Dellavarra is deep enough, so that the largest vessels can come up close to the bank, which is but about a stone's cast from the city.

Another English Company have laid out the new town of *Frankfort*, five miles above Philadelphia, at which, now so flourishing and pleasant place, they have already established several good mills, a glass-house, pottery, and some stores and trading-houses.

New Castle lies forty miles from the ocean, on the Dellavarra, and has a very good harbour.

The town of *Uplandt* is twenty miles above New Castle, on the river, and is a fine large place inhabited mostly by Swedes.

On the twenty-fourth day Octobriis, anno 1685, have I, Francis Daniel Pastorius, with the wish and concurrence of our Governor, laid out and planned a new town, which we called Germantown or Germanopolis, in a very fine and fertile district, with plenty of springs of fresh water, being well supplied with oak, walnut and chestnut trees, and having besides excellent and abundant pasturage for the cattle. At the commencement, there were but twelve families of forty-one individuals, consisting mostly of German mechanics and weavers. The principal street of this, our town, I made sixty feet in width, and the cross street forty feet. The space or lot for each house and garden, I made three acres in size ; for my own dwelling, however, six acres.

Before my laying out of this town, I had already erected a small house in Philadelphia, thirty feet by fifteen in size. The windows, for the want of glass, were made of oiled paper. Over the door I had placed the following inscription : —

Parva domus, sed amica bonis, procul este prophani;

at which our Governor, when he paid me a visit, laughed heartily, at the same time encouraging me to build more.

I have also obtained 15,000 acres of land for our Company, in one tract, with this condition, — that within one year at least thirty families should settle on it ; and thus we may, by God's blessing, have a separate German province, where we can all live together in one. . . .

We Christians acknowledge as our Governor and chief magistrate the oft-named and excellent, the Honourable William Penn, to whom this region was granted and given as his own, by his majesty of England, Carolus II., with the express command that all the previous and future colonists should be subject to Penn's laws and jurisdiction.

This wise and truly pious ruler and governor did not, however, take possession of the province thus granted without having first conciliated, and at various councils and treaties duly purchased from the natives of this country the various regions of Pennsylvania. He, having by these means obtained good titles to the province, under the sanction and signature of the native chiefs, I therefore have purchased from him some thirty thousand acres for my German colony.

Now, although the oft-mentioned William Penn is one of the sect of Friends or Quakers, still he will compel no man to belong to his particular society, but he has granted to every one free and untrammelled exercise of their opinions, and the largest and most complete liberty of conscience. . . .

Our German society have in this place now established a lucrative trade in woollen and linen goods, together with a large assortment of other useful and necessary articles, and have entrusted this extensive business to my own direction; besides this they have now purchased and hold over thirty thousand acres of land, for the sake of establishing an entirely German colony. In my newly laid out Germantown, there are already sixty-four families in a very prosperous condition. Such persons, therefore, and all those who still arrive, have to fall to work and swing the axe most vigorously, for wherever you turn the cry is, *Itur in antiquam sylvam*, nothing but endless forests; so that I have been often wishing for a number of stalwart Tyrolians, to throw down these gigantic oak and other forest trees, but which we will be obliged to cut down ourselves, by degrees, and with almost incredible labour and exertion; during which we can have a very forcible illustration of the sentence pronounced upon our poor old father Adam, that *in the sweat of his brow he should eat his bread*. To our successors, and others coming after us, we would say, that they must not only bring over money, but a firm determination to labour and make themselves useful to our infant colony. Upon the whole, we may consider that man blessed whom the devil does not find idling. In the mean time, we are employing the wild inhabitants as day-labourers, for which they are, however, not much inclined; and we ourselves are gradually learning their language, so as to instruct them in the religion of Christ, inviting them to attend our church services, and therefore have the pleasing hope that the spirit of

God may be the means of enlightening many of these poor heathens, unto their souls' salvation.   To Him be honour, praise, thanks, and glory, for evermore.   Amen.

Francis Daniel Pastorius, *Geographical Description of Pennsylvania*, in Pennsylvania Historical Society, *Memoirs* (Philadelphia, 1850), IV, Pt. 11, 88–104 *passim*.

CHAPTER XXV—NEW JERSEY

164. "Concessions and Agreements of the Proprietors of East Jersey" (1665)

BY JOHN LORD BERKELEY AND SIR GEORGE CARTERET

These two proprietors of East Jersey were also included among the favorites of Charles II, who received the grant of the Carolinas (No. 78). — Bibliography: Winsor, *Narrative and Critical History*, III, 449–456; Channing and Hart, *Guide*, § 106.

THE Concessions and Agreement of the Lords Propriators of the *Province* of *New Cesarea* or *New Jersey* to and with all and every the *Adventurers* and all such as shall settle or plant there.

Imprimis wee doe consent and agree That the Governor of the said Province hath Power by the advice of his Councell to Depute one in his place and Authority in case of death or removall, To continue untill our further order unless wee have Com'issionated one before.

Item that hee hath (likewise) power to make choice of and to take to him six Councellors at least, or twelve at most, or any even number between six and twelve with whose advice and consent, or with at least three of the six, or foure of a greater number (all being sum'oned) hee is to governe according to the limitac'ons and instructions following during our pleasure. . . .

Item That all persons that are or shall become subjects to the King of England and sweare or subscribe Allegiance to the King and faithfulness to the Lords shalbe admitted to Plant and become ffreeman of the said Province and enjoy the ffreedomes and Im'unities hereafter expressed untill some stopp or contradiction bee made by us the Lords or else the Governor Councell and Assemblie, which shalbe in force untill the Lords see cause to the contrary, Provided that such stopp shall not any way prejudice the right or continuance of any person that hath been received before such stopp or order come from the Lords or generall Assemblie.

Item That noe person qualified as aforesaid within the said Province at any time shalbe any waies molested punished disquieted or called in Question for any difference in opinion or practice in matters of Religious concernements, who doe not actually disturbe the civill peace of the said

Province, but that all and every such person and persons may from time to time and at all times truly and fully have and enjoy his and their Judgments and Conciences in matters of Religion throughout all the said Province : They behaveing themselves peaceably and quietly and not using this liberty to Licentiousnes, nor to the civill injury or outward disturbance of others, any Law Statute or clause conteyned or to be conteined usage or custome of this Realme of England to the contrary thereof in any wise notwithstanding.

Item That no pretence may be taken by us our heires or assignes for or by reason of our right of Patronage and power of Advowsen graunted by his Maties Letters Pattents unto his Royall Highnes James Duke of Yorke, and by his said Royall Highnes unto us, thereby to infringe the generall clause of Libertie of Conscience aforement'oned WEE doe hereby graunt unto the Generall assembly of the said Province power by Act to Constitute and appoint such and soe many Ministers or Preachers as they shall think fitt, and to establish their maintenance, Giving liberty besides to any person or persons to keep and maintaine what Preachers or Ministers they please.

Item That the inhabitants being ffreemen or cheife Agents to others of the Province aforesaid doe as soone as this our Com'ission shall arrive by Virtue of a writt in our names by the Governor to be for the present (untill our Seale comes) sealed and signed make choice of Twelve Deputies or Representatives from amongst themselves who being chosen are to joine with the said Governor and Councell for the makeing of such Lawes Ordinances and Constitutions as shalbe necessary for the present good and welfare of the said Province, . . .

AND that the planting of the said Province may be the more speedily promoted.

i WEE doe hereby Graunt unto all persons who have alreadie Adventured to the Province of New Cesaria or new Jersey or shall transport themselves or Servants before the first day of January which shall be in the yeare of our Lord 1665. These following proporc'ons viz! to every ffreeman that shall goe with the first Governor from the Port when he imbarques (or shall meet him at the Randevouze hee appoints) for the Settlement of a Plantac'on there ; armed with a good Muskett boare twelve bulletts to the Pound, with Tenn pounds of powder and Twenty pound of Bulletts, with bandeleers and match convenient, and with six months provision for his own person arriving there 150 acres of Land English measure And for every able man Servant that he shall carry with him armed and provided as aforesaid and arriving there, the like quantity of 150 acres of land English measure, And who-ever shall send Servants at that time shall for every able man Servant hee or she soe sends armed and provided as aforesaid and arriving there the like quantity of 150 acres And for every weaker Servant or Slave male or female exceeding the age of ffourteen yeares which any one shall send or carry arriveing there 75 acres of Land And to every Chris-tian Servant exceeding the age aforesaid after the expiracon of their time of service 75 acres of Land for their own use.

2 *Item* to every Master or Mistres that shall goe before the first day of January which shalbe in the yeare of our Lord 1665, 120 acres of land and for every able man Servant that hee or she shall carry or send armed and provided as aforesaid and arriving within the time aforesaid the like quantity of 120 acres of land, and for every weaker Servant or Slave male or female exceeding the age of 14 yeares arriving there 60 acres of land, and to every Christian Servant to their owne use and behoofe 60 acres of land.

3 *Item* to every ffreeman and ffreewoman [who] shall arrive in the said Province armed and provided as aforesaid within the second year from the first day of January 1665 to the first of Jan'y 1666 with an intenc'on to plant 90 acres of land English measure, and for every able man Servant that hee or she shall carry or send armed and provided as aforesaid 90 acres of land like measure.

4 *Item* for every weaker Servant or slave aged as aforesaid that shall be soe carried or sent thither within the second yeare as aforesaid 45 acres of land of like measure And to every Christian Servant that shall arrive the second yeare 45 acres of land of like measure after the expiracon of his or their time of Service for their own use and behoofe.

5 *Item* to every ffreeman and ffreewoman Armed and provided as aforesaid That shall goe and arrive with an intencon to plant within the third yeare from January 1666 to January 1667 60 acres of land of like measure And for every able man Servant that he or they shall carry or send within the said time armed and provided as aforesaid the like quantitie of 60 acres of land, And for every weaker Servant or Slave aged as aforesaid that hee or they shall carry or send within the Third yeare 30 acres of land and to every Christian Servant soe carried or sent in the Third yeare 30 acres of land of like measure after the expiracon of his or their time of Service. All which Land and all other that shall be possessed in the said Province are to be held on the same termes

and Condic'ons as is before menc'oned and as hereafter in the following Paragraphs is more at lar[g]e expressed. . . .

Documents relating to the Colonial History of the State of New Jersey (edited by William A. Whitehead, Newark, 1880), I, 28–39 *passim.*

---◆---

165. Town Meeting in the Province of New Jersey (1666–1668)

FROM THE RECORDS OF NEWARK

This town, settled by New Haven people, introduced for itself the New England system of town government. — Bibliography: Channing and Hart, *Guide*, §§ 106, 118, 122.

IMPRIMIS, In the Province of New Jersey, near to Elizabeth Town, and the Town Plotts on Passaic River, made choice of by friends from Milford and other neighboring plantations, thereabouts from New England, on the twenty first day of May, one thousand six hundred and sixty six, the above mentioned persons had a meeting, together with the agents sent from Guilford and Brandford to ask on behalf of their undertakers and selves with reference to a township or allottments, together with friends from Milford; at this meeting it was agreed upon mutually that the aforesaid persons from Milford, Guilford, and Brandford, together with their associates, being now accepted of, do make one township, provided they send word so to be any time between this and the last of October next ensuing, and according to fundamentals mutually agreed upon, do desire to be of one heart and consent, through Gods blessing with one hand they may endeavor the carrying on of spiritual concernments as also civil and town affairs according to God and a Godly government, . . .

At a meeting Touching the Intended design of many of the inhabitants of Branford, the following was subscribed:

1st. That none shall be admitted freemen or free Burgesses within our Town upon Passaick River in the Province of New Jersey, but such

Deut. 1–25. Planters as are members of some or other of the Congre-
Exod. 18–31. gational Churches nor shall any but such be chosen to
Deut. 17–15. Magistracy or to Carry on any part of Civil Judicature, or as
Jerem. 36–21. deputies or assistants, to have power to Vote In establishing
Laws, and making or Repealing them or to any Chief Military Trust or

Office.   Nor shall any But such Church Members have any Vote in any such elections ; Tho' all others admitted to Be planters have Right to their proper Inheritance, and do and shall enjoy all other Civil Liberties and Privileges, According to all Laws, Orders, Grants which are, or hereafter shall be made for this Town.

2nd. We shall with Care and Diligence provide for the maintenance of the purity of Religion professed in the Congregational Churches. . . .

Item — the Town agreed, that any Man that would take Pains to kill Wolves, he or they for their Encouragement should have 15s. for every grown Wolf that they kill, and this to be paid by the Town Treasury.

Item — Thomas Richards had granted him, that his Lott by the Landing place should be made up Six Acres, if it may be there had without Prejudice to the Town. . . .

. . . The Town freely Consented, by their Jointly Voteing to Give freely to Mr. Parson, the Charges off diging and Finishing his well Hitherto ; with the Rest of his Transportation Charges.   Item — the Town Consented to pay Mr. Parson Eighty pounds for the first Year, Which is to Be Laid out in Building his House at Moderate prises for their Labour ; . . .

Records of the Town of Newark, in New Jersey Historical Society, *Collections*, VI (Newark, 1864), 1–10 *passim*.

——————◆——————

166. A Sketch of the Complications in New Jersey (1679)

BY SIR JOHN WERDEN

Werden was Attorney-General in England, and this sketch is part of an opinion on the conflicting land grants. — Bibliography : Winsor, *Narrative and Critical History*, III, 449–454; Channing and Hart, *Guide*, § 106.

. . . THE Dutch West India Company were possessed of a Lardge Tract of Land in America (called new Netherlands, for the Governement whereof, among other things, they Imposed a Custome of $\frac{10}{100}$. upon Merchandises of Straingers or Inhabitants there, & collected y^e Same many Yeares.

In. 1664. His Maj^{tys}' Forces under Coll. Nicholls invaded those Territoryes & conquered y^m yet admitting Articles of Surrender (on delivery up of the ffort at New-Amsterdam, now called New-Yorke) wherein the same Payments were consented to, & generally the Priviledges of the Inhabitants (then most Dutch) reserved to y^m.

Coll. Nicholls continued in Possession many Yeares as Governour under His R^{ll} High^{sse} (to whom the K^g by Pattent had graunted the whole Tract, with Power to make Laws &c. for y^e Good Governem^t thereof, soe as they were not repugnant to the Lawes of England) And after him Coll. Lovelace succeeded in the Governement till (1672) dureing all which tyme y^e s^d $\frac{10}{100}$ Customs were duly collected without Interruption.

Soone after y^t y^e Duke had Passed his Pattent, He graunted to Sr George Carteret & Ld John Berkelay, A Parcell of the Premisses, which is since called New Jersey, which they enjoyed Jointly as Proprietors of the Soyle ; untill. (72) when by the Chance of warre, The whole Territory fell againe into ye hands of the Dutch.

Whilest ye Dutch were in Possession of it (& in warre wth England) Mr Fenwicke, Mr Billing &c (most of y^m Quakers) agree with Ld John Berkelay for his Right to One Moity of New Jersey.

Afterwards in (1673) the Peace being made 'twixt England & Holland ; the whole Territory was restored to vs by virtue of y^t Treaty, & all men presumed to be in Possession againe ; in Statu quo.

The Duke being affresh entitled from the Kings New Graunt to him; in. (73) or. (74) sends over a New Governour (Sr Ed^d Andros., who is now there) & a Company of Souldiers to repossesse the Forts & resettle the Country ; but in kindnesse to y^m & encouragem^t to English Traders, Lowers (or abates) the $\frac{10}{100}$ to $\frac{5}{100}$ Customes.

About y^e same tyme Sr G. Carteret & y^e Quakers obtaine New graunts from the Duke of New Jersey, in the same manner, as it was formerly granted to Sr G. Carteret &. Ld Berkeley.

And afterwards the Quakers agree with Sr G. Carteret to divide New-Jersey betwixt y^m by certaine Metes & bounds soe as each might know theire owne Share ; & this is done by drawing an Imaginary Line crosse the Country (but Visible in theire Map) to which all partyes being agreed ; the Duke upon theire desire adds his Confirmation of this theire Partition.

Sr Edm^d Andros y^e present Governour continues to demand & Collect y^e $\frac{5}{100}$ Customes (as his Predecessours did y^e $\frac{10}{100}$) & y^e Quakers exclaime agst it, pretending y^t they ought not to pay Any.

Quære ? whether by the Graunt to the Quakers (& to Sr G. Carterett) of the Soyle, &c. They be empowred to set up distinct Governements, Principallityes, or Commonwealths, within theire Respective Lands ? or whether they are not still lyable, as all other Inhabitants in these Territoryes are, to the Lawes established in New Yorke, for yᵉ whole Territory depending on it?

Documents relating to the Colonial History of the State of New Jersey (edited by William A. Whitehead, Newark, 1880), I, 290-291.

———◆———

167. An Account of East Jersey (1684)

BY DAVID BARCLAY, ARTHUR FORBES, AND GAVIN LAURIE

This extract, written by three settlers in Jersey, is colored by their desire to attract immigrants. Other accounts of the Jerseys will appear in Volume II of this series. — Bibliography: Winsor, *Narrative and Critical History*, III, 449-450; Channing and Hart, *Guide*, § 106.

KNOWING you do expect from us an account of this Countrey, we have for your encouragement, and for the encouragement of all our Countrey Men who may be inclinable to come into this Countrey, given you this brief and true account of it, according as we have seen and are credibly informed, . . . a great deal of it is naturally clear of wood, And what is not so, is easily cleared, the trees being but small and a good distance from one another, so that the Land yet untaken up, so far as we can understand, is easier to clear than that which is taken up, the Towns that are already seated, being seated in the woodiest places. The Merchants in *New York*, both *Dutch* and *English*, have many of them taken up Land and settled Plantations in this Countrey, and severall from that Collony are desiring to come and take up land among us, though they might have land in their own Collony without paying Quitt rents. The wood here is not so hard to clear as many think, they do not pull it up by the Roots, but [cut] them about a foot or more from the ground, and one man may cut down many in a day; four of our men the first day they began, cut down seventy the best trees they could find, fit for building. . . . There will be many houses built there quickly, for many have taken up lots and all that have taken are obliged to build within a year. There is good encouragement for Tradesmen to come over, such as Carpenters, Masons and Bricklayers, for they build not only of Wood, but also of Stone and Brick, yet most of Countrey Houses are built of Wood, only Trees split and set up an end on the ground, and coverings to their Houses are mostly Shingles made of Oak, Chesnut and Cedar Wood, which makes a very neat Covering, yet there are some Houses covered after the *Dutch* manner with pantikles. . . .

We shall now answer, so far as we are capable, your *Queries* sent over to us.

To the first, we cannot positively answer, to give an account of the whole length and breadth of the Province, But we are informed that it is a great deal broader than ye expected, for those that have travelled from the extent of our bounds on Hudson's River, straight over to the *Delaware* River, say it is 100 myles or upwards ; we shall know that certainly after a while, for the Line betwixt us and *New York* is to be run straight over to Delaware River, about 3 weeks hence, and after that the Line betwixt us and *West Jersey;* After which we shall be able to give a true account of the bounds of that Province.

2ly. When the bounds is so exactly laid out, we can the easier guess at the number of Acres, and by that time may be able to give an account what number of Acres is already taken up, but there is no fear of want of Land.

3ly. The quantity of Meadow ground we cannot determine, having travelled as yet but little in the Province, but the way we have travelled, there is meadow [in] abundance, both on the water sides and on the up Land.

4ly. There is also other good ground in some places, great quantities free of wood, which is fit either for Corn or Grass, and the ground all over brings forth good English grass naturally after it is ploughed.

5ly. There are also Commons upon the Countrey, but what quantity we cannot tell, there is little kept in them save wild horses, which the people take up when they have occasion. There is also Land fit for pasturage for Sheep, and there are Sheep in the Countrey, but what number the ablest planters have we know not, but some we see have good flocks.

6ly. An exact Mapp of the Countrey is not yet drawn nor can you quickly expect it, for it will take up a great deale of time, charge and pains to doe it.

7ly. There are also hills up in the Countrey, but how much ground they take up we know not, they are said to be stony and covered with wood, and beyond them is said to be excellent land.

8ly. To the Eight we cannot answer as yet.

9ly. There be People of several sorts of Religion, but few very Zealous. The People being mostly *New England* men, doe mostly incline to their way, and in every Town there is a meeting house where they worship publickly every Week : They have no publick Law in the Countrey for maintaining public Teachers, but the Towns that have them make way within themselves to maintain them.   We know none that hath a settled Preacher that follows no other Imployment, save one Town *Newark*.

10ly. The method of building their houses is mentioned already.

11ly. There are not many Out Plantations that are not within the bounds of some Town, Yet there be some, and these are the richest; what number are there we know not, some have great quantities of Land and abundance cleared.

12ly. The richest Planters have not above 8 or 10 Servants; they will have some of them, 1 Dozen of Cows, yea some 20 or 30; 8 or 10 Oxen, horses more than they know themselves, for they keep breading Mares, and keep no more horses at home than they have occasion to work; The rest they let run in the wood both Winter and Summer, and take them as they have occasion to use them.   Swine they have in great flocks in the wood, and Sheep in flocks also, but they let them not run in the woods for fear of being destroyed by wolves.   Their profit arises from the Improvement of their Land, and Increase of their Bestial.

13ly. There will be in most of the Towns already settled at least 100 Houses, but they are not built so regular as the Towns in our Countrey, so that we cannot compare them with any Town we know in Scotland. Every house in the Town hath a Lott of 4 *Acres* lying to it: so that every one building upon his own Lott makes the town Irregular and scattering.   Their Streets are laid out too large, and the Sheep in the Towns are mostly maintained in them: They are so large that they need not trouble to pave them.

14ly. Betwixt *Sandy Hook*, and *Little Egg-harbor lye 2 Towns Middletown and Shrewsbury*.   There is no Land taken up that way but what is in the bounds of these two Towns; what kind of land it is, we know not, having never travelled that way.   *Barnegate or Burning Hole* is said to be a very good place for fishing, and there are some desiring to take up land there, who inform us that it is good Land, and abundance of *Meadow* lying to it.

15ly. There are no *Fisher-men* that follow only that trade, save some that salt *Whales* upon the Coasts, and other Fishes; there is abundance to be had every where through the Countrey in all the Rivers, and the People commonly fish with Sives or long netts, and will catch with a Sive 1, sometimes 2 barrels a day, of good fish, which they salt up mostly for their own use, and to sell to others.

16ly: There is no Ships belonging to this Province particularly, or built here, save one which *Samuel Groome* built here the last Summer, which stands yet in the Stocks (a stop being put to it by his death). There is conveniency enough to build ships. The Ships in this part trade mostly to the *West Indian Islands,* and some to *New found Land,* where the Provisions of this Countrey vends.

17ly. There is land here in several places, after it is cleared and brought into a farm sett out for Rents as in our Countrey, at 5, 8, and 10 shil: *per Acre* According to the goodness and situation of the said Land; and those that will be at charge to clear land may get good tennants to take upon good termes. But whether it will turn to good account or not, because little experienced as yet with the Charge of clearing of Land, I will not positively inform.

18ly. There is several places of the Countrey fit for mills, and several both Corn and Saw mills already sett up, and good encouragement to sett up more.

19ly. The Acres are here reckoned according to the *English* Account: There is 16 foot goes to the Rood, and 20 Rood long and 8 Rood broad, makes an Acre. One English butt of Wheat which is 8 *English Gallons,* or *Scots Quarts* commonly sows an Acre, and 2 bushells of Oats an Acre, and half Acre; [One] *English* peck which is 4 *English* quarts or *Scots Shopens* of *Indian* Corn plants one Acre.

20ly: There are but few *Indian Natives* in this Countrey. Their strength is inconsiderable, they live in the Woods, and have small towns in some places far up in the Countrey. . . . They have *Kings* among themselves to govern them. For *Religion,* they have none at all, they do not refuse to sell Land at occasion. The prices of Grain and other Provisions here at Present *Indian* Corn, 2s 6d the Bushell; Wheat 4 shill: Rye, 3 shill: Oats 1s 8d the Bushell; Beef 1d; Pork 2d; Venison 1d; Mutton 3d the pound; — this *English* Measure and Weight. But mark, these things being valued in this Countrey money, there is a fifth part difference betwixt it and Sterling Money, So that Wheat being valued here at 4s. the Bushell, is but 3s 3d Sterling, and so of the rest proportionally.

Here you have an account of things so far as we are capable to give you at present, with which we hope you will be satisfied, untill further opportunity and better experience give us occasion to write more. And so we rest your Friends and well wishers to all our Countrey Men. . . .

[George Scot], *The Model of the Government of the Province of East-New-Jersey in America* (Edinburgh, 1685), reprinted in New Jersey Historical Society, *Collections* (1846), I, 288–293 *passim.*

168. An Account of West Jersey (1698)

BY GABRIEL THOMAS

This is an extract from one of the most sprightly and individual of colonial writers, himself a colonist in West Jersey. — Bibliography: Winsor, *Narrative and Critical History*, III, 450–451; Channing and Hart, *Guide*, § 106.

WEST-NEW-JERSEY lies between the Latitude of Forty, and Forty two Degrees; having the *Main Sea* on the South, *East-Jersey* on the North, *Hudson's Bay* on the East, and *Pensilvania* on the West.

The first Inhabitants of this Countrey were the *Indians*, being supposed to be part of the Ten dispersed Tribes of *Israel*; for indeed they are very like the *Jews* in their Persons, and something in their Practices and Worship, . . .

The *Dutch* and *Sweeds* inform us that they are greatly decreased in number to what they were when they came first into this Country: And the *Indians* themselves say, that two of them die to every one Christian that comes in here. . . . my chief aim, in the next place, is to acquaint thee how, and after what manner the Christians live there   And I hope I have pleased thee so far, as it may prove a means to encourage me to give a larger Description hereafter.

The next who came there were the *Dutch*; which was between Forty and Fifty Years agoe, though they made but very little Improvement, only built Two or Three Houses, upon an Island (called since by the *English*) *Stacies-Island*; and it remained so, till about the Year 1675. in which King *Charles* the Second (or the Duke of *York* (his Brother) gave the Countrey to *Edward Billing*, in whose time, one *Major Fenwick* went thither, with some others, and built a pretty *Town*, and call'd it *Salam*; and in a few Years after a Ship from *London*, and another from *Hull*, sail'd thither with more People, who went higher up into the Countrey, and built there a Town, and called it *Burlington*, which is now the chiefest Town in that Countrey, though *Salam* is the ancientest; and a fine *Market-Town* it is, having several *Fairs* kept yearly in it; likewise well furnished with good store of most Necessaries for humane Support, as *Bread, Beer, Beef*, and *Pork*; as also *Butter* and *Cheese*, of which they freight several Vessels, and send them to *Barbadoes*, and other Islands.

There are very many fine *stately Brick-Houses* built, and a *commo dious Dock* for *Vessels* to come in at, and they claim equal Privilege with *Burlington* for the sake of Antiquity; tho' that is the principal Place, by reason that the late Governor *Cox*, who bought that Countrey of *Edward Billing*, encouraged and promoted that Town chiefly, in settling his *Agents* and *Deputy-Governors* there, (the same Favours are continued by the *New-West-Jersey* Society, who now manage Matters there) which brings their Assemblies and chief Courts to be kept there; and, by that means it is become a very famous Town, having a great many stately *Brick-Houses* in it, (as I said before) with a delicate great *Market-House*, where they keep their Market: It hath a noble and *spacious Hall* over-head, where their *Sessions* is kept, having the Prison adjoining to it. . . .

There are many Fair and Great Brick Houses on the outside of the Town which the Gentry have built there for their Countrey Houses, besides the Great and Stately Palace of *John Tateham* Esq; which is pleasantly Situated on the North side of the *Town*, having a very fine and delightful *Garden* and *Orchard* adjoyning to it, wherein is variety of *Fruits*, *Herbs*, and *Flowers*; as *Roses*, *Tulips*, *July-Flowers*, *Sun-Flowers* (that open and shut as the *Sun* Rises and Sets, thence taking their Name) *Carnations*, and many more; besides abundance of Medicinal *Roots Herbs*, *Plants*, and *Flowers*, found wild in the Fields.

There are kept also in this Famous Town several Fairs every Year; and as for Provisions, *viz.* Bread, Beer, Beef, Pork, Cheese, Butter, and most sorts of Fruit here is great Plenty and very Cheap; all those Commodities are to be bought every Market-Day.

A Ship of Four Hundred Tuns may Sail up to this *Town* in the River *Delaware*; for I my self have been on Board a Ship of that Burthen there: And several fine Ships and Vessels (besides Governour *Cox*'s own great Ship) have been built there.

There are also two handsom Bridges to come in and out of the Town, called *London* and *York-Bridges*. The *Town* stands in an *Island*, the Tide flowing quite round about it. There are *Water-Men* who constantly Ply their Wherry Boats from that Town to the City of *Philadelphia* in *Pensilvania*, and to other places. Besides there is *Glocester-Town*, which is a very Fine and Pleasant Place, being well stor'd with Summer Fruits, as *Cherries*, *Mulberries*, and *Strawberries*, whither Young People come from *Philadelphia* in the Wherries to eat *Straberries* and *Cream*, within sight of which City it is sweetly Situated, being but about three Miles distance from thence.

There are several *Meetings* of *Worship* in this Country, *viz.* the *Presbyterians, Quakers,* and *Anabaptists:* Their Privilege as to Matter of *Law,* is the same both for *Plaintiff* and *Defendant,* as in *England.*

The Air is very Clear, Sweet and Wholesom; in the depth of Winter it is something colder, but as much hotter in the heighth of Summer than in *England.* . . .

. . . The Countrey inhabited by the *Christians* is divided into four Parts or *Counties,* tho' the Tenth part of it is not yet peopled; 'Tis far cheaper living there for Eatables than here in *England*; and either Men or Women that have a Trade, or are Labourers, can, if industrious, get near three times the Wages they commonly earn in *England.*

Courteous Reader, As yet I have given thee no Account of *East-Jersey,* because I never was there, so in reality cannot properly or pertinently speak to that Matter. I will not pretend to impose any thing on the World, but have all along, and shall still declare nothing but Verity; therefore one Word of that by and by. I might have given thee a much larger Account of this Countrey, and have stretch'd this (now) Pocket Volume to an extraordinary Bulk and Size; and yet without straining or deviating in the least from the Principles of my Profession, which are Truth it self. I have no Plot in my Pate, or deep Design, no, not the least expectation of gaining any thing by them that go thither, or losing by those who stay here. My End chiefly in Writing, nay, indeed my great Aim, is to inform the People of *Britain* and *Ireland* in general, but particularly the Poor, who are begging, or near it, or starving, or hard by it (as I before took notice in my Preface) to encourage them (for their own Good, and for the Honour and Benefit of their Native Countrey, to whom they are now a Scandal and Disgrace; and whose *Milk* and *Honey* these *Drones* eat up, and are besides a heavy Burden to the Commonwealth, in the Taxes paid by every Parish in *England,* &c. to support them.

Law-Causes are here (as in *Pensilvania*) speedily determined, in the second Court at least, unless in some difficult Business. One Justice of the Peace hath Power to try a Cause, and give Judgment therein, if the Original Debt be under forty Shillings. And for Thieves and Robbers (as I hinted before in the Preface) they must restore fourfold; which, if they are not able to do, they must work hard till the injured Person is satisfied. . . .

Gabriel Thomas, *An Historical Description of the Province and Country of West-New-Jersey in America* (London, 1698), 1–31 *passim.*

CHAPTER XXVI — LIFE IN THE MIDDLE COLONIES

169. A Dutch Clergyman's Experiences (1628)

BY DOMINE JONAS MICHAELIUS

(TRANSLATED BY HENRY C. MURPHY, 1858)

Michaelius had been a minister of Dutch churches in Holland, Portugal, and Guinea, before the experiences here related. — Bibliography: Winsor, *Narrative and Critical History*, IV, 421; Channing and Hart, *Guide*, § 104.

. . . THE voyage continued long, namely, from the 24th of January till the 7th of April, when we first set our foot upon this land. Of storm and tempest we have had no lack, particularly about the Bermudas and the rough coasts of this country, the which fell hard upon the good wife and children, but they bore it better as regards sea-sickness and fear, than I had expected. Our fare in the ship was very poor and scanty, so that my blessed wife and children, not eating with us in the cabin, on account of the little room in it, had a worse lot than the sailors themselves; and that by reason of a wicked cook who annoyed them in every way; but especially by reason of the captain himself, . . .

Our coming here was agreeable to all, and I hope, by the grace of the Lord, that my services will not be unfruitful. The people, for the most part, are all free, somewhat rough, and loose, but I find in most all of them both love and respect towards me; two things with which hitherto the Lord has everywhere graciously blessed my labors, and which will produce us fruit in our special calling, as your Right Reverend yourself well knows and finds.

We have first established the form of a church (gemeente), and, as brother Bastiaen Crol very seldom comes down from Fort Orange, because the directorship of that fort and the trade there is committed to him, it has been thought best to choose two elders for my assistance and for the proper consideration of all such ecclesiastical matters as might occur, intending the coming year, if the Lord permit, to let one of them retire, and to choose another in his place from a double number first lawfully presented by the congregation. One of those whom w have now chosen is the Honorable Director himself, and the other is the storekeeper of the Company, Jan Huyghen, his brother-in-law, persons of very good character, as far as I have been able to learn; having both been formerly in office in the Church, the one as deacon, and the other as elder in the Dutch and French Churches, respectively, at Wesel.

We have had at the first administration of the Lord's Supper full fifty communicants — not without great joy and comfort for so many — Walloons and Dutch; of whom, a portion made their first confession of the faith before us, and others exhibited their church certificates. . . .

In my opinion it is very expedient that the Lords Managers of this place should furnish plain and precise instructions to their Governors that they may distinctly know how to regulate themselves in all difficult occurrences and events in public matters; and at the same time that I should have all such Acta Synodalia, as are adopted in the Synods of Holland, both the special ones relating to this region, and those which are provincial and national, in relation to ecclesiastical points of difficulty, or at least such of them as, in the judgment of the Reverend Brothers at Amsterdam, would be most likely to present themselves to us here. In the mean time, I hope matters will go well here, if only on both sides we do the best in all sincerity and honest zeal; whereto I have from the first entirely devoted myself, and wherein I have also hitherto, by the grace of God, had no just cause to complain of any one. . . .

As to the natives of this country, I find them entirely savage and wild, strangers to all decency, yea, uncivil and stupid as posts, proficient in all wickedness and godlessness; devilish men, who serve nobody but the devil, that is, the spirit, which, in their language, they call *manetto;* under which title they comprehend everything that is subtle and crafty and beyond human skill and power. They have so much witchcraft, divination, sorcery and wicked tricks that they cannot be held in by any bands or locks. They are as thievish and treacherous as they are tall; and in cruelty they are more inhuman than the people of Barbary, and far exceed the Africans. . . .

The promises which the Lords Masters of the Company had made me of some acres or surveyed lands for me to make myself a home, instead of a free table which otherwise belonged to me, is wholly of no avail. For their Honors well know that there are no horses, cows, or laborers to be obtained here for money. Every one is short in these particulars and wants more. The expense would not trouble me, if an opportunity only offered; as it would be for our own accommodation, although there were no profit from it (save that the Honorable Managers owe me as much as the value of a free table); for there is here no refreshment of butter, milk, etc., to be obtained, although a very high price be offered for them; for the people who bring them and bespeak them are suspicious of each other. So I will be compelled to pass through the winter without butter and other necessaries, which the ships did not bring with them to be sold here. . . . I began to get some strength through the grace of the Lord, but in consequence of this hard fare of beans and gray peas, which are hard enough, barley, stockfish, etc., without much change, I cannot become well as I otherwise would. . . .

The country yields many good things for the support of life, but they are all to be gathered in an uncultivated and wild state. It is necessary that there should be better regulations established, and people who have the knowledge and the implements for gathering things in their season, should collect them together, as undoubtedly will gradually be the case. In the meanwhile, I wish the Lords Managers to be courteously inquired of, how I can have the opportunity to possess a portion of land, and at my own expense to support myself upon it? . . . They fell much wood here to carry to the fatherland, but the vessels are too few to take much of it. They are making a windmill to saw the wood, and we also have a grist-mill. They bake brick here, but it is very poor. There is good material for burning lime, namely, oyster-shells, in large quantities. The burning of potash has not succeeded; the master and his laborers are all greatly disappointed. We are busy now in building a fort of good quarry stone, which is to be found not far from here in abundance. May the Lord only build and watch over our walls. There is a good means for making salt; for there are convenient places, the water is salt enough, and there is no want of heat in summer. Besides, as to the waters, both of the sea and rivers, they yield all kinds of fish; and as to the land, it abounds in all kinds of game, wild and in the groves, with vegetables, fruits, roots, herbs, and plants, both for eating and medicinal purposes, working wonderful cures, which are too long to relate, and which, were it ever so pertinent, I could not tell. Your Right Reverend has already obtained some knowledge thereof in part, and will be able to obtain from others further information. The country is good and pleasant, the climate is healthy, notwithstanding the sudden changes of cold and heat. The sun is very warm ; the winter is strong and severe, and continues full as long as in our country. The best remedy is not to spare the wood — of which there is enough — and to cover oneself well with rough skins which can also easily be obtained. . . .

. . . Concluding then herewith, and commending myself in your Right Reverend's favorable and holy prayers to the Lord.

Honored and learned Sir, Beloved Brother in Christ, and Kind Friend ;

Commending your Right Reverend and all of you to Almighty God, by his Grace, to continued health and prosperity, and to eternal salvation of heart.

From the island of Manhatas in New-Netherland, this 11th August, Anno 1628, by me your Right Reverend's obedient in Christ,

JONAS MICHAELIUS.

New York Historical Society, *Collections*, 1880 (Publication Fund Series, New York, 1881), 376–387 *passim*.

———◆———

170. A New England Opinion of the Dutch (1653)

BY THE COMMISSIONERS OF THE NEW ENGLAND CONFEDERATION

On the New England Confederation, see No. 129 above; on the Dutch, see chs. xxii, xxiii, above.

INFORMACŌN was sent by an Indian Squaw to an English Inhabitant in Wethersfeild that the Duch and Indians generally were confeaderated against the English Treacherusly to cutt them of the time of execution to bee vpon the day of election of Majestrates in the seuerall collonies because then it is apprehended the plantations wilbee left naked and vnable to defend themselues the strength of the English collonies being gathered from the seuerall townes ; And the aforsaid Squaw aduised the said Inhabitants to acquaint the Rest of the English with it desiring they would remember how deare theire Slighting of her former Informacōn of the Pequatts coming vpon the English Cost them ; The Comissioners vpon these and other Informations and euidences thought fitt to draw vp a declaration of former greiuances and of this conspiracye as p^rsented to them ;

That the Indians whoe know not god but worshipp and walke after the prince of the power of the aire serving theire lusts hatefull and hating one another should grow Insolent and sundrey wayes Injurius to strangers of contrary Judgment and practise can not seem strange to any whoe duly consider what proportion and agreement there is ordenaryly betwixt the fruit and the tree ; but the vnited English collonies expecting a Just and Naighbourly corespondency and entercourse from and with the Duch liueing att and about the Monhatoes which they call new nether-land (though the place fall within that þte or tract of america called New England lying and being in breadth from forty to forty eight degrees of Northerly latitude which both in Europe and heer is well knowne by ancient pattent to bee graunted by the Kings of England to theire Subiects to settle and plant vpon) haue mett with a constant course of opposition Injuries and many hostile affronts ;   But the Euidence wee haue of theire treacherus practices are of high and mor dangerus consideracõn

The English before or when they began to build seat or plant in these þtes did generally purchase to themselues from the Indians the true pro-priators a Just Right and title to the lands they ment to Improue if they found not the place a Vacuvm Domicilivm but from the Duch att sun-dery times haue mett with many desturbances ; And that not by the prid and distemper of one man at one time but in the succession of one Goû^r after another vpon seuerall occations for many yeares ;

first letting passe an hostile wronge and Injurie capt : howes [Howe] and his companie Receiued from the former Goû^r *first* [Kieft] att longe Island in Ann : 1640 ; The English att New hauen vpon a Just title both by pattent and purchase built within theire owne Just limits a smale towne or village called Stanford but about 2 yeares after the said Goû^r Keift sent men armed to challenge the place as within the Duch limits and Jurisdiction and did most Injuriusly cause the Prince of Oringe his armes to bee sett vp there which armes were by the English p^rsently Remoued ; the Duch hauing never had possession of any þte of the place nor to this day could euer shew any shadow of Right to it ;

In the same yeare 1640 the English att Newhauen sent men to view and Purchase þte of Delaware Bay but with expresse Direction not to meddle with any thing the Duch or Sweds had Right vnto ; as the Eng-lish vessell passed by the Monhatoes the said Monser Keift made a protest but vpon enformacōn of the order giuen hee was satisfyed and wrot to John Jonson the Duch Agent att Dellawar to hold good corespondency with the English there which accordingly hee did att first and shewed them how fare the Duch and Sweds title or claime Reached ; the Rest hee told them was free for them to purchase ; and offered his assistance therin which offer (though kind accepted) was not entertained ; but the Indians being free the English agents att seuerall times from the seuerall propriators purchased large tracts of land on both sides Delaware Bay and Riuer and began to plant and to sett vp houses for trade within theire owne limits ;   But in Anno i642 without cours [cause] or warning giuen without shewing any title to the place or hearing what the English could say for [themselves] the said Duch Gouʳ sent armed vessels and men and in hostile mannor when they were altogether vnprepared for defence, as expecting nothing but peace seized theire goods carried away the men prisoners and with such violent hast burnt downe theire trading houses that two houres Respect [respite] for entreaty or consideration could not bee obteined ; nor soe much time as to Inventory the goods taken out of theire charge ;

And after in another þte of the Riuer they seized theire boat and two other men in it carrying the men and goods first to the Monhatoes and thence Returning the þsons and þte of the goods to Newhauen ; as by letters and other euidence may appeer

In Anno i64i Robert ffenner an English man then liueing at Stanford within Newhauen Jurisdicton haueing purchased a þcell of land near and vpon the west of Stanford for a plantation and freely by his deed in writing put himselfe and the said plantation called Greenwidge into consosiation and vnder the English Gouernment in Newhauen Jurisdiction ; But the said ʌ Keift did soon after take capt : Daniell Patricke an English man of a turbulent sperit and course (whoe then liued att greenwich into his protection and vnjustly wrested the whole plantation from Newhauen ; and still Injuriusly and contrary to the pʳsent Gouʳs sollemne promise (as shalbee more fully declared) The same is withholden and kept from the English

Mʳ Lamberton agent for the English att Newhauen coming from Delaware Anno i642 by the Monhatoes the Duch Gouʳ aforsaid compelled him by threatenings and force to giue an account of what beauer hee had traded within the English limits att Delaware, and to pay Recognition or Costom for the same and a protest sent from Newhauen against those Injurius proceedings proued altogether fruitles

The Duch Gou^r aforsaid sent armed Vessels to Delaware to seize Mr Lambertons Vessell by force or to driue him out of the Riuer but hee þceiueing theire Aime stood vpon his gaurd and att that time Mainteined the Right and honnor of the English

In Anno 1643 John Jonson agent for the Duch att Delaware conspired with the sweds against Mr Lambertons life they traitreously seized and Imprisoned his þson charged him to haue ploted with the Indians to cutt of both Duch and Sweds brought him to tryall vsed means to engage and corrupt witnesses against him ; but all by wise and ouer ruling hand of God, fayling they sett a large fine vpon him for trading within the English limitts in all which the Duch agent sate as one of the Judges in court with the Swedish Gou^r and as is conceiued shared with him in the fine ;

Richard Callicott somtimes agent for the companie of adventerars for the lake Lyconnia allowed for the generall court for the Massachusets complaineth that about the yeare 1644 hee did p^{r}sent to the said Duch Gou^r, letters from the Court of the Massachusets wherin liberty for the English vessell to passe vpp Dellaware Bay and Riuer by the Duch ffortt for Discouery ; and in further procecution *and in further procecution* of the said companies occations was desired and by a verbale promise freely and fully graunted by the Duch Gou^r

Notwithstanding w^h in an vnderhand and Injurius way hee p^{r}sently sent a vessell well maned to the Duch fort att Dellaware with comaund to John Jonson his agent that [there] rather to sinke the said vessell then to suffer her to passe ; by meanes wherof Richard Callicott and his companie were forced to Returne and therby theire whole stocke which att lest was seauen hundred pounds was wasted and theire Designe overthrowne besids the hope of future trade and bennifitt as by the said Duch Gou^{r}s [letter]. Read before the Swedish Gou^r and Interpreted into English did plainly appeer

In Anno 1646 som English of Newhauen haueing purchased land of the Indians propriators within the English limitts and far*e* from any of the Duch plantations or trading houses did there build a smale house for trade wherof the Duch Gou^r aforsaid being Informed hee sent a protest dated august 3^d 1646 Stilo nouo ; charging those English marchants to bee Injurius breakers of the peace and threatened to proceed against them by force

When the Comissioners for the vnited English Collonies mett att Newhauen in Anno 1646 and wrote to the said Duch Gou^r about the for-

mencioned trading house hee in his answare againe declares his Resolution to procequte his vnjust claime against the said English by armes ;
and in a proud and most offenciue mannor protests against the comissioners for the vnited English Collonies as breakers of the league and
violaters of the Right of his Lords for being soe bould as to meddie
[meete] att Newhauen within the Limitts of New Neatherland &c

The Duch for many years together layed a þticulare claime to Conecticott Riuer by him [them] called the fresh Riuer with the land on both
sides of it as by them duely purchased from the Indian propriators and did
much complaine of the English on the Riuer especially Hartford for vsurp-
ing and withholding theire Right in those lands ; To which the said English
returned answare clearing theire Right and proceedings But the Duch
Gouʳ not therwith satisfyed ; by letter dated July 20ᵗʰ i643 stilo novo :
and directed to the honered Gouʳ of the Massachusetts continnued his
complaint wherupon the whole counsell of the collonie considered the
Duch claime from the Peqouts as themselues pretended It i640 with
the answare Returned by the English att hartford and Receiued further
light from Mʳ Winslow one of the Comissioners for Plymouth whoe
descouered the said fresh Riuer when the Duch had neither trading
house nor any pretence to a foot of land there and vnderstood that the
English within Plymouth Pattent Reseated Attawonott and others the
true propriators of the lands in question ; . . .

Monsiour Peter Stewesant in Anno i647 Succeeded Will'am Keift as
Gouʳ ouer the Duch plantations and began with some mixed comple-
ments both to the Gouʳ of the Massachusets and to the Gouʳ of Newhauen he proffessed a Resolution to hold good correspondency with the
English collonies ; but euen then layed claime to all the land betwixt
Dellaware and conecticott Riuer as the Indubitate Right of his lords and
masters the states generall of the vnited provences or the westjndia companie which his predessor either never did or did more obscurly, and
soone after in September i647 in a shipp belonging to Newhauen as sold
by himselfe to Mʳ Goodyeer and by him there to bee deliuered hee sent
armed men and without aquainting any of the Majestrates of Newhauen
with the cause or grounds therof seized a Duch shipp trading in that harbour and by force charged [carried] her and her ladeing thence as a prise
to the Monhatoes ; and soone after by a protest in Duch dated October
i2 i647 Stilo nouo hee enlargeth his claime to all the land Riuers streames
&c from Cape hinlopen (which may bee about Verginnia) to Cape Cod
from which drawing any line to the North, Norwest and west hee wholy

takes in or encroaches far*e* vpon all the vnited collonies and about the same [time] by way of protestation or comaund hee requires from the Gou^r of Newhauen y^t the both [Dutch] marchants and their goods with Reconition and that som of his fugetiues bee returned ; as if Newhauen Collonie were vnder the Duch Jurisdiction ; Against these claimes Injurius and Imperius proceedings of the Duch Gou^r not onely the Gou^r of Newhauen protested but the Gou^r of the Massachusets and all the Comissioners for the vnited Collonies duly witnessed as theire seuerall letters will shew ;

The Duch for private gaine from yeare to yeare haue furnished Indians with great store of guns powder and shott (a damnable Trade as the p^{r}sent Duch Gou^r in a letter cales it which makes them Insolent Injurius and apte to disturbe the peace of all about them besids what hath passed betwixt the English Collonies and Will'am Keift before mencioned ; the Comissioners att seuerall times complained of this mischeuivs trad to the p^{r}sent Gou^r as carried on not onely in [a] private vnderhand way by þticulare trad[ers]. . . .

Wheras the Duch had constant free trad with the English in these þte [parts] without paiment of costom or any such charge and free libertie to anker where they would in any of the English harbours ; the English marchants and marriners haue been put vpon much Inconvenience and forced to pay heuy Costoms or Reconition att the Monhatoes ; a ∧ hath been there sett vp in a place hazardus and English vessels forced to anker there or deeply fined for contempt though som of them could safely take theire oath they knew not the order ; and larg Recognition hath been Required and paied not onely for goods traded att the Monhatoes but for goods traded elsewhere, and onely passing by the Monhatoes, Namely 15 Stivers for each beauer Moose or other skine ten stiuers for each halfe beauer skine and 2 or 3 Stiuers for each dear skine ; of which greivances the Comissioners haue sought Redresse from the Duch Gou^r but without Sucksesse or lasting fruite . . .

lastly to add waight to the p^{r}mises Treachery and crewelty are in bloody coullers p^{r}sented to vs and charged vpon the Duch Gou^r by many concurrent Strong and *and* pressing Testimonies of the Indians att least sence the hollanders in times of treaty begane the vnexpected warr vpon England and sence instead of giveing Just Satisfaction they have proclaimed theire Resolution to continnue It ; The Duch Gou^r and his ffiscall (as by the euidence following may appeer) haue been at worke by gifts and promises to engage the Indians to cutt of the English within the vnited Collonies and wee heare the Designe reaches alsoe to the English in Verginnia they may have vsed more Instruments and baites then are yett descovered but the Indians Round about for diuers hundred of miles cercute seeme to have drunk deep of an Intoxicating cupp att or from the Monhatoes against the English whoe have sought theire good both in bodily and sperittuall Respects

. . . And the Duch Gou^r acknowlidgeth that whateuer is concluded betwixt the English and him can hold noe longer then till hee Receiue som contrary comaund from his Superiors which by the p^{r}mises may welbee Interpreted to bee when hee hath strength and opertunitie to doe vs mischeife whether as the state of affaires either in Europe betwixt the common wealth of England and the Netherlands or heer betwixt the Collonies and the Duch wee may safely admitt a Treaty or what course wee are called to take for the honner and Satisfaction of our nation the Reparation and safety of the English Collonies is matter of serius and waighty consideration; The gracius and wise God guid vs to conclude and doe what is Right in his sight without turning aside for any Respects either to the Right hand or to the left; . . .

Records of the Colony of New Plymouth in New England (edited by David Pulsifer, Boston, 1859), X, 12–25 *passim*.

---

171. A Schoolmaster's Duties (1661)

BY SECRETARY ADRIAEN HEGEMAN

(TRANSLATED BY H. R. STILES, 1867)

This petition throws an interesting light on education in New Netherland; it was written by the secretary of the town government of Brooklyn. The Dutch colonial government made a small annual grant, as here requested. — Bibliography as in No. 166 above.

TO the Right Honble Director-General and Council of New Netherland : The Schout and Schepens of the Court of Breuckelen respectfully represent that they found it necessary that a Court Messenger was required for the Schepens' Chamber, to be occasionally employed in the Village of Breuckelen and all around where he may be needed, as well to serve summons, as also to conduct the service of the Church, and to sing on Sundays ; to take charge of the School, dig graves, etc., ring the Bell, and perform whatever else may be required :

Therefore, the Petitioners, with your Honors' approbation, have thought proper to accept for so highly necessary an office a suitable person who is now come before them, one Carel van Beauvois, to whom they have hereby appropriated a sum of fl. 150, besides a free dwelling; and whereas the Petitioners are apprehensive that the aforesaid C. v. Beauvois would not and cannot do the work for the sum aforesaid, and the Petitioners are not able to promise him any more, therefore the Petitioners, with all humble and proper reverence, request your Honors to be pleased to lend them a helping hand, in order thus to receive the needful assistance. Herewith, awaiting your Honors' kind and favorable answer, and commending ourselves, Honorable, wise, prudent, and most discreet Gentlemen, to your favor, we pray for your Honors God's protection, together with a happy and prosperous administration unto Salvation. Your Honors' servants and subjects, The Schout and Schepens of the Village aforesaid. By order of the same, . . .

Henry R. Stiles, *A History of the City of Brooklyn* (Brooklyn, 1867), I, 116–117.

———◆———

172. Condition of New York in 1679

BY JASPAR DANKERS AND PETER SLUYTER

(TRANSLATED BY HENRY C. MURPHY, 1867)

For Dankers and Sluyter, see Nos. 58, 146 above; for New York, see ch. xxiii above.

HAVING then fortunately arrived, by the blessing of the Lord, before the city of New York, on Saturday, the 23d day of September, we stepped ashore about four o'clock in the afternoon, in company with Gerrit, our fellow passenger, who would conduct us in this strange place. . . . He first took us to the house of one of his friends, who welcomed him and us, and offered us some of the fruit of the country, very fine peaches and full grown apples, which filled our hearts with thankfulness to God. This fruit was exceedingly fair and good, and pleasant to the taste ; much better than that in Holland or elsewhere, though I believe our long fasting and craving of food made it so agreeable. . . .

24th, Sunday. We rested well through the night. I was surprised on waking up to find my comrade had already dressed himself and breakfasted upon peaches. We walked out awhile in the fine, pure morning air, along the margin of the clear running water of the sea, which is driven up this river at every tide. As it was Sunday, in order to avoid scandal and for other reasons, we did not wish to absent ourselves from church. We therefore went, and found there truly a wild worldly world. I say wild, not only because the people are wild, as they call it in Europe, but because most all the people who go there to live, or who are born there, partake somewhat of the nature of the country, that is, peculiar to the land where they live. We heard a minister preach, who had come from the up-river country, from fort Orange, where his residence is, an old man, named Domine Schaats, of Amsterdam. . . .

This Schaats, then, preached. He had a defect in the left eye, and used such strange gestures and language that I think I never in all my life have heard any thing more miserable ; indeed, I can compare him with no one better than with one Do. Van Ecke, lately the minister at Armuyden, in Zeeland, more in life, conversation and gestures than in person. As it is not strange in these countries to have men as ministers who drink, we could imagine nothing else than that he had been drinking a little this morning. His text was, *Come unto me all ye, &c.*, but he was so rough that even the roughest and most godless of our sailors were astonished.

The church being in the fort, we had an opportunity to look through the latter, as we had come too early for preaching. It is not large ; it has four points or batteries ; it has no moat outside, but is enclosed with a double row of palisades. It is built from the foundation with quarry stone. The parapet is of earth. It is well provided with cannon, for the most part of iron, though there were some small brass pieces, all bearing the mark or arms of the Netherlanders. The garrison is small. There is a well of fine water dug in the fort by the English, contrary to the opinion of the Dutch, who supposed the fort was built upon rock, and had therefore never attempted any such thing. . . . It has only one gate, and that is on the land side, opening upon a broad plain or street, called the Broadway or Beaverway. Over this gate are the arms of the Duke of York. During the time of the Dutch there were two gates, namely, another on the water side ; but the English have closed it, and made a battery there, with a false gate. In front of the church is inscribed the name of Governor *Kyft*, who caused the same to be built in the year 1642. It has a shingled roof, and upon the gable towards the water there is a small wooden tower, with a bell in it, but no clock.

There is a sun-dial on three sides. The front of the fort stretches east and west, and consequently the sides run north and south. . . .

27th, Wednesday. Nothing occurred to-day except that I went to assist Gerrit in bringing his goods home, and declaring them, which we did. We heard that one of the wicked and godless sailors had broken his leg; and in this we saw and acknowledged the Lord and his righteousness. . . .

As soon as we had dined we sent off our letters; and this being all accomplished, we started at two o'clock for Long Island. . . .

. . . We went on, up the hill, along open roads and a little woods, through the first village, called Breukelen, which has a small and ugly little church standing in the middle of the road. Having passed through here, we struck off to the right, in order to go to *Gouanes*. We went upon several plantations where Gerrit was acquainted with most all of the people, who made us very welcome, sharing with us bountifully whatever they had, whether it was milk, cider, fruit or tobacco, and especially, and first and most of all, miserable rum or brandy which had been brought from Barbadoes and other islands, and which is called by the Dutch *kill-devil*. All these people are very fond of it, and most of them extravagantly so, although it is very dear and has a bad taste. . . .

. . . On my return home, the son of our old people asked me if I would not go to their usual catechizing, which they held once a week at the house of *Abraham Lanoy*, schoolmaster, and brother of the commissary in the custom house. I accompanied him there, and found a company of about twenty-five persons, male and female, but mostly young people. It looked like a school, as indeed it was, more than an assembly of persons who were seeking after true godliness; where the schoolmaster, who instructed them, handled the subject more like a schoolmaster in the midst of his scholars than a person who knew and loved God, and sought to make him known and loved. They sung some verses from the psalms, made a prayer, and questioned from the catechism, at the conclusion of which they prayed and sung some verses from the psalms again. It was all performed without respect or reverence, very literally, and mixed up with much obscurity and error. He played, however, the part of a learned and pious man, *enfin le suffisant et le petit precheur*. After their departure, I had an opportunity of speaking to him and telling him what I thought was good for him. He acknowledged that I convinced him of several things; and thus leaving him I returned home. . . .

We went from the city, following the Broadway, over the *valey*, or the fresh water.   Upon both sides of this way were many habitations of negroes, mulattoes and whites.   These negroes were formerly the proper slaves of the (West India) company, but, in consequence of the frequent changes and conquests of the country, they have obtained their freedom and settled themselves down where they have thought proper, and thus on this road, where they have ground enough to live on with their families.   We left the village, called the *Bouwerij*, lying on the right hand, and went through the woods to New Harlem, a tolerably large village situated on the south side of the island, directly opposite the place where the northeast creek and the East river come together, situated about three hours journey from New Amsterdam, . . .

11*th, Wednesday.*   We embarked early this morning in his boat and rowed over to Staten island, where we arrived about eight o'clock. . . . There are now about a hundred families on the island, of which the English constitute the least portion, and the Dutch and French divide between them about equally the greater portion.   They have neither church nor minister, and live rather far from each other, and inconveniently to meet together.   The English are less disposed to religion, and inquire little after it, but in case there were a minister, would contribute to his support.   The French and Dutch are very desirous and eager for one, for they spoke of it wherever we went, and said, in the event of not obtaining Domine Tessemaker, they would send, or had sent, to France for another.   The French are good Reformed churchmen, and some of them are Walloons.   The Dutch are also from different quarters. . . .

When we arrived at Gouanes, we heard a great noise, shouting and singing in the huts of the Indians, who as we mentioned before, were living there.   They were all lustily drunk, raving, striking, shouting, jumping, fighting each other, and foaming at the mouth like raging wild beasts.   Some who did not participate with them, had fled with their wives and children to Simon's house, where the drunken brutes followed, bawling in the house and before the door, which we finally closed.   And this was caused by Christians.   It makes me blush to call by that holy name those who live ten times worse than these most barbarous Indians and heathen, not only in the eyes of those who can discriminate, but according to the testimony of these poor Indians themselves.   What do I say, the testimony of the Indians !   Yes, I have not conversed with an European or a native born, the most godless and the best, who has not fully and roundly acknowledged it, but they have not acknowledged it salutarily, and much less desisted, disregarding all convictions external and internal, notwithstanding all the injury which springs therefrom, not only among the Indians, but others, as we will show in its proper place. How will they escape the terrible judgment of God; how evade the wrath and anger of the Lord and King, Jesus, whom they have so dishonored and defamed, and caused to be defamed among the heathen? Just judgment is their damnation. But I must restrain myself, giving God all judgment and wrath, and keeping only what he causes us to feel therefor. Such are the fruits of the cursed cupidity of those who call themselves Christians for the very little that these poor naked people have. Simon and his wife also do their best in the same way, although we spoke to them severely on the subject. They brought forward this excuse, that if they did not do it, others would, and then they would have the trouble and others the profit; but if they must have the trouble, they ought to have the profit, and so they all said, and for the most part falsely, for they all solicit the Indians as much as they can, and after begging their money from them, compel them to leave their blankets, leggings, and coverings of their bodies in pawn, yes, their guns and hatchets, the very instruments by which they obtain their subsistence. This subject is so painful and so abominable, that I will forbear saying any thing more for the present. . . .

Journal of a Voyage to New York in 1679–80, in Long Island Historical Society, *Memoirs* (Brooklyn, 1867), I, 109–274 *passim*.

INDEX

2 Q